1001 BICYCLES
TO DREAM OF RIDING

1001 BICYCLES
TO DREAM OF RIDING

GENERAL EDITOR
GUY KESTEVEN

FOREWORD BY
CHRIS BOARDMAN

UNIVERSE

A Quintessence Book

First published in the United States of America in 2014 by
UNIVERSE PUBLISHING
A Division of Rizzoli International Publications, Inc.
300 Park Avenue South
New York, NY 10010
www.rizzoliusa.com

2014 2015 2016 2017 / 10 9 8 7 6 5 4 3 2 1

ISBN: 978-0-7893-2724-6

Library of Congress Control Number: 2014931456

QSS.BIKE

This book was designed and produced by
Quintessence Editions Ltd.
The Old Brewery, 6 Blundell Street
London N7 9BH
www.1001beforeyoudie.com

Senior Editor Ruth Patrick
Editors Ruth Patrick, Henry Russell, Frank Ritter
Designer Tea Aganovic
Editorial Assistant Zoë Smith
Production Manager Anna Pauletti

Editorial Director Jane Laing
Publisher Mark Fletcher

Color reproduction by KHL Chromagraphics, Singapore
Printed in China by Midas Printing Ltd.

Contents

Foreword | Chris Boardman

When I was young and couldn't sleep, I used to build bikes in my head until I eventually drifted off. It was both more engaging and more effective than counting sheep. It was while doing this that I realized just how diverse the bicycle is, so much so that I don't think I ever managed to finish an imaginary machine before falling asleep. In fact, it is now forty years since I started practicing that slumber-inducing activity and I still haven't run out of two-wheeled possibilities.

Since then, I've been the proud owner of a vast array of real machines, many only slightly less fanciful than those of my imagination. It all started with a blue Raleigh with fat white tires. I can vividly remember the Sunday morning when, aged six, I took off my stabilizers and rode down our little cul-de-sac on two wheels for the first time.

In my early teens, things got a little more serious and I was introduced to track racing at Kirby Stadium. My steed for this new activity was a frame of unknown origin, since it had been reclaimed from a dumpster by my eagle-eyed father. I won my first regional championship on that hand-painted frame, and I regret to this day that I didn't hang on to it.

As I rode faster and started to win things, my bikes became more sophisticated. My very first encounter with that wonder material, carbon fiber, was in the form of a Vitus 979 frame supplied by Graham Weigh Cycles. It was shod with the very latest Campagnolo C Record equipment and was my pride and joy.

At this point, very few people had looked outside the sport and seen the true potential of this super-cloth; the few carbon bikes that existed were basically mirroring the form of the traditional frame, with the carbon unimaginatively rolled into tubes. That was until a guy by the name of Mike Burrows produced his revolutionary wing-shaped Windcheetah. He probably didn't realize it, but Mike had just changed the way bike designers would think of their art forever. The Windcheetah would be the basis of the Lotus Superbike I rode to win Gold in the 1992 Olympic Games.

Mike's design completely ignored the traditional practice of using cylinder shapes to link together the component parts of the bicycle and the convention of building bikes for lightness. Instead he addressed the true demands facing the racing cyclists, the biggest of which was and still is air resistance.

Up until this point, aerodynamics had been all but ignored by a sport blinkered by tradition, even at the highest echelon of riders. Even the legendary final time-trial ride by Greg LeMond that won him the 1989 Tour de France by just 8 seconds over Frances Laurent Fignion was achieved on a very traditional round-tubed bike. LeMond had understood the need to minimize the frontal area of his body using a revolutionary tucked "skiers' position," but there were no fundamental design changes to the bike itself.

In 1994, I found myself on a team with LeMond himself, and to his credit, Greg was one of the first to appreciate Mike Burrows' work. In fact, he insisted that the whole team ride the new Lotus 105 frames (the road-going version of the bike I rode to Olympic track success) in that year's Tour de France.

I didn't realize it at the time, but my few visits to the MIRA wind tunnel with the Lotus team had got me fascinated by the aerodynamic aspect of bicycles, an obsession I was able to indulge some ten years later when I led The Secret Squirrel Club, the clandestine group that would design all the track bikes ridden by Team GB in both the Beijing 2008 and London 2012 Olympic Games. It was a fascinating journey with many weeks spent in wind tunnels trying to understand the interactions between rider and machine.

During this period I founded Boardman Bikes, and as exciting as it has been to have had Gold-medal-winning athletes astride my machines, the company brought me into an arena even more rewarding: the use of bikes as a simple, efficient, everyday means of transport.

As the pages of this book illustrate, the diversity of the bicycle is almost limitless and I have no doubt that new ideas and designs will continue to flow long into the future. For myself, I still design bikes while falling asleep, but now when I wake up in the morning, I get to make them real too. I can't imagine a more satisfying thing to do.

Introduction | Guy Kesteven

Bicycle: Two-wheeled, pedal-driven personal transport.
By cycle: Any feat or entertainment achieved on a bicycle.

However you choose to view it, the bicycle is an incredible and genuinely revolutionary invention. We're not just talking about the revolutions of wheels and pedals either, but the way it has changed lives.

The first brief wobbling moment of both feet off the ground as a child. Scuffed knees, torn clothes, and a thorough telling-off traded for the exhilaration of the first flight off a plank and brick ramp, or a few seconds of wheelie glory. Turning the corner of your street with a brief backward glance and a bag of sandwiches on your first adventure. The joy of tailwinds and descents, or the hard labor of headwinds and hill climbs. The prickling fear of being lost or the rush of finding unknown landscapes as you head farther afield. The pride of polishing and oiling a new bike, the anguish of punctures or the guilt of neglectful rust. Braving traffic previously only seen from the protection of a parent's car. Through this rich tapestry of experiences, bikes are the first real taste of independence, self-reliance, and responsibility that most of us have.

The bike hasn't only provided individual freedoms. It has given previously unimaginable freedoms to groups as diverse as nineteenth-century women and twenty-first-century African people. It has saved countless lives, taken people to almost unbelievable places, helped people travel at unbelievable speeds, or just got them to work without clogging roads or causing pollution. It's underlined some of sport's most famous—and infamous—moments and carried kings, queens, popes, and guerrilla armies on its saddles. Throughout its history it has been both bewitchingly pure and simple or at the cutting edge of constructional technology, and bike-bred innovations have spread their DNA throughout the mechanical gene pool.

In compiling this book I have sought to include every significant bicycle from the historical to the here right now. From the truly humble to the highest-tech and in every diverse form from tricycle to tandem, scooter to flying machine, hand-built classics to wind-tunnel-honed weirdness, death-defying freeride machines to death-provoking designs of the early years.

It's no joke that mortality was under real threat for some of the pioneers of cycling. The early draisines or hobbyhorse striding machines were extremely heavy, they handled badly, and most worryingly of all, had no brakes. Things got a little better when early treadle-powered bikes were superseded by "ordinary" or "penny-farthing" bikes, the mere mounting of which was a potentially disastrous maneuver. Even these earliest machines gave their riders a sniff of the addictive aroma of cycling, though. At a time when carriages and horses were the transport of the truly rich, here was a machine that could multiply the distances and speeds possible on foot without any need for stables or straw. A machine that opened horizons and minds, and even divided skirts to give women their first taste of truly free and independent travel.

The early years of cycling were a time of incredible innovation, ingenuity, and in some cases, insanity. Air-filled "pneumatic" tires; pioneering chains and shaft drives; helical wound tubing; two-wheeled, three-wheeled, four-wheeled, or multi-wheel-sized; side-by-side, staggered, in-line, or solo seating; suspension; built-in security; folding, shrinking, racing, or relaxing designs all wobbled onto the increasingly busy streets in the late nineteenth century. It is often said by the wisest modern bike designers that there is no bike-related design—practical or lunatic—that wasn't tried and likely patented before the start of the twentieth century.

It was the arrival of the chain-driven, air-tired, and easily mounted, dismounted, braked, and steered "Safety" bike of the final years of the nineteenth century that changed the world of personal transport forever. Suffragettes in rational dress found the perfect vehicle to outrun misogynistic conventions, and courting couples left chaperones eating their dust. Athletes set records still impressive today, stuntmen chased trains at mile-a-minute pace, and workers, soldiers, and everyday escapers alike saw their horizons expanded far beyond walking distance. The freaks of the early years disappeared as the bicycle evolved rapidly in the first decades of the twentieth century. Glistening, gold-highlighted luxury bikes fit for duchesses, delivery bikes for traders, and stripped-down racers all flourished on largely car-free roads.

Rakish young bloods tackled the mountains and massive mileages of first editions of classic events. Bike brands became national household names sold with posters and slogans that are still iconic today. Famous landmarks like the Henri de Toulouse-Lautrec advertising posters are shown, and epic stories of riders such as Eugène Christophe are told in the pages of this exhaustive encyclopedia, but hopefully even the most avid enthusiast will find fresh food for thought while flicking through. Ultra-light French "Concours" touring bikes shaved within grams of collapse interleave with kids' bikes decorated in the style of transatlantic heroes or the steadfast steeds of contemporary celebrities like fitness heroine Billy Dovey. Bolted-together aluminum bikes decades ahead of their time appear alongside short-lived gear-change and wheel-fixing systems. Interestingly, the classic forms and features that would remain the default designs for the rest of the century were all on the road in the interwar years.

The Second World War changed the pedaling landscape as radically as it did the political one, however. In the postwar United States, bikes became as caricatured as the cars: Tasseled, chromed, and fake-fuel-tanked toys, discarded as soon as you were old enough to drive. In Communist China, the Flying Pigeon bicycle mobilized millions of

Mao's people to become the most-produced vehicle ever. In Europe, small-wheeled folding bikes from the likes of Moulton and Raleigh replaced traditional "sit up and beg" roadsters as the fashionable way to ride, while hip kids rode motorbike-style Choppers designed for style, not speed. Ironically while built-in radios, color-coded tires, stick-shift transmissions, and multi-rider seats revolutionized kids' bikes, and the BMX craze got bike-shop tills clattering faster than ever before, the bloodlines of the serious thoroughbreds largely stagnated. From the 1930s to the 1980s, national heroes like Coppi, Anquetil, Merckx, Moser, and Hinault fought—sometimes to the death in Tom Simpson's case—to win the monument races on bikes that barely changed. Tires were still sewn together by hand and glued onto rims, gears had to be fumbled for in crucial moments, and nearly every race bike in the world was made with Reynolds trusty 531C chrome molybdenum steel tubing.

Luckily for me, that all started to change just as my riding world opened up in front of me. I still idolized the Raleigh team stars who rode the Reynolds-tubed bikes in the same colors as my beloved 5-speed Ace from the proper bike shop at the other side of town. I even cut out 531 frame-tubing stickers from Reynolds catalogs and glued them onto my frame. Dreaming of one day upgrading to a single Campagnolo Nuovo Record shift lever but always seeing my pocket money swallowed by puncture repair kits, grease, and "get-me-home" Mars bars. The bikes of the stars were changing though. Peugeot was using carbon fiber to float Robert Millar up hills and Cinelli was flattening its tubes and smoothing its welds to cheat the wind. Look and LeMond added more carbon and revolutionary aero bars to snatch last second victories. My friends and I started to hear the first murmurings of "mountain" or "all-terrain" bikes in imported magazines like *Winning*, too. I knew nothing about Repack racing, but the idea of overgrown BMXs that would stop at nothing sounded fantastic to a youth already rattling his racer apart exploring rough moorland trails.

Cups of tea in the local bike shop turned into a spanner in my hand to pay for the biscuits I'd eaten and the spares I'd "borrowed" and my life in the bike industry began one puncture repair at a time. The bikes we were unboxing were also changing radically, as mountain bikes became the must-have accessory, and soon I'd sold and ridden carbon fiber, fat aluminum, and full-suspension bikes in an increasingly broad and often weird shapes. At college, I wobbled down to rowing training on "The bike from Atlantis," a rusting sit up and beg fished from a canal that introduced me to the joy of sneaky single-track short cuts through the wood. Saturdays were worked and college funds diverted into a proper mountain bike, and the inevitable leapfrog of addiction began as I vanished deeper into the valleys, forests, and moors with freakishly neon friends. A man in trunks lured me into trying my first Scott tri bars on a weirdly handling varnished bike designed for the brand-new sport of triathlon. Mike the bike shop manager helped start my lifelong obsession with tandems by taking me out to test ride a repaired bike and coming back an hour later crying with laughter as we speedily replaced two sets of pedals fractured from overexcited cornering before the owners arrived. Over the next few years, I surveyed the forests of the Yorkshire moors on an indestructibly hand-built Dave Yates Diablo mountain bike that's still going strong as far as I know. I commuted 20 miles each way to work at a bike parts warehouse on low-profile aero bikes, and even bought Carnac shoes like Chris Boardman's to get me there in time to snatch a second breakfast. I rode, raced, broke, repaired, and loved bikes in every spare moment I had, and was unbelievably lucky to turn that hobby into a career when I joined the world of bike magazines as a freelance kit tester in 1996. Since then, I've been privileged enough to enjoy (and occasionally endure) riding thousands of all the latest types of bikes, meeting everyone from eccentric designers to legendary riders. A journey that's still as wonderful and surprising as that very first day wobbling along with one stabilizer and a fizz in my heart.

This journey of the bike from its origins as a rudimentary toy of aristocrats to its current high-profile position at the cutting edge of technological, humanitarian, and ecological revolutions is celebrated in the pages of this unique book, too. Flicking through its exhaustive selection of every significant bike ever built, you'll be intrigued by the early years of diversity. The crude cam-pedal Michaux machine or the bewildering complexity of the telescopic axle Plectocycle, confusing to the point where even the towering Ordinary or Penny-Farthing bikes almost make sense. You'll see the early Safety bikes emerge remarkably well-formed from this chaos of invention, with bikes like the Sunbeam rapidly gaining pneumatic tires, chain cases, locks, and other refinements that mean they would still sell well in a modern bike shop. You'll find bikes ridden by household names as well as ingenious cargo machines designed to do the household shopping or deliver the kids to school. You'll find bikes designed for lazy laid-back cruising and the bike of a rider who famously died rather than stopping. Bikes with radios, sirens, and flashing lights and others stripped to the sculptural, speed boosting minimum so effectively that they had to be banned. Bikes where every weld is sweated over in an artisan workshop and workhorses that ease the sweat and toil of staying alive and healthy in sub-Saharan Africa. Bikes you'll remember fondly and bikes you'll barely believe, but above all, 1001 bicycles that truly are worth dreaming of riding.

Index of Bikes by Manufacturer

14 Bike Co.
Custom 608

18 Bikes
Pinion Hardtail 874

2 Stage
Elite 9 418

Abici
Velocino 632

Acer-Mex
Windsor 132

Airborne
Carpe Diem 390

Airframe
A frame 821

Airnimal
Joey 821

Alchemy
Arion 642

Alliance
Steel Coupled Allroad 788

Allsop
Softride 224
Softride Power V 288

Alpine Stars
Cro-Mega 222

American Eagle
Semi-Pro 128

Ammaco
Team 156

AMP Research
B2 265

Anderson
4 Seasons Stainless 789

Appleman
Custom CX 789

Argon 18
E-118 624

Argonaut
Carbon 773

Atomic Zombie
Aurora Delta Racing Trike 819

Audi Worthersee
E-Bike 735

Augspurger
One-Off 480

Avanti
Quantum 515

AVD Windcheetah
HyperSport Series II 747

Award
E Stay 692

Azub
Max 746

Bacchetta
Carbon Aero 2.0 516

Baines
VS37 Flying Gate 72

Bakfiets
Cargobike Short 310

Banshee
Chaparral 410

Barra
Randonneuse 85

Basso
Laguna 538

Battaglin
50 212
Pirana 198

Ben Wilson
Monocycle 525

Benotto
Cambio Corsa 99

Beru
Factor 001 526

Bianchi
928 Mono-Q 506
Army Issue 60
*Mega Pro XL Reparto
  Corse 347*
Oltre Super Record 641
Paris–Roubaix 290
Reparto Corse 89

Bickerton
Portable 128

**Bicycle and Tricycle
Supply Association**
Plectocycle 30

Bigfoot
E-Stay 265

Bike Friday
New World Tourist 319
Pocket Llama 829

Bilenky
Ephgrave Tribute 778
Townie 904

Biomega
MN01 364

Bionicon
Golden Willow 417

Birdy
Speedy 277

Biria
*Easy 7 Comfort
  Bike 828*

Bishop
Road 779

Bixi
"Boris Bike" 580

Black Market
Killswitch 649

Black Sheep
UIMA Phat Bike 783

Blaze
29er 780

BMC
Fourstroke FS01 29 665
Gran Fondo 775
SLT01 431
Time Machine Road TMR01 774
Timemachine TM01 664
Trailfox 665
TM02 911

BMW
Q6.S 358

Boardman
AiR 9.2 Di2 947
AiR 9.8 620
AiR TT 9.8 620
FS Team 536
Pro Carbon 542
SLR 9.8 726
Team Carbon 472

Bob Kellar
Fat Bike 783

Bobby Hunt
Minivelo 827

Bontrager
Race Lite 236

Boo
Glissando Townie 785

Bottecchia
Equipe 262
Emme2 772

Boulder
Defiant 266

Breadwinner
Arbor Lodge 781

Breezer
Beamer 243
MTB 140

Brian Rourke
Custom 953 Stainless
Oversize 887

Brick Lane Bikes
La Poivra Air Frame 878

British Cycling
Olympic Bike 708

Brodie
Holeshot 912

Brompton
M3L Folder 205

Brooklyn MWorks
TMX 361

Brothers
117 876

BSA
Airborne 83
Mark IV General Service 51
No. 15 Standard 63

BTR Fabrications
Belter 601

Buddy Bike
Twin 338

Caletti
Adventure Road 786

Calfee
Bamboo 423
Dragonfly Gravel 784
Team Z 240

Caminade
Caminargent 64
Caminargent 76

Canfield
Big Fat Fatty Fat (BF3) 345

Cannondale
Bad Boy 402
CAAD3 313
Delta V 253
EST 244
F3000 398
Freeride 386
Gemini 391
Jekyll 354
Raven ELO 325
Scalpel 375
Simon 518
Six13 412
Slice 483
Slice RS 892
SM-500 193
SM900 223
ST-500 Tourer 215
Super Six 454
Super V3000 316
Super V Fulcrum 318
Super X Disc 760
SuperSix Evo 631
SuperSix Evo Tourminator 656
Synapse Carbon 450
Synapse Hi Mod 916

Canyon
Aeroroad CF 602
F10 434
Nerve AL 555
Nerve AL 29 644
Spectral AL 29 928
Speedmax CF 755
Ultimate AL 848
Ultimate CF SLX 754

Carlton
Carbon 124
Jewel 103

Carrera
Vulcan 733

Castle
Singlespeed 792

Cervélo
Baracchi 285
Eyre 301
P2 313

P3 381
P5 827
R5CA 825
S1 534
S5 697
Soloist 392

Challenge
Concept XT 488

Charge
Duster 556

Chas Roberts
Dogsbolx 264
Women's Audax 880

Cherubim
Ranger 824

Christiania
Cargo Trike 188

Christini
Venture 443

Chromag
Samurai 485

Cielo
Sportif Racer 667

Cilo
MTB 236

Cinelli
Corsa 105
Saetta 706
The Absolute Machine 237

Cinetica
Giotto 234

Cipollini
Bond 830

Clarkes
Leader 61

Claud Butler
Avant Coureur 84

Cleland
Aventura 153

Co-motion
Periscope Torpedo 791

Colnago
Arte 544
Beppe Sarroni 179
Bititan 297
C40 338
C42 Pista prototype 285
C50 Cross 439
C59 Disc 725
Carbitubo Pista 215
Freddy Maertens 163
K.Zero 725
Mexico Gold 155

Columbia
Superb 82

Commençal
Meta 4X 459
Meta 5 441
Supreme DH 607

Condor
Pista 707

Conference
Circular 457

Cooper
T100 Spa 652

Cotic
BFe 518
Soul 480

Cove
G-Spot 590
Hooker 597
Hummer 364
Stiffee 350

Coventry Eagle
Royal Prince 74

Coyote
Ultralite HT3 361

Crema
Rapha Continental 792

Crypto
Bantam 40

Cube
Aerium HPC
Pro 565
Agree HTC Race 531
Litening 698
Stereo HPC SLT 861

Cunningham
Indian 158

CW
Phaze One 180

CWS
Commuter 122

Cycles Maximus
Cargo Trike 840

Cyfac
Absolu 872

Da Vinci
Carbon Tandem 688

Dahon
Curve SL 497

Dave Yates
Diablo 267
Wayfarer 450

Dawes
Countryman/Ranger 206
Discovery Twin 790
Kingpin 119
Super Galaxy 169

De Rosa
Corum 433
King 372
King 3 501
Titanio 283

Dean
Ace FS4.0 787

Decade
Virsa 580

Decathlon
Rockrider 635

Dedacciai
Nerissimo 699

Dekerf
853 SL 369

Delta 7
Arantix 566

Demon
Hermes 693
Manhattan 894

Derny
Moped 77

Desalvo
Steel Cross 670

Detroit
Madison Street
Bike 736

Devinci
Dixon 767
Wilson 485

Diamond Back
Arrival 221

Dick Power
Track 90

Didi Senft
World's Biggest
Bike 444

DMO
Element
Bivvy 738

DMR
Trailstar 442

Dolan
Tuono SL 847

Don Walker
Crazy Legs Cycle
Cross 808
Stayer Bike 895

Donhou
100 mph Bike 822
Tourer 882

Donkelope
Steampunk 795

Downland
Chris Hodge 748

Dunlop
Pneumatic 57

Dursley
Pedersen 54

Dynamic Bicycles
Easy Step 8 818

Eagle
Ordinary 36

Early Rider
Spherovelo Juno 834

Eddy Merckx
Motorola 282

Electra
Flatfoot 868

Elettromontaggi
Zoom Bike 299

Ellis Briggs
Favori 234

Ellis Cycles
953 512

Ellsworth
Dare 407
Moment 410

Elswick Hopper
Model W 95
Vampire Convincible 106

Empire
AP-1 424

Engin Cycles
Ti Singlespeed 29er 795

English Cycles
Custom TT 490
Nuvinci Cruiser 797
Single Sided 895

Enigma
Excel 886

Ernest Russ
Super Resilient 66

Evil
Revolt 522
Undead 651
Uprising 759

Faggin
Primavera 877

Falcon
Olympic 142

Fat Chance
Yo Eddy 233

Fatback
Snowbike 913

Feather
Cross 903
Rapha Continental 694

Felt
AR1 843
B2 240
DA 869

Festka
Motol Chrom 800

Field
Cross Classic 894
Takashi 824

Fietser
WAW 566

Fiorelli
Coppi 115

Fisher
CR7 217

Fisher/Kelly
MountainBike 150

Flandria
Competition 123

Flat Frames
Wooden Frame 640

Fleet Velo
Joust 559

Flying Pigeon
Utility 95

Focus
Cayo Evo 1.0 22-G
Chorus 651
Chrono 511
Team Replica Izalco 756

Foes
DHS Mono 379
Inferno 408
LTS 273

Forme
Vitesse 551

Formula
F1 250

Fuji
Altamira 668

Funk
Pro-Comp 257

FW Evans/Pashley
SE 595

Gafni
Cardboard Bike 940

Gallus
Paris Brest Randonneur 607

Gangl
Record Strada 753 798

Gary Fisher
Big Sur 344
Goldenfly 362
Grateful Dead 300
Mount Tam 390
ProCaliber 198
Rig 474
Roscoe 504
Superfly 29 492

Gary Fisher/Lawwill
RS-1 245

Gaulzetti
Cazzo 799

Gazelle
Alu-Pro Race Frame 325

Geekhouse
Mudville CX 799

Genesis
Croix de fer 550
Fortitude Race 642
High Latitude Alfine 640
Volare 953 748

Geoff Longstaff
Trike 176

George Elrick
Chrome 74

Ghost
Lector AMR 9500 766

Giant
Anthem X 478
ATX 340
Box One 334
Cadex CFM 3 244
Defy 491
DH Comp 418
Escaper 223
Glory 554
MCM 335
MCR 343
Propel Advanced SL 921

Reign 447
Reign X 464
TCR 314
TCR Advanced SL ISP 643
TCR Composite 401
TCX Advanced 1 941
Trance 920
Trance 29X 898
Trinity Advanced SL 605
Twist Esprit Power
   Double 641
VT1 400
XTC Advanced SL 290 753

Gios
Torino Super Record 149

Gitane
Anquetil 110
LeMond 181

Gladiator
Tandem 42

Globe
Work 3 863

Gnome-Rhône
Alloy 70

Goodies
Trandem 139

Gossamer
Albatross 150

Graeme Obree
Beastie 723
Old Faithful 294

Greenspeed
Anura 623
X5 735

Groovy
Frankenstein X 800

GT
700D Tachyon 222
DHi 465
Fury 512
I-drive 340

Lobo STS DH 348
LTS 290
Olympic 308
Quatrefoil 248
RTS 1 256
Sensor Carbon Pro 918
Stay Strong 701
STS 318
Timberline 287
Vengeance 345
Zaskar 245
ZR2000 351

Guru Bicycles
Photon 882

Hampsten
Strada Bianca 356

Hanebrink
X1 347

Haro
Freestyler 172
Porter 576
Sport 191

Harry Quinn
Milk Race
   Special 109

Harvey Cycle Works
Rapha Continental 618

Hercules
Eileen Sheridan 101
OA21 69
Roadeo 670

Herobike
Bamboo 804

Hetchins
Lightweight 76
Magnus Bonum 124

Hirondelle
Retro Directe 61

Hobbs
Blue Riband 85
Continental 77

Hobo
Weirdy Beardy 872

Holdsworth
Professional 130

Honda
RN01 411

Hope
Glory 24 463

Hoy
Sa Calobra
.002 762

HP Velotechnik
Grasshopper 614
Scorpion FX 743
Streamer 720

Huffy
7 Eleven Track 186
Convertible 86
Fat Bike 761
Penguin Dragster 115
Radiobike 92
Special Roadster 110

Humber
Standard
Special 53

Ibis
BowTi 337
Mojo 458
Hakkalügi 316
Szazbo 312
Tranny 584

Ice
Sprint 908

Imperial
Custom 4-Stroke 560

Independent
  Fabrications
Corvid 523

Inspired
Skye 553

Intense
951 Evo 915
Carbine Carbon 715
M3 442
Tracer 378
Tracer 275 900

Ira Ryan/Trucker
Ned Ludd 889

Iride
Volatore 807

Isaac
Muon 617

Islabikes
Beinn 479
Creig 26 570
Rothan 497

Jack Taylor
Curved Tube 99

Jamis
Xenith 788

Jeff Jones
Spaceframe 535

Jeff Tiedeken
Gravity
  Bike 908

Jernonimo
Slütter Ti X 711

JMC
Black Shadow 174
Darryl Young 180

Juliana
Origin Primeiro 701

Kalkhoff
Endeavour 697

Karpiel
Apocalypse 381

Kelson
R.A.D. 672

Ken Rogers
Clubman 145

Kent Eriksen
Titanium 527

Kessels
Eddy Merckx 132

Kestrel
Airfoil 305
Nitro 221
R4000 207
RT 800 531

KHS
Montana Comp 261

Kiddimoto
Scrambler 700

Kinesis
Maxlight XC130 583
Sync 937

Kirk
Magnesium 261

Kirk Pacenti
650B 471

Kirklee
29er Dream
  Machine 661

Kish
650B Mountain
  Bike 805
Titanium MTB 806

Klein
Adroit 252
Attitude 226
Mantra 300
Palomino 388
Pulse 332

Koga
Miyata Team
  Edition 499
Miyata Elevation
  12000 279

Kokua
LIKEaBIKE 329

Kona
Afrikabike 646
Bass 484
Carbon
  Operator 921
Cinder Cone 230
Entourage 647
Explosif 216
Hei Hei 248
Honzo 751
Humu Humu Nuku Nuku
  Apua'a 315
Kula 323
Lacondeguy
  Inc 553
Stab Supreme 464
Stinky 342
Stinky 2-4 462
Ute 508

Kona/FSA
Major Jake 484

KTM
Lycan 652 719
Strada 5000
  Di2 910

Kuipers
Sawyer 606

Kuota
Kueen-K 569

Kuwahara
KZ-2.5/E.T.
  bike 174

La Gauloise
Bi-Chaîne 57

Labor
Spécial Corse 63

Labyrinth
Agile 655

Land Rover
Nitride 2012 ED 703

Land Shark
Andy Hampsten 212

Landescape
Direct Lateral 679

Lapierre
S-Lite 200 514
Spicy 466
Xelius FDJ 602
XR 729 770
Zesty 465

Last
Herb 160 707

Lawwill
Pro Cruiser 141

Legend
Queen 880

LeMond
Zurich 396

Lexus
F Sport 942

Linear
Limo 448

Litespeed
Archon 469
Blade 367
Ghisallo 394
Trike 329

Liteville
301 803

Littleford
Daily Driver
  3.0 810

Longwise
EU Bike 846

Look
585 439
Bernard Hinault 202
KG196 277
KG396 CLM 376

Lotus
Type 108 258

Lynskey
Cooper CX 454
Pro 29 557
Pro29 FS-120 708

Malvern Five Star
Track Racer 101

Manège
Scooter 112

Manitou
FS 298

Mantis
Flying V 237
Pro Floater 255
XCR Composite 189

Marin
Attack Trail 930
B-17 331
East Peak 297
Mount Vision 930
Mount Vision
  FS 322

Matsuda
Keirin 674

Matthews
Touring
  29er 674

Maverick
ML7 374

Mawis
Custom 870

MCR
Descender 192

Mead
Ranger 60

Mercian
King of
  Mercia 825

Merida
Big.Nine 728
Ninety-Six Carbon
  Team-D 546
Scultura 856

Merlin
Extralight 856
Newsboy 301
Mountain 209

Metrofiets
Cargo 488

Michaux
Michaudine 26

Microbike
Folder 206

Mijl Van Mares
Stretch Cycle 628

Moda
Interval 776

Mondraker
Factor XR 750
Podium 634

Mongoose
Motomag 136
Supergoose 164
Teocali Comp 769

Monty
Hydra 378

Moots
IMBA Bike 810
Vamoots RSL 881
YBB 220

Morewood
Sukuma 560

Mosaic
XT-1 Small
  Batch 676

Moser
Pista 191

Moulton
F Frame 114
Land Rover APB 299

Mountain Cycle
San Andreas 250

MSC
Blast 865

Muddy Fox
Courier 196
Intereactive 332

Muse
Mezzaluna Mixte 676

Neal Pryde
BURAsL 690

Nicolai
Helius FR 586
Pinion 736
Tandem 546
UFO-ST 545

Niner
Air 9 RDO 649
JET 9 RDO 598
RIP 9 753
WFO 506

Nishiki
Alien 218

Norco
Aurum 662
Range Killer B 764
Shore One 467
Sight SE 663
Torrent 411

NS
Soda Slope 653
Surge 597

Nukeproof
Mega AM 660
Scalp 556

Oak
Touring Bike 884

Offroad
Pro-Flex 239

Ogre
Monocoque 875

Olympia
Ego 727
Rex 862

On-One
Dirty Disco 630
Inbred 355

Onderwater
Family Tandem 678

Onix
RH 658

Orange
222 388
Clockwork 230
Five 414
Five 650 931
P7 288
Patriot 371

Orbea
Alma G 601
Orca 573
Ordu 536

Orbit
Routier
  Ultimate 839

Ordinary
Penny-
  Farthing 39

Ordonnanzfahrrad
Modell 05 55

Otto
Dicycle 28

Outland
VPP 298

Overburys
Pioneer 226

Owen
Softride Wood 808

OYT
Gelati 741

Pace
405 477
DPD 262
RC100 218
RC127 942
RC129 623

Paketa
D2R 716

Parlee
Z-Zero 760

Pashley
Classic 667
MailStar 375
Pickle 161
Princess 562

Passoni
Top Force W 892

Patterson
Pro Long 172

Paul Hewitt
Grampian
  Rohloff 870

Paulus Quirós
Reynolds 953 622

Pausey
Pioneer 33

Pawtrekker
Rufftrax Evolution 718

Peacock Groove
Voltron Red Lion 897

Pearson
Hammerandtongs 743

Pegoretti
Responsorium 638

Peka
531 199

Pelizzoli
Curdomo
  Pista 648

Peugeot
Christophe 58
PY10FC Carbone 186
Sitting Bull 205
Tom Simpson 120

Phillips
Duplex Tricycle 45

Pierce
Arrow 50

Pinarello
Banesto 274
Dogma 559
Dogma Visconti 853
Graal 568
Montello
  SLX 194
Paris 308
Prince 395
Swan 326
Sword 295

Pipedream
Sirius 650B 610

Pivot
429C 759
Les 757
Mach 5.7
  Carbon 655
Vault 945

Planet X
Jack Flash 312
Kaffenback 430
Pro Carbon 514
Stealth Pro 468

Porsche
FS Evolution 384

Pratik Ghosh
Cycle Rickshaw 716

Premier
A93 41

Puch
E-Bike 8 545

Punnett
Sociable 48

Pyga
OneTen29 840
OneTwenty650 929

Qhubeka
Buffalo 842

Quadrant
Cross Roller 47
Dwarf 32

Quintana Roo
Illicito 730
Superform 224

Racer
Rosa 639

Ragley
Blue Pig 519
Marley 763

Raleigh
531 Team 148
Activator 254
Arena 143
Banana 258
Bomber 166
Burner 181
Chopper 120
Clubman 200
Commando 136
Crane Special 199
Grifter 139
Kite 118
M Trax Team Edition 306
Maverick 200
Pro Burner 175
Randonneur 195
Record Ace 71
Record Ace 170
Runabout 116
Superbe 93

Shamrock
Celtic Cross 814

Shand
Stoater 638

Shed 6
Stroopwafel 815

Shelby
Lindy Flyer 65

Sinclair
A-Blke 460
C5 188

Singer
Gentleman's
  Roadster 48

Sironval
Sportplex 80

Six-Eleven
CX/Brevet 681

Skoot
Case 386

Slingshot
MTB 239

Smith and Co
Long John 182

Smith Starley
Ariel 28

Soensport
TT Special 116

Soulcraft
Tradesman 797

Souplesse
Bamboo 900

Spa Cycles
Audax 664

Sparkbrook
No. 7 Racing Safety 42

Specialized
Allez 171
Big Hit DH 404
Cancellara 575
Crux Pro 612
Demo 8 443
Egger 211
Enduro 29 939
Enduro SX Trail 437
Epic FSR 403
Epic Ultimate 247
Epic S-Works Kulhavý 705
Epic World Cup 938
McLaren S-Works
  Venge 604
P Slope 712
Roubaix SL2 498
S-Works Demo 8 711
S-Works FSR 286
S-Works Roubaix 915
S-Works Tarmac E5 419
S-Works TTR 528
Shiv 532
Status 713
Stumpjumper 179
Stumpjumper FSR
  Evo 582
Stumpjumper M2 247
SX Trail 525
Tarmac SL4 944
Transition 511
Turbo 702
Venge Cav 100 855

Speedhound
Only One 681

Speedwell
Titalite 134

Spin Günter
Mai Special 483
Spitfire 628

Standard Bykes
STA 243

Stanton
Slackline 706

Star
Combination Roadster 45

Steve Potts
Mountain Bike 816

Stevens
Sonora 731

Steyr
Waffenrad 51

Stijl
Lear's All Fast Mountain
  29er 850

Stinner
29er Rohloff Belt Drive 682

Storck
Aernario Platinum 852
Raddar 612

Strida
1 211

Strong
Twentieth Anniversary 682

Sun
Solo 156

Sunn
Radical Plus 337

Surly
Karate Monkey 427
Krampus 730
Pugsley 420

Swallow
Toucan 302

Swatch
S Bike 227

Swift
Detritovore 837
Safety Bicycle 35

Swiftwalker
Velocipede 25

Swobo
Sanchez 575

Sycip
Java Boy 683

Tensor
Rudi Altig 201

Tern
Swoop 700

Terra Nova
Strawberry 131

Thanet
Silverlight 97

The Light Blue
Kings 613

Thorn
Explorer 420
Me'n'U2 741

Thorn
Raven 848

Ti Cycles
CarGoAway 879

Tifosi
CK7 643

Time
Speeder Veloce 589

Titus
Exogrid 519

Tokyo Fixed
Wide Open 890

Tom Ritchey
MTB 140

Tomac
Diplomat 610

Tommasini
Carbolight
  XLR 486

Tonic
Epic 1 Crusher 906

1820–1978

FROM HOBBYHORSE
TO THOROUGHBRED

The start of a personal transport revolution

SWIFTWALKER Velocipede

1820 • Early strider • Germany • Foot-propelled wooden two-wheeler

It was a beginning of sorts, but the forerunner of the bicycle was ungainly, dangerous, and doomed to fail.

Commonly referred to as the Swiftwalker, it was a wooden human-powered two-wheeled vehicle that first appeared on the footpaths of Mannheim, Germany, in 1820. The wheels were in-line, and propulsion was provided by the rider, who pushed himself and the contraption along with his feet. There were no pedals, and the handlebar was connected to the front wheel to provide steering.

The Swiftwalker concept also arose more or less simultaneously in various corners of mainland Europe and Great Britain, including a version by the London coach maker and inventor Denis Johnson, who fashioned an elegantly crafted wooden frame with large wheels. In the United States, on June 26, 1819, a patent was awarded to W. K. Clarkson, Jr., of New York for a two-wheeled human-powered vehicle, but a fire in the U.S. Patent Office in 1836 destroyed the only known drawings, and Clarkson never built a prototype of his invention.

Interest in this new mode of transport, capable of more than doubling the average walking speed across level ground to around 10 mph (16 kph), was high. However, the Swiftwalker's popularity turned out to be more of a passing fad, as this recreational toy for the wealthy was the cause of a seeming pandemic of collisions with pedestrians. In New York City, a law was passed banning the Swiftwalker from all pathways and public places.

Heavy, cumbersome, and inefficient over bumpy ground, the Swiftwalker had almost disappeared by the end of the 1820s. Nevertheless, this failed experiment evidently contained the germ of an idea. History shows that the Swiftwalker was the parent of all the other bikes in this book and many more besides. **BS**

"The rider perched on a seat between two similarly sized wheels, and using the feet, propelled the bicycle a bit like a scooter."

David Fiedler

◄ The earliest bikes were a cumbersome combination of cart and hobbyhorse.

MICHAUX Michaudine

1867 • Roadster • France • First pedal-powered bike

By 1867, many daring young Frenchmen had been introduced to the draisine or dandy horse—a two-wheeled "running machine" on which riders used their feet to scoot along and brake. If they gained enough momentum, they could sit on the seat and roll for a while. Some draisines even had primitive steering.

It seems that in that year, Pierre Michaux transformed this pavement toy into the forerunner of the bicycle. In his Paris workshop, he added a simple pedaling system to the front wheel of a draisine.

Then, with the brothers Aimé, René, and Marius Olivier, Michaux formed a company to produce the Michaudine velocipede. This had an elegant serpentine cast-iron frame, handlebars, vertical forks, and a "spoon" brake. The wheels—the front slightly larger than the rear—were made of wood; the tires were iron, like those on horse-drawn carriages. The rider perched uncomfortably on a leather pad.

Bike historians, however, aren't sure the pedal idea was Michaux's. It could have been the concept of his son Ernest or of Pierre Lallement, a French carriage builder from Nancy, who also worked with the Oliviers.

What is certain, though, is that the Michaudine was the first pedal-powered bike to be mass produced. It prompted the world's first bicycle craze, which spread from France through the whole of Europe and across the Atlantic to the United States. These primitive boneshakers were all the rage for a couple of years, until the complaints of frightened pedestrians largely punctured the first bicycle bubble. **SH**

VELOCIPEDE Tricycle

1870 • Tricycle • Europe • Early treadle-powered three-wheeler

In 1815, an eruption of the Indonesian volcano Mount Tambora created a plume of ash so large that the Northern Hemisphere was plunged into darkness, making 1816 "The Year Without Summer." Across Europe, crops failed, the price of oats soared, and horses were slaughtered for their meat. The last development created a need for new modes of transportation, and in June 1817 German inventor Karl von Drais unveiled his Laufmaschine, the world's first balance bicycle. The following year, the word velocipede ("fast foot") was coined by French inventor Nicéphore Niépce, whose development of Drais' original incorporated an adjustable saddle.

By 1851, most velocipedes were three-wheelers with rear-wheel drive, tiller steering, and rear-sprung suspension. The advent of the pedal and front-wheel drive saw their popularity explode, and by the mid-1870s they were firmly established in Europe, Britain, and the United States. Two-wheeled velocipedes—nicknamed "boneshakers"—emerged in France in 1863 and were popular in the United States from the late 1860s. With wooden seats, steel frames, and wooden wheels with iron tires, they were so difficult to ride that they were used almost exclusively indoors on flat, even surfaces. The new sport of velocipede cycling certainly had its risks, with the rider poised, according to Charles Pratt in his 1879 manual *The American Bicycler*, "in an unnatural position, thrusting out his feet before him for propulsion, only able to keep his equilibrium by constant and laborious effort." **BS**

SMITH STARLEY Ariel

1871 • Roadster • UK • First bike with wire-spoked wheels

OTTO Dicycle

1880 • Roadster • UK • Treadle-powered twin-track bike

Early bikes had wooden wheels with metal tires like those on horse-drawn carriages. They were heavy to push and uncomfortable to ride.

James Starley had a gift for mechanical problem solving, which he first demonstrated in his work with sewing machines. In 1871, he saw an early French boneshaker bike and had the idea of increasing its comfort by adding wheels with spokes that were individually tensioned between hub and inner rim.

Wire-spoked wheels had been invented sixty-two years previously by British engineer George Cayley for use in gliders, but Starley was the first to fit them on a bike. This development accelerated the transformation

> *". . . he will be remembered as the man chiefly instrumental in establishing [the industry]."*
>
> *James Starley obituary, 1881*

of bikes from curiosities and toys for the rich into a viable transportation option. Starley thus has a reasonable claim to be the father of an industry.

His Ariel had a much larger front wheel than the old boneshakers, and was the first bike to be steered with a center-pivot system. Bikes of this type later became known as penny-farthings, but were called at the time simply "ordinary" or "high" bicycles.

Despite the inefficiencies of its design, the Ariel was very popular. Starley's wheel design was soon being licensed to other manufacturers.

Starley went into business with watch maker William Borthwick Smith to make Ariel bikes (and sewing machines). Wire-spoked wheels rapidly became the norm for bikes, automobiles, and trucks. **SH**

In one workshop in London, the Quadrant Cycle Company was trying to make improvements to the basic design of the bicycle. In the building next door was the Otto Cycle Company.

If Quadrant was experimental, Otto was completely bizarre. Some historians have since suggested that the two companies were probably connected—they must each have known what the other was working on.

Edward Otto invented and patented the Dicycle as a safer alternative to the towering terrors of the ordinary bicycle (later known as the penny-farthing). His bike had two huge 56-in. (142-cm) wheels that were mounted side by side and connected by a sturdy axle. For balance, the rider used a slender trailing arm with a rubber roller on the end to stop himself (or, more unusually for the period, herself) from toppling over backward.

The rider sat between the wheels, above the axle, and pedaled using a treadle-style system fixed to the axle by long rods. The treadles turned pulleys at each end, which drove the road wheels via rubber belts.

Within reach of the rider were two levers with which either of the pulleys could be disengaged. This basic form of steering was achieved by stopping the drive to one of the wheels while the other continued to turn. There was a simple hand brake lever for each hand too, each connected to a different wheel.

Edward Otto's creation was indubitably safer than the ordinary bike—although that was by no means an extravagant claim. When the Birmingham Small Arms Company branched out from its main line in producing weaponry for the British army to build Dicycles commercially, they became the most popular bikes to date in history. **SH**

BICYCLE AND TRICYCLE SUPPLY ASSOCIATION Plectocycle

1884 • Tricycle • UK • Innovation-loaded telescopic tricycle

". . . by loosening a set screw it will pass through an ordinary doorway without taking any portion apart."

Vade Mecum *1885*

The Plectocycle is historically significant as a transitional product between the doomed ordinary bike and the emerging safety bike, and for its use of technology that was later adopted throughout the motor industry.

Based in Holborn, London, the Bicycle and Tricycle Supply Association that marketed the Plectocycle declared itself "so confident that our machines rank among the very best made, that we have determined to send them out, trial free, before purchase."

Its faith in the product was not misplaced. Smooth-rolling 40-in. (101-cm) ordinary-sized wheels were teamed with patented rubber cushions on the 20-in. (50.8-cm) front wheel and steering handles so that the "comfort and even health of the rider are vastly increased." Pritchard's patent "double driving gear" differential transmission allowed tight turning with two driven wheels; the wheels could also telescope inward to get through narrow doors or gateways.

Because there was no crossbar to catch in skirts, tricycles were particularly popular with women. In 1881, even Queen Victoria purchased a brace of tricycles (Salvos, not Plectocycles). Ultimately, though, three-wheelers could not compete with two-wheeled safety cycles, and over the following decade the third wheel came to be regarded as redundant. As Professor H. Ansot wrote rather harshly in the *Overland Monthly Journal* (1895): "The tricycle has never at any time been recognized as a useful or beautiful thing. It looks too much like an instrument more fitted for invalids or poltroons than a sporting outfit." What Ansot could not have foreseen, however, was that original Plectocycles—and the numerous facsimile reproductions—are still ridable with pleasure today. The same cannot be said of most of the two-wheelers of the time that he claimed to prefer. **GK**

QUADRANT Dwarf

1885 • Roadster • UK • Intriguing tricycle with horizontal forks

The brothers William and Walter Lloyd originally established the Quadrant Cycle Company in Birmingham, England, in 1883.

Their company produced bikes with shaft-driven rear wheels, seats with trapeze-style suspension systems, and ingenious lever-operated braking solutions. The Quadrant tricycle of the early 1880s had a chain-driven rear axle and a well-sprung seat over the rear wheels.

Most significantly, the Lloyds also produced this prototype safety bike, which, when viewed in the light of subsequent history, appears to mark the start of the great leap forward in bike design and technology.

The front wheel of the Quadrant Dwarf was slightly smaller than the rear wheel, and both wheels had an elaborate spoke pattern. Pedaling drove the rear wheel via a chain, and a handlebar-mounted lever operated a brake on the back wheel. The seatpost had a 90-degree bend backward to enable the sprung seat to be positioned over the back wheel.

The handlebars steered a vertical front tube, which acted via a complex arrangement involving a pair of horizontal front forks.

This alternative to the center-pivot system being developed by the Starleys was excessively elaborate and did not catch on with the bike-buying public. Undeterred, however, the Lloyds continued with experiments that included the attachment of a Minerva petrol engine to the down tube of a heavy-duty bicycle. **SH**

PAUSEY Pioneer

1886 • Cross-frame dwarf safety bike • UK • Innovative alternative to diamond-framed safety bikes

Herbert Pausey may not have been the first manufacturer to design the cross frame, but on September 6, 1884, he and his business partner Charles Crowden became the first people to patent it.

The simplicity of the design was evident, with a tube joining the rear hub to the steering head and crossed at right angles by a vertical tube with the saddle at the top and crank bracket below. The frame, however, was not braced or strengthened. When under heavy pedaling, the pulling on the chain tended to bring the centers of the driving wheel and the crank axle together, thus laying bare the frame's inherent structural weakness.

The designers soon recognized the need for chainstays and seatstays to triangulate the frame, and within a year these features had been installed on a new model, the Pioneer Safety, which was slimmed down and further improved by reductions in both the diameter and the thickness of the tubes.

The Pausey Pioneer struggled to attract publicity because it appeared at almost exactly the same time as Karl Benz's three-wheel Benz Patent-Motorwagen, which first appeared on July 3, 1886, on the Ringstrasse in Mannheim, Germany, and hit the headlines all over the world. Although journalists correctly anticipated that the automobile was the shape of things to come, the bike was in its way almost as momentous because it was the first pedal-powered machine to make use of the great innovative device that only subsequently became known as the cross frame. **BS**

SWIFT Safety Bicycle

1886 • Roadster • UK • One of the first safety bike designs

By the 1880s, ordinary bikes were well established but remained dangerous to ride. If cycling was ever to develop from an eccentric indulgence of the rich into a universal transportation method, the odds against completing a bike journey without mishap or injury needed drastic shortening. This urgent requirement inspired a flurry of new designs as the safety bicycle rapidly evolved to eclipse the big-wheelers.

It was generally agreed that bikes needed smaller wheels, and that the rear wheel should be chain-driven. Although chains would make such bikes heavier, they would be easier to ride and could be braked more efficiently. The term "safety bicycle" was coined by John Kemp Starley (nephew of James Starley, creator of the Ariel), who would go on to build the Rover, the first commercially successful bike of this type.

The Coventry Machinists Company used this configuration and this name on its Swift brand safety bicycles. Acclaimed then and now as works of art, these machines had sleek geometrical lines and a diamond frame setup of the type that still features on most bicycles today. Front and rear mudguards were part of the frame build, and the saddle was spring-loaded, offering the rider an unprecedented level of comfort on rough surfaces.

Swift was ahead of its time in other ways too. It was one of the first bike manufacturers to promote the now commonly acknowledged link between cycling and physical fitness. This machine was promoted with ads featuring the slogan: "Gold that buys health can never be ill spent."

While the design of and the materials used for performance bikes have since moved on exponentially, most utility bikes still share much of their DNA with these early safety bicycles. **DB**

TRIGWELL & CO. Regent

1886 • Tricycle • UK • One of the earliest unisex tricycles

In Britain in the late 1880s there were more tricycles than bicycles—not because tricycles were inherently more popular, but because, in part, they were more expensive than bicycles, and so the upper classes perceived them as exclusive. Husbands also considered them safer for their wives to ride than two-wheelers. Industrial tricycles had been used since the 1870s by tradesmen across England to transport goods in storage boxes mounted between the rear wheels. By the mid-1880s, more than 120 different models of tricycles from in excess of twenty bicycle companies were crisscrossing the nation.

Trigwell's Regent full-sized tricycle came with a supporting cross frame that gave strength to the

". . . the makers claim it can be ridden 1,000 mi [1,600 km] without oiling or adjusting."

Stanley Show review

seatpost without the need for a top bar. The unisex design obviated two different models. It had 26-in. (66-cm) wheels front and rear, with semi-oval rims, pneumatic tires, and a rarely seen 1-in. (2.4-cm) pitch block chain. It also had an anti-vibration handlebar on a special ball-bearing head that minimized friction. Its durability was demonstrated in 1893 by Frederick Thomas Bidlake, who rode one nonstop for twenty-four hours around a London velodrome and covered 410 mi (656 km)—a world record—at the end of which the bike required no maintenance.

The days of the tricycle were numbered, however, by the imminent arrival on the market of the safety bicycle for which both sexes had been longing. **BS**

◁ Foot pegs allow the Swift's rider to take their feet off the pedals for downhills.

EAGLE Ordinary

1888 • Reverse penny-farthing • USA • Small front-wheeled design

The ordinary bikes that were all the rage at the end of the nineteenth century had a major safety flaw: Riders could easily be flipped forward over the handlebars. Such spills—known as "headers"—could cause serious injury, as the rider was perched high above the front wheel and had around 5 ft (1.5 m) to fall.

The enthusiasts in Stamford, Connecticut, who created the Eagle solved this problem quite simply by reversing the positions of the wheels and putting the large one at the back and the small one at the front. The rider sat above the big wheel and pedaled it through a direct-drive system at the hub. The front tube was enormous, extending at 45 degrees down to meet the backward-curving forks and the small front wheel, which steered the bike.

Features included a saddle with adjustable suspension, a handbrake, a one-piece "cow-horn" handlebar, and ball bearings on every moving joint. The whole machine weighed 44 lb (20 kg).

Although there was no danger of headers, riders could fall off backward when going uphill. The Eagle was also hard to mount and dismount. To get on board, riders had to push the bike hard and run alongside it, jump onto the pedal when it reached the down position, and, as the pedal rose, lever themselves onto the seat as they rolled along. Dismounting involved the same process in reverse, again using the pedal as a step while on the move.

The Eagle soared briefly, but was soon grounded by the advent of the safety machine. **SH**

ROVER Safety

1890 • Roadster • UK • First chain-driven rear-wheel bike

After John Starley joined his uncle James' company in Coventry, England, they and William Sutton set about improving the original design of James'ordinary bike.

After James' death in 1881, John and William produced three new models. The first, in 1884, had an awkward steering system; the second, in 1885, had unequal-sized wheels. Their third, the 1888 model, became the classic Rover Safety.

This was the bike that established many features still used on bicycles today, including pedals below the saddle that powered the back wheel through a sprocket and chain, and handlebars controlling a fork-supported front wheel.

With equally sized 26-in. (66-cm) wheels, a low seating position, and a strong, compact triangular tubular frame, the Rover Safety transformed bicycles from dangerous contraptions into comfortable machines that people of all ages could safely use for everyday transportation.

Soon Rover bicycles were breaking long-distance speed records and enjoying a sales boom. Within a few years, ordinary bikes had become rarely seen oddities.

Indeed, the make was so successful that John Starley changed his company's name to that of the bike. Rover went on to produce motorbikes and cars. John Starley did not live to see this, as he died in 1901 at the age of just 47.

Rover stopped making bikes in 1926, but its name survives today in Range Rover and Land Rover, which are now subsidiaries of Tata of India. **SH**

ORDINARY Penny-Farthing

1891 • Ordinary • UK • The penny-farthing's exciting ride outweighed its many inherent risks

In Victorian Britain, they called them spider wheels, high-wheelers, or, most commonly, "ordinary" bicycles. Their common characteristic was a leading wheel that was several times larger than the trailing wheel.

Although the first bikes to be configured in this way were produced by James Starley in 1871, it would be anachronistic to call his creations penny-farthings. The term was not invented until the bikes were almost out of fashion and rendered redundant by the advent of the safety bicycle.

The name was derived from two British coins of the period with comparably different sizes—the nineteenth-century penny was 1³⁄₁₀ in. (34 mm) in diameter; the farthing (value: one-quarter of one penny) was only just over ⅘ in. (22 mm) across.

The penny-farthing bicycle design was inspired by the wish to develop a pedal-powered machine that covered the greatest distance in the fastest possible time. Prior to the advent of gears, the only way to achieve this was to increase the size of the front wheel. The big wheel on Starley's original measured 5 ft (1.5 m) across; trailing wheels could be as little as 12 in. (30 cm) in diameter.

The Pope Manufacturing Company of Boston described its Columbia penny-farthing as an "ever-saddled horse that eats nothing." One ad claimed that it could cover a mile in 2 minutes and 43 seconds; another boasted "205 miles [328 km] in 22 hours." One rider, C. Waller, covered 1,404 mi (2,246 km) on a penny-farthing in six days.

Clearly penny-farthings could cover vast distances in record time, but their design was too unstable to succeed. They were ungainly and hair-raisingly dangerous; that anyone ever rode them is testimony to the undesirability of the only pre–safety cycle alternative: the dreaded boneshaker. **BS**

"Hence the origin of the term 'breakneck speed,' since a crash often produced devastating results."

David Fiedler, Bikes—An Illustrated History

◁ The start of a penny-farthing race in a New York stadium in the 1890s.

CRYPTO Bantam

1893 • Roadster • UK • Ingenious front-wheel drive bicycle

The Crypto Bantam was a milestone in bicycle design; the evolutionary link between the giddy heights of the penny-farthing and the coming era of the safety bikes.

It first appeared when wheeled transport was beginning to take off everywhere. In 1891, 150,000 bicycles were sold in the United States alone, doubling its cycling population. Here at last was a bike that was easy to mount and dismount without the need for a step, and with a lower center of gravity too. This was all made possible by a single glorious piece of engineering: a revolutionary epicyclic geared hub designed in 1892 by William Shaw and William Sydenham, which could be "altered from the higher to the lower power . . . in an hour or so by any competent mechanic." With one full turn of the crank, the front wheel could make up to two and three-quarter revolutions, and the adustable gearing ratio—forerunner of the modern three-speed—allowed the introduction of a smaller front wheel. This lowered the Bantam's overall height, thus making it safer for all those who preferred to leave the penny-farthing to the young and adventurous.

The Bantam, with its weldless tubular steel frame and hollow rims, was one of the last hurrahs of the front-drive chainless bicycle, which was soon eclipsed by the rear-wheeled chain-driven machine. Three years later, Crypto Cycles proprietor I. W. Boothroyd released the Alpha Bantam, his final attempt at holding back the inevitable tide that saw front-wheel drive bicycles reduced to a footnote in cycling history. **BS**

PREMIER A93

1893 • Roadster • UK • Early helical tube-framed bike

The Premier Cycle Company of Coventry, England, was the first bike maker to fit a frame with helical tubing, which reduced weight and increased strength.

Premier's first helical bikes were experimental; their frames were too light and thin for extensive practical use. But the A93 was an altogether sturdier production weighing 32 lb (14.5 kg) and with 28-in. (71-cm) wheels shod with Dunlop 1¾-in. (4.4-cm) detachable tires.

The model pictured here features a radical design with leaf springs connecting the six spokes in each wheel to the outer rim to provide a smoother ride. The geometry of the frame was certainly modern, but the details were somewhat period. For example, the front forks featured a protruding footrest on either side. Premier's advertising proudly listed the A93's roller chain, mudguards, and brake. The last was a strange contraption involving a long lever parallel to the handlebars: Pull the lever up, and it pushed on a rod that pressed down a disk on top of the front tire.

The A93 was one of a range of Premier bikes that was heavily promoted. The slightly more expensive A1 model came with an all-encompassing chain case that had to be unscrewed to access the mechanical parts of the bike. It was so sturdy that it acted as a back-stay tube. Premier boasted of the lightness of its Racer model—just 20 lb (9 kg)—and claimed that this was because of the use of patented helical tubing throughout. What the company didn't mention, however, was that the weight reduction had been achieved by dispensing with a brake altogether. **SH**

SPARKBROOK No. 7 Racing Safety

1893 • Roadster • UK • Early race-tuned safety bicycle

Founded in 1893 in Coventry, England, the Sparkbrook Manufacturing Company quickly gained a reputation for quality bicycles with an uncommon attention to detail and a high-grade finish. It began by building ordinaries (penny-farthings) and tricycles, and then released the Sparkbrook No. 7 Racing Safety.

The No. 7 featured some tantalizing hints of sports accessories to come, such as the lightweight saddle and extended swept-back handlebars that compelled the rider to lean forward, thus foreshadowing the racing-style posture many years before the first organized competitions.

There was an oiler at the end of the down tube (a nice touch), the frame was an early diamond shape,

". . . will satisfy every cyclist whose ambition is to possess a sound and trustworthy mount."

Sparkbrook brochure, 1893

the chain was on the left-hand side, and there were no brake lights, lamp brackets, or mudguards—intentional streamlining, perhaps?

The 1890s saw a quantum leap in cycling technology: The freewheel signaled the end of fixed gears and enabled coasting; caliper rim brakes increased braking efficiency, and the first multi-gear derailleur systems appeared. The Sparkbrook No. 7 Racing Safety came with Dunlop pneumatic racing tires. It would be another two years before pneumatics became standard in the safety bicycle industry, and they did much to increase the popularity of the No. 7. They were such an improvement on the old solid rubber tires that they heralded the dawn of the Golden Age of Cycling. **BS**

GLADIATOR Tandem

1896 • Track bike • France • Five-seater pace setter

The Gladiator Tandem's main claim to fame is its appearance in the promotional poster—a detail of which is shown here—commissioned by the makers from the celebrated Art Nouveau painter Henri de Toulouse-Lautrec.

The Gladiator featured an intriguing lever chain, designed by William Simpson, that comprised a string of linked protruding triangles. The inside of the chain was driven by the chainring in the normal way, but the rear cog was driven by the protruding tips of the triangles. The triangles amplified the pedaling energy.

For several years, Simpson promoted his idea vigorously, hiring Toulouse-Lautrec to paint it and the top cyclists of the day to ride it. Constant Huret was the solo rider shown in Lautrec's poster, drafting behind the tandem. Both bikes were clearly fitted with the Simpson chains even though they were not strong enough for tandem use.

What cannot be seen in the painting, however, is that the Gladiator was a quint—a five-seater that was used to create a massive windbreak for the following riders and thus give them an advantage over rivals in the competition.

In one race witnessed by 20,000 spectators in London in 1896, Simpson put the five-seater at the head of his Gladiator Pacers team to pit their lever-chain-driven bikes against rivals on machines with conventional chains. Taking advantage of the tandem's slipstream, the Gladiators won, but most experts realized that the team had triumphed not because of the inherent superiority of the chains, but because the other team's leading tandems had been smaller three- or -four seaters. Within a few years Simpson's extravagant claims were largely discredited and his chain was forgotten. **SH**

Henri de Toulouse-Lautrec publicity poster from the late 1890s. ▶

STAR Combination Roadster

1896 • Tandem • UK • Two-seater bike with rear steering

While the conventional modern arrangement is to put the larger rider at the front of a tandem, this hasn't always been the case. Some early bike builders thought that the design would work better with the stronger rider in the rear and the less powerful rider in front.

Founded by Edward Lisle, an early and successful cycle racer, and based in Wolverhampton, England, the Star Cycle Company was highly successful in the 1890s, and by the turn of the century it was producing around 10,000 cycles a year. The Star slogan was: "Light, graceful, and strong."

In addition to a range of men's and women's solo safety bicycles, Star offered a pair of two-seaters: a normal, single-steering tandem, and this Combination Roadster, which was one of the first machines of its type to cater for a less powerful cyclist (usually a woman or a child) at the front. This design allowed the man behind to assist with the steering and the pedaling. Positioning the lady in front was thought at the time to allow her more dignity and honor than being at the back—communicating the same cultural sentiment as "ladies first."

The design included a set of rods connecting the second handlebars with the sides of the front forks. A model of this early bike is currently on display in the National Cycle Collection in Llandrindod Wells, Wales.

Shortly after the appearance of Star's Combination Roadster, similar rear-steering tandems were produced in the United States, first by Geneva in Ohio and then by Stearns of New York.

By the end of the nineteenth century, Star was experimenting with motorized transport. The outbreak of the First World War in Europe in 1914 curtailed the company's interest in bicycles; Star subsequently concentrated on motorbikes and automobiles. **SH**

PHILLIPS Duplex Tricyle

1896 • Tricycle • UK • Side-by-side tandem trike

Sometime in the 1890s, British engineer Ephraim Phillips of Birmingham, England, invented and patented the Duplex Tricycle. Like the Sociable bike being developed around the same time in Canada, it allowed two people to cycle side by side. While the Sociable's single rear wheel struggled to cope with the weight of two riders, the Duplex had two rear wheels, which overcame both this and the problems of mounting and dismounting.

Phillips' tandem trike was a practical design. The front wheel did the steering via a set of handlebars held by both riders. They sat on separate seats at the back, each above a rear wheel as on a normal bike, and each with pedals and a chain driving the rear axle.

> *"Its ease in running is really remarkable—along level roads no effort is required to propel it."*
> Nineteenth-century buyer's testimonial letter to Phillips

Manufacturers were excited about the potential of two-people bikes. They were seen as "courting bikes" on which men and women could be together in couples without arousing adverse comment in an age when unchaperoned meetings between members of the opposite sex were frowned upon. And being side by side was more intimate than one behind the other. With one hand free, the more daring couples may even have been able to hold hands while riding.

Phillips built the Duplex to order, adapting the design to the measurements of each purchaser. Sadly, however, the Duplex was commercially unsuccessful and is now extremely rare. One of only two known still to exist is displayed at the UK's National Cycle Collection in Llandrindod Wells, Wales. **SH**

◁ The Combination Roadster was one of the first tandems.

QUADRANT Cross Roller
1897 • Roadster • UK • Shaft-driven race bike

In the late nineteenth century, few standards had been established for bikes. Engineers were experimenting and testing every aspect of the "safety" bicycle to see if they could improve on the design and thereby steal a march on their commercial rivals.

Walter Lloyd and William Priest of the Birmingham, England-based Quadrant Cycle Company came up with their chainless bike in 1897. The duo secured a patent for a shaft-drive system for the bike.

Their "cross-roller gear" transferred the pedaling action via a bevel gear into a rotating shaft that met another bevel gear at the rear hub. This in turn transferred the twisting motion through 90 degrees again to directly power the rear wheel. The rear cog was arranged with a roller clutch on the rear hub and this acted as a freewheel, but there was no differential gearing. Backpedaling could act as a brake, although there was also a front rod-operated rim brake.

This configuration had several advantages over earlier systems: there was no chain to break or come loose, it was more immediately responsive, it was low maintenance, and it was very quiet. Nevertheless, it eventually lost out to the chain because the bevels or cross rollers sapped some of the rider's power and the rear wheel was more difficult to remove. The cross-roller units were smaller than normal chain sprockets and had to be far more precisely manufactured. This meant they were more expensive to make, and therefore to buy.

Three versions of the Quadrant were produced: a Full Roadster, a Light Roadster, and a Road Racer. The last named was supplied with a Brooks B10 saddle, rat-trap pedals, and narrow racing tires. It cost a hefty £16 and 16 shillings ($26), a fortune at a time when the national average wage in Britain was less than £50 ($80) a year. **SH**

"It is a fact that the Quadrant is the best hill climber ever constructed, which fact is attested by all riders of it."

Quadrant publicity, 1900

◁ Shaft-drive bikes have appeared throughout cycling history.

SINGER Gentleman's Roadster

1899 • Roadster • UK • The smoothest ride one could hope for in the bumpy 1890s

George Singer (1847–1909) served an apprenticeship with the marine engineering company John Penn & Sons based in Greenwich, London, and then moved in 1869 to Coventry, England, where he worked as a sewing machine finisher with the Coventry Machinists Company. He developed an interest in bicycles, and in 1875 set up his own bicycle-building business, Singer & Co. He sold one of his early machines to the Queen of Portugal, and thereafter prospered financially and socially. In 1896 he renamed his business the Singer Cycle Co. Ltd.

Singer's earliest products were ordinaries (penny-farthings), the first models of which he called his

"Singer was one of the three biggest bicycle manufacturers in England."

Maarten Bokslag

Challenge series. These were made from hollow steel tubing and had rubber-filled U-shaped metal rims.

Singer then came up with the idea of raking the rear forks of his bicycles—first backward, a design advance that made steering easier and gave greater stability, and then forward on the front forks, which minimized the shocks and bumps of late-nineteenth-century roads. Singer's curved forks remain in use to this day.

Singer's 1899 26-in. (66-cm) Gentleman's Roadster had his patented fork design, and came equipped with mudguards front and rear, cruiser-style swept-back handlebars, a rear rack, a rather chunky-looking chain, a steering lock bolt housed within a leather strap attached to the handlebar, and a cylindrical map holder below the saddle. **BS**

PUNNETT Sociable

1899 • Tandem • UK • Side-by-side two-seater

A two-seater bike doesn't have to place one person behind the other; it was possible, as early bike builders discovered, to make cycles that accommodated two riders side by side.

The origins of the idea are hazy. A rare side-by-side tricycle was built by Ephraim Phillips in England in the 1890s, and one image from sometime in the nineteenth century appears to show German inventor Karl Jatho and his sister sharing a journey on a bizarre contraption with a small front wheel and a giant rear wheel that is taller than either rider. The riders sit on either side of the huge wheel, each with their own set of handlebars. It looks as if Jatho is supplying pedal power directly to the rear wheel.

A more practical proposition was shown in a charming nineteenth-century photo of a pair of newlyweds departing for their honeymoon bedecked with flowers on a side-by-side bike. This could be the Sociable, which was patented in 1896 by Albert Weaver of Ontario, Canada, and built by the Punnett Cycle Company of Rochester, New York.

The picture shows an anonymous Sociable that uses a single conventional bike frame. The two seats are mounted on sub frames cantilevered off either side of the frame. Of the twin handlebars, only one set moves and steers the bike with a fixed rod and lever system. Both riders pedal in unison via a cunning extended bell crank mounted through a conventional crank bearing.

The design was by no means perfect. Mounting and dismounting required a series of tricky moves, and the demands put on the rear tire made it susceptible to frequent blowouts. On the plus side, Punnett claimed that a single person could ride the bike, by moving one of the saddles into a central position and steering with the inside grip of each handlebar. **SH**

This Sociable was one of the first bicycles made for two. ▶

TRIBUNE Blue Streak

1899 • Roadster • USA • Charles "Mile-a-minute" Murphy's bike

PIERCE Arrow

1900 • Roadster • USA • Innovative bicycle without a chain

It had a single high-speed 104-in. (264-cm) gear; a slim, lightweight steel frame; narrow, slick race tires; early drop handlebars; and no brakes at all. The Tribune Blue Streak was the bike chosen by daredevil amateur cyclist Charles Murphy for an attempt to ride a mile in a minute in 1899. Murphy had boasted that no locomotive—the fastest vehicle in the world at the time—could go faster than him on his Tribune. It seemed a ludicrous claim, and a Long Island railway operator challenged him on it.

Murphy, who had a basic understanding of aerodynamics, insisted the train's rear car should be fitted with an extra cowling to create a massive windbreak. The center of 3 mi (5 km) of track was given a smooth wooden path. Murphy would try to pedal in the slipstream of the 60-mph (96-kph) train.

At first, Murphy stayed a few feet behind the train but was distracted by a shout and slipped back 15 ft (4.5 m) into turbulent air behind. Somehow he pedaled hard enough to catch the train again and was inches behind as it crossed the mile marker. The train slowed and Murphy crashed into it.

He recovered to hear his time for the mile was 57.8 seconds. From that moment until he died in 1950, he was known as "Mile-a-minute Murphy." **SH**

The end of the nineteenth century was an exciting period of innovation in the world of the bicycle. The cushion frame and the coaster brake were introduced in 1898; in 1899 came collet-type adjustable bearings for seats and handlebars; and in 1900 a new shaft-drive mechanism appeared. This employed beveled gears to turn the rear wheel without the need for a chain (a big selling point in an era of trousers and long, heavily frilled skirts) and promised a quieter and cleaner ride.

The George N. Pierce Cycle Company of Buffalo, New York, incorporated this new technology into its new 1900 chainless bike. It also included most of the other refinements of the time, including coaster brakes, a nickel-plated steel frame, and leaf springs on either side of the front fork (a Pierce innovation). A telescopic section containing a coil spring in the upper end of the upper rear fork also gave rudimentary rear-wheel suspension. The spring, the patented invention of the Hygienic Wheel Company, lay behind what Pierce called its "hygienic cushion frame."

The Pierce Chainless is now understandably sought after by collectors for its array of features (shaft drive, rear suspension, leaf springs) and because of its connection with the Pierce-Arrow automobile company. **BS**

BSA Mark IV General Service
1901 • Utility bike • UK • First World War army-issue bicycle

STEYR Waffenrad
1902 • Utility bike • Austria • Austria's iconic national army bike

Having originally formed to build the finest weapons of war, a short outbreak of peace after the Boer War saw the Birmingham Small Arms factory turn its production lines and craftsmen toward the manufacture of bicycles and their fittings. With the clouds of war gathering once more, it seemed they might have to build both.

In 1901, the army adopted a standard bicycle, General Service, complete with fittings including a bell, lamp, pump, tool kit, and rifle clips. This was produced to the same specification and soon several companies including BSA, Swift, Sunbeam, Raleigh, Humber, and Royal Enfield were supplying complete bicycles to equip the newly formed Army Cyclist Corps.

The speed and mobility of the Cyclist Corps would be of great importance in the early part of the First World War, achieving great advantage in reconnaissance missions and being vitally important for communication. Indeed the first British fatality was a cyclist, Private John Parr. However, as the war developed into trench warfare, many cyclist battalions were absorbed into the infantry. In the final 100 days of the war, tactical surprise was again delivered by the unexpected advance of bicycle troops, often leading the advance toward Germany after the lines had been broken. **KF**

Steyr wasn't the first armaments company to make bikes, but it was by far the most successful. The original Waffenrad appeared in 1902. Waffenrads continued to be built and improved upon until 1987, when Steyr's bicycle division was sold to Piaggio, thus ending one of the longest production runs in cycling history.

Although often thought of as a "Hollandrad"—Austria's answer to the celebrated Dutch bike—the Waffenrad initially drew most of its influence from the Roadster produced by Britain's BSA, another gun company that had diversified into bikes.

Steyr was not content to rest on its laurels, and Waffenrads were never the same for long. In the first year of production, a new model appeared with special clips on the top rail to accommodate military officers' rifles, swords, and briefcases. Between 1908 and 1911, the bikes came with a crankshaft engraved with "Waffenrad" in elaborate lettering. Almost every Austrian rode them.

The fundamental shape of the Waffenrad altered little. Even in the 1980s, models retained the basic prewar design, along with a dynamo-powered headlight, a graceful teardropped taillight on the rear fender, a double kickstand, porteur-style handlebars, and coaster brakes. **BS**

HUMBER Standard Special

1903 • Roadster • UK • Safety bike sold on the strength of its brakes

Humber's Standard Special had, according to its manufacturer, the "best band brake on the market," one that gripped the drum all the way around and lifted off it when released. The band was suspended over the stud on a concealed spiral spring, but there was enough clearance to prevent the brake being accidentally applied when riding on rough or uneven surfaces. This was all very reassuring for the novice cyclist, and was spelled out in detail in a Royal Letters Patent, which meant that the design was Humber's alone. At a time when frames had become more or less standardized, components such as gear hubs and brakes were keeping the patents office busy.

"That green three-speed Humber! That would be my baby! I knew it."

Seegobin Ragbeer, Imperishable Memories

The Humber Standard Special #14 Gent's Roadster was manufactured in the company's factory in Coventry, England, and came emblazoned with the distinctive corporate "Wheel of Life" chainwheel logo, depicting five human forms linking hands with their feet outward and their heads joining in the center. This striking motif had been introduced on Beeston Humber models in 1902 and extended throughout the range in 1904. The bike also came with Dunlop pneumatic tires and narrow 15-in. (38-cm) handlebars. It had a 24-in. (61-cm) frame and 28-in. (71-cm) wheels. Humber had high hopes for this model, and it was exported in large numbers, mainly to distant outposts of the British Empire, but also in smaller quantities to the United States. **BS**

RUDGE-WHITWORTH Crescent

1904 • Roadster • UK • Early premium-quality women's bike

In 1904, the "Crescent lady's bicycle"—an elegant machine named for its stylishly curved top tube—was introduced by Rudge-Whitworth, a manufacturer in Coventry, England. One of Britain's earliest high-quality women's bikes, it entered a market that was becoming saturated with inferior machines.

Although there are no published sales figures, according to the company's 1907 catalog: "Its success has been unprecedented, due to the fact that ladies for the first time had offered to them a machine fully guaranteed in every detail." This claim provided a lead-in to the launch of a mildly updated version of the Crescent, the announcement of which was accompanied by a warning to buyers against "the unreliable machines of obscure jobbers and builders."

Rudge-Whitworth made its own high-quality parts and was able to offer a guarantee that, according to its own publicity material, "the commonest specimens" could not match. The premium appeal was increased by the incorporation of nickel-plated steel rims, solid rubber pedals, delicate dress-guards, a full metal chainguard, front and back lever-operated rim brakes, gently upturned handlebars, and a frame finished in shiny black enamel. The Crescent came in four different frame sizes, all of which used big 28-in. (71-cm) wheels.

The updated bike appears to have been at least as successful as the original, partly because Rudge-Whitworth was able to keep the price low enough to compete against any of the cheaply made rivals.

In the year of its launch, the Crescent cost £6 and 12 shillings ($10), and potential customers were encouraged to take advantage of the manufacturer's then unusually generous offer to pack it for them and deliver it at no extra charge to any railroad station in Great Britain. **CJ**

◁ A new bike was an event worth celebrating in 1903.

DURSLEY Pedersen

1905 • Roadster • UK • Extremely innovative bike with distinctive hammock saddle

In 1893, Danish inventor Mikael Pedersen moved from Denmark to England to monitor his new invention, a centrifuge that separated the cream and whey from milk. While in England he also invented a method of jointing lightweight multiple triangulated tubing, which was perfect for bicycle making.

A few years later, Pedersen received a patent to manufacture what would evolve into the Dursley Pedersen bicycle. What he is best remembered for, however, is not the introduction of his patented three-speed hub gear, his ball-bearing headset, or his determination to produce adjustable handlebars. The most distinctive feature of the 1905 Dursley Pedersen— apart from its diamond-shaped frame, continuing the departure from the unstable penny-farthing—was its

unique woven-cord hammock-style saddle. This was strung from the top of the seatpost to just underneath the handlebars. Wide at the rear and tapering toward the front, it was supported by a leather strap that could be tightened or slackened off depending on the weight of the rider, and was made from 45 yd (41 m) of silk cord.

The seat was the keystone and centerpiece of Pedersen's bicycle. The bicycle was invented to fit the seat, the frame following in its wake. "The part of the machine," he later wrote, "which I found especially imperfect was the seat. There have, it is true, been many attempts to make better seats, but none were what I thought completely successful. I made several attempts before I could get exactly what I wanted, but finally my efforts were crowned with success." **BS**

ORDONNANZFAHRRAD Modell 05

1905 • Utility bike • Switzerland • Long-running workhorse of the Swiss army

One of the principal reasons for the massive popularity of bicycles in their early years was that they gave ordinary people a freedom of movement normally reserved for wealthy horse riders. The armed forces also benefited from these "mechanical horses," and military-issue bikes soon became a common sight. Nowhere were bikes used more extensively for military purposes than in Switzerland.

The Ordonnanzfahrrad Modell 05 was used from 1905 to 1989, making it the longest-serving military vehicle of all time. It was built in a single size with 26-in. (66-cm) wheels and a gearing ratio obviously designed for use on Switzerland's valley floors rather than its Alpine slopes. While a drum brake replaced the back pedal coaster brake on bikes from 1941 (medics also got a front drum brake to cope with the extra equipment), descents must have also been hair-raising on a bike that weighed between 48 and 52 lb (22 and 24 kg) unladen. With a frame bag that filled the whole frame, a helmet bag and blanket roll on the handlebars, a tool kit on the saddle, and a food bag on the rear rack, plus optional weapons racks, some riders were lugging more than the same weight again in equipment. Twin wheel trailers could be attached to the bike for extra cargo or even stretchers.

Things finally got slightly easier for Swiss military cyclists in 1993 with the arrival of the 7-speed MO-93, but metal machine gun and mortar carriers meant that gravity remained the major enemy of Swiss Army bikes until the arrival of the 33-lb (15-kg) MO-12 in 2012. **GK**

DUNLOP Pneumatic

1906 • Roadster • UK • First bike with air-filled tires

In the early years of the bicycle age, tires were made of wood, leather, or solid rubber. Not until 1888 was a bike given a pneumatic tire—by Scottish veterinarian John Boyd Dunlop.

Dunlop was living in Belfast, Northern Ireland, which had many bumpy cobblestone streets. After watching his nine-year-old son jarring along such a thoroughfare on a tricycle with solid rubber tires, Dunlop suddenly had the idea that a tire filled with air would give a softer ride. He therefore created crude inflated tubes made of linen and liquid rubber with a nonreturn valve. He filled them with compressed air and they worked rather like air-filled pillows attached to the wheels.

Historians point out that such tires had first been used forty years previously by engineer Robert Thompson, but that was before the emergence of bicycles, so the invention went undeveloped—it was an idea that had yet to find its time.

A generation later, Dunlop realized the importance of his new tires. He coined the word "pneumatic," enlisted the backing of a rich businessman, and persuaded a Belfast firm, W. Edlin and Co., to manufacture frames to go with the new tires. Local racing cyclist Willie Hume bought one of the safety bikes fitted with the new tires. He promptly demonstrated its potential by winning a series of races in Ireland and England.

At first people mocked them as "pudding tires," but the first ads for Dunlop's bike boasted: "Vibration impossible." An Irish journalist rode one from Dublin, Ireland, to Coventry, England—home of the new safety bikes. Dunlop's pneumatic tire became a crucial element in the bike's development, and his name is now printed on tires the world over. **SH**

LA GAULOISE Bi-Chaîne

1909 • Roadster • France • Early multi-gear bike

Once the classic double-diamond frame layout and pneumatic tires of the safety cycle had consolidated at the start of the twentieth century, many inventors spent their time trying to find an efficient and easy way to change the gearing ratio of the bike. The Bi-Chaîne was a far cry from later derailleur bikes, but it was a start.

Paul de Vivie—better known among contemporary cyclists as "Velocio"—was a long-distance cyclist and bike store owner who thought nothing of riding up to forty hours nonstop. He also built a range of complete La Gauloise bikes from a variety of prebuilt frames, many with experimental gearing and handlebar systems.

". . . an interesting attempt at multiple gearing before derailleur technology took over."

Bill Bryant, Randonneurs USA

The Bi-Chaîne used two chains, one on each side of the bike. Three different-sized chainrings were also fitted, one on the normal driveside and two on the far side, plus two different freewheels on each side of the rear wheel. This gave the rider a choice of six gears, but changing between them was not the instant shifter-click or push-button affair it is on modern bikes. The rider had to get off the bike and split the chain using specially designed removable links. The rider would then move the chain to the desired chain-and-freewheel combination by hand, and rejoin the chain after making it the correct length.

While most stems used a closed pinch clamp to hold the handlebars, the faceplate on the stem of the Bi-Chaîne could be unbolted to allow the handlebars to be inverted for a taller riding position. **GK**

◁ Pneumatic tires made cycling comfortable for all ages.

PEUGEOT Christophe

1913 • Roadster • France • The bike with the most infamous broken fork in bike history

Eugène Christophe, the "Old Gaul," had set a hard pace since the beginning of the 1913 Tour de France after finishing second the year before. Now he was halfway up the 4,100-ft (1,250-m) Col du Tourmalet, the highest peak in the Central Pyrenees, an hour ahead of Belgian race leader and reigning Tour champion Odile Defraye. Defraye suddenly pulled out, exhausted, and the race was Christophe's for the taking. But as he went over the summit of the Tourmalet and began to pick up speed, the front forks of his Peugeot snapped.

Forbidden to accept outside assistance by the race rules, with his broken bicycle slung over his shoulder, Christophe trudged 6 mi (10 km) across the Pyrenees

"All the riders I had dropped during the climb soon caught me up. I was weeping with anger."

Eugène Christophe

toward the village of St. Marie de Campan. There he met a young girl who took him to the village blacksmith.

Obliged to effect his own repairs to the fork, Christophe toiled away under the blacksmith's watchful eye, before rejoining the race and finishing the stage. However, the race officials temporarily disqualified the already massively delayed rider on the grounds that the forge bellows used during the repair work had been operated by a young boy, which they classified as outside assistance.

After an appeal he was reinstated, but he had already lost too much time to regain the lead. Peugeot, wanting to avoid bad press, confiscated the roughly repaired fork, and only returned it to Christophe shortly before his death. **BS**

ROYAL SUNBEAM Roadster

1913 • Roadster • UK • Luxury gentleman's bicycle made of steel

For those who could afford the best bikes in 1913, Royal Sunbeam was one of the premium names of early English cycling. This Roadster was produced twenty-five years after John Marston converted his business from high-quality metal lacquering and painting to making cycles. And it was the quality of the renowned gloss paint finish that actually gave the Royal Sunbeam its name, after Marston's wife, Ellen, saw the sun reflecting off the sparkling new frame of the first bike the company produced.

For the Roadster, ball bearings in the steering mechanism, wheel hubs, and cranks, together with Sunbeam's "little oil bath," were combined to ensure smooth running. The bike also had a back-pedal "Coaster" brake, although ads at the time of its launch offered the alternative of a matching pair of the newly introduced rod-actuated "Stirrup" brakes rubbing on the innovative aluminum alloy rims.

The standard Roadster cost £14 and 12 shillings ($23)—three months' worth of the average wage for the time—but the wide range of extras offered value for money and promised to turn the standard-issue machine into a tailor-made bicycle for gentlemen. Dunlop or Palmer pneumatic tires, different bells, acetylene lamps, cyclometers, monogram or pinstripe paintwork, and even a specific golf-club carrier for the sporting gent were all on the menu.

The descent into the First World War a year later saw Sunbeam redirect its production from bikes to munitions, but the company continued to take orders for the Roadster up until 1918. Sadly, Marston's eldest son, and then John and Ellen, died within a few days of each other in 1918, and surviving son Charles had to pay off death taxes by selling Sunbeam to the group that became ICI. **GK**

Sunbeam offered a wide range of upgrade options to customers. ▶

BIANCHI Army Issue

1914 • Military bike • Italy • First World War folding army bicycle

The distinctive celeste green of Bianchi is said to have originated after the First World War with a consignment of surplus army paint diluted with white to make it seem less military. Regardless of whether that story is true, there was undoubtedly frequent crossover between early cycle manufacturing and the armaments industry.

The Italian military high command had been impressed by the speed and mobility of bicycle infantry. On their instigation, Bianchi developed a military bicycle for the "Bersaglieri" light infantry.

The Bianchi frame had a lightweight, hinged, folding design, with a fixed-wheel drive system. Two sprockets on the rear wheel gave a choice of gears, and the complete bike weighed around 31 lb (14 kg). The frame also featured revolutionary front and rear suspension— the use of solid rubber, rather than pneumatic, tires made some form of damping vital to retain effective control. The front fork was equipped with spring-damped drop-out pivots, and the rear seatstay of the frame carried a wishbone-mounted spring-compression suspension system, very similar to those introduced in some modern soft-tail mountain bikes ninety years later. The system reinforces the argument that there are rarely any new ideas in cycling. **KF**

MEAD Ranger

1916 • Roadster • USA/UK • Product of one of the first global bike companies

Rather than making bikes, the Mead Cycle Company, launched in 1894 in Chicago during the U.S. cycling boom, marketed rebadged bikes from manufacturers such as Swift and Premier.

James Mead's company offered to ship a Mead Ranger without payment to anyone in the United States for a ten-day trial: "If it does not suit you in every way and is not all or more than we claim for it . . . ship it back to us at our expense."

In 1901 Mead became one of the first companies to spread its operations to Europe. It established a branch in Liverpool, England, at the same time buying the British Cycle Manufacturing Company, which was based in the same city. Mead's U.S.-style mail order, hire purchase, and franchise deals were unfamiliar in Britain at the time. By 1907 Mead was advertising for British "rider agents" who would buy machines from Mead on favorable hire purchase terms and in return would promote Mead bikes and secure further orders.

One such agent was London-based Frenchman Marcel Planes, who won the 1911 "Century Competition" by riding more than 100 mi (160 km) on his Mead on 322 days of that year. His record total of 34,666 mi (55,787 km) in a year stood for twenty-one years. **SH**

CLARKES Leader

1920 • Roadster • New Zealand • Premium
rider-designed Kiwi road racer

HIRONDELLE Retro Directe

1920 • Roadster • France • Bike featuring a
clever but counterintuitive gear-change system

New Zealand imported more than 800,000 bicycles in the 1900–1950 period. By the end of the 1930s there were more than 250,000 on the country's roads—one for every six people. This was largely because a glut of secondhand bicycles brought the price of a bike down to less than half of what it was at the turn of the century.

In 1920, Leo Clarke established Clarkes Cycle Works in Auckland, marketing his bikes under the Leader brand. Clarke liked to associate his bikes with the country's best riders, but during the interwar years some of them had questionable reputations that did not help the business.

Despite such problems, Clarkes became renowned for fine workmanship. Its products were available both off the rack and customized. Leader race bikes were characterized by very straight forks, elaborate lugging, and tight-fitting rear wheels. By the mid 1930s, Clarkes Cycle Works had grown into one of New Zealand's most influential and respected race-frame builders of the interwar period.

Leo Clarke also trained and started the careers of renowned builders such as Slater Hayes, who left Clarkes in 1937 to establish a successful brand of his own, Comet Cycles. **BS**

Before French company Huret designed and introduced the definitive sideways-shifting derailleur after the Second World War, several other French manufacturers produced their own gear-changing systems.

The Retro Directe single-chain system, patented by French bike builder Hirondelle in 1903 and used on its bicycles until the start of the Second World War, had a unique reverse-pedaling gear change. Through a visually confusing but cunningly engineered chain arrangement, the Retro Directe engaged two different-sized freewheels simultaneously. The action of the two freewheels was reversed, though, so that pedaling forward engaged one gear, while pedaling backward engaged the other, easier gear. The drive cogs were separate from the freewheel mechanism, so they could be changed easily to fine-tune the gears.

This Hirondelle also featured a chain-tensioning roller, operated via rods from a lever on the crossbar, that allowed the rider to take up the slack in the chain when switching between the two front chainrings. The back brake had long arms that pushed onto the rim with an expanding scissor mechanism, similar to that later seen in Campagnolo's famous Delta brakes. Both truly cemented Hirondelle's reputation as an innovator. **GK**

BSA No. 15 Standard

1922 • Road bike • UK • One of the classic English bicycles

BSA—the Birmingham Small Arms & Metal Company—was the result of a collaboration of independent gunsmiths formed to manufacture service rifles en masse for the army in the aftermath of the Crimean War.

After fulfilling early orders, the factory fell quiet for a short time. However, the enterprising owners realized that their state-of-the-art production-line facilities and standardized manufacture of interchangeable parts lent themselves well to the burgeoning cycle trade. So began a diversification that gradually expanded far beyond merely keeping the firearms facilities busy.

After making a small number of complete bicycles, BSA concentrated on providing parts and components to be added to other manufacturers' frames. But by 1908 the cycle market was booming, and BSA once again began to make complete cycles. The company made the bold decision to produce only machines of the highest quality, and pegged its branding at the upper end of the market. Rapidly establishing an outstanding reputation, BSA bikes soon attracted a premium over other brands. It was perhaps a lesson that later British manufacturers would have done well to learn.

Built of weldless steel tubing, with steel rims and rod brakes, this interwar model was equipped with a 48-tooth "BSA" stamped chainset; the 18-tooth rear cog gave a comfortable gear ratio. The bike was available with either coaster brake or freewheel, and even a three-speed hub for additional money. The bike was delivered equipped with mudguards and chainguard, pump, tool bag, and spanners.

These classic bicycles were sold for around £9 ($13.50). By way of comparison, a well-skilled tradesman was earning around £3 ($4.50) a week, so the bike was a significant investment, but comparable to the price paid for a quality machine today. **KF**

LABOR Spécial Course

1922 • Race bike • France • Bridge design technology transplanted onto a race bike

The Labor Spécial Course road bike is well known ninety years after it appeared, thanks in part to a series of French advertising posters showing a troupe of chimpanzees attempting to reproduce the bike in sketches. The purpose of the posters was to highlight the fact that no one could copy the genius of the famous Labor truss bridge frame. Even so, this bicycle, marketed with the phrase "Trust the Truss," bore an uncanny resemblance to an earlier U.S. truss-head bicycle manufactured by the Iver Johnson Arms and Cycleworks company in 1910.

Clever advertising such as this helped Labor bicycles acquire an almost cult status in French cycling in little more than two years. Inspired by a design common

"They look almost identical. I think Labor most likely copied the design from Iver Johnson."

Old Bike *review*

to railroad truss bridges, the torsion-resistant arc underneath the Spécial Course's top tube was added specifically to help deal with the rigors of the annual Paris–Roubaix road race, which was first held in 1896.

Paris–Roubaix began in the French capital and ended in Roubaix, Belgium. One of the oldest road races in professional cycling, it was ridden along the typical but punishing cobblestoned sections of the day. The race had very few inclines, hence the Spécial Course's minimal gearing. The rider would change gear by undoing a wing nut on the rear wheel and flipping the wheel to use the cog mounted on the offside. Despite its simplicity, the bike still weighed a hefty 27 lb (12.3 kg), thanks to its burly varnished steel frame and beautifully crafted wooden rims and fenders. **BS**

◁ BSA offered their bikes with several rear hub options.

CAMINADE Caminargent

1926 • Road bike • France • Groundbreaking modular aluminum bike designed for mass production

Slotting tubes into socketed junction sections or lugs is a simple and effective production method that has been used in frame building for more than a century. The practice, which allows different materials to be combined in the same frame, is still used today, even on super-prestigious Tour de France yellow jersey-carrying bikes such as Colnago's glued-tube C59.

Made in France by Caminade, the interwar Caminargent bike was unusual in its early use of aluminum tubes and lugs, and also in its impermanent tube and lug connection. Each tube was clamped into its lug using pinch bolts, just as many bicycle seat tube clamps work today. The tubes and internal lugs were octagonal in section to lock them into place and prevent the tubes from twisting in the frame. The intricately decorated lugs at the head, crank, seat, and rear-wheel corners of the bike were all cast from aluminum too, which made construction of a range of bike types very simple and cost effective.

Bike maker Pierre Caminade also developed and built a whole line of lightweight parts, including very modern-looking sidepull brakes, handlebar stems, alloy wheels, and even wing nuts. Their all-aluminum build made them very light for the time, although the Caminargent's bolted junctions must have been overly flexible when it was pedaled or steered hard. Flex has always been a potential problem for "lug and plug" bikes, which is why the best aluminum and carbon fiber bikes now feature direct welds or glued tube connections, or are molded monocoque designs. **GK**

SHELBY Lindy Flyer
1928 • Roadster • USA • The first in a genre of quirky "character" bikes

When, in May 1927, twenty-five-year-old U.S. Air Mail employee Charles Lindbergh flew solo nonstop from New York to Paris in his single-seat single-engine monoplane, "Spirit of St. Louis," he gained instant fame. In no time he was approached by a conga line of manufacturers, all desperate to get his name onto one of their products. Lindbergh accepted very few of the commercial offers, but he did accept the "Lindy Flyer," an idea put to him by representatives of the Shelby Cycle Company in Shelby, Ohio.

Shelby had been making bicycles since the boom years of the 1890s. It proposed what would be the first in a new trend of so-called "character bikes," or bicycles with obvious connections to well-known personalities. The Flyer's links to Lindbergh's astonishing feat included

a replica petrol tank under the top rail, plus a model of his famous aircraft mounted on the front fender with a propeller designed to rotate as you pedaled along. One of the first U.S.-made bicycles to adopt chrome plating extensively, the Lindy had seamless steel tubing and was available only in a boy's or male framed design. It had a varying levels of trim and colors, mostly a patriotic mix of red, white, and blue.

Other character bikes included Shelby's "Donald Duck" in 1949, with a bust of the famous duck mounted on the head tube, and Rollfast's "Hopalong Cassidy" in 1952. Surprisingly, sales of the Lindy failed to meet expectations, and fewer than ten—the majority of them now in relatively poor condition—are known to have survived to the present day. **BS**

SELBACH Path Pacer
1928 • Road–track bike • UK • Top-end race bike

The son of a Polish countess, Maurice Selbach moved to England and became a successful race cyclist before the First World War. After the war, like several other big cycling names, Selbach launched his own bike company. He was so successful that when the motor tycoon Henry Ford visited England, he was presented with a Selbach as the "best British bicycle of the day." (Selbach himself, incidentally, was famous for traveling around London not on one of his own bikes but in a big American Buick.)

Selbach's bikes were made from Reynolds tubing and showed the fashionably relaxed frame geometry of the time. He was among the first to use tapered tubes in his frames and roller bearings in his headsets. Fittings

". . . possibly the best examples of the lightweight bicycle makers' craft from that period."

Ben Sharp

were the cream of the era too, with buyers choosing from BSA, Chater Lea, Brampton, and Abingdon parts.

Bike tracks in the 1930s were often called "paths," hence the name "Path Racer." A path racer was a track bike with road geometry, usually with 28-in. (71-cm) rims and no gears. Selbach bikes and frames were used by many of the top racers of the day. Harry Grant took the World Motor-Paced One Hour Record on a Selbach, achieving 56½ mi (91 km) in the hour, and Albert Richter won the World Amateur Sprint Championship riding a Selbach in 1932. Richter, a German who opposed the Nazis, was killed by the Gestapo in 1940.

Selbach himself died even earlier. After catching the wheel of his bike in a London tramline in 1935, he fell and was hit by a truck. **SH**

ERNEST RUSS Super Resilient
1930 • Road bike • UK • Innovatively tubed and forked road race machine

Ernest F. Russ is a man whose name will forever be associated with his famous Super Resilient Russ fork. The fork, which was straight except for a forward throw over its final few inches, was used by a wide range of cyclists from weekend club riders through to world champions throughout Europe and the United States. Russ also perfected the rapid-taper chainstay, and both innovations were widely copied throughout the rest of the bike industry.

Russ was born in 1906. In his teens he joined the Velma Road Club, a mostly track-based club that provided him with the foundation for a successful racing career. He opened a cycle store in London in 1928 and lost no time in developing a reputation for craftsmanship and a keen attention to detail. Two years later, he unveiled his remarkable fork blade design to the world.

Over the course of his career as a frame builder, Russ constructed in excess of 4,000 frames for tricycles and tandems, as well as for conventional two-wheelers. He stopped working full-time in 1958, but came out of retirement on a couple of later occasions, including once in 1960 to produce a frame for a U.S. Navy sailor.

Identifying a genuine Russ frame is not always easy because so many makers used his trademark fork. However, if you want to be sure, just look under the bottom bracket or behind the front fork crown. That is where Russ always left its number, which was often randomized just to make life difficult for anyone who may have been tempted to make a fake one. His son, Edward Russ, now runs a model store in his dad's old cycle store on Battersea Rise, London, and still has all of Ernie's old frame-building plans up in its attic. He wants to get them all down and organized, but it is a herculean effort better left, he says, for retirement. **BS**

Actual Ernest Russ bikes are rare, but the forks were widely used. ▶

Rudge-Whitworth
Britain's Best Bicycle

A GREAT BICYCLE
WITH A
GREAT REPUTATION

RUDGE-WHITWORTH
COVENTRY

CARRIAGE FREE &
CARRIAGE PAID
GUARANTEE

WORKS·AND
HEAD·OFFICES:— COVENTRY
OXFORD
16·GEORGE STREET

BY·SPECIAL
APPOINMENT
TO·H·M
THE·KING
AND·H·R·H
THE·PRINCE
OF·WALES

RUDGE-WHITWORTH Roadster

1930 • Utility bike • UK • All-round bike with an enviable pedigree

Daniel Rudge, inventor of the adjustable ball-bearing hub, built his first bike in 1870 in Coventry, England. In 1894, his company merged with the Whitworth Cycle Company of Birmingham. Rudge-Whitworth Cycles is best remembered for its foray into motorcycle development and racing. While achieving considerable success on the track, the company maintained a separate division responsible for the manufacture of bicycles, one of which was the Gentleman's Roadster.

The design—typical of upright British bicycles of the time—included a crossbar-mounted quadrant gear changer and all-weather angular mudguards. The chain case was also standard in roadster design, but Rudge's

"Rudge-Whitworth . . . an excellent reputation for beautifully made machines."

Hilary Stone, Classic Rendezvous

version was hinged at the front so it could be folded down for easy maintenance of the gear and drive chain. Built around a one-size-fits-all 24-in. (61-cm) lugged steel frame, it came with rod brakes front and rear, and the newly developed and wonderfully ingenious 3-speed Sturmey-Archer sun-and-planet cog hub gears. While gears of other types were available previously, the new Sturmeys were remarkably efficient, reliable, clean, and quiet, and enabled riders of all fitness levels to tackle any hill.

With its long crank, long wheelbase, and shallow frame angles, the Gentleman's Roadster was a stable and confident machine that prioritized strength above light weight. As a result, it was often used by policemen and post office workers. **BS**

HERCULES OA21

1930 • Ladies' tourer • UK • Female-specific bike from Britain's most prolific bicycle manufacturer

The Hercules Cycle & Motor Company began inauspiciously in a small rented house in Birmingham, England, in 1910, as the creation of brothers Ted and Harry Crane. Within just a few months, however, demand for its bicycles was proving so strong that the company was forced to relocate to larger premises. By the mid-1920s, the company led the cycling industry in the application of the techniques of mass production, and by 1928 was exporting one in five of all bicycles made in the United Kingdom.

By the 1930s in England, bicycles had become a prized female fashion item, and Hercules responded to this trend with the OA21 Lady's Tourer. This dropped-top-tube bike was a direct descendant of early loop-framed bikes designed to encourage the wearing of what was called "rational dress"—clothing that would permit women to engage in a full range of activities, including sport, without being excessively revealing or exposing the wearer to ridicule. While this concept had been firmly established since the 1880s, Hercules evolved existing standards even further with the addition of a specially designed chain cover, dress-guard, and box mudguards.

Like all Hercules bicycles, every joint of the OA21's all-British frame was pegged and brazed, silver-polished, rustproofed, and given four coats of enamel. Its chain wheels, cranks, hubs, and flywheels were all made on site. Dunlop-supplied rims, tires, and waterproof sprung saddles were also fitted at the factory. There was a large rear rack and an outsized dynamo-powered headlamp. Although well built, the OA21 lacked refinement and cosmetic extras, and as a result was one of the most affordable bicycles on the market. Hercules continued trading independently until 1946. **BS**

GNOME-RHÔNE Alloy

1930 • Road bike • France • Early aluminum-framed bike

The delightfully named Gnome-Rhône company was a leading French aircraft builder until the First World War, after which it branched out into motorbikes and bicycles. After the Second World War, it was nationalized as part of the Snecma group but carried on making bikes until the early 1950s.

Using its aircraft-making expertise, Gnome-Rhône launched this aluminum bike that stayed in production for twenty years.

Aluminum had been used for bike frames since the 1890s, but its popularity increased in the 1930s. Among the other French bike companies that experimented with it were Aviac and Duravia. They all used the same construction process. The main triangle was bolted together, then lugged with steel sleeves. The bolt holes were covered with the brand logo, which in Gnome-Rhône's case was a whirling propeller.

Gnome-Rhône bikes were left unpainted, showing off their silver frames and matching wide alloy mudguards stamped with the brand "GR." There were pump pegs on the back of the alloy seat tube.

The most distinctive parts of the GR bike were the decorative aluminum chainguard and the lightweight alloy that was also used for the cranks, chainring, carrier, pedals, handlebars, and brake levers. Even the futuristically-styled lights were made of aluminum.

As on most bikes of the period, the rear of the machine and the forks were steel, which allowed brazed-on fittings for the aluminum cantilever brakes, dynamo, mudguards, and luggage racks. **SH**

RALEIGH Record Ace

1934 • Road bike • UK • State-of-the-art road racer/tourer

The Raleigh Record Ace (RRA) was a top-end, state-of-the-art road bike, featuring elegantly curved drop handlebars with an adjustable extension and forks made from "extra resilient high manganese" with solid forged ends. The front wheel used distinctive radial spokes, the rear wheel more conventional tangential spokes. Both wheels featured quick-release wing nuts.

The frame was small, as interwar thinking was more concerned with saving weight than providing a perfect fit. It was made from brazed and lugged steel tubing, with a parallel top tube and Raleigh's own caliper brakes.

The Record Ace was advertised as a "racing machine," but by modern standards it was set up for touring: with brazed bosses for mudguard eyes and a down-tube holder for the Bluemel's Featherweight bike pump. It also came with a classic Brooks saddlebag and lamp brackets on the forks and bars plus a rear reflector. Bluemel's No Weight mudguards were fitted, along with a brown leather Brooks Champion saddle and Dunlop Sprite tires.

Charming decorative details included the Raleigh heron motif appearing as a part of metal light holder and on the spokes of the chain wheel.

The whole bike weighed an impressive 19½ lb (8.8 kg) in "road racing trim," but was somewhat heavier with the mudguards, saddlebag, and lights. Raleigh was on the cusp of discovering customization too: "Optional specification to suit the needs of the ultra-discriminate speedman will always be considered," its publicity announced. **SH**

BAINES VS37 Flying Gate
1935 • Road bike • UK • Innovative short
wheelbase and characteristic suspended seat tube frame

SCHULZ Funiculo
1935 • Road bike • France • Unique,
innovation-loaded large-tubed derailleur-geared roadster

One of many memorable bicycles produced by small British prewar manufacturers, the VS37—commonly known as the Flying Gate—was built to an unusual design with a separated seat tube layout that was also adopted on two other models from the same manufacturer, the Whirlwind and the International.

Based in Bradford, England, W. & R. Baines began building bike frames in 1935. All the company's products were individually hand built using lugged steel.

In common with many other companies of the period, Baines preferred bikes with short chainstays that would help stiffen the bottom bracket and the rear end, to reduce frame flex. Over the years, numerous methods have been adopted in pursuit of this objective, including curved seat tubes and monocoque frames. However, few solutions have been more radical, or visually striking, than Baines' vertical seat tube. This was based around the suspension of the saddle via a dummy tube mounted on an additional set of seatstays. The layout adds stiffness with a minimal increase in weight, because of the use of smaller-diameter tubing.

With the resulting efficient power transmission and a short, responsive wheelbase, many felt the VS37 was the ideal speed machine. The "gate" design was raced to victory in track, time trials, and road races. After the Second World War, a single Whirlwind model was built with a wheelbase to suit the individual rider. Some chose a more relaxed geometry, to create an excellent long-distance frame.

Although Baines ceased trading in 1953, the design gained a new lease of life in the late 1970s, when Trevor Jarvis obtained permission to restart production of the Flying Gates, which are still being hand made to order at his works in Worcestershire. **KF**

Many road race bikes of the interwar period are obvious forerunners of later racers and tourers, but other less conventional bikes of the 1930s also included many features that would reappear subsequently. The remarkably modern-looking outsized T-frame of the Shulz Funiculo is particularly rich in features that remain in use today.

While oversized frame tubes were later used to increase frame stiffness, French bike builder Jacques Schulz sold his supersized flexible frames by offering increased comfort and custom sizing to their riders.

The main tube had internal routing for the twin cables operating the specially designed rear brake; a

"Schulz was a master innovator who redesigned virtually every detail of his bicycles."
Michael Embacher

pump was also stowed inside the frame. The front brake used an equally innovative sidepull cable to expand a telescoping crosspiece that forced the pads onto the wheel rims with particularly powerful leverage not seen again until the advent of mountain bike V-brakes in the 1990s. The rims were aluminum rather than steel.

The Funiculo gear system was a forerunner of later derailleur systems. A spring-loaded lever arm carried two "jockey" guide wheels to take up chain slack. A cable-operated mechanism moved them sideways via a frame-mounted shift lever to engage one of four different-sized rear sprockets. The largest sprocket could contain up to forty teeth, giving a mountain climbing ratio that was not matched until the appearance of SRAM's 11-speed XX1 mountain bike chainset. **GK**

COVENTRY EAGLE Royal Prince

1935 • Road bike • UK • Three-speed all-weather roadster

The Coventry Eagle Royal Prince was an attempt to create a more durable type of road bike in the style of bikes then supplied to British policemen.

It was advertised as an "all-weather roadster," and all its parts were rustproofed by bonderizing—a process of applying a phosphate solution prior to painting, which improved corrosion resistance. Then the whole of the Royal Prince was enameled in thick black paint (unless you were buying the women's version, in which case the parts were chrome-plated).

The Royal Prince's 28-in. (71-cm) wheels sported chrome brake tracks with black-enameled centers. The tires were Dunlop Roadsters. The long mudguards

"The Royal Prince's reign was brief, but its time is affectionately recalled by all who rode it."

Ed Munton-Greene

and a comprehensive chainguard helped deal with wet weather, and every buyer received a free pump, a bagged tool kit, an oil can, and a reflector. Optional extras included an even deeper mudguard set and a 6-volt weatherproof dynamo system, which powered front and rear light units.

Differently built buyers were catered for with a steel tube frame that came in three sizes; standard fitments included rubber pedals and a well-sprung Aero saddle. The Sturmey-Archer three-speed gears were controlled from a lever on the top tube.

One delightful variant was the Royal Prince Tradesman's Carrier, a specially designed delivery bike with a large front wickerwork basket in a steel frame supported by specially strengthened front forks. **SH**

GEORGE ELRICK Chrome

1935 • Race bike • UK • Classic frame from a shed in the heart of Scotland

No one knows where George Elrick learned his craft, but learn it he surely did. The frames he made over a forty-year period in his small workshop, which began as little more than a glorified shed in Stirling, Scotland, suggest that he may have been apprenticed to an English builder, possibly one near his birthplace in Castleford, Yorkshire.

Elrick's beautifully filed and finished lugwork, which seemed almost to disappear into the frame, complemented by his use of British-made Chater-Lea components such as lugs and bottom brackets—among the finest available at the time—are eloquent testimony to his devotion. He built literally thousands of frames, specializing in racing bikes, and a typical day saw him start work after breakfast and often not re-emerge from his workshop until late in the night, exhausted by his labors.

In 1935 Elrick produced his fifth bicycle, this beautiful chrome racing bike, complete with all the usual Chater-Lea accessories, flowing lugwork, and his traditional "Geo. Elrick" transfer.

Although Elrick carved out an enviable reputation among cycling cognoscenti for his attention to detail, he never rose to national prominence. He seldom paid for and never sought publicity—perhaps because he lacked marketing savvy, possibly because he lacked the budget for advertising, but more likely because he believed that his work should speak for itself.

Elrick produced his final frame in the mid-1970s, when urban redevelopment forced him to close his workshop. He was one of the last in an honorable line of Scottish frame builders—most of whom, like Glasgow's Flying Scot, had been forced to close their doors decades earlier as bikes increasingly lost out to the internal combustion engine. **BS**

Chrome plating isn't a pleasant process, but it can look amazing. ⊙

HETCHINS Lightweight

1936 • Road–track bike • UK • Iconic wavy-tubed frame

Some of the most distinctive bike frames of the twentieth century were made by Hetchins of Tottenham, London. Russian immigrant and bike shop owner Hyman Hetchin teamed up with local frame builder Jack Denny in the 1920s to create beautiful bikes that had chainstays with a curl.

There were two reasons behind this distinctive feature. First, Denny believed that bent stays would absorb road imperfections in the same way as curved front forks, thus providing leisure cyclists with greater comfort and helping racers to go faster over cobblestones.

Second, the concept of amateur status was protected so strictly in the 1930s that competition bikes were forbidden to carry the name of their makers in case it worked as an advertisement. The curly stays made Hetchins bikes instantly recognizable regardless of the lack of name. So when World and Olympic sprint champion Toni Merkens was photographed winning the British Championship in 1934, cycle fans could easily see that he was riding a Hetchins Lightweight.

Hetchins bikes also had very elegant and decorative frame junction pieces or lugs. This 1936 model has the most beautiful of all. **SH**

CAMINADE Caminargent

1936 • Road bike • France • Innovative octagonal alloy-tubed road bike

Caminade specialized in lightweight steel tubing in the years leading up to the First World War, then switched to Dural (an aluminum alloy) in the 1920s. Though the use of aluminum in bicycles was not new, Caminade put the first lightweight bicycle into serious production in France in 1936. The company's revolutionary new bike, the Caminargent, was so popular that it remained in continuous production for twenty years.

Initially promoted by a French trade council, the Société du Duralumin, the Caminargent was available in a range of models built around a common octagonal frame that gave it a wonderfully industrial appearance, its sections held together by ornate cast aluminum lugs that were bolted to permit easy disassembly. Cables and wiring were internal, there was a long, tapered seat, and the mudguard, chainguard, alloy rims, and hubs were all supplied by Lefol Le Paon.

But the significance of this machine was far more than the sum of its parts. Here at last was a road bike made from a material that was light and rustproof. On the debit side, the lug method of binding caused the frame to twist, a fundamental design flaw that kept the bike off the race track and led to criticism that it rode "like a piece of spaghetti." **BS**

HOBBS Continental

1937 • Road bike • UK • Classically stylish
road race bike

Albert Hobbs started business in the Barbican, London, in the 1930s, and soon gained a reputation for classy bikes with well-made frames featuring some of the most delicate and attractive lug work of the era.

The Continental was one of his finest creations. He claimed it was the first bike made in Britain with oval-section forks. Reynolds specially made these for Hobbs from the famous 531 alloy steel tubing. It was a style that would soon catch on, with the oval section tapering to a round section on the lower part of the blade to provide steadiness and resilience on good surfaces and bad.

The Continental was beautifully constructed, with the chainstays and seatstays particularly rigid thanks to smoothly tapered butted tubing.

The more expensive Continental Superbe model had an even higher level of craftsmanship. This was a limited-edition bike built only by Hobbs' top mechanics. Each lug was hand cut and neatly filed before and after brazing.

During the Second World War, the Barbican was almost totally destroyed by bombing, and Hobbs moved out of London to Dagenham, Essex, where he shared a factory with the makers of the Sterling submachine gun. **SH**

DERNY Moped

1937 • Track tug • France • Pedal-assisted
motorbike for race pacing

Motor-paced cycling events—cycling behind a pacer car or a motorcycle—began in the 1890s. Motorcycles were fitted with rollers behind their rear wheels to prevent crashes caused when the front wheel of a bicycle contacted the rear of the motorbike. Early pacers had engines as large as 2,400 cc, but in 1920 standards were introduced to limit engine size. In 1938, a Paris-based manufacturer, Roger Derny et Fils, produced a light motorbike powered by a 98 cc Zurcher two-stroke motor pedaled via a fixed gear, with seventy teeth on the front chainring and eleven on the back sprocket, and a petrol tank over the handlebars. The company ceased trading in 1957, but the Derny name survived to become a generic term for all such vehicles.

A derny has a fixed rear wheel and has to be bump-started. A derny rider sits close to the back of the bike in an upright position, so as to create a slipstream for the cyclists behind it. Derny races are nowadays a rarity, but derny vehicles still appear in keirins, sprint races that originated in Japan. Involving six or eight riders, keirins begin behind a derny that paces the riders for the first few laps before pulling off the track, leaving the riders to sprint eight laps to the finish. In a variant form of the keirin, the derny remains on track for the whole race. **BS**

SCHWINN Paramount

1938 • Race bike • USA • State-of-the-art lightweight race bike

Bespectacled Belgian immigrant Emil Wastyn was a well-respected frame builder, mechanic, and Schwinn bike dealer. His shop and workshop were not far from the Schwinn factory on the west side of Chicago.

Frank Schwinn wanted to produce the ultimate world-class, money-no-object race bike to promote his brand, and he hired Wastyn to build it. The Belgian was told to spare no expense, so the Paramount was built with the very latest techniques and materials. Many parts and ideas were imported from Europe.

Wastyn used imported aircraft-grade chrome-molybdenum for the tubing, which was constructed using brazing with carefully carved and styled brass

"We . . . are satisfied that you have the best bicycle that can be bought anywhere."

Al Crossley and Jimmy Walthour, in Schwinn's catalog

lugs. Some parts were hand made by Wastyn and his machinists to the finest tolerances possible at the time.

The frame geometry featured a short wheelbase and steep head angle to give the rider better acceleration and sharper handling. But the ultra-lightweight bike was so expensive that most customers could not afford it.

So Schwinn gave free bikes to a dozen top pro racers, including Chicagoan favorite Joseph "Jerry" Rodman. While the Schwinn team was out on the tracks winning races on their Paramounts, the company displayed its other bikes in front of the grandstands. This successfully promoted the Schwinn brand, although the Paramount model itself never sold in great numbers. **SH**

RUDGE-WHITWORTH Ladies' Tourer

1938 • Road bike • UK • Bike of "fitness girl" Billie Dovey

In the years leading up to the outbreak of the Second World War, British women faced a barrage of attempts by politicians and advertisers to get them out into the fresh air, cycling around and keeping fit. One 1930s' magazine article, "The Modern Eve and her Cycle," suggested that it was easy to see which were the cyclists in any group of office girls. They were the ones with "erect figures," "graceful walks," and "schoolgirl complexions."

Such assumptions—which to modern readers may seem an extraordinary combination of forward-thinking health consciousness and retrogressive sexism—form an important part of the background to the extraordinary career of Billie Dovey, "the Keep-fit Girl." Dovey first made a name by undertaking long-distance bike rides. She then became famous as a symbol of the new independent and athletic woman. She featured in ads for bikes, Hovis bread, and Cadbury chocolate (she is reputed to have carried a bar or two in her saddlebag at all times for energy).

The pinnacle of Dovey's cycling fame came in 1938, when she rode 29,899 miles (48,117 km) around the UK on a Rudge-Whitworth tourer.

In each city and town en route, Dovey would call at local cycle shops, take rides with cycling clubs, and give talks about fitness. Her marathon ride set a record that wasn't broken until after the Second World War.

The bike itself was a steel ladies' frame using parallel main tubes and fitted with front and rear lights. Dan Rudge had been building bikes since 1870 before merging with Whitworth in 1894 to make high-performance cycles and motorcycles. The company was bought by EMI in 1938, and later sold to Raleigh, which adopted some of its innovations—such as fork crowns—for its own bikes. **SH**

SAXON Twin Tube

1939 • Road bike • UK • Radical frame design from interwar England

The late 1930s saw many subtle changes in the design of British road bikes, even though road racing was still in its infancy. Many improvements of the period were aimed at satisfying the demands of club riders and time trialists. Frame angles were steepening, and riders were increasingly seeking greater efficiencies in the transference of power from leg to wheel, which in the main involved finding ways to make stiffer frames that didn't soak up precious energy. This approach typically led to shortened wheelbases, in the belief that shorter frames and chainstays would make the bottom bracket more rigid and thus produce a more energy-efficient bike. The quest to reduce wheelbases, however, brought

"Saxon catered for those who needed a well respected, budget machine."

Hilary Stone

the rear wheel uncomfortably close to the seatstay, and the need to maintain a proper distance between rear wheel and seatstay resulted in some rather unorthodox innovations in frame design.

Saxon's remedy to the problem of flexing—first tried in the 1890s and again by Saxon itself in 1937 on its Wings of the Wind tandem—was to replace the seat tube with two smaller-diameter tubes the size of stays—its famous Twin Tube—brazed along the edge of the bottom bracket shell, thus creating a gap that enabled the rear wheel to be moved forward 2½ in. (6.4 cm).

Founded in 1919, Saxon was a popular alternative to Hercules and Raleigh. London bike dealer Claud Butler purchased the Saxon name in the 1940s, and made twin stay frames under the Saxon badge into the 1950s. **BS**

SIRONVAL Sportplex

1939 • Four-wheeled velocar • France • French prewar four-wheeled pedal car

Quadricycles had first been exhibited at the Exhibition of the Industry of All Nation's World's Fair in New York City in 1853. To some extent, they had been popularized in the mid-1920s by French engineer Charles Mochet's enclosed, pedal-powered, automobilelike velocars.

In the 1930s, another Frenchman, Victor Sironval, experimented with several forms of velocar, including various two-wheeled varieties and a motorized four-wheeler before producing this Sportplex, a two-seater quadricycle. His designs were neither as advanced nor as "carlike" as Mochet's, although it's likely they would have evolved along the lines of Mochet's vehicles had it not been for the outbreak of the Second World War in 1939. The Sportplex therefore represented more of a resurgence than an emergent new trend.

The Nazi invasion of a large part of France in the following year brought an end to normal life in the country for the duration of the conflict. One of the privations was a severe shortage of gasoline. Although this adversely affected most businesses, it worked to the advantage of the Sportplex because it needed no fuel—it was one of the hits of the period.

With the right marketing, Sironval's people mover—or something like it—could have even greater appeal today. Impossible to tip over, the Sportplex has two sets of steering wheels and two sets of pedals, which thus necessitate a degree of coordination between its riders. The handbrake in the center between the seats is accessible to both occupants. It has two large chromed headlamps, rearview mirrors, pressed metal fenders, and comfortable plush seats with attached backrests, all on a tubular steel frame. In fact, everything you'd get in a "proper" automobile—apart from an engine and a fuel tank. **BS**

Rear-steer tandems, velocars, sidecars; it all happened in the 1930s. ▷

COLUMBIA Superb

1941 • Deluxe cruiser bike • USA • A bike ahead of its time becomes a retro classic

One of the most gorgeous-looking cruiser bikes ever conceived failed to make it off the drawing board because of the outbreak of the Second World War. The Columbia Superb would have represented the zenith of prewar designer bicycles, with a chromium-plated dashboard housing an odometer, clock, and speedometer; a rear luggage rack with built-in light; and a front headlight that echoed Art Deco streamlining and the rocketships of Flash Gordon. The ladies' version was designed to have flamboyant wire skirtguards on the rear wheel, and the striping and detailing would have been second to none. Unfortunately, the original design was one of many casualties of the Japanese attack on Pearl Harbor in 1941, as Columbia production turned to more pressing matters.

However, in 1997, in the wake of the reissue of Schwinn's famous Black Phantom, Columbia decided to revive Superb and take advantage of the resurgent interest in retro cycles. Production was at the original Columbia factory in Westfield, Massachusetts, and even some of the same tooling was used where possible. But again the project was doomed. Suppliers failed to deliver the fenders, some of the clocks wouldn't fit neatly into the dashboard (and many simply didn't work), there were problems with the powder coating, and early headlights had defective bulbs.

Once more, the Superb was shelved. This is a sad fact, because style like this comes along all too rarely: Even at rest, the Columbia Superb is poetry in motion. **BS**

BSA Airborne

1943 • Folding bike • UK • Folding bicycle issued to paratroops during the Second World War

During the Second World War, bicycles were an obvious answer to the need for a cheap and lightweight method of giving speed and mobility to infantry, especially at a time when gasoline supplies were restricted. This was particularly true for troops landing from parachutes, who were severely limited in the size and number of vehicles that could accompany them into action.

British airborne forces had a unique bicycle cleverly designed to fold in half. After initial trials proving that the bike could effectively be parachuted from aircraft, in 1942 the government placed an order with BSA for an eventual total of 70,000 such bikes.

Two models were made: one with a separate twin seat tube, the other with a more conventional design. Both bikes had hinges on their twin top and down tubes that fastened with a wing nut, along with another hinge that allowed the bars to be folded, and a simple bare rod pedal that would push through without protruding, along with cable-operated front and rear brakes.

The bicycle was used by British and Canadian troops in Norway in 1942 and Sicily in 1943. By the time of D-Day in 1944, the availability of Horsa gliders, which could carry jeeps, gave Allied forces a far greater airlifting capacity. As a result, rather than being dropped from the air, the bikes were issued to troops landing from ships on the beaches of Normandy, although they were back in airborne use for the disastrous drop on Arnhem.

After the war, many BSA Airborne bikes continued in civilian use, and copies are still made in the UK today by Pashley. **KF**

RENÉ HERSE Concours

1947 • Road bike • France • Award-winning lightweight tourer

René Herse was one of several French builders—others included Nicola Barra and Alex Singer—who competed in an annual technical trials competition for the lightest touring bike. Because the bikes had to be fully functional, dynamo lights and a luggage rack capable of carrying a 9-lb (4-kg) load were obligatory.

Winner of the competition in 1947, the Herse Concours used ultra-thin-walled Reynolds 531 tubing fillet, which was brazed rather than lugged, to minimize weight. The rack and fixing bolts were aluminum. The leather saddle was drilled out. The resulting weight of the complete bike, including accessories, was a remarkably light 17½ lb (7.9 kg).

"Of all the bikes I've had, my René Herse was the best. It was the ultimate in quality."

Roger Baumann

Among the many other awards and competitions won by Herse's bikes were the eight French national female championship victories achieved by his daughter, Lyli.

Herse's later innovations included a hub where the wheel could be removed while the freewheel stayed attached to the frame so that the rider didn't have to handle an oily chain when repairing a puncture.

In 1962, Herse introduced the Demountable split frame with quick-release frame tube junction; this paved the way for Ritchey's Breakaway and S & S Couplings frames. Between then and his death in 1976, René Herse built frames for numerous successful racers, including Geneviève Gambillon, who won the road world championship in 1972 and 1974. **GK**

CLAUD BUTLER Avant Coureur

1948 • Road bike • UK • Postwar bike with a new style of frame engineering

One of the best-known names in British cycling belonged to a humble club cyclist from south London. Claud Butler worked as a bike salesman and opened his own shop in 1928. More shops followed and Butler began building his own bikes. He also began sponsoring leading riders of the day and his bikes were used to compete in four world championships and the Olympic Games.

Just before the Second World War, Butler began to experiment with steel frame construction techniques being pioneered on the continent. After the war these ideas came to fruition in the Avant Coureur bike.

This road machine had a bronze-welded jointing system, without the use of the usual lug castings to strengthen the joints. This construction method became a feature of the Claud Butler range. Lugless welded frames had previously been regarded as an inferior alternative to lugged brazed frames, as the lugless frames required less labor.

Undeterred, by 1948 Butler had developed his technique for jointing into a bilaminated construction system. This used decorative sleeves pressed from flat-sheet steel that were applied around joints instead of lugs. It needed a mixture of bronze-welding and capillary-brazing techniques. The end result was distinctive and ornate fake-lug designs (like the ax-heads on the Coureur). They looked good and were stronger than most established methods of joining lightweight steel tubing.

The bike itself sat on 27-in. (69-cm) rims with a 40½-in. (103-cm) wheelbase. The frame featured lightweight 531 butted steel tubing, sturdy large flange hubs, and 3- or 4-speed Simplex gears. There were also alloy bars, stem, mudguards, and brakes. It was advertised as "the inevitable choice of the connoisseur." **SH**

Ornately decorated lugs created Butler's signature. ▶

BARRA Randonneuse

1948 • Road bike • France • Ultra-light and innovative distance machine

In 1934 members of the French cycling club Groupe Montagnard Parisien introduced special *concours de machines* (technical trials) for bikes to encourage the minimization of weight (and hence the maximization of speed). The winner of the inaugural competition, Nicola Barra, did not then rest on his laurels. He finished first equal in the following year with André Reyhand and kept on innovating right up to and after the Second World War.

Most of these advances were made through the use of aluminum tubing with ever-thinner walls, but Barra also created a range of ultra-light components. These included in 1936 the first modern cantilever brakes with adjustable toe-in pads—an advanced piece of technology that did not find its way onto mass-market bikes until the 1980s.

In addition to its aluminum tubes and customized stem, the most distinctive features on this particularly beautiful Randonneuse are its internally sprung Cyclo rear gears and Le Chat front derailleur, French Stronglight chainset and Mavic rim, and Maxicar hubs. None of which added significant weight to an outstanding long-distance machine that weighed only 20 lb 15 oz (9.5 kg) when fully equipped. **HK**

HOBBS Blue Riband

1948 • Road bike • UK • With the Blue Riband, no component was too exotic

If ever a manufacturer built bikes on the premise that "it's the little things that count," it was Hobbs. There wasn't a bike maker around in the late 1930s who could match the beauty of the lugs crafted by artisans whose even application of brazing material approached perfection on the hand cut, exquisitely ornate, Continental Superbe.

Albert Hobbs began making bicycles in the Barbican, London, in 1930, but moved to the Sterling Works in Dagenham, Essex, after the factory suffered extensive damage during the Blitz.

Desirable though not especially innovative, the Blue Riband, first launched as a prototype range in 1948, had KROMO (chrome-molybdenum) steel tubing and was full of exotic period components, including undrilled Harden "bacon-slicer" hubs, Constrictor Conloy sprint rims, and lovely BSA double-fluted chainsets. Hobbs also made its own range of sought-after components under the Lytaloy brand. These included headsets, bottom bracket bearings, brakes, mudguards, and lamp brackets, as well as elegant personalized touches like the HB-branded pedal plates and rare British alloy Catos toe clips. In sum, the Blue Riband was a treasure trove of the very Best of British. **BS**

RIH SPORT Champion

1948 • Road bike • Netherlands • Classic bike from leading Dutch builder

In 1921, the brothers Joop and Willem Bustraan of Amsterdam named their bicycle company after Rih, a horse in one of nineteenth-century German author Karl May's adventure books. The name means "faster than the wind."

Three years later, RIH won its first championship when a local butcher rode a Bustraan frame to victory in the sprint and 1-km event in the Dutch National Championships. Over the life of the company, RIH would go on to win sixty-three World titles.

In 1948, the brothers handed over their business to Willem's son, Willem, Jr., who in 1955 brought in a young untried apprentice, Wim van der Kaay. Van der Kaay eventually took over the company, and continued building RIH frames until the business finally closed in May 2012.

RIH was the first Dutch manufacturer of lightweight frames, and its bikes were always traditionally styled, with lugged steel and not an oversized tube to be seen anywhere. In the 1940s and 1950s, RIH customers read like a Who's Who of Dutch cycling: World champion Gerrit Schulte, Olympic champion Arie van Vliet, and World Professional track sprint champion Jan Derksen. **BS**

HUFFY Convertible

1949 • Road bike • USA • Children's bicycle with rear training wheels and foot steps

Huffy's roots can be traced back to 1887, when George P. Huffman bought the Davis Sewing Machine Company of New York and moved the works to Dayton, Ohio. In 1892, the company diversified into bikes, which it marketed as Daytons until 1949, when it adopted the Huffy name for its flagship model, the Convertible.

The Convertible's crucial innovations were rear training wheels (stabilizers) and a foot step. These apparently minor modifications to the basic bike design had major consequences: They opened up a whole new market by making mass-produced cycles attractive to younger riders.

Demand was massive and immediate, but luckily Huffman had already led many advances in the improvement of the production-line process, so he was ideally placed to capitalize on the Convertible craze.

By 1953, all bikes produced by the Davis company were marketed as Huffys. Several decades of commercial success followed, but at the start of the twenty-first century the makers fell on hard times. They struggled for several years before being filing for bankruptcy in 2004. However, the brand name still exists to this day, producing bikes in China, and in 2006 the company issued its hundred millionth bike. **DB**

BIANCHI Reparto Corse

1949 • Race bike • Italy • Fausto Coppi's Bianchis become as recognizable as the man himself

In just ten years, Bianchi bicycles—which the twenty-one-year-old Edoardo Bianchi started from scratch in 1885 in a tiny shop on the Via Nirone in Milan—went from obscurity to being asked to provide an open-framed bicycle for Italy's Queen Margherita. The company also taught her how to ride it.

Thereafter Bianchi would never again be far from royalty—at least, cycling royalty—as the company's sponsorship of race teams attracted a succession of great European cyclists. Its first champion was Giovanni Tomaselli, who in 1899 won the Grand Prix de Paris, the world's top track racing event.

Perhaps the greatest name on Bianchi's books was Fausto Coppi, whose rivalry with aging champion Gino Bartali, the leading rider for Legnano, became the stuff of legend.

Coppi reached the peak of his cycling prowess in 1949, when he became the first rider to win both the Giro d'Italia and the Tour de France in the same year. Both victories were achieved in the unmistakable celeste green colors of Bianchi on a bike assembled in the company's Reparto Corse (racing department) factory in Treviglio.

In all, Coppi would win five Giros d'Italia and two Tours on a Bianchi Reparto Corse. In 1953, he secured the World Championship on a modified model of the same bike with an integrated headset that was decades ahead of its time. These wins helped to consolidate Bianchi as one of the greatest and most enduring bike manufacturers, unmatched for the quality of its carbon fiber and titanium frames strengthened with foam injection. Its reputation remains unrivaled to this day: Among its recent champions have been Julien Absalon, Vera Carrara, and Danilo Di Luca.

At the time of publication, Bianchi was the oldest bicycle manufacturing company still in existence. **BS**

" . . . the Bianchi brand survived wars, economic crises, mergers, and takeovers to remain 'the name' to this day."

David Rapley, Racing Bicycles: 100 Years of Steel

ⓒ Fausto Coppi was a true legend of postwar cycling.

WALLER Kingsbury

1949 • Road bike • UK • Postwar British frame builder does the best with what he can find

Born in 1913, Albert Waller learned to weld and braze in the late 1930s while serving in the Royal Horse Guards regiment of the British army. A motorcycle despatch rider during the Second World War, he was invalided back into civilian life after suffering a leg wound. In 1945, he decided to try his hand at bicycle making in premises at 325 Kingsland Road in Hackney, London.

Waller's first bike, the Kingsland, reflected his abiding interest in hill climbs: It had a short 40-in. (102-cm) wheelbase of girder construction to minimize whipping and drag. But he wanted even less. "We later managed to reduce the wheelbase to 37½ in. [95.25 cm] with 27-in. [69-cm] wheels, and still maintained a good riding position," he wrote in a letter in 1982. He named this model the Kingsbury.

The Kingsbury had a truncated seat tube that was supported by two tubes of smaller diameter that ran from the seatstays to the seat tube, and a single beefier tube that ran between the twin verticals to the underside of the top tube. The top tube, seat tube, and down tube all used 531 butted tubing, but the nature of the material that Waller used to make the verticals remains unknown.

Although the quality of Waller's brazing work can only be described as uneven, he developed a loyal clientele. But he never marketed his bicycles through other cycle shops, only his own, and his business remained a one-man operation that lasted less than five years, throughout which his customers were limited to the loyal cyclists of East and North London. Shortly before Waller closed his door for the last time, his son predicted: "They will at some future date restart building these frames, but unfortunately they may be manufactured abroad and imported into this country." To date the prophecy remains unfulfilled. **BS**

DICK POWER Track

1950 • Track bike • USA • Classic New York-built style leader

In the 1940s and 1950s, Dick Power played a pivotal role in the development of the New York cycle scene. The owner of the Sunnyside Bicycle Shop in Queens, Power helped many young New Yorkers achieve their best in the world of cycling, and he spent long hours designing and tinkering with road and track bikes. His ongoing involvement in cycling shifted to coaching following the death of his son in 1951, but he never stopped building custom bikes. These numbered between 400 and 500 in his lifetime, but only a tantalizing fifty or so remain. One of those is the now-classic Dick Power 1950 Track.

Often built around the Higgins frames Power imported from England along with Webb racing

". . . elegant pinstriping and fine craftsmanship . . . a link to an almost forgotten time."

Sean Farrell, The New York Times

pedals, Chater-Lea cranks, and Brooks or Mansfield leather saddles, Power's track bikes were designed and built to be raced on banked tracks at speeds in excess of 45 mph (72 kph). They were practical bikes, designed to be raced hard and often, and to remain totally competitive at the end of the longest track day. That is why, if you're fortunate enough to lay eyes on a Dick Power bike these days, its decals will be tattered and its handmade lugs worn, and it'll be probably be very much the worse for wear. But don't let that stop you from making an offer—Dick Power custom bikes are prized by collectors such as Edward Albert, who, when asked if he rode them, replied: "Do you ride your Picasso? Your Mondrian? No, I hang it on the wall. These are pieces of history." **BS**

Track racing flourished in the postwar United States. ▶

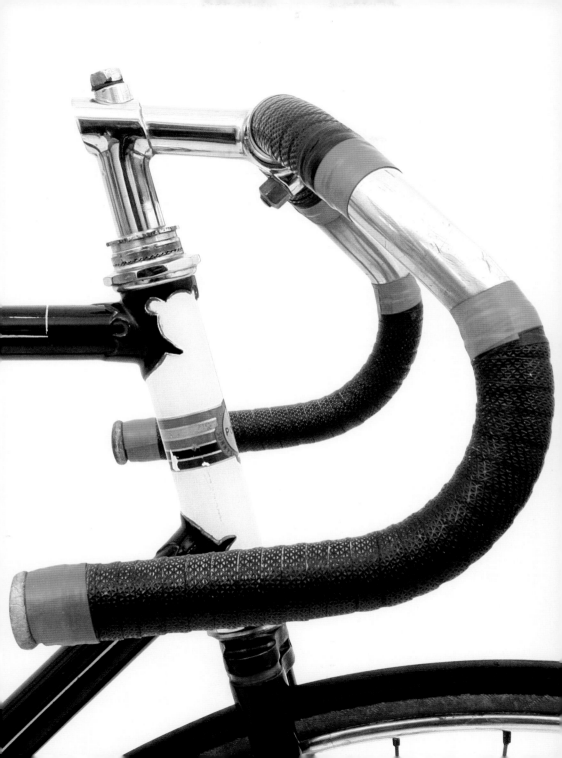

HUFFY Radiobike

1950 • Kids' bike • USA • Kids' bike with a radio in the frame

By the time the Radiobike was produced in 1955, Huffy was already riding on the crest of a wave with its iconic and highly popular Convertible children's bike.

The Convertible featured innovative stabilizers, but Huffy's next move was even bolder. At a time when science fiction and technology in general had grabbed the imagination of nearly every child—and many adults—Huffy's new bike came with an amazing built-in accessory: a transistor radio in the purposely outsized top tube or "gas tank" section of the frame.

Like the Convertible, the Radio was produced in flamboyant red, blue, or green with black-and-white trim, but the three-vacuum-tube valve radio was undoubtedly the big attraction. The radio was designed by Huffy but manufactured by the Yellow Springs Instrument Company, which—like Huffy itself—was based in Ohio.

The radio was powered by a battery pack toward the rear of the bike, and the antenna was located on the curved down tube. The tuner could apparently pick up stations up to 100 mi (160 km) away, which it broadcast via a speaker located in the tank. The original bike was produced in a single-speed version, but there was also an option for a two-speed Bendix rear hub with coaster brake.

Like the Convertible, the Radiobike was produced for only a few years before being taken off the market. Surviving examples look as eye-catching and stylish as they did in 1950, and are a reminder of how innovative Huffy was in its heyday. **DB**

RALEIGH Superbe

1950 • Road bike • UK • Raleigh's iconic all-steel bicycle

If you like bicycles and have a mind to become a collector, you could do worse than start with a 1950 Raleigh Superbe. The fact that they were plentiful means there are enough around to make them reasonably affordable if one comes up, which in turn means that spare parts can still be had. Plus, of course, these "All-steel Bicycles," famously "built to last a hundred years," have weathered the passing decades well.

Raleigh Superbes in good condition are capable of generating some real bidding wars between their many admirers, especially if they have all their original features still intact. These included a full chain case for clean, quiet running; robust if relatively weak rod brakes; and a DynoHub lighting system. Upgrade models may also have a handmade Brooks saddle and

a matching black leather Brooks tool pouch hanging off the back of it.

The Superbe and its stablemate, the Sports, were the workhorses of the Raleigh line, and they incorporated many neat practical features, including a key-lockable front fork that would immobilize the steering and make theft a very dangerous business. Full-length mudguards protected the rider from the worst of the British weather. The substantial weight was made easier to shift by Sturmey-Archer three-speed hub gears, selected by their iconic slim-bodied single-lever handlebar trigger shifter.

None of these features was new, but the Superbe brought them all together in a package that became a byword for reliability. More than a million of these bikes were produced in 1951. **BS**

FLYING PIGEON Utility

1950 • Utility bike • China • The most-produced wheeled vehicle ever

ELSWICK HOPPER Model W

1951 • Tradesman's bike • UK • Classic delivery bike

If ever a consumer item was guaranteed popularity, it was the bicycle in the wake of the rise to power in China of Chairman Mao Zedong and the Chinese Communist Party in 1949. Automobiles were practically unobtainable by all but the wealthiest party officials. Consequently, the bicycle so embedded itself in the emergent culture of the new People's Republic that it became the focus of an entirely new tradition—*san zhuan yi xiang* ("three rounds and a sound"), the four precious gifts that every groom presents to his bride. The rounds would be the spindle on a sewing machine, the face on a watch, and the wheel of a bicycle; the sound would be that of a transistor radio.

The only make of bicycle available in China at the time was the domestically produced, state-approved Flying Pigeon. In the absence of the consumer choice that residents of capitalist countries take for granted, Flying Pigeons quickly became the most numerous vehicles in the history of humankind.

Designed by a worker at a pre-Communist bicycle factory in Tianjin to look like the classic English Raleigh Roadster of 1932, the first Flying Pigeon came off the production line on July 5, 1950. For Mao Zedong, the bike was far more than just a mode of transport: It was a symbol of China's new egalitarianism.

The first models were the PA-02 and the PA-06 for men and the PB-13 for women. Designed to be almost indestructible, they were all-steel and gearless, with push-rod brakes, a rear rack, 28-in. (71-cm) wheels, and a sprung leather saddle. They could also be equipped with a dynamo light.

Even today, a new, fully automated factory in Tianjin with just 600 employees (down from 15,000 in 1950) still produces more than 800,000 Flying Pigeons every year. **BS**

Throughout the first half of the twentieth century, bikes were used by a wide variety of workers, from chimney sweeps and delivery boys to policemen.

In Lincolnshire, England, Elswick Hopper made many such tradesmen's bikes. Its Model W—a classic that appeared in factories, streets, and markets worldwide—was a sturdy, corrosion-proof bike with a hefty tube cage bolted to the steel frame to hold a large wicker basket. Mounted in the middle of the frame triangle was a metal sheet on which could be painted the name, address, and slogan of the owner's business.

It was clearly a working machine, not a leisure item; it was all black, even the grips. The Model W was single

> *"I like this bicycle a lot. It's good to ride . . . I've had a few Elswicks . . . [they're] quite underrated."*
>
> Oldbike

speed, with front and rear rod-operated brakes, heavy-duty front forks, strong wheels with heavy-gauge spokes, and substantial mudguards.

The Utility model was a variant with a smaller front wheel that left space for a bigger, deeper basket, and a retractable two-legged front stand. The latter was useful for loading and unloading or for tradesmen such as knife grinders, who would put the bike up on the stand and then pedal it stationary to turn a whetstone.

Tradesmen's bikes were treated roughly as tools rather than cherished as beloved possessions. Thus, relatively few have survived. Those that are still extant, however, are again becoming sought after as retro city bikes and as static outdoor advertising boards. **SH**

THANET Silverlight

1951 • Road bike • UK • Elegantly designed road bike

British cyclist Les Cassell named his company after his birthplace, the Isle of Thanet in Kent.

Thanet Bikes ended up being based on the other side of England in Bristol, which is where most of its distinctive Silverlights were produced. These bikes had a unique frame design that lived up to the company slogan, "Ease with elegance." The Silverlight used narrow-gauge Reynolds 531 double-butted tubing to create a frame that cradled the bottom bracket above the joint of the down tube and the seat tube in imitation of the way that aircraft engines of the time were supported.

The chainstays were dainty, and the seatstays had an unusual configuration, crossing over the seat tube to join the top tube. This created an extra-small triangle and added to the frame's structural strength. It's a feature that has since reappeared in bike designs at regular intervals, including GT's "triple triangles," but Les Cassell and Thanet did it first. There were decoratively shaped lugs around the joints, and a fine paint finish. Look closely and you'll even find tiny T shapes cut from some of the lugs as a company signature.

Early Thanet models used a silver brazing technique that wasn't entirely reliable but, by 1951, Silverlights had evolved into sought-after upmarket products. They came with either a single fixed sprocket or a four-speed Sturmey-Archer hub. As handmade, custom-built machines, they featured state-of-the-art on-board kit, including Hobbs Lytaloy pedals, a Brooks saddle on a Reynolds aluminum seatpost, and Brooks brakes made of hiduminium—the word is a portmanteau of "high duty aluminum," which was an alloy originally developed by Rolls-Royce for aircraft, and declassified after the Second World War for use in civil engineering. **SH**

WEARWELL Mountain King

1951 • Road bike • UK • One of Britain's oldest cycle manufacturers never lost the ability to innovate

The Cogent Cycle Company was founded in Wolverhampton, England, in 1868 by soldier and former blacksmith Henry Clarke, who had first seen a bicycle in France while being repatriated after being wounded in the Crimean War (1853–1856). In 1889, four of Clarke's sons—William, Jack, Henry, and George—started the Wearwell Cycle Co. Ltd. The business changed hands in 1928 but continued on, and by the late 1940s three-quarters of its production was being exported to some thirty-eight countries. Business had never been better, and in this golden age the Mountain King was born.

The Mountain King had Reynolds 531 butted frame tubes and in-vogue 72-degree parallel angles, with Cyclo

"I was rather pleased to see a bicycle of this quality . . . made throughout in Britain."

Cycling Magazine

Benelux Super 60 10-speed gears, bold lugwork, and a finely brazed lamp bracket. Its wheels were Dunlop Special lightweight high-pressure rims with large flange hubs and road racing tires, and its Brooks saddle came with a chromium-plated frame. Finishing options included chromium-plated fork ends, and the bike came with a blue paint job and a variety of lighter blue contrast areas. It was, simply, a beautiful machine. And it was all British.

It was undeniably light, of course, but nevertheless left an impression of being dependably solid and stable in the recollections of many who rode it. And the good news was the golden age wasn't over—two years after the release of the Mountain King, the Wearwell cycle team won the 1953 Tour of Britain. **BS**

BENOTTO Cambio Corsa

1952 • Race bike • Italy • From Venezuela to Mexico, Benotto never lost sight of its Italian heritage

Benotto Bicycles was founded in Turin, Italy, in 1931 by Cesare Benotto and his brother Giacinto. Unlike most other histories of humble European frame-building beginnings, however, the Benotto story took an odd twist in 1948 after the family read of the vast oil reserves that had been discovered in Venezuela. They packed 200 bicycles on a boat and set sail for La Guaira, where they were met by customs officials who told them: "Here in Venezuela, we don't ride bicycles, we drive Cadillacs."

Undeterred, the Benottos went on to build Venezuela's first folding bicycle and its first tandem. In 1952, Benotto racing bikes came equipped with

"In the late 1980s, Benotto handlebar tape was the thing to have on a racing bike."

Michael Kone, Harris Cyclery

Campagnolo Cambio Corsa derailleurs, Ballila brakes, and Benoot stamped cranks.

In 1953, the brothers learned of the potential benefits of setting up a factory in Mexico, and transferred most of the company's production of lower-end frames there, although the high-end examples continued to be made in Italy. In the 1980s, Mexico-made Benottos came with frames and forks of lightweight, durable Mannesmann Oria steel tubing with an abundance of chrome, superb detailing, and Benotto pantograph gears.

Benotto has won eleven world championships, and in 1968 Ole Ritter set an hour record on a Benotto in Mexico City. The company also originated the Celocinta textured handlebar tape that helps champions maintain their grip on their machines. **BS**

JACK TAYLOR Curved Tube

1952 • Road bike • UK • Curved seat tube, ultra-short wheelbase racer

For racing cyclists, comfort has always been secondary to speed. In the early 1950s, racers thought that a shorter wheelbase meant shorter rear tubes, and more power reaching the back wheel for faster climbing and acceleration. The curved tube frame also managed to shrink the distance between the wheels by curving the seat tube around the wheel, creating a more nimble-handling, faster-reacting bike. That stiffness also meant the bike would absorb road bumps less well.

Jack Taylor's frame didn't have much wheel clearance, either. The 27-in. (69-cm) wheels and high-pressure tires left no space for mudguards. The clearance was so tight that the wheels could only be fitted with track ends that allowed the wheels to be removed to the rear.

As a result, this bike was targeted at particularly aggressive, masochistic riders. Ads said it was perfect for hill climbs and time trials. Whatever the merits of the ride and handling, it was certainly an eye-catching and stylish look. The specification shows that the Curved Tube model of 1951 was a single-speed machine for serious racers, with alloy rims, DF large flange hubs, Lyotard Platform pedals, and a Brooks Competition leather saddle.

The curved-tube models were built with lugless frames because of the difficulty sourcing steel lugs in postwar Britain, where rationing remained until 1954. Instead, Taylor bikes became renowned for their high-quality fillet-brazing technique.

Jack Taylor dates back to 1936, when the company's founder started building them in his mother's garden shed in Stockton, England. In 1945, he set up a business with his brothers Ken (a fine wheel builder) and Norman (an expert welder). To promote their bikes, the trio even competed as a race team. **SH**

HERCULES Eileen Sheridan

1953 • Road bike • UK • An early celebrity-endorsed bike

Eileen Sheridan was an English cyclist who specialized in breaking road records. She was so successful that in 1951 Hercules Bikes signed her on to break as many distance and place-to-place records as she could.

This is the bike the company produced to celebrate the end of Sheridan's time with Hercules. It was a tough, speedy long-distance road tourer roughly based on the bikes she used with outstanding success.

"Roughly" is the right word, because the actual bike Sheridan used was not, in fact, a Hercules. Standard Hercules frames were considered too heavy for her, so the bike was secretly made elsewhere and relabeled. Nevertheless, the Eileen Sheridan autographed bike

> *"[Sheridan] helped to lead to a change in attitude to women's sport in general."*
>
> Road Records Association

was definitely made by the company. It came with a Reynolds 531 frame, available in two sizes: 21 and 23 in. (53 and 58 cm). The frame was spray bonderized before enameling for rust resistance. A 3-speed hub was an optional extra. The tyres were Dunlop Speeds, 26 in. (66 cm) in diameter and 1¼ in. (3 cm) wide; the brakes were GB alloy with hooded levers. In addition, the bike had racing "rat-trap" pedals and brazed-on eyes holding white celluloid mudguards.

Some of Sheridan's times are still remarkable. These include London–Edinburgh—332 mi (534 km)—in 20 hours, 11 minutes and 35 seconds, and Land's End (the southwestern tip of England) to John O'Groats (the northern tip of Scotland)—603 mi (970 km)—in 2 days, 11 hours, and 7 minutes. **SH**

MALVERN FIVE STAR Track Racer

1954 • Track bike • Australia • Lightweight Australian racer

It arrived with typical Australian bravado. "The lightest thoroughly reliable track bike ever built," said the ads at the time.

The Malvern Five Star Dural Track Racer was certainly a dedicated speed machine. In "ready-for-the-track" form the steel-framed race bike weighed just 14 lb 14 oz (6.7 kg). And the price of this world-beater? In 1939 it was sold at only £18 and 18 shillings ($30).

Malvern Star had been making bikes in Victoria, Australia since 1902. The company had links with British component manufacturer BSA and used many of its parts, which were regarded in Australia as "the world's finest fittings."

In the postwar Malvern range the Five Star was the flagship. Each bike had five stars proudly brazed to the front of the head tube. By 1948 the Five Star had been fitted with ingenious additional features, such as the fat handlebar grips, which were made from old wartime gas mask hoses. The frame was hand-painted with logos, decoration, and highlighted decorative lugwork. The bike included a water-bottle holder and front brake, as racers of the day would use their track bikes for road training too.

The Five Star was exported around the world for racing specialists. It was ridden to the World Sprint Championship in 1949, the World Pursuit Championship in 1950, and the Professional Pursuit Title in 1952 and 1953. A Malvern tandem even won a gold medal at the 1956 Australian Olympics.

Malvern Star enjoyed another international moment of glory in 1984, not from any further spectacular sporting triumph, but when one of the teenage stars of the hit film *BMX Bandits* rode a Malvern Star SuperMax. The young unknown actress with a ginger Afro was Nicole Kidman. **SH**

CARLTON Jewel

1954 • Race bike • UK • When it came to outshining its competitors, the Jewel was in a class of its own

Fred Hanstock began making bicycles in 1896 in Carlton-in-Lindrick, a small village in Nottinghamshire, England, and over time developed a reputation for superb handcrafted bicycles with outstanding hand-cut lugs and flamboyant paintwork. Carlton Cycles became one of the truly exceptional British frame makers, thanks in no small part to craftsmen like Bob Keeling, who had already been hearth-brazing frames at Carlton for around twenty years when he turned his hand to the first example of what would become its top-of-the-line bicycle of the mid-1950s, the Jewel.

Keeling recalled making only "about six or seven" Jewels. Although their ornate appearance and nice touches, such as customized chainwheels and cranks, made them more attractive than most other bikes of their own—or, in the view of some, any other—time, they were nevertheless, even by Keeling's own admission, "a little overpriced," costing ten percent more than even the intricately lugged, gold-outlined Hetchins Magnum Opus. The Jewel was the most expensive British lightweight of its time.

It was a "one man, one machine" bicycle, made under the strict supervision of the works manager and created to fit its rider. A wide range of optional kit included Dupra cranks, TA rings, Chater Sprint pedals, Simplex 543 mechs, a Brooks B17 Swallow saddle, FB hubs, Conloy Asp rims, and Le Roi "Bartali" levers.

Completed frames were washed and given phosphate baths before receiving two primers: first a gray, then a silver. The final color was applied using two coats of resin-impregnated Epigloss for a shine second to none. Then came its additional colored panels, linings, and transfers, followed by a final coat of protective lacquer. The aptly named Jewel outshone every bicycle around it and the remaining examples glister to this day. **BS**

"All Carlton chromium plating, their well-known speciality, is to a standard well above the 'severe service' specification."

Cycling Magazine, *November 1961*

◁ Carlton's 1954 flagship really was a Jewel.

VIKING Tour of Britain

1956 • Road bike • UK • High achiever in a talented stable of lightweight racers

In 1908, railway worker Alfred Davies began repairing bikes in a small wooden shed in Wolverhampton, England. Forced by his employer to choose between the day job and his new business, Davies opted to work for himself. He excelled in building lightweight racing bikes, and increasing demand over thirty years saw two moves to larger premises.

When Davies died in 1941, his son, Victor, took over, and in 1951 the company—Viking Cycles Ltd—introduced a new series of road racer, the Tour of Britain, which Scottish cyclist Ian Steel rode to victory in the inaugural competition of the same name. The Tour of Britain became the new flagship of the Viking range.

> "Davies built the business up to a concern producing around 20,000 cycles a year."

Viking Cycles Heritage

Every bike that bore the name was made from Reynolds 531 butted tubes and had a reinforced rear brake bridge, pump pegs, and Nervex professional lugs. The wheels were made from bought-in rims, hubs, and spokes. The locally applied chromium plating was of such magnificent quality that some customers tried to insist that the entire frame be finished in this material!

Although the Viking catalog states that no Tour of Britain models were made beyond 1956, there are riders who claim to have owned later examples. What cannot be denied, however, is that the 1950s was the high-water mark of Viking's popularity, with the SS Master series, the Mileater, the Ian Steel model, and the Tour of Britain forming a stable worthy of the most legendary models in the business. **BS**

CINELLI Corsa

1957 • Road bike • Italy • Iconic race bike with a steel frame

With attractively slim steel tubes, chrome lugs, and superb attention to detail, the Cinelli Corsa is in many ways an iconic Italian lightweight road bike from a golden age. It was the all-purpose road machine that everyone wanted but few could acquire.

The Cinelli company was founded in 1948 by former professional racer Cino Cinelli, a past winner of the Milan–San Remo classic. As a result of the mechanical problems he had endured while racing, Cinelli took an interest in bicycle design. He failed to get existing manufacturers to work with his ideas, so decided to go it alone.

Cinelli worked on the theory that race bikes needed to be made more rigid, so he designed a fork crown with sloping shoulders and internal lugs that went onto some Corsa frames. This crown allowed him to make the fork legs shorter and stiffer. He altered the design of the seat collar too, attaching the seatstays behind the lug rather than alongside it in order to add strength and prevent unwanted movement at the back of the bike.

The quality of workmanship found on many Cinelli Corsas is outstanding, with excellent mitering and brazing throughout, and visually the Corsa is a classic of its time. It manages to sum up Italian style and has inspired countless copies, few of which capture the genius of the original. On top of that, many enthusiasts regard the Corsa's ride quality as bordering on faultless.

Cino Cinelli produced his frames in small quantities—no more than a few hundred each year. Most went to high-level racers of the era and were ridden to great success. Today the relative scarcity of the Corsa has helped make it one of the most sought-after of all vintage race bikes, with a massive international following. **MB**

ELSWICK HOPPER Vampire Convincible

1957 • Road bike • UK • Unique sliding chainring and double tube frame

Few production bikes are as scarce as this bizarrely named offering from Elswick Hopper. Until recently only one prototype was known to exist. It had been found in pieces by an English bike enthusiast and carefully restored.

Then recently an American bike historian stumbled on this perfectly intact version of the machine. It's the only known complete production model of the Elswick Vampire Convincible.

Mysteriously, the bike built in the village of Barton-in-Humber in England was found hanging from the ceiling of a garage attic in an elderly disabled man's house in New York State.

And what a strange machine it is. The frame had a very short wheelbase to appeal to racers and featured a sliding front chainwheel. This unique mechanism involved a long axle at the bottom bracket so the front chainwheel could move from side to side to stay in line with whichever rear sprocket was chosen.

The Reynolds 531 frame needed to be specially designed to accommodate this sliding chain system and the 37½-in. (95.25-cm) wheelbase. It required a special double down tube and seat tube design. The twin seatstays met the seatpost and top tube in a strange complex junction.

Nevertheless, the idea caused a minor sensation at the 1955 Bike Show at Earls Court in London. Sadly it was soon rendered redundant by rapid developments in the flexibility of chains. The extra weight, cost, and maintenance of the Elswick system made the bike not worth its £39 ($62) price tag.

Elswick's North Lincolnshire factory had been all prepared to churn out thousands of the innovative new bike. A stock of almost 2,000 "Convincible" decals were later found, unused. Elswick employees recall making "no more than six" of the bikes. **SH**

". . . this machine is such a rare collector's item that it has been included amongst Classic Builders."

Peter Underwood

Elswick's Vampire is as elusive as its namesake. ▶

SCHWINN Corvette

1959 • Cruiser bike • USA • The classic model year of a classic American bike

Schwinn was the biggest bike manufacturer in the United States in the post-Second World War period, and its bikes followed a similarly isolationist design path as the U.S. automotive industry. These bikes were characterized by curved lines and chrome fixtures that aped aircraft and automobile design in the 1950s and 1960s, and the Schwinn Corvette borrowed its name from the Chevrolet sports car of the time.

Throughout its ten-year production run from 1954, the Corvette was a case of "all show rather than all go," and most Schwinn aficionados agree that the 1959 model was the best. The S-bent alloy front rack was a feature from the original, and the two-tone saddle appeared

> *"It was a nicely equipped model that was appealing to most kids back in those days."*
>
> nostalgic.net

at the same time as Clint Walker—star of cowboy TV show *Cheyenne*—was used in Schwinn adverts. The 1959 model had "S seats" with two-tone top and chrome springs at the rear. The bars, factory-fitted high/low-beam headlamp, cranks, and mudguards were chrome plated. The handlebar grips featured a green teardrop with the white Schwinn logo in the center, although the green color has worn off on the example opposite. The Corvette could be bought with a 3-speed hub gear and caliper brakes, a 2-speed Bendix hub gear with coaster brake, or a single-speed coaster brake hub, in 24- or 26-in. (60- or 66-cm) wheel sizes with white wall tires.

The result was a stunning-looking green, red, blue, white, or black and chrome dream machine, but at 55 lb (25 kg) in weight it was made for cruising not racing. **GK**

HARRY QUINN Milk Race Special

1959 • Race bike • UK • Bill Bradley's Milk Race winner

Leading racer of the day Bill Bradley won the 1959 Milk Race Tour of Britain on a Harry Quinn 531 Milk Race Special, custom made by the little-known specialist for the demands of the classic British road race. Bradley was riding for the England team, and went on to represent Great Britain in the Olympic Games in Rome a year later.

The exact specs of this machine are lost in the road dust of time, but experts have made educated guesses about what Quinn used for the one-off build. It was a Reynolds 531 steel frame with a 10-speed gear system. Quinn's hand-built frames were well known for their short wheelbase and steep angles.

Quinn's family business, originally named Coronet Cycles, had been turning out high-end bikes from its Liverpool workshop since 1890. Harry Quinn was the son of the founder. Other famous cyclists who rode competitively on Harry Quinn frames include Colin Sturgess, winner of the 1989 world professional pursuit title. Harry Quinn bicycles have also won many major international races, including in the Olympic and Commonwealth Games.

Although there is little certainty about the technical specification of Bradley's bike, its purchase price is known: $100 (£68). This was expensive for the time, and the high cost was justified because bike experts thought that racing bikes could never get any lighter than this.

Harry Quinn was an influential figure in the UK cycling scene, and he trained successful frame builders Terry Dolan and Billy Whitcomb. In 1977 his business was sold to Frank Clements, brother of famous bike builder Ernie Clements. Happily, Quinn was kept on as master frame builder until he retired shortly before his death in 2009 at the age of ninety-two. **SH**

◁ The 1959 Schwinn Corvette was the pinnacle of its stylish aesthetic.

HUFFY Special Roadster

1960 • Cruiser bike • USA • Classic style-over-speed cruiser with clear parallels with car design

---

Legendary U.S. bike manufacturer Huffy has had a Special Roadster in its range since 1899. By 1960, the Ohio-based company was the third-largest producer of bicycles in the United States and well on its way to making its millionth bike. The vast majority of sales were cruiser models such as the evergreen Special Roadster flagship.

In the same way that U.S. automotive design followed its own unique path and character in this period, so did American bike design. There are many parallels between the Cruiser bike and the cars of the day, too. Large white wall tires and broad, sprung saddles produced a similarly smooth ride to the softly sprung cars they shared the roads with. Tail fins, chrome, and cream and red detailing were equally popular in bike styling as they were on contemporary cars. Lazy swept-back handlebars produced a similarly laid-back steering feel that was far from sporty, and back-pedal brakes brought eventual stopping to the low-speed cruisers.

Advertising campaigns in the United States and Europe were also very different. In the States, bikes were advertised using TV celebrities from cowboy shows and other household names who had nothing to do with sport, whereas European marketing was all about top road riders and teams. Even the geared, drop-handlebar racing bikes that were produced in the United States tended to be much heavier and less refined than their European counterparts, and any U.S.-based person who was serious about riding imported their race weapons.

For all the Special Roadster's style over speed, bikes like this became the basis for the Repack racers that were to give birth to mountain biking and revolutionize the bike world in the process. **GK**

GITANE Anquetil

1960 • Road bike • France • Jacques Anquetil helped make Gitane the most recognized name in racing

---

When it comes to French racing brands, few manufacturers have a stronger claim than Gitane to the title of "The Greatest." The company's founder, Marcel Brunelière, began his frame-building career in 1925 at his workshop in Machecoul. The Gitane name (French for "gypsy") didn't appear on a bike until 1930, though, and mass frame production didn't begin until 1940. However, the slow start led to great things, and since the late 1950s Gitane bikes have won countless world and speed titles, including eleven Tour de France victories.

Gitane's greatest champion was Jacques Anquetil, the first rider to win five Tours de France (1957 and 1961–1964) and a total of more than 200 race victories

"I was impressed by the way girls were attracted to [Maurice] Dieulois . . . so I joined the club."

Jacques Anquetil

for the brand. This model is named in his honor. Anquetil switched to Gitane from Helyett after his win in the 1957 Tour. Later that year, he rode a Gitane-branded bicycle to victory in the French National Championships. (It should be noted, however, that although marked as Gitanes, Anquetil's earliest racing bikes were hand made by Bernard Carré.)

Other outstanding Gitane riders include Rudi Altig (1960 World Amateur Pursuit champion), Rolf Wolfshohl (World Cyclocross champion in 1960 and 1961), and Jean Stablinski (1962 World Road Race champion).

In 1960, Marcel Brunelière changed the name of his company to Micmo S.A., although he continued to produce more than 500 bikes per day with the Gitane brand name. **BS**

Jacques Anquetil (right) was a true cycling great. ▷

SCHWINN Varsity 8-speed

1960 • Road bike • UK • The most-produced derailleur bike of all time

Although its electro-forged frame made the Schwinn Varsity one of the heaviest lightweights ever produced, by the time production ceased in 1987 it had become the world's most-manufactured derailleur bicycle. Its success was in no small part due to shrewd advertising in comics based on the *Captain Kangaroo* CBS TV series and in *Boy's Life* magazine, which put the bike in the vanguard of the U.S. "lightweight revolution."

The Varsity 8-speed (and its sister, the Continental) extended Schwinn's derailleur line, which became so popular that soon there were no fewer than forty-eight multigear-equipped lightweight Schwinns to choose from. At the peak of its popularity, sales exceeded the company's forecasts by a factor of five. In 1961, the Varsity was upgraded to a 10-speed that took further advantage of the North American bicycle boom.

In the years to come, other lightweights would emerge from the Schwinn stable: the Super Sport, the Sprint, the Sierra, the Caliente, and the company's first Japanese-made bicycle, Le Tour. This expansion of the range was both a cause and an effect of the resurgence of cycling as both a recreation and a transportation mode of choice. As Tom Shaddox of Harris Cyclery said: "The Varsity was the foundation of reintroducing American adults to the joys of cycling, and a cornerstone in building the modern cycling infrastructure of events ... clubs, businesses, etc."

Metallurgical advances in tube elongation and weldability would eventually render electro-forged frames obsolete, but not before Schwinn had sold more than two million Varsities. The company fell on hard times, and filed for bankruptcy in 1992, but the brand was later revived as a subsidiary of Pacific Cycle, which is owned by the multinational conglomerate Dorel Industries. **BS**

MANÈGE Scooter

1960 • Kids' bike • France • This sculpted scooter helped shape a new generation of chic kids

This kids' bike was made by the French toy company Manège, and its design was perhaps influenced by the Lambretta/Vespa motor scooters manufactured in Italy by Fernando Innocenti.

Its body was made of steel, and it rode on 12-in. (30-cm) solid tires. The brochure that accompanied it mentioned nothing about brakes, nor was there a reference to its rather extreme seat height. This feature must have caused considerable anxiety to parents, although their fears may have been allayed to some extent by the rail that extended around the back at waist height to hold the rider in place.

The Scooter had just one speed—it went as fast as little legs could propel it—and it wasn't without a

"If the big wide world wants to engage with children . . . it has to make itself smaller scale."

Michael Embacher, The Embacher Collection

few dashes of childlike whimsy, including a chrome airplane attached to the front mudguard (perhaps a nod to 1950s car hood ornaments), a spare wheel to get you home should you get into trouble at the end of the driveway, a dummy headlight on the front fairing, and some streamlined chrome ornamentation over the rear "air intakes" reminiscent of the detailing on Thunderbird or Cadillac Escalade automobiles.

At 23 lb (10.5 kg), the Manège Scooter was less than half the weight of its average rider. This was in telling contrast to the extensive contemporaneous range of facsimile full-suspension mountain bikes for children that weighed more than their full-sized equivalents for adults. **BS**

The Manège Scooter was the ultimate pedal-free transport for the sixties child. ▶

RON KITCHING Milremo

1962 • Road bike • UK • Rebadged
Euro-parts collection

Tired of disputes with various suppliers, English cycling impresario Ron Kitching came up with a scheme to rebadge a wide selection of the best pro-standard European parts as his own. He chose the name Milremo from an abbreviation of the Milan–San Remo race that sounded suitably continental.

His new brand used many manufacturers' products, all rebranded as Milremo: hubs were Maillard; pumps and minor accessories were Zefal, Silca, and REG; chainrings and water bottles were TA; handlebars and stems came from Belleri and Atax/Philippe; toe clips and straps were by Christophe.

Using these rebranded parts, Kitching built up whole bikes around frames constructed by his business partner, French cyclist André Bertin, who also helped locate suppliers all over Europe.

Although Kitching's bikes were mainly motley creations, they featured a few original innovations. The brakes and pedals, for example, were more than just blind copies, and they were improvements on the originals on which they were based.

The Milremo trademark declined over the years, but it still exists. It is now registered to Shimano, which uses it to brand custom cycling clothing. **SH**

MOULTON F Frame

1962 • Lightweight commuter bike • UK •
The bike that proved that small is beautiful—and quick

In 1956, prompted by the imposition of petrol rationing as a result of the Suez Crisis, Alexander Moulton (an automotive suspension engineer and a colleague of Alex Issigonis, designer of the Mini automobile) conceived a new design for a small, lightweight bicycle. He constructed a prototype and offered it to Raleigh, but it told him that a bike with 16-in. (40-cm) wheels would never sell. So Moulton set up his own company.

Cycling historian Tony Hadland later described Raleigh's decision as "the equivalent of Decca turning down The Beatles." Raleigh had predicted that a bike with such small wheels would be too slow, but the company failed to take account of Moulton's redesigned rubber suspension system. A month after the launch of the Moulton F frame, British cyclist John Woodburn rode one in record time from London to Cardiff, Wales, and thus silenced critics.

Moulton successfully challenged the traditional diamond-frame-and-large-wheels approach to bicycle design. In 1966, Raleigh belatedly released its own Moulton-like lightweight, which the press deemed grossly inferior to Moulton's. Lesson learned. Moulton struck first and struck best, creating a mini bike for the era of the Mini car and the miniskirt. **BS**

FIORELLI Coppi

1962 • Road bike • Italy • Posthumous tribute to champion of champions

Fausto Coppi's first bike race victory as a fifteen-year-old butcher's boy won him only twenty Italian lira and a salami sandwich, but it was the start of an incredibly successful career. After turning professional in 1938 Coppi won the Tour de France twice, the Giro D'Italia five times, and the World Road Race Championship—he was *Il Campionissimo* (champion of champions).

Coppi was also a shrewd businessman. Although he rode Bianchi bikes for most of his professional career, in 1958 he struck a deal with frame builder Fiorelli to produce bikes under the Coppi name.

Coppi died of malaria two years later, but Fiorelli kept on producing the branded bikes. This was both a tribute to the racer's memory and a sound financial move. Unsurprisingly the bikes were largely similar to Fiorelli's existing designs with some very eye-catching and indulgent details. These included polished Nervex lugs for the top and bottom of the head tube, polished metal caps on the crown of the forks, and chromed panel sections on the seat tube, fork tips, and rear stays of the Columbus-tubed frame. Gears from Campagnolo and other components from Cinelli completed the bikes, which were advertised and sold all over the world and are still highly collectable today. **GK**

HUFFY Penguin Dragster

1962 • Kids' bike • USA • The bike American teenagers could ride with pride—and a little attitude

Huffy had always been aware of children's requirements. In 1949, the company was the first manufacturer to add training wheels to a kids' bike, the Huffy Convertible. It tapped into the psyche of the American child again with the help of bicycle distributors who inspired the creation of the iconic Penguin Dragster.

Peter Mole, an executive at distributors John T. Bill & Company, reported to Huffy the emergence of a new kind of bicycle with a long sweeping seat and high-rise handlebars. Children were increasingly customizing their factory bikes, Mole told Huffy, with accessories such as butterfly handlebars and new-styled Polo, or "banana," seats, to such an extent that supplies of that particular seat had all but dried up. Kids wanted something different, something with attitude, something that looked like it had a little muscle—and if they couldn't get it from a dealer, they'd simply make it themselves. Huffy wasn't immediately convinced, but after some months it agreed to produce the bike.

The high-rise banana-seat dragster was a hit, and the moment Huffy knew it was a hit the company dropped John T. Bill as its sole distributor. After all, business is business. **BS**

SOENSPORT TT Special

1962 • Time trial bike • UK • Classic time trial bike built by famous coach's son

This wonderful time trial bike featured chromed Reynolds 531 tubing and came equipped with a complete Campagnolo Grand Sport kit that included chainset, pedals, and gearing.

Its creator, Bill Soens, built it in his workshop in Liverpool, England, where his family had run cycle shops for many years. His uncle, Jimmy Soens, had excelled since 1936 as a frame builder, producing tourers, racers, and tandems in both lugless and lugged styles.

Bill opened a cycle shop in 1957 and traded under the name of his father, Eddie Soens, who in the 1930s held the British 50-mi (80-km) tandem paced track record. Though much admired as a rider, Eddie Soens is better known as a coach, and particularly for his

"He trained through instinct; he knew exactly how hard he could push and exactly when to stop."

David Lloyd on Eddie Soens

discovery of a new star. In 1970, Eddie saw a cyclist who struck him as promising but had an awkward position in the saddle. "Bloody hell," Eddie exclaimed, "you look like a monkey up a stick!" Once the unknown had agreed to lower his seat by 3 in. (7.5 cm), Eddie started work on him.

The rider, who started cycling only the previous year in an attempt to quit smoking forty cigarettes a day, went on to race in the 1972 Munich Olympics, set a 50-mi (80-km) road record, and twice win the National 5000-m (5,468-yard) Pursuit Championship. His name was David Lloyd.

Eddie Soens' unorthodox methods would take cyclists to more British, World, and Olympic championships than any other British coach. **BS**

RALEIGH Runabout

1963 • Moped • UK • Mass-market moped from leading bike manufacturer

This was the era when mopeds were cool. Mini-skirted women in plastic macs and dandy men with hair long enough to touch their collars took to the swinging streets on what were essentially motorized bicycles.

Britain's biggest bike maker, Raleigh, had previously built motorbikes, but as this new craze took hold, it imported foreign expertise. Raleigh licensed the right to build French Motobécane Mobylettes in Nottingham. At first these were called RM4s but, as demand grew, the bike was revised and renamed.

The Runabout was launched at the Winter Gardens in Blackpool in 1963 and was an immediate hit.

It was made to a tight budget from pressed steel, with a rigid fork and chunky mudguards. The engine was a humble 1.4 bhp unit and the bike had a tiny 11-pint (6.25-liter) fuel tank. Top speed was just 35 mph (56 kph). This helped the Runabout significantly undercut rivals on price, yet it had a reputation as a reliable, practical machine.

And the Runabout was easy to ride. Small 23-in. (58.4-cm) wheels kept the riding position low, and wide 2-in. (5-cm) tires gave good grip. There was no suspension, but the fat tires and sprung saddle helped keep the ride comfortable. It had cycle-style brakes to stop and a simple throttle to go. There were no gears. It was as easy as riding a bicycle. Perhaps easier—you didn't have to pedal.

Optional extras included a speedometer, chrome rear carrier and panniers, electric horn, leg-shields, and a windscreen.

The Runabout was very successful until the end of the 1960s, when suddenly the moped bubble burst and they weren't cool any more. All Raleigh moped production stopped in 1971 and the company returned exclusively to bike manufacturing. **SH**

RALEIGH Kite

1965 • Kids' bike • UK • Unique convertible unisex bike

Low-slung step-through frames might be more convenient than crossbar designs, but one of the worst insults self-conscious school children could receive about their bikes during their formative years was that their machine had been intended for a member of the opposite sex. Raleigh's innovative solutions to this problem were the little-known but charmingly quirky unisex Kite and Dart bikes. Their unique selling point was crossbars that could be unbolted, so one bike could suit either a boy or a girl.

Raleigh wisely incorporated several grown-up-looking features that disguised the fact that the Kite was a child's bike—this was a smart way to appeal to end users who generally wanted to appear older than they really were.

The fake fuel tank design of the removable crossbar is borrowed straight from the motorbike styling of contemporary North American cruiser bikes. The Kite introduced a further departure from the downsized adult approach normally applied to kids' bikes. Its early use of 16-in. (40.6-cm) wheels with white balloon tires confirmed its position as the junior representative of the RSW (Raleigh Small Wheel) range inspired by the success of the Moulton mini-wheeled bikes. The fat, all-white balloon tires also mimicked U.S. designs that British children were increasingly becoming aware of through television. This influence would become stronger in the ape hanger bars, banana seat, and truck-style gear shift of the later Chopper, but the Kite certainly started the trend. **GK**

DAWES Kingpin
1965 • Folding bike • UK • Small-wheeled folding bike

The Kingpin came in folding and "separable" versions. Although widely regarded as a copy of the Raleigh Twenty, it actually predates its rival. Both bikes were produced in response to the trend-setting Moulton.

Dawes' unisex bike had 20-in. (50-cm) wheels and a more elegant design than the chunky Raleigh, with slender tubing holding the internal brake and gear cables and a ride quality that was discernibly sportier. The frame was carefully bronze-welded, and there were stainless steel mudguards, alloy brakes by Weinmann, and an alloy stand.

Standard Kingpins had three-speed gears; premium Sprint models had five. Other features included height-adjustable handlebars, "cushion" semi-balloon tires, a dynamo bracket, and reflector pedals.

The most important component of any folding bike is its hinge. Raleigh's was sturdy and overspecified, and while the Dawes version appeared less robust, it has stood the test of time well and has influenced many subsequent folding bike designs.

The Kingpin was available in purple, blue, brown, or green. The folding version came only in brown and green. It folded down to measure just 36 x 12 x 20 in. (91 x 30 x 51 cm), but the weight remained something of a hindrance: The whole bike tipped the scales at a hefty 33 lb (15 kg).

The separable model was soon withdrawn, but the folding bike carried on through Dawes' many changes of ownership. It is still in production today, and is the best-selling folding bike in the current catalog. **SH**

PEUGEOT Tom Simpson

1967 • Race bike • France • Bike used by tragic Tommy Simpson

Tommy Simpson was one of the most successful British racing cyclists of all time, but also one of the most tragic. He has become known as the racer who literally rode himself to death.

The miner's son from County Durham, England, was known for his utter determination. He won many one-day races, become Britain's first World Road Race champion, and triumphed all over Europe.

Repeated continental successes earned him a place in the prestigious Peugeot BP Michelin team, riding a state-of-the-art Peugeot bike. As with most bikes of the period, it used a Reynolds 531 frame with chromed tips on the rear stays and the notably curved forks. The cable and water-bottle cage clips were also chromed, while Simpson stayed patriotic with a handmade saddle by Brooks of Birmingham. Another distinctive feature of Simpson's bike was the gear shifters mounted at the end of his bars in cyclocross style rather than on the down tube. This made them easier to reach quickly in a sprint or climb. Simpson also used center-pull brakes.

Unfortunately, it wasn't his successes that gave Simpson his cycling fame, but the manner of his death.

In 1967, he was battling up the infamous Mont Ventoux, on the 13th stage of the Tour de France. He collapsed in the heat, but despite the pleas of his mechanic, Harry Hall, to quit, he gasped, "On, on, on"— so they put him back on his Peugeot. A little further down the road he fell again, unconscious but still gripping the bars. He was helicoptered to the hospital but pronounced dead on arrival. Amphetamines were found in his bloodstream and back pockets, and he had also been drinking brandy. A memorial erected on the site of the tragedy has since become a place of pilgrimage for many cyclists. **SH**

RALEIGH Chopper

1969 • Kids' bike • UK • Iconic and much-loved design classic

The Raleigh Chopper's tall upright position, long spring-loaded saddle with metal bar cage, and thick wheels made it one of the most iconic children's bikes of all time. Its appearance owes much to Ogle Design, which created concept art for the Raleigh design department, headed by Alan Oakley. But it was Oakley himself who, after a tour of the United States, penned the true dimensions of the bike on his flight home to the United Kingdom. His sketches—made at a time when the movie *Easy Rider* (1969) was reviving interest in Harley-Davidson motorbikes—changed the children's bicycle market forever.

Raleigh patented the Chopper and put it on sale in England in the run-up to Christmas 1969, but the

"It conferred instant cool on its young owners . . . In effect it was the Apple iPad of its time."

David McKittrick, The Independent

small quantity produced—only 500 at first—reflected uncertainty about the bike's appeal.

The fears were unfounded: Almost immediately, the Chopper became for many children the ultimate mark of coolness. Twelve months later, the bike caused an even bigger storm on its arrival in the United States.

Safety issues afflicted the Chopper throughout its history, particularly in the United Kingdom. The MK1 was pulled because of concerns that the front wheel might lift from the ground if the rider sat too far back. The majority of the safety issues were addressed, and in 1971 the MK2 was released on both sides of the Atlantic. Then, after a gap of almost twenty-five years, the MK3 was launched in 2004. **DB**

Raleigh's Chopper is an iconic image of the late 1960s and early 1970s. ▷

CWS Commuter

1969 • Utility bike • UK • Small-wheeled city bike

Established in Britain in the nineteenth century, the Co-operative Wholesale Society (CWS) is a socialist organization that returns its profits to its members. Its grocery stores and supermarkets, known as Co-ops, are still widespread throughout the country.

The Birmingham branch of the Co-op made and sold its own bikes for much of the twentieth century, and in 1965 produced the first Commuter, an interesting little machine designed to compete with fashionable city bikes such as the Moulton.

Like the Moulton, the Commuter had a small-wheeled–fat-tire design. In addition, the CWS bike had a long unsupported seatpost (topped by a well-sprung saddle) and a sturdy rear luggage rack. There were outsized mudguards but a daintily shaped chainguard.

Unusually, the Commuter's frame had a mixte-style double top tube and stirrup brakes controlled by a rod and cable system.

The wheelbase was just 39 in. (99 cm), so it required two firm hands to control the handling. The slender frame was lighter than that of its rivals, but the big soft tires soaked up the bumps and holes of bad surfaces.

In 1968, the Commuter cycle was the basis for a rare motorized version called the Clark moped. A small petrol tank was fitted on the rear rack and the engine fixed to the rear stays. It wasn't a great success, and left-over Clarks were converted back to bikes to be sold off.

This final version of the Commuter, produced in 1969, had a three-speed Sturmey-Archer hub with a twist grip changer and caliper brakes. **SH**

FLANDRIA Competition
1970 • Road bike • Netherlands • Classics-winning Dutch racing bike

In 1926, the brothers Alidor, Aimé, Remi, and Jerome Claeys founded Claeys Brothers Ltd., which sold the bikes it built under the brand name Flandria. After the Second World War, Aimé emerged as the driving force of the company, pushing hard to purchase new machinery from the United States and the United Kingdom, and thereby increasing sales by 1952 to more than 250,000 a year.

A bitter family feud led in 1956 to the company being split up—literally—by the construction of a brick wall through the middle of the factory. Aimé continued to prosper, sponsoring the Flandria Cycling Team from 1959 onward. His 1970 catalog proudly showed his latest models in the hands of two World Champion riders and the Dutch champion.

In common with many bike companies, Flandria traded on this pro cycling success by releasing a team replica model, the Competition. Like most contemporary bikes, the frame was Reynolds 531 steel tubing with Campagnolo frame and fork tips. The componentry was Campagnolo-dominated too. The Competition was a semi-custom bike, hand made to order, and available in five finely spaced sizes and any of three colors.

Flandria also produced a second-tier replica bike, the Professional. It still had a quality steel frame with Campagnolo fork and frame tips, plus "sew-up" tubular race tires. But the 10-speed derailleurs were made by Huret, and there were only three frame sizes, although buyers had a choice of four colors. **BS**

CARLTON Carbon

1970 • Concept bike • UK • One of the first-known carbon fiber frame bicycles

Much of the early research into carbon fiber technology was conducted at the British Royal Aircraft Establishment (RAE) in Hampshire, England. Its discovery, in 1969, of a way to produce highly oriented crystalline fibers was a big technological breakthrough, but some uncertainty about its practical application remained. A House of Commons select committee demanded: "How is the nation to reap the maximum benefit without it becoming yet another British invention to be exploited more successfully overseas?"

Then Carlton of Worksop, Nottinghamshire, used carbon-reinforced polymer to produce around twenty bike frames, which were among the first examples of

"They thought it might be the oldest carbon bike in the world; we think they're probably right."

road.cc

crossover between aeronautics and cycle manufacture. The Tube Investments group (owners of Reynolds and Raleigh) then diverted this new technology across to its Carlton Ti race team's cycle manufacturers, who produced a bike with cast lugs and glue bonding, carbon mainstays and seatstays, brazed steel chainstays, classic 72-degree geometry, and an alloy fork—total weight, 16½ lb (7.5 kg).

The technology was then allegedly sold on to a U.S. company, possibly Graftek. Meanwhile, Carlton took a back seat to Raleigh, which created a Specialist Bicycle Development Unit (SBDU) headed by former Carlton manager Gerald O'Donovan. Following this development, the Worksop factory was closed in 1981, and the Carlton brand was wound down. **KF**

HETCHINS Magnus Bonum

1970 • Road bike • UK • Classic and distinctive all-round road machine

By 1970, the Hetchins workshop had built nearly 10,000 frames, but Harry and his son Alf Hetchin's reputation for extremely high-quality, very distinctive machines had only been strengthened rather than diluted. The Vibrant stay design, first patented in 1934, was still as popular as a signature of any genuine Hetchins in 1970, as this fine example shows.

These Vibrant stays used an instantly recognizable S-bend profile to allow the rear of the bike to soak up the vibration of rough road surfaces rather than pass them onto the rider. As the 1935 Hetchins catalog stated: "The vibratory action caused when riding over uneven ground lessens the retarding force on the rear wheel, resulting in less loss of speed. In the test made regarding rigidity on the chainstays, we found that owing to the rake in stays, the resistance put up was a fraction over 4 percent more than straight stays of the same gauge tubing, the triangle is not intended to spring, only to vibrate at the rear ends and take off all dead shock from the apex."

As well as this comfort- and speed-sustaining rear end, Hetchins frames are renowned for the elaborate lugs used to strengthen and correctly align the tube junctions of the frame. On this model, they are particularly obvious at the fork crown and the head tube, since the main tube junctions are relatively conservative. Chrome fork tips and stays combined with gold and purple paintwork still make it a suitably eye-catching machine and no doubt a joy for the owner to behold before every ride. Contemporary wide-range gearing from Campagnolo and TA Industries means no restriction on the gradient it could tackle, and it also sports an innovative lightweight sheet-alloy framed, cutaway-top version of the legendary Brooks saddle. **GK**

Curly "Vibrant" stays make a Hetchins unmistakeable. ▶

RALEIGH Twenty

1971 • Folding bike • UK • Early folding bike

Raleigh of Nottingham, England, launched the Twenty as a cheap, unsophisticated rival to the innovative Moulton, which had by this time become an international best-seller.

In the early 1970s, sales grew in this sector of the market as demand for small-wheeled bikes increased. A design that had been derided only a few years previously had transformed its image and become just about the most desirable machine on two wheels.

The makers added all sorts of Twentys to the range, including a kids' version, the Commando, and a "Shopping" model with a front basket and wheels 2 in. (5 cm) bigger than the standard 20-in. (50-cm) diameter. All this helped the Twenty become Raleigh's top-selling bike by 1975. A total of 140,000 were made in that year alone.

Introduced at the same time as the Twenty, the Twenty Folding (originally called the Stowaway) had a sturdy locking hinge in the middle of the down tube. When folded in half, it was small enough to be carried on a train or bus—even though it was heavy to lift.

The Twenty Folding was generally a better bike than many small-wheeled rivals at the time. The frame and hinge were very solid and durable, and the bike handled surprisingly well. Its wheels were shod with fat low-pressure rubber, and the steering operated through an unusual plastic headset bearing.

Apart from the hinge, the folding version retained the attributes of the standard Twenty. Both were simple and cheap, and easily adapted and repaired. The Twenty and its derivatives remained in production until 1984. They were popular in international markets—especially in Canada, where it has more recently acquired a cult following online—and were sold under many of Raleigh's other brand names, such as Triumph, Sun, Hercules, and BSA. **SH**

" . . . ideal for boaters, campers, fliers, apartment dwellers, even commuters who want to take their bicycle with them."

Raleigh sales brochure

◀ This upgraded Twenty still looks fresh over forty years after it was made.

AMERICAN EAGLE Semi-Pro

1971 • Road bike • Japan • Pioneering
Japanese import to the United States

The American Eagle Semi-Pro was the first Japanese bike imported in the United States that made cycling experts sit up and take notice. This wasn't just a cheap copy undercutting the established brands—it was a fine bike in its own right.

The American Eagle brand was manufactured by Kawamura and given a new name by importers West Coast Cycles in 1968, which wanted to make it more appealing. By the 1970s, however, the reputation of Japanese manufacturing had risen so much that it was an asset to have an identifiably Japanese name. So American Eagle became Nishiki in 1973.

Nishiki means "gold brocade," the making of which in Japan is considered one of the highest forms of craftsmanship. Over the next few years, some world-class frames appeared from Kawamura under the Nishiki label, which was finally discontinued in 2001.

With the change of brand name, the Semi-Pro became the Competition. Although the latter was highly rated, the Semi-Pro was the pioneer—a well-made, well-equipped 10-speed road bike costing just $150 (£100).

The frame was double-butted chromoly tubing with wraparound seatstays. Components included Suntour gears, derailleurs, down-tube-mounted shifters, and center-pull brakes. The wheels were light but strong, with Araya 27 x 1¼-in. (69 x 3.5-cm) light alloy rims, thirty-six stainless steel spokes, and sturdy Sunshine high-flange hubs. Other parts included Kyokuto Pro Ace pedals, a Fujita seat, and KB Champion touring-style handlebars.

A large alloy disc drilled with holes was fitted just behind the largest gear on the rear wheel to protect the spokes if the derailleur became misaligned. **SH**

BICKERTON Portable

1971 • Folding bike • UK • Star of
TV advertising

The lightweight Bickerton portable earns its place in bicycle history for its innovative design and its ingenious advertising strategies.

After working as a designer at De Havilland and Rolls-Royce, Harry Bickerton had extensive experience of the latest materials and construction techniques. In 1968, he was banned from driving automobiles and thus forced onto a bike. He wasn't happy with his handmade road race bike or any of the heavy folding machines he could find, so he set about using his own expertise to create a bike that combined the best of both machines.

An extruded box section mainframe with a central hinge created a weld-free, easily collapsible, and very

"In all the world there is only one folding bicycle to consider seriously—the Bickerton."

R. Ballentine, Richard's Bicycle Book

light chassis. The extra-long seatpost and U-shape "Chopper" handlebars could then be folded or removed to let the bike pack into its own handlebar bag.

Bickerton's first bikes were forged in his own kitchen oven, so production was slow, but interest exploded with the launch of the Bickerton Portable Bicycle in 1976.

Bickerton was one of the first bike companies to use television to promote its products. The famous "Go bag a Bickerton" ad featured bowler-hatted City gents, happy couples, glamorous girls, and even a nun riding the bikes or carrying them from boats, helicopters, or trains with an animated final sequence showing the bike folding into the bag. The factory closed in 1991, but the Bickerton exerted a major influence on the Brompton design. **GK**

Bickerton set new standards in portability. ▶

HOLDSWORTH Professional
1971 • Race bike • UK • Classic steel bike from UK frame builder

Britain's most successful road racing squad of 1970 enjoyed an impressive twenty-three wins that year. The Holdsworth Team was pictured standing triumphantly in matching red-and-blue shirts alongside its Ford Corsair support vehicle loaded with bikes.

The company—founded in 1926 in London by insurance salesman Sandy Holdsworth—was at first better known for its cycling garments, but its bike sales took off after the Second World War through the skilful use of marketing and the success of the Holdsworth Professional team, run by Roy Thame, who also managed the British national team.

After Sandy's death in 1961, Holdsworth went from strength to strength under his widow, Margaret. The end of the 1960s was its heyday. The team was jointly sponsored by Campagnolo, as Holdsworth was the UK distributor for the Italian components. In 1970, Holdsworth scooped most domestic race titles with a team that included Les West and Colin Lewis. Sadly, Margaret died later that year, and from that point the company split and went into decline.

The Holdsworth Professionals used by the 1970 team went on sale the following year with Reynolds 531 butted tubing and Campagnolo gears, brakes, hubs, chainset, and pedals. The freewheel and chain were Regina, the pro rims were Super Champion, the spokes were Berg Union, the road tires Canetti, the saddle YFC, and the stem and handlebars Fiamme.

Falcon later revived a modernized, carbon fiber and aluminum version of the Professional. **SH**

TERRA NOVA Strawberry

1971 • Road bike • USA • A fine model from a legendary U.S. custom builder

Terra Nova bikes are designed for road sport and racing, track racing, city cruising, and commuting. There are no off-roaders.

The Strawberry is one of the finest creations by Andy Newlands, a metalworker from Portland, Oregon, who is one of the leading lights of the flourishing cycling community in the U.S. Northwest.

Strawberry frames are hand-built using an oxy-propane torch to join Reynolds steel tubing brazed into hand-cut lugs. Newlands creates all his custom frames by this traditional method.

The brazed lugged steel framesets have exquisite joints, and they all feature a Strawberry-designed wishbone specially cast in Taiwan, together with an integrated topstay–seatpost binder.

After graduating in 1970 from the University of Washington School of Civil Engineering, Newlands traveled to England to tour and race bikes. His interest in frame building was inspired after visiting English bike retailers with frame shops out the back.

Returning home, Newlands replicated the English way of operating, which he calls "the one-man, two-dog" working method. The approach may be old tech, but it has earned Newlands unparalleled renown. His workshop now features some of the most sophisticated equipment, and he acts as U.S. sales agent for Italian company Marchetti, which manufactures bicycle wheel-building machines, tube processing machinery and tools, welding fixtures, and bicycle frame alignment equipment. **SH**

ACER-MEX Windsor

1972 • Track bike • Mexico • A spicy Mexican for the "Cannibal" racing king

There were many models in the Acer-Mex Windsor series produced under the guiding eye of former Cinelli frame builder Remo Vecchi, but the best known today are the rather Cinelli-like Professional and Competition. They had similar frames, but the difference was in their components: the Professional had Campagnolo Nuovo Record parts; the Competition used Suntour.

Both bikes had Columbus SP double-butted tubing. This was top grade but had a thicker-than-normal gauge, which made for a rigid and powerful ride but was far less lively than most other frames.

One piece of cycling folklore with which the Windsor will always be associated is the Hour Record

"Acer-Mex wanted to bring recognition for their bikes into the world market."

Daniel Jansen Torres

ride by Eddie Merckx in Mexico City in 1972. Somehow it got around that Merckx had ridden a Windsor, and Acer-Mex had even produced advertising depicting the Belgian champion on one of its Windsors. In fact, however, he had ridden a Colnago. The advertising may have been an attempt by Acer-Mex to trump Benotto, a rival Mexican bike company, but in any case everyone who witnessed the ride knew it had been made on a Colnago.

The Windsor's main strength was value for money. The Professional was one of the best deals going for a bike with Campagnolo Record features—it was hundreds of dollars cheaper than its Italian-made rivals, a saving that compensated for what might otherwise have been seen as an attempt to disguise its origins. **BS**

KESSELS Eddy Merckx

1972 • Road bike • Belgium • Signature spin-off bike of the racing "Cannibal"

Belgian Eddy Merckx won an incredible thirty-five percent of the races he entered, and in 1972 he was at the peak of his form, winning both the Giro d'Italia for the third time and the Tour de France for the fourth.

Merckx seized the opportunity to capitalize on his success with a signature bike built by the Kessels company and finished in the distinctive orange and yellow colors of his trade team Molteni. As with most high-class Belgian, Dutch, and English bikes of the time, the Kessels frame was built from English Reynolds 531 steel tubing, which was butted to give it thicker, stronger ends and a thinner, lighter central section. Just like Merckx himself, the frame showed its class through performance rather than with flashy touches, and the only indulgent features are a chromed fork crown cap and front and rear drop-outs. Angles were the now-classic 73-degree parallel arrangement—in fact, none of the dimensions would look out of place on a brand new road bike today.

The features were all Italian: componentry was from Campagnolo's top-of-the-range Record and Nuovo Record groups, while the saddle, bars, and stem were from Cinelli. These production parts differed from Merckx's own race bike equipment, however: he himself used extensively drilled and milled componentry to reduce weight. While this later became a common practice used widely on production groups, the legendarily fastidious Merckx was one of the first riders to start machining fluted cut-outs into stems and seatposts, hollowing out gear levers, and drilling brake levers and chainrings so that they looked like sieves.

Given the emphatic nature of most of Merckx's victories, it's hard to think the few ounces lost this way made a great difference in reality though. **GK**

The "Cannibal" devours another Alpine climb. ▶

SPEEDWELL Titalite

1973 • Race bike • UK • One of the first production titanium frames

Titanium, a wonder metal that is lighter and stronger than steel, does not rust, and can be polished to a mirrorlike shine, has an almost mythical status in the minds of many cyclists.

While titanium bike frames were first seen in England in 1956, when Phillips exhibited some experimental prototypes, the earliest commercially available examples were these products of the Speedwell Gear Case Company of Birmingham, England. Its wide experience in the use of corrosion-resistant metal for the chemical and aerospace industries allowed the company to put effort into the structural application of titanium. Having perfected

"Every specialist . . . described it as 'the most revolutionary development in twenty years'."

Speedwell publicity

methods of welding the metal in oxygen-purged chambers, it used the techniques to produce motorbike racing frames and engine parts for BSA.

Speedwell had been developing Titalite frames since the late sixties, secretly at first, but by 1973 word was spreading. The company's sales director personally took a sample to Lyon, France, for Bic's Luis Ocaña to test. The rider's mechanic built it up overnight.

Ocaña used the Speedwell in the Dauphiné Libéré, and then on the mountain stages of the Tour de France, when it replaced his team's sponsored Motobecane frame. The Spaniard's victory in that year's Tour quickly popularized titanium, which subsequently became the main material for lightweight racing bike frames and was adopted by more and more professional riders. **KF**

RON KITCHING Custom

1975 • Race bike • UK • Legendary racer Beryl Burton's bike

Long before the advent of disc wheels, skinsuits, and even helmets, a hearty English housewife became Britain's best-ever woman cyclist.

Beryl Burton is hardly a household name today, but her career involved an amazing domination of the sport in Britain for twenty years. She won more than ninety domestic championships and seven world titles. Her women's record for the twelve-hour time trial exceeded the men's, and some of her records still stand. Burton and her daughter Denise even set a new British 10-mi (16-km) record riding a tandem together.

Yet the details of the bikes Burton used are as little known as she was. Deciphering her equipment shows how hard it is for bike historians to get full information about amateur riders of the time.

What is known is that Burton usually got her bikes from fellow Yorkshire cycle enthusiast and parts supplier Ron Kitching. Originally he sponsored Burton with bikes based on Jacques Anquetil frames. But the French star cyclist's name appeared on frames made by many builders. In the mid-1970s, Burton appeared to switch to one of Kitching's own frames, also built by various workshops in their shared home town of Harrogate, with a custom build of parts imported and distributed by Kitching.

Burton occasionally helped out at Kitching's warehouse, and she regularly picked up new parts to try. (She also worked on a rhubarb farm nearby.)

Burton was known as a fiercely dogged competitor who spent hours training on rollers. Her 1967 victory in a twelve-hour time trial was perhaps her greatest achievement, as she beat all the men and the men's record. Famously, she offered the leading man a Liquorice Allsort sweet as she sped past him because "he seemed to be struggling." **SH**

Beryl Burton blasting the track in her heyday. ▶

MONGOOSE Motomag

1975 • BMX bike • USA • First-generation BMX machine

Founded in 1974 by former drag car racer Skip Hess to sell his revolutionary cast-aluminum Moto-Mag wheels, BMX Products soon turned to producing frames—and the Mongoose was born. What Hess couldn't have anticipated was that the Mongoose moniker was about to become one of the most widespread and influential BMX brand names ever.

The first Mongoose BMX race frames were constructed in Chatsworth, California, in early 1975. The Heliarc welded design used a double head tube gusset with a distinctive pierced hole, and flared rectangular seat and chainstay bridges to connect the front triangle to the back end. The Mongoose design incorporated a coaster brake tab on the chainstay, with several rare early examples also sporting a single pierced gusset plate

above the bottom bracket shell. The three main front tubes were made from 4130 chromoly steel; elsewhere mild steel was used. Options included chrome plating and epoxy-coated colors.

The 1975 Mongoose frame weighed 6½ lb (2.9 kg), twice as much as a modern aluminum or carbon equivalent. Geometry has changed too: the first adult-sized BMXs sported a 71-degree head angle, rather than the 74 degrees typical today, and a short 36-in. (91-cm) wheelbase, the instability of which was counteracted by a low 10¾-in. (27-cm) bottom bracket height.

The Mongoose was so popular that in the following years around 600 frames were manufactured daily, and output increased further in 1984, when the company moved to larger premises in Irondale. **MK**

RALEIGH Commando

1975 • BMX bike • UK • Raleigh joins the chopper craze

As soon as *Easy Rider* (1969) hit the screens, every British youngster wanted a low-slung bike with high handlebars in the style of the Harley-Davidsons ridden by Dennis Hopper and Peter Fonda.

Raleigh's BMX-style chopper came from an unlikely lineage. The Raleigh Twenty had appeared in the late 1960s as a small-wheeled Moulton rival. It sold well in various guises, including the Shopper, with a front basket, and the Eighteen, with 18-in. (45-cm) wheels.

To this basic design, the Nottingham, England-based company added a cool molded-foam-rubber chopper-style seat and high chrome handlebars. The Commando also featured a kick propstand, and a tiny front mudguard and bigger rear mudguard. According to Raleigh publicity, the three-speed Sturmey-Archer

twist-grip gear change meant that riders could "take their choice of speeds without taking their hands off the handlebars."

The steel wheels were small—18 in. (45 cm) or 16-in. (40 cm)—and the steel frame was lifted straight from the Eighteen. A tough-looking chrome chainguard was bolted on, and the chainwheel was chromed steel, but the bike kept the Eighteen's handy little carrying rack behind the seat—just in case the rider had to pop down to the shops on an errand.

Camouflage paint completed the transformation of the Twenty into a trendy street machine aimed at the young. It was "as tough, tenacious, and stylish as they come," according to the sales material, which for some reason carried a photo of a Harrier jump jet too. **SH**

RALEIGH Grifter

1976 • Kids' BMX • UK • Young persons' BMX meets ATB

Raleigh certainly came up with some genuinely iconic children's bikes in the 1970s and 1980s. The Grifter was another "must-have" bike for British children. In Raleigh's semi-BMX range, it sat between the Chopper and the Burner.

Its low-slung looks were everything to the youngsters of the day, who overlooked the fact that this was a heavy, cumbersome machine that handled more like a motorbike than a bicycle. With a frame made from high-tensile steel tubes at a time when imports were providing welded tubes, the Grifter weighed around 35 lb (16 kg), yet gave many young riders their first experience of stunts such as wheelies and jumps.

The Grifter survived in various forms until 1983. The earliest versions came in either metallic blue or red, leading to many disputes among teenagers about which color was the faster. The Grifter also spawned the Boxer and the Strika, spin-offs for younger riders.

The Grifter's features included a 3-speed twist grip for the Sturmey-Archer gears, 36-spoke, 20-in. (50-cm) steel wheels, Raleigh's branded "Raincheck" brakes, mudguards front and rear, a kick-down propstand, and a primitive foam-covered metal saddle that invariably disintegrated.

Later models added exotic features including a foam handlebar protector, a properly padded saddle, different color schemes, flashy graphics on the frame, and even flashier chunky tires. Many Grifters were fitted with extravagant rear-view mirrors by the owners.

To many British youngsters, the Grifter was as much a part of the late 1970s and the 1980s as Rubik's cube and the *Back to the Future* films. It still has a cult following today, and some versions have become rare and sought-after collector's items. **SH**

GOODIES Trandem

1977 • Three-seater • UK • Novelty bike for British TV comedy trio

A trio of British comedians—Tim Brooke-Taylor, Graeme Garden, and Bill Oddie—created, wrote, and starred in *The Goodies*, a surreal TV comedy series of the 1970s and early 1980s. One of their gimmicks was to ride a special three-seater triplet bike they called the Trandem.

It first appeared in the pilot episode, when the trio left their office to go on an assignment and seemed to be about to get into a Mercedes, but then wheeled the Trandem out from behind it. Tim fixed a flashing safety light to his head, Graeme raised a Goodies flag on the back, and Bill pumped up two tires at once. They got on the bike and promptly all fell over sideways. There were actually three generations of Trandem over the

> *"Batman had his Batmobile, James Bond his Aston Martin, and we had . . . a bike."*
>
> *Tim Brooke-Taylor*

nine series of *The Goodies*. The first was simply a vintage tandem with an extra seat tagged on to the rear. This was always occupied by Bill Oddie, who was referred to as "the baggage." This seat had no handlebars or pedals, which made it very difficult to balance. For subsequent BBC series, a true three-seater was built.

After *The Goodies* series finished, the Trandem was sold in a BBC props auction to three friends who rode it across Africa raising money for charity. Their adventure is recorded in the book *Three Men on a Bike*.

A third Trandem was introduced when the Goodies switched channels to London Weekend Television. This blue bike had been built in 1980 for a Kleenex TV commercial featuring featured the threesome. It was sold in a 1987 Sotheby's auction. **SH**

BREEZER MTB

1977 • Mountain bike • USA • One of the
original purpose-built mountain bikes

Joe Breeze was among the fastest downhill racers
at Repack, mountain biking's pivotal race held west
of Fairfax, California. He won ten of the twenty-four
Repack races, which took place between 1976 and
1984. He is also widely acknowledged as the first
person to build a mountain bike from scratch, rather
than simply converting an old beach cruiser, as had
previously been the custom.

In 1977, Charlie Kelly—who went on to create the
MountainBikes company with Gary Fisher—asked
Breeze to build him a mountain bike frame. While
working on the project, Breeze won that year's Repack
race on a prototype Breezer 1. The following year,
he built nine more Series 1 bikes, which he supplied
complete, with twin top tube frames made from
chromoly steel.

Breeze shared his later design ideas with
other frame builders, including Tom Ritchey, who
supplied MountainBikes. In 1983, Breeze helped
found the National Off-Road Bicycle Association,
the first sanctioning organization for competitive
mountain biking. Breezer 1 is now in the collection
of the Smithsonian Institution's National Museum of
American History. **SW**

TOM RITCHEY MTB

1977 • Mountain bike • USA • The root of
mountain bike DNA from a legendary innovator

Tom Ritchey is a linchpin in the development of
mountain biking in California; he sparked a revolution.

At age eleven, Ritchey started repairing tubular tires
to pay for a $99 (£60) racing bike of his own. He built his
first racing frame in his garage in 1972 when he was only
sixteen years old, and used it successfully in road races.
In the 1970s he built three fillet-brazed versions of the
Repack off-road racer, and sold one of them to Gary
Fisher, who was so impressed that he hired Ritchey to
build for his new MountainBikes shop. Mike Sinyard sent
a couple of the bikes to be copied in Japan as the original
Specialized Stumpjumper bikes. The Specializeds came
back with TIG-welded frames and overlong forks, but
it was Ritchey's basic frame design that ignited the
mountain biking explosion that followed.

By 1980 Ritchey had built nearly 1,000 frames
in his Skyline California workshop, most of them for
mountain bikes. In the early 1980s Ritchey went solo
as Ritchey Designs. He developed in collaboration
with Columbus and then Tange lightweight varying
wall thickness steel tubesets that could be TIG-welded
rather than brazed. These became the Logic tubes that
formed the backbone of classic designs such as the
Ritchey P22. **GK**

LAWWILL Pro Cruiser

1977 • BMXTB • USA • Hybrid BMX–MTB off-road machine

SABATINI Pista

1977 • Track bike • Italy • Family-built Italian track bike

At around the same time as Joe Breeze and others were building the first custom mountain bikes, motorcycle racer Mert Lawwill produced 600 Pro Cruisers, bikes that bridged the gap between BMX and MTB. Retailing at $500 (£300) apiece, they were essentially the first production mountain bikes, but since they appeared before Gary Fisher and Charlie Kelly coined the term, they were originally known as tracking bikes.

Lawwill's bikes were based on a Schwinn Varsity frame design that Don Koski had fabricated from electrical conduit. They were built by Terry Knight of Oakland, California, with reverse drop-outs and a gear hanger that could be fitted with either a single sprocket or a derailleur gear. The high-rise cow-horn handlebar and relaxed frame geometry emphasized a relaxed approach to riding, but made the bikes incredibly hard work uphill. Large motorbike-style brake levers made the Sturmey-Archer drum brakes surprisingly efficient for downhilling, though, and the introduction of Ukai 26-in. (66-cm) aluminum rims began to make the Pro Cruiser look like a contender among the early mountain bikes. But it wasn't to be. Other designs were more efficient as all-round off-roaders, and the Pro Cruiser fell by the wayside. It is now a highly valued collectible. **SW**

Sabatini was a family affair. The father, Francesco, made each frame by hand at his home in Perugia, Italy, while his wife took care of the decals and built up the wheels. To help them, they had three daughters, who all thoroughly immersed themselves in the business.

Sabatini's Pista came with custom features such as slots cut into the fork blades and seatstays. When the family stopped making bikes in 1987, their final products were snapped up by Gino Bartali, winner of the Tour de France in 1938 and the Giro d'Italia in 1936, 1937, and 1946—a great champion who plainly knew a quality bike when he saw one.

So too did Canadian Brent Avery, prime mover in 2006 of the Vancouver Bicycle Meet-up Group, which currently has a membership of 1,500. Avery bought his first Sabatini in 1978 at the International Cycling Center shop in Calgary, Alberta. He recalls: "There were at least twenty Sabatini road and track bikes there, and I used to go out with a group, including the shop owner, on rides when they were training. The owner had a gold-colored version with SL tubing and full Super Record."

Sabatinis have gone, but they still burn brightly in the memories of the lucky few who own them and the thousands more who would like to. **BS**

FALCON Olympic

1978 • Road bike • UK • Reasonably priced 1970s racer

Falcon took over Coventry Eagle after the Second World War, and maintained that brand's reputation for good-quality road bikes at a reasonable cost.

The Olympic was a typical mid-range bike from the Falcon catalog in the 1970s. It had a plain gauge Reynolds 531 tube frame with oval forks and distinctive wraparound stays, 5- or 10-speed Shimano gears controlled from a lever on the down tube, and 27-in. (69-cm) wheels shod with Falcon's own tires.

Frame geometry was by Ernie Clements, two-time British amateur road racing champion in the 1940s, and later chairman of Falcon. He was famous enough to be celebrated with "designed by Ernie Clements" decals on all Olympics. His brother, Frank, was Falcon's managing director and ran the Falcon Race Team.

Like many bikes of the 1970s, the Olympic constantly changed as its makers struggled to match production demands to the availability of parts. Catalogs were often vague about what make of components were fitted—just in case the makers had to switch to another supplier in a hurry. No matter what parts were fitted to the Falcon Olympic, buyers found it to be a great-handling bike, but because of the simple tube work, it weighed 24 lb (10.8 kg).

The strong but heavy frame gave a comfortable ride and tracked well, even over poor surfaces. Some of the original kit was fine at the price: the Brooks B17 saddle was a particular highlight, and the Weinmann center-pull brakes and alloy rims, plus Japanese drop bars, were all aspirational kit. **SH**

RALEIGH Arena

1978 • Road bike • UK • Affordable 5- or 10-speed UK racer

The Raleigh Arena was a soft-core racer aimed at cyclists on a budget or starting off with their first drop handlebars. It was often sold via catalogs, usually on installment plans. In the age before mountain bikes, this sort of machine was the choice of many general commuters and gentle leisure cyclists.

The Arena came with a more relaxed lugged steel frame than serious race bikes, but this made it more comfortable. There was little attempt to create a serious lightweight bike to trouble proper road racers, but it was a bike that would give years of service.

The fitted mudguards betrayed its softer side. The standard ones were tiny, and there only to protect the bike rather than the rider, but eyelets were provided to fit full-size fenders. The Arena also had a rather quaint lamp mounting on the right fork blade, and an enormous rear reflector mounted on the back brakes. One sign of some slight ambition for the bike was that Raleigh fitted Weinmann caliper brakes rather than its own in-house units, perhaps because the Weinmann brand was associated with top-end race bikes and a cosponsor of Raleigh's continental pro team.

There was a simple down tube shifter for the 5- or 10-speed gears, and Raleigh's own derailleur.

The Raleigh team had won the Tour de France in 1977, the year before the Arena's release, and the company was trying to cash in on its new sporty image. The badging showed the five-ring Olympic symbol, although the bike itself was unlikely ever to be a medal winner. **SH**

SE RACING PK Ripper
1978 • BMX bike • USA • Legendary aluminum Floval-tubed race bike

The radical box section 6061 aluminum PK Ripper, the brainchild of SE Racing founder Scot Breithaupt, is the most famous and celebrated BMX of all time.

Today we are so accustomed to outsized aluminum frames that it's hard to imagine how much of a departure the design was from other steel-tubed products of the time. Breithaupt's genius was not only in making aluminum a viable BMX option, but also in shaping the unusual chassis into a sleek, elegant silhouette, especially when he had almost no bike-making experience.

In addition to its oval tubing, the PK Ripper incorporated several other key features, including a novel triangulated head tube gusset between the top and down tubes, an outsized box section lug behind the bottom bracket shell for stiffness, and a looptail rear

triangle. The frame had burly outsized "Landing Gear" forks—another success story for SE Racing.

In 1977, Breithaupt experimented with a T6 aluminum BMX prototype. After a year of trial and error and intensive study of alloy construction, he concluded that a round top and bottom would provide excellent compression load strengths, while the flat sides would give incredible top-load tolerances. The tubing was dubbed Floval, and the bike was an instant success.

The frame was originally designed for hotshot racer Jeff Utterback and labeled the JU-1. When Utterback left the team shortly afterward, a head tube gusset was added to the frame at the request of Perry Kramer, the successful SE Racing Pro whose initials were incorporated into the Ripper's name. **MK**

KEN ROGERS Clubman

1978 • Tricycle • UK • Sought-after racing trike

Some of the best frames for trikes emerged from the workshop of Ken Rogers in Hounslow, London.

The Reynolds 531 butted steel tubes formed a fairly standard front triangle and forks, with the rear end adapted to deal with the axle and two wheels instead of one. The chain, however, drove just one back wheel—the near-side one. The rider had to compensate for this imbalance by leaning outward for corners to keep all the bike wheels on the ground. This skill required much practice to acquire.

With a shorter wheelbase and simplified transmission, Rogers trikes were lively and fast—very fast. Unusually for a trike, the Clubman came with race-style alloy drop handlebars and skinny high-pressure racing tires. It was clearly designed for rapid road work.

The double braking system on the front wheel used Mafac Criterium cantilever brakes plus Mafac Racer center-pull brakes, arranged one in front of the other. A rear Shimano disc brake system was an optional extra.

Men's and women's versions were available, and one option had a large carrying frame between the rear wheels, complete with two big reflectors. As an alternative trike, Rogers also offered a small-wheeled Utility Bike, which looked a little like a Moulton trike and could be fitted with a child seat behind the rider.

Rogers also supplied trike conversion kits for two-wheelers. The replacement axle fitted into the rear drop-out, and was held secure with special bolt-on stays. At just $75 (£49), the Ken Rogers Clubman was a budget way into trike ownership for many cyclists. **SH**

1979–1998

The dawn of dirt and the sunsest of steel.

THE OFF-ROAD REVOLUTION

SEKAI 4000

1979 • Road bike • Japan • Osaka-built road bike that rivaled the best Europe could offer

The Sekai 4000 was designed in Seattle but made in Japan. It was almost certainly built by a virtually unknown frame builder named Miki who worked on the 4000s in a small factory in Osaka for Sekai. Miki, like other frame builders at Sekai, built bicycles of a quality that rivaled many of the top frame builders of Europe, with features that included a chromed double fork crown and wrapover seatstays.

The 4000 was available as a road and track model. The frame, of a geometric design not dissimilar to a Raleigh International, came with Shimano SF rear drop-outs and Tange TF front drop-outs. Some were fully chromed with Italianesque long-point lugs, finished in transparent red or blue lacquer. The steel tubing was double-butted Tange Champion 2 of a composition almost identical to that of Columbus SL.

In 1980, thanks mainly to the rising Yen, the Seattle-based owners of Sekai relinquished control of the brand, and its Japanese owners sold it to Norco of Canada. Unfortunately, this led to a decline in quality, with the result that a host of dealers, particularly in the United States, decided to drop the Sekai brand. It was a sad demise for a brand equal to the famous Keirin frames for which the Japanese are better known. **BS**

RALEIGH 531 Team

1979 • Race bike • UK • Classic Reynolds 531 road race bike used by international professional teams

The Raleigh 531 Team, with its handmade, high-quality frame, proved that Raleigh could still create road race-winning bikes as well as cornering the market in trendy fashion bikes for youngsters.

The frame was made from specialist 531 steel alloy tubing, a product of the Reynolds company in Birmingham. Until the advent of more complex alloy tubes, Reynolds 531 was the pinnacle of bike tubes. Technically it is a manganese-molybdenum medium-carbon, steel alloy tube, strong enough to be used for E-Type Jaguar subframes. The material was top grade, and the construction was specialist too. The frame was lugged, which meant using steel sleeves brazed over the joints, and butted, having thicker steel in the tubes toward the joints and thinner, lighter steel in the central sections. All this produced a strong, responsive frame that weighed little more than 6 lb (2.7 kg).

The Raleigh Team series grew with the release of Team Pro bikes (made in a specialist factory in Ilkeston, Derbyshire) and lesser Team Record and Professional Team variants. Versions with Reynolds 753 tubing frames were even lighter. Raleigh Team bikes still have loyal fans, and the original bikes from this period are still sought after on the secondhand market. **SH**

SE RACING Quadangle

1979 • BMX bike • USA • Unique, legendary, and exotic BMX mount

The SE Racing Quadangle has been the object of obsessive gazing and fascination for several generations of BMXers. In the 1980s, it was the most lusted-after bike on the market with its radical crisscross tubing, loop-tail rear triangle, beautiful powder coating, and sky-high price tag.

The Quadangle was dreamed up by Scot Breithaupt, a precocious, energetic teenage BMX innovator and the founder of SE Racing. The frame started life as his even more radical mild-steel STR-1 variant, with a downtube constructed from one continuous bent-steel tube that looped under the bottom bracket shell to the rear dropout before bending back up to the underside of the top tube. This metalworker's nightmare was built for legendary racer Stu Thomson, who had been breaking regular BMX frames. It was eventually tweaked and renamed the Quadangle.

The newer frame had interrupted down tubes in 4130 chromoly welded to a U.S.-style bottom bracket shell with a mild-steel looptail rear end. The dual triangulated design created four triangles in all, hence the "quad" part of the name. Despite costing $500 (£335) in 1979, the complete bike was so popular it sold consistently for two decades. **MK**

GIOS Torino Super Record

1979 • Race bike • Italy • Truly classic Italian race bike

Established in 1948 by Tolmino Gios, an Italian cyclist and a member of the 1936 Italian Olympic Cycling Team, Gios bikes began in a tiny workshop outside Turin, Italy. Ten years later, the founder's son, Alfredo, joined the family business. Then, at the Milan 1971 Cycle Show, Giorgio Perfetti, owner of the Brooklyn chewing-gum brand, was looking for a bike supplier to help launch his professional cycling team. The Brooklyn team, on Gios bikes, went on to become one of the most successful teams in cycling history.

The Super Record came with Campagnolo Super Record everything: crankset, headset, brakeset, seatpost, front and rear derailleur, hubs and pedals, even toe clips. The classic design was revived for the sixty-fifth birthday of the company. The limited-edition steel frameset Super Record Gios Vintage was exhibited at the 2003 Milan Cycle Show. It featured special limited-edition chainwheels, bolts, and dust caps, and Globe logo brake-lever hoods. With its eye-catching Cinelli Giro d'Italia handlebars wrapped in classic white perforated leather, suede-leather Selle Italia Criterium saddle, and fabulous array of decals and Gios coin inlays, the Super Record was a symphony in blue and a fitting tribute to the Brooklyn team's glory days. **BS**

FISHER/KELLY MountainBike

1979 • Mountain bike • USA • Purpose-built for the first "mountain bike" store

When Gary Fisher and Charlie Kelly pooled their cash, all of $300 (£200), to set up a company called MountainBikes, they had little idea what they were starting. However, they can definitely be credited with starting the rise of mountain bikes, which would ultimately completely relaunch the social identity and easy accessibility of bikes. They tried unsuccessfully to protect the name but it soon became the ubiquitous term for any knobbly-tired off-road cycle.

It all started when Gary Fisher ordered a few custom frames from a 20-year-old racer-frame builder called Tom Ritchey, who would eventually go on to create his own bicycle business empire. Tom had ridden the now-legendary Repack downhill race, so he knew exactly what was needed. After the first three frames, he built nine more, at $450 (£300) each for a frame and fork. They were built into complete bikes that Fisher and Kelly sold for $1,300 (£870) apiece.

Soon marketeers were calling them "all terrain bikes," but the mountain-bike tag stuck firmly enough to launch an industry. As the market boomed, Fisher and Kelly started buying frames from other builders. When Japanese component company Shimano started to sell suitable brakes and drivetrains, and rim makers Araya and Akai started to make lightweight 26-in. (66-cm) aluminum rims, the turning point was reached. The rims resulted in a big weight saving and greatly improved the stopping power of the popular Mafac cantilever brakes, and Shimano's new gears meant the bikes were good for going uphill as well as down. When good tires arrived on the scene, the early mountain bikes were brought down to 28 lb (13 kg) in weight.

Kelly left the company and Fisher sold it on a few years before it was acquired by Trek. Fisher remains an extremely active bike advocate to this day. **SW**

GOSSAMER Albatross

1979 • Winged bike • USA • Half bike, half airplane that flew across the English Channel

On June 12, 1979, in a celebration of the first-ever flight across the English Channel by French aviator Louis Blériot in 1909, the Gossamer Albatross recreated Blériot's flight using only human power.

Designed and built by a team of aeronautical engineers, and flown by Bryan Allen, a self-taught hang-glider pilot and avid cyclist, the Albatross was pedaled across the English Channel at a height of just 5 ft. (1.5m). It was a feat that demonstrated to the world just what pedal power could achieve.

The Albatross was a canard design, meaning that it had a secondary wing forward of the main wing to assist with lift, not dissimilar to the Wright Brothers'

"Construction [was] interesting since carbon fiber [was then] a somewhat exotic material . . ."

Bryan Allen, pilot

original Wright Flyer. The airframe featured an ultra-light mix of carbon fiber and expanded polystyrene in the ribs of its wings. Despite a wingspan of 98 ft. (30 m), the Albatross weighed only 70 lb (32 kg)—that is, only half of the weight of the pilot.

Allen had to pedal at a rate of 75 rpm for two hours—the Albatross required 0.4 hp to maintain steady flight, and Allen was producing half as much as that again. What the pilot did not expect was to lose his radio early on in the flight. The lack of it meant that his support team had no idea how he was coping with the increased headwinds that were lengthening the flight time and increasing his fatigue. But Allen's resolve kept the Albatross skimming the waves, and he gained the French coast in two hours and forty-nine minutes. **BS**

The Gossamar Albatross took cycling into another dimension. ▶

SCHWINN Spitfire 5

1979 • Mountain bike • USA • A bike that demonstrated Schwinn's inability to change with the times

The Schwinn Spitfire 5 was a pseudo mountain bike. It had a commonplace electro-forged cantilever frame with standard Schwinn cruiser handlebars, an Atom drum brake to the rear wheel, and heavy-duty spokes. The 5-speed Shimano Positron gear-shifting mechanism was an early attempt at index shifting; a controller with a series of discrete stops adjusted the derailleur via a solid wire cable. The Spitfire came with Weinmann brake levers, caliper brakes on the front wheel, a standard Schwinn cruiser saddle, and Carlisle studded balloon white wall tires.

Schwinn wanted to ride the crest of the mountain bike wave started by enthusiasts in northern California, who had been experimenting with new-look frames of butted chrome-molybdenum steel alloy. But Schwinn marketing executives saw the mountain bike craze as little more than a fad and advised against complex and expensive retooling. Schwinn initially called its "new" bike the Klunker 5, but failed to market it and never even bothered to put it in the Schwinn catalogue. That was probably just as well. The bike could not stand up to the rigors of off-road riding, the new name did nothing to improve performance, and the Spitfire 5 was dropped from production.

The 1979-model Spitfire 5s were manufactured from November to December 1978, but if you want to find the rarest of the breed, keep an eye out for the rare Klunker 5 label. That original name had to be abandoned when it was realized that a rival manufacturer already owned it. **BS**

CLELAND Aventura

1979 • Mountain bike • UK • Early UK mountain bike

Whereas U.S. pioneers on converted beach cruisers can lay claim to the commercial invention of mountain bikes, there were plenty of other tinkerers around the world creating their own versions of perfect rough-stuff bikes. Throughout the 1970s, UK off-road pioneer and eventual bike event organizer Geoff Apps was slowly evolving his cycles into off-road bikes.

The Cleland Aventura frame was created in 1979 to cater to Apps' riding demands and short upright designs. Apps' ideas, unusual at the time, would reach general acceptance much later in the world of mountain bikes: braking centered at the hubs and not the rims; high, wide handlebars; small chainrings; and protective plates for clearing obstacles on the ground. Perhaps most crucially, Apps favored the smoother roll of 27½-in. (70-cm) wheels instead of the 26-in. (66-cm) wheels that were standard on mountain bikes at the time. In fact, the 1979 Cleland Aventura was built around the 700C European road bike size of wheels, with Nokian tires, but at the time the bigger wheels did not catch on because of limited tire supplies.

The Aventura was intended for slow-speed technical riding, whereas mainstream mountain bikes were soon focused on higher speeds. Apps was certainly one of the founding fathers of mountain biking in the United Kingdom, but Cleland lacked the right mix of coincidences to become a commercial success and was wound up in 1984. Frame builder Jeremy Torr of English Cycles, who made many of the early Clelands, eventually made an English-badged version. **SW**

COLNAGO Mexico Gold

1979 • Road bike • Italy • A bicycle built for Pope John Paul II

In September of 1979, at a highly unusual meeting in St. Peter's Square—the huge plaza located directly in front of St. Peter's Basilica in the Vatican City—the Italian bike manufacturer Colnago had the honor of presenting Pope John Paul II with a bike. This was the event that officially confirmed Colnago as the most blessed bicycle manufacturer in the world.

John Paul was already a cycling fan, and this rare opportunity was a chance for company founder Ernesto Colnago to present the leader of the Catholic Church with something special. While the Pope was a resident in Krakow, Poland, he reportedly cycled 24 mi (38 km) twice a week and he continued to ride during his summer vacations. In a 2002 interview with *Cyclingnews*, Colnago remarked, "I remember that the Pope said to me, 'You are in the midst of all the cyclists and the sport, and I want to bless cycling and all the riders.'"

Colnago gave the Pope a truly outstanding bike. The manufacturer plumped for a 24-carat gold-plated version of its top Mexico Oro model. The company's hope was that the Pope would use its gilded beauty in the gardens of the Vatican. Unfortunately, it seems likely that the Pope never rode the bike any great distance, because after a year the Vatican called and asked if the bike could be returned, to be replaced by a new one with flat handlebars. Colnago dutifully accepted, building a white Colnago Arabesque Gentleman suitable for use during the Pope's vacations at Castel Gondolfo, 15 mi (24 km) southeast of Rome in the Lazio region of Italy.

The original bike, now residing in the Colnago Museum in Cambiago, Milan, testifies to one of the proudest moments in Ernesto Colnago's career; one that has seen him provide bikes for most of the biggest champions in professional cycling. **DB**

"The Pope picked up this bike and told me . . . that he wished he had one like it a long time ago."

Ernesto Colnago

AMMACO Team

1980 • BMX bike • UK • BMX race bike
from 1980s stalwart brand

The Ammaco brand name appeared on hundreds of BMX bikes in the 1980s. The company was run by two brothers called Jarvis and their brother-in-law, and the name was an odd contraction of their first names: "A Malcolm, Malcolm and Chris Organisation."

Ammaco imported and sold Mongoose bikes. These distinctive frames were soon superseded in the lineup by bikes Ammaco designed and made themselves. The Team race BMX seen here used slim tubes for low weight as well as continuous loop rear stays. However the change in BMX focus from racing to freestyle trick riding in the mid-1980s meant the Team was overshadowed by the Freestyler and Hi Styler trick.

The BMX business was so successful that the Jarvis family was able to sponsor a racing team, Ever Ready Ammaco. One of the riders was Tony Doyle, who went on to win the World Pursuit Championships in 1980 and 1986, plus various European championships. He was awarded the MBE in 1989.

Wanting to use Doyle's success to increase sales, it produced a special model, the Champion. This collectible bike used a classic-looking frame and Suntour gearset with down-tube shifters and Shimano 105 levers operating Exage brakes. **SH/GK**

SUN Solo

1980 • Road bike • UK • Classic affordable
racer revived by Raleigh

The Sun company, originally a brass foundry, made bicycle parts in Birmingham from 1885 and had a full range of bikes available by 1906. After the Second World War, the company was absorbed into the British Cycle Corporation, which gradually evolved into becoming part of Raleigh. In the 1960s the Sun Solo gained a reputation as a reasonably priced good-quality road bike. In the 1980s Raleigh revived the name by launching a budget race bike with the Sun Solo name.

Any stylish new bike with drop handlebars was called a "racer" in those pre–mountain-bike days, but the Sun Solo had frame geometry actually aimed at comfortable touring, including forward-slanting forks that extended the wheelbase. The frame, forks, and chromed 27-in. (70-cm) wheels were made of steel.

Equipment varied; many Sun Solos were simple 5-speed machines, but all were fitted with Weinmann alloy caliper brakes with "suicide" front-facing levers and Raleigh cottered cranks. Other possible standard components on these second-generation Solos included 10-speed Huret gear systems, a fitted dynamo, Maillard alloy hubs, and chromed-steel "cage" pedals. The supplied seat was a simple affair made of molded foam rubber. **SH**

SCHAUFF Aero

1980 • Time trial bike • Germany • Radical low-profile track bike

In 1932, Hans Schauff Senior, the founder of Schauff, created his first race frame in the original company factory alongside Cologne's famous Six Day Track. In the Second World War, an allied bombing raid destroyed the factory and forced the company's relocation to Remagen, 31 mi (50 km) to the south. The Schauff company has remained in the family to this day.

The Aero represented a significant leap forward in bicycle design. The bi-axial Powertwist tube design added torsion strength and gave the frame an exceptional degree of rigidity, as well as a sloping top tube to help minimize drag. Also very different were its unique nonadjustable handlebars, which attached directly to the top of the fork crown. The handlebar-fork was available in a number of lengths and heights to suit the individual cyclist, and the bike positioned the rider in an ultra low-profile, minimum-drag position.

The previous year Aero designed a high-speed racing tandem. Under French rider Jean-Claude Rude and a blind stoker, it topped 90 mph (145 kph) on an autobahn outside Alsace. The Aero did not grab those sorts of headlines, but Freddy Schmidke won a Silver Medal in the 1,000-m pursuit on an Aero at the World Championships in Prague in August 1981. **BS**

ZIELEMAN Special

1980 • Race bike • Netherlands • Little-known but highly desirable custom-built racer

The race bikes of the long-retired frame builder Ko Zieleman, who lived his whole life in Amsterdam, are a well-kept secret, even in the Netherlands.

The handcrafted Zieleman Special (also sold as a bare frameset) of 1980 was a typical Dutch classic racer. It was built with a selection of Columbus steel tubes handpicked according to the rider's size, power, and riding priorities. The tubes were joined with beautiful lugs from Cinelli, which also supplied the stems and bars of Zieleman's complete bikes. Campagnolo dropouts were used to hold the silky smooth Campagnolo Super Record hubs, which spun courtesy of a complete Super Record transmission upgraded with heavily drilled chainrings. Mavic rims were fitted with the customer's choice of top-quality hand made tubular tires.

Zieleman began his cycling life as an amateur rider before taking over the shop his father owned. Riders who knew him from those days, and were lucky enough to have had him customize their bikes, recalled him never making a distinction between customers. All who walked into his shop were equal, and he welcomed everyone with the term "gentleman." But he was not big on sponsoring—not a single frame ever left his shop without being paid for. **BS**

CUNNINGHAM Indian

1980 • Mountain bike • USA • Pioneering Californian alloy mountain bike

Charlie Cunningham is a career inventor from Fairfax, California. He started to build bikes, initially purely for himself, in 1977. This was around the time of the first mountain bikes, but Cunningham bikes were very different from the early mountain-bike models. He built the frames using heat-treated 6061 aluminum at a time when everyone else was using steel, which was heavier but much cheaper. Cunningham also tended to favor dropped handlebars, albeit uniquely shaped ones on a gooseneck stem designed mainly for riding the trails around Mount Tamalpais. Cannondale, which is often credited as an early adopter of aluminum frame building, did not start making its name with aluminum frames for another few years, when they introduced a touring bike in 1983.

Cunningham became a founding partner of the Wilderness Trail Bikes brand, and his influence crossed from frames to designs of tires (he codesigned the original Specialized Ground Control tire) and many other bike components. He was responsible for the evolution of 5⅓-in. (13.5-cm) rear hubs (dishless for extra strength), Grease Guard hubs and bottom-bracket bearing systems, and linear spring—later just known as "V"—rim brakes.

The Indian was almost certainly his most desired bike, ironically because it came closest to looking like a conventional mountain machine, albeit much lighter and much more costly than its rivals. Cunningham is significant in bike building for being probably the first frame builder to introduce the concept of the compact, triangled, low-standover, heat-treated, lightweight, but surprisingly tough aluminum frame in the days when steel was perceived as king. It is rarely recognized now that the likes of Cannondale and Klein owed much to those early hand-built Cunningham frames. **SW**

TUR MECCANICA Bi-Bici

1980 • Tandem • Italy • An ingenious gearing setup paired with Italian elegance

Tur Meccanica's design for the charming, Italian-made, short-wheelbase Bi-Bici race tandem is sometimes referred to as a "donkey back" because the rear seat is placed directly over the rear wheel; the result is a bike of the same length as a standard bicycle. The short length keeps weight to a relatively low 37 lb (17 kg). More than just a curiosity, the compact 5-speed Bi-Bici (Italian for "double bike") concedes nothing in practicality because its carry rack is moved from the back of the bike to the front, remaining a wonderfully conceived piece of Italian design.

The design of the chain drive makes it all possible. The stoker's cranks are connected to an axle that runs

> *"Tur Meccanica's 1980 Bi-Bici . . . actually measures only slightly larger than a single bike."*
>
> Michael Embacher, collector

through the center of the rear hub (without driving it); the stoker's chain runs forward toward the leading chainset, which acts as a transmission crossover to a second chain that runs back to a standard set of sprockets on the back wheel. Because the "alternate, other side drive" has chainrings the same size as those on the front rider's side, the two sets of pedals rotate together in synchronized harmony.

Tandems with stokers mounted over the rear wheel are not new. A green Tally-Ho, dating from around 1897 and hanging from the ceiling of the Three Oaks Bicycle Museum in Michigan, is a reminder of a time when "donkey backs" were popular for pacing track cyclists before the days when track clubs started acquiring triplets, quads, and quints. **BS**

The Bi-Bici offered twice the seating without any extra length. ▶

WILHEMINA Itera Plast

1980 • Utility bike • Sweden • Innovative almost totally plastic bike

Just what one could do with plastic was a hot topic in the late 1970s. Composite materials such as polyester resin had the potential to lower production costs significantly on almost any manufactured item, including bicycles. In 1980, thanks to a sizeable grant from the Swedish National Board for Technical Development, the Itera Development Center was born with one very specific brief: to produce a plastic bike. In 1981 a survey indicated more than 100,000 Swedes were ε agerly awaiting this new development in bicycle technology, and in early 1982 the first polyester resin-filled Itera Plasts came off the production line.

What its designers had conceived, however, was ungainly looking and boxlike, and, try as Itera did, the Plast never caught the imagination of the average Swede. The bike sold poorly and projected sales figures had to be halved. There was even talk of the Swedish government stepping in and taking the whole thing over. Sure, the Plasts did not rust and never required painting, but their resin-filled interiors made them 10 percent heavier than the average bike, and people were complaining about its strange, "spongy" ride.

Despite its limitations, the concept did have its supporters; plastics giant DuPont claimed that almost any part of a bicycle could be made using thermoplastics. One company in West Germany was even making a plastic bell. But when people began to return their bikes because plastic parts had snapped where metal would merely flex, the intriguing Itera Plast experiment melted away. **BS**

PASHLEY Pickle

1981 • Kids' trike • UK • Well-built re-creation of the trike representing a perfect childhood

The current price tag of almost $680 (£450) may seem extortionate for a small child's tricycle, but the sort of wealthy buyers that have been attracted to the Pashley Pickle over the past thirty years do not seem to mind. This is, after all, a beautiful re-creation of the classic kids' trike. For many parents, just to see it is to be transported back into their own childhood.

The bike, launched in 1981, has a timeless and durable design. The frame is made of lugged and brazed steel tubing in the traditional way. The sturdy forks are hand brazed too, as are the "Junior" handlebar assemblies. The Pickle has nothing as newfangled as modern gears; just a single-speed freewheel cog. Today's model does have proper pneumatic rubber tires with valves for comfort, though. These are fitted to

16 x 1⅜-in. (41 x 3.5-cm) alloy wheels with proper ball-bearing tricycle hubs. The braking system is a single-alloy caliper on the front wheel operated by a lever beneath the right-hand handlebar grip. The pedals are made of plastic and feature built-in safety reflectors. The Pickle's seat height is adjustable and the seatpost is L-shaped to support the thickly padded black saddle and allow some forward-to-back adjustment too.

The trike comes complete with three mudguards and a full chainguard. The whole is painted golden yellow with bright red trim or midnight blue with red trim. The final touch? Buyers can choose between a classic wicker basket or a wicker holder for a favorite doll or teddy bear, both available as optional extras. **SH**

ROSSIN Space Bike

1981 • Time trial bike • Italy • Classic sloping top tube "low-profile" bike

Rossin bikes debuted on the world stage only in 1977. Founder Mario Rossin was the former head frame builder at Colnago. The five other builders he gathered around him—represented by the five stars on the wonderful Rossin polygon—were extremely skilled too. With championships such as the Paris–Roubaix, Milan–San Remo, and the indoor Hour Record secured, it was becoming clear that Rossin race machines were fast as well as pretty.

Rossin bikes carried a line of champions to victory during the golden age of Italian steel racing in the late 1970s and early 1980s. The bikes were of Columbus SL tubing with Campagnolo everything: gears, pedals,

"Ever since [the company began] the Rossin name has been one of innovation and racing success."

Grupetto Italia

wheels, brakes, crankset, gear levers, bottom bracket, headset, and drop-outs. The company was stealing a significant march over its more entrenched competition, and rarely was that stolen march seen to greater effect than in the Rossin Space Bike, the distinctive appearance of which was inspired by the recent adoption of the company's bikes by East German team riders.

The bike had horned handlebars, but a more noticeable departure from convention was its horizontal frame tube, which sloped downward. Amateurs test-rode the new design on tracks in Turin and declared their enthusiasm, claiming that as much as a second per kilometer was being cut off established times. Belgian riders Nico Edmonds and Rudy Rogiers rode the Space Bike to several European amateur time trial wins. **BS**

COLNAGO Freddy Maertens

1981 • Road bike • Italy • One-off high-performance race bike

Ernesto Colnago came from a small rural village in northern Italy. He worked as a welding assistant at a Milan bike company by day, while racing bikes in his spare time. After a creditable string of victories, Colnago broke his leg in a crash. During his two-month recuperation, he started building his own bikes. In 1952 he opened his first bike workshop. It was a humble beginning: his father cut down the family mulberry tree to make the workbench.

But Colnago's reputation grew and in 1954 he became a mechanic for the Nivea team. Within a year he built a bike that enabled Fiorenzo Magni to lead the Giro d'Italia. In 1957 one of his bikes won the race with Gastone Nencini on board.

Throughout the decade of the 1960s, Colnago was a mechanic for the Italian national team. More race wins followed, including Eddy Merckx winning the Milan–San Remo race on a Colnago bike. By 1980 he had joined the highly successful GIS Gelati team. The 1981 season saw both Beppe Saroni and Freddy Maertens riding their own customized versions of Colnago bikes.

The controversial Belgian rider Maertens had a great season, winning five stages of the Tour de France on the bike. The Italian Saroni won three stages of the Giro d'Italia, and three other titles including the Giro di Romagna.

The two Colnago riders met in the World Road Racing Cycling Championships in Prague. They both made it through to the final. In a breath-taking sprint finish, Maertens pipped Saroni by a few inches. Colnago's bikes had taken the first two positions.

It was Maertens' last race victory, while Saroni went on to win the title the following year . . . on a Colnago bike, of course. **SH**

◁ Mario Rossin was the design genius behind the company.

MONGOOSE Supergoose

1981 • BMX • USA • Classic BMX race bike from a classic BMX brand

Like most BMX companies, Mongoose began in a garage in California in the mid 1970s. Mongoose founder Skip Hess started by making only his iconic single-piece, die-cast "Motomag" wheels. By 1975 Hess had moved into complete bike building as well.

Massive demand led to Mongoose bikes being produced on a piece-rate basis, with a carefully controlled production line operating both day and night shifts. Soon demand for frames was outstripping the number of available TIG welders, so torch wielders were trained in-house to maintain build quality. Forks and handlebars were also made in-house, and Mongoose started to produce its own components, too. Tube bending and pre-cutting were outsourced to speed up production, and soon as many as 600 frames

per day were being made by the eighty-five-strong workforce. Mongoose managed to remain a leading-edge innovator, rolling out its classic flagship race frame, the Mongoose Supergoose, in 1980.

Produced only by the most skilled welders in the team, the 1981 Supergoose had very thin-walled chromoly steel tubes, yielding a superlight frameset. Strength was kept high with the use of distinctive gusset plates between the top tube and down tube, behind the head tube. The two plates had a signature circular "porthole" that made the bikes instantly recognizable. The original Supergoose frames, forks, and cranks were nickel plated for a tough, eye-catching, mirror finish. Color-coded rims, seat posts, and bars completed the standout looks. **GK**

RALEIGH Vektar

1981 • Kids' bike • UK • Bike with built-in radio and siren

It was styled like something from the *Star Wars* movies, with technology straight out of the *Knight Rider* TV show. No wonder the Vektar became yet another successful Raleigh marketing ploy to capture the imagination of British children in the 1980s.

The Vektar's defining feature was its computer system mounted on the bike's top and head tube. Many of its functions could be controlled on the move, using the left twist grip on the handlebars. The battery-powered electronics were enough to make any youngster of the era drool: a sound generator with eight different siren noises; an AM radio with three preset stations; and a digital speedometer with a trip counter and stopwatch function that told you how far you had cycled. The on-board speaker had a typically tinny sound but was surprisingly loud. The Vektar was, of course, really just a standard Raleigh children's frame with some plastic bits screwed on, but these allowed Raleigh to call it an "electronic street machine" and "the most technically advanced machine around."

The bike was featured on the front page of the huge-selling UK comic magazine *The Beano*, with a story featuring the popular character Dennis the Menace. His posh nemesis, Walter, was given a "spiffing Vektar" bike, so Dennis made his own by sticking a transistor radio to the handlebars. Dennis ended up crashing into some rocks because he had forgotten to fit any brakes. Thankfully, the real Vektar was fitted with tough, grippy tires and Raleigh raincheck sidepulls to keep any real Menaces from getting mangled. **SH**

RALEIGH Bomber

1981 • Road bike • UK • UK copy of U.S. cruiser bike

"Possibly the meanest machine on the street," proclaimed the Raleigh catalog. The American street cruising-style bike had arrived in the United Kingdom, and it inspired a generation of young people.

If you were after a tough image, this was undoubtedly the machine to be seen on in the early eighties. Owners tilted the handlebars back until the grips were horizontal, and cruised their local streets and playgrounds feeling like they were riding Harley-Davidson motorbikes.

Sadly, the Bomber was a flawed icon. The forks bent, twisted, and broke with appalling ease. Paintwork peeled and bearings broke. The bolted-on seatstays were a serious weak point. Owners reported a wide range of frame malfunctions.

Yet nothing dampened the desire for the Bomber. It was the bad boy of British bikes, and many teens saved their pocket money or begged for it as a present.

Some Bombers had no gears, some had three-speed Sturmey-Archer gears, others had five gears. But they all had the distinctive frame with a bent top tube and big French-made chrome 26 x 2³⁄₂₀-in. (66 x 5.4-cm) wheels with fat tires. Other kit included Sturmey-Archer caliper brakes and levers, plus a Sugino chainset.

Raleigh called the handlebars "wide rise"; kids called them "cowhorns." The sprung saddle was chunky foam with a rear reflector; the upright handlebars came with foam-rubber grips, and the frame was adorned with bright graphics. According to Raleigh, "The owner of a Bomber is not to be tangled with." **SH**

SCHWINN Sidewinder

1982 • Mountain bike • USA • Half-hearted introductory mountain bike from U.S. giant Schwinn

Schwinn was a late arrival on the mountain bike and BMX scenes, and its early offerings to this market were ill-conceived bikes that failed to meet the requisite design and engineering requirements. The Sidewinder—Schwinn's first entry into the mountain bike market—had a Varsity frame that had been halfheartedly modified to accept wider tires. However, many owners found them comfortable, although heavy, and still a lot of fun to ride.

To most of the riders from Marin County, California—where mountain biking and adventure sports were born—the Sidewinder certainly looked odd. With its beach cruiser seat, BMX-styled tubular fork and handlebar, and commonplace road bike frame, it was definitely a hybrid, not a thoroughbred. But this was a

period of experimentation, with the idea of just what makes a good mountain bike still in the early stages of being worked through. Schwinn wasn't the only manufacturer experimenting with components from other bicycles in its effort to find the right mix.

The Sidewinder had single-speed, five-speed, and ten-speed options, was available in sierra brown or frosty silver blue, and came with cushioned grips and balloon tires. It was well intentioned, but destined never to generate more than a passing interest among enthusiasts as coming developments—such as the use of lightweight aluminum and the production of specialized mountain bike frames in Japan and Taiwan—quickly took over and forced Schwinn to catch up with what it had initially regarded as only a passing fad. **SH**

DAWES Super Galaxy

1982 • Touring bike • UK • Updated version of the classic Galaxy

One version of the Galaxy touring bike would never be enough for Dawes once it discovered what a winning formula it had.

By 2009, the company's touring bike range included the Galaxy, the Galaxy Plus, the Super Galaxy, the Ultra Galaxy, the Ultra Galaxy Ti, and the Galaxy Twin tandem. At the time of publication of this book, there was a choice of eight models: Classic, Cross, Plus, AL, Classic Ladies, Super Galaxy, and Ultra Galaxy, as well as the basic Galaxy itself.

In a sparkling universe of Galaxies, the Super has always been one of the brightest stars, topped only by the Ultra. The general profile of the Super was basically

". . . the utmost in riding comfort combined with . . . superior handling characteristics. . ."

Dawes catalog, 1982

the same as that of the standard version of the bike, but with even greater attention to detail and the addition of higher-quality components.

Yet the subtle handling differences between a Galaxy and a Super might be fully appreciated only by the most serious riders and connoisseurs. To ordinary buyers, the two machines seemed almost identical in every particular other than price: Both had parallel 72-degree 531 frames in the same four sizes, 27-in. (69-cm) wheels, and Randonneur handlebars. The brakes of both bikes were center-pull units from Weinmann.

The additional cost of the Super was justified by the inclusion of upgraded derailleurs, chainset, saddle, and pedals. The Super also benefited from the addition of front and back luggage racks. **SH**

RALEIGH Wisp

1982 • Road bike • UK • Popular women's mixed-style racer

Yvonne Rix was a resourceful and trenchant marketing chief at Raleigh who assertively promoted the interests of women cyclists. It was she who dreamed up the idea for the Wisp, a women's casual sports road bike with drop handlebars.

The Wisp was a reasonably priced popular bike with sensible components and a durable build for cycling to and from work or college. The frame was made of heavy high-tensile steel, and used a mixte configuration that combined a traditional skirt-friendly step-through with a twin top tube running from the head tube right back to the rear axle. This design helped to add structural rigidity. On the Wisp, this twin tube was matched by double seatstays.

The Wisp was offered with either 5- or 10-speed Sachs Huret gears and standard Weinmann brakes. It also had the Custom chainset that was fitted to many Raleigh sports bikes at the time. Wheels were 27 x 1¼-in. (69 x 3-cm) chromed steel, and the bike came with alloy mudguards and a luggage pannier.

It was clearly designed for young or occasional leisure riders rather than for real enthusiasts. A two-tone blue paint job was complemented by smart graphics, a navy "suede" saddle, and matching fabric handlebar tape.

Thanks to one of the stylish advertising campaigns for which Raleigh was renowned, the bike was a big success. From its base in Nottingham, England, the company sold around 50,000 Wisps in the first year alone. It was particularly popular in France, where it acquired a nickname—*la petite reine* (the little queen). Two variant models also sold well—the Cameo and the Misty, which were promoted more as fashion items than as bikes. The Wisp proved a long-lasting bike too—as the large numbers still around today demonstrate. It is still a low-cost, durable entry-level machine. **SH**

RALEIGH Record Ace

1982 • Road bike • UK • Steel-frame tourer built for comfort and speed

Some touring cyclists want to potter along; others want to move with speed. Raleigh's Record Ace targeted both types, but principally the latter.

This superior hand-built bike had double-butted parallel frame and forks, tapered back stays, and light competition-grade thin-walled Reynolds tubing. There were Sun Tour forged drop-outs, brazed and hand-finished lugs, and a hand-sprayed finish with lacquered paintwork. A tourer–racer crossover, the Ace made concessions to comfort—mudguards, water-bottle holder, suede saddle—and had lots of go-faster kit too.

Standard kit included 27 x 1¼-in. (69 x 3-cm) Weinmann alloy rims with double-butted spokes, plus small-flange quick-release hubs.

Style highlights were delicate engraving between the brown taped drops on the Italienne alloy handlebars, and the frame's Hayden Royal Sovereign semi-decorative lugs.

Other details included a Vagner Crown Fork, Weinmann side pull QR brakes with hooded levers, SR Custom alloy cotterless cranks, and Campag Gran Sport gears and shifters, which were fitted onto the down tube. The 25½ lb (11.5 kg) bike came in four frame sizes but only one color—a subtle ice green. **SH**

VITUS 979

1982 • Road bike • France • Aluminum-magnesium frame points to the future of race bike design

The Vitus 979 was built in the workshops of French companies Angenieux-CLB and Ateliers de la Rive. The first Vitus-branded Duralinox aluminum-magnesium alloy frames—which included tubesets, forks, head tubes, and rear triangle stays—were developed by Atelier in 1978. Angenieux provided drop-outs, rear brake bridges, cast-alloy lugs, bottom brackets, and fork crowns. Lugs were glued to the frame using a dry heat–activated epoxy. Vitus' customer list included Peugeot and Gitane.

The 979 had a classic racing frame, was very light for its time, and possessed a tight geometry with next to no clearance between tire and tubeset. Sean Kelly, the Irish "King of the Classics," rode a Vitus 979 to victory in the 1988 Vuelta a España, and to the green jersey in the 1989 Tour de France. One abiding criticism, however, was that the frame was overly flexible, particularly at its bottom bracket, which might not suit a heavier rider.

The 979 was available in five colors—red, royal blue, gray-blue, silver, and black—that were anodized, not painted, and applied only to the tubing. Everything else was polished aluminum. It came in two models: the MK I, with a binder bolt securing its seatpost, and later the MK II, with an aero-profile seat and down tubes. **BS**

SPECIALIZED Allez

1982 • Road bike • USA • The first of one of the world's most popular road bike ranges

Specialized was founded in 1974 by Californian bike enthusiast Mike Sinyard, who sold his VW camper for $1,500 (£900) to launch a bike component business. In 1981, the company launched its own bikes.

One was the Stumpjumper, the world's first production mountain bike. This celebrated machine helped launch the sport of off-road biking but rather overshadowed the release, at the same time, of Specialized's low-priced steel-framed road bike built in Japan. But the Allez has since become one of the world's most popular road bikes.

The original Allez frame was designed by Tim Neenan, an established West Coast bike builder. The first 100 Allez road bikes were due to be made by a local custom builder but he couldn't meet the demand so Neenan spent a month supervising production at a Japanese factory. The frames were well made, using good-quality Japanese steel tubing; Neenan's geometry was good and the parts were either Specialized's own or top-quality components from other manufacturers.

The range grew to include higher-end models, and the Allez name received a huge boost in 1985 when Kevin Costner rode one in the movie *American Flyers*. **SH**

UNIVEGA Alpina Pro

1982 • Mountain bike • USA • One of the first mass-produced mountain bikes

Univega and Specialized were the first companies to sell complete off-the-peg mountain bikes. The Univega Alpina Pro was made by Miyata of Japan for Lawee Inc., Univega's parent company, and offered for sale at $695 (£430). The Specialized Stumpjumper cost $850 (£525).

The Pro had a good-quality lugged frame and a Sugino crankset designed like TA's European Cyclotourist model. It was the starting point of moderately priced mountain bikes for the masses.

Both companies later released variant models of the same bikes. One of the early subsequent Univega bikes, the Alpina Sport, was cheaper than the Pro and sold more than any other production mountain bike at the time.

Univega founder Ben Lawee ran a bike shop in Long Beach and had been the U.S. importer for French brand Motobecane while at the same time manufacturing bikes in Italy under the Italvega name.

In the 1990s, Univega was absorbed by Derby Cycle, but the Alpina lives on, although the latest models bear no resemblance to the originals. While Specialized and Fisher received most of the kudos for their first mountain bikes, Univega did more than either company to bring mid-priced mountain bikes to the masses. **SW**

PATTERSON Pro Long

1982 • BMX bike • USA • Race BMX from the first family of bicycle motocross racing

Few companies can claim to be as race bred as Patterson Racing BMX. Vance Patterson had already invested in Speedo, another bike company who had stated an intention to make a race BMX frame for his increasingly successful sons Brian and Brent Patterson. Tired of waiting for their frame, Vance took matters into his own hands and produced the extremely clean-looking Patterson Racing Sentry frame in 1978. With its box-section wishbone between the curved rear chainstays, overlapping seatstay-to-top-tube junction, minimalist chopped tube (rather than plate) rear drop-outs, and large flat plate brake bridge, the Sentry was instantly recognizable and set the bar high for subsequent bikes.

The first was the signature Anderson Avalanche, which was developed for team rider Richie Anderson. This used more conventional plate gussets behind the bottom bracket shell and deep plate drop-outs to hold the rear wheel. The head tube used extra reinforcing rings at the top and bottom to keep nose-heavy landings from distorting the frame on landing. While Anderson and others were massively successful in racing the new bike, the Patterson brothers literally hit gold with the appropriately named Patterson Long later in 1978, which was joined by the evolved Pro Long in 1982. This used a longer top tube and front end than the Anderson and Sentry, allowing bigger riders—such as 6 ft 1 in.- (1.85-m) -tall Brent—to get more power into the ground. Apart from this, the design was very similar to the Anderson Avalanche, except for the fractionally more overlapped seatstay–top tube junction it owed to the original Sentry. The evolved design proved ultra-successful too, helping the Pattersons become the only brothers to both hold the National No. 1 Pro title in BMX. **GK**

HARO Freestyler

1982 • BMX bike • USA • Influential freestyle-specific machine

One of the most innovative and legendary BMXs, this bike is the creation of Bob Haro, a Californian rider who was dubbed the "Godfather of Freestyle."

Manufactured in collaboration with sponsor Torker BMX of Fullerton, California, the Haro Freestyler adopted several key features geared specifically to trick riding: a steeper head angle; thicker drop-outs; an outsized triangulated down tube gusset for strength; a double top tube trick platform; and a coaster brake mount on the chainstays for backward rolling tricks. The 4130 chromoly responded well to Haro's needs, as he pioneered BMX "no rules" expression. Before designing the first BMX dedicated to this new branch of the sport,

> *"I thought it was time to create a freestyle-only bike, instead of a BMX used for freestyle."*
>
> Bob Haro

Haro had already won fifty motocross trophies by the age of seventeen and teamed up with R. L. Osborn to form the first freestyle BMX team in the United States. He was also chosen to perform as a stunt double in the movie *E.T.: The Extra-Terrestrial.*

Haro the brand was pivotal to the early development of the graphic identity and fashion look of BMX Freestyle, and remains one of the most popular apparel and accessory companies today. Founder Bob Haro has since left the company, but he remains universally revered in the BMX world. He has designed all the national outfits for the U.S. Olympic BMX teams to date, and orchestrated the elaborate Dove bicycle sequence at the opening ceremony of the 2012 London Olympics. **MK**

Bob Haro's Freestyler was an influential machine on the BMX scene. ▶

KUWAHARA KZ-2.5/E.T. bike

1982 • BMX bike • USA • Bike immortalized in
a famous movie chase scene

JMC Black Shadow

1982 • BMX • UK • Iconic long and lightweight
race BMX

Kuwahara was a relatively unknown Japanese company until it was chosen to provide twenty-five BMX bikes for the Hollywood film *E.T.: The Extra-Terrestrial* (1982). The subsequent worldwide licensing deal to sell replica machines resulted in the brand becoming one of the most popular in BMX in the early 1980s.

Director Steven Spielberg had seen hundreds of kids riding around California on the small-wheeled bikes and decided to include some BMX action scenes in his latest project. Uncertain which brand to choose, he asked his young nephew, who opted for a Kuwahara.

E.T. became one of the highest-grossing movies ever, enabling Kuwahara to mass-produce three different types of E.T. bikes at its Osaka factory. Two were "proper" BMXs, with chromoly frames, loop-tail rear triangles, and double head-tube gussets. The more expensive Original version sported Sugino, Suntour, and Dia Compe parts, plus Ukai alloy-rimmed wheels. A cheaper Replica version used Taihei and Kusuki Taiwanese copy parts. The third version, the Apollo—the so-called "toy store model"—had a high-tensile steel frame and cheaper components. In 2002, Kuwahara issued a twentieth-anniversary model, the KZ-2.5. **MK**

JMC Racing began when Jim Melton started selling restored bikes and components from his home in 1969.

The Jim Melton Cyclery shop opened in 1974. By the following year it had a race team, which at first rode Webco BMXs but soon adopted own-brand JM Special frames. These came in two versions, long and short, and went into production in 1976 as JMC 1 and JMC 2. JMC Tear Drop forks were added to the frames in 1978, and these proved so popular that Melton sold his shop to focus solely on frame production.

In 1980 the company launched first the JMC Mini for junior riders and then the Black Shadow. The latter—an all-black frame designed for powerhouse racer Kim Jarboe—used custom 4130 chrome molybdenum steel alloy tubes and the sharp-steering, extended top tube geometry of previous long JMC frames. A lighter-gauge tubeset was then used for the short version, which was named the 3.1XL by the winner of a magazine contest.

The original Black Shadow became an instant must-have bike, no doubt helped by multiple top-class wins by riders such as Jarboe, Darrell Young, and Jason Wharton including a team world championship in 1982. By this time the frame was available in multiple colors as well as chrome. **GK**

RALEIGH Street Wolf

1982 • Kids' bike • UK • Electronically enhanced first "proper" bike

The Street Wolf was part of Raleigh's plan to conquer Britain's children's bike market, with a model for every age range. The Street Wolf was targeted as the first bike without stabilizers for six-to-seven-year-olds.

The Street Wolf's little brother, the Wolf Cub, was famous for being one of the costliest bikes with training wheels on the market. The Street Wolf had no training wheels but was even more expensive.

Much of the cost was because of the extras. One of Raleigh's early attempts to get into the booming BMX market, the Street Wolf was built on a solid frame but adorned with a range of plastic bolt-on fairings, guards, and gadgets.

Most Street Wolves were painted red and black and had fashionably chunky tires, but the most distinctive add-on was a handlebar-mounted box containing a battery that powered a push-button three-toned siren, which kids loved and adults hated. The box also featured a mock radar display with a moving wolf's head logo.

Raleigh claimed the Street Wolf was "BMX at its toughest." The frame was a sturdy—and heavy— steel affair, and the muscular wheels had five chunky spokes, with a 6-speed gear system controlled from a twist-grip shifter. **SH**

RALEIGH Pro Burner

1982 • BMX bike • UK • Pro-specification race-ready Burner

In 1982, Raleigh sold a range of seven Burners to satisfy the demands of the BMX craze sweeping the United Kingdom. The Pro Burner was the flagship of the lineup, costing more than double the standard specification bikes and, at just over 25 lb (11.3 kg), weighing 7 lb (3 kg) less than a regular Burner.

Sporting a silver-and-blue color scheme, the Pro frame and forks were 4130 chromoly steel, fully chrome plated, and manufactured in Japan by Koizumi. A U.S. equivalent race-ready machine was also issued by Raleigh and labeled the Rampar. Both models shared a distinctive double head-tube gusset. Only a few of them were made, and it is thought that no more than fifty are left in existence worldwide.

Since the Pro was Raleigh's answer to the high-end boutique U.S.-made frames that dominated the BMX race scene at the time, the kit list reads like a Pro start-gate specification: perforated Kashimax Aero saddle, genuine Japanese Mitsubishi Comp III tires, sealed bearing Suzue hubs laced into Araya 7C two-tone rims, and a fluted aluminum seatpost.

Today, a first-generation Pro Burner is a serious collector's item that may fetch thousands of dollars in mint condition. **MK**

GEORGE LONGSTAFF Trike

1982 • Tricycle • UK • High-performance artisan-built tricycle

British bike enthusiast George Longstaff founded his company in 1982. Previously he had experimented with various designs, and built one-off custom bike frames in the garage of his home.

At his company workshop in Chesterton, Staffordshire, Longstaff built all sorts of bikes, including handmade tourers and tandems, but became best known for his tricycles. These top-end three-wheelers soon acquired a global reputation for touring, commuting, and racing. They were also used by many Paralympic cycling teams, including those of Great Britain, Canada, Australia, and Spain. Longstaff gained a reputation for ingenious solutions for disabled cyclists. Eventually his workshop expanded and took over a Salvation Army building next door.

The heart of Longstaff's trike was a drive system with a chain that worked the center of the rear axle using a two-wheel-drive cassette that turned both back wheels. Driving both wheels equally would make cornering difficult—a problem that is dealt with in motorized vehicles by a differential system. Longstaff's solution involved a double-freewheel system that directed the drive to the slowest wheel, the one with the most traction. This made the trike's handling stable.

Many of Longstaff's trikes featured rear disc brakes; some used a rim brake system too. His front forks were available in carbon or steel, and in either unicrown or traditional style.

Longstaff died in 2003, but his company still produces some of the world's most acclaimed trikes. **SH**

RALEIGH Trail Rider

1982 • Mountain bike • UK • Early mountain bike with BMX influences

In the mistaken belief that mountain biking was a fad that would soon pass, Raleigh concentrated mainly on the BMX market.

Its Trail Rider was an attempt to cash in on what seemed to be no more than a temporary craze for off-road bikes without doing much research and development. Engineers simply chose a bunch of BMX parts, fitted them to a copy of one of the early U.S. mountain bike frames, and added some knobbly looking tires and chopper handlebars.

Such was the lack of investment in the project that there was little discernible attempt to make the bike more suited to off-road riding. The double crank, stem, handlebars, and straight-bladed forks used on the Trail Rider were taken straight from the Raleigh BMX

parts bin. Even the caliper brakes were those used on Raleigh's BMX range.

The frame was more adventurous. It was made of 4130 chromoly tubing, and featured a strange extra double set of tubes from the head to the rear drop-outs. But it was simply a copy of a design that had been created by Joe Breeze's early mountain bikes in the United States a few years before.

Breeze later claimed that this "cheap imitation" was so crudely done that the Trail Rider's twin laterals didn't help structural rigidity: While Raleigh's curves around the back tire significantly reduced the stiffness of the tubes, Breeze's laterals were arrow-straight. Whatever the truth of this claim, the fact remains that, by this time, Breeze had already abandoned this frame design. **SH**

SPECIALIZED Stumpjumper

1982 • Mountain bike • USA • The first mass-produced mountain bike

COLNAGO Beppe Saronni

1982 • Road bike • Italy • Handmade bike for Beppe Saronni

At the 1981 bicycle show in Long Beach, California, around fifteen custom builders exhibited mountain bikes in various forms, but Specialized was one of the first to go into mass production with this modestly priced machine, which was manufactured in Japan.

The Stumpjumper was based on the design of the Tom Ritchey-built bikes sold by Gary Fisher and Charlie Kelly, but with slightly longer forks. Although it is unclear whether this modification was intentional, the result was a very laid-back geometry that contributed greatly to the success of the first batch. Five hundred were produced at $750 (£450) apiece; put on sale in mid-1982, they had all sold out by the end of the year. This was about the same number of bikes as Fisher, Kelly, and Ritchey had assembled and sold between them in the whole of 1981.

Specialized had struck a rich seam: It went on to become one of the biggest and most influential bike brands on the planet. The Stumpjumper name remains, but modern manifestations of the bike have nothing in common with the originals, apart from the fact that they still have two wheels, and even then they are 3 in. (7.6 cm) bigger than this historic trend-setting mountain bike. **DB**

In the final of the 1981 World Road Racing Championships, when Eddie Maertens beat Giuseppe "Beppe" Saronni by a few inches, both riders were on Ernesto Colnago's steel-framed bikes. The Italian manufacturer was a byword in the cycling world for sporting achievement.

Maertens faded somewhat after that victory, but the young Italian Saronni was at his peak. In the following year he returned to the world championships to attempt to go one better. His new Colnago was made from brazed and lugged Columbus steel tubing, and had a Campagnolo Super Record groupset, Martano rims, and Cinelli parts.

Saronni's astonishing sprint finish in the last 200 m left previously leading riders Greg LeMond and Sean Kelly trailing in his wake. After the victory Colnago celebrated by building a collection of steel-framed road racing bikes badged "Saronni." These specials are still highly sought after by collectors.

Behind the scenes, however, Colnago was already working on prototype carbon framed bikes that would one day replace steel. Even today, Colnago retains a steel-framed bike in its range, and it is still available in the historic Saronni red. **SH**

CW Phaze One

1983 • BMX bike • USA • Quirky "lightning bolt" down tube oddity

Nothing but a cool-looking gimmick, this quirky design with its zigzag down tube offered (and claimed) no structural benefits, and few of the original frames survive today because the "Z" part was so prone to cracking.

CW started out in the 1970s as Coast Wheels, a bike shop in Yorba Linda, California. Owner Roger Worsham focused on BMX products, and CW racing frames and components expanded rapidly. The flat-topped CW racing handlebar is one of the most popular and recognizable BMX products of all time.

Originally made as a one-off for Billy Griggs, who went on to win two Amateur World Championships before turning pro, the Phaze One wasn't intended as a commercial product. However, a few mentions in BMX magazines prompted massive customer interest. Production started in 1984.

The frame, intended for racing, was made from 4130 chromoly tubing and heli-arc welded with the same geometry as CW's ZX Pro frame. The fad for the lightning-bolt design was short-lived, and CW discontinued it soon after producing extremely limited (and now highly sought-after) Mini and Cruiser editions. It was revived briefly in 2012 as a cruiser with 24-in. (61-cm) wheels, but purists will always prefer the original. **MK**

JMC Darryl Young

1983 • BMX bike • USA • Limited-edition signature frame and forks for BMX racing

Jim Melton started selling restored bike parts from his home in 1969 and set up the JM Cyclery shop in Azusa, California, in 1984. At the same time, Jim started the shop's involvement with BMX.

By 1976, JMC had a very successful BMX race team and was starting to produce its first frames, with the company's innovative Teardrop forks following shortly afterward. The range expanded in the early 1980s with Mini and Long versions of the Standard frame as well as the must-have Black Shadow frame.

Up-and-coming racer Darrell Young joined the team in 1981 when he was only fifteen years old and was crowned Expert World Champion for his age group the following year. Keen to capitalize on his success, JMC introduced a signature Darrell Young race frame and forks in 1983.

The frame featured a seat tube that penetrated through the extended top tube for extra strength. The seat tube also had a built-in clamp bolt to hold the seatpost rather than a separate seat clamp. The rear stays were formed from a single looped tube with the rear drop-out plates welded onto the radius. Sadly, competition from cheaper overseas-built bikes saw Jim wind up the company and the team in 1985. **GK**

GITANE LeMond

1983 • Road bike • France • Championship-winning bike for American rider

Greg LeMond joined the Renault-Elf-Gitane (REG) pro team after winning the World Amateur Championships in 1979. In 1983 he became the first American to win the Professional Road Race Championships. His victory was a turning point in a sport that had previously been dominated by Europeans.

Gitane was renowned for high-performance bikes. Lemond's win was the company's second World Road Race World Championship in three years. In 1983 it also provided rides for Laurent Fignon's victory in the Tour de France and Bernard Hinault's in the Vuelta a España.

LeMond's blue and yellow Gitane was a production bike, equipped mainly with French parts from Simplex, Mavic, and Maillard, but also with Cinelli bars and Columbus tubing. Tires came from Michelin and Wolber.

It was a short-wheelbase design with period down-tube shifting levers and high curving brake cables, although the internally routed rear brake cables are a touch of modernity.

The bike is now displayed at the United States Cycling Hall of Fame in Los Angeles, California. It looks a bit grubby, and rumor has it that the machine was never cleaned after the event and was merely put into storage by LeMond right after the race. **SH**

RALEIGH Burner

1983 • BMX bike • UK • Mass-produced ubiquitous icon

In an era when Nottingham, England-based bike company Raleigh ruled the roost in Britain, the Burner was the most popular kids' ride. A high-profile launch of five different models and a BMX race team led by number-one rider Andy Ruffell ensured tons of publicity, and the Burner, retailing for only around $145 (£90), became an overnight success.

In terms of equipment and construction, the cheapest Burner wasn't much to write home about, but, crucially for Raleigh, the BMX craze was at its height. When the company launched the range, parents recognized and trusted the brand; sales soared.

The 32-lb (14.5-kg) Mark I Burner mainframe was made from high-tensile steel, rather than heat-treated chromoly, and used a series of gussets and thick tubes to ensure the frame was tough enough for rough treatment. Also for durability were heat-treated one-piece cranks with a chrome-plated chainwheel guard to protect the sprocket and gold chain. To make the bikes easy for smaller children to pedal, they had an unusually low 40–16 tooth (2.5:1 ratio) gearing setup.

Finished in blue or red, with matching pad sets and tires, the Burners really looked the part and were instantly recognizable. **MK**

SMITH AND CO Long John
1983 • Cargo bike • Denmark • Ultra-stable low-loader cargo bike

Although its precise origins are shrouded in the mists of time, it appears that the first Long John-styled cargo bikes were manufactured in Denmark around 1923 by Nordisk Cykelfabrik. The company certainly built the celebrated example exhibited at the British Empire Exhibition in London in 1924.

A type of bike rather than a specific model, Long Johns continued to be built in Europe by a succession of manufacturers, including another Danish company, Urania Cykler, and later by Smith & Company, whose owner took over Urania Cykler in the 1960s. The Long John name has been synonymous with Smith and Co. ever since.

Two-wheeled load bikes with large cargo areas set between the steering tubes and the front wheels, the Long Johns of the 1960s had a sturdy load-carrying area with a capacity of around 220 lb (100 kg). Other characteristics were a long wheelbase, an extremely low center of gravity, and a front wheel that was steered via a rod linkage running below the carrier. The 1983 Long John shown here was the longest two-wheeled cargo bike of its day, able to transport loads of just under 309 lb (140 kg). This was a lot for its poor Sachs drum brake, so later models were upgraded to feature hydraulic brakes.

In 1997, Smith & Co. was taken over by Swedish company Monark Exercise, which ceased production of the Long John in 2003 before starting it up again in 2007. Despite all the changes of ownership, current Long Johns still bear an uncanny resemblance to early postwar models, with the basket protruding only a little way beyond the pedals, allowing the bicycle to be ridden almost anywhere. Vintage Long Johns are highly sought after, and they are still as practical today as they were eighty years ago. **BS**

TREK 850
1983 • Mountain bike • USA • Trek's first mountain bike effort

It's hard to imagine the massive Trek corporation dithering about whether to build a proper mountain bike. But even the company that became the world's biggest name in mountain bikes had to start somewhere. And this was its first attempt.

Of course, in the 1983 Trek catalog, the 850 was the only non-road bike. It came right at the end, and was described as a "rough terrain" bike, as if it were some sort of oddity that Trek was unsure about.

The 850 was certainly basic by modern mountain bike standards, but it did the job when it was launched—indeed, it was pretty cool for the money. The pioneering off-roader featured a lugged and

> *"This rough terrain bicycle has been designed to overcome the toughest riding conditions."*
>
> *Trek 1983 catalog*

butted chromoly frame and fork from Tange. The tubing was pretty moderate by today's standards. The 850's geometry featured relaxed frame angles, plus some of the most hardcore parts Trek could find, including a 15-speed Suntour gearset and sealed-bearing hubs, with a Sugino forged alloy crank, SR alloy pedals, DiaCompe cantilever brakes, and Araya 26-in. (66-cm) rims clad in Trek's own branded 2⅛-in. (5.4-cm) tires.

The Avocet Touring saddle was adjustable fore and aft by means of a quick-release lever, allowing it to slide on rails along the top of the seat post. The bike even came with a cage and a water bottle.

The sole color scheme was black metallic with a red panel logo on the seat tube. The bike cost only $580 (£367). **SH**

The 850 was Trek's first foray into the world of mountain bikes. ▶

TRUSSARDI War & Peace

1983 • Folding replica bike • Italy • Paratroop bike rebuilt as a 1980s fashion statement

The Trussardi design legacy began in 1910, when master glove maker Dante Trussardi set up his first shop in Bergamo, Italy. In 1983 Dante's nephew, the late Nicola Trussardi, brought elegance and functional quality to items other than clothing and leather accessories, including aircraft interiors, motorcycles, automobiles, and bicycles.

Manufactured in a limited run of 3,000 in 1983, the War & Peace was based on the folding military bicycles of Italian army paratroopers. The curved steel frame had wing nut-secured hinges in the tube centers. The cream dream machine was dressed up by Trussardi's designers with leather logo panels and other leather accessories, such as rear saddlebags that doubled as chic shoulder

> "Today we have the pleasure of reintroducing a new Citybike, the Trussardi 1911."

Trussardi Group, 2013

bags. The bike came in two versions: one simply pedal powered, and the other (now becoming impossible to find) with a tiny 2-cubic-inch (35-cc) motor.

Trussardi's exercise in nostalgia was one of the few folding bicycles with 26-in. (66-cm) wheels, so it could be seriously contemplated for a longish journey. However, its wonderfully swoopy varnished steel frame contributed to an overall weight of 42 lb (19 kg), putting it firmly in the chic cruiser category.

A more recent version of the bike—the Trussardi 1911 Citybike, designed by Milan Vukmirovic—was released in 2013. Among its trendy accessories are water-resistant leather baskets, a camera case-shaped bag in traditional camouflage, and 1940s-era brass detailing on the headlamp, kickstand, and spokes. **BS**

RIDGEBACK 601

1983 • Mountain bike • UK • Early British mountain bike

Along with the likes of Saracen and Muddy Fox, UK company Ridgeback was among the first to recognize the commercial potential of mountain bikes in the early 1980s. Richard Ballantine and Richard Grant had shipped a few Ritchey mountain bikes into the United Kingdom in 1980 but it took another few years for UK brands to realize that this was going to be more than just a U.S. phenomenon. While a lot of riders had learned their skills by riding bikes in the woods as kids, the only vaguely formalized interest until that point had been through cyclocross as an off-road race discipline, and via the Rough Stuff Fellowship for off-road touring along bridleways.

The Ridgeback 601 was released in 1983, and it was probably the first UK production mountain bike. While a few MX-inspired bikes, like the Raleigh Grifter, and later the Bomber, had emerged during the 1970s, the Ridgeback 601 was among a new wave of genuinely trailworthy machines to come equipped with triple cranksets. It had a big range of gears, as well as cyclocross/touring-style cantilever brakes, knobbly tires, and some lightweight parts (like aluminum rims) that made it lighter than the earlier steel-clad bikes. The lugged frame was hefty compared to modern mountain bikes but the long, relaxed geometry and generous mud clearance made it far better for off-road use than earlier "tracking" bikes.

While Ridgebacks were built in East Asia and sold at very affordable prices, they ironically influenced a lot of the UK custom builders, who were soon producing copies that were very nicely put together.

Ridgeback has celebrated its thirtieth anniversary, developing from this one bike into a successful brand creating machines for many riders including mountain bikers, tourers, and children. **SW**

◁ Trussardi's history in leather goods shows in the quality of the War & Peace's accessories.

PEUGEOT PY10FC Carbone

1983 • Road bike • France • Iconic carbon fiber bike

Peugeot claimed that its PY10FC Carbone was the first carbon bike, but the marketing was misleading; Mossberg, Graftek, and Vitus all had production carbon bikes in 1983, and firms such as Carlton had carbon fiber prototypes more than a decade beforehand. But this was definitely one of the first mainstream brand-name bikes with all its main tubes made of carbon fiber.

As for construction, Peugeot made use of leading French alloy and aerospace companies to build the Carbone. The rear stays were all duralumin alloy developed by the French aerospace company Bador under the Vitus brand name. The lugs and other cast frame sections came from another company, CLB.

The frame was popularized as a very successful racer by the Peugeot Shell team, particularly when it was led by Scottish climber Robert Millar. In 1983, Millar, at only twenty-three years old, used the lightweight frame of the Carbone to great effect, winning a tough Pyrenean mountain stage of the Tour de France. The following year he won another mountain stage and went on to finish fourth overall and win the polka dot jersey of best climber. He also took the Carbone to second place in the Tour of Spain in 1985, cementing a classic rider-and-bike combination. **GK**

HUFFY 7 Eleven Track

1984 • Track bike • USA • Huffy-branded U.S. Olympic bike

The Huffy Corporation, one of America's biggest mass-market bike brands, has a heritage dating back to George Hoffman building bikes in 1892. The company became known as Huffman in 1925 and by 1940 had the first U.S. bike conveyor-belt production line. By 1979 Huffy had made 30 million bikes.

So when the 1984 Los Angeles Olympics arrived, the Huffy Corporation was in a position to score a promotional coup. It managed to arrange that the U.S. team rode Huffy-branded bikes. In total, these "Huffy" bikes were ridden to two gold, two silver, and a bronze medal at the 1984 and 1988 Games.

The bikes were not actually made by Huffy; even today, the bikes branded as Huffy are made in a factory in China. But back in the 1980s, Huffy bosses believed that sponsoring leading U.S. riders in the Olympics and the American pro 7-Eleven team could give them a huge public relations boost. They employed some of the best U.S. specialist bike builders, like Ben Serotta and Mike Melton, to build the Huffy track machines. But as a PR exercise it partly backfired. Andy Hampsten, for example, ditched his Serotta team bike before the 1988 Giro d'Italia, saying he did not want a bike that might break under him; he then went on to win the race. **SH**

Alexi Grewal sprints to 1984 Olympic gold on his Huffy. ▷

SINCLAIR C5

1984 • Tricycle • UK • Revolutionary pedal-assisted electric tricycle from a computer guru

Sir Clive Sinclair forged his reputation for mass-market consumer electronics with desk calculators and the first popular home computers, the Sinclair Spectrum and ZX81. But Sinclair had been designing and developing electric vehicles since the early 1970s, and with an $18 million (£12 million) share sale in his computer company, he began in earnest. Sinclair teamed up with English sports car manufacturer Lotus and vacuum cleaner superpower Hoover to produce the design, and the angular open-topped plastic electric tricycle, named the C5, made its debut in 1984.

The 200-watt electric motor and battery could propel the C5 at a maximum speed of 15 mph (24 kph), but the battery life suffered in cold weather, and the short nonadjustable single-speed pedal transmission, designed just as a backup to electric propulsion, was essential to propel it up even gentle hills. The low driver position reduced visibility in traffic, and the lack of weather protection soon made the C5 a focus of widespread ridicule rather than Sir Clive's anticipated revolution in personal urban transportation. Production stopped only six months after it started, and Sinclair Vehicles shut down shortly afterward with fewer than 20,000 C5s sold. **GK**

CHRISTIANIA Cargo Trike

1984 • Utility trike • UK • Cargo tricycle that started a revolution in urban transport

On May 16, 1984, Lars Engstrom presented to his wife, Annie, a box cycle he had fashioned himself. Within one hour, over morning coffee, an order was received for a second. "Ever since," says Lars, "it has been a chase."

Named after Copenhagen's alternative (and automobile-free) Christiania squatter community, Christiania trikes are less bikes and more a range of load-carrying tricycles. The most popular, thanks to its large 35 x 34-in. (89 x 87-cm) all-purpose box, is the Cargo Trike. Despite its 68 lb (31 kg), it is easy to ride, turns on a dime, and can stop in a stride, thanks to mechanical disc brakes at the front. Riders accustomed to two wheels find that a pivot allows them to continue to "lean" into corners. There is nothing that cannot be customized: high or low gearing; steel or aluminum frame; short, long, or extra-long box; hydraulic or cable disc brakes. Hoods are waterproof and snowproof and come in various shapes and colors. There is even a motorized version of the trike with a maximum speed of 12 ½ mph (20 kph) for extra-long rides.

Thirty years ago, Copenhagen was just another car-clogged city, but now 36 percent of the population pedal their way to work—a statistic that gives Lars and Annie a sense of quiet satisfaction. **BS**

MANTIS XCR Composite

1984 • Mountain bike • USA • Innovative steel and alloy frame bike from a mountain bike legend

The history of Richard Cunningham's Mantis brand is loaded with pioneering designs that went on to be licenced—or just shamelessly copied—by other manufacturers. That is certainly the case with the XCR Composite. This machine appeared just when Cannondale and Klein were beginning to introduce the idea of oversized alloy framesets. Both companies were struggling with the problem of how to wrap big alloy tubes around big tires without crimping or compromising tube strengths or causing clearance problems with chainrings.

Cunningham dodged the problem in a typically left-field way. The front triangle was built from oversized alloy tubes to create a very light and stiff chassis. A separate steel-tubed subframe was then bolted onto the alloy front. Thus, materials that were easier to bend could be manipulated through the curves necessary for adequate tire and crank clearance. The steel rear subframe also gave a more compliant ride than a full alloy frame. Not only was the XCR later licensed by Gary Fisher (who named his bike the CR7), but it also became the basis of Cunningham's very influential experiments with raised-chainstay bikes, which led to his iconic Alien design for Nishiki. **GK**

RALEIGH Team Cadet

1984 • Road bike • UK • Less-expensive copy of Raleigh's specialist Team bikes

Although it was painted in the new Raleigh Continental Panasonic and Pro Team colors of white, yellow, red, and blue, the technical details of the Team Cadet were less exciting. The Cadet's parallel frame (its top tube ran parallel to the ground) was made of "Aero Tubing," but unlike the real pro bikes with their 531 or 753 frames, the Cadet's Aero Tubing frame was made of heavier high-tensile steel tubes, contributing to a total weight of around 27 lb (12 kg). Optional frame sizes were 21, 23½, and 25 in. (54, 60, and 64 cm).

The new bike came with a comprehensive set of components that included the Tange MA 60 headset, 24½-in. (62.2-cm) steel rims, Maillard alloy hubs, 14G Rustless spokes, and Gumwall tires. The brakes were Weinmann 500 alloy with plastic quick-release levers, and the derailleurs were from Huret, including a Club front set brazed to the frame. The Cadet 10 version featured 10-speed Huret gears, while the later Cadet 12 added a couple of extra cogs.

The specs may have been downgraded from the top-end pro bikes, but Raleigh ensured that the Cadet buyer had everything necessary to get straight out on the road. It even came with water bottle and holder, "wide angle" reflector set, and toe clips and straps. **SH**

MOSER Pista

1984 • Track bike • Italy • A one-off creation built for one-hour glory

In cycling there is no greater speed record than the Hour Record; the distance someone has ridden an upright bicycle in sixty minutes. On October 25, 1972, in Mexico City, Belgian cyclist Eddy Merckx set an Hour Record that many thought would never be beaten: 30.71 mi (49.431 km). The record stood for twelve years until Italian rider Francesco Moser pulverized it by more than a kilometer in the same city in January 1984.

Moser, however, achieved his victory on a bike that had several technological advantages over Merckx's. Conceived by designers at Ferrari and Sassi, made under Moser's name, and born in a wind tunnel, the bike was created to achieve just one thing: get Moser the Hour

"The unspoked wheels bring such an advantage . . . because they modify the air resistance."

Jean Wauthier, Belgian Cycling Federation

Record. With a bullhorn handlebar, no seatpost, and an oval steel-tubing frame with a rather conventional front end, it had streamlined double-disc wheels designed to minimize the air resistance inherent in spoked wheels. People began to question the legitimacy of the contest, which was, after all, meant to pit rider against rider, not rider against technology.

Merckx, who had beaten Moser in every previous time trial the two ever had, was unimpressed. "For the first time in the history of the Hour Record," he said, "a weaker man has beaten a stronger man." The authorities, eventually agreeing, went on to establish a clear distinction between conventional and aerodynamically assisted rides, and placed Moser's ride in the latter category. **BS**

HARO Sport

1984 • BMX bike • USA • Affordable bike that brought freestyling to a mass market

Former freestyle BMX rider and founder in 1978 of Haro Bikes, Bob Haro chose perhaps the most direct marketing strategy possible to ensure the category-leading position of his signature brand. Haro had started out in 1978 by making number plates for BMX, but his own passion and talents lay not in racing but in the more radical discipline of stunt riding or "freestyling." Soon Bob was touring the country with his own unique stunt show. As a support act for conventional racing it was increasingly popular in its own right as a daring demonstration of a form of cycling that nobody had seen before.

After receiving initial sponsorship from Torker BMX, Bob designed his own Haro Freestyler frame, one that was specifically intended for flatland freestyle stunts. But the bike that really bought Haro into the big league was the 1984 Sport. Deliberately marketed as a bike that was affordable rather than aspirational, the Sport put the signature aspects of both the Freestyler and Haro's top-of-the-range Master bikes within reach of shallower pockets. It featured the same broad-stance, kinked seatstays, which formed a foot platform behind the seat tube. It also had the same large box gusset underlining the junction of the head tube and the down tube, to help cope with the stress of ends, stoppies, front hops, and other front-wheel-only moves. The Sport's seatstays, rather than extending right forward to the head tube, as on the Freestyler, joined a conventional top tube a few inches ahead of the seatpost. The mass-produced, Torker-built frameset was also based on a more affordable tubeset.

The affordability of the complete bike saw an immediate explosion in the popularity of freestyle-type bikes and riding, and the Sport became the template for similar bikes from all the major BMX brands. **GK**

YETI FRO

1984 • Mountain bike • USA • Iconic debut mountain bike from a new Colorado brand

MCR Descender

1984 • Mountain bike • USA • Original rear-suspension mountain bike

Yeti founder John Parker was a born competitor who set up Yeti cycles after being involved in a serious motorcycle race accident. Appropriately, his first bike was called the FRO, meaning "For Racing Only."

Like many bikes of the early 1980s, the original FRO shared characteristics with BMX bikes. The headset and head tube had BMX dimensions, and the single-piece looped rear stays ended in BMX-style horizontal (rather than vertical) wheel holders. The first bikes were also built from a single wall thickness of 4130 chromoly steel alloy, a material chosen for its crashproof strength rather than its light weight. They were all built on the same layout jig, too, so while their heights differed according to size they all had the same wheelbase.

The early FROs were hefty and slightly cumbersome, but their stiffness and strength, plus Parker's passionate support of the race scene, made them an immediate success. The FRO continued as a linchpin of the Yeti lineup, lending its corners and rear end to the radical C26 semi-carbon bike before losing ½ lb (0.2 kg) through a change to Tange tubing in 1991. Since then, the FRO has been built in aluminum alloy state-of-the-art steel and, most recently, carbon fiber versions; all have retained that signature "looptail." **GK**

Around 1982, cyclist and motorbike racer Brian Skinner formed his MCR (Mountain Cross Racing) company to promote downhill and cross-country mountain bike races in southern California. As a motorbike rider, Skinner found the lack of suspension on contemporary mountain bikes very restricting. Offered the chance to create a custom-built race bike, he immediately thought of adding a shock absorber to the rear end.

Skinner's "Fire-road Racer" prototype used a full-sized Honda XR200 Pro Link motorbike shock in a customized BMX-style steel frame. This gave a massive 6½ in. (16.5 cm) of rear-wheel travel before the tire hit a rubber bump stop on the frame. The Descender had a small 24-in. (61-cm) rear wheel to give more clearance; a 26-in. (66-cm) wheel was used at the front because suspension forks were not yet available.

An article in *BMX Action* magazine led to Skinner designing a more refined linkage-driven version with fellow innovator Dan Hanebrink. BMX frame maker Champion agreed to produce seventy-five frame and fork sets, and Brian bought the whole stock of a bankrupt air shock company called MotoSports. Thus, the MCR Descender became the first mass-produced rear-suspension bike. **GK**

CANNONDALE SM-500

1984 • Mountain bike • USA • Innovative twin wheel-sized fat-tubed alloy-framed bike

TRIDENT BMX

1984 • BMX bike • USA • Affordable U.S.-made race BMX for a famous UK shop

Cannondale's first product, sold from 1971, was not a bike but a bicycle trailer, called a Bugger. It was only in 1984 that its first bicycle, the ST-500 road tourer, produced a hint of things to come. Gary Klein and other small-scale builders had already used oversized TIG-welded aluminum frame tubes, but Cannondale managed to capture the imagination of more riders.

Its first oversized aluminum-frame mountain bike, also introduced in 1984, was the SM-500, and it set trends for almost every bike maker. It was unique among mountain bikes in having a 26-in. (66-cm) wheel up front and a 24-in. (61-cm) wheel in back. It also had a very high bottom bracket, and was adopted by many riders wanting to ride slower-speed, highly technical terrain. A couple of years later, Cannondale made a mountain bike with two 26-in. wheels, and later dropped the 24-in. rear wheel and high bottom bracket.

In 1989 Cannondale started to make more "conventional" mountain bikes. In 1991 it was among the first to sell a full-suspension model, the EST (Elevated Suspension Technology), albeit initially with a flex stem up front instead of a suspension fork. It launched its own suspension fork, the Delta V (later to be known as the Headshock), a year later. **SW**

While BMX burst into life in the Los Angeles area of California in the 1970s, it soon spread to become a global craze, the like of which hadn't been seen in cycling before. This was the buzzing atmosphere into which the Trident BMX was launched.

It was a collaboration between UK south coast-based bike shop Hot Wheels in Bournemouth and BMX component and frame manufacturer VDC in Santa Ana, California. After making the first available 17-tooth cog for Bendix hubs, VDC moved on to bigger components and then component parts for other manufacturers, including top names such as Hutch, Powerlite, and Robinson. The company then began to build its own frames and create complete frames for other brands.

The aim of the design was to produce a lightweight but affordable frame for budding racers on a budget. This was achieved by using a relatively conventional frame layout but made with chrome molybdenum steel alloy. This gave it a clear selling and racing edge over the much heavier high-tensile steel tubing used in most of the highly popular Raleigh Burner BMX frames it was competing against. As a result, it became a great first race bike and can count subsequent superstar riders such as Neal Wood as original owners. **GK**

PINARELLO Montello SLX

1984 • Road bike • Italy • Classic multi-race-winning frame

The Pinarello bicycle company was established by Giovanni Pinarello in Treviso, Italy, in 1952. Some thirty years later, Pinarello's Montello SLX was considered to be one of the best road race bikes available. In the mid-to-late 1980s it helped riders to achieve wins in some of the world's biggest races, including the Vuelta a España, the Giro d'Italia, and stages in the Tour de France.

The Montello SLX was made from Columbus SLX butted steel tubing. This was one of the most advanced lightweight tubesets of the time, featuring internal spiral reinforcements to provide greater rigidity at the joints, as well as lengthwise reinforcements to offer greater stiffness. The bike industry is now used to bikes with cables that run inside the frame tubes, but at the time it was considered unusual that the Montello's rear brake cable passed through the top tube. The bottom bracket was cast with the Pinarello logo, and the frame and fork featured the GPT logo at various points—GPT standing for Giovanni Pinarello, Treviso.

The Montello SLX is still popular today, and regarded as a hugely collectable classic by vintage bike enthusiasts. Bradley Wiggins and Chris Froome of Team Sky both rode Pinarello bikes to victory in the Tour de France in 2012 and 2013, respectively. **MB**

SALSA A La Carte

1985 • Mountain bike • USA • Classic high-class semi-custom frameset

Ross Shafer honed his frame-building skills on Santana tandems, then started Salsa in 1980. Initially he built just a few frames for friends. In 1984, he built small production runs of A La Carte frames and forks. Each was supplied with a custom Moto stem, which soon became part of the Salsa brand identity.

The A La Carte frame design became a classic among a growing new breed of tough but lightweight semi-custom mountain bike frames that stood out from the crowd of big Asian-built productions from mainstream brands. The long top tube, short chainstays, strengthening gussets, and composite forks were ahead of their time, and A La Carte remained in the Salsa range long after a larger company took over the brand.

Shortly after the A La Carte's original launch, Keith Bontrager took this particular steel-framed art form to its logical extreme with the Race Lite, but Shafer set the precedent. The early A La Carte frames may have set the scene, but it could be argued that the early TIG-welded Columbus-tubed version, with the Bontrager fork and custom stem, was the real collector's item. This sold for $900 (£560) and had what was to become the perfect geometry for serious riders in presuspension days—71 degrees at the head, 72 degrees at the seat. **SW**

RALEIGH Randonneur

1985 • Touring bike • UK • Reynolds 531 ST-framed classic tourer

Dawes touring bikes had been the market leaders for too long, and Raleigh wanted to produce its own super tourer. The Raleigh Randonneur, released in 1985, established Raleigh's credibility as a touring bike maker.

The 18-speed Randonneur carried every feature that Raleigh Special Products Department in Nottingham could think of, including top-quality "extras" like a Brooks saddle, Blackburn carriers front and rear, bottle carriers, and a distinctive spare spoke-holder brazed on the inside of the chainstay.

The first Randonneurs were painted a deep eggplant-green color, with a white headtube. The frame was made of 531 ST Reynolds tubing (the ST stood for "Super Tourist," a specialist gauge midway between standard and competition tubing). A thicker down tube combated speed wobble when the bike was heavily loaded. The forks were standard 531 steel tubes. The Randonneur also featured Shimano Biopace chainrings, which were especially fashionable at the time. These oval cranksets were designed to smooth out the variation in pedaling power that occurs at the different positions as the pedals rotate. Later dropped by Shimano, asymmetric rings are still used today, notably by Olympic winner Bradley Wiggins. **SH**

WOODRUP Lightweight

1985 • Road bike • UK • Classic steel-framed lightweight road bike

Woodrup Cycles is one of the longest-standing UK custom bike builders. In 1947 Maurice Woodrup set up his bicycle company in a small workshop in Leeds in the industrial north of England. Its specialty was good-quality, made-to-measure racing frames. In that era of club rides, Woodrup and his wife Jean often rode with their customers to monitor their feedback. The meticulously refined bikes started to win races, and by the 1960s Woodrup was successful enough to sponsor its own team. Woodrup's son, Steve, took over in 1970.

In the mid-1980s a typical Woodrup road bike would be constructed of hand-brazed double-butted Reynolds 531 chromoly steel tubing with neatly filed Cinelli cast lugs. The frame usually featured wraparound seatstays and, of course, down-tube shifters. In 1985 the groupset, unless especially ordered, typically comprised Campagnolo Nuovo Record gears, a Super Record headset, and a Cinelli bar and stem.

Over the years Woodrup bikes have been ridden by some of the United Kingdom's bike greats, including Sid Barras and Barry Hoban. The latter rider rode at least one of his Tour de France stage wins on a Woodrup, and he continued to ride repainted Woodrups as a professional with the French Mercier team. **SH**

MUDDY FOX Courier

1985 • Mountain bike • UK • Iconic mass-market mountain bike

SCHWINN Pee-wee Herman's DX

1985 • Beach cruiser bike • USA • Vintage bike customized for the American comic

Affordable mountain bikes for the masses were launched into the UK market in 1982 by Cypriot accountant Aristos Hadjipetrou and marketing man Drew Lawson. Muddy Fox started life as S & G Distributors, and early bikes bearing that badge were well built. But the push for a lower price point resulted in frames that, while well designed in terms of geometry and fun to ride, had very average build quality.

Lawson's London-centric marketing resulted in budget mountain bikes becoming the must-have item for the new breed of cycle couriers as well as fledgling trail riders. The Courier was presented more as a fashionable all-purpose bike than as a thoroughbred

"For some reason [the Courier] was deceptive—it looked too simple to cut the mustard."

Max Glaskin, cycling journalist

mountain bike, yet the marketing of the Muddy Fox Courier, along with the Saracen Tufftrax, made people sit up and take notice. Eye-catching advertising campaigns included a picture of Jacquie Phelan, U.S. mountain bike race champion at the time, with her bare back decorated with a line of the distinctive Muddy Fox pawprints. A TV ad showed a "couch potato" bursting out of his couch on a mountain bike and pedaling off toward the horizon.

The original Muddy Fox business setup failed, possibly because it relied on marketing style over building substance, but the brand has been relaunched several times since. It now exists as MuddyFox (one word), and offers a range of bikes aimed at even lower price points than before. **SW**

U.S. TV comedian Paul Reubens was trying to write a new movie at a studio complex when he noticed that everyone else on the set seemed to have a bike to get around on. The comic, who is better known as Pee-wee Herman, the name of his on-screen alter ego, complained to producers.

The result was that one day not long after, he found a fabulous, fully restored 1947 Schwinn DX Cruiser waiting for him outside his office. In a speech at the 2010 Hammer Museum Bike Night, Reubens recalled: "It was chained to a post with a sign that had my picture on it and it said, 'Parking for Pee-wee Herman Only.'" He continued: "I ran inside, pulled the paper out of the typewriter and starting typing: 'Pee-wee Herman loves his bike more than life itself.' The movie wrote itself in about three weeks."

The movie that the bicycle incident inspired Reubens to write was *Pee-wee's Big Adventure*, released in 1985 and often cited as one of the best cycling films of all time. His customized cherry-red-and-white DX Cruiser was converted to look like a cartoon bike. Aside from its beautiful paint job, it was enhanced by streaming tassels from the handlebars, rear-view mirrors, metal panniers, and a tiger's head sound-effects speaker mounted on top of the head tube.

The Schwinn plays a starring role. At the beginning of the movie it is stolen while Pee-wee visits his girl in a bike shop, and the rest of the story follows his comical attempts to recover it. The director was Tim Burton, whose own profile was increased by the movie's success. It has since become a cult attraction.

Several identical versions of the bike were built by the studio for shooting Pee-wee's movie. One of them eventually resurfaced in 2007 on eBay, where it reached $17,000 (£11,000) at auction. **SH**

BATTAGLIN Pirana

1985 • Time trial bike • Italy • Carbon fiber
bike that was never raced

The Battaglin Pirana is one of the oddest-looking bikes ever, thanks to its aerodynamic carbon fiber frame and bulbous front wheel, designed to reduce drag. Italian bike designer Giovanni Battaglin intended Roberto Visentini of the Carrera race team to ride it against the clock in the prologue of the 1985 Tour of Italy, but things did not work out. Officials refused to allow Visentini to race on it because they believed it provided an unfair advantage. Tests were said to show that the Pirana was three seconds per kilometer faster than conventional designs of its era.

Rather than comprising conventional tubes, the Pirana's frame was a monocoque molded to cut through the air. In some ways it was years ahead of its time, with a rear brake and rear derailleur sheltered by the frame, and cables that were routed internally. That the front wheel was smaller than the rear wheel was not uncommon—the idea was to lower the front end for a more efficient riding position—but the wheel's bulging shape certainly was unusual, as was the wide-legged fork built to accommodate it.

The Pirana contravenes many of the equipment rules that have since been put in place by the International Cycling Union. **MB**

GARY FISHER ProCaliber

1985 • Mountain bike • USA • Pioneering
race-specific mountain bike

Using lightweight Tange Prestige tubes, probably the first tubeset specifically designed for mountain bikes, the Gary Fisher brand created one of the first pure cross-country race bikes. This was long before a suspension fork could be almost as crucial as the frame in terms of performance. In 1985 it was all about getting a well-controlled ride from the frame, fork, and tires, and the ProCaliber managed to do that superbly.

At a time when Fisher-sponsored riders were winning more than 50 percent of all U.S. off-road events, the ProCaliber helped racer Joe Murray toward enormous success. This was one of the first mountain bikes to have Shimano's indexed gear shifting (Fisher riders helped Shimano develop this), and one of the first to put a brake behind the bottom bracket, under the chainstays. (This was not such a good idea in muddy areas, and soon went out of fashion again.) With its unicrown, rather than T-style, fork—another innovation from Fisher—its short back end, and a relatively long reach to the bars, it set the scene for a new era of race-bred mountain bikes. In 1987 *Mountain Bike Action* magazine voted the ProCaliber as one of its "Top Ten All-Time Best Mountain Bikes," and the frame format was much mimicked in later years. **SW**

PEKA 531

1985 • Road bike • Netherlands • Classic
Amsterdam road racer with an interesting history

Amsterdam frame builder Peter Serier was a significant name among Low Countries bike connoisseurs in the 1980s, creating bikes under both the Peka and Presto names. The Reynolds 531 tubing of this striking bike was still the number one choice for premium bike frames in the 1980s too. It was built not just with Reynolds butted main tubes, but also rear stays and fork blades. The down tube shifter and top tube cable bosses were brazed directly onto the main tubes in 1980s style, rather than with the bolted wraparound clips used previously.

Things get interesting when you look closely at the lugs. They are French Nervex lugs, which suggests a much earlier 1960s or 1970s date for the original frame. This was indeed an earlier bike that had been campaigned long and hard by a well-seasoned Dutch amateur racer. During his ownership, the original frame (built by Jabo or RIH) was updated with new shifter and cable mounts and then repainted in Peka livery by Serier.

The eclectic equipment also shows the intriguing history of this bike. Campagnolo Nuovo Record gears and shifters are driven by a Sugino crank and stopped with Shimano first-generation Dura Ace brakes. It is still a classic bike that's already been used in the historic L'Eroica retro race around the vineyards of Tuscany. **GK**

RALEIGH Crane Special

1985 • Mountain bike • UK • Custom built for
Nick Crane's "journey to the center of the Earth"

As a young man, English TV presenter Nicholas Crane was an intrepid adventurer whose exploits included cycling up Mount Kilimanjaro and riding the fourteen highest peaks in Wales in a day. In 1986, he and his cousin, Richard Crane, set out to ride to "the center of the Earth"—the point in Asia farthest from any sea.

The pair had special bikes made by Gerald O'Donovan, head of Raleigh's Special Bicycle Development Unit in Ilkeston. After measuring the riders, he built a pair of high-spec ultra-light Reynolds 753 manganese molybdenum steel-tubed frames, with a long wheelbase and relaxed seat and head tube angles for an easier ride. The frames were ultra-tough, with every joint lugged, butted, and silver-soldered. The bikes were finished in Raleigh Team colors.

The wheels had to withstand thousands of miles of rough roads, so they were specially made from top-notch components: Mavic M3 CD rims with stainless-steel spokes on Campagnolo small-flange hubs. They lasted the whole 3,293 mi (5,301 km). Weight savings were drastic—the bikes even lacked a front derailleur.

The Cranes' resulting book, *Journey to the Center of the Earth* (1987), was a great adventure yarn—and also a testament to the durability of Raleigh bikes. **SH**

RALEIGH Maverick

1985 • Mountain bike • UK • Raleigh's first
mountain bike

After Raleigh's product manager, Yvonne Rix, persuaded
the company that mountain bikes were the next big
thing, it launched the Maverick and then tried to win
over traditionally conservative British cyclists with a
simple ad: Above a photo of the bike covered in mud
was the legend, "Essential for a dirty weekend."

The new range comprised the Maverick 5, 15, and
18, which referred to the number of gears. The budget
5 had primitive caliper brakes front and back and thick
steel rims; the premium 15 and 18 had Sachs Huret
gears, and Dia Compe cantilever brakes and alloy wheels.

All the bikes were a mix of old and new: They
had heavy chromoly tubing and long 43-in. (109-cm)
wheelbases. The gearing was not as low as that on most
later mountain bikes, but Raleigh was convinced that most
buyers would cycle off-road only occasionally. The bikes
were imported from Japan, where they were made by
traditional methods with brazed metal joints. The seat pillar
was not a quick release, but fixed using an Allen wrench.

Figuring that "all-terrain" sounded better than
"mountain," because most British riders were nowhere near
a mountain, Raleigh classified the Maverick as an all-terrain
bike. But the British didn't embrace mountain biking until
the 1990s, and sales of the Maverick were poor. **SH**

RALEIGH Clubman

1985 • Road bike • UK • Classic 531
all-rounder

Many British cyclists were club bikers who went out
regularly in organized groups—some on time trials,
others on long tours.

To cater to these varied requirements, the original
Clubman, launched in 1948, was a versatile machine at
a popular price. It was lightweight, with a Reynolds 531
frame, but easier to ride than an out-and-out racer, and
had mudguards and lighting equipment for all-year
use in any weather. It sold well in both Britain and the
United States.

In the 1980s, the range was still going strong,
and it hadn't changed much. Components had been
upgraded but the frames were the same as ever. On
this Clubman 12, they started at 21 in. (54 cm), with
three other sizes up to 25 in. (64 cm).

The Clubman's high-tensile steel stays and forks
were cheaper than Reynolds equivalents, and its
Raleigh high-pressure tires were another cost-cutting
item. Weinmann alloy rims with small-flange quick-
release hubs kept the ride lively and responsive.
The bike came with plastic mudguards and reflectors,
bottle cage mount, toe clips with leather straps,
and a lightweight rear carrier. It was truly ready for
anything. **SH**

TENSOR Rudi Altig

1985 • Road bike • Germany • Mass-market
bike named after famous racer

Rudi Altig—German pursuit and road race World
Champion, Vuelta d'España winner, and Tour de France
yellow jersey-wearing sprinter of the 1960s—capitalized
on his success with a range of bikes produced by Schauff.

As is often the case with licensed products, the
quality of bikes bearing the Altig name varied greatly.
Some of the early bikes were definitely race-worthy,
hand built from Reynolds 531C steel alloy or Italian
Columbus steel tubing. Some were even built with
a mix of Reynolds tubing and Columbus forks for
optimum ride quality. These premium Altig bikes
were appropriately equipped with top-level Italian
Campagnolo—or in later years Japanese Shimano—
equipment and hand-built wheels.

Twenty years later, however, Altig brand standards
had slipped. The frame here is still steel tubing with
brazed lug junctions, but it's basic, high-tensile
construction steel rather than lightweight manganese
steel alloy. The gears have been downgraded to French
Huret equipment, although the distinctive square-
tipped two-tone plastic gear levers controlling the
12-speed close-ratio steel chainset, rear freewheel
block, and Weinmann sidepull brakes remained a
source of pride for Altig owners. **GK**

TREK 2000

1985 • Road bike • USA • Standard setter in
frame technology and strength-to-weight ratios

Established in 1976 in a barn in Waterloo, Wisconsin, by
Richard Burke, a former accountant, and Bevil Hogg, the
owner of a chain of bicycle stores, Trek always targeted
the prestige market with its hand-built bikes. From
modest beginnings with start-up capital of $25,000
(£15,500), the company grew rapidly.

In the 2000, Trek first made use of True Temper T-2
aluminum tubing, which, after a complex series of heat
treatments and cold working processes, resulted in a
frame that produced considerable gains in strength-to-
weight ratios. Rigorous tests on the prototype revealed
that it was almost twice as resistant to fatigue as frames
made from conventional aluminum tubing.

Trek also developed a high-tolerance internal lug
system and borrowed the latest bonding techniques
from the aerospace industry to help eliminate
structural deficiencies caused by conventional
welding. No longer was it necessary to heat-treat joint
areas, a process that degrades tensile strength. Other
refinements included Shimano Dura Ace componentry,
a brake that increased output while reducing friction,
and a new-style pedal that improved cornering
clearances. The Trek 2000 set new standards in strength,
responsiveness, and durability. **BS**

LOOK Bernard Hinault

1986 • Road bike • France • Prototype carbon bike on which Greg LeMond won the Tour de France

"It was revolutionary and pretty avant-gardist for the time . . . The Tour de France was the best place to launch such a product."

Bernard Hinault

French company Look had already made a massive technological impact on the Tour de France in 1985, when Bernard Hinault won the race on its bike with radical "clipless" pedals.

The French star again featured in Look's equally innovative success the following year, when its prototype Bernard Hinault carbon fiber frame was ridden to overall victory in the Tour. In so doing, the KG86 became the first carbon-tubed frame to win the most important road race in the cycling calendar.

Controversially, though, the rider wasn't Hinault himself but his La Vie Claire teammate, American Greg LeMond. While Look would go on to use full monocoque frames, KG86s comprised a combination of naked carbon and Kevlar-weave tubes glued into minimalist alloy lug junctions at the corners of the frame. The results were thus lighter than contemporary steel frames, although handling could suffer in extreme situations, because of flex, and Lemond eventually moved to custom carbon frames built by Calfee.

While Look was the official team sponsor, and had its name on the frame stickers and embossed into the drop-outs, other stickers show that TVT was the actual manufacturer. TVT was an established producer of fiberglass-based composites, and therefore ideally placed to harness the greater strength and lower weight of carbon fiber.

While TVT achieved its greatest success in collaboration with Look, it also sold frames under its own name. Look moved on to create its own in-house carbon fiber chassis, such as the radical KG196 and KG396 road racing and track racing frames.

Look is still at the cutting edge of both clipless pedal and carbon frame development today, more than three decades after its historic back-to-back wins in the Tour de France. **GK**

Greg LeMond and his distinctive Look at the 1986 Coors Classic race. ▶

BROMPTON M3L Folder

1986 • Folding bike • UK • Highly innovative ultra-compact commuter bike

Britain has an unparalleled history of developing folding bicycles that can be packed down for easy transportation. When Andrew Ritchie relocated the fledgling Brompton Bikes company to a workshop under a London railway bridge arch in 1987, he became part of a tradition that had started in the nineteenth century, and progressed through the BSA paratroop bike of the Second World War to the revolutionary Moulton and Bickerton bikes of the 1960s and 1970s.

The Brompton shares many features with the original Moultons and Bickertons. The frame is a single-beam design, with rubber bumper suspension, an extended seatpost, and tall handlebars to create a one-size-fits-all chassis. Small wheels allow the bike to be folded into an extremely compact package. Above all, the Brompton's detail and practicality have ensured its amazing success: It is currently exported to forty-two countries.

The first prototype of 1976 had 18-in. (45-cm) wheels, the rear one of which could be folded under the frame—this was Brompton's unique innovation. Prototype 2 used 16-in. (40-cm) wheels to reduce pack size, but the simplified folding mechanism and lighter overall design of Prototype 3 became the template for the classic Brompton shown here. No major companies wanted to commit to licensed production, so Ritchie started building the bikes himself part time in 1981. Interest grew, and the distinctive kinked-frame Brompton entered full production in 1987.

Since then, the ultra-compact "fold into its own handlebar bag in seconds" design has won multiple awards and been to Buckingham Palace, the South Pole, and most places in between. There's even a Brompton World Championships to prove that these highly practical bikes can also be serious fun. **GK**

PEUGEOT Sitting Bull

1986 • Mountain bike • France • Early French mountain bike

California was the main breeding ground for mountain biking, but it was not the only one. In France, automobile and bike maker Peugeot produced the Sitting Bull to cater to growing local interest in mountain bikes.

The construction of the Sitting Bull was entirely traditional. Steel frame tubes and fork legs were set into cast lugs with tapering A-frame stays welded onto the seat tube. In common with most mountain bikes of the time, the wheelbase was extremely long for extra stability and reliable handling. The forked, direct-welded Bullmoose bar-and-stem combo was a classic late-1980s fashion item. Shimano M700 gears were one of the earliest mountain-bike specific

"A versatile machine for rough track touring or pothole-ridden commuter journeys."

Wilton Hargreaves

component groups, and were clearly good enough to draw Peugeot away from its traditional reliance on French equipment. The cantilever brakes and massive motorbike-style four-finger levers were budget Lee Chi items from Taiwan.

Peugeot later sponsored some of Britain's most successful cyclocross racers as they crossed over into mountain biking. Tim Gould and David Baker both rode in the team's distinctive black-and-white checkerboard kit. Their bikes were White Spiders, built by London specialist Chas Roberts, but Peugeot subsequently developed its own Reynolds 531-tubed Grand Canyons and Columbus steel-framed Magnums. By the mid-1990s, however, Peugeot was focusing its resources on low-cost, high-volume bikes such as the Anaconda. **GK**

◁ Brompton's innovative M3L Folder.

MICROBIKE Folder

1986 • Folding bike • Sweden • Popular
second-generation minute city folder

In 1986, Sven Hellestam was standing on a platform in Gothenburg, Sweden, after just missing his tram because his connecting bus was late—again. So he bought a folding bike. But his purchase wasn't compact enough, took too long to fold away (forty-five seconds), and was hard to carry without getting him dirty. Frustrated, he decided to design one himself.

However, the recent commercial failure of a high-profile folding bike company in Sweden made it difficult for Hellestam and his business partner, Otto Linander, to find financial backing. Fortunately, they secured a large enough loan to build ten prototypes of their Microbike. Production began in 1987, and two years later they had to move to larger premises. Their Microbike was a hit.

Hellestam never forgot the limitations of that original 1986 folder. His aluminum-framed bike weighed just 23 lb (10.5 kg) and was 39 in. (1 m) long when folded. Its entire frame comprised just six joints; it had 12-in. (30-cm) plastic wheels; best of all, it took only five seconds to fold and three seconds to unfold. Early models came with a cog belt-drive, though later models had Kevlar belt-drives. By the time the Microbike ceased production in 1993, it had sold more than 16,000 units. **BS**

DAWES Countryman/Ranger

1986 • Mountain bike • UK • Lazy-riding early
mountaineer from touring bike specialist

The Humphries and Dawes Company set up in 1906 in Birmingham, England. Twenty years later, Humphries went off to start a motorbike company, and Dawes Cycles emerged.

Dawes was always best known for touring bikes and, like many bike companies during the 1980s and 1990s, was sold (several times) to bigger parent companies. But in the early years of British mountain biking, it created a selection of touring-style all-terrain bicycles, so called because there were old-school elements in the British bicycle industry who didn't want to refer to these new-fangled U.S. contraptions as "mountain bikes."

The Countryman and the Ranger were Dawes' most respected early offerings. They were usually equipped with full-length mudguards, a rack, and often a dynamo. The long back end was incorporated reputedly "for all-terrain stability," but more likely because Dawes based this 26-in. (66-cm) wheel bike on its long-wheelbase touring bikes, and it was not easy to put bends in chainstays to accommodate fat tires on wheels of this diameter.

Although Dawes resisted initial interest in mountain bikes, it was eventually among the earliest, and best, of the British mountain bike pioneers. **SW**

KESTREL R4000

1986 • Road bike • USA • Revolutionary carbon fiber monocoque bike

When Kestrel showed up to the Long Beach bike show in 1986, it stopped the bike industry dead in its tracks. Carbon fiber had been used for bike frames since the 1970s, and bikes using carbon tubes joined together with alloy lugs were already taking wins in top races like the Tour de France. Kestrel's R4000 introduced a host of modern features that have become default settings for road race bike design in subsequent years.

Rather than using separate carbon tubes and alloy lugs to form the frame, the R4000 frame was a true monocoque. That meant the left and right halves of the frame were laid up in individual molds using carefully aligned sheets of carbon fiber. Alloy inserts for the bearings and wheel mounts were added into the corners, then the halves were baked and joined together to create the finished frame. It's a commonplace method now, but in 1986 it seemed more like science fiction.

The smooth lines of the frame also allowed Kestrel to mold aerodynamic profiles into the "tubes" of the R4000. The down tube used a thin ovalized section with internal cable routing for the gear shifters. The rear stays were blade-shaped to reduce drag. The seat tube was a full teardrop aero section, pioneering the "wheel hugger" cutout to shroud the rear wheel from the wind. **GK**

ZERONINE Pro XL

1986 • BMX • UK • Race-winning BMX that grew from a sticky start

Back in 1978, Owen Scheppman was gradually taking over his parents' house in Illinois. Not with the usual teenage debris but with two-color screen-printed vinyl numbers for BMX number plates. Soon, demand for these stickers—numbered zero through nine, hence the company name—was so high that Owen drafted in his family to help cut them out to sell at weekend races.

In the process of expanding his range to include number boards, pads, visors, and custom race kit, Owen picked up sponsorship of several top riders. Understanding the power of his brand name, he realized he needed to introduce a bike frame to complement the product lines: thus the Pro XL was born.

This was a pure race frame using slim 4130 chrome molybdenum steel tubing in a conventional layout that was only easily recognized by the rear drop-outs. Rather than the normal plate that both stays are welded onto, the Zeronine used extended chainstays with the drop-out plates hanging below like small flags. Their light weight gave them outstanding acceleration, and soon it wasn't just Zeronine number plates crossing finishing lines first all around the world. Unfortunately BMX popularity waned in the late 1980s, and Zeronine's bikes became a short-lived but highly collectible memory. **GK**

TREK 2500

1986 • Road bike • USA • One of the biggest leaps toward the perfect bike

Founded in 1975, it took Trek just eleven years to grow from making bikes in a Wisconsin barn into the largest U.S. producer of hand-built, silver-brazed, quality framesets. "Change makes the world go round, not money," Trek's cofounder Bevil Hogg once said, and the 1980s saw the company make many major advances. By 1980, it had its first automatic painting machine, followed by automatic brazing in 1983, and in 1985 the world's first—and at the time the only—robotic device that assembled, aligned, and then brazed away in one single, fluid motion. Next came the internally lugged, adhesive-bonded model 2000, which took Trek tantalizingly close to Hogg's personal concept of the perfect bike. And finally, in 1986, Hogg's designers and engineers stole the limelight with one giant

stride toward what was as close to cycling perfection as anyone had come: the three-tube carbon fiber composite model 2500.

Hogg was in awe of carbon fiber, and the 2500, which first appeared in the 1987 Trek catalog, was the culmination of everything he knew the material was capable of. It marked the beginning of Trek's development of carbon fiber technology. The 2500 was a pivotal piece of cycling engineering: Its Matrix graphite-epoxy double-butted composite tubes were bonded onto aluminum alloy lugs, a stepping-stone on the way to the many ultra-light and rigid frames of molded carbon fiber to come. Hogg had left Trek by the time the 2500 was released, but his driving force and vision made it happen. **BS**

MERLIN Mountain

1986 • Mountain bike • USA • The most aspirational mountain bike frame of mountain biking's heyday

Merlin Metalworks was founded in 1986 in Cambridge, Massachusetts, by a bunch of Fat City Cycles employees who wanted to build in titanium rather than steel. When Fat City owner Chris Chance wasn't too receptive to the idea, they set up their own workshop almost next door.

Merlin's founders were Gwyn Jones, Gary Helfrich, and Mike Augspurger. They quickly established their company as a market-leading titanium frame supplier, and to this day early Merlins are still highly regarded for their relatively plain but highly desirable aesthetics and ride characteristics. The bare metal finish would buff up like new every time you cleaned it; there would never be issues with corrosion; and the low-weight, high-strength, fatigue-resistant build appeared to be offering a bike for life.

Such advantages helped to offset the high initial investment costs. Sprayed in team colors, the Merlin Road was used by a select few road pros, including Greg LeMond and a young Lance Armstrong. The Merlin Mountain then introduced mountain bikers to a frame with a ride character that dealt with rough terrain with a genuine spring in its stride, even when compared to the very best custom steel frames currently on offer. This was important in the days before suspension forks.

The Mountain was actually the first frame Merlin built, specifically for U.S. National Champion Joe Murray. He continued to win races on it. Merlin has since been through several reincarnations, and some of its key personnel moved on to form Seven Cycles. **SW**

STRIDA 1

1987 • Folding bike • UK • Super-neat triangular-framed folder

In 1984, Mark Sanders, a mechanical engineering graduate of Imperial College, London, designed a folding bicycle that won the following year's Royal College of Art Giorgetto Giugiaro Award for Concept Bikes. A year later, it was being geared and tooled up for its first production run. Sanders formed his own company, but struggled to decide on a name. After turning down a string of suggestions from marketing consultants, he went with Strida, which was proposed by the nine-year-old son of one of the company directors. Its iconic first production bike was unveiled at Harrods store in London in 1987.

In 1988, Strida won Best New Product, Most Innovative, and Best British Design at the UK Cyclex

" . . . unique . . . due to its shape, simplicity, and the fact it can be wheeled along when folded."

Mark Sanders

Bicycle Innovation Awards. Over the next four years, the Strida 1 would sell more than 25,000 units worldwide.

Its success was not difficult to explain. Aimed at commuters and urban dwellers with limited storage space, the Strida 1 was a breeze. It was easy to fold, and a cinch to maintain, and belt-driven, which meant that you could confidently leave it in your living room overnight without worrying about waking up to grease stains on the carpet the following morning.

The simplicity of the Strida 1's folding mechanism made it both practical and an aesthetic delight. "The bike is basically three tubes and three joints," Sanders said in an interview. "I feel lucky that they also formed such a distinctive visual statement—a triangle with wheels at its corners." **BS**

SPECIALIZED Egger

1987 • Concept bike • USA • Unique show bikes for the Specialized brand

As a child, Robert Egger wanted nothing more than a bike. One day his father came home from work and told him to come out front and look in his pick-up truck. When the boy saw a trailer full of old parts from a whole load of discarded bikes, he thought he'd been duped. But his father also gave him all the tools from which to construct a machine of his own.

Having learned how to build a bike, Robert Egger knew that he would never have to buy one. He went on to take a degree in industrial engineering at the University of Wisconsin-Stout, and when he graduated in 1984 he sent out only one résumé—to bike manufacturer Trek. When he started there as a designer, he loved the work but felt isolated, as just about the only hardcore rider on the staff.

In 1987 Egger left Trek to join Specialized, to which he had been attracted by the mantralike slogan "Innovate or die." His first creation for his new employer was this extraordinary show bike, designed to attract attention to the company's stands at trade exhibitions.

Looking back, this bike looks like a statement of personal intent; a lifetime career manifesto. In the quarter of a century that followed, Egger has produced a succession of one-off bikes for the same promotional purposes, and every one of them has had three significant features in common. First, they all appear, when stationary, as if they are moving fast. Second, they all weigh less than 15 lb (6.8 kg). Third, they are all calculated to create in observers the desire to own one—or, at least, something similar—themselves. Egger himself has described his rationale thus: "Your job as a designer is to say, this thing is so cool and so kickass, whoever sees this thing is going to want it. You're kind of creating lust, creating a want for something that people have to have." **GK**

◁ Few bikes fold smaller than the Strida 1.

BATTAGLIN 50

1987 • Road bike • Italy • Stephen Roche's Tour de France-winning bike

The superstar Irish racer Stephen Roche has two main claims to cycling fame. The first is that in 1987 he was only the second competitor ever to win the Triple Crown of the Tour de France, Giro d'Italia, and World Road Race Championship.

And if that wasn't enough, Roche is also renowned for uttering one of cycling's most memorable quotes. During one epic stage of his 1987 Tour de France victory, he produced one amazing death-defying burst of climbing through the mountains that ended with him passing out at the finish line. He was given oxygen to help revive him and when medics asked if he was okay, he replied: "Oui, mais pas de femme toute de suite." ("Yes, but I am not ready for a woman straight away.")

The 1987 Tour had twenty-five stages, the largest number ever at that point, and Roche was victorious over Pedro Delgado by just 40 seconds overall. Roche was riding for the Carrera team on a bike made by Italian specialist Battaglin, a company that is run by former Italian racing star Giovanni Battaglin, winner of the 1981 Giro d'Italia.

Fittingly for an Italian firm, Roche's Battaglin was built with a top-of-the-line Columbus SLX steel tube frame and forks, fitted with premium Campagnolo Record components. Later in his career he rode for the Motobecane team on a bike of the same name, but it was on the Battaglin that he had his greatest success.

Roche was known as a colorful, tough, and uncompromising competitor. Once he broke team orders to pull away to beat teammate and race leader Roberto Visentini. This earned Roche the hatred of the Italian's fans, who would spit at him as he passed, despite him riding an Italian bike with Italian equipment. **SH**

LAND SHARK Andy Hampsten

1988 • Road bike • USA • Rebadged Giro d'Italia-winning bike

Andy Hampsten was the first American to win the Giro d'Italia. The highlight of his 1988 victory was a tough mountain stage where he left the field behind, ascending the Gavia Pass through fierce snow and over sheet ice before speeding boldly down the other side.

Although Hampsten was officially riding a Huffy bike, his red, green, and white frame was actually custom made for him. His new bike replaced a standard Serotta team bike that had broken beneath him. Hampsten lost confidence in the team machines, and was given permission to ship in his own new bike.

He employed American bike builder John Slawta of Land Shark to build the ideal machine for the Giro.

"Slawta certainly has an old-world style of making bikes that go up and downhill properly."

Andy Hampsten

The equipment included Shimano Dura Ace brakes, headset, gearset, seatpost, and pedals rather than the usual Campagnolo equipment. Cinelli 16½-in. (42-cm) bars, grips, and saddle gave control and comfort, while Wolber tubular rims and tires just under 1 in. (2.5 cm) wide added crucial traction.

Hampsten used an Avocet computer for mileage and speed feedback, and opted for a frame in Tange steel tubing (although the stickers read "True Temper") that, though not light—19 lb 10 oz (8.9 kg)—gave high stiffness for stable handling to cope with the worst surfaces and weather conditions that the Italian Alps could throw at him. Hampsten reasoned that a super-light bike might have saved seconds on ascents, but he could lose more time on icy potholed descents. **SH**

CANNONDALE ST-500 Tourer

1988 • Touring bike • USA • Fat-tubed touring
bike that started Cannondale's cycle range

Cannondale is best known for its fat-tubed aluminum frames, but it launched in 1971 with a utilitarian luggage-hauling bike trailer called the Bugger, which culminated in the Bugger III child-carrying trailer about ten years later. Meanwhile the company developed a range of practical touring bags and clothing for cyclists, so it was no surprise that its first bike, the ST-500, was a tourer. More shocking, to many, was that the frame was built from TIG-welded fat aluminum tubing at a time when almost every other bike was based on steel tubes.

The ST-500 was marketed as "ideal for long-distance touring, time trialing, and everything in between." Its combination of stiffness and a long wheelbase produced a mix of efficiency in drive power and stability when loaded with baggage. It could be bought as a complete bike or as a frameset, and the facts and figures that Cannondale used in the marketing went a long way toward suggesting that skinny steel tubed frames would soon be things of the past. Also, at a time when many big brands were moving production to Asia, the "Hand Built in Pennsylvania" tag had some sway among enthusiasts. What Cannondale definitely achieved was to get bike riders thinking about different desirable frame properties. We were entering the age of aluminum. **SW**

COLNAGO Carbitubo Pista

1988 • Race bike • Italy • Early Ferrari tech
carbon fiber racer

Ernesto Colnago began manufacturing bikes in 1954. Over the next twenty-five years, he built a reputation as one of the finest producers of customized road race frames, including the super-light steel creation that took Eddy Merckx to the Hour Record in 1972.

In the 1970s, Colnago faced criticism that his frames were not stiff enough. He looked at alternative materials, such as titanium and particularly carbon, which led to the unveiling at the 1988 IFMA bike show in Cologne, Germany, of the magnificent Carbitubo Pista.

The Pista's carbon frame was developed by Ferrari, and the complete bike featured the latest lightweight Campagnolo components. Even its chainrings had holes drilled through them to reduce weight! Carbon tubes were attached using aluminum lugs, but working with carbon was still in its infancy, so the lugs were susceptible to movement and even cracking under stress. As a result, only twenty Pistas were produced before Colnago turned its attention to titanium tubing. The resulting Bititan frames still retained the double down-tube design of the Carbitubo, and, although they were produced in larger numbers than the Pista, they were every bit as collectible. **BS**

◁ Cannondale pioneered oversized TIG-welded alloy frames.

KONA Explosif

1988 • Mountain bike • USA • Mountain bike that loved punishment

When Dan Gerhard and Jake Helibron set up Kona with experienced designers Paul Brodie and Joe Murray, they made an Explosif impact with the unmistakable aesthetics and vibrant ride of their first bike.

With its tall head tube, sloping top tube, and tall seatpost extension, the Kona Explosif immediately looked more dynamic than the short head tube, horizontal tube norm of the time. Wider front end triangulation, and the tighter, lighter back end meant it steered noticeably better and kicked harder than any of its contemporaries. Kona's Project Two rigid fork and the long seatpost extension soaked up more sting and slap from the trail. The sloped top tube also saved eye-watering rider-on-frame contact if you had to straddle it suddenly.

This all created a bike that positively demanded thrashing. The original mint-green Explosif was an immediate hit, but Kona really established the following it still commands today with the 1990 model, which used Tange Prestige Concept heat-treated steel with ovalized and tapered main tubes. The top tube was also dropped further, creating the stub of extended seatpost that became a Kona signature. The plain paint jobs were replaced with the legendary spatter paint over white, and the flagship Explosif sailed at the head of a fleet containing other classic Konas, such as the Cinder Cone and the Lava Dome.

Explosif has been in near-continual development ever since, but the latest models still stick to the proven formula of infectiously agile ferrous fun. **GK**

FISHER CR7

1988 • Mountain bike • USA • Radical alloy and steel hybrid frame

Six years before the mighty Trek Corporation acquired the services of the Gary Fisher, his brand was coming up with innovative ideas in mountain bike design. The unique CR7 was a collaboration between Fisher and Richard Cunningham of Mantis Cycles. It used fat aluminum tubes for the mainframe and thin chromoly steel tubes for the bolted-on rear triangle. (This was in the days when it was very difficult to manipulate aluminum tubes well enough to use them fully effectively for the more fiddly shapes that were needed for seatstays and chainstays, so most frames were built in steel.)

The idea was to combine what Fisher later described as "different resonating frequencies"—essentially, excellent straight-line tracking in the mainframe—with enough "give" in the back end to boost comfort. It was also a perfect platform for Fisher to use his new 1¼-in. (3-cm) Evolution outsized headset and seatpost, not to mention a whole new range of Fisher-branded componentry, including the Bulge Bar and—groundbreaking on mountain bikes at the time—press-fit bottom bracket bearings.

The idea worked in terms of ride feel, but problems with the bolts that fastened the two halves of the frame together at the bottom bracket and the seatstays meant that it wouldn't last long as a concept. Also, it was released at a time when aluminum tube-shaping techniques were improving, so complete aluminum frames (with big tires for more comfort) were starting to make more sense. **SW**

PACE RC100

1988 • Mountain bike • UK • Radical integrated design that was way ahead of its time

Although Pace Cycles—founded by motorbike racers Adrian Carter and Duncan MacDonald, and based in Yorkshire, England—would become known for its carbon-legged forks, the RC100 complete bike first brought the company to prominence.

In an era when most mountain bikes were just collections of round tubes with bolted-on off-the-peg components, the RC100 was planned to the last detail. Its box-section aluminum frame was trimmed to minimize weight, while creating the right mixture of drive stiffness, tracking stability, and trail resilience.

The bike was laden with function-specific custom-machined components. Its unique long top-tube–

> *"The Pace RC100 was a very trick bicycle. It looked like nothing we had ever tested before."*
>
> Mountain Bike Action

short stem-frame geometry eventually became the industry standard after being popularized by Gary Fisher's Genesis. Pace was among the first brands to use Magura's hydraulic rim brakes and its own single-piece, threadless stem-steerer-headset assembly.

The hollow spline-axled Bullseye cranks were custom machined to fit Pace's wide press-fit-bearing bottom bracket, again setting a standard that would evolve into the industry norm. The RC30 aluminum-crowned Reynolds 531 steel-legged forks also became classics, and the inspiration for the RC35 suspension fork.

After selling its fork business, Pace went back to designing frames, but henceforth had them made cheaply overseas rather than in the United Kingdom, where production overheads had soared. **SW**

NISHIKI Alien

1988 • Road bike • USA • U.S.-designed, Japanese-built one-hit wonder

Throughout bike design history, but particularly in the mountain biking era, some designers have been sought to apply their special touch to mainstream brands and take them right to the limits of performance. That's what happened when Nishiki hired renowned innovator (and later magazine editor and Hall of Fame inductee) Richard Cunningham to design its Alien bikes.

Nishiki was a U.S. brand based on Giant frames made first in Japan and later in Taiwan. As the popularity of mountain biking increased, Nishiki president Howie Cohen wanted a shortcut to the front of the pack. Cunningham had already used an elevated rear stay design to create the then fashionable ultra-short back end to improve climbing and reduce chain jam issues on his own Mantis bikes. He had also been experimenting with bolting steel rear frames onto aluminum mainframes to create a lightweight but easily reparable whole.

However, the first Cunningham-designed Aliens were not bolted together but fully welded with lightweight Tange Prestige steel tubing. It wasn't until the arrival of the radical Alien ACX that Nishiki achieved the showstopper it sought. The frame of this bike bolted a modified version of the original Alien rear end onto a square-section alloy-tubed mainframe in a range of vivid colors.

The finished product retailed at $1,249 (£764) and was an instant success. Today the bike is still much sought after by retro bike collectors, and while Nishiki didn't maintain its market leadership for long—technological advances in the 1990s made competition keener than ever before—it had a memorable one-hit wonder with its genuinely out-of-this-world Alien. **GK**

Nishiki's radical-looking Alien was aptly named. ▷

MOOTS YBB

1988 • Mountain bike • USA • Pioneering and ultra-successful soft-tail frame

Moots, based in Steamboat Springs, Colorado, started building bikes in 1981, and really found its niche with the YBB soft-tail. At first glance, the YBB (Y Be Beat) looked like just another steel or titanium hardtail, albeit a beautifully built one. Closer inspection of the rear end, however, showed an interesting aspect to the slightly offset wishbone tube at the top of the rear seatstays.

Inside the fixed upper section of the tube was a short section of solid-state urethane elastomer spring and a short collar section containing a smooth-sliding bushing ring. Into this socket went a short "shock shaft" that was clamped into the seatstay bridge at the lower end. Slim chainstays, and the inherent spring of the 3Al 2.5V titanium alloy tubing, allowed the back end to move vertically without the need for heavy, complex pivots. With just 1⅛ in. (2.8 cm) of stroke, the movement was not much more than that gained from a fat tire.

The built-in damping of the firm foam spring was not exactly high-tech, but it kept the back end following the ground better than a hardtail. It added only 4 oz (115 g) to the bike weight, and avoided the bob and bounce inherent in longer-travel pivoted-suspension designs. The YBB, still a Moots staple, has won multiple national championship events. **GK**

TRIMBLE Carbon Cross

1988 • Mountain bike • UK • Innovative cross-frame carbon composite mountain bike

During the 1980s, Brent Trimble designed frames for Kestrel. The first of his unique "beam" designs was the Carbon Cross, which was constructed from a composite of 30 percent carbon and 70 percent fiberglass.

The "one-size-fits-all" design offered a massive amount of standover height, and allowed the chain to be taken off whole. Raised chainstays also meant no chain-slap noise. But the unsupported bottom bracket caused too much flex, so in 1989 Trimble released the Inverse 4 with an extra carbon section between the main beam and the bottom bracket unit.

Trimble's most famous mountain bikes were produced between 1989 and 1991. As the design progressed, other options were introduced, with model numbers relating to a maximum recommended rider weight: inevitably the limits were ignored by riders, and before long the frames had a reputation for breaking.

In 1993, Trimble showed a full-suspension version using a Gizbag rear shock made from a folded inflated inner tube contained in a nylon webbing bag. The design did not survive, and the brand faded until 1998, when Dean Bicycles licensed the design and built some frames. Around a decade later, Trimble started selling the frames again, using a new carbon composite. **SW**

DIAMOND BACK Arrival

1988 • Mountain bike • USA–Japan • Pioneering mass-market aluminum-framed mountain bike

The cover of the 1988 Diamond Back catalog showed a rider with no helmet, just a sweatband; and although there were mountains in the background, he was riding on a dead flat grass trail. Diamond Back was influential in opening up the sport to nonspecialists.

The Arrival was Diamond Back's star turn. It had a 7000-grade aluminum frame that was hand-built in Japan, with brazed-on fittings for two water bottles, mudguards, and load carriers. The bike's components included state-of-the-art late-1980s kit, including a Shimano Deore XT drivetrain with thumb shifters, Tooga T-Bone stem and alloy bars, Araya RM-20 alloy rims (with quick release), and a Vetta Turbo Italian saddle. Buyers loved the hardcore mountain bike details, such as the sealed headset and bottom bracket, the knobbly Tioga Farmer John tires, and the Tange chromoly reinforced fork. The Shimano front brakes were cantilever, and at the back was a U-brake system attached to the chainstay.

The Arrival undercut the custom steel bikes that had previously dominated the mountain-bike market. It came in two distinctive 1980s color schemes: polar white with a lilac clear coat, and gloss black with yellow splatters. It cost only $860 (£540), but today collectors pay many times that for a good original example. **SH**

KESTREL Nitro

1988 • Mountain bike • USA • Groundbreaking carbon-wrapped suspension mountain bike

U.S. West Coast carbon frame specialist Kestrel, formerly known as Cycle Composites, was the first in the bike industry to make bladder-molded carbon frames. Its MX-Z was the first carbon mountain bike frame. This Kestrel Nitro was among the first carbon-wrapped mountain bike frames (it actually had an aluminum skeleton, divided between the front and rear subframes). It was also one of the first mountain bikes with front and rear suspension, complete with compression and rebound damping.

The bike's name was inspired by its nitrogen-charged shocks. Keith Bontrager built the frame, then collaborated with Paul Turner to develop the fork, which was effectively the first-ever product of RockShox, which launched officially around a year later.

The Nitro made a big impression at that year's trade show in Long Beach, California, but never really saw the light of day. The mountain bike world was ready for suspension forks, but robust and efficient rear suspension systems would have to wait a few more years, and the Nitro was not a rideable sample. Kestrel exhibited a more viable version at the next Interbike show, but its principal interests increasingly focused on super-light hardtails like the sub-20-lb (9-kg) CS-X. **SW**

GT 700D Tachyon

1989 • Mountain bike • USA • Early
experiment in mountain bike wheel size

ALPINE STARS Cro-Mega

1989 • Mountain bike • USA • Iconic
motocross-inspired E-stay bike at an affordable price

The Crossover may have been a good idea, but it never really got the chance to prove itself. According to GT's publicity, its 27½-in. (70-cm) wheels combined "the strength and dependability of 26-in. [66-cm] mountain bike wheels with the efficiency of a 700C wheel."

The rims of the 700D were smaller than the 700C rims of road bikes, but both were the same size when the former was fitted with medium-sized tires (fatter than road tires but thinner than mountain bike tires). The idea that the frames should have room for fatter 700D tires too was theoretically great, but it would have made more sense to use the already established 650b rim and tire size. Twenty years later, the 650b would finally catch on as the ideal compromise between 26 in. (66 cm) and 29 in. (73.5 cm). The drop handlebar-equipped 700D Tachyon from the Crossover range was essentially the first occupant of the growing Monster Cross bike niche. GT also produced a tandem, the Quatrefoil, with the same wheel size.

If GT had gone with 650b wheels, the Crossovers may have become the first production big-wheeler mountain bikes. Many riders who bought 700Ds later fitted them with 650B wheels. **SW**

Alpine Stars, originally makers of hiking footwear and ski boots, later diversified into mountain bikes. It had a strong professional race team in the early 1990s, and many riders lusted after the then-unique frames with raised chainstays and very short back ends. While the fat aluminum-tubed Al-Mega was the choice of many racers at the time, frames made from this material lacked durability. There was a (relatively rare) titanium-tubed version too, but its bottom bracket flex was so pronounced that the chain might shift to the next chainring if you stood up and sprinted hard.

The cheaper steel-framed Cro-Mega better stood the test of time. The flexible bottom bracket was a problem, but the high chainstays gave good traction on steep climbs and eliminated chainsuck (chains stuck to the underside of the chainrings jamming under the frame). Elevated Oversize System frames gave a sub-16-in. (40-cm) chainstay length and, with their curved seat tubes, far more mud room than any other bikes at the time. There was also a tiny 12-in. (30-cm) framed version with a fat top tube that connected straight into the rear stays. Alpine Stars was also one of the few brands to commit to Gary Fisher's 1¼-in. (3-cm) Evolution headset. **SW**

CANNONDALE SM900

1989 • Mountain bike • USA • Radical sloped-frame trials-specific mountain bike

By 1989 Cannondale had been producing oversized alloy-framed mountain bikes for five years. The frames featured filed welds that made the junctions between the massive tubes look totally seamless. Big, hooped brake cable anchors and rear-mounted quick-release seat collars had been joined by rearward-extending "cantilevered" wheel drop-outs for easier wheel changing. Cannondale's big tubes were also coated in a gloriously rich paint finish that gave the radical new SM900 its "Red Shred" nickname. But the standout features of this bike were much more than skin deep.

Cannondale's SM2000, SM800, SM500, and SM400 frames had a conventional level top tube, low bottom bracket, and steep seat angle for racing. The SM900—and cheaper SM600—were designed with a deliberately high bottom bracket to increase ground clearance under the cranks. The top tube was also sloped to increase clearance between the rider and the frame so they could throw their body weight around more easily to maintain balance. The frames had a more relaxed head angle than normal to increase stability, and they were fitted with powerful roller cam brakes as standard. As a result of their agility and extra control, they became really popular with radical riders. **GK**

GIANT Escaper

1989 • Mountain bike • Taiwan • The editor's first mountain bike

One thousand of the bikes in this book are here for their technological, historical, or aesthetic significance. This machine is an unashamed editorial indulgence: It features because it was my first mountain bike.

In summer 1989, a college rower, tired of running 6 mi (9 km) to the boat club and back for training sessions, noticed the sun glinting on a chromed rim and weed-wrapped pedal at the bottom of Exeter Ship Canal in Devon, England. He embarked on an unorthodox fishing trip with a single scull as a trawler and a woodworking G-clamp as a hook, and caught a long-submerged 5-speed flat-bar Peugeot roadster. He called it the bike from Atlantis.

Within months, the wobbling wheels and grinding gears had seen every bit of local trail before finally succumbing to the inevitable effects of their watery past. Savings were pooled, college loans diverted, and I became the proud owner of a Giant Escaper.

The chromoly frame was lively enough, and the heavy and complicated rear U-brake of the previous year's model had been replaced with plastic-coated cantilever brakes. I replaced the standard tires with grippy Specialized Ground Controls, and a whole new world opened up to me. The rest is history. **GK**

QUINTANA ROO Superform

1989 • Triathlon/Time trial bike • USA • The original triathlon-specific bike

After making the first triathlon-specific wetsuit in 1987, Dan Empfield turned the attentions of his new Quintana Roo company to a triathlon-specific bike, and the revolutionary Superform was born in 1989.

His lightweight, highly mobile swimming wetsuits weren't the only new idea he pioneered in the young sport though. Many riders were already using aero extension "tri" bars to improve comfort and aerodynamic efficiency on their bikes. The low bent-forward position caused issues with breathing and pelvic angles, however, which intensified when the athletes jumped off their bikes to run. Dan became one of several riders to start pushing the saddle of his bike forward to open up the angle of his legs, effectively creating a bike that worked with aero bars rather than vice versa.

After taking measurements of all the leading professional triathletes' bikes in the transition area at races, Empfield decided to continue with his experiments of building the bike backward from the bars. The result was the creation of the first Superform, with an 80-degree seat tube angle that is still radical by today's triathlon standards. The Superform also adopted the contemporary fashion for smaller 650C wheels, which were thought to reduce drag due to their smaller frontal area.

On its first major competitive outing in the 1989 Ironman, New Zealand, Ray Browning came off the bike and comfortably onto the run 30 minutes ahead of joint favorites Scott Tinley and Richard Wells. Lance Armstrong also used a Superform before he switched to road racing, and the success of this bike and the later Kilo model cemented Quintana Roo's position as a leading triathlon bike supplier that still holds to this day. **GK**

ALLSOP Softride

1989 • Mountain bike • USA • Radical cantilever-seat suspension mountain bike

The Softride's bicycle suspension system was the product of Mike and Jim Allsop. The first Softride mountain bike was shown at the 1989 Interbike show. The suspension beam was constructed from two foam-filled fiberglass boxes bonded together with a layer of viscoelastic so that, as ground shock was transmitted through the wheels and mainframe, the beam could deflect and allow the rest of the chassis to rise under it. This added comfort and shock absorption with no obvious loss in pedal power.

The first Softride production bike, the PowerCurve, debuted in 1991. Its beam was twinned with a first-generation suspension stem called the Frankenstem

"The idea was to 'suspend the rider and not the bike,' and Allsop did that perfectly."
Simon Kolin

that Team Ritchey pro cross-country riders later used instead of suspension forks. Danish professional off-road racer Henrik Djernis won three World Championships on a Ritchey fitted with an Allsop stem.

However, the beam idea and the stem quickly faded from popularity as other suspension systems offered more appropriate shock-absorption for rough trails, leaving the Softride system mainly to long-distance road riders. In 1993, Gerry Tatrai won the Race Across America by more than twenty hours on a Softride beam. The design also became popular with triathletes, who wanted floaty comfort and could use the minimalist frame to improve aerodynamics. As a result, several big Ironman triathlons were won on a long-running line of Softride machines. **SW**

Allsop's beam bikes were certainly distinctive. ▶

KLEIN Attitude

1989 • Mountain bike • Italy • Iconic fat-tubed alloy mountain bike

Gary Klein was a free-thinking bicycle designer who decided that outsized aluminum tubes were the way to go. He produced his first bike frame from this material in 1975, and his first Mountain Klein bike ten years later.

Several Klein bikes were exceptional, but for mountain bikers the best of all was this Attitude. Its uniquely outsized, almost cartoonlike, neon multi-colored aesthetics kickstarted the really fat (rather than just fat) mountain bike revolution, but the Attitude wasn't all about looks: The press-fit bottom bracket bearings, hidden headset, and one-piece bar and stem were distinctively original too. Klein completed what he called "the fuselage" with his own Deathgrip tires, which, at 2⁷⁄₂₀ in. (6 cm) in width, kept riders loyal to the fully rigid chassis at a time when suspension forks were becoming the norm. British racer Dave Hemming won a silver medal in the World Junior Downhill Championships on his fully rigid Attitude.

Press-fit hidden headsets and bottom brackets became the industry norm on top-end bikes about fifteen years after they had first appeared on bikes like the Attitude. In the late 1990s the Klein name was bought by Trek, which employed Gary until 2007, when he went off to design telescopes. **SW**

OVERBURYS Pioneer

1989 • Mountain bike • UK • Distinctively painted and slope-tubed mountain bike

Overburys was, until recently, a bike retailer with a frame-building workshop in Bristol, England. As a frame brand, it acquired almost legendary status in the early days of British mountain biking as the custom builder of what were probably the first fillet-brazed raised chainstay frames in Europe.

Raised chainstay frames were becoming popular because they avoided the problems of chains jamming and slapping up and down on the frame in rough conditions, and they enabled riders to remove the chain without splitting it.

The Overburys builder was Andrew Powell, and most of his frames and forks were fillet-brazed using Columbus or Reynolds tubing. While these E-stay frames were attention grabbers and often painted in wild colors, the Overburys Pioneer became the classic with racers and more casual trail riders alike. It was one of the first British mountain bike frames with a sloped top tube for standover clearance, and an extended seat tube sleeved and supported by skinny "fast-back" seatstays. Early Pioneers ranged from ready-to-race models to fully equipped bikes for luggage-laden tours. They were reasonably priced, starting at around $800 (£500) for a complete bike. **SW**

S&M Dirt Bike

1989 • BMX bike • USA • Mid-School dirt jumper

Greg Scott Swingrover and Chris "Mad Dog" Moeller founded S&M bikes in 1987. The Dirt Bike evolved from Mad Dog's signature frame when Moeller "got sick of everyone riding a bike with my name on it." Essentially just a stronger race frame capable of handling dirt jumping and street riding, the chassis is a simple, straight-up creation that typifies the BMX Mid-School era.

Early S&M designs avoided the platforms, pegs, and accessories on trick bikes of the day. Clean lines and simplicity were key to the brand's style, and the approach is epitomized in this "back to the roots" machine with thick-gauge 4130 tubing.

The Dirt Bike was a response to the emerging branch of BMX riding known as "trails" or "dirt jumping." In this purist form of freestyle, riders hit consecutive takeoffs and landings, and jumped across gaps of up to 30 ft (10 m).

An important stage in BMX development, the Dirt Bike (and its peers) grew out of an independent, punk-style, DIY attitude that led to the foundation of rider-owned bike companies and media fanzines, all staffed by hardcore BMXers. S&M still adheres to this philosophy. An air-hardened custom geometry Dirt Bike option has been offered since 2008. **MK**

SWATCH S Bike

1989 • Mountain bike • Switzerland • Iconic box-frame mountain bike

The Swatch S Bike was an attempt by the super-fashionable watchmaker—and longtime cycling sponsor—to carve itself a bigger slice of the mountain bike action.

With most mountain bikes still made from slim steel tubing, the massive red-painted rectangular mainframe of the S Bike made it one of the most distinctive bikes of the period. The braced crucifix frame layout looked clean and sharp, and synced with the contemporary vogue for elevated chainstay bikes designed to reduce wheelbase length and stop chains jamming against the frame in mud. Essentially the same design was used for chromoly steel bikes produced in Taiwan, and the alloy-frame bikes made by Verlicchi in Italy.

In 1992, the S Bike followed Verlicchi's lead by modifying its frame to create a suspension bike. A pivot into the rear end of the mainframe was attached to a modified version of the existing swingarm, with a short coil shock behind the seatpost to create a new model called the S Bike Fully.

The S Bike had some success on the downhill circuit—including a Junior World Championship win under Laetitia Holweck in 1992—but its heavy frame tended to develop cracks in the swingarm. **GK**

WINDCHEETAH Speedy

1989 • Tricycle • UK • High-performance recumbent trike

Mike Burrows designed the carbon fiber Lotus that helped Chris Boardman to Olympic gold in 2012. He also created a folding bike, a very thin bike, and a freight-carrying bike, as well as carbon composite road bikes and wheels for Giant Bicycles. Another product was the Speedy recumbent tricycle that he originally designed for his own use in winter near his home in Norfolk, England. It was a simple off-season training vehicle with a lightweight aluminum-bonded chassis.

This machine, later refined and put into limited production, gradually became one of the best-known recumbent trikes in the world. There was always a long waiting list for the small number of Speedys produced

"Every time someone gets out of a motorcar, and onto a bicycle, the world [is] a better place."

Mike Burrows

annually. As demand grew, Burrows shifted production from his own engineering company in Norfolk to the Seat of the Pants Company in Manchester. The trike was renamed the Burrows Windcheetah, and the size of the front wheel was increased from 17 in. (43 cm) to 20 in. (51 cm) to meet U.S. customer requirements. Meanwhile, endurance cyclist Andy Wilkinson rode a highly developed Windcheetah 861 mi (1,386 km) from Land's End to John O'Groats in 41 hours 4 minutes, beating the bicycle record by four hours.

Production models now include sophisticated components including carbon fiber springs, titanium bolts, and wheel covers made from microlight aircraft fabric. The original Speedy is still available, with Shimano 105 gears, fiberglass seat, and drum brakes. **SH**

YETI C26

1989 • Mountain bike • USA • Iconic but fatally flawed "future of mountain bikes"

Few images have captured the mountain bike community's imagination like those of U.S. race legends ripping down trails or styling jumps on their carbon-tubed Yeti C26s. Magazines hailed the C26 as the future of mountain bikes, yet sadly the bike in question never made it into production, leading to mythical stories of lost tubesets and black-market bikes built from butchered frames.

Yeti was a key player in the early U.S. mountain bike race scene, but its FRO bikes were bombproof plain steel tube heavyweights that put their riders at a significant disadvantage in competition against nimbler machines. Desperate to reduce weight, Yeti designer Chris Herting hit upon the idea of inserting his new C9 carbon fiber-wrapped tubeset into the front and rear sections of the existing FRO frame.

The resulting C26—the letter stands for "Chris," the number for Herting's age in years at the time—was significantly lighter than its predecessor and, perhaps more important, looked amazing. Prototype frames were handed out to Yeti riders Juli Furtado (who won the World Championships on hers) and John Tomac, and the legend was born.

However, things were not as great as they appeared to be. The tight fit of the tubes into the steel lugs squeezed most of the bonding glue out of the joint, and thus created some uncertainty about whether the parts were firmly stuck or just hanging together. Thankfully for the riders and Yeti's reputation, none of the bikes actually broke in use, but as soon as the season was over all the race bikes were recalled. This made the C26 one of the most sought-after bikes ever: when forty sets of unused Easton tubing were later unearthed in a factory move, some collectors even chopped up steel FRO frames to create fake C26s. **GK**

John Tomac's Yeti is as iconic as he is. ▶

KONA Cinder Cone

1989 • Mountain bike • USA • Affordable, aspirational classic

Founded in 1988, Kona hired race ace Joe Murray as product designer and manager. The Murray signature Cinder Cone was the company's first attention-grabbing bike. Its sloping top tube, compact triangles, long head tube, and Project Two straight-bladed fork formed the template for mountain bike frame designs from that point onward. It was relatively cheap, looked unlike anything else, and worked extremely well. Many riders now say that the Cinder Cone—along with other early Konas, such as the more costly Explosif and the titanium-framed Hei Hei—was the bike that first made them fall in love with single-track riding. The bike frame's steepish geometry was fairly

> *"At the time it made other bikes seem a bit cumbersome in their handling traits."*
>
> Steve Worland, bike journalist

revolutionary for the time, and may have helped to popularize the application of epithets such as "lively" and "inspired" to the performance of bikes on technically demanding trails.

Although Canadian Paul Brodie, and perhaps American Charlie Cunningham, were the first builders of low top tubes and compact frame triangles, Murray and Kona first popularized and mass produced bikes for riders on lower budgets. A quarter-century down the line, the Cinder Cone is still a part of Kona's range, but it now uses Scandium aluminum alloy tubes instead of the original quality chromoly steel that set the scene all those years ago. An original Cinder Cone in decent condition will still fetch about the same amount of money in real terms as its original purchase price. **SW**

ORANGE Clockwork

1989 • Mountain bike • UK • Classic steel mountain bike

The story of the Orange Clockwork proves that inspiration for the creation of a legend really can blow in from anywhere. One day, Championship windsurfer Lester Noble became bored while waiting around for strong winds, so he grabbed a Muddy Fox mountain bike to keep fit. He was hooked straight away, and after racing the 1984 World Championships on only his second ride he convinced the managing director of his employer, Tushingham sailmakers, to augment their business by making bikes.

Noble takes up the story: "I started designing bikes because Muddy Fox had turned their range into an urban fashion item and we were only interested in riding off-road. We sourced them from Taiwan and called them Tushingham bikes. Then windsurfing went flat and I met up with metal worker Steve Wade and we agreed to start our own range of bikes."

While most bikes of the time were either sold complete or built from expensive custom frames, Orange took a course that went straight down the middle. The frames were bought in from Taiwan, but built up to customers' requirements in the United Kingdom. Sales of their lively-riding steel frame literally went like Clockwork. The maker's reputation for no-nonsense toughness and great customer service, plus a successful race team dressed in Orange's signature black and orange, soon made this refreshingly affordable bike a must-have for UK riders.

While the Orange range rapidly expanded to include the aluminum alloy 02, the titanium Vitamin T, and the heavier-gauge P7, the Clockwork remained as the brand's unshakeable foundation. It returned to the Orange lineup in 2013 with larger, 29-in. (73.5-cm) wheels and an alloy frame. Best of all, it was still as affordable as ever. **GK**

Orange's Clockwork is an instantly recognizable classic. ▶

FAT CHANCE Yo Eddy

1990 • Mountain bike • USA • Iconic hand-built mountain bike

Chris Chance had been quietly impressing enthusiast riders with his robust but fast Fat Chance mountain bikes since the mid-1980s. Frames like the Yo Eddy and the Wicked in the late 1980s and early 1990s made many riders appreciate that there was still room for classy small-batch-built steel creations in a market that was increasingly swaying toward aluminum frames.

The Yo Eddy had a fairly racy geometry, with very short chainstays, but still had room for 2½-in. (6.3-cm) tires. With 1½ in. (3.6 cm) of rake in a brutal-looking but surprisingly compliant straight blade fork, the machine quickly set the standard at the time for hard-riding, race-bred mountain bikes. The 1992 Yo Eddy Team quickly became a collectable classic, with its quad-butted tubing, distinctively different Yo Eddy fork, silver-to-violet paint fade, and titanium head badge.

Variously vivid alternative colors, usually overlaid with or incorporating striking graphics, emerged on the standard Yo Eddys of the mid-1990s, and these bikes still look stunning today.

The original Fat City Cycle company eventually closed shop in 1994, when the brand was sold to a holding company that had also acquired the Serotta bike brand. The Yo Eddy remained in production for a few years, until a bunch of Chris Chance's employees left the company and created Independent Fabrication. This was a case of history repeating itself: Their migration reminded some observers of a similar scenario that had occurred in the early days of Fat City, when a few of the frame builders who wanted to create titanium frames went off and started a new company, Merlin Metalworks.

Eventually, Chris Chance also moved on, reportedly to be a holistic healer and massage therapist in San Francisco. The guys who set up Independent Fabrication are still trading. **SW**

"The only way to describe it is to say it's . . . a way of life that you'll understand once you ride one."

Ted Costantino, Bike Magazine

◁ The Yo Eddy's flamboyant design attracted flamboyant riders.

CINETICA Giotto

1990 • Race bike • Italy • Beautiful single-monocoque carbon-loop frame

The unique carbon-loop, single-monocoque frame of Cinetica's Giotto was at least 1 lb (0.5 kg) lighter than even the most lightweight steel frames of the late 1980s, and its torsional rigidity left all other frame concepts of the time trailing in its wake. Its designer, Andrea Cinelli—son of the great Italian rider and bicycle designer Cino Cinelli—worked with researchers from Campagnolo, Ferrari, and the University of Milan to add high-tech refinements, such as a computer built into the saddle to provide an extensive range of performance data, and aesthetic touches like its gorgeous carbon-varnished frame, a symphony in red thanks to the boys at Ferrari.

Despite all this, only around fifty of these beauties were ever made, although there were plenty of potential buyers and the company was eyeing a serious high-end production run. Two conflicting stories have been told to explain this odd situation. According to one version, the molds that produced the Giotto's signature frame were accidentally destroyed. In the other account, it is stated that the cost of producing the exquisite frame proved prohibitively high. The truth may never emerge.

Although the failure of the Giotto to make it into production may be regretted, it's an ill wind that blows no one any good. The cycling world had an instantly ultra-rare collector's item that truly deserved to share its name with the famous Florentine Old Master. The fact that Giotto himself is widely credited with starting the Italian Renaissance also resonates with the position of the Cinetica in Italian carbon bike history. Finding one of the "missing" Giottos is not easy these days, with the whereabouts of only a dozen or so being known. One was used as a prop in the action movie *Terminator 2: Judgment Day* (1991). **BS**

ELLIS BRIGGS Favori

1990 • Race bike • UK • Intriguing English-made but Italian-style frame

This sleek, hand-built Italian-style race bike emerged from the unlikely birthplace of a small workshop at the back of a cycle store in Shipley, Yorkshire. But make no mistake, the Favori was a fine piece of work, using double-butted Reynolds 531 tubing and decorative lugwork all hand-brazed in the traditional way by experts who were already lifelong bike builders.

It was a good-looking bike, with the frames usually finished in a metallic champagne gold and the curvy lugs picked out with white. The 531 forks and forged drop-outs were left as bare polished steel and the frame also featured brazed-on bottle cage bosses and bottom-bracket cable guides. The Favori

> *"Ellis Briggs started to sound a bit old-fashioned compared to all the exotic Italian names."*
> Paul Gibson, Ellis Briggs

was considered a professional or serious amateur road racer's machine, and components were usually top-flight Campagnolo Record. Of course, the Italian name was an attempt by the homely Yorkshire company to appear sportily exotic and continental, and it also helped with exports across the Atlantic.

In 1971, Yorkshire racer Danny Horton won the British National Road Championship as part of the leading Falcon team. But his bike that was proudly labeled "Falcon" was really an Ellis Briggs underneath, according to Ellis Briggs today. If that is true, it would have been a very similar frame to the Favori.

The Ellis Briggs company, established in 1936 by Len Ellis and Tom Briggs, is still owned and managed by their descendants. **SH**

The Favori sounded Italian but it was Yorkshire born and bred. ▸

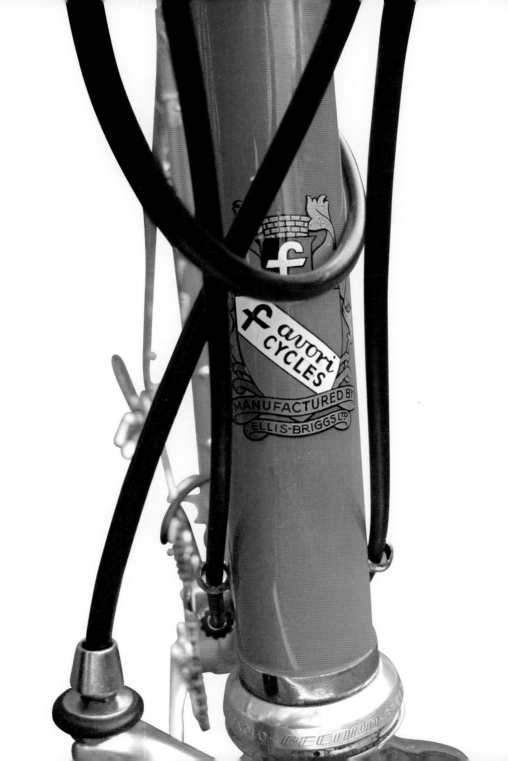

BONTRAGER Race Lite

1990 • Mountain bike • USA • Steel frames combining lightness and strength

CILO MTB

1990 • Mountain bike • Switzerland • Franco Ballerini's Paris–Roubaix-winning bike

Former motorbike racer and engineer Keith Bontrager is a champion of "simple" steel frames, and there are still plenty of ultra-modern frames that reference his work in the early 1990s, particularly the Bontrager Race Lite. Bontrager combined various marginal gains to create the ultimate steel frames, adding gussets to strengthen the joins of light tubes, and using bonding and/or riveting to boost strength and resilience in parts that might have been weakened by welding or brazing.

The seatstays of the Race Lite were of a twin "sleeved" tube design, with fatter tube diameters for braking support at the top, and thinner tube diameters lower down to keep weight low and muffle trail shocks. The Race Lite frameset, which still retains kudos as a collector's item today, would come with Bontrager's Switchblade forks, with his patented composite fork crown bolted into straight steel legs. This design became a foundation of RockShox suspension forks.

After a few difficult years of trying to increase frame production and develop further into building component parts, Bontrager was bought by the mighty Trek Bicycle Corporation in the mid-1990s. Bontrager himself continues to help Trek to develop product designs bearing his name. **SW**

Cilo, one of the very few Swiss bicycle manufacturers, was established on the shores of Lake Geneva. The name was an acronym of the founder's initials and its base in the Lausanne-Oron region.

While mountain bikers remember Cilo for its vivid Day-Glo colors, which gave it a strong brand identity in World Cup mountain biking in the early 1990s, the brand was actually established with some beautiful road bikes during the 1940s and 1950s. Finely detailed brazed lugs and lavish paintwork were always at the forefront of Cilo's identity, but the road frames were subtle compared to the mountain bikes.

Swiss downhill racing star Phillippe Perakis attracted attention to the Cilo brand at the 1990 World Championships in Durango, Colorado, where he qualified as second-fastest on a Cilo equipped with the ATZ swing-link suspension fork. Unfortunately, Perakis broke his wrist and could not take part in the final. Shortly after that, Cilo became one of the first brands to use rear suspension for downhill racing.

The original Cilo brand failed in 2002, but lives on as a label on bought-in carbon frames, and as a popular red, white, and black retro road jersey from the time when Cilo was linked to the Aufina pro road team. **SW**

CINELLI The Absolute Machine

1990 • Mountain bike • Italy • Stylish off-roader with Cinelli-labeled carbon fiber handlebar

MANTIS Flying V

1990 • Mountain bike • USA • Early semi-monocoque-construction mountain bike

If Cinelli's reputation in mountain biking was developed by The Machine, it was cemented by The Absolute Machine. This bike was made from smooth-welded Columbus Max EL (extra-light) steel tubing that was elliptically shaped to provide strength where it was most needed. For example, the down tube was tall and slim at the top end, but short and fat by the time it reached the bottom bracket.

The Absolute Machine's chromoly steel fork, slim by today's standards but considered oversized at the time, was intended to stand up to the high forces encountered when riding off-road. The Cinelli-labeled handlebar was typical of its era in being flat and virtually straight (riser bars were out of favor at the time) but was unusual in being made from carbon fiber. The front brake cable entered the chromoly steel stem via the clamp bolt, and exited directly above the cantilever brake, which was a really neat touch.

The 7-speed Deore XT groupset, Shimano's top-level off-road groupset at the time, sat at the top of many mountain bikers' wish lists, and the black finish and minimalist graphics helped too. Cinelli's attention to detail—such as the gold cable outers and gold decals—added to the cool factor. **MB**

Richard Cunningham was one of the most prolific and respected innovators of the early mountain bike scene. His Mantis Flying V was an extension of previous twin-material Mantis designs and the elevated-stay designs he did for Nishiki in 1988, and it also ushered in the new construction technique of the monocoque.

In engineering terms, a monocoque is a structural member that carries all the stress through its outer skin while joining separate components together to form a homogenous structural piece. In bike construction it is used more broadly to describe a hollow box-section frame member. If it is formed from two halves welded together, it is referred to as a clamshell monocoque, and that is exactly the basis of the Mantis Flying V.

Cunningham took a steel rear subframe and mated it to a hand-hammered clamshell monocoque to produce the first Flying V bikes. Their extremely low frame weight of under 4 lb (1.7 kg) and outstanding looks brought them immediate success. The hand-hammered frames were then replaced by stamped sheet frames, and soon many other manufacturers were making pressed-sheet mainframes. The identical construction method was also used on Cunningham's iconic Mantis Pro Floater suspension bike. **GK**

SLINGSHOT MTB

1990 • Mountain bike • USA • Unique wired suspension frame

Slingshot Bikes began to produce original designs back in 1980 with a BMX bike. The company made its first mountain bike in 1985, but a 1990 re-design made the enthusiasts really sit up and take notice.

Depending on the definition of suspension being invoked, the 1985 models made Slingshot one of the first companies to offer a mountain bike with a full chassis suspension system, albeit without a suspension fork. The Slingshot approach to suspension is unique in both its design and ride feel in that it consists of a mid-chassis suspension configuration.

Instead of a conventional down tube, it has a tensioned steel cable suspended on a spring. The 1985 design featured two springs and two cables, with the springs located at the bottom bracket, but the more highly regarded versions of the mid-1990s had a single cable with a spring behind the head tube. As the spring stretches and rebounds in response to bumps, and to a lesser extent to the rider's pedaling and body movement, a flexible hinge at the saddle end of the top tube moves to accommodate the extension and rebound of the whole traveling chassis. The fact that the wheelbase is constantly extending and retracting creates a strange but surprisingly comfortable ride sensation. It is at its strangest in climbs, where riders learn to use the "inchworming" effect, a feeling that some riders love and some hate.

The Slingshot was one of the first "soft-ride" mountain bikes, and it proved that full-suspension bikes are difficult to categorize and unpredictably quirky. While many of Slingshot's frame-design details have changed over the years, the basic idea of mid-frame suspension remains. Since a change of ownership, Slingshot now offers more conventional frames as well as its wire-and-spring designs. **SW**

OFFROAD Pro-Flex

1990 • Mountain bike • USA • Lightweight all-terrain bike

The first Offroad-branded "all-terrain bicycle" was shown in 1988, but really it was just another rigid-framed, rigid-forked mountain bike. Two years later, designer Bob Girvin of KG Engineering produced the Offroad Pro-Flex, a bike with a high-pivot single swingarm suspension system using an elastomer bumper as a spring at the rear. A bump-absorbing hinged "Flex Stem," again with an elastomer bumper, was then fitted up front instead of a suspension fork. This first Pro-Flex, offering 1 in. (2.5 cm) of rear-wheel travel, was a taste of bigger things to come.

The Flex Stem was a fairly short-lived alternative to the suspension fork, although in 1993 the Pro-Flex

"*It was incredibly light, and I liked it so much I kept it for over a year.*"

Steve Worland, bike journalist

range was offered, slightly bizarrely on reflection, with both a Flex Stem and a suspension fork. Then, in 1993 Girvin created his own Girvin linkage fork, consigning the Flex Stem to the parts bin. With both fork and rear end working together, the Pro-Flex became one of the first widely accepted and popular full-suspension bikes.

The Offroad brand officially changed its name to Pro-Flex in 1994. The bike's rear suspension configuration remained the same: a basic single-pivot design with a big elastomer donut as the spring. It was a lightweight setup that worked well in terms of shock absorption and pedaling efficiency. The same type of donut was used in Girvin's linkage fork. The complete bike's low weight began to interest many cross-country racers in the concept of full suspension. **SW**

⬅ Wire replaces tube on the radical Slingshot.

FELT B2

1991 • Triathlon bike • USA • First bike from the now-legendary triathlon brand

Jim Felt started his cycle-making career as an ace mechanic on the U.S. motocross circuit. When top rider Johnny O'Mara asked him to build a bicycle frame, Felt was busy building his reputation for race-winning technical innovation while working for the motocross teams of Japanese manufacturers Honda, Kawasaki, Suzuki, and Yamaha.

Triathlon was still in its infancy, but O'Mara found the new discipline perfect for building his fitness for arduous motocross races. He proved fast enough to win the California state time trial championships on Felt's bike in 1990, and that was enough to get Felt recruited by metal experts Easton for its newly created bike division.

Felt then found himself building a bike for multiple-Ironman triathlon champion Paula Newby-Fraser. He named his matte black aero bike the B2 after his country's angular new stealth bomber project, and Newby-Fraser promptly used it to blow away the opposition and take her fourth Hawaii title.

Felt continued to build race specials at Easton, including frames for mountain biker John Tomac, duathlete Ken Souza, and Ironman Wolfgang Dietrich. He launched Felt as a separate company first in 1994 and then again in 2001 after the resolution of a dispute with his distributors, Answer. Felt now produces every sort of bike, from beach cruisers to carbon fiber mountain bikes.

However, Felt has remained true to its roots. Triathlon is still a core focus of the Felt brand, and the B2 is still a key bike in the lineup. The latest versions of the B2 even use the same frame mold as the earlier flagship bikes, retaining their radical cutaway aero shaping. A wind-cheating drinking bottle is among the standard-issue accessories. **GK**

CALFEE Team Z

1991 • Road bike • USA • Pioneering full-carbon road racer

Craig Calfee is one of the great innovators of recent bike-design history. His career began with a potentially serious accident, as he narrowly escaped injury when he and his old Schwinn bike hit a car that had run a red light. Calfee luckily escaped unscathed, but his bike was written off.

As the recently graduated sculptor was working for a composite rowboat builder at the time, he tried to build his own braided carbon fiber tubed frame, fork, and stem. The first bike was an extremely rough, vaguely straight mess, but its distinctive webbed-joint design was inherently very light and much stiffer than other carbon fiber bikes. Calfee realized its potential and

> *"LeMond was blown away. Without even riding it, he said 'This is amazing.'"*
>
> Craig Calfee

moved to California to make bikes by night and work as a carpenter by day.

News of his lightweight hand-built bikes reached top U.S. racer Greg LeMond in early 1991. LeMond had already won one Tour de France on a carbon-and-alloy Look Cycles frame, but he was not happy with the performance of the TVT carbon alloy frames his "Z" Team was using. LeMond asked Calfee to build him a custom bike and he was impressed by the lightweight climbing and sure-footed descending ability of the 3-lb (1.4-kg) frame. Twenty frames were completed to equip the team for immediate success in the season-opening Paris–Nice race, and Calfee's position as the leading carbon fiber craftsman was confirmed at the highest level. **GK**

Greg LeMond was a pioneer of carbon fiber race use. ▶

BREEZER Beamer

1991 • Mountain bike • USA • "Rider-suspending" bike

Joe Breeze was one of the first to build mountain bike frames for racing down the fire roads of Tamalpais, which overlooked his home in Fairfax, California. His beautifully made Breezer bikes, with their classic painted diamond panels, were already established as among the ultimate dream rides for dirt riders when he turned up to the Interbike trade show in 1991 with the show-stopping Beamer.

Its Softride visco-elastic beam consisted of a sandwich of different materials in a cantilevered arm with the saddle attached directly to the far end. The rider bounced up and down independently of the pedals and frame in a seesaw form of suspension. Breeze made the

> ## "Joe Breeze is one of the central figures in the development of mountain biking."
>
> *Mountain Bike Hall of Fame induction citation*

rest of the bike look stunning by cutting away the now-redundant upper part of the seat tube and dropping the top tube down to form a super-low seatstay wishbone. The steel tubing was joined and painted in Breeze's meticulous style, with the subtly curved steel fork painted to match. Unfortunately, on top of the fork was one of the heaviest and ugliest stems ever produced. The box parallelogram Softride stem had a diagonally mounted internal coil spring to match the twanging rider position with a similarly bouncy connection between frame and bars.

Happily, the Softride beam and stem system was soon consigned to long-distance road-bike use by properly controlled suspension systems and forks that suspended the frame from ground shock. **GK**

STANDARD BYKES STA

1991 • BMX bike • USA • Heavy-duty "street" BMX pioneer

Founded by hardcore BMX riders Rick Moliterno and Kurt Schmidt, Standard Bykes was one of the key "second-generation" rider-owned companies pivotal in dragging BMX out of its late-1980s stagnation.

The STA's initials stand for Stronger Than All, an apt description of the modern freestyle frame's tanklike attitude and more than 7-lb (3.1-kg) weight, backed by an unconditional "no questions asked" lifetime warranty. The STA was the first freestyle frame to have the new threadless fork–stem combination borrowed from mountain bikes. Its performance proved so superior that other BMX manufacturers followed suit, and it literally changed the industry overnight.

Pioneering modern construction ideas such as thicker-walled tubing and oversized materials, Standard designed the 20-in. (51-cm) top-tubed chromoly STA to provide the strength and durability needed for the emerging street and skatepark style of riding. A key frame feature was super-thick rear drop-outs capable of handling the forces exerted by the use of axle extenders, or "pegs." These accessories are used when "grinding" or sliding down rails and edges, and were being adopted widely for a new style of tricks blossoming in the sport at the time.

The Standard marque subsequently introduced several construction and material production techniques to BMX, including double-welded drop-outs and air-hardened OX Platinum steel tubing. However, by the late 1990s Standard became just another fish in an ever-growing pond of rider-owned companies, and market share fell off dramatically. Still owned by Moliterno today, Standard continues to hand weld bikes in Davenport, Iowa, and remains true to the concept of rider-developed and -tested products built on a small scale in the United States. **MK**

◁ Nice frame, shame about the beam.

CANNONDALE EST

1991 • Mountain bike • USA • Early elevated-
stay suspension bike

The EST was Cannondale's first single-pivot offering. It
emerged at a time when suspension forks were barely
available. The first Elevated Suspension Technology
(EST) bikes came with a Flex Stem up front, a swingarm
with a very high pivot (well above the crankset), and a
big coiled spring instead of seatstays.

Unfortunately, the pivot positioning combined
with weight shifts, pedal forces, and a primitive shock
to create the sort of nodding-donkey bobbing that
gave suspension a bad name. Because cantilever
brakes were not possible on the frame, the rear brake
was a pulley-operated affair that was fiddly to set up
and spongy in use. The tiny swingarm pivot developed
play and did not prevent the front and rear of the frame
from flexing independently on rough terrain.

Even so, the EST deserves brownie points just for
being the first production suspension bike. The frame
weighed less than 6 lb (2.7 kg) and the rear shock,
despite its limitations, was one of the first coil-sprung
oil-damped rider weight-adjustable units on a mountain
bike. In 1992, Cannondale added its revolutionary Delta
V head tube-based suspension fork (which later became
the Headshock) to the EST, and in 1993 the company
really found its mojo with the launch of the Super V. **SW**

GIANT Cadex CFM 3

1991 • Mountain bike • Taiwan • Early carbon
fiber mountain bike from major Taiwanese manufacturer

Giant produces bikes for other prestige brands as well
as frames under its own name. It is one of the most
advanced makers of aluminum frames, but also has long
experience in carbon fiber construction. Its first carbon-
tubed road and mountain bikes hit the market in 1991.

Giant has since gone on to become the only
manufacturer to produce and resin-impregnate its
own carbon fiber construction sheets from bundles of
carbon filament, but the first Cadex fiber bikes were of a
plug-and-lug format. Preformed carbon fiber tubes were
inserted into metal socket junctions (lugs) and held in
place by aircraft-strength glue. Most bikes of the time
only had carbon tubes for the main triangle of the bike,
but Giant also used carbon for the rear tubes. The upper
and lower stays consisted of advanced square-section
tubes, with an alloy bridge above the rear wheel joined
to the frame by another short carbon fiber section. The
cable stops were also glued onto the tubes. In a cunning
example of industrial efficiency, the Cadex's lugs were
also used for alloy-tubed bikes available at a lower price.

Riders were more skeptical about composites and
glue than they were about the TIG-welded alloy bikes
that were now also appearing. Yet Giant continued to
evolve its carbon construction methods. **GK**

GARY FISHER/LAWWILL RS-1

1991 • Mountain bike • USA • Radical fully suspended disc-braked integrated machine

Most early attempts at rear-suspension systems on mountain bikes were simple affairs, with front suspension in the stems instead of the forks, but the first Gary Fisher full-suspension bike had its suspension at both ends. It was designed by Mert Lawwill, who had costarred in the movie *On Any Sunday* (1971).

Lawwill designed the Gary Fisher RS-1 using his own leading-link fork design. His was one of the first bikes to use disc brakes front and rear, with a floating caliper at the back to prevent the brake from interfering with shock function. The rear hub, made by Campagnolo, had an oversized axle to help stiffen the four-bar-linkage swingarm assembly, and the bottom-bracket shell was wider than was normal at the time for extra crankset and swingarm support. The shock itself was a Lawwill-designed stack of damped elastomer blocks, offering 2½ in. (6.5 cm) of travel, with a very early Risse Racing air shock supporting the fork linkages.

Gary Fisher made 750 of these bikes, and they were all sold despite having nonstandard parts that were hard to upgrade. In 1993, the company tried to update the RS-1 design with the Alembic. The carbon frames were made in Japan, but early problems with the design meant only seven prototypes were ever made. **SW**

GT Zaskar

1991 • Mountain bike • USA • Iconic mountain bike from leading BMX brand

GT Bicycles was founded as a BMX brand in 1979 by Gary Turner, who gave his initials to the brand. When mountain bikes started to become popular, GT set itself apart by developing mountain bike versions of its distinctive triple-triangle BMX frame design (the third triangle was created by the seatstays crossing the seat tube before joining the top tube). The design was said to disperse trail shocks at the back of the bike better than more conventional designs, while making all the frame triangles more compact and consequently stiffer.

GT's aluminum-framed Zaskar used the triple-triangle design and was among the first recognized all-round "hardtail" mountain bikes. Hardtail means front suspension only, while "all-round" signified that it was suitable for more than just cross-country trail riding.

The Zaskar's competition results established its image. In its many and varied incarnations over the years it has become the only bike model that has achieved World Cup wins in cross-country, downhill, slalom, and trials. Julie Furtado, usually riding a Zaskar, became one of the most successful racers in history, and trials legend Hans Rey used it for almost everything. It was a cult bike, it is still sold, and is now available in carbon and bigger-wheel versions. **SW**

SPECIALIZED Epic Ultimate

1991 • Mountain bike • USA • Carbon-tubed titanium-junction flagship superbike

For more than a century, bike-frame construction depended on tubes being plugged into cast lugs at their corners. The method has many advantages. Tube ends do not have to be meticulously shaped for a perfect join with other tubes, as they do with fillet-brazed or TIG-welded frames. The same lugs can be used for different-sized frames just by changing the measurements between them. The tubes can be secured with melted metal filler (normally bronze or silver), or bonded with a glue if the material has a low melting-point and cannot withstand high temperatures. And different materials may be used for the tubes and lugs themselves.

Innovators such as Carlton, Vitus, Alan, and Peugeot plugged aluminum or carbon fiber tubes into metal lugs in the 1970s and 1980s, but the technique reached its pinnacle with Specialized's Epic Ultimate road and mountain bike frames of 1991. Specialized had created versions with steel lugs the previous year, but in 1991 it topped the range with titanium lugs. The ultra-light frame design retained its position at the head of the pack until 1995, thanks to the successes on it of legendary racers such as Ned Overend, 1990 World Mountain Bike champion and six-time winner of the National Off-Road Bicycle Association (NORBA) championship between 1986 and 1992.

Advances in carbon fiber fabrication soon meant that carbon tubes could be bonded to carbon lugs. Completely seamless monocoque frames were also appearing. The plug-and-lug technique was debased slightly by heavy carbon-and-alloy bikes such as the Giant Cadex and Raleigh M Trax, but, because of its position in the hierachy when it was launched, the Epic Ultimate is still one of the most sought-after—and expensive—frames for retro bike fans. **GK**

SPECIALIZED Stumpjumper M2

1991 • Mountain bike • USA • Early advanced metal matrix alloy mountain bike

Steel bikes had dominated bicycle construction for a century when Gary Klein and Cannondale in the United States developed the first oversized aluminum frames. Development of steel alloys for bikes was stagnant, with the fifty-year-old Reynolds 531 still the benchmark. In contrast, aluminum bicycle tubing development was frenzied, with heat-treated 6000 and 7000 series frames vying for top honors as more and more manufacturers saw the potential of their low weight and high stiffness.

Specialized took an altogether different route when it used Duralcan's Metal Matrix Composite for its super-light M2 flagship. This material—aluminum oxide "whiskers" mixed into a 6061 aluminum alloy

> *"The revolution had started . . . word had begun to spread . . . inspired by the Stumpjumper."*
> Max Glaskin

base—made a truly cutting-edge chassis; with various gusset and tube-shape changes it remained the default material for Stumpjumper M2 hardtails for a full decade.

Specialized introduced another innovation in 1991. The M2 was the first bike in its S-Works series, an elite-level bike-and-dealer program in which flagship stores sold the most expensive and advanced models in the Specialized lineup. The M2 was rapidly joined by an S-Works steel frame and S-Works road bikes, and soon lightweight S-Works tires were made available.

The S-Works stores were a direct ancestor of the current Specialized Concept stores, which have turned the idea of a store selling top-of-the-line Specialized products into one of a general Specialized store selling its complete range of branded products. **GK**

◁ Specialized's Epic upheld its "Innovate or die" ethic.

GT Quatrefoil

1991 • Mountain bike tandem • USA • Radical wheel-sized tandem off-roader

The Quatrefoil tandem was part of GT's Crossover range, which saw the first attempt to introduce intermediate-sized wheels into mainstream mountain biking. While the size is now termed 650B or 27½ in. (70 cm), in 1991 GT (and sub-brand Mt. Shasta) referred to it as 700D.

The idea was that the in-between wheel size would form the ideal "crossover" between large-diameter thin-tire road wheels and small-diameter fat-tire off-road wheels for light dirt riding and rough road use. The wheel size was introduced on only a few models in the ranges of each brand, and they all shared the same center ridge-style tires and Araya rims.

"The Quatrefoil . . . is dressed in . . . Midnight Aurora, Daktari White, and Deep Purple."

GT Quatrefoil catalog, 1991

While the idea never really took off, an enduringly popular result of the experiment was the Quatrefoil tandem. The frame used a steel tubeset, and the exaggerated oval cross-section of the boom tube between the bottom brackets and top and lateral tubes gave torsional stiffness while allowing vertical compliance. GT's triple-triangle overlapping rear stay and interlocking pierced top tube–seat tube join was also opened up to allow room for a rear Shimano U brake. Shimano also provided the Deore gearing, which included a very rare, super-durable, smooth-shifting "crossover" drive. Models of the Quatrefoil from 1992 also saw the introduction of GT's innovative flip-flop stem, which had a double-ended internal tightening bung to allow easy changes in handlebar height. **GK**

KONA Hei Hei

1991 • Mountain bike • Canada • Sandvik-built titanium mountain bike

Kona's titanium-framed Hei Hei was an object of almost obsessional desire for mountain bikers for more than a decade. *BikeRadar* described it as an "über-lustworthy dream machine." The pedigree of the Hei Hei is not entirely straightforward, however, but rather exemplifies a trend of "borrowing" other designs that was very noticeable throughout the boom years of mountain biking.

As it turns out, the first Kona, the Kona Titanium of 1990, was not really a Kona at all, but a product of premium titanium bike builder Merlin Metalworks of Cambridge, Massachusetts. While some of the angles were allegedly decided by Kona racer and designer Joe Murray, the layout was very much Merlin's standard-level top tube design. The change to Murray and Kona's sloping-top-tube and extended-seat-tube design came in 1991, when production moved to Sandvik Inc., of Streetsville, Ontario, Canada. It was there that the first true Kona Hei Hei was built.

Aerospace contractor Sandvik was extremely skilled in the difficult art of working and welding titanium, and the Kona Hei Hei soon became a byword of understated but outstanding quality construction. The resilient sprung ride and extremely long fatigue life also suited the naturally agile ride that Kona was famed for in both trail biking and racing, and the Hei Hei became almost universally acknowledged as one of the most aspirational frames of the 1990s. Even today, the Kona Hei Hei still commands a premium price and high levels of interest among retrobike collectors the world over.

Since the 1990s, the Hei Hei name has been passed on to lightweight full-suspension bikes in the Kona range, but Sandvik continues to build titanium mountain bikes for other manufacturers. **GK**

Kona's Hei Hei was truly aspirational. ▶

FORMULA F1

1991 • Mountain bike • UK • Genuine Formula
One technology meets early mountain biking

The Formula F1 was one of the first mountain bikes to emerge from the skill set of Formula One motor racing engineers—in this case, David Price, chief mechanic at McLaren in 1974, the year Emerson Fittipaldi won the World Championship in one of the company's cars, and Phil Sharp, who helped Mercedes win the Le Mans 24 Hours race, who together founded DPS Components of Surrey, England.

The Formula F1's "single size fits all" mainframe was a carbon monocoque construction at a time when even carbon tubes on bikes were remarkable rarities. A Reynolds 531 chromoly-steel rear subframe was bolted on, and the Mark I bikes had rigid aluminum-crowned straight-bladed carbon-legged forks with Magura hydraulic rim brakes. Weighing about 25 lb (11.5 kg), they cost $3,000 (£2,000) and initially were simply ridden around Formula One race paddocks by a few star drivers.

The first few bikes suffered from excessive amounts of flex in the back end, but improved versions were soon being ridden on the UK cross-country race circuit by outstanding performers such as women's champion Deb Murrell. Some were offered for sale to the public at prices ranging from $2,400 (£1,600) to $3,750 (£2,500). These had much stiffer rear triangles, but a year or so later they were finally blessed with RockShox suspension forks.

There was also a highly desirable full-suspension version, using exactly the same mainframe, a very high pivot, a shock unit under the top tube, and a bolted-on rear subframe. This model was once badged as a Saracen for a bike show but it never became a Saracen production model. It was raced by Murrell in the UK Downhill Championships and was not dissimilar in design to a few of the early full-suspension bikes offered years later by some of the big brands. **SW**

MOUNTAIN CYCLE San Andreas

1991 • Mountain bike • USA • Innovation-packed disc-braked monocoque full-suspension bike

Several mountain bikes could claim to be the first to smell of the future, but Mountain Cycle's San Andreas widened the nostrils most. It may even have been the first of what came to be called "all mountain" bikes, putting the focus back on bump-taming fun rather than just hammering along a trail.

Robert Reisinger, the founder of both Mountain Cycle and Pro Stop disc brakes, designed the one-size-fits-all 2½-in. (6-cm) travel elastomer-sprung aluminum chassis. The elastomer stack could be varied to suit rider weights and ride feel requirements and produce the desired shock feel. The top tube–seat angle could be changed completely with the adjustable seat-pod

> *"It's difficult to know where to start explaining the San Andreas; it's almost become a myth."*
>
> Mountaincycle.com

assembly. The monocoque build and rear suspension pivot placement were already forward-looking, but the disc brakes and Mountain Cycle's own "Suspenders" upside-down fork were way ahead of their time. The first fork offered about 2 in. (5 cm) of travel, impressive for the time, and a sturdy bolt-through-axle design also pointed to the future in terms of wheel tracking.

The San Andreas was the first production monocoque frame, and the subframe was a truly innovative feature that allowed the single-size mainframe to be adjusted to fit almost any rider. Mountain Cycle remains the only company to produce a complete line of monocoque frames, and was the first to have a bike included in a permanent collection of the San Francisco Museum of Modern Art. **SW**

Mountain Cycle's San Andreas was way ahead of its time. ▶

KLEIN Adroit

1991 • Mountain bike • USA • Radical integrated-steering outsized aluminum frame

Gary Klein built his first outsized aluminum-tube bike frame in 1972 as a student at the ultra-prestigious Massachusetts Institute of Technology, and in the process created chassis technology that would dominate the bicycle world for forty years.

It took Klein more than a decade to set up Klein Bikes and begin to produce this radical super-light model. The first "Mountain Klein" mountain bike, built in 1985, had distinctive square-section rear tubes, which avoided having to crimp round tubes to get them around the back wheel. Gear cables were routed inside the frame to keep lines neat, and the quality of the welding and paintwork was stellar.

In 1991 his outsized tubed frames reached perfection in the Adroit. The "fuselage," as Klein always

referred to frames, was centered around a 2-in. (5-cm) main tube made from 6061 T6 heat-treated aluminum, with patches of boron carbon fiber sheet added for reinforcement. Massive-diameter front forks, a one-piece welded stem and handlebar plugged into the outsized front end, and thrust-load taper bearings in the steering made the Adroit instantly recognizable. The bikes were finished in eye-threateningly bright multi-color airbrush-fade paint jobs, which even extended to color-matched bottle bolts and suspension forks (when they were fitted).

At just over 20 lb (9 kg) for a complete bike, and with a brutally stiff knockout punch under power, the Adroit was equally an in-your-face ride and a worthy flagship for this iconic brand. **GK**

CANNONDALE Delta V

1992 • Mountain bike • USA • Innovative mountain bike with unique internal head tube suspension

Much of the fascination with bike makers and their histories lies with those who deliberately decide to be different. A case in point is U.S. company Cannondale. Named after the railway station that stood opposite its first Pennsylvania headquarters, Cannondale was one of the first two companies to develop frames made from welded large-diameter aluminum tubes. These outsized tubes made one of its other long-lasting innovations possible too.

Having first appeared in 1989, suspension forks were still in their infancy in 1992, when leading brands like RockShox, Manitou, and Marzocchi had already established motorbike-style twin telescopic leg designs as their default design. But keeping the upper and lower tubes stiff enough to steer well, while able to

slide up and down smoothly, one inside the other, was an identified problem with the telescopic fork idea.

Enter the Cannondale Headshok, a radical design that put the suspension inside the head tube of the frame. This left the bottom of the fork as a completely rigid unit, but with the advantages of a low weight and superior stiffness. To stop the fork twisting around, the maker used a faceted shaft running on sheets of roller bearings at the top. Over time the Fatty suspension grew from a 2-in. (5-cm) stroke to a 3-in. (8-cm) one, which matched telescopic forks of the time. Space between fork and frame limited maximum travel, however, so Cannondale transferred the same technology into its equally radical one-side-only "Lefty" fork, which first appeared in 1999. **GK**

RALEIGH Activator

1992 • Mountain bike • UK • Early super-cheap suspension mountain bike

The Activator was the first mountain bike for generations of British cyclists. Designed and built by Raleigh, it was a budget machine thanks to its simple in-house suspension. Setting no new standards for quality or technology, the Nottingham-made bikes helped to popularize mountain biking in the United Kingdom.

The bike was Raleigh's bid to be taken more seriously by the mountain bike market. It came in two versions: the first had front suspension; the second also had rear springs. Both had grip-shift systems and basic cantilever brakes. Raleigh's sales slogan for the bikes was: "Activator—the suspense continues."

In reality, the Activators were very heavy machines by today's standards. The high-tensile steel frame was much more dense than modern chromoly steel,

making the bike not only awkward to handle but also difficult to progress uphill. The Raleigh-designed simple telescopic front forks certainly looked good, but they were only partially effective. Limited damping inside the forks made for a very bouncy ride, and their accompanying flexibility led to vague steering.

In 1993, the Activator II was launched, fitted with Raleigh's own basic rear suspension. The company selected a system that looked uncannily like the one it had manufactured for the small-wheeled Moulton Mk III, which, despite its undoubted virtues, is not everybody's immediate idea of a mountain bike. However, the Activator II's price point—at just $300 (£200)—definitely stood in its favor, making it a popular present for youngsters at the time. **SH**

MANTIS Pro Floater

1992 • Mountain bike • USA • Classic early suspension mountain bike

Not many bike designs were effectively killed by their own success. The Mantis Pro Floater full-suspension mountain bike, designed by long-time editor of *Mountain Bike Action* magazine Richard Cunningham, was one such two-wheeler.

With less than 3 in. (7.6 cm) of rear-wheel travel, the Pro Floater had just the right amount of chain growth to keep suspension bobbing to a minimum and still provide a smooth ride over the bumps. The front section was made of aluminum, as was the swingarm, while the compression strut (seatstay) was chromoly. There were no reliable shock-absorber makers available at the time, so Clark Jones, a friend of Cunningham at Noleen Racing, a motocross suspension business, developed a coil-spring shock for the bike.

The suspension arrangement was very lightweight, which proved a huge advantage. Cunningham was sure that rear suspension was going to replace the hardtail, but even his best friends laughed at that notion, so to hedge his bets he also made a new hardtail. A summer later he could count the times he had ridden it on the fingers of one hand, so he sold it.

The Pro Floater was far from perfect, but it was probably the first dual-suspension bike to break the hardtail barrier and gain widespread acceptance among elite riders. Unfortunately, sales instantly outstripped production and frustrated customers and dealers had to wait months for their bikes. Two years later, all the top brands fielded dual-suspension bikes, and, sadly, Mantis' roller-coaster ride was over. **GK**

GT RTS 1

1992 • Mountain bike • USA • Very successful
early suspension mountain bike

GT's first full-suspension bike was launched at a time when few trail riders were thinking about rear suspension. Most were just starting to get used to the idea of suspension forks, and saw rear suspension as something for hard and fast downhill riding only.

But the RTS 1 was never meant to be a downhill-biased bike; its unique suspension configuration was designed to attract ordinary cross-country trail riders. The high swingarm pivot produced very pronounced pedal feedback and should not really have worked, but the lower linkage attached to the shock in a way that meant hard pedaling actually almost locked the shock. As a result, a generation of riders still wary of bob-prone designs were drawn to the RTS "solution."

RTS stood for Rocker Tuned Suspension. A small rocker arm at the base of the shock unit connected the mainframe to the swingarm, so the shock was not a structural part of the frame, and there was no obvious flex between the mainframe and the swingarm. The tiny 2-in. (5.5-cm) amount of travel, and the fact that the bike felt rigid when climbing, attracted a lot of riders to the RTS. It spawned a whole family of budget models, making it one of the first full-suspension bikes intended for mass-market sales. **SW**

VERLICCHI DH

1992 • Mountain bike • Italy • World
Championship-winning mountain bike frame

When downhill racing became the trend in mountain biking in the early 1990s, many companies risked missing out because they lacked a full-suspension bike.

Italian motorsports fabricator Verlicchi had made a reputation building the premium S Bike models for Swatch. At the same time, Italian suspension maker Marzocchi was looking for a frame to showcase its new rear air shock and Star and XC suspension forks. The pair teamed up to produce a dedicated suspension frame. It ended up being a conventional-looking 7000-series aluminum mainframe with an extra diagonal tube across the bottom corner to carry the pivot for the monocoque swingarm, whose tip extended past the main pivot to squeeze the short-stroke air shock.

The frame, immediately adopted by the Iron Horse Brand as its "FS Works" model, achieved a real coup by winning the Downhill World Championship race under former BMX racer Dave Cullinan. Verlicchi immediately renamed the frame as the Bromont in reference to the Canadian location of the World Championships. The win also saw the frame adopted by Sintesi, Diamond Back, Mongoose, Rudy Project, Carraro (with a coil-sprung rear shock), and Haro (with a modified mainframe) as "their" full-suspension option. **GK**

YETI AS

1992 • Mountain bike • USA • Kamikaze race-winning full-suspension bike

The Kamikaze race is staged on the steep shale access road of Mammoth Mountain ski resort in California, and is as insane as it sounds. The Yeti bike brand once totally dominated the event, starting with its AS suspension bike and racer Jimmy Deaton, a pairing that achieved three back-to-back wins, in 1992, 1993, and 1994.

Like many early suspension bikes, the Yeti AS was a simple machine. Basic pivots behind the cranks and a small urethane rubber bumper at the top of the stays gave a measly 1½ in. (4 cm) of wheel movement on an otherwise conventional frame. This limited movement, and elastomer springs in the forks that tended to melt and disintegrate halfway down the hill, did not stop Deaton from fitting a monster 66-tooth chainring and charging down at more than 50 mph (80 kph).

The 1993 AS LT (Long Travel) extended the stays into the mainframe to give room for a Risse shock and double the wheel movement. It came at the price of softer rear-brake performance and more pedaling bounce. Deaton used the AS for the Kamikaze that year, but when in 1994 he fitted his monster chainring to the AS LT, he took his third win. Myles Rockwell and Missy Giove, in Yeti's distinctive turquoise-and-custard kit, have since taken over victory honors. **GK**

FUNK Pro-Comp

1992 • Mountain bike • USA • Alloy E-stay bike with square-section forks

Today Funk is a state-of-the-art custom titanium bike builder based in Colorado. Twenty years ago, however, Daryl Funk was producing this memorable bike oddity, which can still excite riders from that era.

The Pro-Comp is one of the most striking examples of the fashion for E-stay bikes. These off-roaders had elevated chainstays that did not head straight to the bottom bracket, as on conventional frames, but crossed the seat tube and joined the down tube about a third of the way up. E-stay bikes were claimed to offer better mud clearance and easier chain removal, and prevent "chain slap" against the stays after a riding over a bump. It also eliminated the problem of "chain suck," in which the chain snags on the chainring teeth when dirty or worn.

The Funk Pro-Comp had an outsized thin-walled Easton 6061 T-6 aluminum-tubing frame, was TIG welded, and came in bright neon color schemes with two brazed-on water-bottle mounts. As an optional extra the bike featured Funk's own chunky square-section fixed alloy fork and a titanium steerer. It weighed a comparatively hefty 29 lb (13.2 kg), but the weight varied, as it was almost always sold as a frameset for customers to build up themselves. **SH**

RALEIGH Banana

1992 • Road bike • UK • Famously fruity race replica bike

When it comes to cycling, Raleigh has been a household name in the United Kingdom for almost a century, with a network of local dealers always proudly displaying images of the current Raleigh-equipped professional racing team. Through the 1970s to the 1990s, Raleigh was headline sponsor of a succession of leading continental teams such as TI Raleigh, Creda, Panasonic, and Castorama. It also sponsored professional home teams such as Raleigh Weinmann, and the team that used the distinctive bike featured here: the Raleigh Banana.

The actual team bikes, in their distinctive banana-flavored color schemes, were hand built by some of the finest UK craftsmen in the Raleigh Special Products Division frame shop, using Reynolds 753, the premium lightweight tubeset of the time. The bikes were equipped with the latest Shimano Dura Ace equipment and lightweight hand-built wheels, with Italian Ambrosio rims and glued-on tubular race tires. Unsurprisingly for a team sponsored by the banana marketing board, the Selle Italia Turbo saddle was also bright yellow, as was the tape on the 3T handlebars.

The Banana race bikes, like many of the team bikes of that era, were mimicked and marketed as race replicas. Instead of just one model, however, Raleigh actually produced two Banana race replicas. The first was a Reynolds 531-framed machine of a decent quality; with Shimano 105 gears, no one could say it was not a good bike in its own right. However, the more common model was built from Raleigh's proprietary 18-23 steel tubing. With basic Huret gears, it was very much a look-alike bike, but that did not prevent it from being extremely popular. When Falcon took over sponsorship of the Banana team after Raleigh, it released a similar model. **GK**

LOTUS Type 108

1992 • Track bike • USA • British cycling legend born in a wind tunnel

In 1992 it was almost unheard of for teams of engineers and designers to meet in a wind tunnel with a bicycle prototype and try to determine the rider's optimum riding position. But that is what cyclist Chris Boardman, designer Mike Burrows, and the Lotus team did with Boardman's new time bike. Knowing that between 80 and 90 percent of a rider's energy is expended in the struggle to overcome wind resistance, they wanted to minimize drag as much as possible.

Burrows, himself an enthusiastic amateur cyclist, spent years trying to figure out how he could maximize his own speed. "Why does a frame," he once questioned, "need to be a collection of tubes; why not like a wing?"

"British Cycling has Lotus to thank for its current run of world-beating success."
Richard Aucock, MSN Cars

His frame, of a carbon fiber monocoque type, was really more like an aerofoil cross-section. It had a distinct winglike look, along with tri-spoke and disc wheels. Extended aero handlebars allowed Boardman to hunch forward with his arms stretched out in front.

Boardman rode Burrows' sci-fi Lotus at the 1992 Barcelona Olympic Games, winning the gold medal in the 4,000-m pursuit. A virtual unknown, unemployed, and with little money to his name, he was wracked with nerves before the race: "Even when I was sitting on the startline and I'd won the rounds previously, set the fastest times, done a world record in training, I never actually thought I was going to win it." In the end, only fifteen Type 108s were built, all timeless examples of how design can enhance performance. **BS**

The Lotus Type 108 screams pure performance. ⟩

KHS Montana Comp

1992 • Mountain bike • USA • Classic ultra-light steel mountain bike

Some bikes are perfect snapshots of a specific time in mountain bike development, snapshots "taken" just when one era was coming to an end and a new wave of innovation was about to come roaring in and wash away all previous benchmarks. The early 1990s were such a moment of "calm before the storm," just when fully rigid steel bikes were reaching their pinnacle of low-weight, cost-effective performance. There are few finer examples of this type of bike than KHS's Montana Comp. KHS (which stands for Knowledge, Health, and Strength) Bicycles is a joint U.S. and Taiwanese company related to the larger KHS Inc.

The Montana Comp layout was totally conventional, its horizontal crossbar and curved fork legs contrasting with the sloping top tubes and straight-leg forks of vogue brands like Kona. The pink-and-blue paintwork was right on trend, though, and the use of the latest True Temper AVR varying-wall-thickness steel in a TIG-welded (rather than lugged and brazed) format produced a remarkably light, well-sprung frame. A mixed selection of Shimano Deore DX and LX provided twenty-one gears through the latest Rapid Fire trigger shifters, and Deore LX cantilever brakes did the stopping.

Carefully chosen Kalloy, Zoom, and Bontrager kit with period favorite Panaracer Smoke and Dart tires completed a lightweight build—25 lb (11.3 kg)—at an affordable price. The Montana was a massive success, with multiple magazine test wins and sales to match.

But within a couple of years, aluminum alloy had replaced steel as the top material and suspension forks were becoming a must-have component. Threaded steering bearings with inserted stems were replaced by clamp-on Aheadset-style cockpits, and suddenly the Montana looked like it was from another era. **GK**

KIRK Magnesium

1992 • Road bike • UK • Unique cast-magnesium bike

Engineer Frank Kirk was inspired to make cast-magnesium bikes while working for the Ford car company on new fender moldings for a Ford Sierra. He knew magnesium alloy to be among the lightest metals, and although it is less rigid than steel, it is also cheap and environmentally friendly—a cubic meter (35 cu ft) of seawater contains enough magnesium to make a bike frame. Kirk showed his first prototypes at international bike shows in 1986.

The frame was made by blasting molten magnesium alloy into a mold under 1,000 tons of pressure. The process reportedly took only eight seconds, but there were teething problems. At

> "The computer could predict just what we could afford to change, and what we couldn't."
>
> Frank Kirk, engineer

first the bike was only available in white and in one size—22 in. (56 cm). Kirk claimed the magnesium frame would accommodate riders between 5 ft. 5in. (1.5 m) and 6 ft. 2in. (1.8 m), thanks to adjustable steel seatposts and handlebar stems. He publicly demonstrated the frame's strength by driving his Mercedes over them.

But problems continued. Kirk teamed up with Norsk Hydro, a big Norwegian power company, robot production lines were launched, and marketing was handed to Dawes Cycles. A range of bikes evolved and there were even seven colors available. But the partnership with Norsk Hydro was not happy. After repeated reliability problems, Kirk's big backers pulled out and the bikes disappeared from sale. Even so, they remain a fine example of material innovation. **SH**

BOTTECCHIA Equipe

1992 • Road bike • Italy • High-end steel race bike

The Bottecchia Equipe was a steel race bike used by Greg LeMond, American three-time winner of the Tour de France, and his Belgian ADR team, and it featured in the Italian brand's range for several years.

The Bottecchia company was founded in Cavarzere, near Venice, in 1926 by Ottavio Bottecchia, a rider who had won the Tour de France himself in both 1924 and 1925 and the first Italian ever to win the race. Bottecchia died shortly afterward, but his business partner, Theodor Carnielli, continued to grow the brand.

The Bottecchia Equipe, like nearly all bikes of its era, was made from steel, double-butted to bring the weight down while maintaining strength, and

"[He had] skin like an old saddle, wrinkles . . . like scars, and the awkwardness of a peasant."

Contemporary description of Ottavio Bottecchia

reinforced to provide the stiffness that professional racers require when riding hard. The bike featured curvy chrome lugs, down-tube shifters, and an elaborate Bottecchia "B" on the fork crown. The fork, seatstays, and chainstays were chrome, too.

Like most of the high-end Italian bikes of this era, the Equipe had Campagnolo components, including the Delta brakes, which were produced for several years from 1985. These were some of the most distinctive ever made, with a clever linkage system hidden away underneath an aerodynamic cover. Deltas were not light, they did not work especially well, and they were difficult to adjust, but they were certainly beautiful to look at. They are regarded as classic today, and remain of great interest to vintage bike enthusiasts. **MB**

PACE DPD

1992 • Mountain bike • UK • Downhill bike that was a long way ahead of its time

Duncan Macdonald and Adrian Carter are the English engineering duo who produced the iconic square-tubed Pace RC100 hardtail in the late 1990s. But in summer 1992 another of their machines, the forward-looking Duncan's Purple Descender, or DPD, hit the downhill race slopes. Named for Macdonald, its designer and rider, and the vivid purple anodized paint on the square-tubed frameset, the DPD was an awe-inspiring machine that introduced many features years before they would appear on mass-produced bikes.

Starting from the front, the lower legs of the Pace suspension forks were wrapped in carbon fiber for lightweight strength. The legs were extended upward through two clamps in a motorbike style for extra stiffness. The handlebar was then bolted directly on top, another standard feature on motorbikes but a totally new idea on a mountain bike.

The long, low cross-braced frame had a separate bolt-on seatmast and an asymmetric swingarm with a raised-drive side strut to clear the chainset. A tiny air shock controlled rear-wheel movement around a low forward-position pivot, which gave a great balance of smoothness and positive pedaling. From the outset, the DPD was designed to use Pro Stop hydraulic caliper disc brakes controlled by conventional cable pulling levers, even before the standard style of disc-brake mount had been decided upon. The wheels themselves were bolted in place as they are on a modern downhill bike, rather than secured by standard quick-release attachments.

While the entire bike was way ahead of its time, only one DPD was ever produced. Pace spent several frustrating and ultimately unsuccessful years trying to perfect various versions of the RC500 suspension bike before Macdonald left the company. **GK**

Duncan from Pace races his eponymous Purple Descender. ▶

CHAS ROBERTS Dogsbolx

1993 • Mountain bike • UK • Premium steel mountain-bike frame

It was an outrageous name for an outrageous frameset. The Chas Roberts Dogsbolx was a steel hardtail mountain bike with distinctive rear-tapered horseshoe seatstays and a frame geometry targeted at serious all-terrain bikers. Before the Dogsbolx, the Roberts company was creating more conventional handmade custom bikes and frames one at a time in its workshop in Surrey, England. The bike range included road, track, time trial, audax, touring, commuting, mountain, tandems, and folding bikes. These carried more restrained names like "Clubman" or "Road Classic."

The new machine's name turned heads before people had even seen the bike. Roberts was not alone in using attention-grabbing names: Dave Yates had produced the Donkisknob, and Kona the Sex range.

The Dogsbolx may have adopted new standards in branding, but the detailed spec reveals how much attention to detail went into the design of the frameset. It was a composite of specially selected tubing: The top tube was Reynolds 753, the down tube was custom oval Dedacci, and the seat tube and chainstays were various grades of Columbus tubing. The seatstays were different again, Reynolds 725, while the rear horseshoe was Roberts' own chromoly. **SH**

RALEIGH Torus

1993 • Mountain bike • UK • Innovative titanium hardtail with X-Lite Trimnell fork

The Raleigh Torus owes much to former motorbike racer Rex Trimnell, who founded X-Lite in 1991. His ultra-lightweight bar ends were an instant success, so production moved from the Trimnell family garage into a purpose-built unit in 1993. There Trimnell developed his best-known innovation, a unique twin-crown fork—first in aluminum, then in titanium. It was a rigid twin-leg design with integrated Ti bars and stem.

Raleigh saw the potential of Trimnell's creations and its pro racers, such as Barry Clarke and David Baker, were soon using X-Lite Ti frames and, on smoother courses, the rigid fork. Trimnell licensed the rights to his forks to Raleigh's Special Products Division, which led to the release of the Raleigh Dyna-Tech Torus (Dyna-Tech was a short-lived high-tech branding from Raleigh).

The Torus boasted a "plasma arc-welded titanium frame and direct control fork." It was a rare top-end machine with a bonded titanium frame, very light, but with the smooth, controlled ride of a heavier steel bike. The brakes and gears were all Shimano; the bar and bar ends were X-Lite, of course. But the headline attraction was the direct-control fork with its sophisticated Timken roller-bearing headset. At first this fork was impossible to buy as a stand-alone component. **SH**

AMP RESEARCH B2

1993 • Mountain bike • USA • Introducer of the most widely used mountain bike suspension system

BIGFOOT E-Stay

1993 • Mountain bike • UK • Specialist mud-friendly UK mountain bike

The mountain bike frame and fork division of AMP Research emerged from a company, ATK Motorcycles, begun by Austria-born motorcycle racer and suspension designer Horst Leitner. In the early 1990s, Leitner turned his attention to developing a mountain bike chassis. The resulting AMP Research B series bikes were characterized by their unique Mert Lawwill design, which articulated four-bar linkage forks and what became known as a Horst Link chainstay pivot at the rear wheel drop-outs. Early AMP Research offerings, notably the B2 in 1993, were nimble trail bikes, which was unusual because most of the early full-suspension bikes were aimed at downhillers.

Licensing rights for the Horst Link four-bar linkage design were acquired by Specialized very shortly after the original AMP Research models were launched, and a few other companies paid sub-licensing fees to use the Horst Link setup, which remains popular. But the early complete AMP Research frames and forks tend to be remembered by riders for negative reasons. Their low-weight build inevitably involved compromises in durability, especially in the pivot bushings. AMP Research has continued to supply spare parts for those early frames, which are now collectibles. **SW**

The Bigfoot E-Stay was an aluminum elevated-chainstay bike developed by Graham Foot, who ran a bike store in Gloucestershire, England. Its massive mud clearance was a big selling point, and the short chainstay helped considerably on climbs.

Unfortunately, the Bigfoot logo did not last for long after Muddy Fox claimed rights to the name. (Muddy Fox already had a Bigfoot in its range, with a fairly similar paw-print logo.) Instead, Bigfoot re-emerged as Ozone, with designs mirrored by offshoot company Smokestone, named for an earlier Bigfoot model.

Bigfoot frames changed little over their production period, staying true to the original concept with fat 6061 heat-treated aluminum tubes and (usually) 1¼-in. (3-cm) Evolution headsets. The outsized down tubes resisted bottom-bracket flex far better than many other elevated-chainstay frames, and the flat plated drop-outs were replaceable on both sides.

Foot says that Bigfoot made about 200 frames over the course of a few years. Foot himself went on to other things, but there is still a lot of enthusiasm for raised chainstay frames, and they make a lot more sense now that new frame-building techniques can prevent the bottom-bracket area from flexing. **SW**

BOULDER Defiant

1993 • Mountain bike • USA • Innovative mountain bike with concealed shock absorber

The story of Boulder Bicycles' mountain bikes started in 1989 with the Rogg, a design that had either a flex stem or no suspension at all up front, and a shock built into the end of the top tube out back. The movement of the whole rear triangle could be locked out with a thumb shifter on the handlebar.

Two years later, Boulder launched a bike called the Gazelle, built on the same basic principle as the Rogg but this time with the all-new RockShox fork up front and a smaller raised-chainstay rear triangle. Crafted in the United States, this 26½-lb (12-kg) bike was probably the lightest and the best of the early full-suspension mountain bikes. Then Boulder's Richard Williams built a 52-in. (132-cm) long-wheelbase version of the Gazelle with zero stem reach for the Kamikaze downhill race.

In 1993, Boulder produced an updated all-rounder called the Defiant, with a choice of a 5¾-lb (2.6-kg) steel frame or a 4½-lb (2-kg) titanium frame. By then, suspension forks were getting better and the Defiant's integral top-tube shock offered up to 3 in. (7.6 cm) of rear-wheel travel. But arguably an even better frame was the Starship, and especially the titanium Starship. This had a standard chainstay configuration rather than the slightly more flexible raised chainstay swingarm, and there were versions fitted with the highly regarded Risse air shock, with a choice of 3, 4, or 5 in. (7.6, 10, or 12.7 cm) of suspension travel. The 4-in. version became the classic bike to own, although the most collectible bike from Boulder may well be its short-travel titanium Paris–Roubaix suspension road bike. **SW**

DAVE YATES Diablo

1993 • Mountain bike • UK • Classically built UK steel mountain bike

In 1993, the Dave Yates Diablo was one of the last flags flying at the end of the story of UK-built steel bikes, and its history is revealing in terms of the whole global industry. Dave Yates started to build touring frames for M Steel Cycles in Newcastle, England, in 1976, at exactly the same time as Trek Bikes started building touring frames in a barn in Wisconsin. Yates said, "We even had the same number of people working for us, although our workshop was actually bigger than their barn." Like Trek, Yates was not shy to innovate, producing some of the first UK mountain bikes, as well as elevated-stay designs and dedicated disc-brake specials.

Yates' live frame-building displays came to be a regular star turn at bike shows, but homegrown, hand-filed, and fillet-brazed bikes were increasingly coming

under threat as East Asian bike factories got into their stride supplying companies like Specialized and Trek with efficiently produced TIG-welded frames.

The Diablo was born as a direct result of this competition, offering buyers an off-the-shelf rather than custom-shaped frame, using an affordable Nivacrom tubeset from Italian steel maker Columbus. But as much as riders loved its solid strength and honest character, East Asian products inevitably swamped the market, with Trek becoming a huge brand on the back of Taiwanese technology.

Yates has stuck proudly to his hand filing and brass brazing, and if you can find him in his rural Lincolnshire workshop he will build you a totally modern Diablo, or even teach you to build it yourself. **GK**

RALEIGH Tomac

1993 • Mountain bike • USA • Cutting-edge race machine for legendary all-round mountain bike athlete

"Like the boat Columbus sailed on . . . Tomac's Raleigh will find its place in history."

Mountain Bike Action, *February 1992*

Nobody typified the explosive impact of mountain biking as a leading force in the growing "extreme sport" world more than U.S. racer John Tomac. Competing in both cross-country and downhill events, Tomac dominated both disciplines with his distinctively aggressive "attack" style and continuous experimental use of cutting-edge prototype componentry.

His forceful image and race record turned him into a marketing executive's dream, and having raced for Yeti cycles he transferred to Raleigh in 1992. The frame that Raleigh provided was a truly experimental machine that had carbon fiber main tubes set into a titanium rear end and head tube section.

The first bikes that Tomac raced on were built by Merlin cycles and had innovative features such as press-fit bottom brackets, but none of these were available to the public. It was in the following year that production was handed over to Litespeed, which was commissioned to create sixty limited-edition bikes. These were of a very similar semi-carbon design but with a conventional screw-in bottom bracket and signature features such as twin-hole drop-outs. The Litespeed frames were given a bead-blasted finish rather than the satin finish of the Merlin bikes, which makes them instantly recognizable to collectors.

Raleigh's headline sponsorship was backed up by leading mountain bike brand Tioga, which supplied bars, stem, bar ends, headset, and its distinctive Kevlar-strung Disk Drive Geodisc Webbing rear wheel. Tomac's Tioga race setup also included a Japanese suspension fork and signature Farmer John or Farmer John's Nephew tires.

After retiring from racing, Tomac ran his own bike brand for a while. He retains a range of signature tires, now made by Kenda rather than Tioga. He remains an iconic figure and an outstanding rider to this day. **GK**

Tomac's semi-composite Raleigh also used a semi-composite wheel. ⊡

TURNER Burner

1993 • Mountain bike • USA • Early full-suspension bike

Suspension fork and bike shock designs were in their infancy when the Burner first appeared, but Dave Turner's classic was so right that it became the first true do-it-all suspension bike. Whether on a weeknight muck-about downhill race or a cross-country event on a Saturday or Sunday afternoon, this neatly compact design, with its widely imitated rocker linkage-driven shock, was more than a match for anything else that was available at the time.

Turner had conceived and refined his designs while simultaneously pursuing a pro racing career and working for suspension guru Horst Leitner. This varied background gave him the expertise required to develop a top-performance bike that was still totally practical for everyday tasks.

While many other bikes of the period were fragile prima donnas, the Burner was a proper workhorse from the start. Grease injection ports were even built into the main pivots for easy maintenance—a feature that Turner's bikes retain to this day. The original Horst Leitner suspension design was modified with a horizontal rocker linkage driving a vertical shock to create what became—and remains—a classic outline for full-suspension bikes. The design was highly versatile too: The basic Burner model was easy to adapt into the longer-stroke, reinforced-frame Burner DH, which became one of the most rebadged and copied gravity racers of the mid-1990s.

The Burner also consolidated Dave Turner's reputation as the most fastidious designer around, a man who sweats all the weld and tube details himself and personally tests even the smallest proposed geometric modifications before allowing them to be incorporated into his bikes. The latest 650B Burner incarnation still smokes with hand-built attention to detail, and few bikes have a comparable claim to true classic status. **GK**

"The Turner Burner is a faster, smoother, trail-inspired machine ready to take your riding to the next level."

Turner Bicycles advertisement, 2013

⊲ Turner's Burner introduced a classic design.

VENTANA Marble Peak

1993 • Mountain bike • USA • Classic full-suspension mountain bike

While many mountain bike pioneers such as Gary Fisher, Tom Ritchey, and Dave Turner have gone on to become celebrities in the dirt world, Ventana founder Sherwood Gibson has always deliberately kept a low profile. But anyone who has ridden one of his quietly innovative bikes, such as the Marble Peak of 1993, is likely to have become a lifelong fan of his work.

Gibson's interest in building bikes began when he was a high school BMX racer in 1974. He produced component parts for friends and racers while he qualified in mechanical engineering. He remained involved in the rapidly growing mountain bike race scene, and finally produced his first steel frame in 1985. He set up Ventana in 1990, and the first Ventana-badged product was an alloy race frame named the Cone Peak. Ever since, Gibson has stuck with aluminum tubing, along the way refining the flawless "Electric Sex" welds for which he has become legendary.

The classic lines of the Marble Peak took Ventana to the forefront of suspension design in the early 1990s, and bikes like the 9-in. (23-cm) travel El Cuervo of 2010 and the El Ciclón of 2012 have kept it there ever since. And, unlike many of his contemporaries who now have their frames built overseas, Gibson has stayed totally true to his roots. He still hand builds his frames in limited numbers in the coastal region of northern California and custom paints them in myriad colors. He is a true artisan who totally deserves the unparalleled reputation he has built up over the past quarter-century of quiet innovation. **GK**

FOES LTS

1993 • Mountain bike • USA • Radical long-travel, hardcore mountain bike

While Fox Racing Shocks are now leaders in mountain bike suspension, the manufacturer wasn't the first motor sport company to make an impact by controlling impacts. Brent Foes was already a successful designer of off-road racing trucks for Ford and Nissan when he turned his attention to mountain bike design. He immediately saw that the one or two inches (2.5–5 cm) of movement in early suspension bikes was of little use, and that mountain bike frames would be well suited to the advanced monocoque structure techniques that he was using in his race truck chassis.

After a year of prototyping, Foes unveiled the groundbreaking LTS design at the Interbike trade show in 1993. With a full 6 in. (15 cm) of rear wheel movement, the LTS had well over double the suspension stroke of contemporary brands. The mainframe was a pressed-aluminum welded seam monocoque that created a stiff and strong, yet relatively light, structure. Knowing that bearing quality and the stiffness of the suspension struts were crucial to the smooth operation of the system, Foes also gave the LTS a robust swingarm at a time when most rear ends looked like angle-poise lamps. He also gave the bike full triple-chainring compatibility for climbing, thus creating the original all-mountain bike years before competitors caught up.

The puny suspension forks of the time meant that the Fab—so called for its stickers bearing the legend "Foes Fab" (short for "fabrications")—did not fulfill its potential until the arrival in 1995 of the equally revolutionary Foes F1 fork. **GK**

PINARELLO Banesto
1993 • Race bike • Italy • Double Grand Tour-winning bike of Miguel Indurain

Giovanni Pinarello began racing bicycles in 1939 at the age of seventeen. In 1947, after winning more than sixty amateur titles, he turned professional and went on to win five further titles. In 1952, his sponsor, Bottechia, told him he had to stand down from the Giro d'Italia in favor of up-and-coming Pasqualino Fornara. Crestfallen, but with a big payoff from Bottechia to ease his pain, Pinarello turned his attention to building bikes himself.

It would be another five years before the first Pinarello bicycle appeared in national competition, but thereafter the company became involved in a number of great sponsorships, beginning in 1960 with Mainetti. Then came Jolly Ceramica, and, in the 1980s, Banesto and the great Spanish champion Miguel Indurain.

Indurain and Banesto helped Pinarello to five Tour de France wins, two Giro d'Italia victories, world time trial championships, an Hour Record, and Olympic gold.

The 1993 Pinarello Banesto team bike was the first machine with TIG-welded Oria steel tubing to win both the Giro d'Italia and the Tour de France. Pinarello later recalled: "We lowered the top tube by 2 cm [¾ in.] to make the triangle more compact and rigid. Indurain never changed his position in the fifteen years he raced on Pinarello bicycles."

Indurain's bike also sported Spinaci aero handlebars, a pointed head tube, and aluminum aero rims for drag-reducing efficiency. Two years later, Pinarello won both Tour and Giro again with the first-ever aluminum TIG-welded bike. **BS**

SEROTTA T-Max

1993 • Mountain bike • USA • Aspirational mountain bike with Italian steel tubing

As mass-produced Asian mountain bikes increasingly dominated the market in the early 1990s, only a few products stood out as beacons for the continued relevance of handmade steel frames. Serotta's T-Max was one of them.

The T-Max was built from outsized Italian Columbus Max OR tubing with variously shaped cross-sections and tapers to increase strength and stiffness in high-load areas without adding weight. Rather than using junction lugs to join the tubes together, Max OR was brazed together in a smooth "lugless" construction everywhere except on the seat cluster.

Although TIG welding was also used by Taiwanese manufacturers, the T-Max was much more than a steel reflection of alloy fashion. Buyers of these highly desirable Colorado-made machines could choose between a suspension fork and Serotta's own beautifully made unicrown fork. Tapered and ovalized tubes gave the bike an immediately distinctive look, which was further emphasized by the application of the sunburst fade paint jobs that were popular at the time. The most dramatically shaped tubes were the tapered rear chainstays, which ensured that all the power went straight to the rear wheel, and thus helped Serotta to compete with lighter, stiffer alloy options.

The result was a classic bike that has not only stood the test of time, but also carried Serotta through periods of economic recession. The company still produces low-volume, ultra-high-quality steel and titanium bikes for discerning riders. **GK**

LOOK KG196

1993 • Road race bike • France • Epoch-making monocoque carbon fiber–Kevlar frame

Look—the company that gave the world the clipless pedal—created a revolutionary bike with the KG196. While carbon fiber technologies had been toyed with in bicycle design since the 1970s, the KG196 had one of the first mold-formed monocoque—rather than tube and lug-built—frames. At 20 lb (9 kg), it was not the lightest bike of its day, but the continuous fiber strands made the frame stiff and strong. The carbon fiber and Kevlar construction was also exploited to create one of the first aerodynamically enhanced road race bikes.

The wind-cheating features started with a unique bayonet-style fork, in which the main structural section extended up in front of the mainframe, while a thinner

". . . remains very rigid so that all the cyclist's efforts are transmitted directly to the road."

Look KG196 manual

steerer tube slipped inside the head tube. The tops of both tubes were then joined with a specially designed stem top piece. The bar was held by an adjustable articulated stem that looked unorthodox, but enabled the rider to achieve ideal height and reach positions without having to change the componentry.

The tube sections were teardrop profiled for minimum drag, and the seat tube curved back over the rear wheel in an extended fin before the seatpost junction. The down tube extended below the crank bracket to shroud the rear wheel, and the rear brake cable was hidden inside the top tube.

When Swiss road racer Alex Zulle and his Spanish ONCE team rode KG196s, they used Mavic's 841 gear and brake groupset and Cosmic wheels. **BS**

BIRDY Speedy

1993 • Folding bike • Germany • Super-light high-performance foldable

Folding bikes have generally had to compromise performance to shrink down to a suitably unobtrusive pack size. The Birdy Speedy from prodigious innovators Markus Riese and Heiko Müller of Darmstadt, Germany, proved that a folding bike could be every bit as light and nippy as a conventional bike, and yet fold up small enough to tuck under an arm.

A compact aluminum-beam mainframe and 18-in. (46-cm) wheels make the complete Birdy weigh only 24 lb (10.8 kg). For folding, the bike uses a "tuck-under" rear swingarm design to keep the chain under tension but unable to put oily marks on the folder's clothes.

The real genius of the bike is in its fork, which uses a leading link design with urethane rubber block "anti-dive" suspension. This then simply unhooks and folds back under the frame to lie alongside the folded rear wheel. The telescopic seatpost slides down into the frame, while the hinged handlebars flip down to lie alongside the wheels. Various bags and airline regulation suitcases are available to make the machine portable and stowable in cabin.

A range of gears and specification levels, including hub gear, road race derailleur, disc brakes, and rack and luggage options, are now available. Riese and Müller even produce a titanium-framed version, primarily for the Japanese and Australian markets. The complexity of the frame and suspension makes even the most basic models more expensive than other folding machines, but their acceleration and smooth, suspended speed are still a benchmark for high performance.

The Birdy first flew in 1993 at two German trade shows, Intercycle in Cologne and Eurobike in Friedrichshafen. It was so well received that Riese and Müller put it into production for a full international launch in 1995. **GK**

ⓒ Look's KG196 was loaded with innovations.

TREK OCLV

1993 • Mountain bike • USA • The first mass-produced mainstream brand all-carbon mountain bike

While U.S. West Coast carbon frame pioneer Kestrel developed its first carbon frames about four years earlier, Trek was the first mainstream big-production firm to commit to them. Impressively, it invested about $1 million (£670,000) in OCLV (Optimum Compaction Low Void) in-house carbon molds rather than taking the superficially easier route of outsourcing its carbon molding elsewhere. Trek's earlier carbon mountain bike frames, from 1990, had mimicked their bonded aluminum-tubed frames, with carbon tubes glued into aluminum lugs. The bikes felt good to ride but seemed to offer no major advantages in terms of weight saving or strength. The bonding failed on many of those early offerings too, but Trek continued to make and improve them alongside the development of the OCLV bikes.

The OCLVs, made from high pressure–formed carbon sheets sealed in resin, effectively took carbon composite science into stores and onto the roads and trails as competitively priced, very light, and surprisingly tough frames. They were constructed as separate tubes and "lugs" rather than as "monocoques," and became instantly popular on the race scene because of their low weight and smooth ride feel. The medium-sized mountain bike frame was 1 lb (0.5 kg) or so lighter than almost any aluminum frame at the time.

Meanwhile, suspension forks were flooding the market, and this trail-softening effect allowed Trek and others to go lighter than ever in their carbon frame designs. In 1995 the revolutionary Trek OCLV "Y frame" full-suspension bike joined the OCLV range. **SW**

KOGA Miyata Elevation 12000
1993 • Downhill bike • Netherlands • Greg Herbold's NORBA Championship-winning bike

This is the bike on which Greg Herbold won the 1993 NORBA Downhill National Championship.

It had a front triangle built of carbon tubing that was APA-bonded to aluminum lugs at either end. The rear triangle was fashioned from chromoly steel, and a simple Swinglink, attached at the end of the top tube below the seat clamp, connected the two triangles. The suspension was simple at best and offered only 2 in. (5 cm) of rear-wheel travel. The shock itself was designed and supplied by Yamaha, and consisted of a spring and an oil cartridge for damping. The only aspect that had potential for adjustment was the tension of the spring, which was controlled by two rings on the shock body.

Herbold's bike was fitted with hydraulic rim brakes and a full-disc rear wheel for speed, and was covered in various anodized purple, blue, and red parts. Herbold attacked each course at speeds no one else was willing to attempt. He won the first-ever dual slalom race at Mammoth Mountain in 1987, and although he was accused of cutting the course to win the very first International Cycling Union World Downhill Championship in Durango, Colorado, in 1990, he went on to become the NORBA National Downhill Champion three times, and gain over twenty-five victories in his ten-year racing career.

The Koga Miyata Elevation 12000 was a long way ahead of its time in its use of carbon fiber for a downhill bike. In fact, it took the mountain bike industry more than fifteen years to use carbon routinely in the manufacture of mainstream downhill bikes. **CJ**

SANTA CRUZ Tazmon

1994 • Mountain bike • USA • The first Santa Cruz full-suspension mountain bike

Santa Cruz Bicycles was founded in 1994 in Santa Cruz, California, by pro skater Rob Roskopp, who happily admits to being mentored by Richard Novak of Santa Cruz Skateboards. The company's first bike was the Tazmon. Not many companies at that time started with a full-suspension bike, and Santa Cruz has continued to set trends ever since.

The Tazmon had a simple single-pivot aluminum girder swingarm to give 3 in. (8 cm) of suspension travel. Along with Pro Flex, this first Santa Cruz bike proved that a well-made single-pivot suspension frame was hard to beat in terms of weight and all-round ride efficiency. Majority opinion seems happy with the idea that Santa Cruz was the first to put the swingarm pivot in a position that appeared to achieve a nearly perfect compromise of pedal efficiency and shock absorption. While pedal pressure tries to extend the shock slightly, and therefore prevents the shock from being fully active during hard pedaling, this results in a taut ride feel that pleases a lot of competitively inclined trail riders. Using a pivot is still the most straightforward way to fit a frame with rear suspension.

Unsurprisingly, other manufacturers soon began to mimic the Tazmon, which a year later was redesigned with another inch (2.5 cm) of suspension travel to become the first of the better-known Heckler family. A full twenty years later, Santa Cruz was offering an evolved version of the Heckler in the 27½-in. (70-cm) wheel size. The simple beauty of a single-pivot swingarm with a middle chainring-centered pivot position remains. So, too, does Santa Cruz's *raison d'être*: in a 2011 interview in *BikeRadar*, company founder Rob Roskopp spoke passionately of his strength of motivation. "Who wants to turn out junk?" he demanded to know, then added: "We make bikes we want to ride!" **SW**

"Our first bike. It was solid and dependable, and performed better than almost anything at the time. It put us on the map!"

Rob Roskopp, Santa Cruz Bikes

Santa Cruz still uses this classic swingarm design. ▶

EDDY MERCKX Motorola

1994 • Race bike • Belgium • Top-end steel-framed competition bike

Belgian rider Eddy Merckx is one of cycling's all-time greats, with a unique record of race wins, including five Tours de France victories, five Giro d'Italias, and three World Championships. He owed part of his success to obsessive bike maintenance, famously often stopping mid-race to make minuscule adjustments to his seatpost before going on to win.

After retiring in 1978, Merckx set up his own bike-building business with the aid of the Italian Ugo de Rosa, who had built many of Merckx's winning racing bikes. In 1980, de Rosa helped Merckx set up the new factory in a former stables in Belgium. Merckx, living in the farmhouse next door, called on some old friends from the Molteni race team to work there.

Merckx's bike business was as successful as his race career had been, and the bikes that his company has created are now among the ranks of the world's most prestigious and sought-after machines.

Within a few years of starting, Merckx was turning out bikes for the world's top professionals, and between 1991 and 1994 his company sponsored the successful American Motorola (formerly 7 Eleven) team. The riders' red, white, and blue Merckx Motorola bikes have since become classics of their era. They were steel framed, made from Italian Columbus tubing, with Shimano Dura Ace or Campagnolo groupsets. The young Lance Armstrong won his first Tour de France stage on an Eddy Merckx Motorola. **SH**

DE ROSA Titanio

1994 • Road bike • Italy • All-conquering titanium race bike

The De Rosa Titanio—made, as the name suggests, from titanium—was one of the most successful bikes in professional cycling in the mid-1990s, and it still retains a place in the Italian brand's range to this day.

Ugo de Rosa had been building bike frames in Milan since 1953, but it was not until 1990 that he began to investigate and develop titanium tubing to make high-end frames. Titanium has much to recommend it as a material for building bikes, and even more so in the years before carbon fiber became a viable alternative. Light and extremely hard-wearing, titanium can be built into framesets with very high strength-to-weight ratios. Indeed, titanium hit the height of its desirability during the 1990s, becoming the frame material of choice for many discerning riders.

De Rosa spent more than three years working with titanium before delivering the Titanio in 1994. The frame had slim tubes and a short head tube to put the rider into a low, aerodynamic riding position. Distinctive De Rosa graphics made the bike easily recognizable and it became an instant classic.

The Gewiss-Ballan professional team achieved extraordinary results on the Titanio in 1994. Italian Giorgio Furlan scorched to victory in the Milan–San Remo classic, for example, and Russian Evgeni Berzin won both Liège–Bastogne–Liège and the Giro d'Italia. In all, Gewiss-Ballan gained a total of more than forty victories that year. Although the team became associated with doping, its huge success helped to cement the place of the Titanio in cycling history. **MB**

COLNAGO C42 Pista prototype

1994 • Road bike • Italy • Rarely used bike designed to tackle the Hour Record

For Ernesto Colnago, bike design is not just about formulaic geometry or weight reduction; it is an elegant synergy of rider and bike. The curved and sleek frameset of the C42 Pista prototype set the bike apart as a unique piece of machinery.

Colnago built the frame to enable Tony Rominger to attempt the Hour Record in 1995. Much like the Pinarello Sword, used by Miguel Indurain to set the record in 1994, the C42 Pista prototype was an all-carbon monocoque frame with a Colnago-built monocoque handlebar setup. The rear end of the frame extended over the back wheel to improve aerodynamics, and the seat tube also hugged the curve of the rear wheel. The dimpled disc wheels predated the airflow boundary layer innovations of manufacturers like Zipp by several years, while Rominger's choice of a 61-tooth chainset was a bold move, even for an Hour Record attempt.

In the end, Rominger never used the bike—the International Cycling Union's clampdown on design was partly to blame for that—but in 1995 Abraham Olano used a road version. Part of the C42 Pista's charm is that it was never used as much as it should have been, and it remains an intriguing example of cycling art. **DB**

CERVÉLO Baracchi

1994 • Aero bike • Canada • Insane-looking aero bike that started a cycling superpower

Few people who saw the freakish green Cervélo Baracchi in a tiny one-bike booth at the 1994 Milan trade show realized that they were witnessing the birth of what was to become a biking superpower.

Phil White and Gerard Vroomen were already working on radical bicycle and human-powered vehicle designs when Italian double world champion Gianni Bugno got in touch with a request for the fastest-possible aero machine. The pair went back to first principles, abandoning all conventional aesthetics and double-diamond frame precedents to produce a truly unique machine. Not content with bolting a stem and bar on top of the forks, Cervélo made a totally integrated front end that joined the distinctive straight-legged front forks to what normally would be the tri bar. In this case it was a forward-projecting prow complete with molded armrests and a deep, flat-sided extension block that made the Baracchi look like some kind of freakish lime-green riding rhino.

Because the Baracchi turned out to be at odds with UCI regulations, the bike was never raced by Bugno or anyone else. But it put Cervélo on the cycling map, and twenty years later, its direct descendant the P5 is still one of the fastest, most radical aero bikes available. **GK**

SPECIALIZED S-Works FSR

1994 • Mountain bike • USA • Early high-performance mass-market full-suspension bike

When Californian mass-market pioneer Specialized launched its original S-Works FSR full-suspension bike in 1994, it was described as "fully active, fully independent, fully intense." Almost instantly, Specialized team riders were winning major races on it. Jason McRoy won the UK downhill championships, and "Insane" Wayne Croasdale flew the flag in the United States.

The S-Works was the top model in a new family of full-suspension bikes carrying the FSR tag. FSR, slightly confusingly, stood for "Future Shock Rear." These were the first of the big-name full-suspension bikes to appeal to the retail consumer market rather than just downhill racers, with the main hype centering on the chainstay-mounted Horst-Link design of the rear suspension configuration.

While a lot of riders used the bike to bomb flat-out downhill, the bike's efficient cross-country riding credentials set it apart from a lot of earlier downhill-biased bikes. Numerous imitations of the bike seduced many into thinking that a vertical-axle-path Horst-Link bike was the only possibility, and at the time it was certainly hard to beat. Today, with many equally desirable bikes offering lightweight all-round performance, the S-Works FSR holds its place as one of the most aspirational bike families around.

Heeding its company mantra, "Innovate or die," Specialized has introduced whole new orthopedic-ergonomic concepts for saddles and shoes with its Body Geometry range, as well as pioneering the idea of single-brand "concept" stores in the bike industry. **SW**

GT Timberline

1994 • Mountain bike • USA • Classic affordable triple-triangle-frame steel mountain bike

In the early 1990s, Californian BMX bike maker GT was trying to shift its focus into the burgeoning new mountain bike market. Knowing the importance of brand identity, it made sure to carry its trademark triple-triangle frame over onto the new off-road format.

What GT described as "triple-triangle technology" referred to the main triangle of the frame, the rear triangle of stays, and a frame geometry in which the seatstays crossed the seat tube and joined the top tube to create a small triangular shape beneath the seat. Reviewers at *MBUK* magazine were skeptical, saying: "It's more visual trademark than ride-enhancing engineering, but few bikes are as instantly recognizable as a GT hardtail." In fact, although the triple-triangle design is now synonymous with GT, it

dates back almost 100 years to very early safety bikes. The protruding section of top tube beyond the seat tube was the perfect place for an embossed GT logo, however, and on the Timberline an oval cross-section top tube was used for an even more distinctive look.

The extra triangle may have been a causative factor, but the early GT Timberlines of 1994 had a notably stiff ride. The bike had a TIG-welded chromoly 4130 steel tubular frame, available in five sizes. The unicrown forks were chromoly too. The 1994 Timberline had a 21-speed Shimano Alivio gearset and brakes. The wheels had Alivio hubs too, with 26 x 2-in. (66 x 5-cm) tires. Some examples of the time were also supplied with a reversible flip-flop steel stem that was painted to match the frame. **SH**

ORANGE P7

1994 • Mountain bike • UK • Original hardcore workhorse mountain bike

Bikes that deliberately stand out from the crowd often become instant classics. That was the case when Orange launched its punishment-proof P7 for the 1994 season. By this point Orange was already on its sixth generation of bikes built from ultra-light Tange Prestige tubing, and its whippy ride was extremely popular.

Mountain biking habits were already starting to change, as more people started to use suspension forks to let them hit stuff harder and faster. That required a different sort of bike to cope, and Orange consciously designed the P7 as a British bulldog of a bike. It used a larger-diameter steel tube with a similar wall thickness to produce a tougher, more muscular-

"The P7 is a smooth and friendly way to whip along single-track and technical trails."

BikeRadar.com

feeling ride. The Orange catalog of the time refers to "a solid hammerhead platform suitable for suspension addition. A true all year ride till death bike." Magazine reviewers agreed: Comments such as "for the hardcore mountain biker, the P7 is the ultimate steel chassis" helped cement Orange's reputation as a builder of tough machines.

The new P7 also showed some cunning sleight of hand from this extremely marketing-savvy brand. While the company described it as "the seventh generation of our original Prestige frameset," the tubing was actually a custom steel alloy very similar to Prestige but at a significantly lower cost. Orange's customers were obviously unconcerned, though, and the P7 went on to become the Orange's best-selling bike. **GK**

ALLSOP Softride Power V

1994 • Triathlon bike • USA • Radical bike with a suspended saddle beam

Triathlon bikes, designed for riders who travel for hours in a single position with a swim behind them and a marathon run ahead, are often a compromise between the most efficient aerodynamics and comfortable ergonomics. However, Allsop's radical Softride Power V frame of 1994 managed to achieve both aims.

By locating the saddle at the end of a "Softride" visco-elastic carbon fiber sandwich beam, Allsop suspended the rider from road shock, giving a very comfortable ride. The saddle could be adjusted forward and backward along the beam to mimic the steeper seat angles used in triathlon. But where Allsop's Power V, and also the Power Wing and Road Wing alloy machines, really benefited was aerodynamically—the vertical seatpost and seat tube section of traditional frames with its attendant drag was entirely missing.

The Softride bikes were immediately adopted by forward-thinking triathletes such as Jürgen Zäck. They were also popular with riders in the ultra-grueling 3,000-mi (4,828-km) Race Across America, and at one point in the race's history 80 percent of the field were using a beam bike of some type. Elsewhere, the radical carbon frame design looked outstandingly futuristic in a field that continued to be dominated by simple round-tubed alloy and steel frames.

Unfortunately, the bikes did have certain disadvantages. The primary one was weight, and even the carbon machines generally weighed more than 20 lb (9 kg), which impacted their climbing ability. And because the saddle was in constant contact with the rider, saddle sores could become an issue. Ultimately, this caused the bikes' popularity to decline over the next decade. Today, Allsop concentrates on office computing accessories, and the Softride name is now used for bicycle racks, not the bikes themselves. **GK**

The Softride was very popular among triathletes. ▷

BIANCHI Paris–Roubaix

1994 • Road bike • Italy • Radical full-suspension road bike for classic cobble race

The legendary road race from Paris to Roubaix, Belgium, which takes place over just one day, is universally accepted as the most difficult "Spring Classic" of them all. While the route is mainly flat, it takes in numerous sections of traditional cobbled farm roads. These are highly destructive to both bikes and riders, and consequently a huge range of technologies have been applied to "tame" the punishing *pavés* (paved roads, named for the loaf-sized blocks used to build them). The most radical approach was taken by the Bianchi company's one-off Paris–Roubaix machine, built with suspension to carry top rider Johan Museeuw in the 1994 edition of the grueling race.

The radical steel frame was built around a special-edition road wheel-sized RockShox suspension fork, and had a fully active full-suspension 2-in. (5-cm) travel rear end. The frame featured designed-in flex in the rear stays as an alternative to a rear pivot, a technique widely copied in lightweight mountain bikes ever since. But the flex was unfortunately a fatal Achilles heel in this case. In an interview with technical guru James Huang from Bikeradar.com, designer Matt Harvey explained: "A chromoly rear end can flex thousands of cycles [by a] small amount, whereas the Italian factory, against my pleading, made it out of 6061 [aluminum] without heat treating it." The larger-diameter alloy tubing also caused clearance problems compared to Harvey's original steel swingarm design: "The Dura Ace bottom bracket was so narrow that the inner chainring was rubbing on the stay so they put a rag in the vise and squeezed it." In the event, the rear chainstay snapped 15 mi (24 km) before the finish line, and a botched bike change cost Museeuw his chance of a win. Bike sponsor Team Mapei then dropped Bianchi, and the bike has since languished in infamy. **GK**

GT LTS

1994 • Mountain bike • USA • Benchmark-setting fully active suspension design

GT's RTS had been a clever attempt at creating a full-suspension bike that would adequately reward leg power as well as offer reasonable protection from rough trails. The problem was that it behaved very differently depending on whether the rider was standing or sitting, and pedaling or not pedaling, which limited the travel to about 3 in. (7.6 cm).

The GT LTS (Link Tuned Suspension), released in 1994, was a four-bar linkage design that went a long way toward isolating the shock performance from pedaling and, to some extent, from minor rider weight shifts too. Actively following the terrain, the suspension effectively protected the rider from the

"To this day, every so often, I ride my old LTS and I'm always amazed how good it feels."

Hans Rey, mountain biking legend

hard edges of bumps. The shock was isolated from frame stress and side loads, so there was no obvious wear or initial stiction (static friction). This bike offered more than 4 in. (10 cm) of rear-wheel travel, and far more ride-feel adjustability than most of its suspension-bike rivals. Despite suffering from a certain amount of braking interference with the suspension action, the design was good enough to last through to the launch of the early I-Drive bikes about four years later. But the use of bushing rather than bearing units in the pivots caused problems, and the relatively underbuilt back end suffered from a certain amount of twisting force from pedal power. So, on reflection, the LTS was a compromise, but probably one of the best compromises in that four-year period. **SW**

GT's LTS was fast uphill and down. ▶

VENTANA Conquistador de Montañas

1994 • Mountain bike tandem • USA • Full-suspension mountain bike tandem

If the idea of riding a bike up and down steep mountain trails seems crazy to some people, then attempting to do the same thing on a tandem will seem crazier still. But Ventana's aptly named El Conquistador de Montañas completely rewrote the rulebook on what is possible with one wheel per person—plus lots of skill and guts.

Fitting full suspension onto a mountain bike tandem might seem overkill at first, but it actually makes far more difference on a twin than a solo. This is because the stoker (rear rider) cannot see rocks, ditches, logs, or any other obstacles on the trail. Stokers are completely reliant on constant communication from the pilot to prevent a permanent pounding from the

"The culmination of Ventana's superior design capabilities [and a] work of beauty besides."

www.pinoymtbiker.org

saddle. In contrast, a full-suspension tandem takes care of the bumps before they get to the stoker. Also, full-suspension tandems are limousine-smooth because their sprung mass (riders and frame) is much higher in proportion to the unsprung mass (wheels) than that of a solo bike. The Conquistador thunders across the roughest terrain with total ease, and the launch photographs showed exactly that: two riders flying out of a jump on a bright green one.

Ventana has evolved the Conquistador over time to ensure it keeps pace with technical developments. For example, ingenious S&S couplings were added to the frame so that it could be packed down into more transport-friendly sections. It is also available with 29-in. (73.5-cm) wheels for even smoother, faster riding. **GK**

SCOTT Waimea

1994 • Triathlon/Time trial bike • Switzerland • Early mass-produced triathlon bike

The Ironman Triathlon sandwiches the bike section between a 2½-mi (3.9-km) swim and a full 26⅕-mi (42-km) marathon run, and at 112 mi (180 km) it is the longest section of the race. Unsurprisingly, racing three disciplines in a line places unique stresses on the triathlete's body, and triathlon bikes have evolved to accommodate that. Scott was one of the first big brands to enter multi-sport water, and its Hawaiian-named Waimea checked a surprising number of boxes for a modern triathlon bike.

The most obvious characteristic of a triathlon bike is its steep seat-tube angle, which pushes the rider farther forward over the pedals. When the rider drops onto the armrests of the tri-bar handlebar extensions, the angle between the legs and body is more open. The athlete is thus better prepared for the sudden leg-muscle lengthening that occurs when the time comes to rack the bike and start to run. Scott had already pioneered mass-market aero/tri-bar extensions when ski coach Boone Lennon designed the company's first "DH" handlebar for U.S. racer Greg LeMond (who famously took advantage of it when he won the Tour de France in 1989, in the race's closest finish ever).

At the time that it was built, many manufacturers were experimenting with smaller 650c (26 x 1¾/66 x 4.4 cm) wheels because it was thought that their reduced frontal area would reduce drag. However, it has since become known that the extra rolling drag of small wheels outweighs any aero efficiency they might have, and now small wheels tend to be used only to keep small-sized frames in proportion.

The Waimea model has long since given way to Scott's Plasma family, but it still definitely deserves its place in bike history as one of the first triathlon bikes to be made widely available. **GK**

◁ Two springs, two riders, and twice the fun.

GRAEME OBREE Old Faithful

1994 • Track bike • UK • Groundbreaking Hour Record bike ridden to success by its inventor

By 1994, the ultra-prestigous world Hour Record had stagnated for ten years. One man against the clock on an oval velodrome, seeing how far he can ride in sixty minutes, is seen as the ultimate test. Normally only the top names in cycling even dream of a serious attempt on the record, but the impetus of a failing business and deep personal troubles drove hitherto unknown amateur time trialist and inventor Graeme Obree from the Scottish club circuit onto a world stage. Unfazed by the prestige associated with the record, he decided to put everything he had into an attempt—fueled by marmalade sandwiches and a kitchen turbo trainer.

With no big brand sponsor, Obree set about building a radically different bike for the attempt. Its most controversial aspect was the handlebar, lying under his chest in an unconventional "ski-tuck" position; this gave him a significant aerodynamic advantage and increased his power output by changing his point of balance. The bike also featured a single-bladed fork and elevated chainstays. But most famously, in an attempt to reduce the "Q-factor," or distance between the pedals, a standard bicycle bottom bracket was replaced by bearings from the family washing machine.

With an almost superhuman effort, Obree took the record at the second attempt, immediately launching a cat-and-mouse battle with British rider Chris Boardman. The Hour Record swapped between them several times before the International Cycling Union changed the rules to ban first the ski-tuck and then subsequent "Superman" pedaling positions devised by Obree. **KF**

PINARELLO Sword

1994 • Track bike • Italy • Full-carbon monocoque frame designed for an Hour Record attempt

Spaniard Miguel Indurain is one of the world's top cyclists. His *palmarès* is trumped only by the likes of Eddy Merckx and Bernard Hinault, and he remains the only man to win five consecutive Tours de France.

When Indurain set out to secure the world Hour Record, Pinarello designed a bike that would optimize his aerodynamics and power. The bike was developed in 1994—when there were still no International Cycling Union rules on bicycle design—in collaboration with Ing Giacchi, an aerodynamics engineer who had worked extensively in Formula One. Pinarello, which was already supplying Indurain with road frames, ditched traditional metal materials for a carbon frame.

The result was the Pinarello Sword (Espada Carbon), a one-piece carbon monocoque frame that was every bit as beautiful as it was groundbreaking. The sleek curves and one-piece design were completed by full disc wheels and time-trial extension bars. Three versions were made: two for the road and one for the track. For the first track version, Indurain used front and rear full-disc wheelsets and an aerodynamic handlebar.

Indurain, whose bike was made to measure, went on to break the Hour Record in Bordeaux, France, on September 2, 1994, covering a distance of 32.958 mi (53.040 km) and edging out Graeme Obree's distance of 32.132 miles (52.713 km), which had been set in April of that year. Indurain later went on to use a modified version of the Sword during his fifth and final Tour de France win in 1995. He attempted the Hour Record again in Colombia in 1995, but failed in his attempt. **DB**

COLNAGO Bititan

1995 • Road bike • Italy • Full-titanium road frame with double-spar down tube

In a period when many bike manufacturers were jumping on the titanium bandwagon, Colnago's Bititan was a typical breath of fresh air from the Italian innovator. The key aspect of the frame was the double (hence "Bi Titan") butted-down tube construction, which boosted the frame's rigidity without sacrificing the supple, sprung ride for which titanium was prized.

Ernesto Colnago, who had set up business in the 1950s, was already a leading light in race bike manufacture, but the Bititan was certainly one of his most classic designs. The down tube design meant that no fewer than five separate titanium tubes sprang from the bottom bracket, a design that tested the skills of his team of Italian welders to the limit. The bike exuded Colnago's style and Italian panache in spades, and proved a very successful race machine too.

The Bititan was used during two successful Tour of Spain bids by the Swiss rider Tony Rominger, but its most legendary and entertaining win came at the World Championships in Columbia in 1995, when it was ridden by Spanish rider Abraham Olano. When Olano broke clear with teammate Miguel Indurain and Italian Marco Pantani, it was clear that the medals would be decided by the three riders. Olano eventually forged clear, with the dutiful Indurain blocking Pantani's hope of a pursuit. Although Olano enjoyed a clear gap in the closing miles, a flat tire threatened to ruin his chances. But the smooth ride of the Bititan enabled the Spaniard to carry on and he survived to give Spain, and Ernesto Colnago—who was by his own account a big Olano fan—a huge victory.

In later years carbon became the material of choice for top race cyclists, but the Colnago Bititan remains one of the seminal titanium frames from a decade of innovative design and technological expansion. **DB**

MARIN East Peak

1995 • Mountain bike • USA–UK • One of the first great affordable full-suspension bikes

By the mid-1990s, Marin's Mount Vision full-suspension bike was so popular that riders at trailhead cafes were puzzling as to which one was theirs in a heap of identical mango and silver-colored machines. But not everyone could afford its $2,400 (£1,600) asking price; accordingly, for those on a tighter budget, the East Peak was offered with the promise of 90 percent of the original's performance for 60 percent of its price.

With every manufacturer fighting for a slice of the growing suspension market, there were no shortage of $1,500 (£1,000) bikes to choose from, but quality was often dire. To quote a magazine test of a contemporary Peugeot competitor, the frame "appears to be formed

"The East Peak was unanimously loved by climbers and gravity lovers alike."

Mountain Bike Rider *magazine, 1998*

from what scrap metal was handy." The East Peak boasted the same neat cross-braced 6061 aluminum frame as the championship-winning Mount Vision Pro, but it weighed only 29 lb 7 oz (13.4 kg) and cost only $1,492 (£995). The Shockworks coil-sprung rear damper and RST 281 forks were simple and effective, and the Shimano STX components propelled lightweight Mavic rims. Marin sourced its own lightweight bars, stem, seatpost, and saddle, and it even came with respectable IRC tires. In short, this was an affordable bike that was totally up for anything the rider wanted to do. Soon the Marin Mount Visions were mixed with a healthy side serving of East Peaks, and the bike has been a top-value stalwart of the Marin range—and UK mountain biking—ever since. **GK**

◁ Colnagos' Bititan is a titanium masterpiece.

OUTLAND VPP

1995 • Mountain bike • USA • Innovative
design that introduced virtual pivot technology

Outland was the company that kick-started the VPP
(Virtual Pivot Point) rear-suspension concept. The
short-lived company's designs showed that there
was an alternative to the Horst Link four-bar linkage
patent owned by Specialized, or the many single-pivot
solutions. Outland's VPP rear suspension didn't pivot at
a set point between the main frame and the swingarm.
Instead, its pivot point effectively floated in space and
changed position as the rear wheel reacted to impacts.

All suspension bikes have a rear-wheel axle path
that can be traced. On some it traces a simple curve; on
others it is a near-straight vertical line. The axle path on
a VPP setup can be tuned to do pretty much whatever
you want it to do. Most designs balance between using
chain tension and bump force to change the way the
shock is responding. The idea is to give the rider just
the right ride feel as they pedal, while lengthening or
shortening the back end of the bike to accommodate
big and small bumps.

Santa Cruz and Intense now own the rights to
the VPP designs, but many other suspension designs
use configurations inspired by the Outland design.
The Santa Cruz Tallboy and Intense Spyder are good
examples of bikes that use it effectively. **SW**

MANITOU FS

1995 • Mountain bike • USA • Early full-
suspension mountain bike

Manitou was founded by motorcycle racer Doug
Bradbury after he saw "a bunch of idiots going over the
Pearl Pass on bicycles." He tried one a couple of years
later but kept crashing, so he decided to build his own.
The result, in 1985, was Manitou Mountain Bikes.

Bradbury's first bikes were unexceptional, but in
1990 he created the first Manitou suspension fork,
which was immediately adopted by young racer John
Tomac. Five years later, Bradbury designed the first
Manitou full-suspension bike. With fork legs in place
of the seatstays, the design was elegantly coordinated
in design, but less well coordinated in function. Many
of the early frames broke, and within just a year the
"double-forked" design had been superseded.

Bradbury's early bikes have become highly
desirable collector's items, but his other hardtail frames
are actually more interesting from a rider's point of
view. This was mainly because they were extremely
light by the standards of the time, but also because
they were among the first frames to use Easton tubing,
wider hubs on un-dished wheels, wider bottom
bracket units for lateral rigidity, and a long-top-tube,
short-stem geometry that made for extremely stable
handling at both high and low speeds. **SW**

MOULTON Land Rover APB

1995 • Folding all-terrain bike • USA • A bike
that goes anywhere and folds up, too

Manufactured under license by Pashley Cycles in
Stratford-upon-Avon, England, the Moulton All Purpose
Bicycle (APB) was made for everyone: city dwellers, rural
folk, riders on good roads and on bad. Its designer, Alex
Moulton, freely conceded that early APBs did not quite
have the level of sophistication of many other Moulton
bikes. Its high-tensile steel-tubed frame, for example,
made it heavier than the lightest Reynolds-tubed
spaceframe Moultons, but its hairpin construction
required fewer brazed frame joints, making it cheaper
and easier to make in substantial volume.

The folding Land Rover APB of 1995 was just one
of many options released during the APB's thirteen-
year production run, which ended in 2005. Using the
Land Rover name under license, it had leading-link front
suspension with variable damping for different riders
and terrains. It was available in British racing green with
yellow lettering, or golden yellow with green lettering. It
had a unique triangulated stepover space frame, a Sachs
21-speed Centera gear system, mountain bike-type
cantilever brakes, and optional front and rear racks.

In 1997 a group of Cambridge University graduates
made a well-publicized 6,000-mi (9,650-km) expedition
on Land Rover APBs through Mongolia and China. **BS**

ELETTROMONTAGGI Zoom Bike

1995 • Folding bike • Germany • A folding
cycle stick that was big on form but limited in function

Richard Sapper was already a very experienced
designer when Elettromontaggi asked him to design
a bicycle for urbanites. Sapper had lived and worked
on the fourth floor of his apartment in central Milan
for decades and he knew precisely what his time-poor
fellow city dwellers would require.

The Elettromontaggi Zoom Bike took ten long
years of design and development. Intended to be used
as an adjunct to public transport, the bike was made
of lightweight aluminum. The bike's clean, minimalist
frame blended seamlessly with its finely integrated
hardware and triple-geared derailleur, which, when
the bike was folded, recessed neatly into the central
rail, along with the headlight and its battery. The rear
light was a cleverly placed LED; all cabling was internal
and fully flexible; and the brakes were rim-mounted
sidepulls acting on 14-in. (35.5-cm) wheels.

Interest in the Zoom Bike was high at the Frankfurt
Auto Salon, where it was touted as a practical method
of covering the large space of the exhibition area. But
on the open road, having small wheels meant that the
rider felt every crack and bump. In the end, all of sixty
prototypes were produced, but Elettromontaggi's city
bicycle never made it into production. **BS**

KLEIN Mantra

1995 • Mountain bike • USA • Outrageous-looking Sweet Spot suspension bike

Gary Klein was always one of the more enigmatic figures in the bike industry, but even loyal fans of his idiosyncratic innovations got a shock when the Mantra, his first full-suspension design, was unveiled. "Sweet Spot" designs with a single very high pivot uniting the front and rear frame halves had already been introduced by John Castellano on his own bikes. Typically Klein swapped Castellano's tubular steel frame for a massively outsized aluminum beam and alloy swingarm, which included a large-diameter strut for the 4-in. (10-cm) stroke urethane spring. Klein's one-piece signature MC2 cockpit took care of steering, and everything was coated in a sumptuous paint job.

The "fuselage" was extremely stiff and, with the rider standing on the same section as the rear wheel, it pedaled extremely well to exploit fully its low 24-lb (11-kg) weight on climbs. Freewheel descending was a surprisingly smooth experience too, especially when production Mantras were upgraded with an air-sprung Fox damper that gave a vast 7 in. (18 cm) of rear-wheel movement. On the negative side, if you braked hard, the whole bike would shorten and steepen before expanding back out as you let go of the levers, producing a nerve-wracking galloping sensation. **GK**

GARY FISHER Grateful Dead

1995 • Mountain bike • USA • Mountain bike tribute to legendary band by former lighting engineer

Mountain bike pioneer Gary Fisher became acquainted with members of the Grateful Dead band in the late 1960s when he staged some of their light shows. He later supplied mountain bikes to band members, including a custom-painted one for guitarist Bob Weir.

Fisher was then persuaded to produce a limited edition (rumored to be 550 bikes) of his well-regarded middle-range Hoo Koo E Koo with custom Grateful Dead graphics. The designs came from Prairie Prince, illustrator for the Grateful Dead and drummer for rock band The Tubes and later Jefferson Starship. The designs effectively turned the tubes of the frame into skeletal limbs, with the characteristic "Dead Head" skull and roses as part of a "Cog Head" headbadge.

The Hoo Koo E Koo itself was a workmanlike rather than a special frame, and the components were nothing to write home about either. But Grateful Dead aficionados loved the paint and the graphics. Now it is not unusual for original unused versions of the complete bike to sell for much more than the original retail price, in some cases ten times as much. And, as is often the case with bikes like this, the ones with all the original equipment sell for the most, even though it was immediately upgraded by many original buyers. **SW**

CERVÉLO Eyre

1995 • Road bike • Canada • Triathlon-specific aluminum bike

The Cervélo name amalgamates the Italian and French words for "brain" and the French word for "bike." It sums up the small Canada-based manufacturer's creations, which are heavily influenced by clever scientific research and computerized design. The company even uses the San Diego Air and Space Technology Center's wind tunnel to check the aerodynamics of its bikes.

After fulfilling their first commission—to build a pro racer's new time trial bike—founders Phil White and Gerard Vroomen set out to make successful road race and triathlon bikes commercially. The first product was the Eyre, a high-spec road bike that was well suited to triathlon racing. Its aluminum frame was almost as stiff and light as some expensive titanium rivals, but other factors influenced the performance too. The steep seat tube, the stiffened bottom bracket, and the integrated aerobars all helped to create a ride that was acclaimed as fast, responsive, and surprisingly smooth for an alloy-framed machine. Doubtless the outsized aerodynamically optimized down tube (with specially calculated differential butting) also contributed.

The Eyre was soon producing champions, most notably Carlos Sastre, who won the 2008 Tour de France on a Cervélo frameset. **SH**

MERLIN Newsboy

1995 • Mountain bike • USA • Classic cruiser-style luxury mountain bike

Taking its design cues from bikes ridden by U.S. newspaper delivery boys in the 1950s, this curvy cruiser-style frame quickly became sought after by bike nuts everywhere when it was released for the 1995 season.

The Newsboy's cruiser looks were deceiving, for it had the power and handling of a thoroughbred cross-country mountain bike. Its top-quality aerospace-grade titanium-tube profiles created a svelte but beefy and durable chassis that reflected all the best performance traits and low weight of the Merlin Mountain, while encompassing a design ethic that captured the attention of riders uninterested in hardcore race bikes. Subtle detailing included internal cable routing, a WTB Speedmaster Rollercam brake behind the bottom bracket, asymmetric S-bend chainstays with room for a 2½-in. (6.5-cm) tire, geometry suitable for a short-travel suspension fork, and tube join welds that were beautiful and functional.

Merlin's first production run of Newsboys was limited to just 100. There was a follow-up model with disc brakes about seven years later, and a 2004 version called the Roots, but nothing captured the looks and feel of the original Newsboy, which proved that retro style could blend with up-to-date performance. **SW**

SCOTT Endorphin

1995 • Mountain bike • USA • Innovative
composite soft-tail frame

With the Endorphin, Scott first presented its carbon-composite technology in the marketplace at a time when very few other mainstream mountain bike frames were built from carbon. Overlapping layers of carbon-composite cloth were wrapped by hand around a removable solid core to make a one-piece structure that was then placed in a heated mold for compression and curing.

The Endorphin was not intended as just another lightweight carbon hardtail. Its L-shaped rear triangle configuration was designed to flex enough—around ¾ in. (2 cm)—to add noticeable comfort to the ride when the trails got rough. The downside was that the

"Its striking design saw the arrival of carbon as a material for the future."

Nick Craig, long-time Scott pro rider

bike struggled if a heavy rider rode too aggressively. Many earlier ones failed between the mainframe and the rear subframe, a result of the low frame weight and the amount of suspension in the back end.

Today many manufacturers are using layered carbon composites to achieve a good mix of vertical compliance and lateral stiffness in both mountain and road frames. For extra structural durability, Scott's later carbon hardtails dropped the massively elevated chainstay "lever" design of the Endorphin in favor of a more traditional-looking rear triangle.

The Scott Endorphin has been the bike of choice for connoisseurs and celebrities including, most famously, Melanie Brown (Scary Spice of The Spice Girls), who bought one for her husband. **SW**

SWALLOW Toucan

1995 • Tandem • UK • Custom-built tandem
from specialist builder

While Pete Bird has designed and built all sorts of bikes, he's undoubtedly best known for his passionate enthusiasm for tandems. He started his training on a much smaller scale than two-seat bikes, initially learning his metalworking skills as a goldsmith, but by 1980 he had already designed his first tandem for English frame builder Chas Roberts. He then saw a gap in the market to sustain himself as a frame builder, and his parents' garden shed became the global headquarters of Swallow Tandems the following year.

This humble location gave no clue to the level of innovation being conjured up inside as Bird started to develop a full range of tandem-specific components such as air-cooled hub brakes for long double-rider descents. His frame designing and building expertise increased rapidly too, and he soon became the world's youngest frame builder qualified to use ultra-thin-walled Reynolds 753 steel.

Swallow's ambitions and physical requirements soon outgrew the garden shed, so the company moved out of England into the beautiful riding country of mid-Wales, with the annual Tandemania event following on its heels. Constant development and interaction with customers—including several who built their own bikes on Bird's teaching weekends—led to the development of what many cyclists now regard as the greatest of all made-to-measure tandems, the Swallow Toucan.

This beautifully made machine was crafted to the suit the precise needs, desires, and dimensions of each team to provide a glovelike fit, and then loaded with all Bird's frame design and bespoke componentry innovations to give a lifetime of outstanding performance for those lucky enough to take a Toucan into their riding world. **GK**

Pete Bird has been perfecting tandems for nearly twenty years. ▷

RITCHEY P-22 Stamstad

1995 • Mountain bike • USA • Understated bike of an endurance legend who started a whole new sport

Designed and built by Tom Ritchey, one of the first-ever mountain bike frame makers, the Ritchey P-22 steel-frame mountain bike had a Tange Ultimate tubeset that took steel performance to the limit. Its weight was close to that of alloy frames of the time, but the slim, subtly tapered, multiple-wall-thickness tubes gave the P-22 a particularly smooth and compliant ride. This made the bike perfect as the weapon of choice for U.S. Mountain Bike Hall of Famer and endurance riding and race legend John Stamstad.

Stamstad switched from endurance road biking to road biking in the early 1990s, but shot to fame in the legendarily grueling 24 Hours of the Canaan race event in West Virginia. This all-day and all-night race on a highly technical desert course was judged too hard for solo riders, but Stamstad bypassed the teams-only rule by entering under four different variations of his own name. By the time the organizers realized that only one man was riding, not four, Stamstad was well on the way to beating half of the four-man teams, at the same time creating a whole new solo 24-hour racing revolution.

Stamstad also triggered the development of what was to become the Great Divide Race by riding the 2,500 miles (4,000 km) and 200,000 ft (61,000 m) of climbing along the spine of the Rocky Mountains between the Canadian and Mexican border in eighteen days and five hours, a record that stood for five years. The American also won the Iditasport sled–run–bike race—held in conditions of -40°F (-40°C) in Alaska—multiple times before retiring in 2001. **GK**

KESTREL Airfoil

1995 • Triathlon bike • USA • Radical missing-tube aero machine

After nearly twenty years, few bikes prompt as many spectator double-takes as Kestrel's distinctive Airfoil family. Ever since producing its first carbon fiber monocoque bike frames, Kestrel has been at the forefront of fiber frame evolution.

Kestrel's pioneering monocoque construction method has the potential for a much greater range of shapes and frame designs than traditional tube-to-tube construction methods. With conventional road bikes the method does not necessarily create a big advantage, but it has allowed the creation of some outstanding mountain bikes and aero road machines. Being able to shape the frame around suspension components or airflow plays to the strengths of Kestrel's carefully hand-laid designs, but the Airfoil

stretched cosmetic and construction limits to entirely new levels, even by the maker's high standards.

The most obvious aspect of the Airfoil design is not what is present, but what is absent. By strengthening the top tube and seatstays, Kestrel created a loop strong enough to make the normal vertical seat tube strut redundant. It was removed entirely, so the only piece of frame projecting into the inside of the perimeter frame was the short stub supporting the front derailleur. Whether the design reduces overall weight is moot, as the upper tubes are increased in bulk to compensate for the missing seat tube. Aerodynamic gains are also questionable, as the spinning rear wheel is no longer shrouded by the tube in front of it. But the Airfoil offers an extremely stiff frame to ride. **GK**

RALEIGH M Trax Team Edition

1995 • Mountain bike • UK • Bonded alloy-and-titanium-tube mountain bike

Raleigh Special Products Division had announced its intention of making a serious mark on the world of mountain biking, and then came a second-generation M Trax bike, the Team Edition.

The bonded titanium main tubes provided strength and lightness, and the rear triangle, made of hand-brazed Reynolds chromoly, gave a sturdy but compliant feel for traction benefits. The frame geometry of the earlier M Trax was tweaked too—the sloping top tube improved body control and gave a better ride, and the Unicrown chromoly forks were especially tough and resilient.

Raleigh's competitive intentions were seen in the top-tube cabling, which was routed in a triple-cable "guitar" style. The secure chromoly steel handlebar stem and Dia-Compe Ahead set bearings positioned the straight titanium alloy bars forward and low for a more hardcore riding stance.

Standard-fit super-light SRT 400 Gripshifters slickly twisted through the cogs when needed, and the Shimano Alivio groupset gave reliable, affordable performance. This handsome and purposeful bike came in three frame sizes and weighed in at around 26 lb (11.8 kg). **SH**

SARACEN Tufftrax

1995 • Mountain bike • UK • Classic affordable boom-time mountain bike

Starting in 1987, Saracen Cycles was among the first of the UK mass-market mountain-bike brands, and it became a market leader in the early 1990s. It focused on good-quality frames built in Asia but painted and assembled into finished bikes in the United Kingdom.

In fact, the first frames of what became Saracens were built in the United Kingdom. The Saracen brand was then owned by Blumels, better known for its mudguards and pumps. F. W. Evans Cycles also had its name on some of the early Saracens, which were designed by Evans employee Gary Smith. But the brand was soon acquired by brothers Paul and Rick Stanforth. Those early mass-produced Saracen frames were excellent in build quality.

The Tufftrax was not by any means ground-breaking in any design sense, but it completely defined the UK standard for sub-$600 (£400) bikes. It offered a full Shimano groupset and a build said to be so tough that you could "drive a tank over it and hardly scratch the paint." Most riders saw Saracen as value-led, but its intuitive feel for the mass market caused it to set many trends. After going distinctly downmarket for a while in the early 2000s, the brand was bought and relaunched by new owners in 2009. **SW**

SANTA CRUZ Heckler

1995 • Mountain bike • USA • One of the first true suspension trail bikes

Santa Cruz dropped a serious pebble into the mountain biking pond with the Heckler, and its simple suspension is visible in bikes nearly two decades later.

The Heckler used a single top tube rather than two separate tubes spliced together at an angle. The rear shock also pivoted slightly at both ends rather than being fixed rigidly into the frame. Slab-sided machined uprights joined the tubular rear stays to a single pivot mounted above and in front of the bottom bracket. The Heckler delivered 4 in. (10 cm) of rear travel (more than any contemporary fork) to give a very smooth ride that still responded to rider power by stiffening up and "digging in" for more traction.

The alloy frame tubing trod just the right balance between low weight and high strength and the Heckler soon developed a reputation for totally trustworthy toughness and intuitive action suspension and handling behavior. Vibrant color palettes meant that this was one bike that wasn't going to be ignored in the shop or on the trail. As a result, it was an immediate hit with riders who wanted the extra speed and control of suspension but without the limited durability, high weight, and pogo-stick pedaling of other bikes. **GK**

SANTA CRUZ Chameleon

1996 • Mountain bike • USA • Multi-purpose, tough-as-nails hardtail

In the mid-1990s it was unusual for a company to produce a full-suspension bike as its first product. But that's what Santa Cruz Bicycles did in 1994. It wasn't until 1996 that it launched a hardtail. The Chameleon was over-built for extra durability, and designed to accommodate a longer-travel fork than the contemporary norm. It also featured a rear wheel drop-out design that could be run either with derailleur gears or a single sprocket. A large part of the market didn't really understand what it was for, but it was to become a template for real enthusiasts looking for a bike that could be ridden far harder than a regular cross-country machine. Soon the Chameleon was being launched like a jump bike and generally abused in ways that would have been alien to risk-averse riders. The Chameleon was tame compared to the much longer-forked machines that would come later, but it was light for a jump bike, suitable for the growing dual-slalom niche, and fast-handling enough to appeal to a growing breed of trail riders who liked to push the boundaries. Santa Cruz already had a great suspension bike in the Heckler. With the Chameleon it showed that adding a little heft for durability plus a longer-travel fork created all sorts of new riding possibilities. **SW**

PINARELLO Paris

1996 • Road bike • Italy • Metal matrix-frame
Tour de France winner

Pinarello Paris bikes dominated cycling during the 1990s, a feat that was all the more impressive because those years spanned the end of the age of steel in bike making. Pinarello led the cycling world into the age of alternative frame materials.

The 1994 Tour de France was the last to be won by a rider on a steel-frame bike. Spaniard Miguel Indurain's winning machine had a TIG-welded Oria-tubed frame with outsized oval-sectioned tubing. It was badged as a Pinarello Paris but was actually a custom-made bike from Italian builder Pegoretti.

The following year, Indurain won the race again—and again his bike was badged as a Pinarello. But this time it was a very different machine because the frame was made of metal-matrix alloy. The construction technique was borrowed from the military aerospace industry, where metals are routinely combined with other materials to strengthen them. This metal-matrix frame released for the 1996 season used round tubing made out of aluminum impregnated with a state-of-the-art ceramic material. The forks were aluminum and, as was usual for Pinarello in its period of race dominance, the components were supplied by Campagnolo. The bike's claimed weight was around 19 lb 12 oz (9 kg).

In 1996, Pinarello provided the victorious wheels once more, this time with Team Telekom's Bjarne Riis in the saddle of a metal-matrix bike. Only paint and geometry distinguished this bike from the previous year's, and that was because Indurain's bikes always had to be built with his upright riding style in mind.

The following year, teammate Jan Ullrich won the race on yet another Pinarello Paris, albeit with a full Columbus aluminum frame. After one more year of victory for aluminum and a single year for titanium, carbon bikes have won every Tour since 2000. **SH**

GT Olympic

1996 • Track bike • USA • Custom "Superbike"
built for U.S. Olympic team

At a high-tech workshop in Santa Ana, California, GT Bikes led a team of highly-qualified engineers working for two years on the secret million-dollar "Project '96." The aim was to create the fastest-ever track bike to empower the U.S. cycling team to dominate the 1996 Olympics in Atlanta.

At a cost of around $70,000 each, around twenty of these machines were built, each taking around thirty hours to assemble.

The GT Superbike used ground-breaking ultra-light composites to keep total weight down to about 16 lb (7.25 kg). The aerodynamic technology was revolutionary. The seat and down tubes were almost

> *"The GT Olympic tried to be the bike of the gods, but it overreached itself."*
> Ed Munton-Greene

flat, cutting through the air like blades. The attention to detail was unprecedented. For example, the top tube was shaped to optimize the turbulence created between fast-pumping legs.

Each Superbike was adapted to the shape and size of its rider but kept secret until the team arrived in Atlanta, so some team members struggled to adjust to their new ultra-thin bikes. In the event, the U.S. team won only two silver medals on the track (Erin Hartwell in the 1000m and Marty Nothstein in the Sprint).

Although the bike was not a success, GT picked up a significant sales boost from Olympic exposure. However, within four years many of the aerodynamic advances were banned from track racing and a Superbike is a rare sight today. **SH**

GT's "Superbikes" pushed technology to the limits. ▷

BAKFIETS Cargobike Short

1996 • Cargo bike • Netherlands • Innovative child- and cargo-carrying two-wheeler

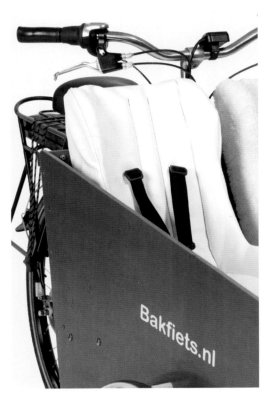

A typical Dutch-style tradesperson's bike, the Cargobike Short was created by Bakfiets of Amsterdam, Netherlands, as an alternative method of urban transport. It is configured so that it can be ridden in work clothes or Sunday best, in all kinds of weather. At its center is a cargo box sturdy enough to carry loads of up to 176 lb (80 kg). The box comes complete with a folding bench (which can be removed if people are not being transported), two sets of seat belts, and even optional cushions. A ride in the Cargobike Short has all the excitement of a backyard go-kart; kids, in particular, are guaranteed never to end the ride prematurely by asking, "Are we there yet?"

When at rest, the Cargobike's specially designed wide kickstand clicks into place, allowing passengers to enter and leave the box safely without fear of the machine tipping over. The steel frame combines with the marine plywood box to make the Cargobike unavoidably heavy, at 84 lb (38 kg), but the low-slung geometric design keeps any load very low to the ground, so passengers can expect a dependable, stable ride. Most impressively, the bike travels on just two wheels, so it follows a single track that can be easily steered through potholes or other obstacles, unlike the more common tricycle cargo-bike configuration.

To cope with the load, ultra-heavy-duty 2-in. (4.7-cm) wide puncture-resistant Schwalbe Marathon tires surround extra-thick spokes with diameters of $^7/_{100}$ in. (2 mm). On overcast days it is wise to pack the bike's tent-style ventilated all-window kiddy canopy to prevent the cargo box from turning into a splash pool.

The Bakfiets Cargobike, and other vehicles of its type, are popular and successful in the Netherlands and Denmark, where there are advanced provisions for bikes in urban areas, and in emergent nations, especially in Africa. **BS**

"The Cargobike carries its load very low which actually makes it much lighter and easier to handle . . . "

Workcycles

The boxy Bakfiets can carry kids or cargo. ▷

IBIS Szazbo

1996 • Mountain bike • USA • Pioneering
Sweet Spot long-travel trail bike

When Ibis Cycles teamed up with suspension designer John Castellano, the bike world got a shock—literally.

The Szazbo was the first of Castellano's Sweet Spot designs and launched a whole genre of bikes that many top manufacturers, including Schwinn, later copied, and that influenced the legendary Ibis BowTi. The Sweet Spot design split the frame into roughly equal halves. The front mainframe was made up of a conventional head tube and top tube, but the down tube pointed toward the rear wheel rather than the cranks. Castellano placed the large suspension pivot just beyond the usual halfway point. The seat tube then curved up and back from the pivot, reinforced with a slim tube that pierced through the top tube and connected the two ends of the seat tube. The rear subframe formed the other half of the bike and comprised a short seat tube stub to mount the front gear, twin struts leading to the main pivot, and a super-compact rear triangle. CNC-machined sections formed a web ahead of the front wheel and chunky rear drop-outs, while a riveted Ibis logo graced the head tube. The Fox air shock that sat between the front and rear halves gave 5 in. (13 cm) of travel.

The Szazbo was an undoubted classic, and the design still lives on as the Castellano Zorro. **GK**

PLANET X Jack Flash

1996 • Jump bike • UK • Hard-as-nails jump
and stunt bike that started a riding revolution

In the mid-1990s, young mountain bikers were beginning to share the local jump spots with BMXers in increasing numbers. The arrival of this simple, affordable, and absolutely bombproof frame launched dirt jumping as a major segment of the sport.

While riders had been converting the tougher mountain bike frames such as GT's legendary Zaskar into what were essentially big-wheeled BMXs, Planet X's Jack Flash (because it's for jumping) was one of the first purpose-built MTB-wheeled dirt jump bikes. Most hardtails were still designed to be as light as possible for racing and climbing and take a similarly light 2⅓–3¼ in. (6–8 cm) fork, but the Flash was created for stunt strength. The thick-walled head tube was reinforced top and bottom to prevent repeated fork landings from distorting the tube and loosening the bearings. Behind the head tube, two big gusset plates joined the top and down tubes, decreasing the stress on the head tube welds. The top tube also sloped down to give maximum clearance for flying feet on increasingly radical "step-through" jump moves. As subtle ride comfort wasn't a concern, the back end could be made equally strong with a massive square-section seat and chainstay, and further gussets reinforcing every corner. **GK**

CANNONDALE CAAD3

1996 • Road bike • USA • First U.S. bike used by European pro road team

Cannondale celebrated its twenty-fifth year in business by launching the latest version of its CAAD bike series.

The CAAD3 was an outsized aluminum-frame machine designed for the Italian Saeco racing team. This was the first American-made bike used by an European pro outfit. The appearance of the unfamiliar chunky frames in the red Saeco colors was a breakthrough moment for modern bike design too—the bikes were used for the first time in the 1996 Tour de France.

All this was great for the Cannondale brand. Saeco was famous for its teamwork built around the sprint strategies of Mario Cipollini, who once, after winning a Tour de France stage, rushed up to the TV cameras and announced, "Cannondale makes the best bikes!"

The CAAD3 had an ultra-lightweight frame made from butted thin-walled 6061-T6 aluminum tubing. The build process included using computer-guided lasers to cut tube ends to the finest of tolerances, making for more durable welds. The frame was repeatedly advertised as being "as light as titanium."

The down tube featured a unique "Power Pyramid" that increased in diameter as it got closer to the bottom bracket, to make the frame as stiff as possible and respond perfectly to Cipollini's sprinting technique. **SH**

CERVÉLO P2

1996 • Aero bike • Canada • Original mold-breaking wind-cheater from the Canadian brand

In Cervélo Phil White and Gérard Vroomen created one of the bicycle world's most innovative and aspirational brands. The bike that took them from concept designers to a game-changing driving force was the P2.

A deep down tube, minimalist top tube, internal cable routing, bladed seatstays, wheel-hugging seat tube, and matching seatpost have become common on many modern aero bikes. Cervélo introduced a lot of these features when it converted the prototype Eyre bike into the first production P2 bike.

As dramatic as it looks, the details really made the P2 a performance piece. Cervélo was the first company to use proven drag-reducing airfoils from the U.S. National Advisory Committee for Aeronautics. Cervélo also paid great attention to how each tube was constructed. Its custom Smartwall design used thicker walls along the sides of the tube to increase stiffness and strength without adding excess weight.

This meant that the P2 slipped through the air and delivered power to the road far better than existing aero bikes. Cervélo later added the P3, P4, and P5 to the lineup, but to this day, the P2 is still an outstandingly fast bike that has a great deal more to offer than its budget price might suggest. **GK**

GIANT TCR

1997 • Road bike • Taiwan • Sloping top-tube design from legend Mike Burrows

British-based designer Mike Burrows was already a legend before he produced the pioneering Taiwanese Giant TCR, an innovative creation that confirmed his place among the most revered bike visionaries of his era.

Burrows first found fame in 1992 as the designer of the carbon fiber 108 time trial bicycle manufactured by Lotus for Chris Boardman, who rode it to gold in the 4-km pursuit at the Barcelona Olympics.

In 1997, Burrows and Giant showed their new development—the TCR—to Manolo Saiz, director of ONCE, the most successful road bike racing team in the world at the time. The Spaniard immediately signed up for it.

Until that point, most road bikes were fairly homogeneous, with long, flat top tubes and relatively conservative geometry. There was little to differentiate one make from another. By contrast, the TCR or "Compact" design used a mountain bike-style sloped top tube for a smaller, tighter, and lighter frame. Increased seatpost extension meant the comfort of the ride was improved, and sizing was also simplified into three standard "T-shirt" measurements: small, medium, and large, rather than the conventional numeric sizing.

Since 1997, Laurent Jalabert, Abraham Olano, Robert Gesink, and Óscar Freire have all ridden the TCR to major success. The size range has now expanded beyond the three original options with several distinct levels of carbon fiber—Composite, Advanced, and Advanced SL—now used in the basic TCR format. **DB**

KONA Humu Humu Nuku Nuku Apua'a

1997 • Leisure bike • USA • The bike with the longest name ever

In the century and a bit they've been around, bikes have been given all sorts of weird and wonderful names, as manufacturers have striven to make their machines stand out from the crowd of competing products. While bike company Kona is actually based in Ferndale, Washington State on the U.S.–Canada border, it has often given its bikes Hawaiian or volcano-related names to reference its brand name (Kona is a district of the Big Island, Hawaii). While Explosif, Cinder Cone, Kilauea and other names have all become classic bikes within the family, one name literally sticks out in the brand history.

Humu Humu Nuku Nuku Apua'a is Hawaiian for "reef triggerfish" (*Rhinecanthus rectangulus*). While there is no discernible link between this marine creature and the relaxed, single-speed beach cruiser shown here, the twenty-one-characters across the top tube immediately marked this bike out as the one with the longest-ever name (a title it still holds).

However, Kona has not always had such great success with the names it's chosen for its bikes. The Sex suspension bikes of 1994 amused some people but outraged many others, with the perhaps predictable consequence that they were withdrawn from sale almost as soon as they went on the market.

Naturally, the name was chosen to attract attention, but there's nothing meretricious about this bike, which is cheap and straightforward to maintain and provides unambitious cyclists with a comfortable (though by no means effortless) upright ride. **GK**

IBIS Hakkalügi

1997 • Cyclocross bike • USA • Extra-versatile high-class cyclocross bike

Ibis Cycles began in founder Scot Nicol's garage in 1981, in the early days of mountain biking. While the company established a reputation for classy and innovative mountain bikes, their crossovers to other types worked well too, with their trials bikes, tandems, and road bikes becoming just as desirable.

At the time, most cyclocross bikes were built for racing, but the designer of the Hakkalügi recognized that, with the addition of a little more tire room, two sets of bottle-cage bosses, and eyelets for a rack and mudguards, a cross bike could be turned into a genuine all-rounder that was equally suited to trails, roads, and even load-hauling.

"I bought one . . . fifteen years ago and it's still going strong . . . and still my favorite bike . . ."

Steve Worland

The etymology of the name of the bike is obscure. Nicol vaguely recalled that it may have been derived from a friend's Ultimate frisbee team, Hock a Loogie. (Most Ibis aficionados use the shortened form, "Lügi".) However, there is no doubt that the butted tubing is named "Moron" as an abbreviation of "more on the ends." The distinctive Ibis cantilever brake cable hanger at the top of the seatstays is known as the Hand Job.

The Hakkalügi was way ahead of its time, with frames like this eventually becoming popular as all-round trail, commute, and touring options. Ibis disappeared for a while before being relaunched as a family of carbon frames. Happily, the Hakkalügi name lives on, most recently as a disc brake-equipped carbon frame and fork. **SW**

CANNONDALE Super V3000

1997 • Mountain bike • USA • Iconic boom-frame superbike from the golden era of the mountain bike

Cannondale's distinctive Super V design first appeared in 1993 and was eventually retired in 2002; it hit its peak of popularity and performance with this model.

The Super V Active SL frame was a lightened version of the previous Active frame. After failure issues with the curving, carbon fiber swingarm that made its debut in the previous year, a conventional alloy rear subframe was reintroduced in 1997. However, the main Y-frame layout was retained—a single main spar with cantilevered seatmast pipe supported on skinny bridging struts. Redesign of the distinctive Fatty Headshock suspension fork allowed Cannondale to squeeze another ⅜ in. (1 cm) of travel out of the unique "inside the head tube" design. This was still significantly shorter than the 4 in. (10 cm) of wheel movement provided by the Fox Alps 5R rear shock, and this disparity was already pushing Cannondale's development of the radical single-sided "Lefty" fork that appeared two years later. There were still some unique components aboard the flagship machine, though. These included the outsized CODA Headshok stem needed to cope with the supersized fork steerer, and an ultra-light machined arm CODA 900M crank designed by "Magic Motorcycle" guru Alex Pong.

Cannondale also pulled in the best components from other world-leading brands. These included the first examples of the holistically designed CrossMax wheelset from French rim legends Mavic. Shimano provided XTR- and XT-level transmission equipment, while Sachs twist shifters were given yellow grip rubbers to match the rear swingarm and decal colors. The result was a seriously good-looking bike that also hung off the scales at under 25 lb (11.3 kg), which was lighter than many race hardtails of the time, and established the Super V3000 as one of the most aspirational bikes around. **GK**

The Volvo Cannondale team and their bikes dominated MTB sport in the late 1990s. ▶

CANNONDALE Super V Fulcrum

1997 • Mountain bike • USA • Highly innovative team-only downhill bike

GT STS

1997 • Mountain bike • USA • Ill-fated thermoplastic-frame mountain bike

Cannondale's Super V DH 4000 was no beauty, but it featured some fascinating innovations that inspired designs that remained current fifteen years later.

Cannondale used the Y-frame, supersized tube layout of its Super V chassis for many years but, as riders became more radical, the frame was reinforced to survive the onslaught. For the Fulcrum, Cannondale changed its suspension system too, from a simple single low-pivot system to two short linkages to control the direction of wheel movement. The linkages worked only with a specific chainring size, so the makers adopted an elaborate system of five different drive chainrings, plus auxiliary drive shafts and idler wheels, to transfer drive to the rear wheel without affecting the suspension. The extended-leg double clamp fork used needle roller bearings on squared sliders rather than conventional solid-state bushings, with Hope hydraulic disc brakes as standard.

Too expensive to put into production, the Fulcrum remained a team-only ride for the Volvo Cannondale squad. Some of the lessons learned from it were used on the subsequent Gemini downhill bike, while twin crown forks and linkage suspension have since become must-have features on any serious gravity machine. **GK**

After introducing the world-beating RTS suspension bike in 1992, followed by the ultra-successful LTS platform, it seemed GT Bicycles couldn't go wrong with mountain bikes. However, the change to composite construction technology for the STS series shows that no reputation is sacred once high speed and hard landings are involved.

Rather than carbon tubes bonded into carbon lugs, as was the standard of the time, the STS used a thermoplastic fiber "rope" threaded through cutaway alloy crank-carrying, seat cluster, and head tube sections. The whole structure was then locked into a mold and baked hard before the back end of an LTS DH bike was bolted onto it. With sci-fi looks from the contrasting polished alloy, the STS became an immediate best-seller, but the incidence of broken frames was so high that STS was said to stand for "Soon To Snap."

GT persisted with the technology for its Lobo downhill bike in 1998 and the flagship XCR 1000 model of the epicyclic I Drive suspension design in 1999. Both bikes were improvements on their predecessors, but ultimately the damage to GT's reputation had been done, and it was more than a decade before the company returned to carbon fiber as a frame material. **GK**

SANTA CRUZ Super 8

1997 • Downhill bike • Taiwan • The first of
Santa Cruz's super-successful DH bikes

The emergence of Santa Cruz's Syndicate as one of the
top-ranked downhill race and World Championship
teams began with the launch of this bike.

    The Super 8 delivered 8 in. (20 cm) of rear wheel
travel using a version of the single-pivot swingarm
layout pioneered on the Tazmon and the Heckler. While
the broad outline was the same, Santa Cruz reinforced
the main tubes and head tube with additional welded
plates (gussets) to accommodate the longest downhill
forks. The rear swingarm was overbuilt with deep
rectangular box-section tubes. The most eye-catching
part of the Super 8 frame was the huge hollow cylinder
that bridged the two spars just inside the mainframe.

    However, the original design was soon changed
for the even stronger frameset pictured here. The
conventional mainframe was replaced by an interrupted
seat tube-style layout based on outsized frame spars
reinforced with saddle gussets, and using a short seat
tube stub and machined vertical brace to hold the
coil-sprung shock. The new swingarm also changed
the signature cross-pipe for computer-machined front
sections with an inset shock mount. The Super 8 sold
well until it was replaced in the Santa Cruz lineup by the
Bullitt freeride bike and the first V10 DH machines. **GK**

BIKE FRIDAY New World Tourist

1997 • Touring bike • USA • Collapsible small-
wheeled tourer

The New World Tourist was designed to ride more like
a conventional bike than its collapsible rivals. It doesn't
compromise ergonomics with an unusually steep head
tube or awkward short wheelbase; instead it is almost
as long as a standard bike.

    Bike Friday offers three chromoly steel frame
sizes, but only 20-in. (50-cm) wheels, usually with no
suspension. Nevertheless, riders report that the long
wheelbase helps create a smooth, comfortable ride and
more relaxed handling than other small-wheeled bikes.

    For transportation, the Bike Friday is less about
folding quickly than carefully breaking down into
separate pieces. The stem and seatpost disassemble
with quick releases, and the front wheel is completely
detachable. The rear wheel stays on, and the rest of the
frame folds when another quick release is unhooked.
The saddle and handlebar height are unaltered in the
packing process. Everything slips into marked sleeves,
then packs into a bag or a case, which can function as
a seat or a trailer.

    The bike is slower to pack than some rivals, but it
is more likely to be bought by long-distance travelers
than daily commuters. The total packed bike is within
the 50-lb (23-kg) limit on many U.S. domestic flights. **SH**

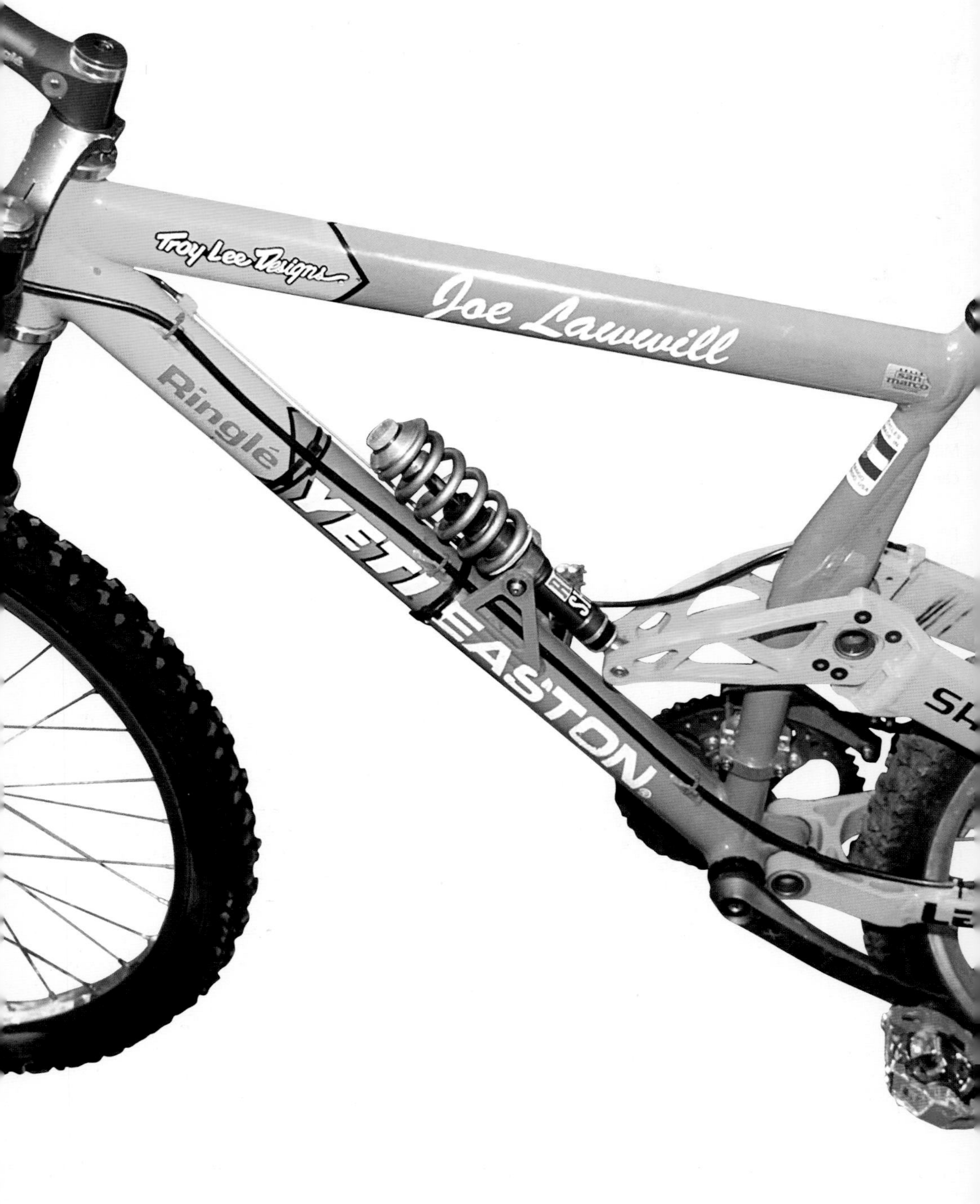
Troy Lee Designs
Joe Lawwill
Ringlé
YETI
EASTON

YETI Lawwill

1997 • Mountain bike • USA • Parallelogram suspension bike designed by legendary motorcycle racer

Colorado-based mountain bike brand Yeti was always innovative when it came to suspension systems. Owner John Parker reached out to a motorcycle-riding legend to develop one of the first full-suspension bikes designed purely for downhill racing.

Mert Lawwill was among the most successful American motorbike racers of the 1960s and 1970s. His first notable victory came in the Sacramento Mile in 1965. In 1969 he was the AMA Grand National Champion, and in 1971 he co-starred with Steve McQueen in the movie *On Any Sunday*. Throughout his career, he rode for Harley-Davidson.

Lawwill was also a top technical innovator. The parallelogram design he brought to Yeti in 1997 proved a high-performance solution to a lot of suspension problems. By mounting the rear wheel to the mainframe on the opposite end of a pivoted rectangle, Lawwill's design allowed the rear wheel to move without serious disruption of pedaling. Depending on the configuration, the system could also deliver huge amounts of rear wheel movement, and while the first Lawwill bikes had only 3 in. (7.5 cm) of wheel travel, later versions moved as much as 9 in. (22.8 cm) to suck up the biggest impacts and landings. The multiple versions in its seven-year lifespan also altered between pull shock and push shock designs from Risse and RockShox to keep all that movement under control.

After Yeti came under the ownership of Schwinn, it was no surprise when the U.S. monster-bike brand adopted essentially the same Lawwill design on its Straight 6 and Straight 8 bikes, which, between them, amassed an impressive tally of race results. The Lawwill system was ultimately too heavy and complex, with eighteen bearings to potentially cause problems; the last Yeti rolled out in 2004. **GK**

TURNER DH

1997 • Downhill bike • USA • Variation on a popular theme

This bike began as a variation on a theme but became the progenitor of a dynasty.

It was originally conceived as a modified form of the Turner Burner. It had the same Horst Link suspension design as the original, but gained a heavily reinforced frame to take longer travel forks that stabilized the steering.

The bike was immediately successful on the amateur and professional race circuits. It was widely used in repainted livery by other brands, with Tommy Misser using one to great effect under a Kona paint job.

The success of the DH started a long line of industry-leading bikes from the tiny U.S. brand. In 1999, Turner

"I started on a Turner, then tried other downhill bikes. I soon returned to Turner."

Chris Sills

released its first single-pivot suspension design downhill machine, the DH Javelin, which was one of the first bikes to come with built-in International Standard Chainguide (ISCG) tabs.

In 2000, the name of this bike was changed to the Turner DH Racer (DHR). The original DHR had a twin top tube design, but in 2004 this was superseded by the latest box-section tubing.

In 2008, Dave Turner began collaborating with suspension designer Dave Weagle, and in 2011 the Turner DHR was released with some of the most extreme geometry of any off-the-peg downhill bike: a slack, 63-degree head angle, and a low, 13½-in. (34.3-cm) bottom bracket, which gave the machine an incredibly stable feel when riding at speed or over rough terrain. **CJ**

MARIN Mount Vision FS

1997 • Mountain bike • UK • First national championship-winning full suspension bike

Marin is a U.S.-based brand, founded in 1986 in Marin County, California, where mountain bikes first emerged in a commercial sense. But Marin's UK distributors, ATB Sales, kick-started the further evolution of the brand into dual-suspension bikes by hiring established aerospace and Formula 1 engineer Jon Whyte, whose access to great motor-sport research and development facilities soon saw the emergence of a whole family of Marin full-suspension machines.

While Whyte later helped to develop a range of bikes bearing his own name, his first single-pivot, full-suspension designs for Marin helped to convert a growing generation of enthusiast riders to the benefits of full suspension. Perhaps more crucially, the marketing emphasis was on normal cross-country

trail use rather than radical downhill riding. The Marin Mount Vision in particular, with its 4 in. (10 cm) of simple swingarm-activated rear wheel travel, is still seen as the spark that ignited massive sales growth in suspension bikes (especially in the UK) at a time when the hardtail (front suspension only) was king. Along with bikes like the Santa Cruz Tazmon, which later became the Heckler, the Mount Vision showed that a reasonably priced full-suspension bike could offer comfort, speed, and traction efficiencies without a big increase in weight. With British cross-country racer Paul Lazenby on board, it was the first full-suspension bike to win a national championship cross-country race in any country. The Mount Vision is still in the Marin range to this day, but as a carbon fiber flex-stay design. **SW**

KONA Kula

1997 • Mountain bike • USA • Fantastically fun soft-fork, big-bar, hard-frame Frankenstein bike

Evergreen trail-riding favorite Kona has always had a refreshingly left-field approach to biking, and even its race bikes have been served with a big heap of fun on the side. The 1997 Kula brought together three seemingly disparate elements, which created a holy trinity of hooligan fun that still brings back brilliant memories to those who rode it.

While many brands had been using aluminum alloy tubing for years, Kona stuck to steel longer than most, so the alloy Kula frame was a departure. The company threw its energy into it wholeheartedly, specifying the premium Elite tubeset from U.S. metal masters Easton.

Rather than match this super-light frame with a similarly weight-conscious and control-compromising race fork, Kona went for the must-have hard rider's fork of the mid-1990s—Marzocchi's Z1 Bomber. With twin coil springs and generous amounts of dual-duty lubricating and impact-damping oil sloshing about inside its chunky "open bath" legs, the Bomber certainly wasn't light. But no other fork provided the same smoothness, grip, and control.

Kona topped off the radical Kula with a wide downhill riser bar, complete with squishy, flanged BMX-style grips. The result was an electrifying and infectiously enthusiastic ride, especially on fast woodland trails. Over time, this unlikely trio of soft fork, big bar, and hard frame have become the classic template for a killer ride, but, back in 1997, the Kula was a true pioneer. **GK**

CANNONDALE Raven ELO

1997 • Mountain bike • USA • Innovative frame and fork design

Even at a time when Cannondale seemed to be creating a greater number of innovative solutions in frames, forks, and componentry than all other bike manufacturers put together, the Super V Raven frame construction was still a big surprise to many. Its unique build used an aluminum skeleton rib with two carbon fiber skins on each side that effectively created a giant carbon and epoxy boom tube as a mainframe instead of a conventional triangular configuration.

The skeleton included fixing points for the componentry, bearings, and suspension pivots, with the carbon skins securely bonded onto it to stiffen the frame torsionally. Its single-pivot suspension design, with 4 in. (10 cm) of travel, was well suited to cross-country riders looking to ride aggressively over rough terrain.

While modern frames and componentry extend their carbon construction all the way into the internal structures, the Raven showed that there's plenty of room in frame construction for interesting material mixes to create what Cannondale marketeers described as a "function-specific skeleton and skin, each uniquely suited to its assigned tasks." Other frame and component part builders have gone on to mix titanium and carbon or even machined aluminum frameworks with carbon in-fill. But the increasingly popular method in top-end products is to use reinforced moldings with nano-carbon whiskers bound in resin for the structural insides, plus variously layered carbon skins to resist horizontal and torsional loads on the outside.

Cannondale's innovative approaches to frame, fork and componentry designs—described by company consultant Mike Cotty as "as iconic as they come"—calmed down slightly when the business was acquired by Canadian conglomerate Dorel Industries. **SW**

GAZELLE Alu-Pro Race Frame

1997 • Race bike • Netherlands • Bike from TVM Pro Team supplier

The distinctive feature of the Alu-Pro was its cross-frame design: the top tube was kinked, and created a third triangle shape with the seatstays crossing over the seat tube to join the top tube.

This stylish but short-lived frame was made from high-strength, low-weight, 7000-grade, outsized and seamless aluminum tubing. Gazelle's own straight front forks were made of Reynolds 531 chromoly steel, while the seatpost was aluminum. The bike was branded a "professional superlight" machine, and tipped the scales at only around 23 lb (10.5 kg).

Most of the bike's equipment was workmanlike rather than world class: a complete Shimano 105

". . . our annual survey found Gazelle to be the most trusted brand in Europe."

Reader's Digest 2010

groupset with integrated dual-control shifters and brake levers. Other features included 28-in. (71-cm) Rigida Ultimate Power double wall rims, Shimano RSX Super hubs, TransX aluminum bars, Look Anatomic pedals, and a Selle Royal saddle.

The fast racing frame bore the logo of TVM Gazelle. Strangely, however, the bike on which the pro team's French rider Laurent Roux won the 1997 Classique des Alpes, the Paris–Bourges, Stage Three of Route de Sud, and the Tour de l'Avenir had a frame made of traditional brazed and lugged Reynolds 731 steel race tubing but with carbon forks.

In 1999, after Roux was involved in a doping scandal and suspended for six months, Gazelle and TVM ended their association with him. **SH**

PINARELLO Swan

1997 • Time trial bike • Italy • Used by Banesto and Telekom Tour de France teams

"One of the all-time 'gets me hot and bothered' bikes. None of the new bikes are close to as sexy as those things."

Gatovolador

This bike was originally built for the Italian track federation and, in particular, for Andrea Collinelli, who was targeting gold in the individual pursuit at the 1996 Atlanta Olympics. The Italian achieved his ambition but the Swan didn't receive the attention it deserved until a year later at the Tour de France.

According to the Pinarello company itself, "The frame was created to improve aerodynamic behavior and create a new higher-performance bike." And it is hard to dispute claims that it is the manufacturer's finest-ever product.

The bike certainly stood out; its arching curvature and lack of a top tube making it instantly recognizable. What it needed was a star to show off its capabilities in high-profile competition. So who better to ride it than Jan Ullrich, and where better for him to perform than at the final time trial of the 1997 Tour de France, with the finishing line at Disneyland, Paris?

By that point in the race, Ullrich was already resplendent in yellow but he wasn't the only rider to utilize Pinarello's latest invention. Abraham Olano of Spain, who had been signed by Banesto to replace Miguel Indurain, was also on the new bike and, having dragged himself through the Tour mountains, he was hoping to cap his race with a stage win.

In spite of a frame that weighed 3 lb 15 oz (1.8 kg) without forks, the Swan carried the Spaniard to his first stage win of the race, with Ullrich sealing overall Tour victory with a second-place finish.

Although these triumphs made the headlines, the day was not a complete success for the bike and its fully monocoque carbon fiber frame. After sustaining a puncture and slipping his chain, Ullrich's Deutsche Telekom teammate and defending Tour champion Bjarne Riis lost his cool with the Swan and threw it to the side of the road. **DB**

Indurain's Pinarello was the swansong of radical monocoque aero bikes on road or track. ▶

KOKUA LIKEaBIKE

1997 • Child's bike • Germany • The original early-learning scoot bike

Few companies have done more to speed up young children's progress from wobbling waddle to confident pedaling than Kokua with its LIKEaBIKE.

Rolf, Alfred, and Beate Mertens of Kokua—which means "harmony" in Hawaiian, even though the company is thoroughly German and based in Roetgen, near Aachen—realized that children found it hard to learn both balance and the principles of pedaling simultaneously. The LIKEaBIKE idea was to create a bike-shaped scooter that was propelled by the pilot striding along in the saddle. As the steps got longer and the bike went faster, the junior pilot naturally balanced and steered more easily. Thus, even children of less than eighteen months could become competent scoot bikers before advancing to pedal bikes.

Built from ecologically sourced wood, LIKEaBIKE had a removable washable cloth seat, padded felt steering bumpers in the fork slots, and handlebar grips with bump guards to stop small fingers getting trapped. While early models had wooden disk wheels with solid rubber tires, these were soon joined by pneumatic-wheeled versions. Different sizes of adjustable frames were then added to the range, as well as spoked-wheel and knobbly-tire options, and accessories such as trailers and wooden baskets. The latest Kokua catalog also features metal-framed, tricycle, and pedal-powered LIKEaBIKEs.

Modern parents have a bewildering choice of balance bikes, including the Bikestar, the Islabike Rothan, the Ketler Speedy, the Puky LR1, the Ridgeback Scoot, and the Specialized Hotwalk. All these machines have their merits, but, in the opinion of most online reviewers, the Kokua LIKEaBIKE is the pick of the crop, and will help a child progress toward adult-style bikes more quickly than any other brand. **GK**

LITESPEED Trike

1997 • Child's tricycle • Taiwan • Charming starter ride from company with top racing pedigree

Litespeed started in 1986 as a side project for the Lynskey family's custom metalworking business. With clients such as Olin Chemical, Kaiser Aluminum, and aircraft manufacturers Boeing and Lockheed, the Lynskeys already had massive experience with titanium. When co-owner David Lynskey suffered a running injury, he built himself a titanium bike to ride for rehabilitation. The bike attracted admiring glances, and it was not long before Lynskey was sidelining other projects in order to create a production model.

Litespeed rapidly became one of the premium titanium brands. It also produced bikes for several other brands, including Eddy Merckx and Bianchi. While

> ". . . Litespeed has the best designed ISP that I've encountered to date."
>
> *Matthew Vandivort, Sixcycle.com*

Litespeed's flagship road and mountain models were among the consummate aspirational bikes, in the view of many, its most iconic product was its smallest.

This limited-edition child's tricycle was the show-stopping item at Interbike in 1997, and the ultimate purchase for any cycling parent, in spite of its $1,000 (approximately £600) price tag. While Litespeed produced only a few Trikes, demand was so great that Lynskey remade the design under its own name several years later, much to the relief of parents wanting the ultimate gift. These later versions feature an alloy of titanium with three percent aluminum and two-and-a-half percent vanadium, new compact geometry, a CNC-milled and anodized aluminum fork, and Cane Creek C2 headsets. **GK**

WTB Bon Tempe

1997 • Mountain bike • UK • Ultra-expensive and eye-catching mountain bike

Steve Potts is the only one of the original California mountain bike innovators still building bikes locally in the second decade of the twenty-first century.

As a "Repack" race gang member, Potts is widely acknowledged as one of the originators of the whole mountain bike revolution in Marin County in the mid-1970s. His legendary skill with the welding torch has sustained a constant demand ever since for fresh frames from his Point Reyes shop, while classic Potts bikes now sell for a fortune on the Internet.

The Bon Tempe, which Potts created in collaboration with fellow Californian component innovators Wilderness Trail Bikes (WTB), is generally agreed to be the outstanding design of his long and distinguished career.

Given that Potts is famed for his flawless aluminum and titanium tube welding skills, it's no surprise that he was responsible for the immaculately built titanium rear half of the Bon Tempe. This was joined onto an extruded aluminum front spar with a single high pivot design based on John Castellano's Sweet Spot concept. This gave a generous 5½ in. (14 cm) of wheel travel from the Fox Racing coil-sprung shock absorber. Pedaling and braking caused a lot of bounce in the system unless the rider was standing, at which point the suspension effectiveness was dramatically reduced. This, combined with the extremely high price and the one-size-only design, meant that the "good times" of the Bon Tempe as pride of the WTB bike range lasted only until 2001. **GK**

MARIN B-17

1997 • Mountain bike • USA/UK • Pioneering lightweight 6-in. (15-cm) travel all-mountain bike

Marin deserves great credit as the first manufacturer to produce simple, affordable, durable full-suspension bikes. These became hugely popular with "weekend warriors," particularly in the UK, where they were designed. The Marin Mount Vision was the first full-suspension bike to win the UK National Championship under Paul Lazenby in 1997.

The B-17 was all about serious fun without costing a fortune or requiring the rider to push it back uphill. The X-braced frame was derived from cross-country bikes: beefed up to take tough treatment, but not so heavy as to prevent mounted ascents.

Marin fitted tough, lightweight components, including Shimano gears and brakes, and a downhill-style RST fork that delivered a 6-in. (15-cm) suspension stroke with double clamps above and below the frame's head tube to add strength and stiffness.

The arrival of the B-17 meant you no longer needed to go to a specialist dealer for a downhill bike or to push your overweight bike up every hill. This aptly named machine was a proper bomber that would drop you right on target, no matter how technical the trail, and still get you home safely afterward.

Perhaps inevitably, the trail-strength frames suffered breakages as the drops, stunts, and jumps for which they were used became bigger and more brutal, and the RST forks had relatively simple polymer spring internals that choked their control when ridden at the limit. Nevertheless, the B-17 remained an affordable stepping stone to more radical riding until 2000. **GK**

KLEIN Pulse

1997 • Mountain bike • USA • Budget option from luxury mountain bike brand

Some people identify Trek's buyout of Klein in 1995 as the start of the latter's decline from a boutique brand into a producer of corner-cutting, price-trimming bikes such as the Pulse. However, closer study of Klein's corporate history reveals that there had previously been several bikes in its lineup that hadn't require house-sized bank loans, and with only one exception they were all great rides.

The first affordable Klein—the 1993 Fervor—came with the trademark square chainstays and MC1 integrated cockpit of the Attitude, and a liquid green-over-black "pond weed" paint job that even extended to the bottle bolts, leaving a conventional (rather than an oversized) fork as the only compromise.

The 1997 Pulse's main tube profiles were similar to those of the flagship Attitude, but with conventional rather than indulgently smoothed welds, and round rather than square rear stays. The paint was more muted, too, and the bikes were sold complete, as Comps or Pros, rather than as frames, as previous Kleins had been. As an exercise in making a premium name accessible to a budget market, it was not unsuccessful.

The cheap Klein that was definitely worth steering clear of was the Karma, unless by chance you happened to want to own what was possibly the ugliest bike ever built. Based on the Mantra Sweet Spot, the Karma incorporated a crude, L-shaped swingarm rather than the elegant triangulated subframe of its more stylish sibling. The most alarming downgrade, though, was the replacement of the Fox Racing rear shock with a triangular block of urethane rubber. This massive and unsightly intrusion seriously compromised performance, and was symptomatic of the dumbing down that tolled the death knell of Klein as a premium brand. **GK**

MUDDY FOX Intereactive

1997 • Mountain bike • UK • Radical interlinked suspension design

The Intereactive is one of the most interesting mountain bike designs ever built; the story behind it is fascinating and sad in equal measure.

The bike was originally called the Intereactive by designer Dave Smart, who built the first twenty prototype frames for Muddy Fox with Grand Prix motorbike fabrication specialist Harris Performance.

The Telelever front fork and monocoque design were radical enough for the time, but Smart's Intereactive design also linked front and rear wheel together under tension, with the result that the shock absorber didn't react to pedaling or braking inputs in the same way as conventional independent suspension.

> "... the Intereactive system did freaky stuff by synchronizing front and rear suspension."
>
> Gizmag.com

This effectively removed the power bob and braking dive problems that are still the main obstacles to efficient suspension design today.

Unfortunately, Smart and Muddy Fox soon parted company over a payment dispute. After the split, both the design and the name of the bike were subtly but crucially changed before it went into production. The resulting Intereactives still looked stunning, but the ratio of interaction between front and rear suspension was dramatically altered. This meant that if the front damper ran softly enough to work well, the rear suspension barely moved. Initial enthusiasm for the bike faded rapidly as rider reports filtered onto the grapevine. Muddy Fox then declined, leaving the Intereactive as a poignant reminder of what might have been. **GK**

Dave Smart's unique Intereactive design never got to prove its potential. ▶

GIANT Box One

1997 • Mountain bike • Taiwan • Low-cost alloy-framed bike

With global sales of more than five million and a near-billion-dollar revenue, to call Giant a mere business is to undermine its position in the market—"empire" would be a better description. In 1997 Giant came up with its attempt at an affordable mass-market full-suspension mountain bike, the Box One.

The earliest models had a welded square-tubed alloy design with an unorthodox seat tube arrangement. Instead of the conventional triangle formed by joining the up and top tubes, the seatpost was held in place by two heavy-duty struts protruding from the top tube. The outline echoed that of Giant's pro-level downhill MTBs. The front suspension was provided by Suntour DC90 magnesium triple-clamp forks.

Rear suspension came from the same GTM7 fully adjustable rear shock used on Giant's more expensive models. The gearing components were trusty SRAMs— ESP 5.0 3 x 9 front and rear derailleurs and ESP 7.0 shifters. Powerful hydraulic braking came from a pair of Magura HS11 rim brakes. The wheels were Alex AL-DV22 double rims fitted with Tioga tires.

The Box One went through numerous specification changes each year, and was joined in 1999 by the Box Two. Both models were aimed at serious beginners. They were good bikes with effective suspension systems, but they were heavy because they were built with cheap materials. Also, the use of bargain components meant the bikes required careful handling to thrive on demanding MTB terrain. **TB**

GIANT MCM

1997 • Mountain bike • Taiwan • Radical-looking carbon fiber monocoque bike

Giant's Cadex mountain bike gave the Taiwanese manufacturer a solid grounding in carbon fiber technology. Traditional "plug and lug" construction—in which carbon fiber tubes are glued into alloy junction lugs—restricted geometry changes and added weight. Wanting to gain an advantage over other major manufacturers, Giant then hired designer Mike Burrows, fresh from his world record-breaking and Olympic gold-winning Lotus Superbike, to apply a new technique of carbon manufacture.

The monocoque mainframe of the MCM was created in two parts by laying multiple carbon fiber sheets by hand into a mold. The sheets—and therefore the fibers within them—were oriented to tune the stiffness and strength of the frame as appropriate to the loads that each section of it would bear. Smooth curved lines were used wherever possible: Sharp edges could cause areas of weakness in what was still a developing technology. Once completed, the two halves were glued together, pressurized to squeeze out excess adhesive between the sheets, and then baked to fix them into their finished shape.

Finally, the monocoque was attached to the aluminum rear end of the bike. Distinctive "banana" linkages then drove a shock absorber under the mainframe, to create an impressively light and effective full-suspension machine for racing and trail riding. It's a tribute to the MCM's design that it wouldn't look out of place on the trails today, and many MCMs are still in regular use. **GK**

IBIS BowTi

1997 • Mountain bike • USA • Cult titanium-frame interlever suspension bike

American bike designer Scot Nicol was always famed for the quirky and humorous touches on his steel and titanium mountain bikes. However, even his signature Moron ("More on the ends") butted steel tubing and fist-shaped Hand Job brake stops paled into insignificance alongside the freaky BowTi.

The idea of using flex in the frame members to provide suspension movement wasn't new, and many designs had already used deliberately thin tube sections instead of a pivot. What made the BowTi different was that the twin titanium down tubes were designed to flex along their whole length from head tube to rear wheel. This gave a full 5 in. (12.5 cm) of rear wheel travel

> ". . . carries the ultimate bling-bling factor, unique design . . . and no pivots to wear out . . ."
>
> MTBR.com

controlled by a Fox Shox racing damper. However, the twin tubes also allowed a lot of twisting and sideways flex in the frame. This created an unmistakably mobile and lively ride to the point where following one down a trail and watching the wheels track independently was a fascinating experience.

The design carried through until 2001 with limited commercial success, but there's no doubt that the BowTi is a cult classic from one of mountain biking's true characters. When photographer Russ Burton was asked about his Ibis, he said, "It was proper out-of-the-box thinking, and it sort of worked. I bought it because Scot talked me into it when I rode with him, and it's still gorgeous. It's still hanging on the wall with dust on it . . . but I'll never get rid of it." **GK**

SUNN Radical Plus

1997 • Mountain bike • France • The most successful downhill mountain bike ever

In the 1990s, France led the field in downhill mountain biking: Nicolas Vouilloz, Anne-Caroline Chausson, Fabien Barel, Cédric Gracia, François Gachet, and Mickael Pascal dominated World Cup rankings, with the first two taking thirteen World Championships between them. Most of these great names rode Radical and Radical Plus bikes.

The Radicals were purpose-built, dedicated downhill race bikes that first appeared at a time when most competitive riders were using all-round aluminum alloy bikes with bigger gears and tires. Sunn introduced long, low-slung, steel-tubed frames similar to those on modern downhill bikes, with shock-absorbers driven by motorbike-style linkage.

The Radical Plus had an idler cog above and two spring-loaded cogs below the normal chainring to isolate the suspension from the pedaling input. Its chassis—a mix of round- and square-section tubes with a split top tube and space frame-style seatmast section—was more complicated than that of its predecessor.

The long stroke shock and the Obsyss fork—custom-built by Max Commençal and Olivier Bossard—delivered unparalleled levels of control and confidence, and helped make Sunn Radicals the most successful bikes the downhill World Cup and World Championships have ever seen.

Unfortunately, Sunn found it impossible to translate sporting triumph into commercial profitability: bikes that soared on mountain trails flopped on the streets of Paris. Since most bike manufacturers can make this transition without difficulty, there can be little doubt that this was a consequence of insufficient investment rather than lack of expertise. Sunn's finances were often a cause for concern, and at the time of publication of this book it was uncertain if the French company remained in business. **GK**

C The BowTi was a truly unique and fascinating machine.

BUDDY BIKE Twin

1998 • Tandem • USA • Side-by-side "sociable" riding twin

The Punnett Cycle Manufacturing Company of Rochester, New York, made the first side-by-side bicycles in the 1890s in an attempt, it said, to develop a more "sociable" bike that had its riders sitting alongside each other rather than one behind the other as with traditional tandems. Seats, pedals, handlebars, and riders were all set side-by-side on a steel tubing frame. There was an extra sprocket on the rear wheel, and the handlebars steered together in unison, attached at either end of a common crossbar.

The modern Buddy Bike is an altogether easier machine to ride. The side-by-side Brooks sprung saddles can be independently adjusted for height via separate

"It is said that a difference of 100 lb [45 kg] weight in the two riders is not noticeable."

Punnett Cycle advertisement, 1896

clamps on the horizontal spar. Ingenious crank-style pedals operate through a shared bottom bracket. To avoid confusion, the brake controls are all given to one rider who steers via a lever arm attached to the base of the handlebars and the top of the conventional fork. With a tighter turning circle than conventional tandems, the Buddy is maneuverable and feels balanced, even with two riders of widely different weights. It can also be ridden solo (though it does tend to lean).

The Buddy Bike should not be used on narrow cycle paths or gates, where its width may cause clearance problems, or anywhere in Argentina, where side-by-side riders may face prosecution—the only tandems that are legal in that country are those that are single file, one rider behind the other. **BS**

COLNAGO C40

1998 • Road bike • Italy • Franco Ballerini's Paris–Roubaix-winning bike

The Colnago factory in Cambiago, Italy, is a treasure trove of cycling memorabilia and history, with bikes from every era a reminder of the manufacturer's colossal success in the sport. However, one bike above all stands out. Encrusted with deliberately preserved mud and dirt from the grueling bike- and leg-crushing cobblestone sections of Paris–Roubaix, Franco Ballerini's Colnago C40 sits in pride of the place at the center of the factory. Ballerini may not have been as prolifically successful as the Belgians Eddy Merckx and Johan Museeuw—two of Colnago's other leading riders—but he always had a special place in the heart of the company's founder, Ernesto Colnago, who was unstinting in his praise of Ballerini as the last great Italian rider to dominate the pavements.

The C40 bike that Ballerini rode to his second Roubaix title in 1998 didn't set any records in weight or design, but it remains nevertheless a masterpiece of styling that evokes the spirit of its golden age. The mud that's caked to the customized frame with its specially increased tire clearance, Ballerini's No. 12 nameplate, his filthy pedals, and his cobble-battered saddle, combine to make an evocative lasting tribute to the legendary rider.

The handmade full carbon frame with Colnago's signature "stiletto" straight-legged fork gives the bike a classic look and feel. The beautifully detailed Art Deco-style Mapei color scheme on the frame is also a reminder of the most dominant team of the 1990s.

Ballerini tragically died in a motor accident in 2010, but his Colnago C40—preserved forever in the heart of a factory that is overflowing with cycling history—is a poignant tribute to one of the greatest-ever performances in the Paris–Roubaix by one of the race's most memorable characters. **DB**

Colnago's C40 was a cobble-conquering classic. ▶

GT I-drive

1998 • Mountain bike • USA • Innovative, eccentric pivot suspension design

GT's I-drive suspension design first saw the light of day in 1998, five years after the four-bar linkage LTS family was launched. Designed by GT's suspension expert Jim Busby, it was a heavily hyped and remarkably complex setup that left lots of riders and bike shops struggling to decide which category of suspension to fit it into.

In fact, it created a whole new category. GT described it as "a modified four-bar linkage" design, but it incorporated an element of unified rear triangle designs, where the crankset and rear gear are directly connected. (Actually, the crankset was connected to both the front triangle and the swingarm, on its own little subframe.) The "I" in the name stood for

> *"Fast, nimble long-travel bike that will let you test your skills to the limit."*
>
> Bikeradar.com

"Independent," so the new suspension category was generally referred to as "Independent Drivetrain."

The bottom bracket and crankset were mounted in a large eccentric housing that rotated on a bearing connected to the swingarm. There were four resulting linkages, but only one main pivot; this kept drive power direct, with very little feedback into the shock, a supple suspension feel, and no braking interference. In use, there was still some bob created by rider weight shifts, so a smooth pedaling action was recommended, but the fact that the I-drive design is still in production is testimony to its genius.

I-drives and shock units have since improved, and similar setups now exist on bikes made by Mongoose, which has the same parent company as GT. **SW**

GIANT ATX

1998 • Mountain bike • Taiwan • Benchmark DH full-suspension mountain bike

During the 1990s, Giant of Taiwan became one of the world's largest manufacturers of mountain bikes. Giant didn't restrict itself to generic products; it was tirelessly innovative, developing carbon-alloy hybrid bikes and full-carbon bikes for both off- and on-road use. Its involvement in team sport increased as it grew, and its boom period climaxed with the introduction of the radical ATX DH.

The instantly recognizable mainframe used a multi-piece rectangular section in a "wonky Y" layout that split to support the cantilevered seatmast and the bottom bracket at the back end. The bottom bracket was further reinforced by a thin "skid plate" tube that curved around like a flat variation of the conventional down tube. Curved chainstays joined a high main pivot to the rear wheel, while rectangular section seatstays joined onto long, banana-shaped linkage plates. In turn, these drove the long-stroke RockShox Deluxe coil shock, which came complete with an extra-volume "piggyback" damper.

The spec of the complete bike was full-on, too: RockShox Boxxer downhill forks with extended stanchions; double crowns at the top and bottom of the head tube, and a bolt-through front wheel axle for extra steering stiffness. Hope C2 brakes and hubs were fitted for maximum control on the increasingly steep and fast World Cup circuit courses.

Giant ATXs were used by pro riders Rob Warner (latterly a presenter on Red Bull TV) and Crawford Carrick-Anderson. They soon became popular with amateur riders, many of whom have publicly attested the manufacturer's claim that these machines' "smart mix of weight, comfort, and affordability" provides "the lifestyle off-roader the ruggedness and comfort of a mountain bike." **GK**

Giant's ATX downhill was a true gravity-assisted racing specialist. ▶

KONA Stinky

1998 • Mountain bike • Taiwan • Benchmark DH full-suspension mountain bike

The Stinky, created by Pacific Northwest brand Kona Bikes, was one of the longest-running freeride machines on the market, leading the field for more than a decade as the best do-it-all aggressive mountain bike.

With a 7005 aluminum frame and 5-in. (12.7-cm) front and rear travel, the Stinky shot to fame after Kona redesigned it to attract the attention of the fledgling freeride movement. Kona started the Clump Team, which first featured *New World Disorder* film riders John Cowan, Bobby Root (famous for extremely long wheelies), and Graham Kuerbis.

As the Clump Team grew, so did the Stinky. By 2004, the bike had gone up to 6 in. (15 cm) of rear travel, and was available with a triple-crown front fork capable of large jumps and drops. Kona Clump rider Dave Watson

demonstrated this by jumping from a cliff over the Tour de France peloton on the famous Alpe d'Huez climb. This audacious move gave freeriding overnight infamy, and the stunt cemented the Stinky's place in biking history.

In 2006, the Stinky got bumped up to 7 in. (17.8 cm) of travel, while maintaining its unique look and four-bar suspension design. The Stinky remained the same in 2007, but in 2008 it lost its triple-clamp suspension and returned to a single-crown fork. It subsequently became Kona's entry-level bike, as the Stinky Dee-Lux, the Stab, and later the Operator, and the Supreme Operator moved to the head of Kona's freeride and downhill lines.

People wonder why the makers call this excellent product "Stinky," but Kona agrees with Shakespeare that a rose by any other name would smell as sweet. **CJ**

GIANT MCR

1998 • Road bike • Taiwan • Radical-looking carbon fiber monocoque road bike

If you've seen Chris Boardman's Lotus Superbike, you won't be surprised to learn that this radical-looking Giant shared the same designer.

More surprising, perhaps, is that the designer in question, Mike Burrows, established his reputation for revolutionary Human Powered Vehicles (HPVs) with recumbent tricycles such as the Speedy.

Burrows' time with Giant was short but incredibly productive. Most of his concepts had previously been introduced by other companies. Mountain bike-style sloping top tube "compact" road bike frames sold in so-called "T-shirt" sizes rather than traditional seat tube lengths had already been used by Salsa and other companies. Kestrel had introduced its carbon fiber monocoque road bike frame at the Long Beach bike

show more than a decade earlier. Super-thick carbon fiber spokes had appeared on wheels from HED, Spin, Spinergy, and Spengle. Aero-profiled seatposts, angle-adjustable stems, and rear brakes hidden by frame cutouts weren't new, either.

But while these features had previously been one-off, custom items, Burrows' achievement was to bring them all into reliable mass production. To showcase these advances, Giant included them all in this radical-looking bike, which was available in shops with exactly the same spec as that used by the super-successful Spanish ONCE team. The result was an immediate hit with those who loved the Sci-Fi looks and state-of-the-art aerodynamics enough to overlook the less impressive weight and drive stiffness stats. **GK**

GARY FISHER Big Sur

1998 • Mountain bike • USA • Bike that changed accepted technical trail handling

Fisher did not invent "genesis geometry"—a method of centering the rider's body weight on the bike through the use of shorter-than-normal chainstays, a longer top tube, and a shorter stem. British MTB pioneers Pace and Doug Bradbury at Manitou did something similar with their frames years earlier, but the Fisher Big Sur first brought the concept to widespread attention, and helped it on the way to the industry-wide acceptance that it subsequently achieved.

The extended top tube stopped the shorter stem from cramping you, the short stem stopped you from feeling like you were going to dive over the bars when the suspension fork compressed, and the overall configuration put slightly more weight over the rear wheel to achieve better traction, which was especially useful for seated climbing.

Not everyone liked it, but its combination of steepish head angles and increased fork offset was found to work well on the increasingly popular new breed of big-wheeled 29ers, on both high- and low-speed terrain. The set-back hand position also helped to weight the body better over the front of the bike, resulting in a smoother fork action and livelier low-speed steering. **SW**

TREK 8000 WSD

1998 • Women's mountain bike • USA • The first properly female-specific mountain bike

Long after it had become acceptable and conventional for women to wear trousers, "ladies' bicycles" continued to feature structurally compromised dropped top tubes that would enable them to ride in skirts.

That remained the general rule until the end of the twentieth century, when Trek introduced the Women's Specific Design (WSD). The bikes in this range had proper top tubes for structural stiffness, and their frames had shorter reach to account for the fact that women typically have longer legs than men in proportion to their upper bodies. The grips fitted to the bars of WSDs were narrower, and the brakes had adjustable reach levers to fit smaller hands better. The forks were also custom tuned, with lighter weight-damping oil to work better with the lower air-spring pressure used by lighter riders. After Trek researchers found that women rode less aggressively but more smoothly than men through technical sections, some WSDs were fitted with faster-rolling tires.

The success of the original 8000 WSD bikes encouraged Trek to produce models across a wider price range. Specialized, Scott, and Giant soon brought out female-targeted mountain bikes, and bikes for women are now part of every major manufacturer's range. **GK**

GT Vengeance

1998 • Race bike • USA • Specialist triathlon bike from a BMX and mountain bike brand

In the early 1990s, Mark Allen won virtually every major triathlon event. His victories included the Ironman World Championship at Kona, Hawaii, every year from 1989 to 1993, and again in 1995. He was awarded Triathlete of the Year six times by *Triathlete* magazine and the title of World's Fittest Man by *Outside* magazine in 1997. When Allen decided to put his name to a bicycle, it was going to have to be something special.

The bike was initially developed for use by the U.S. team for the 1996 Atlanta Olympics. Although banned from road time trial use because it was considered "too aerodynamic," triathlon regulations are more relaxed.

The Vengeance was one of the first bikes to use an aerodynamic seat tube with a "wheelhugger" cutout at the rear. The seat tube also extended up underneath the saddle to minimize drag between the rider's legs, and mounts were provided to hide a bottle in the slipstream. Gear cables were hidden inside the frame tubes, and the fork legs used a deep flared shape to reduce drag.

These features were aerodynamic, but they made the Vengeance very heavy and rigid. This was fine on long, flat, smooth courses, but reduced the bike's effectiveness elsewhere. Nevertheless, the Vengeance influenced the design of many bikes that followed. **BS**

CANFIELD Big Fat Fatty Fat (BF3)

1998 • Downhill/Freeride bike • USA • Super-long-travel gravity machine

Lance and Chris Canfield started Canfield Brothers Downhill Bikes in 1998. This was the first machine that Lance designed. Although there was already an established trend toward bigger bikes—3-in. (7.5-cm) wide tires and travel suspension forks of up to 10 in. (25 cm) were increasingly common—the BF3's 12 in. (30 cm) of rear suspension was unprecedentedly large, but the brothers felt that it would make rough downhill race courses smoother and ultimately faster.

Lance immediately proved his point when he won the very first Bootleg Canyon Downhill race on the BF3, in spite of competitors heckling him with "You can't race that." He went on to take second place in the first-ever freeride mountain bike competition, on the Moab Rim in Utah.

The BF3 was not light: its frame and shock alone weighed nearly 18 lb (8 kg). Built from aluminum, and with a simple single-pivot suspension, it looked like a motorbike missing its engine.

Only two BF3s were made before the Canfield Brothers moved onto more sophisticated designs as they gained experience of suspension design. In 2014, the Brothers were still going strong, with five frame designs being sold across the globe. **CJ**

BIANCHI Mega Pro XL Reparto Corse

1998 • Road bike • Italy • Marco Pantani's double-winning bike

This is the bike Italian rider Marco Pantani used in his 1998 victories in the Tour de France and the Giro d'Italia.

Bianchi's Mega Pro XL Reparto Corse was tailor-made for the pint-sized mountain specialist. Using a Dedacciai doubled-butted 7000-series shaped alloy tubeset, the bike's measurements were precisely dialed in to suit Pantani's explosive character and out-of-the-saddle, on-the-drops riding style.

The bike had to be light too, and, weighing in at just 15 lb 5 oz (6.96 kg), it was among the most sprightly around at the time. A custom paint job befitting a champion was also a must, with the rider's name adorning the top tube.

In the year of its release, the Bianchi Mega Pro was regarded as unconventional. However, standards in unorthodoxy have changed a great deal since then, and to modern eyes some of its features may appear rather staid: the standard-issue, threaded bottom bracket shell, the non-integrated 1-in. (2.5-cm) head tube, the telescoping 1⁷⁄₁₀₀-in. (27.2-mm) seat tube, and the conventional tube shapes that are circular in all but a few, restricted sections. It should be remembered that, in the late twentieth century, aerodynamics was the almost exclusive preserve of time trial bikes.

Sadly, Pantani's 1998 successes marked the pinnacle of his career. He was expelled from the 1999 Giro d'Italia after a dope test revealed a suspiciously high hematocrit level. Although no further action was taken against him, his career subsequently went into a steep decline. He was found dead in a hotel room in 2004. Yet despite the shadow of suspicion that hung over Pantani, he remained a hero to many. Miguel Indurain said, "There may be riders who have achieved more than him, but they never succeeded in drawing in the fans like he did." **DB**

HANEBRINK X1

1998 • Fat bike • USA • Monster-tired bike for conquering unridable terrain

Fat bikes—machines with 3- to 4-in. (7.5- to 10-cm) wide tires on special versions of 26-in. (66-cm) mountain bike rims—are popular today, but the fattest bike of all first appeared in the late 1990s. With massive 8-in. (19-cm) wide tires on tubeless, auto-style, alloy wheels, Dan Hanebrink's X1 was a showstopper that was designed to be unstoppable. By using super-wide tires, the X1 had an incredibly low contact pressure with the ground, so it didn't dig into soft or loose surfaces such as sand, snow, or marsh, and still gripped firmly where other bikes could not.

Fitting the wheels took some ingenuity, and to do it Hanebrink had to develop his own super-wide

> *"Tidy handling, great spec, superb build quality and a lively feel."*
> Bikeradar.com

forks—or custom-modify the crowns on White Brothers downhill forks to fit. The rear stays also had to be super-long so that there was room for the rider's heels to pedal properly before the frame kinked out around the tire to the super-wide rear axle. This gave the X1 a massive 51-in. (129-cm) wheelbase, but normal handling metrics didn't apply to this balloon bike, because it came into its own only where other bikes couldn't go.

At just 35 lb (16 kg), and with a full set of gears, it was surprisingly mobile, even on normal trails. The makers claimed that its only limitations were those of the rider.

The X1 is now produced alongside the electrically assisted Bearcat, the full-suspension X3, and the X5 electric motorbike. **GK**

GT Lobo STS DH

1998 • Mountain bike • UK • Radical carbon-frame downhill machine for the gravity glory days

"The Lobo was kind of famous for, shall we say, 'parting' back in the day."

bikeradar.com

Having started as a dominant brand in BMX in the 1980s, GT Bicycles had worked its way into a similar position in the mountain biking world a decade later. With its Zaskar, Xizang, RTS, and LTS bikes, GT had dominated the popularization of every major innovation from oversized aluminum to titanium, then pedal-proof, and subsequently smoother "full-time" suspension. The company wasn't about to let up in the last years of the century.

GT's engineers had already introduced their STS composite chassis technology on the LTS and I Drive bikes. This unique construction method looped a long "rope" of carbon fiber composite material through hollow alloy exoskeleton sections at the head tube, seat tube, and bottom bracket corners, before being compressed and cured to bake it into shape.

The Lobo STS DH was an entirely new bike, and one of the first purely downhill-dedicated bikes to be produced in significant numbers. 6.5 in. (16.5 cm) of travel was a lot for the time, and the manner in which it was delivered was important. GT recognized that a low center of gravity was crucial for stability, so it used a unique RockShox Deluxe coil-sprung shock that was pulled (rather than squashed) into action with a long truss linkage that joined the squat, heavily braced rear stays to the radically backward-sloped seat tube. The shock could also be moved in the frame to alter geometry and ground clearance.

At 38 lb (17.25 kg), it was impressively light for its time, although unfortunately that was reflected in a reputation for poor frame durability, which earned it the acronym-derived nickname "Soon To Snap." It still achieved some notable race success under riders such as Steve Peat though, and the fragility of the bikes means surviving Lobos are even more valuable as collectible retro bikes. **GK**

GT's Lobo was packed with unique construction and suspension technology. ▶

ROCK LOBSTER TIG Team 853
1998 • Mountain bike • UK • Classic high-value, top-quality steel hardtail

Rock Lobster made some of the most popular shop-built bikes of the 1990s. Its range included several alloy-framed bikes, but the bike that drew most attention was its Reynolds 853 steel flagship, the TIG Team.

At the time, Reynolds 853 was the most advanced steel alloy available, and, unlike most ferrous alloys, it hardened and strengthened at the joins where the stress was greatest. The head tube was ring-reinforced, with handling designed for a standard 4-in. (10-cm) travel fork, and there were full disc brakes and attendant hydraulic hose routing. A sloped top tube gave standover clearance, and a forward-facing seat clamp slot prevented mud getting in from the rear wheel. The neat wishbone rear and tiny cowled Ritchey drop-outs gave classic slim steel good looks under the gem-red paint. The ride was also classic steel—agile, responsive, and dependable.

Despite the frame's lightness—4 lb 6 oz (2 kg)—it had a resilient toughness. The tubing kept the steering stiff, while the slim tapered-tube back end gave a good balance between long-haul comfort and muscular power delivery. When finished as complete trail bikes by collaborators Merlin Cycles, TIG Teams remained firm favorites for more than a decade. **GK**

COVE Stiffee
1998 • Mountain bike • Canada • Hardtail with an innovative twist

The Cove Bike Shop opened in Deep Cove, North Shore in Vancouver, British Columbia, before mountain bikes had really started. But as soon as they did start, Cove founder Chaz Romalis began importing the best of them. Unfortunately, they weren't really tough enough for the sort of riding Romalis and his cohorts wanted to do, so Cove decided to make its own. A new breed of super-tough bikes quickly evolved, with the Stiffee spearheading a trend toward tough, aluminum-frame, long-forked bikes that would soon be known as freeride hardtails. Arguments continue about whether it was the Cove Stiffee or the Santa Cruz Chameleon that got the recipe right first, but they were both historically significant as the earliest made-to-be-different, hard-hitting hardtails that were more than simply a mechanic's personal lash-up with overlong forks.

Significantly, they weren't just jump bikes. Stiffees could happily handle long rides on cross-country terrain and withstand the handling of riders who would break most other bikes. Today there are plenty of cross-country trail bikes designed to work best with 4- to 5-in. (10- to 12.7-cm) travel forks and great geometry, but in the late 1990s Santa Cruz and Cove were bridging the gap between cross-country and more aggressive riding. **SW**

GT ZR2000

1998 • Road bike • UK • Distinctive rear-triangle design

GT is best known as a mountain bike manufacturer, but the Californian company also constructed road bikes, and once sponsored a pro road racing team for a season.

GT mountain bikes were easily spotted by the distinctive way the crossover seatstays created a "triple triangle" frame profile. This supposedly reduced the amount of vibration transferred from the back wheel to the seat. There was no reason why this system couldn't work for road bikes, too, hence this GT ZR bike—an attempt to create a high-end road or triathlon machine using a tungsten inert gas (TIG)-welded 7000-series butted aluminum frame. The extra rear triangle added even more stiffness to the rigid aluminum tubing.

The complete bike came with GT's own Edge ultra-lightweight carbon fiber composite unicrown fork, and a comprehensive set of Shimano Ultegra components, including dual pivot brakes, STI levers and hubs, as well as the full gearset. The GT came in seven sizes, but only one paint job: a red-and-white race-style scheme.

Other state-of-the-art kit fitted to the ZR included Ritchey Pro Road pedals, an American Classic seatpost, and Tange Seiki DX-8 headset. Rims were Mavic CX 23, tires Continental Grand Prix 4000, and spokes DT stainless steel. **SH**

TREK Y-Foil

1998 • Road bike • USA • Road race version of monocoque mountain bike frame concept

A road bike frame design spawned from a full-suspension mountain bike frame sounds like a real Frankenstein mess, but only rule changes stopped this smooth-looking speed machine in its tracks.

Trek's Y22 frame was the ultimate expression of the URT (unified rear triangle) suspension concept that dominated mountain biking in the late 1990s, joining front fork, seatpost, and main pivot with a Y-shaped monocoque structure.

Trek extended the upper stays of the carbon-fiber rear triangle forward to meet the "Y" mainframe. This smoothly blended front and rear, and made the Y-Foil more aerodynamic than traditional round-tubed frames. Because it was cantilevered off the mainframe, the saddle was suspended, giving a very smooth ride over rough surfaces and making it the bike of choice for long-distance racers and riders. Rear brake and water bottle mountings were also built into the bridge section, while a small arm held the front mech in place.

Unfortunately, the aerodynamic advantages of the Y-Foil and other similar Y-framed bikes led the UCI to ban any bikes without a seat tube from competition. Production ceased after only a year. This distinctive frame has since become a collector's item. **GK**

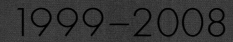

1999–2008

Technology takes bike performance to a whole new level.

PUSHING THE LIMITS

CANNONDALE Jekyll

1999 • Mountain bike • USA • Changeable-geometry mountain bike with radical single-sided fork

This was one of the first suspension mountain bikes to allow riders to subtly change the frame geometry and thereby alter the handling. Cannondale named it after the good Dr. Jekyll, the character in the Robert Louis Stevenson novel who could quickly turn himself into the evil Mr. Hyde.

Cannondale, one of the two companies that had introduced outsized aluminum tubing to the bicycle world a decade previously, had never been afraid to innovate. While the frame of the Jekyll was not very radical, the same could not be said of the Fox rear shock in a threaded mount that could be screwed backward and forward. With the damper wound back, the bottom bracket lifted and the steering angle steepened for greater ground clearance under

spinning pedals and quicker steering on climbs. With the damper wound forward and the fork angle slackened, the ride height of the bike dropped for stabler handling at high speeds.

This created a true all-round mountain bike, but the fork, not the frame, dominated the limelight. Previously Cannondale had used the Fatty Headshock system that hid the suspension damper in the front of the frame but limited the amount of travel it could deliver without pushing the handlebars sky high. The new Lefty fork moved the same needle-bearing internals into a single leg tube with a cone-shaped axle attaching onto a custom hub. Although it looks weird, this light and stiff fork created an enduring family that Cannondale still uses today. **GK**

ON-ONE Inbred

1999 • Mountain bike • UK • Insolently designed blue-collar bargain

On-One was launched as the mountain bike offshoot of the Internet-marketed UK-based Planet-X brand. The brand driver was former *MTB* magazine editor Brant Richards, who was, to quote another *MTB* journalist, "an early and very successful adopter of guerrilla marketing via social media."

The On-One Inbred was often described as a backlash bike. The first one was a single-geared, rigid-forked, steel-framed offering in the days when almost everything else appeared to be going for more and more gears, more suspension travel, and increasingly exotic frame materials. All On-One bikes were, and still are, insolently designed blue-collar offerings sold direct via mail order. What makes them important is that they've always been well designed and nicely built too.

Before setting up On-One, Richards learned a lot from designers such as Keith Bontrager and tested bikes for magazines. As a marketeer, his strengths are anticipation of, and response to, customer requirements. He is also aware that word of mouth can be a more powerful selling tool than advertising.

The Inbred surfed on the crest of a new wave of single-geared, steel-frame bikes. In its 29-in. (73.5-cm) wheel format, introduced in 2003, the Inbred made a lot of big-wheel naysayers sit up and take notice. The Inbred has since evolved to include multi-gear suspension, fork-equipped versions, but it's still one of the cheapest frames on the market, and it's still made from decent-quality, 4130 butted chromoly steel. **SW**

HAMPSTEN Strada Bianca

1999 • Retro race bike • USA • Classic competition-standard road bike

Former pro racer Andy Hampsten and his brother Steve set up their bike-making business in Seattle in 1999. The Strada Bianca is still one of their best-known products: a retro 1960s-style road racer that has acquired a formidable reputation as a competition-level all-rounder.

Named after the Italian for "white road," the Strada Bianca is a classic, characterful fast bike on smooth tarmac. Moreover, it is versatile enough to handle rough stuff like trails, dirt, cobbles, and gravel too. The Bianca could wear skinny tires and race wheels to join a group of enthusiasts testing out a stage of the Tour de France, or slip on fat tires to explore a demanding trail anywhere in the world; the bike is equally at ease in either environment.

That's mainly thanks to its hand-built frame. There's nothing retro about the quality of the modern materials and parts used here. The Strada Bianca tubing is Columbus PegoRitchie Spirit, a triple-butted steel alloy strengthened by the addition of tiny percentages of niobium and manganese.

These Spirit tubes are considered among the top materials for a lightweight but extremely durable competition bike frame. They enable the bike not only to keep up with the leading group but also to be comfortable over a long day in the saddle.

The standard fork is carbon, but a steel fork is an optional extra for around $200 (£133). Buyers also have the option of a straight-gauge titanium or an aluminum fork.

Andy Hampsten himself rides a titanium version of the Strada Bianca with S&S Couplings for easy travel by air. He claims the Bianca's handling is similar to the bikes he used in his race career, which included victory in the 1988 Giro d'Italia. **SH**

TURNER Stinger

1999 • Mountain bike • USA • Innovative pull-shock full-suspension race bike

Dave Turner started his career in mountain biking as a professional cross-country racer, but it was not until his bike company had been in business for five years that he developed his first dedicated speed machine—a minimalist, lightweight creation that was remarkable as much for what was missing as for what was included.

Take, for example, the suspension. Turner's previous bikes had used horizontal "walking beam" linkages to drive a conventional rear shock. The Stinger did without them altogether, and joined the rear struts directly onto a custom Fox pull-shock that seemed to float inside the mainframe.

". . . for people who are hyper-conscious about saving every gram they can."

Dave Turner

The result was a frame that weighed no more than most hardtail race bikes of the time, but which gave 3 in. (7.5 cm) of rear wheel movement to aid traction and control on technical courses. This design was licensed in slightly modified form by K2 for its Razorback bikes.

Unfortunately, the custom shock caused problems, and the Stinger was discontinued in favor of the conventional rocker-linkage suspension Nitrous. Although this bike had some success under Canadian racer Geoff Kabush, it too suffered from flex-related issues caused by heavy braking, and it was replaced in 2005 by the 4-in. (10-cm) travel Flux.

Dave later pushed the limits of pedal-driven off-road speed with his first carbon fiber frameset, the Turner Czar. **GK**

Turner's innovative Stinger was an ultra-light racer for the fastest riders. ▶

TREK VRX

1999 • Mountain bike • USA • Radical-looking
all-round mountain bike

By the mid-1990s, Trek's hitherto successful Unified
Rear Triangle (URT) Y bike design struggled to compete
because the rider stood on the unsprung portion when
descending, effectively creating just a hinged bike, not
a suspension bike.

Trek changed all this with the introduction of
the VRX series. These bikes still used a braced Y-style
mainframe, but the Icon crankset was mounted on the
bottom corner of the mainframe spar, not on the rear
subframe. The rear end used a new swingarm design
based on deep rectangular and triangular welded
extrusions. While the wheel arced around a single pivot,
Trek added a secondary Fully Independent Linkage
(FIL) connected to the mainframe and swingarm via a
small rocker link. This changed the shock rate slightly
and used different shock mount positions to give "cross
country," "all conditions," and "downhill" settings with up
to 5 in. (127 mm) of travel.

The top-of-the-range VRX 500 matched this
frame with equally interesting components, not least
the RockShox SID XL suspension fork. The bike also
featured eye-catching Rolf Dolomite Disc wheels,
Hayes hydraulic disc brakes, and a Fox Vanilla R coil-
sprung shock. **GK**

BMW Q6.S

1999 • Mountain bike • Germany • Folding
mountain bike with BMW motorcycle-style suspension

Bicycles associated with automobile makers come in
two categories: those that are engineered by the auto
makers themselves, and those that are made by bicycle
manufacturers with the badge of a famous carmaker
appended as an afterthought. The BMW Q6.S definitely
belongs in the former category.

While BMW was responsible for the design of the
Q6.S, bicycle company Schauff put it all together. Even
so, there is a lot of BMW in this bike. The main feature is its
front Telelever suspension. This is a quintessentially BMW
innovation that virtually eliminates brake dive—the
tendency of a traditional telescopic fork system to push
downward while braking. The Telelever—an adjustable
coil-spring shock absorber mounted on a swingarm
attached to the mainframe with telescopic sliders on
the front fork—balances braking forces against weight
displacement shifts.

The bike is not weakened by its foldability, thanks to
its beefy X-shaped aluminum frame (available in small,
medium, and large—and all robot-welded, just like their
automotive stablemates). The Q6.S gives a cushy ride,
but is also good downhill and on cross-country trails,
with an efficient contemporary all-rounder weight of
27 lb (12 kg). **BS**

SANTA CRUZ Bullitt

1999 • Mountain bike • USA • Classic heavy-duty mountain bike

Santa Cruz's Bullitt was one of the classic 6-in. (15-cm) suspension bikes that let a whole new generation of freeriders and all-mountain riders push mountain biking way beyond its previous limits.

As is often the case with classic bikes, it was the simplicity of the Bullitt (named after the movie starring Steve McQueen) that made it so successful. The layout was essentially a bigger-tubed, stronger version of the existing Santa Cruz single pivot template. The way the rear stays were curved around to form a reinforcing loop behind the rear shock-absorber was very fresh for 1999, however. Thick machine-cut uprights spanned the stays, and the swingarm swung through extra-large pivots. The Bullitt came with a custom-tuned Fox Vanilla RC coil-sprung shock of the type used in downhill race bikes to soak up big drops and rocks.

Subsequent versions were modified slightly to take bigger rear brake rotors and longer stroke forks, and the Bullitt remained a classic Santa Cruz for many years. Unfortunately, neither the second-generation bike, with altered geometry and suspension, nor the later derivative, the Butcher, recaptured the original's popularity and it's only the 1999–2005 Bullitt that fans will think of when this iconic name is mentioned. **GK**

ROTWILD RFR02

1999 • Mountain bike • Germany • Early all-mountain machine with lots of downhill features

This crossover frame was a no-nonsense machine for no-nonsense riders. The raw finish showcased the beautiful big fish-scale welds that joined the outsized spar sections of the top tube-reinforced Y-frame design together. Rotwild strengthened the frame with two extra tubes straddling the RockShox SID rear shock, while the seat tube was cantilevered off the rear of the top spar. The small-tubed swingarm pivoted off giant cartridge bearings just above the chainring for a full active ride with 5 in. (12.7 cm) of rear wheel travel—little more than 1 in. (2.5 cm) less than Rotwild's RFR01 full-on freeride bike of the time. The shock was fitted into an adjustable trunnion mount on the front and three separate mounts on the rear, giving twelve potential shock mount positions. Other features showed the heavy-duty compliant character of the frame. Small threaded inserts just behind the headstock were added for screw-in fork bumpers that stopped the tubes from being damaged by the extended legs of a triple-crown fork if it whipped round in a crash.

The low pivot setup of the rear end gave smooth performance and stiff tracking. The alloy frame and SID air shock weighed less than 28 lb (12.7 kg), and made the RFR02 a ground-breaker in the all-mountain genre. **GK**

BROOKLYN MWORKS TMX

1999 • Mountain bike • USA • Heavyweight motocross-inspired steel-framed downhill mountain bike

The TMX brought overnight fame to Brooklyn Machine Works, a group of riders and frame builders.

At a time when most bikes were using alloy tubes or box sections, Brooklyn remained faithful to super-strong steel tubes and extra reinforcing plates that they'd learned to trust from riding BMXs. This made the TMX totally bombproof and ready to handle the biggest drops when it was built up freeride-style.

What really made the TMX stand out, though, was the design team's solution to the perpetual problem of how to isolate the suspension movement from pedaling and braking. In most designs, the rhythmic pull of the chain is counteracted by carefully angling the rearward movement of the wheel through careful positioning of the pivot. The TMX totally isolated the two by adding a secondary "jack shaft" that took the chaindrive from the conventional crank and aligned it with the main swingarm pivot. The rear brake was also mounted on an independently moving braking arm so that the suspension reacted only to impacts and other trail-related inputs. The frame angles, swingarm length, and overall bike length could be adjusted to suit the demands of different riders and different race courses. The extra-long Fox Racing shock could also be positioned to change rear wheel movement from 8½ to 10½ in. of travel.

The result could best be likened to the cycling equivalent of a steamroller, with jaw-dropping industrial looks, and the apparent ability to defy gravity and ignore everything in its path. The complex design and steel construction, together with the heaviest components, meant that this behemoth of a bike weighed in at over 50 lb (22.6 kg). Consequently, it struggled to compete on race circuits against increasingly lightweight opposition. **GK**

COYOTE Ultralite HT3

1999 • Mountain bike • Taiwan • Budget aluminum hardtail

Price isn't everything: The frameset of this Coyote cost only around $550 (£350), but the complete bike had plenty of plus points as an entertaining MTB machine.

For starters, the HT3 was built around a very lightweight aluminum tubeset with 7,005-grade double-butted pipes. Both the chainstay and seatstay featured strengthening bridges. The result was an arrangement that flexed just enough to give smooth riding over rough terrain, but retained effective sprinting up steep climbs.

The bike had few if any frills, but its quality was highly impressive because it was built in the same factory as some Specialized bikes. The paint finish and

> *". . . tiny fractions add up to an aluminum bike that doesn't beat you up. Good."*
>
> *Bike Magic*

graphics were considered particularly good at this price point.

The complete HT3 bike came with a "British race kit," a collection of quality components that included very light but capable RockShox SID forks, Profile carbon bar and Stiffee stem, a Uno seatpost, WTB saddle and grips, and the Hope Pro hydraulic disc brakeset. With this sort of kit fitted to a light aluminum frame, the HT3 had all the potential to become a fast mountain bike.

Other features included Mavic wheels shod with Continental CC 1.9 tires. The all-important groupset—supplied by Shimano—was the specialist cross-country XTR system with an 11-34 MegaRange cassette. *Bike Magic* reported that the bike was so light that the bottom-end gears were seldom needed. **SH**

GARY FISHER Goldenfly

1999 • Mountain bike • USA • One-off Olympic race-winning mountain bike

"Yes, I'm shy, but I like the attention. It's a nice recognition. And I still get it sometimes."

Paola Pezzo

Italian racer Paola Pezzo won the first Olympic mountain bike medal in Atlanta in 1996 and immediately became a poster girl for the sport. Her bike sponsor, Gary Fisher, was determined to put another gold medal around her neck in 2000. While the course at Sydney was relatively technical, with both drops and intense rock sections, Pezzo was still concerned with minimum weight rather than maximum suspension travel. This led Fisher to create the Goldenfly soft tail. Because it used an almost undisturbed frame design and Trek's latest OCLV (Optimum Compaction Low Volume) carbon fiber construction, the bike was extremely light. A super-short stroke RockShox SID shock was then placed between the seatstays and the mainframe to create a soft tail to take some of the sting from the trail before it started to beat up Pezzo. The Goldenfly was also built around Fisher's long top tube and short-stem Genesis geometry for maximum agility.

The bike was built in-house by Trek and then delivered to Pezzo in Italy by Gary Fisher himself, and four more evolved versions were supplied before Pezzo went Down Under to defend her Olympic title. The super-light, smooth-riding Goldenfly did its job flawlessly too, putting Pezzo on the top step of the podium for a second time. Trek launched a production version of the frame right away to capitalize, but rather than sporting the Gary Fisher livery, it was launched as the Trek STP with conventional rather than Genesis geometry.

Meanwhile Pezzo retired from racing to raise a family in 2002—she reluctantly came out of retirement for the Athens Olympics in 2004—and she now runs two Olympic Bike Center stores in the Italian Alpine mountain bike hotspot of Lake Garda with her husband, Paolo "Crazy Horse" Rosola. **DB**

Paola Pezzo on her way to Gold in the Sydney Olympic Games. ▷

BIOMEGA MN01

1999 • Utility bike • Denmark • When was the last time you rode a work of art?

Designed without so much as a nod to compromise by renowned designer Marc Newson, Biomega's stunning MN01 has won all the category accolades in the world of engineering, design, and cycling. It was also named one of the ten most innovative products by the Centre Georges Pompidou in Paris, France.

The MN01 is recognizable by its extravagant, exquisite S-shaped frame, which creates a dilemma for the owner: should one ride it, or do what the Carnegie Museum of Art in Pittsburgh and the San Francisco Museum of Modern Art did, and hang it on the wall?

The genius of its aluminum S-shaped frame is the flexing it provides, which is akin to that of the steel-

". . . the creation process is reversed . . . design is driving the geometry of the frame."

Rico Zorkendorfer, designer

frame bikes preferred by riders who spend prolonged periods in the saddle and want to minimize jarring to the body. However, although this bike has all the lightweight strength of aluminum and components borrowed from the aerospace industry, it is clearly not a bike for typical Lycra-clad cyclists, but rather is aimed at urbanites.

The MN01's 18-in. (45-cm) long rack, capable of carrying 26 lb (12 kg), is an aesthetic tour de force—attached only to the seatpost, it creates the illusion of floating above the rear wheel. Its Rohloff 14-speed internal gear hub, carbon fork, and twin Hope hydraulic disc brakes provide all the function you'll need, but if ever there was a bike that put beauty before hardware, this is it. **BS**

COVE Hummer

1999 • Mountain bike • Canada • Canadian titanium hardcore hardtail

Deep Cove bike shop in Vancouver, British Columbia, Canada, found itself at the center of one of mountain biking's most exciting revolutions when freeriding took root among the fallen trees of the North Shore rain forests on the outskirts of the city.

At the time of the Hummer's first appearance, cross-country and downhill racing had become so serious and focused that, for many riders, mountain biking had lost the fundamental cool factor that had formerly made it so attractive. Huge amounts of money were being plowed into bikes and tracks that only the pros could ride, and downhillers were even swapping flamboyant, motocross-inspired clothing for aerodynamic skin suits developed for road racers.

Freeride was exactly the return to totally uninhibited, radical riding that many bikers had been looking for. Because of the amount of fallen timber on the North Shore rain forest floor, riders were building rough wooden trails high in the trees, complete with seesaws, massive jumps, and dizzying drops. These routes were being tamed by a whole new breed of renegades who were more likely to spend time wielding chainsaws than consulting training plans, and who performed stunts they had learned from BMX and trials riding.

The 1998 Stiffee alloy hardtail was a perfect, affordable all-rounder for riders who had insufficient funds for the latest long-stroke suspension bikes, but the Hummer was created for cyclists who could afford suspension but wanted the subtle spring and responsiveness of titanium. Built from highest-grade butted forms of this metal by Sandvik and then later by Lynskey, the Hummer was tough enough to negotiate the biggest drops but light enough to be a contender in cross-country events. Its success inspired the creation of a whole new species of high-class hardcore hardtails. **GK**

Hummer was Cove's flagship titanium take on its classic Stiffee hardcore. ▷

WHYTE PRST-1

1999 • Mountain bike • UK • Unique linkage fork suspension bike

It is inevitable that bike technology doesn't always develop at the same speed for different parts of the pedal-powered puzzle. The Whyte PRST-1 of 1999 is a case of a wild tangent being taken to get around this problem.

Former Formula One designer Jon Whyte was frustrated that no conventional forks matched the smoothness of his new back end. Rather than using a telescopic fork, the PRST-1 used clamshell monocoque fork legs attached to the frame with twin linkages. A Fox air-sprung damper provided impact control, while cartridge bearings were fitted at the frame and fork ends of the structure. The wheels were held in place at either end using axle bobbin and cam-operated "Big Gripper" latches that mimicked Honda's Grand Prix motorbikes.

The result was an incredibly smooth and sensitive ride. The J-shaped path reduced the effect of fork dive when braking and the whole bike was surprisingly light, prompting one contemporary mountain bike magazine to ask "Is this the fastest XC bike ever?" on its cover.

The praying mantis-like bike divided opinion, and the bike also tended to divide itself into its constituent parts if it turned sideways in a crash. Within a year, Fox suspension forks reset performance benchmarks and rendered the PRST-1 obsolete overnight. **GK**

LITESPEED Blade

1999 • Time trial bike • USA • Custom titanium time trial bike repainted as a Trek

In addition to its own premium bike brand, titanium specialist Litespeed built bikes for other brands, both officially and covertly. The most infamous rebadged Litespeed was ridden by Trek-sponsored Lance Armstrong in his 1999 "comeback from cancer" Tour de France campaign. Litespeed founder Mark Lynskey explained how this came about:

"We made bikes for Lance for many years. The link originated through Eddy Merckx, Steve Hed, and later John Cobb. We were building titanium frames for Eddy, and he arranged for us to build bikes for Lance's Motorola team and later U.S. Postal. When Lance won the Worlds in 1993, it was on a bike we had built (labeled as a Caloi). When Trek became Lance's sponsor, he of course used their road frames, but at that time they did not have a really good time trial bike that he liked. Hed and Cobb were Lance's aerodynamic advisors, and Steve had also advised us as we developed the Blade so it was a simple connection for Lance to want us to build him one."

The Blade was extremely distinctive. The deep oval and teardrop aerodynamic profiles on all the mainframe tubes were made from titanium, in spite of the fact that the metal is notoriously difficult to shape. **GK**

◁ Formula One met Heath Robinson in Whyte's PRST-1.

TEX
BRAVO LANCE
Good Job
LANCE
You're The Man!!!
Just do it
Go Boy!
Good luck
WUZ UP LANCE
Hey Lance,
TREK
TREK
TREK
TREK
VECTOR PRO
UNITED STATES
Volkswagen
LANCE,
GOOD LUCK!
OR
BETTER YET
CONGRATULATIONS

TREK 5500

1999 • Road bike • USA • Lance Armstrong's first Tour de France-winning bike

Trek first ventured into the European peloton with the fledging U.S. Postal team in 1997, but it enjoyed only modest success until Armstrong's unbelievable 1999 season. Despite an earlier World Championship win, the Texan was still viewed as a rank outsider when he conquered all at the Tour de France. Armstrong was immediately lauded as a sporting hero: The man who beat cancer and also won the toughest sporting event on the planet. He was an overnight marketing dream and Trek was more than willing to go along for the seven-year ride.

Trek's OCLV carbon road frame, which Armstrong rode to victory in 1999, was first introduced in 1992, when Armstrong was no more than a promising young rider. In the intervening years between Armstrong's World Championship win in 1993 and his Tour de France win in 1999, relatively little changed with the design of the OCLV. The steerer tube was threaded chromoly steel and housed a Cinelli quill stem. Trek claimed that Armstrong also rode a standard stock frame during that year's Tour de France—a point it was also keen to stress during his second comeback in 2009. The 1999 OCLV weighed in at 61¾ oz (1.75 kg), a favorable amount compared to the carbon contemporaries of the day.

Armstrong stuck with Shimano Dura Ace pedals throughout his career, and much of the equipment on his Tour-winning Treks remained the same. In 1999 Rolf provided the wheels, and they were later replaced by other sponsors, but Armstrong's bike is deserving of its place in this book simply for the ride he provided through France that year. We all now know the truth about Armstrong and that era as a whole, but at the time and for seven years, the Trek–Armstrong partnership could do no wrong. **DB**

DEKERF 853 SL

1999 • Mountain bike • Canada • Artisan frame from a Canadian steel specialist

While aluminum and carbon fiber now dominate the bike market, steel has always retained a niche position in the materials menu. The slim lines and trademark sprung ride of steel tubing joined together with traditional building methods have a powerful retro appeal, and the best builders, such as Chris Dekerf, go to extreme lengths to produce bikes that are both almost sculptural in beauty but still loaded with practical advantages.

In 1999, Canadian bikes were in the forefront of mountain bike media coverage thanks to the crazy antics of the Vancouver Freeriders. But the 853 SL was at the opposite end of the mountain bike spectrum to brutish box-section aluminum-framed freeride bikes.

"I learned to make things by hand from a master craftsman, my father."

Chris Dekerf

Reynolds 853 steel alloy was a revolutionary material at the time, but it was how Dekerf put the SL together that made it a pinnacle of steel bike design. While most of the frame junctions were heat treated to maximize strength, the head tube, bottom bracket tube, and short extended seat section were left uncooked. This meant these critical areas could be easily removed and replaced if the bearing threads, headset faces, or built-in seat bolt threads became damaged. The rear stays also used Dekerf's signature penetrated pipe design where the short cross members were pierced by the extended stays for a mechanical as well as a welded joint.

The result was a sublimely smooth ride from an equally sublime-looking bike, and many of the features used in 1999 are still in Dekerf's Team SST today. **GK**

ORANGE Patriot

1999 • Mountain bike • UK • Outstandingly tough hardcore mountain bike

Orange Mountain Bikes co-owner Lester Noble is in no doubt about which of his bikes transformed the company from a nationally recognized manufacturer into a globally sought-after brand: "The Patriot, I suppose, was the start of what we are today. It was made to ride British downhill courses, but made us a bit of a name abroad, too."

After a decade of success building conventional tube-frame bikes, Orange started experimenting with folded sheet frame sections on its X2 bike before using a folded sheet swingarm and mainframe tube for the 1999 Patriot. The bike was promptly adopted by Animal, one of the UK's most successful downhill racing teams, and thanks to the incredible South African junior (and subsequently world) champion Greg Minnaar, the Patriot exploded onto the race scene.

While the 222 frame took over from the Patriot for racing, this simple 6-in. (15-cm) suspension bike was seized on by increasingly radical riders as the ideal heavy-duty gravity machine. It evolved continually until a brief hiatus in 2008, but it was still a very similar bike when it returned to the market in 2012. As Noble says, that's one of the bike's greatest strengths: "We never got caught up in the fashion side of the sport. Our designs wouldn't have been as successful if we hadn't been like that."

Among the Patriot's other strengths are communicative and reactive suspension; excellent all-round weight balance, and exemplary reliability. The three weaknesses that are worthy of mention are: a certain amount of pedal kickback on long descents; the inconvenient absence of International Standard Chainguide (ISCG) mounts and internal routing; and, above all, the cost—British-built bikes can no longer compete with Asian products. **GK**

WILLITS 29er

1999 • Mountain bike • USA • First widely available 29er-wheeled mountain bike

The first big production mountain bikes employed 26-in. (66-cm) rims and tires because of these components' easy availability. However, there were plenty of early experiments with bigger wheels using 650B and 700C rims and tires. If tires and rims had been more readily available in other sizes, those early production mountain bikes may well have had 29-in. (73.5-cm) wheels—a nominal size that relates to the overall diameter of a 700C rim plus a tire fat enough for use on rough terrain.

Many riders were introduced to 29ers by early Gary Fisher models, but prior to their appearance on the market, most mountain bikes were 700C machines.

"Every frame and fork is made by Wes to give you the best-riding, most durable product."

Willits publicity

Marin County mountain bike builder Charlie Cunningham made a 700C rim-based, all-terrain bike for himself in the early 1980s. Bruce Gordon's early Rock 'n' Road bike used road bike rims and modified RockShox forks to accommodate the wheels. Gordon's bikes were a major influence on Wes Willits of Crested Butte, Colorado. During the latter part of the 1990s, Willits developed his own "28er"—the wheels were limited in diameter because there were still no suitably fat tires available at the time. But at the Interbike show in 1999, Willits exhibited several 29ers, complete with modified suspension forks and big tires. The new fat tires turned these machines into genuine 29ers, so Willits deserves the kudos for creating the first 29er mountain bikes. **SW**

◁ Orange's Patriot frame was hand-folded in Halifax, UK.

DE ROSA King
1999 • Road bike • Italy • All-carbon frame

In the middle of an innocuous-looking industrial zone on the outskirts of Milan, there stands a huge neon fascia that declares: "De Rosa Ugo & Figli—Biciclette Speciale." The sign heralds the entrance to De Rosa headquarters, a family business originally founded in 1952 by engineer and amateur cyclist Ugo De Rosa, and now run with his sons Danilo, Cristiano, and Doriano. After building a road bike for Raphaël Géminiani's run in the 1958 Giro d'Italia, De Rosa's cycles gradually became a fixture on the international peloton of the 1960s.

The King model first burst onto the scene in 2000. This full-carbon build became the new flagship of the De Rosa range of road bikes. The frame was a full year in development, and was designed in conjunction with Mizuno of Japan, a world leader in carbon frame construction. As Cristiano De Rosa recalls, "Before we launched the King frame we did a lot of testing to understand just how to derive the best combination of carbon fiber composition and shape. Not only did we have our crew of road testers, but our custom-built test-bed machine really enabled us to refine the King."

Standard models were kitted out with a Mizuno MR50 fork and—not too surprisingly—high-end Campagnola components: record gear- and brakesets plus Eurus wheelsets.

Over the years the King would evolve, most dramatically with the 2008 King 3, where the 43¼-oz (1.23-kg) frame shed almost 20 percent of its original weight. Now that is *speciale*. **TB**

SANTA CRUZ Superlight

1999 • Mountain bike • USA • Slimmed-down race-ready version of the Heckler all-rounder

Santa Cruz was one of the first brands to detect and move into a gap in the market for a lightweight, relatively simple full-suspension bike aimed specifically at riders who had previously ridden only hardtails.

More than a decade later, the single-pivot Superlight remains a part of the Santa Cruz range and, in the right hands, can still outride pretty much any cross-country-biased bike that's come along since.

The introduction of platform damping on modern rear shock units kept the performance up with the best of them. With all the clever multi-pivoted frame designs out there today, that's an impressive feat for a single-pivot frame. Santa Cruz has recently introduced a Superlight for 29-in. (73.5-cm) wheels too. It's in competition with a whole raft of VPP (Virtual

Pivot Point) bikes within the Santa Cruz range, but its relatively simple design helps keep the cost and weight down. A 26-in. (66-cm) wheel Superlight frame weighed about 5½ lb (2.5 kg). The 29-in. (73.5-cm) wheel version weighs around ½ lb (0.25 kg) more. There are certainly lighter frames around today, but not at the same sort of price.

The Superlight is one of the very best privateer racer's bikes ever built. It's still a 4-in. (10 cm) travel bike, but recent editions were tweaked to be suitable for 4½-in. (12-cm) forks. In the 2000 National Off-Road Bicycle Association pro race, Kirk Molday rode a Santa Cruz Superlight to victory at Big Bear, California. According to Rob Roskopp, Molday didn't just beat the opposition, "he smoked 'em." **SW**

SANTA CRUZ Juliana

1999 • Mountain bike • USA • Female-specific
suspension frame designed by a legendary racer

When Californian suspension specialist Santa Cruz
wanted to build a bike specifically for women, it chose
to collaborate with the most successful female U.S.
mountain biker, Juliana Furtado. Furtado was a national-
level skier until knee injuries turned her attention to
mountain biking, which she dominated throughout
the late 1980s and early 1990s, winning three World
Championships. She also won the downhill worlds in
1992, and represented the United States at the Atlanta
Olympics in 1996.

This female-specific version of the popular
Superlight that Santa Cruz developed with Furtado's
assistance was named in her honor. It used the same
layout and lightweight alloy tubing and bolt-on braces
as the Superlight, and had the same 4 in. (10 cm) of travel.

Following its success, Furtado created a whole range
of Juliana Bicycles, including four different machines
based around Santa Cruz's latest suspension and frame
technologies, including a carbon fiber frame and VPP2
suspension on the most expensive Furtado Primiero
model. Furtado also created a supporting selection
of equipment and clothing for female riders, and
continues to be closely involved in racing as a sponsor
of local riders. **GK**

MAVERICK ML7

1999 • Mountain bike • USA • Innovative
mountain bike from suspension-fork pioneer

Paul Turner launched his Maverick design house
after tiring of the big-business side of the RockShox
suspension superbrand he had created.

His first Maverick, this ML7, was loaded with
innovations. The square-tubed, curved-triangle
frame was hand built by aluminum chassis pioneer
Klein. Fox Racing Shocks created a unique, air-sprung,
magnesium suspension strut, and cast magnesium was
employed in the unprecedented Monolink box section
linkage. The maker proudly asserted that he had
"turned the mountain bike world on its ear"—a strange
expression, but by no means an excessive claim.

The Monolink suspension gave a direct drive feel
and accurate traction feedback for excellent climbing,
and sucked up bumps when freewheeling back down.
Klein later licensed the design for its Palomino range.

Unfortunately, elements that worked well on the
prototype proved less durable in real-world usage. The
magnesium shock body was slightly porous and lost air
pressure. The 3D twisting and pedaling loads through
the Monolink caused bearing failure. Similar problems
dogged Maverick's fork and Speedball seatpost
production too, although the brand carried on until
2012 before finally closing shop. **GK**

CANNONDALE Scalpel

2000 • Mountain bike • USA • Ultra-light full-suspension racing mountain bike

The original Scalpel was ridden by Tinker Juarez to his fourth 24-hour U.S. solo national title, helping to quash the notion that full-suspension setups were principally for short, intense efforts or more casual riding. The key for lightweight riders like Juarez was to create a full-suspension bike that was as light as possible. The Scalpel was described by Cannondale as "the world's lightest dual-suspension design," and it became "the most winning dual-suspension design in World Cup history."

At the time, it was a one-of-a-kind machine that managed to mix the ride characteristics of hardtails and full-suspension bikes, adding comfort for rough terrain but with a lockout for climbs.

The Scapel was a fast and surprisingly comfortable cross-country bike. It offered 2½ in. (6.5 cm) of rear wheel travel, and was among the first designs to rely on carbon fiber chainstays. The frame weighed less than 5 lb (2.25 kg) including the shock, making it twenty-five percent lighter than most other cross-country designs of the time.

The Scalpel has since evolved considerably, and now comes with a completely carbon fiber frame, 29-in. (73.5-cm) wheels, and with the shock based within the mainframe triangle instead of behind the seat tube. **SW**

PASHLEY MailStar

2000 • Utility bike • UK • Classic postal worker's official delivery bike

In 1929, Britain's Post Office introduced a bicycle for staff that was to stay almost unchanged for more than eighty years. The sturdy red bikes were required to carry loads of up to 50 lb (23 kg). They were simple machines with a freewheel and two rod-operated brakes, but no gears.

Various manufacturers built these machines, but in 1977 Pashley won the contract to supply all the Post Office's bikes. Having successfully re-tendered around the turn of the millennium, Pashley abandoned the old design in favor of the revolutionary MailStar.

The new bike was designed to operate on all road conditions and in all weathers. It was reliable, easy to maintain, and had an increased load capacity of 53 lb (24 kg), thanks to the addition of front and rear cargo carriers made of tubular steel.

The frame was changed to a step-through design to allow riders to mount and dismount easily. The features were advanced, too. At last, postal workers with hilly rounds could take advantage of a three-speed internal-hub gear system. Also new were a rear light, a chunky and durable saddle, and heavy-duty tires. A sad sign of the times was that the bikes now came with wheel locks with extension cables so that they could be secured against thieves. **SH**

LOOK KG396 CLM

2000 • Track/Time trial bike • France • World beater based on the hugely successful track frame

"The frame-specific fork design certainly guarantees that heads will be turned wherever it's ridden."

Cyclingnews.com

Based in Nevers, France, Look claims an impressive timeline of technological achievement: the company produced the first clipless pedals (1984); the first full-carbon frame (1986); and the first single-piece carbon frame (1990). Then, in 2000, the KG396 frame launched a new era of success on the track, beginning with four gold-medal victories at the 2000 Sydney Olympics.

Having thus established its reputation, the KG396 became a highly desirable acquisition. By the 2003 World Championships, the Chinese, French, German, Mexican, and Russian teams were all using it. A stiff, low-vibration frame, it's remembered as perhaps the best track bike of the early twenty-first century.

The outstanding development occurred in 2004, the year that saw the first appearance of the KG396 CLM frame. The suffix gives the game away here—CLM stands for "*contre-la-montre*" ("against the clock"), which is the French term for time trial.

A monocoque build, the KG396 CLM frame is molded in two halves with a design based entirely on that of the original track bike. The specially created fork is hinged off the front of the frame, mounting above and below the head tube, offering a sharp, aerodynamically sound edge to the wind.

The first professional teams to use the KG396 CLM competitively were Denmark's CSC (now Team Saxo-Tinkoff—which at that time included Laurent Jalabert), and Crédit Agricole (CA) of France; it was the distinctive green-and-white jerseys of CA that won the team trial at the 2001 Tour de France.

Retailing at around $8,000 (£5,000), these frames were clearly aimed at sponsored professionals rather than self-financing amateurs—but the quality and performance were so good that no one questioned the price—clearly, one should expect to pay top dollar for a world-beater. **TB**

Look's radical KG396 was the choice of the French track team. ▶

MONTY Hydra

2000 • Trials bike • Spain • Minimalist bike for
competition trials riding

Bicycle trials and motorbike trials both require machines
that are similar in many details.

Observed bike trials involve the rider tackling
vertical obstacles, drops, and balance sections that can
be natural or man-made. Pedals are rarely used to propel
the bikes. Instead, riders rely on hopping and heaving
the bikes around, often balancing and jumping from
wheel to wheel. As a result, "modified category" bikes
have evolved in a very specific way.

On the Monty Hydra, the saddle was a token gesture
rather than a place for prolonged sitting, and the frame
was dropped as low as possible out of the way of the
rider. Super-wide bars and a tall stem gave the riders the
leverage and lift they needed to launch themselves up
boulders or onto crate stacks, while the aluminum frame
was strong enough to land a big drop, and light enough
to get up there in the first place. Small 20-in. (51-cm)
wheels were used for strength and easy maneuverability,
with fat reinforced tires that could be run at low
pressures for absorbing landings without bursting.
Brakes were hydraulic in disc or rim format. A bashguard
under the front chainring provided a safe landing and
balance point for times when it was impossible to land
on the rear wheel. **GK**

INTENSE Tracer

2000 • Mountain bike • USA • Proudly U.S.-
built suspension bike icon

Jeff Steber constructed the first Intense frame on his
kitchen table in 1991 in California, and his cutting-edge
aluminum frames have been built in the Golden State
ever since.

Intense has come a long way since Steber's
simple original shock-on-the-end-of-extended-struts
suspension frame. This bike, in particular, has become a
timeless flagship for Intense's commitment to maximum
fun on every ride, thanks to creative construction
painstakingly executed by true craftsmen.

The hand-built Tracer frame used larger-diameter
tubes and meticulously machine-cut junction sections
and other structural set pieces to create a much tougher,
stiffer frame than any previous Intense. Steber also
added smooth, rotating, self-contained ball-bearing
pivots in each part of the suspension. These gave
the bike great sensitivity to small bumps, and reaped
traction and comfort benefits from the Fox Racing rear
shock-absorber. The Tracer was also given appropriately
control-enhancing handling to allow riders to exploit the
full potential of the tough yet smooth-riding chassis.

Still a part of the Intense lineup, the Tracer has
moved with the times, and is currently available in three
different wheel sizes to keep it totally on trend. **GK**

FOES DHS Mono

2001 • Mountain bike • USA • Pioneering fork, frame, and shock package

Former-off-road racing truck designer Brent Foes introduced long-stroke suspension to the mountain bike world in 1993 with his original Fab LTS. The success of this revolutionary bike inspired him to develop even better suspension control. His innovations included a motorcycle-style twin clamp "upside-down" front fork with 5 and later 6½ in. (12.75 and 16.5 cm) of stroke.

The DHS Mono incorporated all the Foes Fabrication advances in a single machine. By combining a super-strong, extremely stiff monocoque frameset with an extended version of the Foes F1 fork and a freshly developed Curnutt shock-absorber, Brent created the first totally integrated downhill chassis. The downsized motorsport shock introduced stable platform damping to mountain bikes. By limiting the sensitivity of the shock to small, gradually increasing, loads but then opening up to swallow bigger impacts, the shock left other bikes floundering in its wake. It also gave the Foes an accurate feel on challenging courses, and the bike became the benchmark for downhill race performance.

Other manufacturers seized the concept of platform damping in rear shock-absorbers to cure bounce issues, and it is still evident to this day in Fox's Pro Pedal and RockShox Floodgate technologies. **GK**

X-LITE Downhill

2001 • Downhill bike • UK • Father-and-son company whose products changed the MTB world

On holiday with his family in the United States, twelve-year-old Alex Trimnell spotted a polished Klein mountain bike. His father, Rex, an engineer and a motorbike rider, saw beauty in the outsized tubes and polished chassis, and decided to export one back to his home in England.

There, Rex realized that he disliked the rigid chromoly fork, and created a new, dual-crown fork, as on a motorbike. He then patented his design, which formed the basis of all subsequent downhill forks.

The X-Lite Downhill began around 1996. The first frame Rex and Alex built was based on airplane wing design, and used three pieces of hot-bonded aluminum that were then riveted together for strength and rigidity. The suspension system pivoted around the bottom bracket, and used a motorbike rear shock produced by Kayaba. The dual-crown fork on the bike had dual brake mounts, to allow for a dual-disc brake system, developed with the Hope company, which gave even braking forces to the fork legs.

The bike went through two incarnations, as Alex and his friend Andy Pope raced it all over Britain and refined the design as they went. It was never sold, but the component brand X-Lite became a huge success, and sponsored riders such as Steve Peat. **CJ**

CERVÉLO P3

2001 • Aero bike • Canada • Carbon fiber version of trendsetting aerodynamic frame

Every few years, a new bike appears with a whole host of features that influence all subsequent bikes to such an extent that what began as innovation becomes part of the design landscape.

That's what happened when Gerard Vroomen and Phil White of Cervélo took their obsessive aerodynamic zeal and their usual clean-sheet approach to develop something even faster than their benchmark P2 frame.

The front end of the P3 wasn't radically different. Narrow bladed forks with a conventional, front-mounted brake plugged into a super-narrow, hourglass-profile head tube to split the air as cleanly as possible. Cervélo's unique True Aero airfoil tube patterns shaped the

> ## "I revered the P3C because it was so vastly superior to every other tri bike of its time."
>
> *Aaron Hersh*

straight down tube, and the top tube terminated in a neat, flush-fitting two-bolt clamp.

However, the design element that caused jaws to drop was the seat tube. Curved wheel-hugger cutouts designed to transfer air smoothly onto the spinning rear wheel had long been a feature of aero bikes, but no one had previously produced anything as radical as this tube, which extended right over the top of the wheel before heading vertically upward in a deep fin to sync with a matching vertical aerodynamic seatpost. It's been a signature Cervélo feature ever since.

With the P3 and the carbon P3C, Cervélo reinvented aero bikes. Riders using Cervélo bikes won more time trials and triathlons—including Ironman, World Championship, national, and Olympic titles—than any others. **GK**

KARPIEL Apocalypse

2001 • Freeride bike • Italy • Huge-travel freefall freeride bike

Occasionally a bike and a rider become synonymous. Such was the case with Josh Bender and his Karpiel Apocalypse. The two were the embodiment of extreme during the craziest period of mountain biking history, when it seemed as if the top performers were hell-bent on self-destruction.

When Bender teamed up with Karpiel, he was the hottest property in freeride because of his insane "hucking"—the popular name for the practice of riders launching themselves and their bikes off the biggest possible precipices. Some of his breathtaking exploits were shown in *Double Down* DVD and the *New World Disorder* film series.

Bender hucked bigger and farther than anyone else, tackling drops of up to 60 ft (18 m). His performances spoke for themselves, and for that reason he never had to court sponsors. He always figured: "Just keep doing what you're doing—going big—and they'll come to you."

Karpiel's Apocalypse was one of the strongest, longest-travel downhill bikes around, built specially to soak up massive single-impact loads.

By using two separate shock-absorbers, rear wheel travel was extended to 15 in. (38 cm), with extra damping chambers added to prevent Bender from catapulting over the bars after landing. The seat was also extended forward, hammock-style, to keep alive hopes of future Bender generations. Add a 12-in. (30-cm) stroke fork from Risse Racing, and the Apocalypse was ready to roll off any precipice he dared attempt.

Although Bender has sustained many serious injuries, including a broken back, he is still going big rather than going home. As he said himself: "When you go beyond your equipment's ability, stuff's gonna happen. I'm Bender, not broken." **GK**

SANTA CRUZ V10

2001 • Mountain bike • USA • Radical
suspension-movement mountain bike

Bikes that are built only in small quantities and ridden by only a few people are ideal for testing new technologies. It was on one such bike, the V10, that Santa Cruz introduced the innovative Virtual Pivot Point (VPP) suspension system.

Downhill suspension using a pair of independently moving linkages to join the mainframe and the rear subframe wasn't new; Cannondale used a similar system on the team-only Fulcrum in 1997. The idea of each linkage moving in a different direction as the wheel went through its range of motion was first seen on the Outland bikes of the early 1990s. Santa Cruz bought the rights to the patent for them.

Rather than a short-suspension, cross-country bike, however, the first Santa Cruz VPP bike had 10 in. (25.5 cm) of wheel movement, which enabled it to "sag" almost 4 in. (10 cm)—the normal full travel for a trail bike of the time—under no more than the weight of the rider.

This made the V10 outstandingly responsive when pedaling, and resistant on rough terrain. It became one of the most successful downhill bikes of all time, and was still winning World Championships with a full carbon chassis thirteen years later. **GK**

SANTA CRUZ Blur

2001 • Mountain bike • USA • Iconic, hard-kicking, hard-riding trail bike

---

By the year 2000, most major manufacturers made full-suspension mountain bikes, but such machines struggled for acceptance with buyers who perceived them more as gravity-assisted playthings than as viable bikes for climbing and cross-country. The main problem was pedal "bob"—unwanted suspension movement created by the on–off effect of the rider's pedaling.

Santa Cruz's answer was to apply the Virtual Pivot Point (VPP) suspension architecture it had developed for the 10-in. (25.4-cm) travel V10 downhill bike to an all-new, 4-in. (10-cm) travel design, the Blur.

The VPP system worked by moving the rear wheel around a "virtual" (rather than a frame-anchored) pivot point, which shifted as the suspension went through its stroke. This allowed the increase in torque to be balanced against the sag of the suspension to create a stable and positive pedaling feel.

The Blur chassis also used a single-sided swingarm strut and short linkages to create a stiffer frame than most other bikes of the period.

Its introduction coincided with that of Float forks from Fox Shox. These used outsized legs and a damping circuit for outstanding control. The combination of Fox fork and Blur frame became a classic. **SH**

◀ Santa Cruz's V10 is a multiple World Champion.

PORSCHE FS Evolution

2001 • Mountain bike • Germany • Superbike from supercar maker

Porsche's 2001 version of the Votec mountain bike was a flashy state-of-the-art flagship. The front forks used motorcycle-style top tubes, and direct-mount, two-piece stem plates to attach the forks directly to the bars. At the straight blade bottom end, they gave 5½ in. (14 cm) of wheel travel, and a similar amount of rear wheel movement from a Cane Creek rear air shock. The Spengle composite tri-spoke wheels were as eye-catching as any roadcar alloys.

Votec had made two previous mountain bike designs for Porsche. The first was a hardtail with a distinctive, super-low top tube and a diagonally buttressed seat tube extension. The second was a full-suspension design with the same distinctive profile but a mix of slim tubes and a machined alloy web section

joining the top tube and the down tube. The third bike, the FS Evolution, was undoubtedly the pinnacle of their collaboration. At its heart was the Votec-designed autoclave baked carbon fiber composite monocoque frame. This created a V-profile upper and lower main spar, supported centrally by a machined aluminum upright onto which the rear shock was also mounted. The seatpost and saddle slotted into the cantilevered top-section terminal, while the one-piece aluminum swingarm mounted onto the lower spar.

Many of the components were carbon fiber too, including cranks and lower fork legs and pedals and cantilevered seatpost. Bolt-on stop/go components were also the best: high-end Shimano XTR gears, and ventilated, motorcycle-like Magura disc brakes. **BS**

ROCKY MOUNTAIN Slayer

2001 • All-rounder • Canada • Super-versatile full-suspension all-rounder

In the early years of mountain bikes, their performance was judged on how well the gears and brakes worked and how well the tires gripped. Then suspension forks came along, followed a few years later by rear suspension. Shortly after that, mountain bikes started to be categorized as cross-country or downhill, but demand for a bike that was in between the two soon inspired the creation of the Rocky Mountain Slayer.

With 5 in. (12.7 cm) of suspension at either end and a robust but light Easton aluminum chassis, it was neither a cross-country bike nor a downhill bike. It was one of a new generation of all-mountain bikes, with enough gears to deal with extreme ups and downs, Magura hydraulic disc brakes, and burly tires, but not so much weight that you couldn't pedal it up hills.

When Wade Simmons won the first Red Bull Rampage Freeride competition on a Slayer, it felt like a new sport was born. The beauty of the bike was that you could use it for almost any type of riding. It was one of the first true all-rounders, superb for doing the sort of downhills that were fun for hardcore riders and did not require them to use the ski lift to get back up to the top. By the latest standards, the Slayer was pretty tame, but it started an interest surge in medium-travel suspension bikes that, as suspension became more efficient, would evolve into the lightweight trail bikes that many riders buy today. The Slayer still exists in the Rocky Mountain range, but it's now a very different bike, with far more suspension travel than the original. All Mountain bikes have evolved with rider abilities. **SW**

CANNONDALE Freeride

2001 • Mountain bike • USA • Long-travel trail bike; the first freerider

The end of the 1990s was a boom time for mountain biking, with big businesses sponsoring race teams and increasing numbers of ordinary riders discovering the joys of steep terrain. Cannondale was in the thick of both sides of the action with its Super V family of bikes. While Cannondale Volvo riders were ripping up the race tracks on their team-only Super V Fulcrum bikes, mere mortals could buy the Freeride.

The name—originally a snowboarding term for off-piste riding—was adopted by bikers to refer to machines with more suspension travel and more controlled steering. Above all, freeriding was about style rather than speed: Freeriders were not racers,

"Our goal is to create the perfect ride. There's nothing better than the Cannondale feel."

Cannondale publicity

so the weight of their bikes was not a consideration. Cannondale's new bike certainly looked the part, thanks to a totally new "Moto" fork with a massive hooped cross-brace that mimicked the outsized tubing of the alloy frames. Concertina-style rubber boots covered the exposed fork sliders for motorbike-style looks. The Super V Freeride still used cable-operated rim-pull brakes, which, though surprisingly retro, were probably preferable to Cannondale's own-brand CODA disc brakes, the performance of which was poor.

The worst thing Cannondale did was try to copyright the term "Freeride," a move that succeeded only in alienating exactly the riders it was trying to attract. It is generally agreed that this was the main reason the bike didn't last long in its range. **GK**

SKOOT Case

2001 • Novelty suitcase–scooter bike • USA • Unique folding child's bike–luggage combo

"Traveling with children"—the phrase strikes fear into the hearts of parents everywhere, with its multitude of potential pitfalls too numerous to catalog. How can the headaches of such expeditions be reduced? Where to start? Well, why not start at the beginning, and get your child to pack and carry his or her own suitcase? Not just any suitcase, but a suitcase that doubles as a bike.

The Skoot Case—part luggage grip, part retro scooter—is large enough to carry most of the appurtenances your child will need for a week or two away from home, and, with its own seat and steering wheel, it converts easily into a bike that can be ridden rather than carried to and from the check-in counter.

Best of all, the dimensions of the Skoot Case are airline-approved as cabin baggage, and the whole vehicle fits into overhead compartments, so its rider need never be too far away from his or her favorite toy.

Suitable for children aged from three to around five years, the Skoot Case luggage scooter is made in lightweight but durable plastic, and has removable handlebars and a lift-up saddle. It has internal storage clips to keep things in their proper place throughout the journey, and soft rubber trim on the exterior surfaces to prevent any nasty knocks. It even has a strap for use in the event that ground obstacles prove too difficult to negotiate, and parents have to come to the rescue: they can either carry the bike like an ordinary luggage item, or pull it along with the child on board.

The Skoot may appear fragile, but its hard-gripping rubber wheels can handle loads of up to 110 lb (50 kg)—more, indeed, than a small child can be expected to carry.

This novelty bike may not take all the pain out of family trips, but its popularity suggests that it is widely regarded as an effective analgesic. **BS**

Forget the cab from the airport with the Skoot Case. ▶

KLEIN Palomino

2001 • Mountain bike • USA • Maverick monolink design licensed by luxury manufacturer

There's a limit to the number of ways you can put a bike together, and cycle design history is full of patent claims, counterclaims, and lengthy licensing agreements. There's no stigma attached to tech trading: some of the best bikes have used frame features or suspension systems from other originators. However, Klein's Maverick-licensed Palomino was one of the less happy partnerships.

Trek-owned Klein was already making Maverick's ML7 frame, but wanted to bring its characteristic boutique beauty to its own version of the Monolink. Unfortunately, somewhere in development, the back-swept seat tube required for the unique suspension

"Oh my God, what have they done to my bike? Look at me: I'm Superman!"

Gary Klein

strut placement was tilted back an extra ten degrees. Even more unfortunately, no one spotted this until the bikes were unboxed for the global launch in Garmisch-Partenkirchen, Germany. The sight of Gary Klein spread-eagled across a prototype Palomino in the belting rain of a Bavarian hotel parking lot, as Trek marketing employees tried desperately to wrestle him out of sight, remains one of my most enduring images from twenty years of professional bike testing.

While this issue was easily resolved, the Monolink design was a poisoned chalice. Even after Klein had got the bikes into the right shape, the production Palominos suffered from leaking magnesium air shocks, rapidly loosening bearings, and cracked linkages. The Palomino was put out to pasture very quickly. **GK**

ORANGE 222

2001 • Mountain bike • UK • One of the most successful downhill race bikes ever

Ever since the late nineteenth century, bike brands have used successful teams and riders for two purposes: to help sell their machines, and to provide feedback on design changes.

Orange's involvement with the Global Racing Superteam came about entirely by chance. When Global's supplier failed to deliver a consignment on time, the team's recent recruit, South African wunderkind Greg Minnaar, carried on using the Orange Patriot he had ridden for his previous team. The other Global riders tried it and liked it, and team director Martin Whiteley saw an ideal partner in Orange. As he later recalled:

"We wanted a bike that riders would want to ride, and, after surveying our team, Orange was the clear and obvious choice. A company that was small enough to react and deliver, but big enough to be supportive and creative."

However, the bigger, faster World Cup downhill courses needed a bike with more suspension and a longer, lower handling feel than the Patriot, so work started immediately on the 222.

Despite 8 in. (19 cm) of suspension travel, adjustable geometry, and a massive 1¼-in. (3.2-cm) main pivot, the hand-built monocoque frame of the 222 made the complete bike the lightest, fastest-accelerating machine in the World Cup. By the end of a stunning first season, the 222 had won the Men's World Cup and the Women's European title, as well as the Men's and Women's UK national championships and the Spanish, Swiss, and Austrian national titles. The 222 won the World Cup again in 2002, and the evolved 223 won again in 2004, both times under British rider Steve Peat, thereby cementing the bike's place as one of the most successful downhill machines of all time. **GK**

Orange's 222 was outwardly simple but super-successful on the World Cup scene. ▶

GARY FISHER Mount Tam

2002 • Mountain bike • USA • First mainstream 29er from Trek sub-brand

AIRBORNE Carpe Diem

2002 • Road bike • Netherlands • Affordable titanium all-rounder from direct-sell pioneer

The 27½-in. (70-cm) wheel was standard for bicycles until the increasing availability of bigger tires and suspension forks made it possible for major companies to produce 29-in. (73.5-cm) wheels in bulk.

Still, traditionalists resisted 29ers until Gary Fisher made the mainstream sit up and take notice. Even then, many riders remained confused by Fisher's mix of hardtails and full-suspension bikes, but they gradually came around as they discovered that the softer roll and extra stability of big wheels largely compensated for the small amount of extra weight.

Fisher spent a couple of years developing different ideas on 29ers, all the time trying to keep the back end as short as possible. The first production bikes, fitted with custom Marzocchi suspension forks, were launched to a skeptical press and public in 2001, but the 2002 Mount Tam 29er started to get riders ready to consider the idea that a combination of bigger wheels and altered geometry was worthy of their attention.

It wasn't until 2004, when RockShox produced a Reba 29er fork, that the big bikes really took off. While other brands had produced 29ers with WTB Nanoraptor tires, the combination of Fisher's commitment and Trek's marketing finally won the battle for acceptance. **SW**

Airborne started out selling well-made, Asian-built titanium frames straight to the end users, bypassing retail outlets. Having enhanced its reputation with mountain bikes that took their names from U.S. Air Force jets, Airborne moved into road bikes.

Like every Airborne frame, that of the Carpe Diem—Latin for "seize the day"—was built from 3AL/2.5V titanium alloy tubing which was cold-worked to create tapered shapes in line with the load paths most likely to be encountered on rough cyclocross courses. Powerful cantilever brakes controlled traction on slippery descents. Stable handling angles increased the bike's versatility, delivering trustworthy handling in all situations, while the titanium tubing added spring to the ride feel, as well as keeping weight to a minimum and entirely removing the danger of corrosion.

All these factors made the Carpe Diem a classic, with many loyal fans still riding later versions of the bike more than a decade later. The design line has been carried on since the absorption of Airborne by Dutch distributor Van Nicholas, with its jack-of-all-trades character now evident in the Amazon all-rounder, which the company still promotes under the old established slogan: "the obvious choice." **GK**

SCHWINN Rocket 88

2002 • Mountain bike • USA • Parallelogram-suspension mountain bike

Success on the racetrack tempts designers to transfer suspension systems that have worked well in competition onto their all-round trail bikes. Sometimes these have been successful, but in other cases, such as Schwinn's Rocket 88, the results haven't been as positive.

When Mert Lawwill developed a unique parallelogram suspension system for Yeti Cycles' downhill bike, Yeti's then-parent company Schwinn adopted it for the Straight 6 and Straight 8 bikes. Both bikes proved popular and successful on the downhill circuit. Unfortunately, the transfer of the system into a lighter-weight, shorter-suspension trail bike package proved a serious problem.

The Rocket 88's mainframe was linked to a low-profile version of the Lawwill system that gave 3½ in. (8.8 cm) of wheel movement. However, while Yeti and Schwinn suspension bikes used large-section aluminum pieces for the four parallelogram pieces, the 88 used small tubular stays to reduce weight. This allowed significant flex, which translated into additional twisting and shearing loads on the large number of bearings required by the parallelogram. This led to loosening of the rear subframe and rapid bearing failure. The 88 was withdrawn after less than two years. **GK**

CANNONDALE Gemini

2002 • Mountain bike • USA • Specialist downhill racing mountain bike

By 2002, downhill racing was well established as the craziest biking circuit, complete with a flamboyant cast of thrill- and attention-seeking riders. Few, if any, could compete with the on-track flair and off-track partying of flying Frenchman Cédric Gracia, though, and it took an equally special sort of bike to cope with him.

At first sight, his Gemini may appear staid and conservative. This is particularly surprising in view of Cannondale's reputation as an innovative company. But closer inspection reveals a wealth of remarkable features. The rear wheel is held in place with a 5⁷⁄₁₀-in. (14.5-cm) wide, ½-in. (1.2-cm) diameter hollow axle. The rear swingarm is designed to flex in the final stages of compression to stop the frame cracking.

Gracia and the Gemini faced their toughest test at the infamous Red Bull Rampage freeride event, staged in an amphitheater of desert cliffs in Utah. The rider rose to the challenge in typical style, launching himself off the biggest cliff drops, and even back-flipping his bike over one jump to take the overall win.

Unfortunately, when Gracia tried to repeat the win in 2004, dressed as Captain America, he crashed hard and had to be airlifted to hospital with life-threatening injuries. Happily, he survived, but the event didn't. **GK**

V-PROCESS NV01

2002 • Mountain bike • France • Prototype
World Championship-winning downhill race bike

French downhill racer Nicolas Vouilloz is a legend of the sport, winning the Downhill World Championships ten times in eleven years from 1992 to 2002, and bringing a new professionalism to the mountain bike race circuit.

Having started as members of the Sunn Chipie team, Vouilloz and suspension specialist Olivier Bossard set up an independent race team, V-Process. NV bikes (named after Nico Vouilloz) were focused race machines rather than mass-market products.

The frames were hand built in France from top-quality Easton aluminum alloy, with a single pivot swingarm design to keep them light and reliable. Bossard custom built an advanced rear shock-absorber and motorcycle-style upside-down fork, both of which used separate control circuits to swallow the biggest hits smoothly and retain maximum stability while pedaling or braking.

Having raced the original NV01 bike successfully for two seasons, Vouilloz and Bossard prepared a new NV02 model for the Kaprun World Championship course in Austria. This improved version of the bike featured a swingarm that was extended by ½ in. (1.2 cm) for increased stability.

The choice of gold for the paint job proved appropriate as Vouilloz stormed to a record tenth gold medal win on the bike. He then withdrew from bike racing for five years to pursue a rally driving career with Peugeot and the Bozian team. In 2008, he was the overall winner of the Intercontinental Rally Challenge, with one win, six second places, and five top-five finishes in the season's events.

By then, Vouilloz had returned to the saddle and was dividing his time between the two disciplines. His first professional cycle race on his comeback was in the 2007 World Cup in Champéry, Switzerland. **GK**

CERVÉLO Soloist

2002 • Aero road bike • Canada • Iconic
aerodynamic road bike

When the governing body of cycling imposed a minimum weight limit for racing bikes, it sent innovation in a different direction. Instead of gaining speed and efficiency through losing weight, designers started to increase speed by reducing aerodynamic drag. The bike that started this new phase of design was the Soloist.

While aero road bikes weren't a new concept, first-generation bikes of the 1970s and 1980s just used teardrop-shaped versions of standard, small-diameter steel tubes: drag reduction was minimal. Second-generation bikes such as the Soloist introduced dramatic design changes and clearly measurable advantages.

"As the mechanic (not salesman) said 'this bike looks fast when standing still' and he was right."

Reviewer on roadbikereview.com

Cervélo was certainly well positioned to pioneer this new wave of wind-cheating road race machines. Starting in the 1990s with the Eyre and the P2, then adding the P3 in 2001, Cervélo had come to dominate the time trial and triathlon market in terms of innovation.

The Soloist borrowed heavily from Cervélo's existing True Aero tube shape, which combined with Smartwall construction techniques to produce a frame that shaved several seconds off every mile. This made it perfect for solo attacks on the peloton in races, and within a year of its launch, Cervélo became the bike choice of the top-level CSC team. Strong riders like Jens Voigt, Fabian Cancellara, and Stuart O'Grady loved the brutal power delivery, and these breakaway bikes soon helped CSC to become the number-one team in the world rankings. **GK**

Cervélo's Soloist launched the latest generation of aero road bikes. ▶

LITESPEED Ghisallo

2002 • Road bike • USA • Titanium maestros counter carbon competition with the world's lightest frame

Litespeed led the off-the-peg titanium bike market, with the company's industrial piping experience translated into some of the most technologically advanced bikes available. Yet by 2002, even the best bikes made from titanium alloys were having their ultimate performance status threatened by super-light yet stiff carbon fiber mega-machines.

However, the Litespeed Ghisallo showed the biking world it was still worth putting the pedal to the metal for peerless results. By adopting a compact frame layout, with dropped top tube, extended seatpost, and correspondingly low front and rear frames, Litespeed put the frame dots they needed to connect as close together as possible. It then used the lightest-possible tubeset by working the metal to the absolute limit in terms of

stiffness and strength-to-weight ratio. The result was a frame that weighed just under 2 lb (0.9 kg)—the world's lightest bicycle. Litespeed backed up the featherweight float up climbs with a responsive short wheelbase for a predatory and aggressive ride.

On the downside, the sharp steering angles combined with noticeable flex through the paper-thin tubing to create a twitchy, nervous ride at speed and when the bike cornered too hard. The lack of metal also meant Litespeed had to set a maximum rider weight to stop heavy riders from crushing it. Despite these limitations, the Ghisallo was still consistently regarded as one of the world's most desirable superbikes until the Chattanooga, Tennessee-based company built the last one in 2010. **GK**

PINARELLO Prince

2002 • Road bike • Italy • Aluminum-framed Tour winner

Giovanni Pinarello began building road bikes as a teenager in the 1940s in Catena di Villorba, Italy. A modestly successful professional racer, at the end of his career he launched his own brand that would enjoy enormous success in his native country before bursting onto the world scene with victories at 1984 Olympic Games in Los Angeles.

One of the great road bikes, the Pinarello Prince was the company's marquee model. It quickly achieved high-profile successes in just about every major road race on the calendar—including German Erik Zabel's four consecutive green jerseys in the Tour de France—and supplied the Fassa Bortolo team, for whom in 2003 Italian Alessandro Pettachi notched up twenty-four victories on his Prince SL.

Unsurprisingly, the Prince then became popular with amateur road racers and serious leisure cyclists.

The frames on the original 2001 models were aluminum, but featured a carbon seatstay and fork, plus an integrated headset. Somewhat heavier than most modern road bikes, the Prince suited those looking for a precision ride rather than comfort.

The Prince evolved gradually, and continued to head the Pinarello range until the 2007 launch of a full-blown carbon model. Two years later came the awesome Prince Di2, which was built to work with Shimano's Electric Dura Ace group.

In 2010, the Prince's reign ended when it was succeeded by the Dogma range, which quickly achieved comparable levels of success. **TB**

LEMOND Zurich

2002 • Road racing bike • USA • Bike caught in the middle of a drug war of words

The Zurich was a premium road racing bike with a Reynolds 853 steel frame, a carbon fork, and a Shimano Ultegra groupset. It cost around $2,100 (£1,330) and was marketed under the brand name of Greg LeMond, three-time winner of the Tour de France.

These might seem like the ingredients for an instant hit, but the Zurich's apparently disappointing sales hinted at a huge behind-the-scenes conflict between LeMond and the manufacturer, Trek.

The two parties had originally agreed to collaborate on producing the LeMond range of bikes using the rider's idea of a stretched geometry for the otherwise standard lightweight steel racing frame. The theory was that the longer top tube and wheelbase meant the rider presented a smaller obstruction to

the wind, was more stable, and was able to send more power to the pedals.

The problems came when LeMond made strong public statements against doping in professional cycling and mentioned Lance Armstrong, one of Trek's star riders who had enormous influence in the company. Trek claimed LeMond was breaking his contract by harming the company, and demanded an apology. Both sides went to their lawyers. LeMond claimed that Trek had repeatedly tried to silence him about doping, and had deliberately held back sales of his bikes. In 2008, the two severed their ties.

The unfortunate outcome was that the LeMond brand didn't get the marketing it deserved, although today the Zurich is very sought-after by collectors. **SH**

ROCKY MOUNTAIN Switch

2002 • Freeride • Canada • Seminal bike ridden by freeride legends

The freeride biking scene of the early 2000s was most effervescent in and around North Shore, Vancouver, British Columbia. Almost overnight, the area displaced the West Coast of the United States as mountain biking's hottest location.

Vancouver-based Rocky Mountain Bicycles was perfectly placed to reap the benefits of the region's sudden popularity, and quickly jumped in to sponsor the best up-and-coming riders. Among the most prominent were Wade Simmons, Richie Schley, Thomas Vanderham, and Brett Tippie, a foursome who rapidly became affectionately known as the Godfathers of Freeride.

They cemented their places in mountain biking history on the Rocky Mountain Switch bike. First released in 2002, the Switch came with 5 in. (12.7 cm) of rear travel through a four-bar suspension system and an Answer Manitou front fork with an adjustable 4 to 5 in. (10 to 12.7 cm) of travel up front.

The front triangle was built of Easton RAD tubing, and its distinctive box-section tubes were held together with beefy reinforcing yokes. These, plus the bike's large suspension components, gave it a very distinctive look that made it instantly recognizable in films such as *New World Disorder 3*, and in the flurry of freeride images and features that dominated the mountain bike media for several years.

The Switch was redesigned in 2006 and given 7 in. (17.8 cm) of rear travel. It remained a part of Rocky's range until 2008. **CJ**

CANNONDALE F3000

2002 • Mountain bike • USA • Super-light race-focused hardtail from the outsized alloy specialists

Volvo Cannondale was one of the best-funded and most successful mountain biking teams of the late 1990s and early 2000s. The U.S. bike manufacturer made sure its riders had every possible advantage.

The F3000 hardtail is a prime example of Cannondale's craft. While most bike brands of the period relied on conventional twin telescopic-legged forks from specialist suspension manufacturers, Cannondale had been following its own path for several years. Its Fatty Headshok used a unique outsized head tube and fork steerer that contained the air spring and hydraulic damping circuits of the lower unicrown fork. This was limited in travel to $3\frac{3}{20}$. in. (80 mm) because the free stroke had to fit between fork top and frame, but that was more than enough for cross-country race use. Although actual suspension performance wasn't as smooth as most conventional forks, the unicrown lower section design made the Fatty Headshok stiffer and lighter, particularly when combined with the matching supersized System Integration (SI) stem.

Cannondale's component choices included a custom-built Coda crank using hollow machined arms and an outsized alloy axle for maximum stiffness at minimum weight. As well as giving Cannondale's athletes a genuine pedaling edge, this design—first pioneered by Alex Pong as part of his Magic Motorcycle concept brand—paved the way for Cannondale's innovative use of outsized BB30 bottom brackets, which were made available as an open-source standard.

Cannondale's use of small diameter seatposts and rear seatstays to reduce vibration from the rear wheel on rough terrain has also become a widely adopted frame feature on both alloy and carbon fiber frames, making the F3000 a true design icon. **GK**

SCOTT CR1

2003 • Road bike • Switzerland • The lightest carbon frame road bike on the market

For the first thirty years of its existence, the Scott company had little connection with two wheels. Setting up operations in Sun Valley, Idaho, in 1958, engineer and amateur ski racer Ed Scott originally made tapered aluminum ski poles. Expanding into Europe, the company produced ski and motocross equipment, eventually establishing its base in Fribourg, Switzerland.

In 1989, turning its attention to the bicycle, Scott released the radical clip-on aerodynamic handlebar that Greg LeMond used in his 1989 Tour de France victory. Scott then began to research lightweight frames in the late 1990s, initially for mountain bikes. In 2001 the company came up with the Team Issue road bike, which had a frame weight of less than 2 lb 3 oz

> *". . . plush when you're sitting up and cruising . . . a more racy feel when down in drops."*
>
> Bicycling *magazine*

(1 kg). Two years later, Scott unveiled the CR1 with a frame weighing just under 2 lb (0.9 kg), easily the lightest on the market at the time.

It is constructed from carbon-butted tubes that give strength at stress points. Scott claims that, using its manufacturing process, it takes twenty-six hours to produce each frame. The end result is a bike that is low in mass, stable and precise to ride, and able to accelerate as fast as something slippery off a stick.

The CR1 was used with some success by Saunier Duval, which Scott sponsored until the team became embroiled in drug allegations. More than a decade later, the CR1 is still with us, and has evolved into its own range. **TB**

GIANT VT1

2003 • Mountain bike • Taiwan • Innovative firm-pedaling all-round suspension bike

A pivotal point in the wider acceptance of full-suspension mountain bikes was the introduction of suspension "platforms." Previous development had been concerned with making suspension as fluid as possible, but this led to excess suspension movement related to pedal and body-weight shift. Platforms had a deliberately increased initial resistance to movement that effectively sealed off the shock from pedaling, braking, and body-shift forces. The first successful suspension platforms were introduced by Curnutt on Foes bikes, and manufacturer Manitou rapidly adopted the technology as Stable Platform Valving (SPV). Manitou then teamed up with Giant, one of the world's most experienced bike builders, to produce the innovative VT1.

With fork and rear SPV damping to stop the bike from "bobbing" when pedaled, Giant was able to accommodate much more suspension travel than typical for a trail bike of the time, with 5 in. (12.7 cm) of wheel movement at either end. Exploiting its skill in aluminum frame-building, Giant created a lightweight frame to reduce pedaling effort further, and the bike ushered in a new era of all-rounder bikes that could be ridden fast up- and downhill.

As is often the case with pioneering designs, the VT1 had flaws. The rear shock worked extremely well, but the stubborn-feeling SPV front fork affected comfort and traction. However, riders still remember the VT1 fondly, and it definitely deserves its place in the pantheon of significant suspension designs. **GK**

GIANT TCR Composite

2003 • Road bike • Taiwan • First major brand to use an integrated seatpost design

If you were to choose a name for the world's biggest bicycle business, "Giant" would seem pretty apt. In 2003, the Taiwanese mega-corp introduced a pair of newcomers to its wide-ranging collection, which encompassed trikes for toddlers right up to high-end carbon frame road racers that included the two TCR models: the Composite and the Advanced.

Besides having top specs in their own right, the TCRs were noted as the first mass-produced bikes to feature the option of an integrated seatpost. This idea has raised controversy in some parts of the bike world, and it is not difficult to see why. The classic telescopic seatpost enables the rider to adjust the height of the saddle. Too low? Take it up a bit. Too high? Drop it down a little. Why would anyone want to change such a

simple system? But Giant wanted to, and the company has continued to run with the idea. The reason for its enthusiasm is that integrated seatposts are lighter and more aerodynamic—both important considerations for a serious racer. The downside, of course, is that they need to be set up with great care. The only way to reduce the seat height is to cut the post physically, but chopping off too much is a disaster.

Cosmetically, the only real difference between the two TCR models is that the tubes of the Advanced were squared. However, the Advanced is lighter overall and featured a higher grade of carbon and a full carbon fork (the Composite has an aluminum steerer). The Advanced certainly has its fans: *Cycling Plus* voted the model its Bike of the Year. **TB**

CANNONDALE Bad Boy

2003 • Urban bike • USA • Trend-setting urban spec mountain bike

The official launch of Cannondale's Bad Boy range came a couple of years after team and design department riders at Volvo Cannondale started creating their own unofficial machines from stock Cannondale parts. The basic idea was very simple. They took the existing lightweight CAAD aluminum alloy frame of the race mountain bikes and fitted 27½-in. (70-cm) road bike wheels and tires, rather than the normal 26-in. (66-cm) wheels and tires. This produced a very light and fast-rolling bike for urban and road use, but with all the toughness and disc-brake stopping power of a mountain bike. The bikes were originally intended for training mountain-bike racers who did not have access to proper trails, but it was soon realized that they were extremely versatile and great fun in their own right.

Cannondale immediately started to create a commercial version of the bikes, carefully selecting matte black components to create its signature "Bad Boy" look. The initial models were a huge sales success, and Cannondale expanded the range. This included a premium model that included both 26-in. (66-cm) mountain bike wheels with appropriate tires and 27½-in. (70-cm) road wheels. Cannondale even introduced a slick-tired "Bad Boy" version of the Jekyll full-suspension bike, although that model did not last long in the lineup.

The range as a whole has been a massive seller for Cannondale over the years, and it has spawned countless imitation bikes from other manufacturers. It offers proof indeed that thinking out of the box can sometimes create impressive results. **GK**

SPECIALIZED Epic FSR

2003 • Mountain bike • USA • Unique "Brain" suspension race machine

Recreational riders were quick to realize and exploit the traction, control, and comfort of full-suspension mountain bikes, but racers were much more resistant to the extra weight, complexity, and pedal-related movement of early designs. Specialized tackled most of the issues in a single hit with its ingenious, yet remarkably simple and effective, "Brain" technology and the Epic bike it was built into. The Epic has also become one of the most successful race bikes ever produced, still winning Olympic gold medals a decade after the first prototypes were developed.

Stopping the bob caused by both rhythmic pedal-stroke inputs on the chain, and the inevitable bounce of body weight as the legs churn up and down, headed the agenda in the early 2000s. Every suspension company was trying to kill the pedaling bounce of its bikes, either through the architecture of the suspension systems—Maverick's Monolink, Santa Cruz's Virtual Pivot Point (VPP), Giant's NRS system—or with a "platform" tuned to resist unwanted movement, as pioneered by Curnutt with its R shock.

Specialized took the platform concept further by equipping both the Fox fork and rear shock of the Epic with a Brain. The Brains were small, spring-loaded brass weights that popped up and opened when a wheel hit a bump. The Epic thus became a super-efficient, fully rigid bike on smooth climbs, but a full-suspension bike on rough descents. It immediately became a racers' favorite, and three World Championship titles and an Olympic gold medal later it still is. **GK**

SPECIALIZED Big Hit DH

2003 • Downhill bike • USA • Unique twin wheel-size downhill machine

Specialized's Big Hit was a significant bike in the freeride movement. In 2003, the idea of jumping off cliffs or wooden structures as a sport in itself was beginning to take hold. The very first Red Bull Rampage in 2002 saw Specialized team rider Darren Berrecloth placing third on the very first incarnation of the Big Hit.

The bike featured a Specialized A1 aluminum frame, and 8¹/₁₀ in. (20.5 cm) of rear travel delivered through a Fox Vanilla RC shock. But one of its most radical features was its mix of a 24-in. (61-cm) rear wheel and a 26-in. (66-cm) front wheel. This idea was taken from motocross bikes, which also run smaller rear wheels. The intended advantages were a stronger and stiffer rear end, a lower bottom bracket, and a tighter- feeling rear end through corners. In reality,

though, the mountain bike world resisted the 24-in. (61-cm) rear wheel because it necessitated purchase of different sized tubes and tires, and there was limited availability of good downhill tires in the 24-in. (61-cm) size. Specialized stuck to its guns, however, and kept producing the Big Hit with a 24-in (61-cm) rear wheel until 2006, when it finally changed it to 26 in. (66 cm) both front and rear.

The Big Hit was as unique as Berrecloth himself, who landed one of the first 360 drop-offs on this bike, and came second in the legendary 2005 Crankworx slopestyle event in Whistler, Canada. Although mixed-sized wheels never took off, the Big Hit proved to be a serious contender and a massively popular recreational ride in the freeride world throughout the early 2000s. **CJ**

SCOTT Genius

2003 • Mountain bike • Switzerland • Mountain bike with remote-controlled suspension

Mountain bike advertisers would often claim that a particular model "climbs like a racing bike but descends like a downhill bike." By 2003 the differences in weight, handling, and suspension travel between the fastest climbing and downhill bikes made such a claim seem impossible, but Scott's uniquely innovative and unashamedly named Genius bike certainly came close.

Typically for Scott, the aluminum alloy frame was extremely light, which made acceleration and altitude gain easy. But the real "genius" lay in the Equalizer shock-absorber that designer Peter Denk developed with DT Swiss, the suspension and bike component specialists. To keep the frame compact and reduce extra weight from overlapping components, the shock-absorber sat between the frame and the back wheel. Thus, Denk had to reverse the shock's direction of operation so it was pulled apart rather than squashed together.

He also designed the shock in three distinct sections: one containing the damping oil, and two separate pressurized air-spring sections. A remote-control lever on the handlebar allowed the rider to open one or both air chambers or lock them both closed. This gave the bike an "Open" mode (4¾-in. [12-cm] wheel travel) to cope with rocks and jumps on downhills; a "Traction" mode (3½-in. [9-cm] travel) for climbing; and a "Locked" mode for sprint finishes. The Genius also changed shape in its modes, becoming lower and more stable for downhill in Open mode but steeper and higher for better ground clearance and uphill steering in Traction mode. **GK**

TURNER 5.Spot

2003 • Mountain bike • USA • Original all-mountain bike from a legendary designer

The Turner Burner (1993) was one of the first true all-round full-suspension mountain bikes, and it introduced a design template that is still used today. It then celebrated its tenth anniversary with the launch of this concept of a pedal-powered Swiss Army knife.

The design was based around a 5-in. (12.7-cm) suspension stroke in the heart of Turner's classic four-bar linkage frameset design. All the detailing—including grease-injected pivots and meticulously machined keystone sections between the custom-butted gusset-reinforced tubes—was typically Turner, and the bike's overall appearance was rather understated.

A few yards of trail were all it took to make it clear that, along with similar tough trail bikes such as the Rocky Mountain Slayer, this bike was going to create

a new benchmark for all-round performance. While it doesn't sound like a lot by modern downhill and freeride standards, the front and rear suspension strokes were as long as some World Cup downhill race bikes at the time, and the 5.Spot was an outrageously confident and sure-footed descender. The superbly balanced suspension meant that the wheel movement never undermined its ability to get back up the mountain with minimum fuss, and it never felt short of speed on single-track trails either.

The result was a string of maximum-score reviews in magazines all over the globe, and a renewed wave of enthusiasm for Turner's quietly superlative designs. The evolved 5.Spot still holds a key place in the Turner family album today. **GK**

ELLSWORTH Dare

2003 • Downhill bike • USA • Walking-beam IST-suspension bike

U.S. brand Ellsworth has always occupied a premium position in the hearts and minds of mountain bikers, thanks to iconic bikes such as the aptly named Dare. The Dare was certainly a very distinctive "bike of two halves" in its first incarnation. The front end had a single-piece monocoque, with a big box-section behind the head tube that split apart and curved outward to form a "flying V" layout. The seat tube was welded between the splayed ends of this molar-shaped mainframe, with a large, rectangular section welded onto it to carry the cartridge-bearing pivot for the suspension linkage. The linkage was the largest "walking beam" ever used on a bike, too, with the two precision-machined beams extending right back toward the rear axle, as in a tow truck. This meant the equally massive box-section "seatstays," with their intricately machine-cut pocket and window details and deeply recessed hoop bridge, were almost vertical. Pivots on the oversized chainstays made the back end a true four-bar linkage setup. Finally, Ellsworth laser-etched its name and a tribal tattoo-style scroll design into the big mainframe tubes, and finished the frame in several super-tough anodized color options.

The super-long shock at the far end of the linkage enabled the setup to pump out a massive 8 in. (20.3 cm) of travel, and the front end could handle forks of an equal stroke length. The result was truly a bike on which to dare anything, at a time when the madness levels of mountain biking (and the heights of the drops riders were attempting) were unprecedented. **GK**

FOES Inferno

2004 • Mountain bike • USA • Monocoque alloy frame with hot-rod flames molded into skin

Former off-road racing truck designer Brent Foes first cooperated with motorsport shock legends Curnutt Inc. in 1998 on his DHS Mono downhill race machine. Foes later recalled: "I knew Charlie Curnutt when we were racing trucks in Baja and the Southwest, and Curnutt shocks were the way to go if you wanted to win in the desert."

Curnutt's shock-absorbers became an optional upgrade on most Foes frames, but the Inferno was the first Foes bike to have them as standard.

The Inferno pushed the limits of trail-bike suspension to a whole new level. Its 7½-in. (19-cm) wheel movement was greater than that of most

"Astounding. Seriously. This bike takes technical trail riding and turns it inside out."

GalbraithMt.com

downhill bikes of the time. The circuitry of the Curnutt shock meant that the bike would pedal and climb extremely well, enabling riders to search for the ultimate descents without excessive exertion.

Control of the downhill speeds facilitated by such advanced suspension required an extremely stiff frame, so Brent used an evolved version of his clamshell monocoque frame design. This comprised two pressed aluminum frame halves that were welded along their seam to create a super-stiff hollow structure. Foes' design was made even more spectacular by hot rod-style flames built into the sides of the frame molds. These acted as three-dimensional stiffening ribs to stop the skin flexing under load. The innovation was another chapter in the "ahead of his time" legend of Foes. **GK**

WHYTE 46

2004 • Mountain bike • UK • Perfect review-scoring suspension trail bike

Sometimes the most successful partnerships in manufacturing come from a totally chance meeting or conversation. That's definitely the case with Whyte's multi-award-winning 46 superbike.

British former Formula 1 designer Jon Whyte had already pushed the boundaries of smooth control with his Telelever suspension fork PRST-1 design. When the time came to replace it, making a lightweight long-travel frame wasn't a problem, but he couldn't find a conventional front fork to match.

As luck would have it, on his next business trip to Taiwan, he shared a taxi with Paul Turner, who had just started his Maverick design house and was looking for bikes to match to his new Duc32 fork. With its massive baseball bat-style upper legs, and motorcycle-style upside-down design giving up to 6 in. (15 cm) of suspension travel, Whyte's design was a perfect match for Turner's fork.

The two men saw the synergy at once. Hands were shaken, deals were signed, and the Whyte 46 hit the trails in 2004 weighing less than most bikes with half its suspension, but descending as well as bikes that were twice its weight. Rave reviews and a string of five-out-of-five and ten-out-of-ten reviews in the cycling press helped the first year's production run of 500 bikes to sell out almost immediately.

Whyte himself left the company soon afterward, but the design he had helped develop continued to be refined for several years until 2010, when Whyte bikes released the equally cutting-edge carbon fiber frame 146. This machine was not to everyone's taste, but *Trail* magazine described it in glowing terms: "Fantastic fun to ride . . . [I]ts dramatic reaction to your every move makes it an infectiously enthusiastic—and very usable—playbike." **GK**

Whyte's 46 set new standards for lightweight suspension travel. ▸

ELLSWORTH Moment

2004 • Mountain bike • USA • Evolutionary premium-quality suspension all-rounder

Proprietor Tony Ellsworth started a bike company almost accidentally when he designed and built a full-suspension bike for his wife, and then a few friends of friends started asking for similar designs. The Moment, and the shorter-travel Truth, were the bikes that helped create the Ellsworth identity. Both used a patented Instant Center Tracking (ICT) four-bar linkage design that aficionados regard as one of the most pedal-efficient in the industry. It is unaffected by braking forces and stays fully active no matter what else is happening on the bike. At the time of its launch, the Moment was among an elite few bikes that could offer enough suspension travel for downhill blasts while being light and pedal efficient enough to race cross-country.

The Moment hardly changed at all over the following decade. Subtle tweaks to the design have trimmed the weight, but it was always one of the lightest of its type. The Ellsworth full-suspension bike family has grown, and a variety of machines with different-sized wheels and different amounts of wheel travel are now available, but they all still use the same ICT suspension setup. The Moment is still one of the very few 6-in. (15-cm) travel bikes that never feel in need of a lockout or a platform damped-shock unit. **SW**

BANSHEE Chaparral

2004 • Freeride bike • Canada • Almost indestructible freeride rig made in Vancouver

Banshee was founded by bike-industry legend Pippin Osborne to answer the need for mountain bikes that could withstand the rigors of the North Vancouver mountains. Banshee bikes were claimed "to last longer than you" and boasted a ten-year warranty on their frames. The Banshee Scream, the big-hit freeride bike, is still the only mount that world-renowned big-drop aficionado Josh Bender has not managed to break, and he jumps off cliffs 50 ft (15 m) high.

When the Chaparral was released in 2004, it was to all intents and purposes just a smaller Scream. It was Banshee's answer to a bike you could pedal up hills but still huck big jumps and drops on. It was a big hit with big-hitting riders, and although heavy it had the all-important and relatively rare "strong enough for North Shore" stamp of approval. The same Easton RAD box tubing was used to build the mainframe, while a machined alloy rocker made up the four-bar suspension design, providing 7 in. (18 cm) of rear travel. After 2004, the focus moved toward purpose-built freeride bikes and truly pedalable trail bikes rather than compromise machines. The Chaparral continued until 2007, made lighter with the help of modern "solo air" suspension but still weighing 42 lb (19 kg). **CJ**

HONDA RN01
2004 • Downhill bike • Japan • Honda's only pro World Cup downhill race bike

Honda developed the Honda RN01 G-Cross for the sole purpose of top-class downhill competition. Released in 2004 with a team fronted by Greg Minnaar, then World Champion, the RN01 became the talk of the mountain bike industry for several reasons. Honda created the bike with many purpose-made components not commercially available, including Showa suspension previously only found on motor bikes. The bike itself was not commercially available, nor did Honda ever plan it to be, so it seemed to be purely an interesting design exercise for Honda's engineers. And Honda had used an internal gearbox instead of the traditional derailleur gearing system, with components so secretly guarded that mechanics would take the gearbox out of the bike after a race.

Finally, in 2007, after disbanding its G-Cross team, Honda revealed to the world what was inside the RN01 gearbox. Rather than some radical gear system, it was simply a conventional derailleur, cog cassette, and chainring. The innovative part was that the freewheel was placed in the bottom bracket instead of on the rear wheel, keeping the chain constantly moving so the rider could shift gears ready for the next power section without having to pedal through rocky sections. **CJ**

NORCO Torrent
2004 • Mountain bike • Canada • Super-strong freeride mountain bike

There may come a point in the development of a bike when riders cry "Enough!" Norco's monstrous Torrent was a hardcore hardtail that even the craziest cliff jumpers thought was a leap too far.

In the mid-2000s, it seemed that every small wood had grown its own set of rough-planked trails in imitation of the raised wooden treehouse trails of North Shore, Vancouver, and that every radical rider was mounted on one of the massive freeride suspension machines that were needed to conquer them.

The Torrent, introduced in 2004 by hardcore Canadian brand Norco, was the daddy of them all. Its square-section-headed main tubes were almost big enough to make railroad bridges, but its chassis still had extra reinforcing struts welded onto the back end, just in case. Huge strength was essential, as trying to tear off the front of the bike was Marzocchi's monster 66R fork. With almost 7 in. (18 cm) of suspension stroke, it could dive headfirst into the heaviest landings without spilling its coil-spring and oil-damped guts. Massive, 2½-in.- (6.5-cm) wide Stick E compound downhill tires and 8-in. (20-cm) disc brakes added truck-sized control.

Unfortunately, more agile, smaller "slopestyle" bikes made the overweight Torrent obsolete overnight. **GK**

CANNONDALE Six13

2004 • Road bike • USA • Hybrid carbon-aluminum frame

The Cannondale Six13 made its public debut in prototype form at the 2003 Tour de France. Its revolutionary hybrid frame design has top, down, and seat tubes made from carbon, while the rear triangle is aluminum. The name comes from those two elements' respective atomic numbers on the periodic table. Notable is the "co-molding" method by which the frame is constructed. The soft, "uncured" carbon tubes are positioned inside the aluminum tube clusters, forming internal "bladders" that inflate when heat is applied, resulting in a light frame with extremely powerful joints. Unusually, unlike most carbon designs, the Six13 is offered in no less than a dozen different frame sizes.

In achieving such a remarkably light road bike—the frame weighed no more than 2½ lb (1.13 kg)—Cannondale actually created a bike that was too light for competition. Gilberto Simoni of the Cannondale-sponsored Saeco team was told to add weights to the bike to comply with the "15-lb" rule of the Union Cycliste Internationale (UCI), the sport's international governing body. Simoni still rode the Six13 to victory at the Tour's fourteenth stage. Seizing a neat PR opportunity, the company swiftly launched its "Legalize my Cannondale" campaign.

Cannondale quickly created a range of Six13 bikes to capitalize on the success. The specific number of carbon tubes depended on the price point of the model. The line was later expanded to include the Slice trial bike, which was constructed in a similar way but with aerodynamically tapered tubes. **TB**

SCOTT High Octane DH

2004 • Downhill bike • Switzerland • Innovative downhill race bike with an adjustable seatmast

Scott unleashed the High Octane DH in 2004 at the Interbike cycle show in Las Vegas. The High Octane was ahead of its time in many ways. The frame had an adjustable head angle between a slack 65.5 degrees and a steeper 68.5 degrees. The seat angle was also adjustable, thanks to a carbon fiber seat tower that bolted onto the mainframe. The seat tower had three adjustment points, allowing the rider to dial in his or her preferred seat angle. This was also one of the first times that carbon was used on a downhill bike. The use of carbon instead of alloy also meant that the High Octane could be built up under 40 lb (18 kg), which in 2004 was unheard of for a downhill bike.

The suspension, and consequently the bottom bracket height, were also adjustable, with a choice between 7 and 9 in. (18 and 23 cm) of rear travel. This came via a choice of four mounting positions for the front of the shock. The bottom bracket adjustability came via the mounting plate at the rear of the shock, which had a high and low mounting position. A single-pivot suspension design was used on both the High Octane and its little brother, the Scott Nitrous, a shorter-travel, more freeride-friendly version.

The High Octane continued to be Scott's flagship downhill bike until 2007, with few changes save for different paint jobs and updated componentry. In 2008 it was replaced by Scott's new Gambler DH bike. The Gambler continued with many of the High Octane's technologies, though, including the adjustable travel, bottom bracket height, and head angle features. **CJ**

SANTA CRUZ VP Free

2004 • Freeride bike • USA • Santa Cruz's
Ultimate Freeride Challenge-winning big-drop machine

Santa Cruz Bicycles introduced its Virtual Pivot Point (VPP) suspension design in late 2001. Two short contra-rotating links connected the rear triangle to the frame, allowing the effective pivot point of the suspension to be a moving "virtual" pivot in front of the bottom bracket rather than an actual point on the frame.

After garnering great critical acclaim with this design on the very first Santa Cruz V10, Santa Cruz evolved it into a specific freeride version—the VP Free—in 2004. This was a bike designed to tackle the biggest lines, hit monster jumps and drops, and navigate the highest man-made ladder bridges. Unlike many freeride machines, it was designed to be pedaled

"This bike is very plush and takes the hits and rails the downhills like nothing I have ever ridden."

Reviewer on mtbr.com

to the top rather than pushed or carried by a ski lift. Its 8 in. (20 cm) of rear travel were plushly controlled through the VPP linkage. A super-stiff 6-in. (15-cm) spaced rear axle, bulbous 1½-in. (3.5-cm) head tube, and the over-built chassis combined to give the VP Free the feeling of a tank in bike form. The long wheelbase also added to its stability, even at top speed.

Tyler "Super T" Klassen rode it to win the first Race Face Ultimate Freeride Challenge, earning a $10,000 (£6,700) contract with Race Face. A year later, he was the first rider to sign directly with Santa Cruz, winning the Red Bull Ride, a regular feature of the infamous "Dangerous Dan Flow Show." Known for riding some of the biggest drops ever hit on mountain bikes, Tyler also used the VP Free in the movie *Kranked 5* in 2004. **CJ**

ORANGE Five

2004 • Mountain bike • UK • Legendarily simple but effective mountain bike

Wherever you go in the mountain bike world, you will find fiercely patriotic mountain bikers choosing to ride a home-built brand out of national or regional pride. U.S. riders support Turner, Intense, Ventana, Ellsworth; German riders are likely to buy a Nicolai or a Liteville; in the north of England, the company at the top of every patriotic buyer's shopping list is Orange.

The downtube and the swingarm of the Orange Five, which are literally folded into shape in the heartland of Britain's industrial heritage at Halifax, Yorkshire, have an unashamedly rugged look. The Five is deliberately built as tough as it looks, with a simple suspension system depending on two easily replaced bearings, and paint thick enough to take years of wear. The Five was also one of the first bikes with internal gear-cable and brake-pipe routing, which gives a clean look and helps prevent damage. Most manufacturers are only now starting to introduce this feature.

The first Orange Five appeared in 2004, but its basic layout had been used in the shorter-travel MrXC and long-travel Patriot frames of 1999. The Five itself has been evolving incrementally for the past decade. While other brands have jumped between different designs (and even Orange has dabbled in more complex suspension systems with its ST4 and Blood bikes), the Five has always remained true to its simple toughness. The handling is always closer to that of a downhill bike than a cross-country machine, making it a fantastically fun and communicative bike to ride. It has been voted Trail Bike of the Year in *MBR* magazine several times over, scoring an unprecedented ten out of ten marks in the process. In 2013, the legions of loyal long-term Five riders were treated to a version with 29-in. (73.5-cm) wheels, and it seems that Orange's favorite fruit will be looking fresh for a long time. **GK**

Orange's Five is still a classic trail bike more than a decade after its launch. ▷

BIONICON Golden Willow

2005 • Mountain bike • Germany • Ingenious shape-shifter with goat-influenced suspension

While many bikes are intended to have global appeal, some are especially designed to cater to particular local demands. The German company Bionicon makes bikes that take full account of the preferences of its compatriots, who have long displayed a marked predisposition toward cunning technology.

At first glance the Golden Willow, like other Bionicon bikes, appears to be a modern but conventional enduro bike, complete with downhill-style fork. Closer examination, however, reveals that the shock absorber and the front fork are connected with thin pneumatic hoses that run through a bright orange button on the bars. That's because the designers had been watching the behavior of wild goats in the mountains near Bionicon's headquarters in Rottach-Egern, a town on Lake Tegernsee in the district of Miesbach in Upper Bavaria, Germany, about 35 mi (56 km) south of Munich. Of particular interest to them was the way in which the animals stretch their front legs to go downhill and bend them to gallop up. By joining the air chambers of the front fork and rear shock, Bionicon shunted the air back and forth to make the bike sit up for descents and kneel down for descents, just like their gradient-beating four-legged friends.

The most aggressive riders might find the Golden Willow's suspension action slightly limited, but there's no doubt that the design keeps the rider level-headed at the press of a button. *Bikeradar* was skeptical at first—"Too good to be true?" the magazine's reviewer wondered aloud—but a test ride caused a damascene conversion: "That's what we thought initially, but we've been riding this bike for a couple of months now and we've learned to love it."

There is no doubt that, for cyclists who want a different bike for every part of their ride, this is truly the "goat-to" machine. **GK**

"We experimented, thought a lot and looked around us— nature provided our inspiration, not other bike brands."

Bionicon

◁ Bionicon's Golden Willow is a uniquely adjustable concept.

2 STAGE Elite 9

2005 • Mountain bike • New Zealand •
Innovative twin-shock downhill bike

Downhill mountain biking pushes manufacturers to explore every possible way of making their products the fastest on the circuit. When Dave Evans released his radical 2 Stage Elite 9 bike, it certainly caused a stir. While the design was complex, the up-and-under shocks worked on a very simple principle. Rather than trying to get one shock and suspension system to cope with the very different demands of small bump sensitivity, pedaling efficiency, and big hit absorption, the 2 Stage operated two separate shock and suspension systems simultaneously.

The first shock controlled the first 5 in. (12.7 cm) of mostly vertical travel, which kept the bike feeling smooth without pedaling feeling mushy. The second shock and pivot point pulled mostly backward through a further 4 in. (10 cm) of travel to absorb high-speed landings and big hits such as boulders.

The bike performed better than cynics expected, giving excellent traction and big hit control in rough sections but pedaling well to keep up speed between them. Reviewers also found the twin shocks surprisingly easy to tune. By 2009 the bike had become a regular race winner. However, its weight caused it to struggle as competing bikes became lighter. **GK**

GIANT DH Comp

2005 • Downhill bike • USA • Giant's first
Maestro suspension-equipped downhill bike

The Comp, first released in 2002 with the DH Team, marked the start of a new generation of downhill bikes for Giant. Although it followed the successful DH One of the late 1990s, it was very different from its predecessor. Gone was the box-section frame in favor of the cylindrical tubes of Giant's own AluxX SL aluminum.

A quick glance at the Giant DH Comp would suggest that it was a hardtail without rear suspension, but a closer look reveals a rear shock tucked away behind the bottom bracket at the base of the down tube. At the time, the system was known as a four-bar single pivot, but it would later develop into Giant's Maestro suspension design, which is now used on all the company's full-suspension models. Having the whole suspension linkage and shock tucked away so far down the frame gave the DH Comp a very low center of gravity.

The DH Comp and Team had the same 8¼ in. (21 cm) of rear travel delivered through identical chassis; their differences lay only in componentry and paint. The Comp had a budget build and was cheaper than the Team, which had high-end components. Both the DH Comp and the Team were superseded in 2006 by the Giant Glory, which featured the refined and newly renamed Maestro suspension system. **CJ**

SPECIALIZED S-Works Tarmac

2005 • Road bike • USA • Complete bike version of a team-only frameset

Cannondale led U.S. involvement in the continental pro team scene with its sponsorship of Team Saeco and sprinter Mario Cipollini. Trek then put bikes under the successful U.S. Postal team headed by Lance Armstrong. The benefits in global road bike sales were immediately obvious for both brands, and it was no surprise that other bike manufacturers wanted a slice of the action.

For 2005 Specialized signed up to provide bikes for the German Gerolsteiner team, whose machine of choice was the Tarmac frameset, which was characterized by a massive downtube and integrated bearing bottom bracket area to channel power and steering from bars and pedals to the road.

Seatpost, rear seatstays, and lower fork legs all included Specialized's Zertz technology elastomer gel inserts, which were designed to absorb vibration from the wheels. Specialized's Body Geometry compact curve bar, angle-adjustable stem, and Alias saddle were all innovatively built to provide increased comfort.

In 2005 this top-class frame won stages in the Tour de France, the Vuelta a España, and the Tour of Poland under Gerolsteiner riders. Specialized then made it available in a range of four different complete bikes rather than just Pro level S-Works versions. **GK**

TREK Top Fuel 110

2005 • Mountain bike • USA • Carbon rocket for world-beating solo rider

Twenty-four-hour solo racing is the most grueling discipline in mountain biking. There was no one better at it than Chris Eatough, who in 2005 won his sixth successive world championship in the discipline.

In the same year, Eatough assured Trek a successful introduction for its new full-suspension race bike. An evolution of the Fuel 98, the Top Fuel 110 took its name from the most powerful and explosive fuel category of dragster racing, and its number from the grams per square meter count of the ultra-high-quality carbon fiber used in the frame, which featured an innovative fully carbon OCLV rocker link to drive the RockShox rear shock. It was hand laid and finished by Trek in its Wisconsin composite facility that was also turning out bikes for the all-conquering U.S. Postal Team.

Eatough's bike was loaded with ultra-light carbon fiber parts, plus wheels and tubeless tires from Trek's Bontrager accessory range. Eatough used a more comfortable Bontrager saddle than the stock San Marco item, and swapped conventional grips for three layers of road bike bar tape to reduce vibration and blistering. He also used a stiffer, longer-travel RockShox Reba fork rather than the standard SID unit for extra control on mountain descents. **GK**

THORN Explorer

2005 • Tandem • UK • Budget versatile two-seater for beginners

The Thorn Explorer showed that newcomers to the world of tandems need spend no more than $1,500 (£1,000) to obtain a good-quality two-seater. Without disc or drag brakes and seatpost suspension, and with a frame that was a little limited for extreme load carrying, this was not a bike for long-distance expeditions across mountains, but its responsive handling still made it an excellent, well-built tandem for the majority of teams.

The bike was built on a stiff MIG-welded chromoly frame with chromoly forks imported from Taiwan. It came in three sizes (designated for pairs of riders as small-small, medium-medium, and big-small). The vital boom tube running between the two bottom brackets

"A great value machine with superb handling and lots of options too."

Cycling Plus *magazine*

was particularly big and chunky, giving admirable stiffness to the handling. The Thorn-made 26-in. (66-cm) wheels, however, had light rims held by 36 plain-gauge spokes, and were fitted with low-pressure tires, all targeting less hardcore tandem riders.

Thorn gave buyers a choice of straight or drop handlebars, and options in crank lengths of between 5½ and 7 in. (14–18 cm), depending on the length of the riders' legs.

Other standard features included Shimano V-brakes, SRAM gripshift, and a Shimano drivetrain. The Explorer also came with mudguard fittings, brazed-on mounts for three bottle holders, a front and rear carrying rack, and mounts for front and rear dynamos. The machine weighed 43 lb (19 kg). **SH**

SURLY Pugsley

2005 • Mountain bike • USA • Pioneering production fat bike

While 2-in. (5-cm) wide mountain bike tires work well in most conditions, adventurous riders in Alaska and Canada started to experiment with double-width tires and rims so they could ride on fresh snow. In 2005, left-field bicycle-building company Surly introduced the first off-the-peg fat bike—the Pugsley, named for the eldest child of Gomez and Morticia Addams in the comic horror cartoons drawn by Charles Addams and featured in The New Yorker magazine from 1938.

Fat bikes do not sink into snow, sand, or marsh because their 4-in. (10-cm) wide tires spread the rider's weight over a much greater surface area than normal-width rollers. The tires create a serious clearance problem between the wheels and the frames, though. To solve this, the Pugsley has extra-wide spacing on the rear stays, and the crank bearings are spaced to 4 in. (10 cm) wide rather than the normal 3 in. (7.5 cm). The forks also have a very wide stance, with the same axle width as the rear wheels rather than a typical front-axle width. This has the advantage that a rider can use a spare rear wheel at the front, which is useful in races such as the Iditarod, where temperatures can drop as low as -40°F (-40°C), freezing grease and damaging normally reliable gear mechanisms. If that happens to a Pugsley, the rider can simply switch the wheels and carry on to safety.

This original-production fat bike proved to be remarkably popular among riders looking to explore away from the beaten path—as, for example, some U.S. ski resorts now open their cross-country ski trails to snow bikes in winter. The Surly Pugsley has been much copied since fat-bike fever swept through the U.S. market in 2010, but it remains the original go-anywhere bike, and one of the best of them. Like the boy for whom it is named, it is an energetic little monster. **GK**

Surly's Pugsley was the first production fat bike. ▶

CALFEE Bamboo

2005 • Road bike • USA • Extremely tough, smooth-riding, bamboo-framed road racer

Craig Calfee began building his own bike frames after his Schwinn was crushed by an automobile in 1987. At the start of the 1990s, he pioneered full carbon frame and fork construction, and then produced the sub-2 lb (900 g) Dragonfly frame in 2000.

Meanwhile, in 1995, the sight of his dog's inability to chew through a bamboo stick gave him the idea of using this species of grass as a construction material. Ten years of research and prototype-riding confirmed to him that bamboo, with its long fibers, hollow structure, and high bending strength, is a natural equivalent to carbon fiber. It's also free from the knots and grain inconsistencies of plain wood.

Calfee's experimental bamboo frames with carbon fiber lugs failed as the former expanded and contracted with varying temperature and humidity. He eventually discovered that the best joining material was hemp in an organic resin.

Production began in 2006. While more than double the weight of Calfee's carbon fiber products, the bamboo bikes were acclaimed for their smooth ride, resilience, and cheapness. Their particular suitability for utility bikes in poor countries inspired Craig in 2006 to found the Bamboosero charity project in Ghana. **GK**

TURNER Nitrous

2005 • Mountain bike • USA • Ultra-light but fragile race mountain bike.

As an ex-pro racer, Dave Turner knew that true race performance sometimes demanded an extremely specific machine, and that's precisely what he created in the Nitrous.

Based on the rocker-pivot, four-bar linkage that he'd used since the original Burner, Turner shaved every possible bit of weight out of the frame. The tube walls were super-thin, and had no external gussets around the head tube. That was because the geometry was designed to work with a 3-in. (76-mm) travel fork to match the same amount of travel at the back. Because the fork was so short, the maximum leverage, even at race speeds, was within the strength limits of a conventional, tube-only head junction. The tall triangular shock mount and rocker link were as light as possible, and the rear drop-outs and bottom bracket shell were machine-shaped to carve out every last ounce. The result was a frame weight of only 4 lb 8 oz (2 kg), which is still lighter than many carbon fiber full-suspension frames today.

Unfortunately, even with a rider weight limit of 165 lb (75 kg), Turner had gone too far. Flex in the thin, square-section seatstays caused cracked tubes in many frames, and within two years the Nitrous was withdrawn. **GK**

ROCKY MOUNTAIN RMX

2005 • Freeride–downhill bike • Canada •
Famous freeride "filmstar" bike

Rocky Mountain Bicycles was founded in 1978 as a shop in Vancouver, Canada, and gradually developed into a major manufacturer.

The story of the company's RMX bike began in 2003 with the RM7 that was named for Wade Simmons, its best rider and the winner in 2001 of the Red Bull Rampage in Utah. In 2004, while retaining the Wade Simmons signature frameset, Rocky added three new models: the Team, the Pro, and the RMX. These versions had new front triangles for increased standover height, and Thrust Link suspension systems, which worked as cantilevers that allowed the motocross motorbike-style swingarm to pivot above the bottom bracket while compressing the rear shock.

Between 2005 and its final year in 2008, the RMX barely changed, either in external appearance or technical specification. Nevertheless, it retained a loyal following throughout the period, thanks in no small part to annual appearances in the biggest mountain bike films, such as the *New World Disorder* series and *The Collective* series featuring Thomas Vanderham, Richie Schley, and Wade Simmons, all aboard their RMXs.

A Rocky Mountain rider from 1995, Simmons became synonymous with the brand in general and with the RMX in particular. He was known as the Godfather of Freeride for all his work to bring in sponsors and outside support, and thus enabling future generations of freeride athletes to make careers in the sport. In 2010, Simmons, Schley, and a third Rocky Mountain freerider, Brett Tippie, became the first freeriders to be inducted into the Mountain Bike Hall of Fame. At the time of publication, Simmons was Rocky Mountain's longest-standing athlete, and continued to guide mountain bike trips to Costa Rica each year with Big Mountain Adventures. **CJ**

EMPIRE AP-1

2005 • Mountain bike • UK • Award-winning
radical cast-aluminum frame downhill bike

Engineer Chris Williams mixed his passion for mountain biking with his experience in the research departments of Ford, Jaguar, and motorbike mavericks CCM to create the truly mold-breaking Empire AP-1.

Having used sand casting to create one-off prototype parts for cars and motorbikes, Williams used the process to build his bike. L169 military-grade casting alloy was melted into basic shape, and then precision-machined into the hard anodized frame members. The mainframe was bolted onto the separate seatmast, while the swingarm was attached with motocross-grade bearings.

The resulting frame is heavy, even for a downhill bike, but Williams is not sure weight is a bad thing. He

> *". . . built to withstand anything the world's best downhill riders can throw at it."*
>
> Chris Williams

says, "When looking at suspension performance, it is highly beneficial to have a high-sprung to unsprung mass ratio for superior grip. To this end, lighter machines will be at a significant disadvantage."

On the trail, the AP-1 won the UK Junior National Championship under Lewis Buchanan in 2009, and was hailed as a Superbike in *MBUK* magazine. In 2010, Empire shared Red Dot design awards with leading innovators Apple and Dyson, and in 2011 the AP-1 beat the Bugatti Veyron engine block to Component of the Year in the Cast Metal Industry awards.

In 2010 the AP-1 design was joined in the Empire range by the MX-6 trail bike, which uses a similar cast and machined frame and high-pivot suspension layout. **GK**

Empire's AP-1 frame borrowed technology from automotive prototyping. ▶

TREK 69er HT

2005 • Mountain bike • USA • Radical different-sized wheel single-speed MTB

To help develop its bikes, Trek has always used a team of pro riders who throw up some interesting ideas that actually make it into production. Trek's 69er was exactly such a bike, inspired by single-speed advocate and hardcore racer Travis Brown.

Production single-speed bikes were nothing new: Many brands had been producing single-cog machines for more than a decade. However, Trek's 69er frame design went way beyond the usual fitting of horizontal drop-outs or adjustable bottom bracket for derailleur-free chain tensioning. The 69er did have horizontal drop-outs—complete with threaded axle stops to prevent slippage of the axle if the rear skewer loosened—but it also had an outsized, hydraulically shaped seat tube to make it as stiff as possible when straining the single-gear

ratio up a climb. The frame had no gear cable fixtures, just mounts for the rear disc brake hose along the similarly oversized flared-end top tube.

But the bike's name hints at the really interesting part. Brown was already part of the development team for the 29ers that were being launched under Trek's Gary Fisher label. However, while he appreciated the smooth rolling and stability of the bigger wheels, he didn't like the reduced acceleration that was a consequence of their increased weight. Hence the 69er used a 29-in. (73.5-cm) wheel up front in a modified and color-matched Maverick triple-crown fork, and a faster-reacting 26-in. (66-cm) wheel at the rear. The unbalanced ride proved popular: the 69er remained in the Trek range until 2010. **GK**

SURLY Karate Monkey

2005 • Mountain bike • USA • One of the original big-wheeled mountain bike cruisers

The Karate Monkey was one of the first mass-market bikes to roll onto the trails, and it's a tribute to the original design that it has since remained in production largely unaltered ever since.

Surly has always produced super-strong workhorse bikes that offer great long-term value through simple toughness. The Karate Monkey is based around main tubes made from double-butted 4130 chrome molybdenum steel. Double butting means they are thicker at the ends than in the middle, which gives the frame more spring and saves weight where it's not needed. The default fork supplied with the frame and complete bikes is a rigid steel unit too, with second-generation versions getting a slightly springier and forgiving feel. It's the right length to swap with a 3-in.

(7.5-cm) stroke suspension fork if you want an even smoother ride.

At the back end of the complete bike, the drop-outs feature a conventional gear hanger to open up a full range of drivetrain possibilities. The frame is equipped with threaded mounts for bolt-on racks if you want to take more gear along for the ride, though the expedition role is now filled by the more recent Surly Ogre bike. The introduction of the Ogre also allowed Surly to refocus the Karate Monkey more on the rougher side of riding: The V-brake bosses of the original bike were removed to leave disc brakes only.

The versatility, strength, and entertainment value of the Karate Monkey have made it one of Surly's most popular bikes. It won't get the chop any time soon. **GK**

SANTA CRUZ Nomad

2005 • Mountain bike • UK • Aggressive all-mountain bike

Having set benchmarks for pedal-efficient but chaos-controlling performance in the short cross-country and super-long downhill categories with the Blur and V10 bike, respectively, Santa Cruz turned its attention to the emerging all-mountain genre.

The Nomad was designed to range far and wide over inhospitable terrain, carrying with it everything required to tackle any challenge in its path. In practical terms, that meant 6 in. (15 cm) of rear wheel travel using Santa Cruz's patented Virtual Pivot Point (VPP) suspension. This system—developed from Outland's original—used two short, contra-rotating linkages to join the front and rear halves of the frame. These were

"For sheer broad-based competence, the Nomad can't be beaten."

Bikemagic.com

positioned so that the suspension stiffened slightly under power for a purposeful pedaling feel, but pushed through the stroke easily when not pedaling. This was ideal for a bike that could grunt up the steepest, most technical climbs, and then blast down the far side with total disregard for the rocks and drops in its path.

The instantly recognizable hump-backed frameset made maximum use of the latest high-pressure tube-forming techniques to create a very stiff and strong chassis. As a result, the Nomad could handle the longest-travel trail forks of the time without weighing too much. The alloy-frame Nomad was followed in 2010 by a lighter and stiffer carbon fiber model. This was updated again in 2012 with a rear axle assembly that was even more robust. **GK**

RISIGO Deluxe Cruiser

2005 • Urban bike • Taiwan • Innovative bodyweight-propelled bike

Ever since the appearance of the first velocipede in 1870, inventors have sought improved ways of propelling human-powered two-wheelers. Treadle pedals on rods, direct cranks on front-wheel drive, and shaft drive are just a few of the variant methods that were tried before the start of the twentieth century, when metal-link chains were introduced. Although they immediately became the default drivetrain, they haven't stopped the search for new ways of getting bike wheels to go around.

Among the most persistent innovators is Risigo, a company whose creations have always stood out at U.S. Interbike shows because of their unique and distinctive galloping gait.

Not content with involving just your legs, the Risigo also brings your rump in on the act. Press the paired pedals down, and not only does the bike go forward but the saddle is driven upward by a cam lever. As soon as the cranks go past their dead spot, rider weight takes over, pushing the saddle down and engaging a ratchet drive that further assists the bike's forward movement.

It's certainly a fascinating process to watch as the rider scuds along in a curious slow-motion hopping action. The Deluxe Cruiser's system is truly remarkable, but no other major manufacturer has yet attempted to emulate it, either because of doubts about the safety of riders whose view of the road ahead is constantly altered by the up-and-down movements of their heads, or because, in the view of one commentator, "the world isn't ready for it."

Whatever the truth of the matter, and regardless of whether this bike has a commercial future, of one thing there is no doubt: Interbike just wouldn't be Interbike without Risigo. **GK**

PLANET X Kaffenback

2005 • Road bike • UK • No-nonsense all-round roadster

Before you start looking up battles from the Boer War and wondering what relevance they have to a steel-framed winter bike, understand that this Planet X workhorse is phonetically named after traditional UK winter training ride routines. Riding to the "cafe and back" has always been the bedrock of "getting the miles in" during wet winter months when motivation revolves entirely around a hot cup of tea and slab of cake to reheat and refuel for the ride back home.

Because reliability is more important in winter than outright speed, Planet X built the Kaffenback from Maxwall chrome molybdenum steel tubing. The rear stays have mounts for either disc or cantilever-style brakes, and the Swap-Out drop-outs can be adjusted to take up the slack in a single-cog transmission. That

makes the Kaffenback a great choice for riders who like to increase the smoothness of their pedaling style by using a fixed gear without a freewheel mechanism. Mudguard mounts are also an essential feature, as many UK clubs run a "no mudguards, no ride" policy on their group rides to make sure riders get wet only from the sky, not from the wheel in front. The Kaffenback will also take a full rear cargo rack. Planet X's trademark multi-tube seatstay top wishbone arrangement gives enough room for extra-large 1⅜-in. (3.5-cm) wide tires. That makes it suitable both for heavy-duty touring work and for wearing knobbly tires to race round the park in cyclocross races. In fact, there's practically nothing that this sturdy steel bargain won't take in its stride on the hunt for a cup of tea. **GK**

BMC SLT01

2005 • Road bike • Switzerland • The bike that carried Floyd Landis into Tour de France history

If you've followed the controversies, claims, and counterclaims surrounding the exposure of a deeply ingrained drug-taking culture in the all-conquering U.S. Postal bike team, you might know Floyd Landis better for his off-the-bike antics than for anything he achieved on the road. He was the first former teammate of Lance Armstrong to admit to systematic doping, and was thus instrumental in triggering the initial investigations. However—by fair means or foul—Landis was one of the most successful riders of his generation, and although he was stripped of his 2006 Tour de France title days after riding into Paris in yellow, he remains a central figure in the history of cycle racing.

A year before his now-discredited victory, an eager Landis left the safety and sanctuary of the U.S. Postal team and took over as leader of Andy Rihs' Phonak team, all of whose members rode BMC bikes.

The SLT01 was the top bike in BMC's range, with a production weight of 15 lb 13 oz (7.2 kg). Along with a hefty price tag of 8,199 Swiss Francs ($9,000/£5,640), the bike had numerous eye-catching and memorable features. From the unique and airy seat cluster and the unusual T-section top tube, to the beefy rectangular-section chainstays, the bike certainly stood out in the professional peloton.

Landis kitted out the rest of his bike with an Easton bar and stem, Zipp 404 wheels, and a Campagnolo Record 10-speed. He had just ridden the machine to glory in Paris when he tested positive for testosterone and was banned from racing and fired by Phonak. **DB**

DE ROSA Corum

2005 • Road bike • Italy • Lightweight steel frame using modern construction

During the 1990s, this famous Italian company established in the early 1950s that made bikes for Eddy Merckx and the Molenti team at the height of its powers moved from creating classic, steel-framed racing bikes into the modern materials of the time—titanium, aluminum, and carbon.

In 2005, however, De Rosa returned to its roots, and launched the Corum range of steel-framed bikes. But these were no old-style, lugged and brazed machines clunking their way weightily from the workshop—the new Corums used ultra-modern technology. The bike's frame was constructed using the latest ultra-light oversized Dedaccia EOM 16.5 steel alloy tubing, which was tungsten inert gas (TIG)-welded by hand by a member of the De Rosa family.

The steel frame was light—just 3 lb 8 oz (1.6 kg)—and was supplemented by a carbon fork, seatposts, and bars. Complete bikes weighed around 16 lb (7.25 kg), although might be slightly heavier with certain optional components.

The Corum frame could be ordered to a custom size, but buyers rarely needed to. De Rosa's stock frames were available in a choice of two geometries (regular and more sloped), and a huge range of sizes: thirty different standard Corum frames were available.

Other parts of the design were more traditional: the cables were externally routed, the brakes were calipers, and the bike sported a classic-looking paint job.

The result was a bike that was lively, responsive, and comfortable. "The frame interacts with you," cried one surprised modern reviewer brought up on a strict diet of carbon and aluminum. Other commentators were amazed that the ride was both stable and compliant. Whatever the merits of the bike, the Corum re-ignited the classic cycling debate about the pros and cons of frame materials. **SH**

"I've had Litespeeds . . . but this is the best handling and most beautiful frame I've had the pleasure of riding."

Contemporary advertisement, retrobike.co.uk

◁ De Rosa's steel-frame Corum oozed classic charisma.

SCOTT Plasma CR1

2005 • Aero bike • Switzerland • Ultra-light, carbon fiber aero bike

The Scott company and carbon fiber consultant Peter Denk established a reputation for lightweight composite road machines with their CR1. Taking the same tube-to-tube construction elements into the wind tunnel, they then created this similarly super-light time trial machine.

While the days of angular, integrated, superbike aero machines were still a long way off, Scott devoted considerable effort to making the Plasma as streamlined as possible. The legs of the alloy-tipped carbon fork flared toward the top to create smoother airflow around the front wheel/fork crown area. Unlike many other bikes of the period, the Plasma had a down tube that was pulled up and away from the front tire, allowing its two parts to deal with airflow independently. While the aerodynamic advantages of this were uncertain, it made the Scott a lot less gusty in mixed wind conditions than most contemporary deep tube bikes. The top tube was also ovalized horizontally, rather than vertically, to give precise and responsive steering without excess stiffness. On premium-grade models, the top tube/aero seat tube junction was kept clean by extending the seat tube all the way to the saddle clamp. This seatmast design reduced drag and weight, but required care when originally cut to the right length because there was little room for adjustment once the tube had been chopped. The bladed rear stays and wheel-hugger seatpost were separated more clearly than on than many other bikes.

The Plasma quickly established a formidable reputation. *Bike Radar* praised its "quick-witted handling and aggressive posture," and noted that "it takes a confident rider to get the best from it." It kept Scott at the top end of the time trial and triathlon bike charts for several seasons. **GK**

CANYON F10

2005 • Road bike • Germany • Ultra-light direct-sell dynamite from German bargain-meisters

By the time Canyon launched the F10, the company had come a long way from its inauspicious beginnings with the father of a young racer selling imported Italian components from a car trailer to help pay for fuel and race entries.

Canyon really seized the headlines when its Project 3.7 bike—built around a new frame by legendary carbon composite specialist Hans Christian Smolik—was unveiled at the 2005 Eurobike trade show in Friedrichshafen, Germany. Weighing in at just 8 lb 5 oz (3.78 kg), and ready to ride with pedals, the bike smashed the opposition in the always hotly contested "Lightest Bike of the Show" contest, and ensured maximum publicity for the upstart brand.

". . . a bike that accelerates quickly when you stomp on the pedals is mentally fortifying."

Jeff Jones, cyclingnews.com

Even without the price-no-object component choice, the F10 was still a super-light machine, with the frame weighing in at just under the magic 1 kg (2 lb 3 oz) mark, and the slim carbon forks (the sole Smolik carry-overs from the project bike) adding only another 10½ oz (300 g) to the total weight.

The frame passed the most stringent fatigue tests of the German EFBe safety laboratory. The 2⅖-in. (5.5-cm) diameter downtube made it extremely stiff, while steep steering angles made it as responsive to handlebar input as it was to pedal pushes.

The result was an instant hit in Canyon's German homeland, and the start of a serious global brand expansion that continues to this day. **GK**

Canyon set out its performance ambitions early with the F10. ▶

SCOTT Spark

2005 • Mountain bike • Switzerland • Innovative, ultra-light race and trail machine

Development of Scott's groundbreaking Spark race bike started two years before it first hit the shops in 2007; meanwhile, in prototype form, it had won world-ranked marathon races.

The Spark had a hard act to follow. The previous carbon mainframe G-Zero Strike chassis had been an incredibly light and popular race machine. In order to avoid disappointing its fans, Scott now strove to minimize weight, and produced a mainframe and shock that together weighed just under 4 lb 2 oz (1.87 kg).

Scott also gave the Spark a remote-control terrain-referencing edge that no other bike could match for neatness and effectiveness. The custom-created, carbon fiber-bodied Nude shock, produced by DT Swiss, packed the triple-chamber design of the Genius Equalizer into

a tiny, lightweight package, and linked it to the Trac Loc switch on the bars. In one position, the shock was fully locked and closed for sprinting, smooth climbs or road riding. In Traction modes, the shock used sixty percent of its capacity for a more progressive feel that still allowed sufficient ground-following movement to guarantee good traction. The All Travel mode fully opened both air chambers to allow the maximum 4³⁄₁₀ in. (11 cm) of rear wheel movement for smoother descending.

In spite of all this damping technology, the complete bikes in the Spark range were still much lighter than many hardtails of around the same price.

The remote control gave the Spark the edge on climbs, but reliability was poor, and the shocks felt less smooth than Fox and RockShox products. **GK**

SPECIALIZED Enduro SX Trail

2005 • Mountain bike • USA • Hardcore gravity play bike

Mountain biking has always been a very fast-evolving branch of biking, and it's often evolved new bike genres faster than the brands themselves can respond with a major new model. In some cases, though, a slight tweak to an existing model can create a massively successful niche machine, and that's exactly what happened in 2005 with Specialized's Enduro SX Trail.

Specialized had previously divided the tough-guy end of the riding spectrum between the standard Enduro trail bike and the downhill Big Hit bike. However, many riders, such as sponsored Freeride star Darren Berrecloth, wanted the best of both worlds. The lighter weight and easier handling of the Enduro for busting out the latest stunts, but the extra suspension of the Big Hit to keep them safe on less than perfect landings.

The SX Trail uses the lightweight semi-box-section frame of the Enduro but with a long stroke, coil-sprung—rather than pressurized air-sprung—version of Progressive's Fifth Element shock. A matching 6-in. (15-cm) stroke fork from Marzocchi took care of any unplanned nosedives. The wheels, cranks, bar, and stem were heavier-duty models designed to take the biggest drops, and extra-large brake rotors gave good control.

The resulting bike was an immediate hit with the new generation of riders using "bike park" resorts such as Whistler Mountain in Canada and Morzine and Verbier in the Alps, as well as aggressive trail riders who didn't want the weight of a full downhill bike. Its success also spawned a whole new genre of "mini downhill" bikes and gravity-focused trail centers the world over. **GK**

COLNAGO C50 Cross

2005 • Cyclocross bike • Italy • Early carbon-framed cross bike

Successors to the highly successful C40, the first C50 frames emerged in 2004 and were named to commemorate fifty years since Ernesto Colnago founded his business in Cambiago, Italy. Colnago had worked in the bicycle industry since the age of thirteen, and, after a serious crash ended his racing career, he combined building his own frames with working as a mechanic for some of the top names in the sport—he eventually worked with Eddy Merckx, designing and building the frame on which the Belgian broke the world Hour Record in 1972.

The bike shown here is the cyclocross version of the original Road, Track, Crono, and MTB C50s that

"I consider myself a part of my sport. Colnago equals professional cycling."

Ernesto Colnago

had appeared in the previous year. Its carbon frame has several unusual features, including a down tube that morphs into a box shape as it reaches the bottom bracket, aiding power transfer, and heavily reinforced joints to increase rigidity.

Before its launch, the C50 Cross underwent extreme testing by the Belgian Sven Nijs and the Dutchman Richard Gronendaal, stars of the Dutch Rabobank team (later Belkin). It did all that was asked of it, while retaining something in reserve.

The prime emphasis throughout this bike is on performance—in order to achieve explosive pace when coming out of corners, rigidity takes precedence over comfort. In 2012, the C50 Cross was superseded by the Cross Prestige. **TB**

LOOK 585

2005 • Road bike • France • All-carbon Tour de France winner

Look was established in 1951 in Nevers, France, and for the next three decades manufactured high-end skiing equipment. In 1984, the company entered the world of two wheels by adapting existing spring-loaded ski fittings for use by cyclists. Known as *pédales automatiques* (automatic pedals), clipless, clip-in, or step-in pedals, they require a special cycling shoe with a cleat fitted to the sole, which locks into a mechanism that firmly holds the shoe.

These innovations were used by Bernard Hinault in his Tour de France victory the following year, and soon became de rigueur throughout the sport. In 1986, Greg LeMond used the first Look frame, the handmade KG86, which combined Kevlar with carbon, to win that year's Tour.

The Look 585 range comprised the Origin, the Ultra, and the all-black Optimum. The three had different top and head tube lengths, but were all race-ready production models. Frames were constructed using very high-modulus (VHM) compressed carbon, which combined the weight advantages of this material with the rigidity associated with alloy models.

Norway's Thor Hushovd rode a modified 585 on his green jersey point competition victory for the Crédit Agricole team in the 2006 Tour de France. After later adopting a 595 frame, Hushovd switched back to the 585 for the 2008 Paris–Roubaix "Hell of the North" race. It appeared to be a standard model—there was no additional tire clearance at either end nor any obvious geometry adjustments. When asked the reason for the change of vehicle, Look's head mechanic Pascal Ridel explained that it was merely a question of comfort: "It's a little smoother than the 595," he said. Hushovd's machine was fitted with Shimano Dura Ace controls, cranks, derailleurs, cassette, and chain. **TB**

SCAPIN Style

2005 • Road bike • Italy • Beautiful blend of traditional steel and carbon fiber construction

The Scapin Style wasn't the first bike to use carbon fiber tubes in conjunction with steel structural fixtures. In the early days of fiber adoption, it seemed the obvious way to join the two materials together, but as technology progressed, carbon fiber tubes were joined with matching carbon fiber lugs, and bi-material bikes faded away. Scapin's revival of the idea isn't about making things easier—far from it: It's more designed to employ both materials to their maximum advantage and create something beautiful and original in the process.

Scapin used high-modulus carbon fiber, the phenomenal strength-to-weight characteristics of which underline the performance of the bike best in an outsized down tube and rear chainstays. A more compliant vibration-absorbing carbon tube was then used for the seat tube section to damp road buzz before it reached the rider. In the latest Style designs, this tube extends up to the bottom of the saddle clamp by passing through a sculpted lug that sits between the top tube and the rear stays. The rear seatstays, bottom bracket section, top tube, and head tube are built from a custom blend of Columbus Spirit steel. This makes for more accurate and secure bearing attachment, and adds a sprung element to the top line of the ride. This gives the Style the signature buoyant ride of a top-quality steel frame, and the power transfer of a much less comfortable carbon frame. At 2 lb 12 oz (1.3 kg), it's also significantly lighter than a full steel frameset. Moreover, the frame is gorgeous and available in seven different classic color panel schemes. **GK**

COMMENÇAL Meta 5

2005 • Mountain bike • Andorra • The first bike in a wave of fantastic French fun machines

At Sunn Bicycles, Max Commençal was a key player in the French domination of downhill mountain bike racing in the 1990s. His bikes and suspension designs were used by legendary riders such as Nico Vouillioz, Anne-Caroline Chausson, Fabien Barel, and Cédric Gracia, but this never translated into mainstream success. That all changed when Max set up his own Commençal brand and launched the Meta 5.

In terms of chassis design, the Meta 5 wasn't particularly radical. The rear swingarm was fairly flexible when ridden hard, and the frame weight was relatively high. What turned it into a must-have mountain machine were its suspension and handling angles. The simple, single-pivot swingarm used a pair of triangular linkages to drive the vertically mounted

shock, which kept center of gravity low. Commençal's race experience meant the shock was superbly tuned to glue the rear wheel to the ground. Add the twist and compliance of the swingarm, and the Meta was renowned for its traction. The suspension tune kept the bike feeling very level and consistent when compressed hard through corners. While the stock cockpit equipment tended to be slightly high and narrow, the default steering geometry was outstandingly stable and reliable at speed. Unfortunately, its aptitude for aggressive riding wasn't matched by its strength, and frame failures dogged the Meta 5 throughout its history. It was still a popular bike, though, and it continues to be a top choice of technical trail riders in a stronger new chassis today. **GK**

DMR Trailstar

2005 • Mountain bike • UK • Legendarily tough dirt jumper

Given the size of the massive frame tubes on this bike, you could be forgiven for assuming it was made from aluminum alloy, but in fact the DMR Trailstar was built from BMX and dirt jumper riders' favorite material—steel. The combination of serious oversizing and steel certainly didn't do the weight of this frame any favors—at nearly 7 lb (3.1 kg), it was heavier than many full-suspension bikes and three times the weight of the lightest carbon fiber cross-country mountain bike frames.

But this was a frame built for raging, not racing, and it was detailed to match. Massive reinforcing rings around each end of the head tube prevented big impacts from bending the tube out of shape. Another wraparound gusset plate under the throat of the down tube–head tube junction kept the head tube from being torn off if the bike plowed into the ground. It also enabled the Trailstar to take longer-travel forks for freeride riding.

This versatility was further enhanced by a long frame and chainguide mounts. The Trailstar also introduced DMR's much-copied Swap-Out drop-outs, which allowed a whole range of rear axle and transmission options. And best of all for young riders on a budget, the DMR Trailstar was affordable too. **GK**

INTENSE M3

2005 • Downhill bike • Italy • Ultra-successful monocoque-frame, VPP-suspension DH bike

The Intense M1 first emerged around the turn of the century. At a time when not many manufacturers offered thoroughbred downhill race bikes, it soon became one of the most successful, cloned, and rebadged bikes of this kind ever. But it was the more refined M3 frame that made the most notable breakthrough. While the M1 was ridden to a World Championship silver medal by Shaun Palmer, the M3 won most plaudits from riders and reviewers.

The M3 emerged after Intense Cycles' acquisition of a shared license (with Santa Cruz Bikes) for Virtual Pivot Point (VPP) rear suspension. The M3 was developed during the 2000 World Cup season by Chris Kovarik and Michael Ronning. It was the bike every amateur downhill racer aspired to.

M Series chassis continue to evolve and stun to this day. Their VPP setup uses tension from linkages moving in opposite directions to match rear-wheel axle path and shock responses to different types of bumps to increase pedal efficiency. Most M3s are so well equipped that $10,000 (£6,250) price tags are common. But they are the first downhill race bikes with no obvious failings. In a sport where the slightest underperformance can lose a race, perfection—or proximity to it—is crucial. **SW**

SPECIALIZED Demo 8

2005 • Freeride–downhill bike • USA • Unique twin swingarm freeride–downhill bike

When Specialized released the Demo 9 in 2004, it weighed 48 lb (21.8 kg), had an unprecedented 9 in. (22.8 cm) of rear travel, and could take a 26-in. (66-cm) or a 24-in. (61-cm) rear wheel. It was designed to tackle the biggest cliff drops undertaken by freeriders, whose motto was "go big or go home."

Previously, few major bike manufacturers had bothered with purpose-built, big-drop bikes, leaving them to niche companies such as Brooklyn and Karpeil. But then Specialized decided it wanted a piece of the freeride action.

Then fashion changed to be more about style than size. The Big S responded with this slimmed-down version of the Demo 9, the Demo 8, which lost 1½ lb (0.7 kg) out of the frame alone through a redesigned bottom bracket/shock mount area. The suspension linkage was an innovative take on the FSR Horst Link featuring two rear triangles to control the extra travel, while limiting the chainstay to 16⁷⁄₁₀ in. (42.4 cm). In 2005 that was revolutionary, but it would rapidly become a template for all freeride bikes. Matt Hunter made the Demo 8 famous in films like *The Collective* and *Roam*, riding it off huge jumps in Kamloops, Canada, and road gaps in Morocco. **CJ**

CHRISTINI Venture

2005 • Mountain bike • USA • Ingenious two-wheel-drive mountain bike

If off-road trucks and cars work better with all-wheel drive, then surely driving both wheels of a bike is a great idea too? That's the reasoning that inspired Christini to develop this ingenious double-drive bike that was an engineering masterpiece but a handful to ride.

The two-wheel drive system is almost unnoticeable on the full-suspension frame, as the rear wheel is powered by a conventional derailleur. However, a small worm gear takes drive from the rear hub up a solid shaft hidden inside the seatstays; a second universal joint-connected drive shaft takes the power to another shaft inside the top tube. Further gears inside the head tube drive cogs in the custom-modified crown of the White Brothers suspension fork. These turn a telescopic ribbed shaft that allows for fork compression with remarkably little effect on the suspension smoothness. A second worm gear and driver disc transfer power into the front wheel. The really clever bit is that this front-wheel gear runs fractionally slower than the rear wheel. This means that, in normal use, with no rear-wheel slippage, the front wheel freewheels along as normal. As soon as the rear wheel slides or slows down more than the front, the front-wheel drive engages and you are hauled forward by the front end. Hence traction is outstanding. **GK**

YETI 575

2005 • Mountain bike • USA • Enduring
lightweight design for speed and enjoyment

Mountain bike riding has always been about taking skills and nerves to the limit. Iconic Colorado brand Yeti has never been afraid to push the boundaries, and its 575 bike was a game-changer for trail riders who wanted extra suspension control in a climb-friendly lightweight package.

The neatly laid-out frame provided a rock- and drop-swallowing 5¾ in. (15 cm) of rear wheel movement, and was shaped so that it could take forks with the same stroke or slightly longer.

The handling geometry was also lower and slacker than most bikes of the time, giving the 575 a real down-and-dirty sure-footed authority on the trail in spite of its readily apparent frame flex.

" . . . agile and pedal-friendly 575 platform is an excellent aggro trail bike."

bikeradar.com

By using a flexible carbon knuckle, rather than a rear pivot, and thin-wall aluminum tubing joined with extensively machined junction blocks, Yeti kept weight remarkably low for such a generously sprung chassis. The latest Fifth Element air damper was incorporated to provide resistance to pedal-related movement. The resulting bike pedaled up like a racer but came back down like a raver.

This combination of fast yet fun performance immediately made the 575 a firm favorite with cross-country riders and gravity fiends alike. The bike has been through several subsequent evolutions, but has retained its character and is currently the best-selling Yeti of all time. **GK**

DIDI SENFT World's Biggest Bike

2005 • Novelty bike • Germany • Enormous
world record-breaker

Bearded cycling enthusiast Didi Senft has become famous as the man who dresses as the devil to appear at major cycle races. The eccentric German can often be seen at the trackside near the finishing lines of Tour de France or Giro d'Italia stages, screaming encouragement at passing riders while dressed in a red costume with a black cloak and horns. He also paints his trademark trident symbol onto the road that the riders will use.

Away from the races, Senft is a bike builder who specializes in bizarre novelty machines. He is both designer and constructor of more than 100 different remarkable oddities, which he sometimes takes out on the road but more often leaves on display in a personal bike museum in his hometown of Storkow near Berlin.

Included in his collection is the bike currently recognized by *The Guinness Book of Records* as the largest ever made. It is 25 ft 7 in. (7.8 m) long, 12 ft 2 in. (3.7 m) tall, and weighs 330 lb (150 kg). The wheels are 10 ft 10 in. (3.3 m) in diameter. This machine may sound too big to be true, but it really works: Senft himself has piloted it.

The rider sits astride the top tube pedaling a chain wheel that is attached to the down tube. The chain transfers power to the back wheel via another chain wheel attached to the seat tube. The front forks incorporate ladder steps on either side for climbing up to the top tube.

As if that was not enough, Senft has since surpassed this twice, once with a bike measuring 125 ft (38 m) in length, and the second time with a giant bike in the shape of a mobile guitar that he pedals from underneath. His collection also includes a recumbent two-story tandem and an enormous rickshaw 42 ft (12.4 m) long and 21 ft 10 in. (6.7 m) high. **SH**

Didi Senft is a larger-than-life character with a bike to match. ▷

TREK Fuel EX

2005 • Mountain bike • USA • Innovative and award-winning all-round trail bike

Trek's full-suspension cross-country Fuel had been a popular all-rounder for several years before a complete refresh for 2005 made it a category leader.

With the "EX" suffix, Trek's lightweight short-travel race frame signaled it was ready for rougher, tougher trails, and the new design didn't disappoint. The mainframe came in lightweight, hydraulically shaped alloy or with a super-light carbon fiber front end built in Wisconsin using Trek's proprietary Optimum Carbon Low Void (OCLV) process. Wider tube formats in both designs also created a stiffer frame, despite their low weight. A short Evo link connected the rear stays to the top of the custom-tuned rear shock (RockShox or Fox), with asymmetric chainstays adding tire and crank clearance behind the bottom bracket.

The Fuel EX also boosted shock performance with its Full Floater mounting system, which squeezed the shock between the upper linkage and extended tips of the rear stays, rather than the mainframe. By doing this, Trek produced the equivalent effect of moving your hands backward as you catch a ball, helping to dissipate the impact force. Add an Active Braking Pivot (ABP) rear axle concentric pivot at the rear of the stays to effectively isolate braking forces from suspension behavior, and the Fuel Ex felt like it had far more travel than its actual 4¾ in. (12 cm) on descents, but less on climbs.

With solid componentry—high-quality, home-brewed Bontrager kit, including tubeless-ready tires and wheels—the Fuel Ex really was an exceptional bike. **GK**

GIANT Reign

2005 • Mountain bike • Taiwan • Evergreen all-mountain machine

As one of the largest bike manufacturers in the world, Giant could perhaps be forgiven for just concentrating on solid mass-market products. It's a credit to Giant's creativity and passion for all forms of pedal sport that it has always also had some tasty and innovative machines within its comprehensive portfolio.

After challenging performance expectations with the VT1 trail bike and the early adoption of pedal-bounce-isolating shock-absorbers, Giant really pushed the big-suspension, big-mileage bike concept forward with the introduction of the Reign just two years later.

As well as introducing the Maestro suspension system that is still in use today, the Reign featured a radical single-piece "basket" in the belly of the frame. This ultra-strong, open-walled section enabled Giant to drop the shock absorber and suspension parts very low to create a low center of gravity. The first Reigns also came with Manitou's outsized, clamped-axle Nixon fork for extra steering authority.

The resulting bike was an instant hit. It had significantly more suspension and a much stronger and stiffer frame than the VT1, and riders could tell it meant business as soon as they let rip down a descent.

Over time, the signature basket section with protruding shock was replaced with a curved tubular section, and the frame underwent many changes to reduce weight and increase suspension movement. The Reign later spawned a more radical Reign X version for full-on freeriding, but, in the opinion of many, the original was always the favorite. **GK**

LINEAR Limo

"While not exactly a carbon fiber racer, it is a respectable performer. A lot of this has to do with the . . . frame."

Bryan Ball, Bentrider

The Linear brand began as a part-time venture in Guttenberg, Iowa, in the 1980s. Its first production models featured swept-back, chopper-style handlebars that wouldn't have been out of place on Harley-Davidson motorcycles. Sales, however, were poor, and the company went through several changes of ownership before going out of business in 2002. However, it re-emerged later in the same year under a new name, Linear Recumbents.

New prototypes were built, and engineers and professors at Alfred University in New York used strain gauges and dye-penetrants to test the first prototype for fatigue cracks after an 1,100-mile (1,770-km) test run from Maine to Georgia. The future for Linear looked assured when, in 2006, the company sold its first Limo 3.0 Recumbent Touring Bike.

The Limo has always been characterized by continual evolution in design. This 2006 model came with a rear Avid BB-5 disc brake (later changed to a BB-7 for longer pad life), and a flexible Linear seat (RANS seats are now standard). The latest models have stiffer rear ends for pedaling efficiency, and you can now choose your own color, with a selection of cool decals to match.

While Linear Recumbents has always lacked the market penetration to break into the recumbent bike mainstream, it has built up a loyal following, and in 2011 the company's Roadster was Bentrider Recumbent Bike of the Year.

The Linear Limo is comfortable, and its under-seat steering provides the rider with an unhindered view of the road ahead. It remains the only bike of this type made in North America using box-section aluminum. An ergonomic delight, even over long distances and bumpy terrain, there will be no numb bums on a cross-country Linear Limo ride. **BS**

Linear's single-spar design means a comfortable ride. ▶

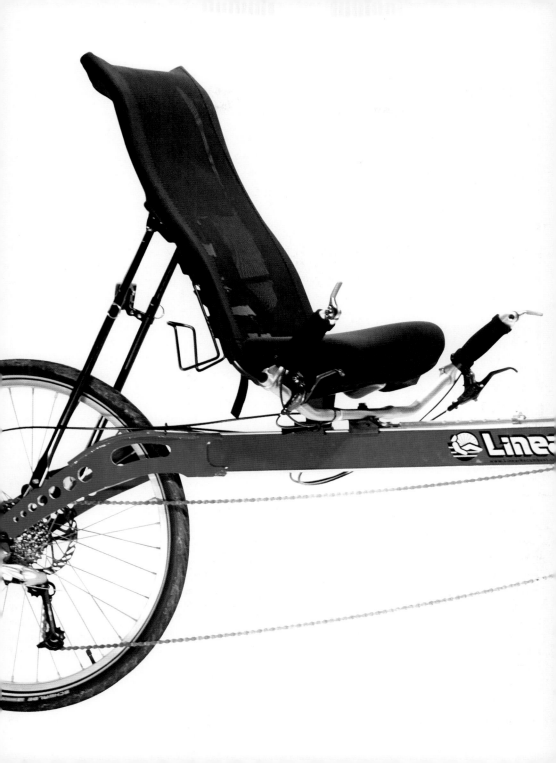

DAVE YATES Wayfarer

2006 • Touring bike • UK • Award-winning custom-built tourer

Starting as a builder for M Steel cycles in Newcastle-upon-Tyne, England, Dave Yates has been turning out acclaimed steel bike frames for more than thirty years. The former school metalwork teacher also runs frame-building courses and does repairs and resprays in a workshop on his farm in Lincolnshire. What he doesn't do is sell complete bikes.

Yates is a passionate long-distance cyclist, having completed many marathon rides, including Land's End to John O'Groats, London–Edinburgh–London, and Paris–Brest–Paris. His touring bikes incorporate features he has tried and tested himself.

His Wayfarer was judged Touring Bike of the Year by *Cycling Plus* magazine in 2006. Its neat fillet-brazed frame, made of Reynolds 525 steel tubes, comes in four sizes—18, 20, 22, and 24 in. (46, 51, 56, and 61 cm)—and a wide range of colors.

The Wayfarer is designed for 26-in. (66-cm) wheels with wide fork crowns. These smaller wheels are stronger, better able to carry heavy loads, and readily available worldwide if you're planning a long-distance adventure. The wider forks allow buyers to fit larger-section, more comfortably riding tires up to 2¹⁄₁₀ in. (5.3 cm) wide.

Frames are made to accommodate dropped handlebars and cantilever brakes, but can be adapted for straight bars and V-brakes. Serious touring riders will appreciate the brazed-on fittings that hold up to three sets of bottle cages, and front and rear panniers. The frames are sold without components, however, as Dave Yates recommends having the bike made up by a trusted cycle shop.

The secret of his success? Yates says: "loads of experience and that extra indefinable feel for frame building to create something really special." Either he doesn't know himself or he isn't telling. **SH**

CANNONDALE Synapse Carbon

2006 • Road race bike • USA • Comfortable yet fast full-carbon frame

Cannondale began in 1971 on the back of a bicycle cargo trailer known as the Bugger. It was another thirteen years before the first Cannondale bike appeared—a fat, alloy-tubed tourer. The next two decades saw such developments as the Headshok suspension system and the BB30 crankset standard, which brought the company great success.

In the late 1990s, however, Cannondale was undermined by a disastrous foray into motorbike production. Facing bankruptcy in 2003, the cycle division was saved by Canadian venture capital.

Following the success of the Six13 composite carbon-alloy frame launched a couple of years earlier,

> "We choose the hard way because we're convinced it's what's right for our customers."
>
> Chris Peck, R & D Cannondale

2006 saw the first appearance of Cannondale's most enduring road bike, the Synapse. This bike—the company's first with an all-carbon frame—borrowed flexible rear stay technology from the Scalpel full-suspension mountain bike in the shape of the Synapse Active Vibration Elimination (SAVE) micro-suspension system. The result was a strong and lightweight road bike that was comfortable on long journeys.

The Synapse ended Cannondale's proud tradition of U.S.-based manufacturing. The company's factory in Bedford, Pennsylvania, lacked the facilities to make the frame, so specialized facilities were used in Taiwan. Three years later, all Cannondale production was moved to the Far East, with the U.S. factory devoted only to final assembly and testing. **TB**

Cannondale's Synapse took its Silk Road concept to new speed and comfort levels. ▶

SCOTT Ransom

2006 • Enduro bike • Switzerland • Radical freeride machine

Peter Denk's radical freeride bike seemed to break all the rules. The mainframe was built from carbon, a material normally associated with cross-country race bike lightness. But the Ransom could not only take a beating; its low weight effectively created a totally new category of bike. A custom-designed, three-stage shock (fully open suspension, taut climbing, and lockout modes) needed careful setup to get the best out of it, but with 6½ in. (16.5 cm) of rear-wheel travel it was capable of keeping up with short-travel, cross-country bikes on climbs, and then totally outriding them on the rough downhills.

The Ransom frame weighed less than 7 lb (3.1 kg), including the Equalizer shock, which was the feature that really set it apart from its rivals. Built with two air

chambers and a separate chamber for damping oil, this was one of the first shocks you could adjust while riding via bar-mounted shifters. While the locked-out setting effectively turned it into a hardtail, the fully open mode offered the full available range of travel. The intermediate traction mode reduced the travel to 3½ in. (9 cm), stiffened the spring, and steepened the geometry for a more agile ride on climbs and cross-country tails. And that wasn't the end of it. There were in-between shock settings for heavier or lighter riders who wanted to tweak ride feel through air pressures and platform damping via controlled oil flow. In short, the Scott Ransom was a technical breakthrough that opened minds to both longer travel and the use of carbon in "normal" trail bikes. **SW**

TREK Session 10

2006 • Downhill–freeride bike • USA • Long-travel isolated chaindrive Session 10

The Session 10 was launched in 2006 at the mountain bike park in Whistler, British Columbia. Andrew Shandro, former downhill-racer-cum-freeride-visionary, played a crucial role in its development.

The "10" in the name refers to the 10 in. (25.4 cm) of rear-wheel travel. Built from Trek's own ZR 9000 aluminum, the monocoque front triangle looks like the hull of a battleship. The high rear pivot is great for suspension action, but not so good for the chain tension, a problem Trek solved by using a Chain Torque Eliminator, which routes the chain above the pivot point, isolating the pedaling action from the suspension action. The 10 in. (25.4 cm) of suspension comes through a purpose-built extra-long 3½-in. (9-cm) stroke Manitou Revox shock.

The long wheelbase gave a stable ride at speed, and, because most of the frame's weight was around the bottom bracket, the bike tracked very well too.

Shandro showcased the Session 10's remarkable ability to ride huge drops and jumps with style and precision in *The Collective*, the seminal freeride film, and in *Roam,* the award-winning follow-up. The success of these movies greatly boosted demand for the Session 10, which remained in production in unchanged form until 2008.

The evolutionary form of the Session 10, the Session 8, has, as its name suggests, 8 in. (20.3 cm) of travel. It is slimmer than the bike shown here in response to the growing popularity of lighter downhill race bikes. **CJ**

LYNSKEY Cooper CX

2006 • Touring bike • USA • The comeback bike of the legendary titanium frame-building family

The Lynskeys sold their titanium bike-building company, Litespeed, in 1999, but after several years pursuing solo projects, they decided to get back into the business in 2005.

In the interim they lost none of the expertise they had previously acquired from more than forty years of supplying titanium and other specialist metals to the aerospace and chemical industries, plus thirteen years of titanium bike construction.

The first official Lynskey Performance bike showed the makers' breadth of experience to maximum advantage. Delivered to Jim's Bicycle shop in Cincinnati, Ohio, on April 3, 2006, it was a custom touring machine that used the road-smoothing flexibility and strength of titanium to produce a properly silky ride.

It has always been Lynskey's practice to customize the geometry and frame fixtures of each of its bikes on the basis of discussions with the buyer, who in this case wanted to use it for exploring.

Lynskey also prides itself on its products' finish, with a range of options from simple bead-blasted to hand-polished laser engraving to sumptuous custom paint jobs produced by local artists.

In addition to its custom machines, Lynskey has become the go-to contractor for other brands that want titanium-tubed flagships for their own ranges. As a result, if you find yourself on a titanium bike that is ostensibly a Marin, a Cove, a Ragley, or a Planet X (or, indeed one of several other brands), you may well in fact be riding a Lynskey. **GK**

CANNONDALE Super Six

2006 • Road bike • USA • Launch of bike that would become legendary

Cannondale had been using hybrid carbon fiber construction in its high-performance Six13 frames for four years when the all-carbon Super Six took the performance of the company's flagship road racer to a whole new level.

This bike was made almost entirely from carbon; the only alloy components were the bottom bracket, the fork bearing inserts, and the patches that protected against scuff damage from rear axles or dropped chains behind the cranks.

The resulting frame was less than 2 lb 3 oz (1 kg), but Cannondale knew that, although it was important to weigh in below this psychological barrier, its efforts would be for nought if the finished bike wasn't propelled properly. Consequently, the main tubes were connected to a bottom bracket and chainstay segment that was molded in a single piece for maximum stiffness under pedaling pressure. The frame also used a massively outsized down tube to match the outsized BB30 bottom bracket standard previously pioneered by Cannondale and crank manufacturer FSA.

The top-of-the-line complete bike got Cannondale's ultra-light, ultra-stiff Hollowgram SL crank to maximize power delivery. Up front, a tapered fork kept handling obedient, with a stable rake making it sure-footed and confident through corners. Feedback from pro riders on prototype bikes inspired Cannondale to fit super-thin pencil stays at the rear to suck sting out of the road and create a remarkably comfortable yet outrageously responsive machine. **GK**

RIDGEBACK Cyclone
2006 • Hybrid bike • UK • Made for the town, but with mountain bike toughness

It isn't just the demands of professional racers that dictate bicycle design. Commuting cyclists are just as important as competitive riders when it comes to bike development. Often more so, because although you can build a race machine with no expense spared, if the bike you're making has to be affordable, then budget becomes a big concern. If it also has to be tough enough to cope with everything the daily commute can throw at it—potholes, curbs, bad weather, and crowded bike sheds—it becomes an even trickier proposition.

A delicate balancing act it may be, but Ridgeback pulled it off with the Cyclone. It is based on a mountain bike design, and aimed at people who wanted a bike they could ride to work during the week and take to the trails on the weekends.

A sturdy gusset-reinforced aluminum frame and chromoly steel fork—which was better suited than a suspension setup to the roads on which the bike would spend most of its time—made the Cyclone a durable, no-nonsense hybrid. An upright position made for a comfortable ride and provided better visibility for seeing traffic, while 26-in. (66-cm) wheels kept the Cyclone nimble enough to nip through it. Most important, it was firmly positioned at the inexpensive end of the price spectrum.

Practicality and price are all well and good, but if you can't have fun on a bike then it doesn't get ridden. The Cyclone will not simply get you to work; its versatile yet rewardingly responsive ride will put a smile on your face in the process. **RB**

CONFERENCE Circular

2006 • Multi-seat bike • USA • The ultimate social ride bike

The Conference Bike (or CoBie for short) is a seven-seater that is steered by one rider and pedaled by everyone on board thanks to an inventive circular jointed driveshaft. Each of the drive sections is joined to the others by a universal joint, and pedaling input is controlled by a crank and freewheeling gearbox under each human engine. The bike can be ridden solo, but the more is certainly the merrier, since it weighs 400 lb (181 kg) unladen, and is 8 ft. 2 in. (2.5 m) long and 5 ft. 11 in. (1.8 m) wide.

The twin rear wheels under the steerer and the two small car wheels at the outer edge of the front ring are designed for strength, not speed. Nevertheless, it's definitely an exhilarating ride, even at 10 mph (16 kph), because only the steerer is heading in the direction of the bike's movement. The steering wheel has a very sharp lock so that the bike can be swung around quickly, and you'll be glad the handlebar ring is fitted with wrist straps because the CoBie becomes a pedal-powered waltzer through turns.

The CoBie is a creation of American 3D artist and sculptor Eric Staller. It is manufactured by the Dutch Bicycle Company, whose client list includes the Jerusalem Science Museum, New York's Alfred University, Google, and Cirque du Soleil. Many Conference bikes are available for hire; they are used mainly by tourists. If you ever get the chance to try one, we certainly recommend it as an experience like no other—especially if you're facing backward when going into a sharp corner! **BS**

IBIS Mojo

2006 • Mountain bike • USA • Beautifully balanced lightweight

When the iconic Ibis brand returned to the scene after a short hiatus, founder Scot Nicol made sure that the relaunch was a stylish event.

In its first incarnation, Ibis had made a name for itself as a manufacturer of gorgeous, slim-tubed, steel and titanium bikes built in the United States, so the news that the company was being revived with Asian-built carbon fiber frames was not well received by die-hard fans. However, most doubters were delighted when they saw the beautiful Mojo. Still in production at the time of publication, it remains one of the best-looking full-suspension mountain bikes around, whichever version you choose.

A reinforced head tube swallowed the integrated headset, while the monocoque frame flowed back in an organic X-braced mainframe layout that's become the instant visual signature of the Mojo family. Further curved and flowing tubes formed the rear swingarm, while cutaway pockets on the frame took the short upper and lower linkages for the Dave Weagle-designed suspension. With 5⅜ in. (14 cm) of rear wheel travel, and matched fork capability up front, the Mojo could tackle most trails without blinking. The frame weight of less than 6 lb (2.75 kg) meant that it could be built into a light and efficient climber too.

Ibis had to fight to meet demand. The basic Mojo was later joined by the 12-oz (350-g) super-light SL frame, and the stiffer, longer-travel Mojo HD. In any form, the Mojo is the last word in "get on and go anywhere" trail bikes. **GK**

COMMENÇAL Meta 4X

2006 • Four-cross slopestyle bike • Andorra • Four-cross all-round favorite of progressive riders

The Meta 4X first appeared under the feet of Cédric Gracia, who was then racing for Commençal in both downhill and four-cross disciplines on the World Cup circuit. He also competed in the Red Bull Rampage, a big-mountain freeride competition, and various urban races around the world.

The Meta 4X was built with rocker-actuated suspension that neutralized pedal forces. As a result, the bike soon became a darling of single-track riders as well as stunt racers. With its fun, aggressive geometry, it could be pedaled all day, and transformed itself on descents into a mini downhill bike.

The Atherton Team—the brothers Dan and Gee, and sister Rachel—joined Commençal in 2007. In 2008, Dan took the Meta to the top of the podium in the World Cup 4X round in Vallnord, Andorra. The Meta continued to be one of the best-selling 4-in. (10-cm) travel hardcore all-rounder bikes, and stayed in its original design until 2013. Then, with help from Thibaut Ruffin of the Riding Addiction Team, Commençal redesigned the Meta, keeping the values of the original bike strongly in place. It was built around a new linkage that put the shock deep in the frame, thus keeping the center of mass low, and creating a playful and controlled ride. The Meta 4X is still a great bike for trail and all-mountain riders, enduro racers, Avalanche downhill competitors, and, of course, four-cross riders. Commençal's Young Guns team rider Brendan Howey even uses his 2013 Meta 4X to compete in slopestyle competitions—it's a true all-rounder. **CJ**

SINCLAIR A-Bike

2006 • Folding bike • UK • Small is good, but there is such as thing as too small

". . . if you have a bicycle which is seriously lighter and more compact . . . it will change the way in which people see bikes."

Clive Sinclair

When it comes to miniaturization, few people know how to get a lot out of a little better than British inventor and entrepreneur Clive Sinclair. In 1958, Sinclair conceived the world's smallest mass-market transistor radio; in 1966 he gave the world its first pocket-sized television. So when he decided to turn his attention to designing a folding bike for urban commuters, you just knew that, whatever else it might be, it would definitely be, well . . . small.

The A-Bike was designed by Alex Kalogroulis, and built by Daka International in Hong Kong. Its chain system is fully enclosed at the rear, and dynamically geared to allow riders to pedal in just the same way as they would a standard road bike, while the adjustable seat can accommodate anyone between 4 ft 9 in. (1.4 m) and 6 ft 3 in. (1.9 m) in height. It has single-gear transmission, optimized for short journeys, and rides on high-performance 90-psi (6.3 kg/sq-cm) tires. The wheels are 8 in. (20.3 cm) in diameter. However, the A-Bike's biggest selling points are its weight—only 13 lb 14 oz (6.3 kg)—and its size: it folds up to just 27 x 12 x 6¼ in. (67 x 30 x 16 cm), small enough to fit in a standard knapsack.

In London, England, the volume of motorized traffic on often narrow streets, and the congestion charge levied since 2003 on automobiles entering the downtown area during weekdays, make the attractions of a folding bike hard to resist. Unfortunately, the A-Bike's tiny wheels make it too wobbly, and its mount has been described by test rider Lance Foster as "definitely the most uncomfortable seat I have ever sat on." British *A to B* magazine went farther, judging the bike "a fabulous folder, but almost unridable."

Sinclair's creation is undoubtedly eye-catching, but it does not have what is required for long commutes, and is good for only short hops. **BS**

The A-Bike folded cleverly but tiny wheels limited its practicality. ▷

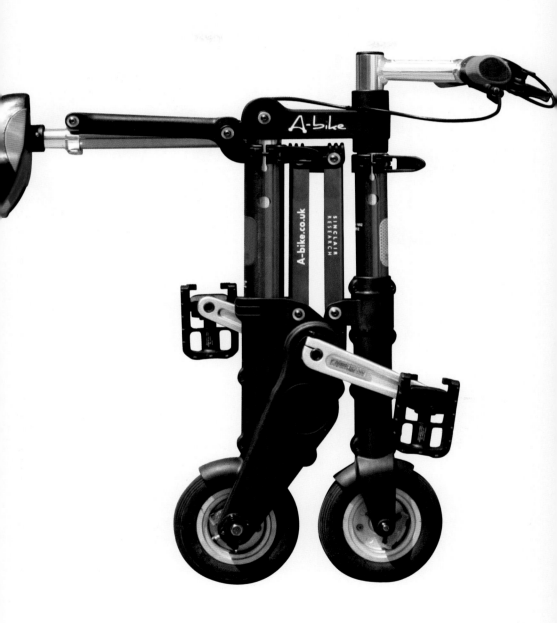

KONA Stinky 2-4

2006 • Kids' freeride bike • Canada • Child-size version of the famous Kona Stinky freeride bike

The original Kona Stinky freeride bike was first released in 1999, when riders had just begun to want bikes that could seriously push jump and drop limits. This radical riding caught the imagination of many junior riders, but it took until 2003 for the Vancouver/Ferndale Washington brand to release the Stinky Jr, a 24-in. (61-cm) wheeled version of the Stinky. This downsized bike still came with full-sized attitude, though, and the same walking-beam suspension, shrunk down to 4 in. (10 cm) of travel, and the same 7005 aluminum tubeset for maximum strength. In 2006, the Stinky Jr became the Stinky 2-4, and continued to mirror its older sibling in both paint jobs and componentry.

The Stinky 2-4 showed Kona's commitment to the next generation of mountain bikers. Before its arrival,

nine- to twelve-year-old kids didn't have a properly designed bike between the BMX-style 20-in. (50-cm) and the adult-sized 26-in. (66-cm) wheel.

It wasn't just a marketing exercise, either. Kona put the same time and energy into developing the Stinky 2-4 as it did into the Stinky itself, and both bikes had custom suspension. Consequently, a vast number of budding little rippers had bikes on which they could flourish, and many professional riders of today have the Stinky Jr and 2-4 to thank for their development.

This model is still in production, and venues such as the Whistler Bike Park in Vancouver, British Columbia, have their own little squadrons of mini shredders, most of them on Stinky 2-4s, competing to be among the new generation of freeride superstars. **CJ**

HOPE Glory 24

2007 • Kids' bike • UK • One-off custom-machined alloy and carbon fiber show bike

Based in Barnoldswick, Lancashire, England, Hope Technology was formed by two Rolls-Royce machinists who wanted more capable components for their own mountain bikes.

Hope started making pioneering cable brakes and then hydraulically operated disc brakes and special hubs to mount them on. As Hope's repertoire grew, so too did its factory, which came to feature ultra-high-tech cutting, shaping, and anodizing facilities. Although its meticulously sculpted but always mountain-tough kit is on the wish list of almost every rider, the company has only ever produced one single bike.

The Glory 24 started as a special project for a member of Hope's staff. Top trials rider and sales manager Woody Hole had a son who needed a new bike; rather than buy another manufacturer's product, it seemed only natural to knock one up in-house.

The bike was a masterpiece of machined sculpture. The whole rear section was mechanically carved from a single piece of alloy using computer-controlled 3D machines. It took more than seventy hours for the I-beam stays and multi-pocketed seat tube and bottom bracket assembly to be completed. Equally complex and time-consuming was the head tube at the far end of the two carbon fiber main tubes.

Hope finished the bike with its own top-of-the-range brakes, stem, seatpost, and bearing components, while a cut-down Pace carbon fiber suspension fork sat up front. SRAM gears drove the lightweight handmade wheels to complete this ultimate Christmas present. **GK**

GIANT

2007 • Freeride-trail bike • USA • Maestro
suspension freeride all-rounder

The 2007 Reign X was a beefed-up, aggressive, freeride-trail version of Giant's Reign trail bike.

Much of its strength comes from its creation on Giant's manufacturing equipment, which is some of the most sophisticated in the industry. Unlike many bike manufacturers who outsource, Giant has its own factories in Taiwan. This allows the company to shape every tube on the Reign X to the exact strength and stiffness required. It also cold-forges various elements of the frame, such as the shock cradle, a process that allows the bottom of the shock to protrude through the down tube. This keeps the center of mass as low and as close to the bottom bracket as possible, and allows the top tube to swoop low beneath the rider. A low center of gravity and a low standover height are essential aspects of freeride bikes because they increase stability and reduce the risk of injury. The Maestro suspension design used on the Reign X involves two short links that attach the rear triangle to the front triangle, isolating the pedaling forces while providing 6⁷⁄₁₀ in. (17 cm) of travel.

Canadian freeride superstar Kurt Sorge signed with Giant in 2007, and rode the Reign X in all its developing forms right through to 2013. **CJ**

KONA Stab Supreme

2007 • Downhill • USA • World and national
championship-winning downhill machine

The Kona Stab range started way back in the dawn of downhill bike development in 1998. The original bike in the series came with a triple-clamp front fork and 6 in. (15 cm) of rear suspension. In 1999, the Stab Dee-Lux came on the scene with a wild, wavy down tube, a 7-in. (17.8-cm) Marzocchi Monster T front fork, and the same length of rear travel. The Stab line continued to develop as Kona's downhill-specific bike line. Each top Stab model had a different second name: Stab Dee-Lux, Stab Primo.

In 2004 and 2005, Kona won two World Championships with Frenchman Fabien Barel. One of the most focused and dedicated racers of all time, Barel put a huge amount of time and effort into the development of the Stab Supreme. So too did his teammate, British rider Tracy Moseley, one of the most talented female downhill riders in the world and the winner of six British National Championships and the 2006 World Cup Downhill Series.

The result was awesome. The Stab Supreme was crafted from AL-7 aluminum, featured 8¼ in. (21 cm) of rear travel through Kona's walking-beam four-bar linkage, and a braking arm that allowed the suspension to remain active under braking. **CJ**

GT DHi

2007 • Downhill bike • USA • Race bike with
I-Drive suspension that eliminates pedal feedback

The GT DHi was one of the lightest off-the-peg
downhill bikes of its day, with the complete build
weighing in at 39 lb 9 oz (18 kg).

The bike featured GT's unique I-Drive suspension.
It was claimed that this system eliminated pedal
feedback by isolating the chain tension, thereby
countering the bottom bracket movement against
the suspension movement. It achieved this through
a link attaching the eccentrically mounted bottom
bracket to the main pivot, so that when the suspension
compresses, the bottom bracket moves backward,
reducing chain growth. The mainframe and the
swingarm were monocoque aluminum that created
a very stiff lightweight chassis. GT used a carbon fiber
seatmast that also housed the shock.

The rest of the build featured a 66-degree head
angle, 14-in. (35.6-cm) bottom bracket height, and a
Fox DHX 5.0 rear shock controlling the 8½ in. (21.6 cm)
of rear travel.

The DHi lasted for two years before evolving into
the GT Fury, a full-carbon monocoque race bike. It will
thus be remembered as the immediate predecessor of
the first full-carbon production downhill bike, and also
as one of the first really lightweight DH race bikes. **CJ**

LAPIERRE Zesty

2007 • Mountain bike • France • Rewrote the
rules of all-rounder trail bike fun

Developed alongside the longer-stroke suspension
Spicy, the Zesty combined high-control suspension,
riotous handling, and efficient pedaling.

While the angles, OST suspension, and cunningly
constructed alloy (subsequently carbon fiber) frames
were the main reasons for the Zesty's award-winning
performance, the details were excellent too.

While some brands demand that riders use rubber
rings and tape measures to set up their suspension,
Lapierre combined a bolt-on pointer on the mainframe
with a small graduated graphic on the swingarm to let
them pressurize the air-sprung shock-absorber without
getting out of the saddle. The alloy pointer is color-
matched to details like the protective caps on the pivots
and the grips and collars, so while the pricing has always
been competitive, the feel has always been premium.

Because Lapierre knows this bike is such fun to ride
flat out that it's bound to push its riders to the limit, the
company added a unique carbon fiber gear-protecting
fin, and custom chain cushions to the rear of the bike.
They were also one of the first companies to introduce
internal brake and gear cable routing on the mainframe
to keep lines safe if a crash sends the bike cartwheeling
riderless down the trail. **GK**

LAPIERRE Spicy

2007 • Mountain bike • France • Benchmark-setting all-mountain enduro bike

When you've got a ten-time downhill World Champion developing your bike, chances are it's going to be pretty good at going downhill. What made the Spicy a benchmark for so long, though, is that it's just as much fun to pedal back up or punch out the miles on while looking for the ultimate descent. French downhill legend Nicolas Vouilloz had previously worked on race bikes for V-Process and Sunn, and, when he teamed up with Lapierre, his input was crucial to the development of the new Spicy.

For this bike, the French designers dropped their Full Power Suspension (FPS2) system for all-new Optimized Suspension Technology (OST). Big, hydraulically-shaped alloy tubes that flared rather than tapered to the tips of the swingarm formed a long, low, frame with relaxed

angles. Thus the Spicy had more in common with contemporary downhill bikes than with trail bikes.

Reviewers raved about the bike's control and composure on the fastest and most technical trails, and Vouilloz proved the Spicy's quality by riding it to victory in the Alpe d'Huez Mega Avalanche Endurance downhill race.

The OST and the relatively light weight meant that the Spicy still pedaled well without gravity on its side, making it perfect for aggressive trail riders. As the design has developed through subtle shape and suspension changes, together with carbon chassis options on the most expensive models, the Spicy has managed to retain top ranking in most polls throughout its existence. **GK**

NORCO Shore One

2007 • Freeride bike • Canada • Beast bred to tackle Vancouver's infamous North Shore trails

Norco is based in Vancouver, British Columbia, one of the most revered mountain biking meccas on the planet. The North Shore Mountains that rise above the city skyline hold trails that have become renowned all over the world. The steep technical root sections below old-growth cedars have graced the pages of magazines for decades. The Norco Shore One was created here in 2006.

This bike was designed to tackle head-on the North Shore's most testing terrain, including the rock-riddled fast straights, the root-laced corners, and the infamous ladder bridges and big drops. It was built from hydro-formed aluminum, and used a licensed version of Specialized's Horst Link, four-bar FSR suspension design to give the bike 6^{7}⁄$_{10}$ to 7^{2}⁄$_{5}$ in. (17–18.9 cm) of rear

travel. The steep, 66-degree head angle gave the bike a nimbleness in the tighter sections of Vancouver's trails. Coming with a giant 7-in. (17.8-cm) travel RockShox Totem front fork meant riders could really hit almost anything they wanted without worry. An overall weight of 45 lb (20.4 kg) meant it wasn't a natural climber, but there were still plenty of people who used to pedal the long climb out of Vancouver to the mountain-top trailheads on their Shore Ones, grimacing as the trail wound up above them, but knowing the taste of the sweet descent would make it worth the effort. In particular Jay Hoots, one of Norco's longest-serving athletes, was a large part of the Shore's continual development over the next four years until the bike was discontinued in 2011. **CJ**

PLANET X Stealth Pro
2007 • Time trial bike • UK • Multiple award-winning time trial and triathlon machine

Some bike manufacturers have built their reputations on cost-no-object innovation, professional team sponsorship, and aspirational rather than affordable pricing. Other brands have developed an equally loyal and devoted following by keeping a keen eye on cost to build a range of excellent bargain machines. Planet X and its mountain bike sibling, On One, have forged a fanatical following the world over with low-cost, high-performance bikes like the Stealth Pro.

Some companies spend hundreds of hours in wind tunnels and thousands more computer-modeling airflow before investing in complex carbon molds that are replaced by faster models only a couple of years later. Unlike them, Planet X asked their national championship winning triathletes and time trialists

Spencer Smith and Ian Cammish to outline their perfect practical speed bike. Their specifications were then combined with wind-cheating aerodynamic profiles in a cost-effective carbon fiber layup to create complete bikes that cost less than many comparable frame-only options from other brands.

As well as recording countless race wins and championship victories, the Stealth Pro won Bike of the Year in reader awards of 2007, 2009, and 2010, while testers at *Triathlon Plus* magazine commented, "Naturally fast and efficient yet very easy to ride . . . if it's high-value velocity you're after, the Stealth takes some beating." In view of its global popularity, it is little surprise that the evergreen Stealth Pro is still a stalwart of the Planet X lineup. **GK**

LITESPEED Archon

2007 • Road bike • USA • Sculpted aero speed machine

The Tennessee city of Chattanooga might be best known to the general public for its choo-choo train, but in cycling circles it's renowned for titanium bikes from Litespeed and Lynskey.

Lynskey actually sold their interest in what had been their family company in 1999, but the new owners, American Bicycle Group, continued to develop titanium frame design to increasingly extreme limits.

Litespeed had already created an ultra-light climbing bike in the shape of the 1 lb 11-oz (0.7-kg) framed Ghisallo, but that chassis was too flexible for heavy or aggressive riders. With that in mind, Litespeed concentrated on maximizing stiffness in the Archon chassis to build a properly aggressive race bike worthy of the most powerful riders. This required the use of 6AL/4V titanium alloy, which is so much harder to work with than the usual 3AL/2.5V alloy that even most top-level titanium frame builders use it only for small laser-cut fixtures, such as wheel-holding drop-outs. Litespeed, however, developed techniques to work this most stubborn material into complex shapes. On the Archon, these included a flared hexagonal top tube and an outsized down tube. An innovative "wrap" design meant both tubes were extended forward around the head tube to increase weld area and torsional strength.

This rigid and precise-steering machine was later upgraded with a tapered fork and outsized crank to push its performance higher still. The latest Archon model (pictured) is the first Litespeed bike to be made from carbon fiber rather than titanium. **GK**

KIRK PACENTI 650B

2007 • Mountain bike • USA • Inbetweener wheel innovator

U.S. bicycle designer and frame maker Kirk Pacenti worked his industry apprenticeship building frames for icons such as Keith Bontrager, Litespeed, and Merlin. He then set up a frame-parts company called Bike Lugs and became a champion for 650B wheels, a rim and tire size that sits in between the 26-in. (66-cm) and 29-in. (73.5-cm) mountain-bike wheel sizes.

While the 650B has been around for a long time and was used in Europe on touring bikes well before mountain bike history started, it took a while for the size to strike a chord among mountain bike manufacturers and riders. Those who showed interest usually felt that neither 26-in. (66-cm) nor 29-in. (73.5-cm) wheels were ideal. In short, bigger-diameter wheels and tires roll more smoothly over rugged terrain than smaller ones, but do not always allow frame and fork manufacturers to achieve exactly what they want in terms of building in particular geometric or suspension characteristics. A smaller wheel is slightly lighter and slightly stronger, and produces slightly livelier handling. The 650B size offers a good compromise between the 26-in. (66-cm) and 29-in. (73.5-cm) options, and looks set to become popular enough to make 26-in. (66-cm) mountain bike wheels obsolete within a few years.

Frames carrying the Pacenti badge are not very common, but a good number of enthusiasts bought his classy steel-tubed 650B frames in order to fit his 650B tires. He was, via Panaracer, one of the first makers to produce a seriously useful 650B mountain bike tire, the 2.3-in. (5.8-cm) Neo-Moto. Since then, other tire, fork, and frame manufacturers have jumped aboard the 650B bandwagon, and Pacenti himself now makes rims in all sizes. He continues to innovate in other areas too, but to industry commentators he will always be known as the champion of 650B wheels. **SW**

"As much as I love 29-in. wheels, I appreciate the fast acceleration of a smaller rear wheel. I own a Pacenti frame fitted with a 29-in. front wheel and a 650B rear."

Steve Worland, bike journalist

◁ Kirk Pacenti created the spark that ignited the 650B explosion.

BOARDMAN Team Carbon

2007 • Road bike • UK • Legendary first value bike from racer turned designer

Famous racers have been cashing in on their names with signature ranges of bikes for decades. But levels of actual rider involvement have varied dramatically, from virtually nil personal input to actually building them by hand themselves.

Consequently, when UK Olympic gold medalist, Tour de France stage winner, and world record holder Chris Boardman linked his name to a new premium brand from UK car and cycle superstore Halfords, many were wary. But as it turned out, Boardman and his small team have secured Olympic gold medals, World Championship wins, and major successes in terms of favorable reviews and runaway sales.

Rather than go for the ego boost of putting his name on the most exotic bikes directly, the straight-talking champion made his name through delivering brilliant bikes at affordable prices. The Team Carbon was one of the first Boardman bikes to really set the Halfords tills on fire and rock the established brand hierachy. The bike's lightweight and smooth-riding carbon frame and fork featured the same sure-footed geometry that was developed for, and used by, multiple World and National Champion Nicole Cooke, MBE. It was then equipped with a carefully chosen range of parts that would be the envy of most bikes costing several hundred dollars more. Even so, the bike still met the price threshold of the UK government's "ride to work" assisted bike-buying scheme for commuters. It instantly became an absolute top-seller and a perfect launch for the Boardman brand. **GK**

TREK Project One

2007 • Road bike • USA • Custom paint job on ultra-light carbon bike

The slogan was simple: "Don't settle for anyone else's bike. Create your very own." Trek's idea was that a full custom paint job would be an added sales incentive to high-end buyers considering one of their carbon frame bikes. Customers visiting the Project One website could choose the fit, wheels, components, and styling, and Trek would build each "dream bike" at its specialist workshop in Waterloo, Wisconsin.

The Project One idea has been a great success and has grown to include a choice of thirteen road and mountain models. Thousands of colors are offered, along with a wide range of preselected designs, including famous team colors and a range of Trek's own colors and logos. Customers paying a bit more can bring their own weird and wonderful designs to life.

Clicking on a design option on the Trek website allows potential customers to see the entire bike of their choice in their own choice of livery. They can also try their chosen frame in the whole range of styles before choosing. If they want a custom signature on the bike, they can simply type in the words they want.

Buyers sitting at their home computers can change the details of every aspect of their bike. They can try different bar-tape colors, stems, wheels, and tires. Buying a bike in this way is not cheap, but the pricing differentials between all the options are clearly shown. At the end of the selection process, the customers simply order their bike with a click of the mouse. The only thing they have not done, of course, is take the bike on a test ride. **SH**

GARY FISHER Rig

2007 • Mountain bike • USA • Simple "second" bike that became a cult classic

Mountain bike pioneer Gary Fisher has always maintained a reputation for left-field thinking when it comes to his bikes and his personal sense of style.

The charismatic Fisher, who set up the first Gary Fisher mountain bike shop in California in the late 1970s, kept up a relentless pace of innovation with his eponymous brand throughout the next decade. When he sold his brand to Trek in the 1990s, he continued to progress its innovations under Trek's wing. Important was his adoption of bigger 29-in. (73.5-cm) wheels. Flagship lightweight race bikes fitted with 29-in. wheels were used by the sponsored athletes of their professional cross-country team, but the simplest bike in the range had the biggest influence in getting the new wheel size accepted.

The Gary Fisher Rig was a single-speed bike with a good-quality aluminum alloy frame and a simple but effective suspension fork. At around $1,000 (£700), the complete bike was relatively affordable. The lack of gears reduced maintenance and made the bike a popular "second" or "winter" choice, particularly among riders wanting to protect more expensive machines from wet and gritty conditions. What surprised some was that the big smooth-rolling wheels and lightweight frame, combined with the attacking stand-up-and-stomp style necessary to get a single-speed up steep hills, made the Rig a remarkably fast ride. The rigid rear end and single-gear ratio also forced riders to think more about what and how they were riding, which increased their engagement with the trail. **GK**

SCOTT Nitrous

2007 • Freeride bike • Switzerland • Slopestyle version of the Scott High Octane DH bike

The Scott Nitrous was first developed in 2004, following the success of the company's High Octane downhill bike. The Nitrous was a reduced-size version, built for freeride and slopestyle applications, and shared the same basic layout and esthetics as the High Octane. The frame and tubeset were the same, and the Nitrous also had the High Octane's unique-looking seat tube configuration. Both frames were of a low, single-pivot suspension design. The first Nitrous had 6 to 6½ in. (15–16.5 cm) of rear travel; this was bumped up to 7½ in. (19 cm) of travel in 2007.

European slopestyle genius Timo Pritzel has ridden for Scott since 2002, and in that time he has used the Nitrous in such films as *New World Disorder 2* and *Kranked 7*. He also came second in the 2004 Crankworx Whistler Slopestyle. In 2008, he broke the World Record High Jump, won Big Mountain Style in Châtel, France, and was named Mountain Biker of the Year at the Action Sports Awards. In 2009, Scott worked with the Coastal Crew—a group of four freeriders from Canada's Sunshine Coast—and Radical Films to produce their seminal film segment in *Kranked 8*. Here, the four riders ride together in an almost choreographed display over jumps and down trails before splitting off into pairs and then rejoining at the end for a crescendo of a finale. Two of the riders, Kyle Jameson and Kyle Norbraten, are riding the Scott Nitrous. The model was discontinued after Scott worked for two years with team athletes Timo Pritzel and Lance McDermott to develop the Voltage FR, their new-generation freeride bike. **CJ**

TRANSITION BottleRocket

2007 • Slopestyle bike • USA • Short-travel do-it-all stunt bike

The BottleRocket is the most famous bike made by Transition Bikes, a company owned and run by riders in Washington State. From its inception as a prototype in 2006 to its termination in 2012, it was a steadfast feature of many local bike parks, trail centers, dirt jump spots, and downhill tracks. Designers Kevin Menard and Kyle Young—both strong riders in their own right—clearly brought a lot of what they wanted into the bike.

In 2007, the trend in bike parks, trail centers, and freeride mountain biking in general was toward jumpy, feature-filled trails that rode like a mini slopestyle course the whole way down the mountain. Trails resembling the Whistler Mountain Bike Park's famous A-Line, in Vancouver, British Columbia, started to pop up all over the world. Everyone wanted an A-line, a trail with more than forty sculpted jumps, berms, and drops. This led to a new breed of bikes capable of being pedaled up to the top of these trails but primarily focused on being as much fun as possible on the way down.

The BottleRocket epitomized this trend. The link-actuated single pivot gave the bike 5½ in. (14 cm) of rear travel and the alloy frame was built to take big landings and bigger crashes in its stride. It is a mark of its success that the BottleRocket never really changed in its six-year history, apart from a slight weight reduction in the frame when excess metal was removed. As suspension has developed, though, bikes with longer travel can now pedal better than the BottleRocket, and it has been superseded in the Transition lineup by the new Double frame. **CJ**

PACE 405

2007 • Mountain bike • UK • Offshore-built bike from famous British brand

Making its debut in the late 1980s with the innovative RC100, Pace Cycles produced distinctive frames from extruded square-section alloy tubes until rising production costs forced the company to concentrate on its suspension fork and clothing lines. However, the founder, Adrian Carter, could not leave frame designing alone, with the result that Pace unveiled its first full-suspension frame in 2007.

The surprise—and undeniable disappointment for some—was that the frame of the 405 was built in Asia before being finished and receiving its shocks and fixtures at Pace's headquarters near York, England. There was no sign of the trademark square tubing either; the externally butted design had been replaced by hydroformed flared and curved alloy tubes.

But the 405 was very practical, with plenty of tire room for muddy conditions, and built-in fender mounts on the down tube. It also featured a fully floating-style mount for the custom-tuned DT Swiss rear shock.

While purists grumbled, those who actually rode the bike were impressed by its impeccable balance and confidence. The beauty of it, as *Bike Radar* noted, was its "lead from the front" style, which enabled it to deal superbly with speed. Also in its favor was a bargain retail price.

An instant classic, the 405 went on to spawn shorter- and longer-travel versions. A couple of years later, DT Swiss, which had formed a relationship with the makers of this bike while it was still in development, bought the Pace's fork business and designs. **GK**

GIANT Anthem X

2008 • Mountain bike • Taiwan • Benchmark-setting short-suspension mountain bike

Rapid innovation of technology and handling needs generally means there is a high turnover of top-ranked mountain bikes. Occasionally, however, a bike takes the top spot and resolutely refuses to give ground to any competitors. Giant's Anthem family is the epitomy of this rare breed, having dominated the cost-effective race and fast-trail mountain bike category for almost a decade.

The original Giant Anthem was an unashamedly aggressive race machine. Its super-light frame made the most of Giant's massive aluminum building experience and was produced by hand-picked welders. A short-stroke version of Giant's proprietary Maestro suspension had a Manitou SPV shock to remove unwanted pedal movement from the system. The result was a blisteringly quick race weapon.

The Anthem legend grew with the introduction of the X frame. Travel was slightly increased, and the Giant aluminum alchemists increased frame stiffness while decreasing weight—it was lighter than many carbon fiber frames. Fox shock-absorbers were introduced for smoother, more controlled suspension. The bike immediately proved far more trail-capable than the vast majority of 4-in. (10-cm) travel "race" bikes on the market.

The Anthem X was joined in 2010 by the X 29, which increased traction and control for better speed sustain on rough terrain. The X 29 continued the Anthem's perfect review score record. Carbon and mid-sized-wheel (650B) versions have also joined the lineup, but many recognize the alloy Anthem as one of the best mountain bikes ever made. **GK**

ISLABIKES Beinn

2008 • Kids' bike • UK • The core bike of an outstanding children's range

As its reputation for outstandingly well-designed kids' bikes has grown, Islabikes has expanded significantly. The original Beinn mountain bike has always been the company's centerpiece on account of its rugged versatility and ability to take its riders as far as their imagination lets them.

Starting with a 20-in. (50-cm) wheeled bike, the range now extends through two 24-in. (61-cm) models to a full-sized, 26-in. (66-cm) mountain bike, and a 29-in. (73.5-cm) wheeled bike for adults.

All Beinn bikes steer clear of heavy, overly complicated items such as lookalike suspension forks that don't work with a child's weight, and confusing, awkward-to-use multiple chainrings. Instead, they use finely crafted rigid forks and aluminum alloy frames with custom-made single chainring cranks. This keeps them light, agile, and fun to ride on long adventures, rather than restricting weight and enjoyment with sheer dead weight. The bikes can also be ordered with mountain bike tires, road tires, mudguards, or cargo racks, making them truly versatile all-rounders.

As with all Islabikes, many of the components are custom made to ensure the best possible fit for junior riders. Just speaking to Isla about the brake levers of the latest Beinn reveals how much detail they go into: "We've designed our own super-slim grips because diameter is such an important factor in getting the child's hand as close to the brake lever as possible. We also have our own brake levers that are much smaller than anything else available." **GK**

AUGSPURGER One-Off

2008 • Mountain handbike • USA • The handbike is given teeth, attitude, and an appetite for hills

Hand-powered cycles are as varied as the disabilities of those who ride them. There are fork-steer models, lean steers, and various handcycle–recumbent hybrids. And then there are "off-road" handcycles like Mike Augspurger's One-Off. This trike, with two wheels up front and one behind, plus a low gear ratio, is the handcycle's answer to the mountain bike.

Most handcycles have crank handles for steering that are mounted on bearings: these tend to swivel and sap confidence. The One-Off has separate left- and right-handed handlebars mounted onto their respective kingpins. This results in minimal bar movement, even over rocky terrain, and the linkages are designed to gain stability as the bike gains speed. High-speed descending is positively encouraged by powerful disc brakes on the two front wheels.

The One-Off's prone rider position allows riders to lift themselves off the sternum support and take their weight onto their arms to power the crank, which is designed with opposed cranks, as on a standard bike. Just with their hands on the crank handles, riders can hold their weight over the sternum support with the handles in the horizontal; their arms are free to work in opposition and thus provide continuous power. **BS**

COTIC Soul

2008 • Mountain bike • UK • Lightweight steel-frame trail mountain bike

Because of its place in history as the original material for bikes, steel has generally been used for more traditional models. All that changed when Cotic founder Cy Turner introduced the Soul, a radical take on technical riding frames. He used Reynolds 853 tubing, made from the first steel alloy that actually increased in strength rather than weakening where welding heat was applied. Thinner tubing walls could be used to create a light but strong frame able to compete with alloy and titanium.

Reynolds produced tubes of a larger diameter than normal to add mechanical stiffness to the 853 frames without sacrificing all the resilient, springy ride feel normally associated with steel frames. To accentuate the flexibility, Turner used particularly slim rear stays in a wide-stance, curved-top layout. This also created ample room for large, knobbly tires.

Cotic designed the handling of the Soul around longer-stroke 5-in. (12.7-cm) suspension forks. With an increased amount of movement in the fork, the shock-absorbing internals soaked up impacts more slowly and smoothly than a shorter-travel unit would. Add the resilient steel frame ride and the potential to use bigger-volume tires without clearance issues, and the Soul rapidly established itself as an infectiously fun ride. **GK**

Cotic's UK-designed Soul uses British Reynolds tubing and Hope finishing kit. ▷

CANNONDALE Slice

2008 • Triathlon bike • USA • Multiple Ironman-winning carbon bike

Riding a bike for 112 miles (180 km) is hard enough. Doing that between a 2½-mile (4-km) swim and a 26-mile (42-km) run is extremely tough, both physically and mentally. Yet many bikes that had purportedly been designed for triathlon seemed to sacrifice easy, relaxed, and restful handling for qualities such as top aerodynamics and power delivery, which are important in some events but not necessarily in this one.

Indeed, a significant body of recent research suggests that these priorities are actually wrong, because riders suffer fatigue much sooner if they have to fight the steering. The more they have to lift in and out of the optimum aerodynamic tuck of lying on the aero bars, the greater the drag that is created, and the greater the effort that is required. The use of increasingly deep aero wheels, which are liable to catch crosswinds, further exacerbates handling problems.

In 2008, in its brand-new, totally carbon fiber Slice, U.S. manufacturer Cannondale made safe, friendly handling an absolute priority. The effect was not easy to achieve: triathletes like to have their saddles a long way forward to make it easier for them to start running straight off the bike, but that can upset the balance of the machine.

Cannondale responded by fitting a very stable handling fork that kept the Slice as steady as a rock, even in windy conditions. A super-narrow frame allowed the Slice to slice through the air, and the carbon fiber construction absorbed tiring vibrations from the road.

The Slice formula certainly worked: the bike became the machine of choice for multiple race-winning, record-setting, British-born, U.S.-resident Ironman legend Chrissie Wellington until her retirement from triathlon in 2012. **GK**

SPIN Günter Mai Special

2008 • Road bike • Germany • World's lightest road bike

Weighing only 6 lb 4 oz (2.85 kg), the Spin was claimed to be the world's lightest road bike.

Günter Mai built this custom machine in 2008, and promptly proved it was a perfect working bike by riding about 15,000 mi (24,000 km) on it over the next two years. The weight was gradually reduced, as Mai found new bits to replace or carve down in size. The featherlight bike was built on a one-off extreme carbon frame produced by Spin, weighing only 1 lb 6 oz (642.5 g). To this was added a one-off carbon fork weighing just 6½ oz (185.9 g), specially made by THM.

The wheels, from AX Lightness, used a type of carbon normally found only in Formula 1 cars. The

"Here's a machine that will make even the most dedicated weight weenies drool."

Bikeradar.com

ultra-light hubs came from Dash Cycles, and the total wheelset weight was just 1 lb 4½ oz (583 g). The German-made brake calipers were carbon too.

The cassette was drilled out to the minimum needed to retain its structure. Mai even machined a few millimeters from the axle end caps. Handlebar tape was stretched thin and used most sparingly.

He saved a few more grams by opting for old-fashioned but lightweight BTP frame shifters mounted on the downtube for the six-speed gears. Even the tiniest bolts and spacers were replaced with specially made titanium or carbon versions.

After proving that his machine worked, Mai stunned the cycling community in 2010 by dismantling it, and selling the parts off individually. **SH**

◁ Chrissie Wellington used the Slice to record-breaking effect.

KONA Bass

2008 • Slopestyle bike • USA • Bike on which
Paul Bass landed first double backflip in natural terrain

The Kona Bass was conceived in 2008 for Kona Clump
Team member Paul Basagoitia, or "Paul Bass" as he is
affectionately known. In 2004, Bass borrowed a bike and
won the biggest slopestyle competition in the world,
Crankworx Whistler. Kona signed him, and the following
year he won again.

The Kona Bass succeeded the Cowen DS, Kona
team rider John Cowen's signature bike. It featured 4 in.
(10 cm) of rear travel through Kona's walking-link four-
bar design. An eccentric bottom bracket and sliding
drop-outs allowed the bike to be set up as single-speed
or geared. Made of Kona Clump 7005 Aluminum, the
robust frame featured tabs on the head tube for riders
wanting to attach a gyroscope for multiple bar spins.
The Bass is everything a slopestyle bike should be, and
Paul Bass has used it to become the most decorated
slopestyle rider of all time.

After winning two Crankworx slopestyles in a row,
he continued his winning streak in 2009 and 2010,
taking top spot at Teva Mountain Games in both years.
In 2011, the Kona Bass was reworked with shorter
chainstays and a zero stack tapered head tube to keep
the front end low. The Bass has gone on to become the
most dominant slopestyle bike in the world. **CJ**

KONA/FSA Major Jake

2008 • Cyclocross bike • USA • Upgraded
version of a classic cyclocross all-rounder

In 2008, U.S. rider Ryan Trebon achieved National
Championship success with the Major Jake, a conversion
of Kona's Jake the Snake cyclocross bike. This had been
an evergreen all-rounder in the Kona lineup for years,
serving as an affordable race bike as well as a super-
tough road and city bike.

Trebon, at 6 ft 5 in. (1.96 m) tall, required a 25-in.
(63.5-cm) frame, which had to be specially created
because the production range topped out at 24 in.
(61 cm). It featured the same Race Light butted
scandium tubing profiles as the production bikes, and
a neat machined section at the fat end of the driveside
chainstay to give maximum chainring clearance,
minimizing chain jam in muddy conditions. Socketed
rear drop-outs provided secure rear-wheel connection,
and a neat hooped stay bridge anchored the rear brake.
The bulk of the bike made the tubes look skinny, but
this was a meaty frame. The Alpha Q CX20 carbon fork
allowed adept steering through cyclocross courses.

Production Major Jakes had a relatively affordable
spec based on a Shimano 105 groupset and Mavic
Ksyrium Equipe wheelsets, but team cosponsors FSA
(Full Speed Ahead) sent Trebon into action with its full
carbon wheels and light cockpit equipment. **GK**

CHROMAG Samurai

2008 • All-mountain bike • Canada • Steel hardtail that can tackle the burliest downhill trails

Chromag is a small company that specializes in hardtail frames and components. The aim of founder Ian Ritz was to create a bike without the complications of a suspension design that could be ridden on any trail by anyone. The Samurai was the result.

The bike's frame, built from True Temper chromoly and 4130 steel, is of fighter jet-level strength. The geometry has been honed over the years by Chromag's professional riders. The 68-degree head angle, 12½-in. (31.75-cm) bottom bracket height, and 16½-in. (41.9-cm) chainstays mark it as a bike for epic rides. One such event was the now discontinued Mount Seven Psychosis 4,000-ft (1,200-m) downhill race, for which the course record in the hardtail category is now held in perpetuity by Kevin Phelps on a Samurai.

The bike has not changed much since its introduction—there have been a few subtle tweaks here and there over the years—but the great thing about a hardtail is that there is only so much the maker can do; the rest is down to the pilot. The Samurai is available only in limited production runs, so there has always been a waiting list, and the time-lag between order and delivery has increased since the bikes became available worldwide. **CJ**

DEVINCI Wilson

2008 • Mountain bike • Canada • Globally popular downhill race bike

Although most mass-market bikes are now made in Asia, particularly Taiwan and China, not every North American and European manufacturer has abandoned domestic production. Among the companies that still proudly fly their own national flags is Devinci of Canada.

The company began in 1987 as Da Vinci (named after legendary inventor Leonardo), with two engineering students at the helm. They were joined in 1990 by entrepreneur and road bike enthusiast Felix Gauthier, who altered the name slightly and helped the company expand its production. Times were tight, and they built their own heat-treating oven to enable their move into aluminum frames, but the hard work paid off and they became successful throughout Canada with a wide range of road and mountain bikes.

The bike that launched Devinci into the big time was this Wilson downhill race rig. The success of Canadian racers such as Stevie Smith on the World Cup circuit helped the rock-solid, well-balanced, and affordable machine to become a hit, and Devinci is now a globally recognized brand.

All Devinci's manufacturing—from raw materials to final complete bikes—is still done under one roof in Chicoutimi, Quebec. **GK**

TOMMASINI Carbolight XLR
2008 • Road race bike • Italy • Carbon and alloy racer

RIDLEY Dean
2008 • Triathlon bike • Belgium • Time trial bike with unique split fork

Tucked away in the historic town of Grosseto in Tuscany, Italy, Tommasini is a small frame-building business with a big reputation. Irio Tommasini was a successful bike racer who, while still an amateur, began to make frames at a bike factory in Milan in 1948. By 1957 he had gained enough experience to launch his own family bike-making operation. Soon his handmade bikes were winning fans and winning races. Top riders started using them and they started to be exported. Today the frames maintain their reputation as being among the world's finest. Tommasini's two daughters mostly run his company now, while he still plays a hands-on role in the workshop.

The Tommasini Carbolight XLR frame was built with XLR8R tubing, a specialist form of high-grade aluminum manufactured by classic tubing suppliers Columbus of Milan. Columbus said that its top-of-the-range tubing was guaranteed "to not disperse the cyclist's exertions in excessive deformations." That presumably means it is very tough, torque-resistant stuff. And the frame itself was a premium piece of engineering. Tommasini personalized the top tube with a distinctive bell-shaped section. Aluminum lugs featuring a "T" logo were machined in their workshop and used to reinforce the gently heated tubing joints. Anything fitted to this exclusive frame had to match its top quality. The fork, for example, also from Columbus, is the Super Muscle carbon integrated monocoque unit with nickel braiding. The seat tube is premium carbon too.

The Carbolight's design was upgraded in 2008 with a subtly flexible T-Flight carbon rear triangle, another exclusive Tommasini creation. At the same time, the frame builder designed and made his own replaceable aluminum rear drop-outs for the bike. **SH**

Just as the wind sculpts sand dunes and exposed trees and rock outcrops, it can also create beautiful shapes when bike designers take its effects into account. But as much as sculptor Henry Moore might have approved of the way the almost melted-looking main tubes of the Ridley Dean drape themselves over the rear wheel and sprout up to form the seatmast, the bike is not designed for the art gallery. No, this frame is designed to give its rider the biggest aerodynamic advantage possible, and it goes about this in a number of very interesting ways.

Every part of the frame is aerodynamically profiled, starting with the almost beak-shaped head tube,

> *"Results from tests show it saves 15 watts of energy when it is ridden at 45 kph [28 mph]."*
> Sydney Morning Herald

which extends forward and down over the front of the fork for a super-smooth join. The F Split fork and stays operate in the same way as split flaps on an airliner, channeling airflow away from the turbulence caused by the spinning wheels (Ridley claims a reduction in drag at racing speeds of up to 10 percent). Sections of deliberately roughened "R-Surface" paint are designed to cause suction at the surface of the frame and prevent the airflow from pulling away from the carefully shaped tubes. The brakes are hidden out of the way behind the fork and cranks. It is an exercise in speed sculpture that has proved as effective as it is eye-catching, winning numerous time trial and triathlon events and playing a big part in the 2008 Tour de France second place of rider Cadel Evans. **GK**

Ridley's Dean is a truly radical race bike. ▶

CHALLENGE Concept XT

2008 • Recumbent trike • Netherlands •
Aerodynamic looks and tanklike toughness

The application of streamlining to a recumbent trike is no easy task. The response of the designers at Challenge was to make the crossbeams of their new Concept XT slope upward from the wheels toward the frame, rather like the wings of a fighter plane, and create a cruciform shape that swept radically forward.

The Concept XT was an impressive entry into the world of recumbent trikes, and it showed beyond doubt that Challenge was a company committed to the creation of a new benchmark design, rather than one that was simply attempting to capitalize on an emerging market trend.

The trike had a stiff frame, light steering, a seat that was both firm and comfortable, and high-performance components that were mainly Shimano and also included Avid BB-7 disc brakes and an FSA Gossamer triple crankset. Short cabling to the discs made braking precise and responsive, and a lot of very cool engineering went into the method of disassembly—an Allen wrench was all that was needed to remove the front wheels and the brake caliper and plate, which were also designed to come off easily. Steering came in both direct and indirect setups.

The leg length was adjustable via a sliding aluminum boom (the trike was available in just one frame size), and the lead derailleur cable was nicely concealed inside the frame.

Ultimately, though, the Concept XT sold well because of its looks and toughness. The 26-in. (66-cm) rear wheel was built to tandem specifications, and the front wheels were 16 in. (406 mm) in diameter. The beautiful, pearlescent green frame came with a ten-year warranty and could carry loads of up to 285 lb (129 kg). Challenge engineers rode it down flights of steps to show reviewers just how tough it was. **BS**

METROFIETS Cargo

2008 • Cargo bike • USA • Box-front
cargo bike

Phillip Ross and James Nichols are bike enthusiasts in the U.S. biking capital of Portland, Oregon, who had the idea of building cargo bikes in the style of the load-carrying bikes used in the Netherlands and Denmark. They devised a two-wheeler with an extended frame to support a large wooden box set between the rider and the front wheel. The handlebar pushes and pulls the shafts that steer the front wheel.

The two Americans improved the handling of the typical European cargo bike by enlarging the front wheel from 20 in. (50 cm) to 24 in. (61 cm). Modern steel tubing produced a lighter frame, and the wooden box is detachable with carrying handles. Including the

". . . sub-compact car, mini-van, and pick-up truck all rolled into a gorgeous hand-built bicycle"

Splendid Cycles

weight of the rider, the Metrofiets bike has a carrying capacity of 400 lb (181 kg).

When Ross and Nichols launched the Metrofiets company, bike reviewers scoffed at their business model, especially because their products were not cheap. But the idea took off, and Metrofiets now produces well-crafted bikes for all sorts of businesses.

Each bike is made to a high spec and customized to individual requirements. Sophisticated components such as hydraulic disc brakes, Shimano internal drivetrains, electric gear shifters, and belt drives may be selected. In Portland, residents are used to seeing Metrofiets machines in action in a huge variety of guises, including as a two-wheeled coffee shop, a mobile bike service station, and a dispenser-bar for a local brewery. **SH**

Dutch practicality is mixed with Portland style in the Metrofiets Cargo. ▶

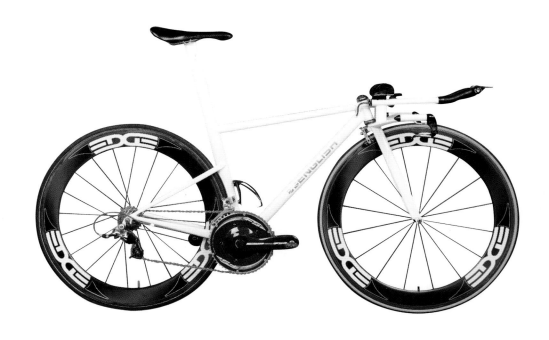

ENGLISH CYCLES Custom TT

2008 • Road bike • UK–USA • Custom low-cockpit TT bike

British bike designer Rob English graduated from Cambridge University with a degree in mechanical engineering, and then spent several years wandering the globe and racing bikes in as many hill climbs, time trials, and MTB competitions as he could enter. Finally he got a job with Bike Friday and settled in Oregon.

When English became Bike Friday's head of engineering and development, he almost immediately set about designing his own time trial bike. When it went into production, demand grew quickly, and as a result he established English Cycles, using his native country's Union Jack flag as a logo. English soon become a cult name in the bike world. The company now makes all types of bikes, from recumbent tandems to folding mountain bikes.

The Custom TT is definitely the model that's closest to English's heart. He built it with a very low cockpit, and there's a theory behind that. As an experienced time trialist, he knew that the most important aerodynamic element in a time trial event is not the bike but the rider. Getting this human wind block into the most aerodynamic position possible is the secret of success for any solo speed machine.

English therefore constructed a bike with an integrated fork and bar that enabled him to lie almost parallel to the ground. The bike weighs just 16 lb (7.25 kg), and has custom-machined aerodynamic brakes. To test his theory, English entered the Oregon State time trial Championships and, riding the bike himself, won it three years running and smashed the course record. **SH**

GIANT Defy

2008 • Road bike • Taiwan • Multi-award-winning aluminum alloy affordable road bike

Giant Bicycles of Taiwan produces vast numbers of every conceivable type of bike under its own brand name, and is also extremely sought after as a contractor for other brands. This has given the company an unparalleled amount of experience and expertise in both aluminum alloy and carbon fiber construction. Giant is one of the very few manufacturers that creates frames from alloy and carbon materials delivered raw to its factories, rather than from prebuilt components supplied by external fabricators. This gives Giant maximum control of quality and consistency throughout the construction process. Buyers do not have to pay a fortune to benefit from all these advantages, and few bikes showcase that fact as well as the Defy "do-it-all" road bike.

Introduced in 2008, the Defy has been improving from one award-winning year to the next. Giant used its advanced tube-shaping technology to produce a frame in the trademark "Compact" sloping top tube layout. This was very close in weight to many carbon bikes. The tapered head tube, big down tube, and front half of the top tube give precise handling, better than that of its comfort-oriented, long-distance "Sportive" rivals. The tapering top tube; slim, multi-shaped seat tube; and thin rear stays are still very effective for taking the sting out of rough road surfaces. Fitted with Giant's own-brand lightweight equipment and good-value transmission options, it feels sprightly on climbs too. No wonder the Defy has won multiple awards in both alloy and various carbon fiber formats. **GK**

GARY FISHER Superfly 29

2008 • Mountain bike • USA • Big-wheeled carbon frame racer

Inveterate innovator Gary Fisher can be single-handedly credited with providing the finance, marketing, and development that moved 29-in. (73.5-cm) bikes into the mainstream market. However, years after the first prototypes and his Paul Smith race display teams were launched, the big wheels were still struggling to gain acceptance, even with his team's pro racers.

The problems were excess weight in the frame, and wheels that dulled acceleration, which was required in aggressive race situations. While 29ers could generally bridge any gaps created by other riders on descents or fast technical sections, their riders would still have to respond to repeated demoralizing attacks from lighter, more responsive 26-in. (66-cm) bikes. However, with the whole development arsenal of parent company Trek and

its Bontrager component division at his disposal, Fisher's big-wheelers soon lost the grams and got the wins.

The breakthrough came with the Superfly, whose hardtail frame was built from the highest grade of OCLV carbon, and weighed only 2 lb 13 oz (1.3 kg). Team bikes were equipped with custom carbon parts and ultra-light tires to get weights down to a podium-standard 22 lb (10 kg), but even production bikes were exotically equipped to help them leap up the trail.

The effects were obvious, not only in the results of the Gary Fisher–Subaru team, but also in the surge of 29er race bike development by other brands. By 2009, most major pro teams were fielding big-wheelers, and if you're not rocking a serious wheel size today, you may as well not bother showing up on the start line. **GK**

TREK Session 88 FR

2008 • Freeride bike • USA • Freeride-friendly version of the Session 88 DH bike

The Session 10 was Trek's flagship downhill and freeride bike from 2006, but in 2008 its gravity family split in two with the Session 88 DH and 88 FR.

The 88 FR—as the suffix suggests, this is the freeride version of the 88 DH—featured a redesigned chassis and suspension system. Every piece of the new frame was made using the latest hydro-forming techniques. The E2 head tube goes from 1⅛ in. (2.85 cm) on the top to 1½ in. (3.8 cm) on the bottom race to allow for the new tapered steerer forks. Trek's Full Floater suspension attaches the shock to two moving linkage points, rather than directly to the frame. This gives the bike the feeling of more travel than its actual 7⅘ in. (20 cm). The bike also features Trek's Active Braking Pivot (ABP) on the rear axle, which allows the

suspension to work freely regardless of whether you are braking.

The Session 88 FR has been developed and ridden by some of the best riders in the world, including Cam McCaul, Brandon Semenuk, and Andrew Shandro. In 2008, McCaul rode a Session 88 FR to fifth place in the Red Bull Rampage, and Andrew Shandro had a segment in Anthill Films' mountain bike short movie *Follow Me* (2010).

The Session 88 FR lasted through 2009, but was replaced in 2010 by the Scratch, a more utilitarian freeride bike for a market that wanted a bike they could pedal all day as well as send off jumps and drops. The Session range survives in its downhill guise, though, and includes the full-carbon Session 9.9. **CJ**

WILIER TRIESTINA Cento Uno

2008 • Road bike • Italy–Japan • Italian flair with Japanese fiber

By 2008 Wilier, one of the world's oldest bike manufacturers, had been in business for over a century at its factory in Rossano Veneto, Italy.

When it came to creating the frame of its new flagship road racer, the company turned to carbon fiber experts at Mitsubishi in Japan to create a whole new chassis with a three-piece frame build.

Unusually for the time, each side of the rear end was built as a complete V-section, and each side was different to deal with the distinct stresses placed upon it when being ridden. These two sections were then bonded and fiber-wrapped onto the monocoque front end. The flowing junction between top tube and rear stays was a point of aesthetic note. Maximum stiffness was assured by the use of a huge rectangular main tube

between the forks and cranks, and the latest outsized, extra-wide press-fit—rather than the conventional screw-in—bottom bracket bearing system. To minimize weight, the seat tube was extended to the base of the saddle rather than using a separate telescopic seat post, so owners had to effectively trim the frame to fit. This was not a job for the faint hearted, with the frame alone costing $4,100 (£2,500).

With the confident and assured handling that Wilier had developed from years of working with top racers, the Cento Uno wasn't just a very efficient race-winning bike—it was also an absolute joy to ride. Unsurprisingly this led to a string of rave reviews in the cycling media and rapturous feedback from those lucky enough to be able to own one. **GK**

SABBATH Mondays Child

2008 • Road bike • UK • Fluidly shaped titanium road bike

The bike pictured here is the latest Mondays Child model from Sabbath, but the development story of this model begins five years earlier. Sabbath bicycles have always been produced by the same manufacturer, but that manufacturer has changed its name since the bikes first appeared.

In 2008, the company now known as Sabbath was designing and selling bikes under the Sunday brand name. Seeing a niche for affordable prestige bikes in a market increasingly dominated by carbon fiber and alloy frames, Sunday had its UK-designed titanium frames made overseas by specialist aerospace manufacturers.

According to the nursery rhyme, "Monday's Child is fair of face," and there's no denying the frame was very

eye-catching. The subtly outward-curving seatstays, designed to give smoothness to the ride, were noticeable in profile. The "New Wave" down tube was the most radical section of the bike though, featuring a S-shaped, shape-changing pipe that curled down toward the front wheel before curving back to the bottom bracket. Malleable 3AL 2.5V titanium alloy was used for this design showpiece, while the head tube and rear drop-outs were made from ultra-hard 6AL 4V titanium alloy for "prang-proof" toughness.

The result is a very dynamic and sprung ride and handling that complement the natural buoyancy inherent in the resilient spring of titanium, but without the overly elastic, wayward feel of many comparable frames. **GK**

ISLABIKES Rothan

2008 • Kids' bike • UK • Fantastically engineered scoot bike

Getting children started in cycling isn't always easy, but nobody has devoted as much time, thought, and effort to the task as Isla Rowntree and her Islabikes team.

Despite being a multiple mountain bike and cyclocross national champion, Rowntree has always struggled to find a bike to fit her own slight build. As a result, she created her own custom frame business, Zinn. But, almost as soon as she had done so, she was recruited successively by several major bike manufacturers as a consultant. One company asked her to develop a children's bike range, but balked at the extensive list of expensive innovations that Rowntree suggested, so the project was shelved. While this might have discouraged a less determined operator, Rowntree decided that if no one would cooperate with her, she'd go it alone. She then founded her own premium junior bike brand.

Islabikes' range starts with the Rothan balance bike breed, in which Rowntree has characteristically invested an admirable amount of research time and energy. As she explains: "The narrow-diameter hubs stop kids catching their legs on the wheel nuts while scooting. And the small-diameter handlebars and grips allow their tiny hands to get a better hold and move them closer to the tiny brake levers. The latter are genuinely usable by a two-year-old. Many balance bikes have brakes fitted, but not many children can operate them."

The tubular heat-treated aluminum alloy frame comes with two choices of seatpost length under the purpose-designed "scoop" saddle to enable the bike to grow with its rider. The twelve-spoke wheels have proper pneumatic tires with enough space to fit a pump head easily. The whole bike weighs a little under 8 lb (3.6 kg), so it's equally easy for little legs to propel and for grown-ups to carry if the junior rider runs out of steam. **GK**

DAHON Curve SL

2008 • Folding bike • Taiwan • Neatly curved folding-frame commuter

The Curve SL is an entry-level introduction to the impressive range from the world's largest manufacturer of folding bikes. Instantly recognizable by its eye-catching elliptical frame, the Curve is considerably shorter than most folders, with a wheelbase of 38 in. (96 cm), which makes it good for public transport-assisted commuting, although it might make you feel that when you're riding it that you're a little too "over the front wheel."

Its compactness may mean it will feel small if you're more than 6 ft (1.8 m) tall, and its 3-speed Sturmey-Archer internal hub—operated via a twist grip—might not have the number of gear ratios you'd like, but it comes fully loaded for city commuting, with fenders front and back,

> *"The Curve SL does everything you'd expect it to . . . fold[s] in seconds, weigh[s] next to nothing."*
>
> Bike Fold

wide mudguards, a rack, and a double kickstand. Tires for the 16-in. (40-cm) wheels are either Schwalbe Big Apples or tougher Marathons. Both will absorb enough bumps to overcome the lack of front or rear suspension. And say goodbye to flats (well, mostly), thanks to Schwalbe's embedded Kevlar puncture protection.

The bike takes 15 seconds to fold into the size of an average suitcase. This makes up for it only folding in half, while other folders are hinged in two places and can fold down in thirds. Just beware: the pedals on the Curve SL are MKS detachable. They're of good quality—better than you'll find on most folders—but don't buy any toe clips or straps because they won't all fit in the pouch provided. And you won't want to lose them: pedaling without pedals is so uncool. **BS**

SPECIALIZED Roubaix SL2

2008 • Road bike • USA • Race-winning, shock-absorbing road bike of Belgian superstar Tom Boonen

With the massive increase in the popularity of mass-start long-distance rides, known as "sportives" or "gran fondos," most manufacturers now produce specific bikes to cater for such events. Because of their more comfortable riding positions and shock-absorbing construction, these bikes have also proved popular with professionals in the Spring Classics—grueling, 125-mi (200-km) plus single-day races in Europe that often include multiple sections of cobbled streets and farm tracks.

The most famous such competition is the Paris–Roubaix. Specialized's bike, one of the first dedicated carbon fiber sportive bikes, was named after the finishing point of this race, and was the first machine of its kind to win it twice in succession, each time ridden by Belgian superstar Tom Boonen.

The SL2 on which "Tornado Tom" outsprinted his rivals was a prototype of the production version. Specialized obviously worked very hard to make it a more competitive machine without sacrificing its shock-absorbing qualities. The biggest change from the previous Roubaix bike was the use of much bigger tubes throughout the lower half to increase stiffness by an average of 10 percent in respect of steering and power delivery. It still retained the curved tube shapes, as well as the jellylike Zertz vibration-damping insets in the fork legs and rear frame to increase comfort and reduce fatigue.

Boonen clearly demonstrated the improvements as he pulled away from his rivals in the last few hundred yards of the Roubaix Velodrome. **GK**

KOGA Miyata Team Edition
2008 • Road bike • Netherlands • Classy, quick, and comfortable aluminum bike

This was the sort of bike that could have graced the legs of racing legends of the past, but in 2009 it became available at a price that ordinary bikers could afford.

The Team Edition was one of Koga's mid-range bikes, but it used much of the construction expertise that the company had gained from building bikes for professional road racing teams. It showed that Koga had been developing the skills of working with aluminum for twenty years. And the Team Edition was an impressive demonstration that the metal was still to be reckoned with in an age when carbon was threatening to dominate.

Koga's triple-butted and triple-hardened 7005 aluminum frame was certainly a masterpiece of light, efficient engineering. It had super-smooth tungsten inert gas (TIG) welds, and, on the road, it felt positive and zippy, with sharp handling in the bends.

Koga founder Andries Gaastra was the first Shimano importer in Europe, and his Team Edition was fitted with the full Ultegra groupset. The understated design was finished in Team Shimano's black, blue, red, and white colors, and came with a matching Koga carbon fork with aluminum steerer.

The alloy bar, stem, and seatpost came from the PRO PLT range, and the saddle was a Special Edition from Selle Italia. Koga supplied the bike in an admirably wide range of seven different stock sizes, from 20 to 24 in. (50–66 cm). Retailing at around $2,100 (£1,350), the Miyata Team Edition was one of the fastest bikes for the money of its time. **SH**

DE ROSA King 3

2008 • Road bike • Italy • Lightweight monocoque version of classic King

Ugo de Rosa's family brand has been responsible for some of Europe's most highly regarded road bikes. De Rosas are built at the company factory in Cusano Milanino in the north of Italy.

In 2008, eight years after the emergence of the original King, the model was given its first significant upgrade. The super-stylish King 3 is a monocoque—or semi-monocoque, if you happen to be an engineering pedant—constructed from premium Mizuno T-700SC carbon fiber and featuring an integrated seatmast. *Bikeradar* struggled to find anything wrong with it—the reviewer's only adverse criticism of his test machine was that the bottom bracket cups needed re-tightening; apart from that it was all hail to the King.

The main visually discernible difference between the King 3 and the original bike is a new sloping geometry, but the redesign also yielded a remarkably reduced frame weight—quoted by de Rosa as being only 2 lb 2½ oz (0.98 kg).

In order to provide that highly prized perfect fit for each individual rider, the frame was made available in ten different sizes. As with any de Rosa bike, such finesse came at a price—the frame and fork alone set buyers back the best part of $5,000 (£3,000).

The new King enjoyed immediate success in competition, being used by the infamous Rock Racing team—the self-styled bad boys of road racing—as well as by Gabriele Bosisio, who took a stage victory in the 2008 Giro d'Italia. As befits a cutting-edge road bike, the King 3 was light and agile, perfect for tackling gradients in a higher gear than you might have expected, and supremely comfortable over long distances. And let's not overlook that oh-so-cute headbadge featuring de Rosa's fabulous heart motif—wasn't it Mies van der Rohe who taught us God is in the detail? **TB**

> *"It's not just about the money, it's more the passion and pleasure, it's a family business with personal service."*
> Ugo de Rosa

◁ De Rosa's King is road bike royalty.

2009–2010

BIGGER, SMARTER,
FASTER, SMOOTHER

Exceeding expectations everywhere.

GARY FISHER Roscoe

2009 • Mountain bike • USA • Tough trail bike that introduced a unique and very successful shock concept

Flamboyant bike fanatic Gary Fisher has been an innovator ever since he came up with the name "Mountain Bikes" for his California bike shop in the late 1970s. When Trek bought his brand, it maintained his pioneering spirit with a string of cutting-edge concepts that found their way onto its own bikes after being proven on Fisher-labeled machines.

These innovations included the Dual Rate Control Valve (DRCV) shock, codeveloped with Fox Racing and first seen on the Roscoe trail bike in summer 2008. This shock used a simple internal push-rod design to effectively provide two shocks in one can. On tamer trails, the shock used only the smaller-volume air chamber that mimicked the tight control and pedaling efficiency of a short-travel cross-country bike. Hit something big or fast that pushed the shock past 40 percent travel, though, and the push rod inside automatically opened a second chamber, giving a seamless transition to a much bigger, more controlled impact appetite. Add the braking force-isolating ABP axle concentric rear pivot, which had already been used on Trek bikes, and the Roscoe ruled rough terrain as firmly as bikes with much more than its meager 5½ in. (14 cm) of travel. Traction, control, and impact protection were also enhanced by extra-large 2⅖-in. (6-cm) Bontrager tires as standard. Both the tires and the Bontrager Rhythm Pro wheels were compatible with inner tube free liquid sealant systems, confirming the Roscoe's position as a significant advance in what rough riders could expect from a state-of-the-art trail bike. **GK**

RIDLEY Damocles Pi

2009 • Road bike • Belgium • Very successful all-carbon race bike

A relative newcomer to the world road scene, Ridley Bikes was founded in 1997 by frame builder Joachim Aerts and quickly established itself as one of Belgium's leading makers of racing bikes. Now a common sight at most of the world's major road events, Ridley sponsored the Russian Katusha team during its inaugural season, and the Lotto-Belisol team at the 2013 Tour de France. The company's brief history has seen a streak of victories, including the Australian, Dutch, Belgian, and British national road race championships, as well as sprint victories for Robbie McEwen in the Tour and the Giro d'Italia.

Soon after the Damocles Pi was launched, it was ridden by Filippo Pozzato in his thrilling battle with Tom Boonen at the 2009 Paris–Roubaix. This was the event at which Katusha, in its first season of racing, served notice that it was a force to be reckoned with.

Based on a carbon frame constructed from individual tubes, the Damocles' chief charm is its versatility on different types of road—anything that can successfully navigate the grueling cobblestones of Roubaix has to have something going for it. The design pays specific attention to the annoying problem of outsized carbon tubes' reverberating surface road noise. The Damocles provides a silent and comfortable ride on any surface, and it is extremely effective in absorbing vibration.

Ridley has since introduced other Damocles models, including in 2010 the Filippo Pozzato ISP model, named in honor of the bike's celebrated patron. **TB**

BIANCHI 928 Mono-Q

2009 • Road bike • Italy • Advanced carbon frame

Reviewers could hardly believe the latest arrival from Italy. Here was a road bike that rode like it had a classic steel frame but which weighed just over 2 lb 2 oz (1 kg). It was Bianchi's new, entry-level, full-carbon machine.

The 928's frame was monocoque piece, with a single mold for each frame size, so it had none of the bells and whistles of Bianchi's high-end flagship HoC and T-Cube bikes, which were built from bonded carbon tubing.

Instead, the Mono-Q's frame was simple and understated, and used smaller-diameter tubing than some of its outsized rivals. However, that slim rear triangle gave the bike a distinctive elegance and a

"Bianchi have created a frame that doesn't ride like a carbon bike at all."

Bikeradar.com

handling precision that some others lacked. Perhaps it didn't offer the professional sophistication of its pricier siblings, but nonetheless the Mono-Q was a fine performer by any standard.

According to *Bike Radar*: "Handling was spot on—it's quick with direction changes, and light enough to climb well." Another reviewer from OutsideOnline.com called it "versatile", "comfortable", and "quick enough for hard efforts on twisty courses."

Detailed specs of the bike included Bianchi's own full-carbon forks, FSA headset, stem, handlebar, and seatpost, and a complete Shimano Ultegra drivetrain. The Mavic Equipe rims were shod with Vittoria Rubino 27½ x 1-in. (70 x 2.3-cm) tires; the saddle came from Fizik, and the bar grips from Bike Ribbon. **SH**

NINER WFO

2009 • Mountain bike • USA • A big-wheeler for the biggest terrain

The WFO totally changed the way people looked at big-wheeled mountain bikes.

Once you know that the WFO name comes from the motorsport racing term "Wide, Full Open," it is easy to comprehend that this bike is designed to let nothing stand in its path.

Its 5½ in. (14 cm) of rear wheel movement and tapered head tube—a first in a frame for a bike with 29-in. (73.5-cm) wheels—could handle a fork with a stroke of up to 6½ in. (16 cm). This feature put the WFO in a long-travel big-wheeler class of its own. (Even at the time of publication of this book, the only competing products were Specialized's Enduro 29 and Trek's Remedy 29.) Given that most riders and reviewers reckon that the larger wheel size equates to an extra ⅘ in. (2 cm) of travel over a 26-in. (66-cm) wheeled bike in terms of smoothness and impact control, that makes the WFO a veritable mountain monster.

To back up the suspension capability, the WFO is supplied with a full suite of big-hit features. The RockShox Monarch Plus rear shock is custom-tuned, and has an additional "piggyback" shock chamber to cope with heat build-up in the damping oil on super-long descents. It's even compatible with a full-on coil-sprung DH rear shock, if that's the fitting that you want to use.

The frame also has direct mounts for a chain guide (so you're always ready to pedal, no matter how rough things get), as well as built-in guides for a remote-control dropper seatpost lever. In other words, if you want a big-wheeler for the biggest terrain, the WFO is more than capable. BikeRumor.com put it even higher than that, judging that the machine delivered "the perfect ride for someone with both technical climbing and challenging descents in their backyard." **GK**

Niner's WFO was the first long-travel 29er and was well ahead of its time. ▶

KONA Ute

2009 • Cargo-carrying bike • USA • Extended-rear-end pannier-carrying specialist

Kona liked to call it "the pickup truck" of the bike world, and the Ute certainly set out to fulfill that role. The extended rear on the bike allowed you to haul your friends, kids, or shopping just like a pickup's load bay.

"Whatever the occasion, duty, or chore, the Ute makes it easy. The Ute is all about moving your life by bike," said Kona.

It was all possible thanks to a sturdy long-wheelbase frame designed specifically for carrying heavier loads. The idea was a progression from Xtracycle's bolt-on frame-extending rear end. The Ute's purpose-built frame delivered a more robust way of carrying cargo than a segmented frame.

From the middle of the bike to the front, the Ute had a fairly standard appearance but it was designed with a chunkier frame, extra-wide-range 8-speed gearing, and powerful disc brakes to cope with heavier loads than a normal bike. The wide handlebars swept back and had cork grips for easy, upright riding, and the Kona Plush saddle was soft and forgiving.

The Ute's frame was aluminum in order to make the bike relatively light, with Kona's own robust P2 steel forks. It was built with pretty relaxed geometry and a low top tube for plenty of stand-over room. An extra-sturdy arrangement of stays at the rear end also coped with the extra load weight.

The extra length and fat 1.9 in. (4.7 cm) tires helped make for a smooth and comfortable riding experience, although the weight and ungainly handling meant that the bike wouldn't win any races. The overall length was 85 in. (215 cm) and the bike weighed around 37 lb (17 kg).

And as a final temptation to buyers, Kona's "long-tail" bike came with all the conveniences included in the price: front mudguard, waterproof panniers, a wood-covered load bay, and a kickstand. **SH**

> *"I absolutely loved this bike. It was great fun to ride and it's immensely practical, straight off the shelf."*
>
> Road.cc

Kona's extended-rack Ute boasts serious cargo capacity. ▶

FOCUS Chrono

2009 • Time trial bike • Germany • Aero time trial bike designed by famous aero custom builder

Marketing ploys have always been a big part of trying to tempt people to part with money for a particular piece of pedal-powered action. In mountain biking, many suspension bikes used by the downhill race teams of household-name brands used to be entirely different specialist builder bikes rebadged with the big-name logo. The same thing happens in time trials and triathlons: Top athletes use specialist custom-built frames painted to look like their sponsor's steed.

Swiss bike builder Andreas Walser has constructed many such machines. When Focus realized that its sponsored athlete and champion time trialist Judith Arndt was using one of Walser's designs, it asked him to

". . . for aggressive athletes prepared to sacrifice comfort for all-out speed."

Bikeradar.com

create its next mass-produced time trial–triathlon bike. The Chrono has a fearsomely efficient wind-cheating chassis. The head tube is waisted dramatically inward to minimize the front area above the skinny front forks. The down tube and wheel-wrapping seat tube are extremely sharp edged, with bladed rear stays to keep airflow as smooth as possible. Adjustable seat positions allow the rider to set up a classic pedaling position or the more radical forward stance favored by many triathletes.

Classic Walser details like a hidden seatpost clamp are also included, along with ultra-aerodynamic components. The aggressive ride position of the Focus is based on Walser's years of creating custom-fit bikes for the world's fastest riders, making it a truly top-level time trial machine that's also available to mere mortals. **GK**

SPECIALIZED Transition

2009 • Road bike • USA • Radical pro team-influenced aero bike

When Cervélo announced that it was launching its own World Tour team for the 2009 season rather than continue supporting Saxo Bank, Saxo's team manager, Bjarne Riis, linked up with Specialized, which was keen to expand its operations in Europe and gain access to a stable of riders that included Andy and Frank Schleck of Luxembourg and World and Olympic time trial champion Fabian Cancellara of Switzerland.

The Transition had previously been ridden by several stars, including Belgian sprinter Tom Boonen, but it was anticipated that, with Cancellara at the controls, the bike would consistently win races against the clock. The prediction proved correct almost immediately, with Cancellara triumphing on a Transition in the prologue to the Tour of California in May 2009.

The Transition was designed with a purpose as steely as the determination of the Swiss champion, and was based entirely on the principle of a minimal front section to cut through the air with maximum efficiency. In addition to deep-section carbon main tubes, the bike was fitted with a narrow, hourglass-shaped head tube. The seat tube and seatpost were also as thin and deep as possible to facilitate the rapid and unhindered passage of air between rider and bike. The chainstays and seatstays behind the rider ran almost parallel to the back wheel of the bike, then flared out just before the rear drop-outs.

Even as Cancellara first mounted the Transition, Specialized was already working with him on the bike that would replace it, the Works TTR, which eventually became the Shiv. Nevertheless, the remarkably cost-effective Transition remains a popular part of Specialized's range and is still an eloquent testament to the company's capabilities. **DB**

ELLIS CYCLES 953

2009 • Road bike • USA • Handmade bike show award winner

The frame was beautifully made from Reynolds chromoly, with brightly polished steel stays and chromed forks. It looked stunning. Ellis Cycles couldn't help bragging: "It's got all the bells and whistles," its publicity proclaimed. That meant the bike featured exquisite details such as polished and carved head lugs, plus internal rear brake cable routing.

The completed bike was a head-turner in a retro kind of way. It had the quality feel of the very best handmade bikes, but also the style of a classic bike from the 1980s. These looks made it a showstopper. Little wonder, then, that it was awarded the Best Lugged Bike at the prestigious North American Handmade Bike Show

"At speed, performed as well or better than any bike we have had . . . this year."

Road Bike Action magazine

(NAHBS) in 2009 ahead of a vast array of established U.S. bike-building talent.

Ellis Cycles is the trading name of Dave Wages, who is based in Waterford, Wisconsin. Wages worked in bike shops from his school days, later learned from Dave Kirk and Kelly Bedford at Serotta, and then worked for Waterford Custom Bikes. In 2008, he started his own business, Ellis (his great-grandmother's maiden name).

This bike used Reynolds 953 stainless steel for the rear triangle and chromoly 753 for the main frame. The head lugs were stainless steel; the seat and bottom bracket lugs were painted steel. Drop-outs were very hard stainless steel. The bike was built up with SRAM groupset and wheels, carbon seatpost, and Ritchey Classic drop bars. Total price was $10,000 (£6,600). **SH**

GT Fury

2009 • Downhill bike • USA • Stage-setting production carbon downhill bike

When the Fury was first released, GT engineers were at pains to emphasize that they had chosen carbon fiber for its resilience rather than for its lightness. They felt the need to broadcast this assertion because, although carbon fiber's strength-to-weight ratio is more than ten times greater than that of aluminum, the material had previously been used almost exclusively for weight reduction, and had gained an unjustified reputation for failure on aggressive trails.

In an effort to show what carbon fiber was really capable of, GT set about designing a bike that would weigh only marginally less than the average aluminum downhill rig—around 38 lb (17.2 kg)—but which would be significantly stronger. The frame thus produced is monocoque, and the single-pivot suspension design offers 8⅜ in. (21 cm) of rear travel with a 64-degree head angle.

In 2012, the Athertons—brothers Dan and Gee and sister Rachel—became GT's World Cup race team, along with long-term GT racer Mark Beaumont. Known as "the first family of downhill racing," the Athertons made the Fury famous almost immediately, and raised the question of when GT would update the now three-year-old design. Apart from a few changes—including an angled headset and a shorter stroke shock—the Furies that the Athertons rode throughout 2012 were stock items. This was the season in which Rachel Atherton won five out of six World Cup events, Gee Atherton claimed silver at the World Championships, and Dan Atherton won the Super Enduro in Finale Ligure, Italy.

In 2013, GT introduced a redesign of the Fury, which the Athertons put on the map by winning both the elite women's and men's races at the season opener in Fort William, Scotland. **CJ**

LAPIERRE S-Lite 200

2009 • Road bike • France • Carbon frame with carbon–alloy forks

Despite more than six decades of producing high-end road bikes, Lapierre is less well known to mainstream cyclists outside France than some lesser European brands. In fact, the Lapierre factory in Dijon produces more than 90,000 cycles a year, and boasts impressive credentials in competition. Founded by Gaston Lapierre in 1946, it was under the ownership of his son Jacky that, having anticipated the vogue for mountain bikes, the business expanded swiftly. Although the family sold its interest in the business in 1996, Gaston's grandson Gilles remains at the helm.

The Lapierre S-Lite frames used a tube-to-tube carbon construction. The mid-range S-Lite 200 model cost around $2,500 (£1,500). For that you got a T3 HR carbon frame fitted with Easton EC90 Superlite carbon–alloy forks, a pair of Mavic Aksium race wheels with Michelin Lithion tires, Shimano 105–Ultegra components (including a 10-speed CS-5600 cassette), and the excellent Marco Ponza steel power saddle.

S-Lite 200s were unprepossessing, but although they didn't stand out in a crowd, they revealed a solid, smooth ride when put through their paces. They were immediately used with great success by the French FDR.fr racing team (formerly La Française des Jeux). **TB**

PLANET X Pro Carbon

2009 • Road bike • UK • Outrageously good-value direct-buy racer

Planet X has been providing high-performance bikes to bargain-hunting on- and off-road riders for nearly two decades. One of its strongest sellers throughout the period has been the Pro Carbon road frame.

While Planet X is by not the only company that direct sells Asian-built frames and complete bikes, it collaborates more closely than most of its competitors with the companies that actually make the merchandise. Such proactivity helps Planet X to seal equipment deals that few other manufacturers can match. Wastage is minimized too, because new frames are developed only after market research has clearly identified a desire for change. Moreover, supply consistently meets demand.

While outstanding value has always been the Pro Carbon's main attraction, the bike's quality has been widely praised. That's because Planet X's owner Dave Loughran and head designer Brant Richards are keen cyclists themselves, and the company has always been closely involved in sponsoring top national and international riders whose feedback has been used to make constant improvements to the design. Many of these riders also work at Planet X, and gladly give their advice to customers on request. **GK**

TREK Remedy Slope

2009 • Slopestyle bike • USA • Custom-built bike for slopestyle aficionado Brandon Semenuk

When one of your athletes is arguably the world's best up-and-coming slopestyle rider, you want to offer him all you can. When the athlete in question is Canadian sensation Brandon Semenuk and you are Trek, the offerings will be substantial. So when the company set about creating Brandon's competition bike for 2009, it began with a blank canvas and asked the rider what he wanted. He asked for something similar to his hardtail, with a long top tube and short chainstays to facilitate 360-degree spins off drops and jumps. In response, Trek took its Remedy trail bike, lengthened the top tube, lowered the bottom bracket, shortened the chainstays, and fitted a hydraulic gyroscope brake system. One final custom piece was a down tube-mounted gear shifter from a time trial bike. This was attached to the top bottle-cage mount rather than the handlebar, to keep it out of the way in crashes and to stop the cable wrapping around the steerer.

Brandon won Crankworx Colorado on this bike, but the machine remained a one-off until 2014, when Trek unveiled the Ticket S version of it shown here. The company produced a limited initial run of 125 units and then fifty different signature color scheme frames in each quarter throughout the year. **CJ**

AVANTI Quantum

2009 • Road bike • New Zealand • Carbon road racer

After four years' development, Avanti launched the Chrono Team, a class-leading carbon time trial bike, in 2008. It then applied the lessons it had learned to a road frame, which was unveiled in 2009. Designed as a dedicated race machine, everything about it was geared toward enabling its rider to generate speed.

At its heart was a massive 3⅖-in. (86-mm) diameter bottom bracket shell to keep the core of the drivetrain solid under the largest pedaling loads. Backing that up was an asymmetrical chainstay design incorporating a larger tube on the driveside to prevent the frame twisting under the force generated by the rider.

It soon showed its class: The Avanti-Subway team rode Quantums into the top four places at the 2009 New Zealand Elite National Road Race Championships.

It was an impressive feat for a company that was less than twenty-five years old and up against bigger names with longer histories. But since its formation in 1985, Avanti has advanced from locally made steel-tubed road bikes to Italian-built carbon fiber mountain bikes. In 2004, Avanti bikes were ridden to gold at the Athens Olympics. These performances spurred on the company to begin work on a project that would eventually become the Chrono Team. **RB**

RAM Nduro

2009 • Mountain bike • Bulgaria • Sturdy
Eastern European mountain bike with custom paint options

In common with many other leading industries in the twenty-first century, bike production is increasingly a global undertaking. Ram came out from behind the communist side of the old Iron Curtain to give Bulgaria a bridge into the wider world of cycling.

The Nduro's frame tubes were hydraulically shaped to increase stiffness and strength in line with peak impact and twisting loads. The extended seat tube was reinforced with an additional square-section pipe, while the head tube had a reinforcing gusset and thicker tube walls to prevent the fork from ovalizing it and loosening the bearings irrevocably.

In spite of these tough-guy touches, rear travel was short, with either 4-in. (10-cm) or 4⁷⁄₁₀-in. (12-cm) arc options, depending on the chosen shock position. The wide bar and short stem of the complete bike confirmed that this chunky 30-lb (13.5-kg) bike wasn't designed to excel heading skyward, but was more concerned with getting to the bottom of any slope as quickly and as entertainingly as possible. Large, heavily treaded tires meant plenty of grip for making the most of the relaxed head angles, and hard riding in tests revealed an impressively stiff and accurate bike when carving hard round corners.

By 2009, however, the initially excellent value of the Bulgarian bikes was on the wane, and reviews of the time commented that there were better bikes available for the same money. Yet although the recommended retail price of around $2,600 (£1,600) was increasingly an obstacle, Bikeradar.com still approved the Nduro as "chaos capable."

What Ram did have on its side, however, was a broad range of two-tone color options for buyers who were prepared to wait a few extra weeks for a truly personal machine. **GK**

BACCHETTA Carbon Aero 2.0

2009 • Recumbent tricycle • USA • Super-fast
recumbent aero trike

Soon after its release in 2002, the original titanium Aero rocketed Bacchetta into the pantheon of recumbent bike designers by winning both the Race Across Florida and the Race Across America. This new version had a lot to live up to; it was not found wanting.

The latest bike is built around an IsoGrid carbon monocoque frame which, despite being painted over, still manages to look immaculate and is significantly more rugged than its predecessor, with a strength-to-weight ratio that can carry a rider weight of 250 lb (114 kg). The components are first-rate, too, from the carbon crankset and SRAM X.0 drivetrain, to the X-Eyed CNC Dual Pivot brakes that easily slow this very

". . . the stiffest, most efficient and best hill-climbing racing recumbent around."

Flying Furniture Cycles

light—21 lb (9.5 kg)—cycle and attract none of the criticisms leveled at the old Aero's stopping power. For hill climbing, every ounce of energy is transferred to the rear wheels, and on most ascents you need never leave one of its middle ring gears. There's plenty of vibration damping, too, thanks to the natural buzz-smoothing properties inherent in its carbon frame.

Available with 650C (22½-in./57-cm) or 700C (24½-in./62-cm) wheels, the Aero 2.0 was voted "easiest recumbent to ride" by Flying Furniture Cycles, which particularly praised the ergonomic Euromesh seat, an unusual feature in high-end carbon fiber racers.

In 2010, Kent Polk won the Race Across America on an Aero 2.0, thereby adding another chapter to the legend of the Bacchetta. **SB**

Bacchetta's Carbon Aero proves recumbents aren't just for cruising. ▶

CANNONDALE Simon

2009 • Mountain bike • USA • Unique bike
built around programmable suspension system

When the Simon prototype first appeared at Interbike
in 2009, it had been in development for five years. It still
hasn't come to market.

The idea is good. By using a flow-control needle
in the damper valve of the fork, Simon can react
immediately to slowdown or speed-up. Position-
and force-measuring sensors on the single-sided
Lefty fork also monitor movement of the suspension,
automatically adjusting it every two milliseconds
according to preset preferences. The onboard computer
can be programmed to create a very linear feel for
maximum travel use, a much firmer setting for pedaling
or cornering efficiency, or any potential suspension feel
in between, thanks to around 10,000 possible control
choices. At any one time it can display four different
modes for instant actuation, as well as a lockout mode.

The simple electric stepper motor-controlled
valve replaces multiple shim stacks and other damping
circuitry hardware, creating a fork that's easily serviced
and light, even with the battery pack included.

While Cannondale has since been quiet on the
project, Lapierre, Ghost, and Haibike have introduced
a similar auto-damper adjusting system in the shape of
their RockShox co-developed EI technology. **GK**

COTIC BFe

2009 • Mountain bike • UK • Heavy-duty
version of the popular Soul steel hardtail

Cy Turner of Cotic hit on a very popular recipe when he
launched his long-stroke fork-compatible Soul hardtail.
Its combination of confident handling angles for secure
control on steep descents, a long reach to offset the use
of a short stem and wide bar for a power-steering effect,
and the resilient spring of the top-quality Reynolds 853
tubed frame chimed with many riders, particularly in the
UK. The impressively low sub-4½ lb (2 kg) weight for a
steel hardtail frame also gave the Soul real pep when the
trail turned upward.

Some riders wanted something tougher and even
more capable, though, and that's when the BFe was
born. The letters stand for "Big Fe" (the chemical symbol
for iron) and, when spoken, can sound like "beefy."

The BFe has the same 853 double-butted down
tube as the Soul. The rest of the frame uses Cotic's own
custom heat-treated steel tubes for extra strength. The
1¾-in. (4.4-cm) head tube can handle a 6³⁄₁₀-in. (16-cm)
travel fork in standard, tapered, or even full 1½-in. (3.5-
cm) steerer formats. Mounts are provided on the bottom
bracket for a chainguide, and the seat tube is the right
diameter for a seat dropper post. At 5 lb 6 oz (2.45 kg),
the frame is still light enough to launch out of corners or
scamper up climbs. **GK**

RAGLEY Blue Pig

2009 • Mountain bike • UK • Radical steel-framed, affordable, all-mountain hardtail

The Blue Pig was the ultimate in the line of increasingly radical hardtails designed by legendary left-field magazine tester Brant Richards. A lot of the inspiration for this cult classic came from the topography around Brant's home in Todmorden, Yorkshire, England, which is dominated by steep slopes leading onto wild, open moors that are rendered slippery for much of the year by the high level of rainfall.

In order to handle such demanding terrain, the Blue Pig's front wheel is pushed a long way out in front, with a long-travel fork and a slack steering angle. A short stem and super-wide bar on top prevent the wheel from folding under the rider, even when turning steep corners on sketchy descents. To help on uphill sections, the bike uses a steep seat tube to keep the rider centered in terms of traction, and stops the front wheel popping up. The forward-placed seat lets riders drop back behind the saddle easily so they can get their weight in the right place on downhill charges.

To maximize grip, the Blue Pig was designed to cope with the biggest tires available through the use of a cunning split-plate "three finger" design at the front of the chainstays to get the right clearance between chainrings and tires. **GK**

TITUS Exogrid

2009 • Mountain bike • USA • Ultra-expensive titanium–carbon fiber hybrid mountain bike

For years, Titus produced some of the most sought-after mountain bikes in the world. Its designs weren't particularly radical—the suspension and layout were similar to those of Specialized—but few brands sweated the details like Titus. Most companies left simple forgings largely unchanged to keep costs down, but Titus devoted hours of hand machining to every segment of the frame. How much this saved in terms of weight or contributed to strength and stiffness is a moot point, but it undoubtedly made the company an outstanding example of cutting-edge craftsmanship.

Titus didn't skimp when it came to the tubes. On the basic bikes, these were extensively manipulated alloy pipes. On the most expensive models, Titus used titanium tubes with custom-formed thickness at either end. Then, in 2009, with Maxm, Titus developed Exogrid, an inner carbon fiber tube bonded into a tight-fitting titanium sleeve that was machined into an open lattice design along its center section. This put more metal at the high-stress areas at the end of the tubes, but reduced weight in the less heavily stressed middle sections.

The process was breathtakingly expensive: the Racer X Exogrid was one of the first complete bikes to break the $10,000 (£6,250) price barrier. **GK**

TREK Madone Butterfly

2009 • Road bike • USA • $500,000 (£313,000) Damien Hirst-designed "butterfly" bike

It's a rare occurrence when contemporary art meshes with the world of professional cycling, but that's exactly what happened in 2009. During his return to the sport after overcoming testicular cancer, Lance Armstrong asked seven of his favorite artists to design paintwork for his racing steeds. Seven designs were chosen, but by far the most famous and most eye-catching work came from British artist Damien Hirst.

The story began when U2's Bono—a friend of Armstrong—put the American rider and Hirst in contact. Armstrong was already a fan of Hirst's work, and the result of this collaboration was a stunning example of both Hirst's unique talent and Armstrong's search for headline-grabbing perfection. Hirst delicately adorned the original Trek with real butterflies, lacquering them onto the whole of the bike from the wheel rims to the complete frame.

The bike itself was an off-the-peg model that used the same components as Armstrong had been using throughout that racing season: SRAM Red groupset, Bontrager cockpit and wheels, and Armstrong's trusted Selle San Marco saddle, which he'd ridden throughout his career.

Armstrong used the Hirst bike for the traditional Paris finish to the final day of racing in that year's Tour de France in which he finished third overall. But the story did not end there. All seven of the Armstrong bikes were transported to Sotheby's in New York for auction. Of the $1.25 million (£780,000) raised in the sale, $500,000 (£313,000) came from the Madone Butterfly, making it at the time the world's most expensive bike. The money went to Armstrong's Livestrong charity; the bike went to an unnamed private collector. In the light of Armstrong's subsequent disgrace, one may wonder what its current resale value might be. **DB**

"How do you take a $10,000–$15,000 bike . . . and turn it into a $500,000 bike? Get Lance Armstrong to ride it."

Tour de France Blogspot, 2009

◁ Damien Hirst's distinctive butterfly livery.

EVIL Revolt

2009 • Downhill bike • USA • The first DELTA-link suspension bike featuring Flip Chip adjustable geometry

Dave Weagle's Evil started as hardtail-only brand. After building the suspension for the outstanding Cove Shocker and Iron Horse Sunday DH bikes, Dave helped relaunch Evil in 2008 with the introduction of the Revolt suspension bike.

This state-of-the-art downhill machine featured Dave's Extra Legitimate Travel Apparatus (DELTA), a brand-new system that provided the suspension with a dual progression curve, the first and last thirds of which were progressive, for pedaling and impact control, while the middle third of the stroke compressed at a flatter rate for consistent traction.

The short and compact links also have a lot of angle and velocity change during the suspension stroke. This allows them to take advantage of the speed-sensitive dampers found in mountain bike rear shocks. The linkage could also be tailored to different tracks using different link kits, a feature that was especially useful to the Evil World Cup race team, which in 2009 featured Matti Lehikoinen, Filip Polc, and Stevie Smith. Smith also featured—along with Evil's freeride representative and key Revolt development rider Thomas Vanderham—in the award-winning film *Follow Me*. Smith appears in a segment of the movie with Brandon Semenuk in both downhill and slopestyle settings. Markus Stöckl—MS Evil downhill team race owner—set a new world record in Chile on the Revolt at 102 mph (165 kph). Cam Zink won the Red Bull Rampage in 2010, landing a 360-degree spin off the Oakley Icon jump aboard his Revolt. **CJ**

INDEPENDENT FABRICATIONS Corvid

2009 • Road bike • USA • Ultra-light carbon bike with decorative crown lugs

This top-end custom road bike from metalworking legends Indy Fab is acclaimed for its visual and technical distinction. It is made in the company's Newmarket, New Hampshire, workshop by a remarkable method that involves the creation of hollow tubes by inflating a specially made bladder within the basic carbon fiber material. The tubing is then permanently bonded using aerospace adhesive and carbon lugs to maximize the strength of the junctions and make the parts virtually inseparable.

The Independent Fabrication (IF) molding process is precisely customized to individual requirements. It adds a unique cosmetic appeal too, as the molded lugs incorporate stylized crown designs that resemble traditional old brazed steel lugwork. Corvid customers can choose either a practical, unidirectional carbon fiber finish or a prettier carbon cross-weave on the tubing. The frame itself weighs only 2 lb (0.9 kg).

Other features include custom-machined titanium drop-outs, ENVE composite forks, and an integrated headset. Among the many distinctive decorative touches are a sterling silver headbadge and custom tints and decals applied in IF's own paint and finish shop. Every Corvid comes with a lifetime warranty.

This all results in a bike that is beautifully strong, light, and classic-looking. Judges at the 2009 North American Handmade Bike Show voted it the Best Carbon Bike, and it has enjoyed a steady stream of positive reviews and customer praise since it went on general sale. **SH**

BEN WILSON Monocycle

2009 • Concept bike • UK • Sculptor's view of future cycling

If you don't find traditional bicycles fun, then London, England-based 3D industrial designer Ben Wilson has some blueprints that might interest you. Wilson has had a long fascination with monowheels, but finding one to produce in his workshop proved difficult. "There are rumors of a production monowheel in China," he said, "but after looking and finding nothing, he did the only thing he could do. "Because we couldn't buy a monowheel, we made one."

Commissioned for the XX1st Century Man Exhibition in Tokyo, Japan, Wilson's single center-seated wheel isn't an attempt to improve upon the bicycle. Instead, its value, as he saw it, was in the discussions

"Over the years, the myth of the monowheel has become a fascination."

Ben Wilson

and ideas that his research and product generated. More theoretical than practical, it has obvious functional limitations: There is no suspension except what is in the tire and in-built beneath the seat; you can't carry anything unless it's in a backpack; it is gearless; you can't fold it, and there's a rim in front of your face. But what does any of that matter when you're pedaling something more eye-catching than a Lamborghini?

Only one prototype was ever made, and it is now tucked away in a private collection. But if you want to see one that looks astonishingly similar to Wilson's, check out the motorized machine—powered by a V8 engine—built by American inventor Kerry McLean, or watch the monocycle chase in *Men in Black 3*—its creators drew inspiration from both Wilson and McLean. **BS**

SPECIALIZED SX Trail

2009 • Slopestyle–4X–Trail bike • USA • Second-generation redesign of hardcore do-it-all favorite

After the five-year reign of the original SX Trail, the directors of Specialized decided that a thorough redesign was required.

Developed from the Specialized Enduro, the SX Trail had always been a favorite among hardcore single-track riders, four-cross racers, slopestyle riders, and just about everyone in between. A Swiss Army knife style of bike, it was made for the jump-loving, trail-riding occasional racer.

When Specialized reformulated the SX in 2009, it wanted to hold onto the bike's do-it-all nature but bring the style and technology up to date. The company gave the new bike beautifully swooping aluminum tubes, but maintained the long front end and short rear end. This retained the nippy feel of the rear end through the short chainstays, the stability of a long front triangle, and a low center of gravity to keep the whole bike feeling small and agile.

The 6 in. (15 cm) of rear travel comes thanks to Specialized's Horst Link and the Fox DHX 5.0 coil shock. The frame design comes from the SX's big brother, the Demo. So, too, does the suspension, which is characterized by a rearward axle path that allows for better square-edge bump compliance.

The SX has been used in slopestyle competition by Canada's Darren Berrecloth, who in 2010 came third overall in the Freeride Mountain Bike World Tour. Berrecloth has been winning freeride competitions on the SX since their inception: he came second in the 2005 Crankworx Slopestyle; won the Nissan Qashqai Tour Championship in 2007; and became the Adidas Slopestyle Champion in 2009.

Specialized took a chance in updating the SX Trail, but the risk paid off as the revised version maintained the dominance of the original. **CJ**

BERU Factor 001

2009 • Road bike • UK • World's most expensive and high-tech road bike

Designed by Formula One motor racing engineers with input from some of Britain's finest athletes, and constructed from the ground up to meet each individual owner's requirements, the Factor 001 was the closest thing to a superbike the cycling world had ever seen when it was unveiled at the Science Museum in London. Originally intended as a one-off concept bike that wasn't hamstrung by the need to conform to Union Cycliste Internationale specifications, there are now more than 300 001s worldwide, with the first production model going to the then-Formula One World Champion Lewis Hamilton.

Its technological punch was certainly worthy of its gasoline-powered cousins: hydraulic carbon-ceramic disc brakes to limit weight, and an onboard LCD touch-screen electronics system capable of providing data on, among other things, body temperature, heartbeats per minute, ambient barometric pressure, crank force, angles of lean, and amount of torque produced by both legs.

It weighs only 16 lb (7.4 kg), and its sculpted aerodynamics mean easy and efficient cruising. Twenty-speed gears and ultra-light high-pressure tires wrapped around Beru's own eight-spoke carbon fiber wheels, and an exceptionally rigid, twin-spar carbon fiber monocoque frame mean no loss of power. It all sounds great—until you spy the price tag: $35,000 (£22,000) or more, depending on the options. How much Formula One can be packed into a bicycle? Is the 001 the pinnacle of road bikes? See your bank manager and find out. **BS**

KENT ERIKSEN Titanium
2009 • Road bike • USA • Classic titanium road bike

Kent Eriksen founded Moot Cycles in the 1980s in Steamboat Springs, Colorado. Moot soon switched from traditional steel frames to titanium, and Eriksen became a pioneering master of the new material. The company grew to become a world-renowned brand in the 1990s.

In 2004, however, Eriksen tired of running what had grown into a large operation. He sold out and quit the company he had established. He spent more time riding bikes and resting, and eventually he founded another bike company.

The new enterprise is a deliberately smaller operation than Moot—it is a bespoke titanium custom frame and component workshop, still in Steamboat Springs. Eriksen's role is more hands on too. He builds

road, cross, and mountain bikes, and races and tests them with his wife, Katie Lindquist, a former 24-hour solo World Champion, as well as a small team of hand-picked helpers. Kent Eriksen bikes have won a host of awards, including Best Titanium Construction, Best Titanium Bike, and Builder of the Year at the North American Handmade Bike Show.

This 2009 Eriksen road bike is a great example of what he can produce and is built to blend speed and subtle smoothness. Like all Eriksen bikes, this carefully color-matched beauty is built from carefully chosen custom-tube configurations that are shaped and sized to ensure a perfect fit for their lucky owners. A curved titanium seat post and ENVE carbon fork complete this achingly aspirational frameset. **SH**

SPECIALIZED S-Works TTR

2009 • Aero bike • USA • Prototype aero bike that became the production Shiv

When Specialized began to sponsor the Saxo Bank professional team, the bike manufacturer took on a massive responsibility in the shape of Swiss powerhouse Fabian Cancellara. "Spartacus," as he was known, was on the form of his life, crushing all opposition in time trial events on the Cervélo bikes he had used with his previous team, CSC. Hence anything less than emphatic victories on a new bike would be disastrous. Add the ferocious reputation of team manager and ex-pro rider Bjarne Riis, and the Time Trial Riis (TTR) team was definitely a high-stakes project.

Specialized's design team didn't play it safe, though. They took International Cycling Union (UCI) legal regulations to the limit with an extended stem "beard," which was ostensibly used to mount the front brake and therefore count as part of the structure rather than an illegal fairing. The integrated handlebar also took legal tube ratio rules to the limit in the hunt for maximum aerodynamic advantage, with Cancellara getting a fully custom-built, fixed-position cockpit. Because of the difficulty of accessing the front brake on the prototype, Specialized had to build a cable adjuster into the brake lever. Segmented metal Nokon cables were used to cope with the tight twists and turns of the internal cable routing. SRAM's latest R2C (Return 2 Center) shift levers ensured that even the tiny carbon fiber shift paddles were always at their most aerodynamic horizontal setting. A vertical aero seatpost with hidden clamp, and a wheel-shrouding seat tube cutout, kept the bike as aerodynamic at the rear as at the front.

Although subsequent changes to UCI regulations meant that the prototype required further modification, by the time it went into production as the Shiv it was good enough to become an extremely successful bike under pro and amateur riders. **GK**

YIKE BIKE Carbon

2009 • Electric bike • New Zealand • Short-range electric urban bike

The Yike Bike is a folding electric carbon fiber bike designed for quick, quiet urban transportation. Created by mega-yacht designers as a super-chic, high-tech way for their clients to nip about onshore from their boutique harbor berths, the Yike is a world away from normal heavyweight utility E-bikes.

The 1.2 kw motor tops out at 12 mph (19 kph). While the battery allows its rider to travel only 5 mi (8 km) before requiring a recharge, that's usually more than enough to get along the promenade from your mooring to the most exclusive venues in town. It takes only twenty minutes to charge back to 80 percent capacity. It's packed with features—built-in head and

> *"We created the Yike Bike to dramatically change urban and suburban transportation."*
> Grant Ryan, CEO, Yike Bike

brake LED lights, an electric anti-skid braking system, and an all-important speed limiter. The accelerator and brake buttons are right there under your thumbs on the handlebars, as are its indicator buttons. Your hands need never leave the handles.

Although the Yike produces zero carbon emissions, it makes a distinct whirring sound that has been left unmuffled so that it can announce its otherwise noiseless presence for safety reasons.

Despite its dizzying cost—$3,600 (£2,250)—this isn't just a posh yacht toy. *Time* magazine ranked it fifteenth in the Fifty Best Inventions of 2009, and *Guinness Book of World Records* listed it as the world's lightest and smallest compact electric bike. A true icon, the Yike Bike has since inspired a host of other E-bikes and scooters. **BS**

CUBE Agree HTC Race

2009 • Road bike • Netherlands • Excellent-value race bike that helped to establish a brand

Cube's Agree HTC frame was a relatively conservative-looking design, with a short head tube that created an aggressive character. The down tube was outsized to create a stiff connection between front and rear. This meant steering and power centers locked together to harness maximum saddle effort, with simple, tapered rear stays taking that effort to the rear wheel. Externally mounted cables kept the frame light and easy to maintain. The 2009 model had lightweight, alloy-topped, carbon-legged forks from Dedacciai; Cube then used Easton forks before developing its own model.

Shimano Ultegra gears in "new for 2009" SL gray provided understated stop-and-go performance, and

> "... it's one of those bikes that encourages you to miss your tea."
>
> Matt Brett, Bikeradar.com

while the default spec saw the chain churned around by a carbon-armed FSA SL-K chainset, a matching Ultegra triple-ring chainset was offered as an option.

German brand Syntace, Cube's long-running partner, provided the cockpit and seatpost equipment, while smooth-rolling Fulcrum Racing 5 Evo wheels were shod with top-quality Schwalbe Ultremo ZX tires. Italian specialists Fizik provided the Aliante Delta saddle.

Despite the excellent seat, most contemporary reviewers of the Cube Agree stood on the pedals as they danced up hills, and praise for the bike's climbing ability was universal in the ride reports. The Agree has continued to impress owners and reviewers ever since, and even today the bike remains the benchmark for affordable performance. **GK**

KESTREL RT 800

2009 • Race bike • UK • Carbon racer with unusual mix of curves and angles

The Rock Racing team's new bikes arrived only shortly before the start of the 2009 Tour of California. Team member Francisco Mancebo of Spain jumped straight onto his untried red, black, and white Kestrel and won the first stage with an early break from the field after only 3 mi (5 km)—104 mi (167 km) from the finish—and an impressive turn of speed at the end, outpacing Italian Vincenzo Nibali (Liquigas) and Belgian Jurgen Van de Walle (Quick Step) over the final 550-yd (500-m) sprint.

It was a headline-making arrival for the new RT800. Kestrel had been making high-end carbon-framed racing bikes in Philadelphia, Pennsylvania, since 1986, when the company was formed by a group of ex-Trek employees. But Kestrel had recently been taken over by Advanced Sports Inc. Previously, Kestrel frames had been well-mannered, smooth designs, but this newcomer had angles and curves all over the place. It looked like it had been working out in a gym.

The RT800 was no beauty, but it was evidently a bike that meant business—a muscular machine. The slightly outsized sloping top tube and teardrop-section down tube almost overwhelmed the stumpy head tube. The seat tube was even stranger, with another teardrop cross-section and abrupt rear-wheel cut-out. The multi-shaped top tube was faintly curved to meet the swooping seatstays, which met the chunky chainstays at an aluminum drop-out. The joints in the lightweight 800k-grade carbon frame were clearly visible throughout.

The spec included a Shimano Dura Ace 7900 groupset and drivetrain, Kestrel EMS carbon forks, a Selle Italia saddle, and Mavic Equipe wheels. Rock Racing's team bikes had Shimano PRO wheels; carbon seatposts, bars, and stem; and Vittoria tires. **SH**

▣ Cube's affordable carbon racer is Agree-able for many reasons.

SPECIALIZED Shiv

2009 • Aero race bike • USA • A genuinely illegal race weapon

"The biggest problem we had was stopping Fabien ripping the handlebars off when accelerating out of corners."

Chris D'Alusio, Specialized

The failure or success of a bike can still ultimately come down to the name it has been given. Few bikes have ever been given a more appropriate—or edgy—name than Specialized's Shiv.

For those unlikely to know, a shiv is a makeshift stabbing weapon used in prison riots, and it thus evokes the brutal world of no quarter given or asked that is endured by people committed to punishment for life. That is also a fairly accurate description of the world's fastest time trialists and triathletes, the people for whom the Shiv was designed.

Specialized aerodynamicist Mark Cote and research and development project leader Chris D'Alusio started with a blank piece of paper for the Shiv project, and went on to recruit any expert or testing method they could find. As well as thousands of hours of computer simulation and more than 100 hours of actual wind-tunnel testing, Cote and the crew were able to get their prototypes validated spectacularly by two legendary athletes: Ironman-dominating triathlete Craig "Crowie" Alexander and Swiss time trial specialist Fabien "Spartacus" Cancellara.

The result was a totally radical aero bike, complete with a "bearded" stem that extended all the way down over the front wheel to smooth airflow, and a custom-built modular handlebar. The exhaustive testing paid off massively too, with Spartacus on a Shiv prototype taking two time-trial wins and the overall in the Tour of Switzerland, plus the opening stage of the Tour de France, and Crowie, also using a Shiv prototype, winning the Hawaii Ironman World Championship.

Like the prison weapon it was named for, the original Shiv was outlawed by the Union Cycliste Internationale in 2010. However, a second-generation Shiv was produced in both UCI-legal and "bearded" triathlon versions. **GK**

World champion Craig Alexander taking his Shiv to yet another victory. ▶

CERVÉLO S1
2009 • Road bike • Canada • Aerodynamically designed aluminum frame

In the cycling world, the bid to achieve aerodynamic advantage began with time trial cycles. In this sport, only fractions of a second separate the top competitors. The principle is that if you can slice through the air with less drag, you will be able to go faster, or expend less energy to maintain the same speed. That idea is now being applied to road bikes.

Based in Toronto, Canada, the Cervélo brand emerged in 1995—the name being a linguistic mix of the Italian word for brain (cervello) with the French word for a cycle (vélo). Cervélo has always used CAD systems and computational fluid dynamics in the design process, with aerodynamic testing carried out in the wind tunnels of the San Diego Air and Space Technology Center.

The Cervélo was among the first of the first generation of aero road bikes, with the "S" series taking advantage of features developed for the company's extremely successful "R" series of triathlon/time trial bikes. That pedigree is immediately evident in the shape of the super-skinny tubes that make up the frame, especially the thin-edged, thick-sided down tube and the hour-glass head tube.

Considering that the S1 overshoots the $3,000 (£2,000) barrier, it is perhaps surprising that it has an aluminum frame, yet race wins at the Paris–Nice, the Critérium International, and the Liège–Bastogne–Liège events confirm that it is a serious piece of kit. For those with deeper pockets and a preference for carbon frames, the S5 becomes the weapon of choice. **TB**

JEFF JONES Spaceframe

2009 • Mountain bike • USA • Unique titanium truss-frame mountain bike

Oregon-based frame designer Jeff Jones builds frame and fork combinations that celebrate the art of free thinking. His philosophy is based on trying to build the perfect "non-suspension" mountain bike—non-suspension being in quotes because Jones works according to the theory that enough suspension can be built into a rolling chassis without resorting to separate sprung shock units. Jones' frames and forks, mainly built in titanium, are an ingenious and purposeful attempt to take the maxim of "form follows function" to its logical conclusion. Relaxed geometry creates easy-riding characteristics, with big wheels emphasizing the bump-absorbing ride of the sprung space-frame and truss fork. If suspension forks had never been invented, there would be more bikes like this.

The truss fork's ride feel is amazing: It copes with rocky, rooty terrain without flexing back on big hits or under hard braking, making you realize how much other forks flex and flutter. To quote Jones: "If you let each part of the bike do what it needs to do to the fullest extent, without interference from other parts, then the bike responds in performance. When parts or systems might interfere with one another, I give priority to the part or system that demands priority, based first on safety, then reliability, then desired performance, then lowest weight. The 3D space-frame keeps lateral flex and twisting to a minimum, putting more of your riding effort directly to the ground while allowing the frame to be laterally stiff for efficient pedaling and vertically compliant for a smooth ride." **SW**

BOARDMAN FS Team

2009 • Mountain bike • UK • Benchmark bargain full-suspension bike

The road bikes developed by former Olympic and Tour de France stage winner and legendary equipment obsessive Chris Boardman were very successful, but a certain pessimism greeted the launch of his first full-suspension mountain bikes. However, their sophistication and keen price have earned them almost universal approval.

Typically for the Boardman brand, there are no obvious signs of corners cut in construction or componentry. The FS Team is made from custom-designed, hydraulically shaped aluminum, with hand-sanded welds on the major mainframe joints to give a smooth, carbon fiber look to the frame. The tried-and-tested suspension layout featured a stiffening

"You won't find a better full-suspension bike than this for under £1,000 [$1,600]."

MBUK magazine

"linkage" hanging from the crossbar to drive the rear shock-absorber, and a secondary pivot ahead of the wheel. This gave a carefully controlled 5-in. (12.7-cm) suspension stroke that, largely independent of braking and pedaling movement, was relatively simple to set up. The pivots had smooth, durable cartridge ball bearings, rather than the fragile nylon bushings used on many competing bikes. A similarly reliable RockShox suspension fork kept the front end under close control.

Italian FSA cranks and 20-speed SRAM gears and brakes were great value, and the Boardman-brand saddle and cockpit kit were canny copies of highly expensive models. The result was a versatile and affordable bike that was very enjoyable to ride. **GK**

ORBEA Ordu

2009 • Time trial bike • Spain • High-speed aerodynamic race machine

The Orbea name first appeared in 1840 in Mallabia, a small town in the Basque Country of northern Spain. After eight decades of specializing in machine tools and rifles, Orbea Hermanos (Orbea Brothers) built its first bicycles during the 1920s. As a cooperative business in the 1970s, Orbea founded its first road-racing teams, and later became an essential component in the success of the Basque Euskaltel-Euskadi team, which, until recently, recruited talent only from that region. Orbea's biggest success so far has been the road race gold medal won by Samuel Sanchez at the 2008 Beijing Olympics.

Orbea has also enjoyed enormous success among triathlon riders, and the Ordu was claimed to be the fastest bike of its type. It certainly looked the part; gone were the smooth curves of the traditional time trial bike—in their place appeared aggressive-looking sharp lines, including a radical diamond-shaped seatpost. Triathlete Andrew Starykowicz underlined the Ordu's high-speed credentials when he shattered the Ironman bike split world record in 2012. His time of 4 hours, 4 minutes, and 39 seconds for the 112-mi (180-km) ride was an astonishing 6 minutes and 54 seconds faster than the previous best. When interviewed after his victory, the American declared: "It wasn't just about winning Ironman Florida. It was about making a statement, start to finish, of 'I'm not just gonna win, I'm gonna dominate.'" And there was no better bike than the Ordu on which to do so.

Unfortunately, only the most dedicated and best-funded time trialists and triathletes can afford to take a serious look at the Ordu. Prices for the most basic model start at around $6,000 (£4,000), and it is more than double that for the top model, the M-Ltd. But you only get what you pay for. **TB**

You see something out of *Tron*; the wind sees almost nothing. ▶

BASSO Laguna
2009 • Road bike • Italy • Stylish sports road bike

Basso had been creating bikes since 1974. The company was founded by Alcide Basso, brother of the 1972 cycling world champion Marino Basso. Alcide made his first bike frame in his garage, but after some racing successes he expanded his business into a small factory.

With its Italian design style and construction expertise, it was no surprise that the glamorous Basso Laguna was shortlisted as one of the bikes of the year by Bike Radar in 2009. *Cycling Plus* loved the Laguna too, citing its directness and fast handling.

This sporty road bike had race pretensions while falling a little short of being a hardcore competition machine. That nervous whippetlike character that was such fun for fast road rides wasn't for everyone, and

several testers criticized the Laguna's lack of comfort and stability, and its jittery front end.

Yet at only around $3,120 (£2,000), the new Basso bike was a well-specified machine for the price. It was Basso's entry-level carbon bike at a time when the company was trying to increase sales internationally.

The frame and forks—made from the same T700 7K grade carbon fiber as was used in more expensive racing bikes—weighed only 2 lb 13 oz (1.3 kg), and the complete Laguna weighed just 17 lb 14 oz (8.12 kg).

The wheels—Khamsin G3s—and the Ergo Veloce ten-speed groupset were from Campagnolo, the acclaimed component manufacturer based in Vicenza, just 6 mi (10 km) down the road from Basso's base in Dueville, Italy. **SH**

WILIER Izoard

2009 • Road bike • Italy • Affordable yet still aspirational carbon road racer

The Wilier Izoard is named after one of the most famous Alpine climbs of the Tour de France, the Col d'Izoard. This 7,740-ft (2,360-m) high mountain pass is close to the border of Wilier's homeland in Italy, and is regularly included in the Giro d'Italia race route as well. While it has seen some titanic struggles between groups of riders, as well as solo battles between human and mountain, the Izoard is slightly overshadowed by larger regional peaks such as the fearsome Col du Galibier, which rises to 8,678 feet (2,645 m) in the Dauphiné Alps near Grenoble, France.

Thanks to the continual evolution of Wilier's construction methods, the Izoard has an upgraded fork shape and enhanced carbon fiber sheet positioning throughout its frame, which keeps the bike extremely competitive without making it crushingly stiff and harsh to ride. The XP version of the Izoard adds a humped top tube and a more upright ride position to increase stiffness and make progress over rough road patches more like gliding than riding.

As would be expected from such an illustrious Italian brand, many of the complete bikes feature equipment produced by other famous Italian manufacturers. Campagnolo supplies the gearing systems, Fulcrum provides the wheels, FSA furnishes the cranksets, and Selle Italia produces the saddle. Thus the Izoard is a veritable banquet of biking *bellezza*. When the bike was reviewed, nearly all *Cycling Plus* magazine's Bike of the Year testers placed it in their top ten, and many counted it as one of their top five. **GK**

TREK Madone

2009 • Road bike • USA • Custom commemorative comeback bike

In professional bike racing, or bicycle manufacturing for that matter, the number 1,274 had no particular meaning. It had nothing to do with bike telemetry, weight, make, or model, and it is not the number of a secret patent. It was quite simply a reference to the number of days that elapsed between Lance Armstrong's first retirement in 2005 and the date of his comeback in 2009.

On a sunny morning in downtown Adelaide, Australia, the former seven-time winner of the Tour de France dusted off his helmet and racing shoes and saddled up with the latest machine from his longtime bike supplier, Trek. But anyone thinking that Armstrong would be allocated a custom-made machine for his comeback was doomed to disappointment. The American was given an off-the-shelf frame picked straight from the factory line in Waterloo, Wisconsin. The only instruction that Armstrong had issued was the need to "Maybe think about how long I've been retired."

The Trek Madone frame was kitted out with the customary SRAM Red, a Bontrager Aeolus wheelset, and Dura Ace pedals. But what really set the bike apart was the custom paint job. Speculation had mounted as to what Armstrong would ride for his return, but, as with so many aspects of his racing career, it was the message ("I'm back") that mattered more than the medium (his mount). Project One took thirty-one hours to complete the brushwork, and the result was one of the most memorable bikes of the racing season, with that number 1,274 and the rider's Livestrong brand decorating the Trek frame throughout.

After Armstrong confessed in 2013 to drug abuse throughout his career, he was stripped of all his titles and became a non-person in the cycling world. Yet although his reputation is ruined, that of this great bike remains untarnished. **DB**

" . . . a solid, dependable £1,000 [$1,600] road bike that can turn its hand to everything from commuting to sportives. . ."
road.cc

BOARDMAN Pro Carbon

2009 • Road bike • UK • Signature budget race bike of impressive quality

Olympic gold medalist Chris Boardman is a legend for his scientific approach to the smallest details of bike training, technology, and setup. When he partnered up with UK bike and auto store giant Halfords, it was always unlikely to be the usual signature range deal.

The Pro Carbon, one of the first bikes in the Boardman range, immediately created a buzz. It was one of the cheaper carbon bikes available from a store rather than an Internet retailer, but the frame was obviously a quality piece. At 2½ lb (1.1 kg), the monocoque carbon frame was impressively light by contemporary standards. The tapered headset and super-light matching fork were seen as innovative, and their stiffness added to the stability of a bike already enhanced by handling angles deriving from

Boardman's racing experience. In fact, when a review suggested the Pro Carbon was too stable for racing, Boardman memorably joined an Internet forum to point out that Nicole Cooke won a gold medal at the Beijing Olympics on it, as well as steering a prototype version to world and national championship wins in the same year.

Boardman Bikes was one of the first brands to adopt the new range of SRAM road components launched into a world dominated by Shimano in Japan and Campagnolo in Italy. The lightweight SRAM Force Groupset, combined with Ritchey wheels and finishing equipment, yielded a bike weight of less than 16 lb (7.25 kg), giving a performance above that of many more expensive machines. **GK**

TREK Equinox TTX SSL

2009 • Time trial bike • USA • Lance Armstrong's comeback Tour of California time trial bike

Almost four years after retiring from the sport in 2005, Lance Armstrong made his return to professional cycling in 2009. He opened his season at the Tour Down Under in January before making numerous appearances at events, including the Tour of Flanders and the Amgen Tour of California.

His U.S. re-debut caused the biggest stir. Race organizers in Solvang, California, whipped the local crowd into a frenzy when Armstrong rode to the start house for his first time trial since returning to the sport. It was Stage Six of the race and, despite his time off the bike, Armstrong was looking impressive.

As in all those Tour de France time trials of 1999 to 2006, for the Tour of California Armstrong was on a Trek-badged bike. The Equinox TTX SSL was resplendent in

Livestrong livery, and beneath the slick paint job was a standard medium-sized frame with aero fork blades, Trek's deep-section down tube and horizontal top tube, and SRAM-supplied components. For the Solvang time trial, Armstrong plumped for a HED H3D front wheel and a deep-section Bontrager Aeolus 9.0 wheel at the rear, as well as Bontrager brake levers and bars.

Armstrong finished the 15-mi (24-km) test in a respectable fourteenth place, behind his teammate and eventual race winner Levi Leipheimer. However, his Equinox caught the headlines later in the race when it was stolen from the team. A police investigation was launched immediately, and eventually the bike was handed in to the authorities by an individual who wished to remain anonymous. **DB**

WILIER Mortirolo

2009 • Road bike • Italy • Top-rated,
affordable, carbon fiber road bike

The classy handling of the Wilier Mortirolo helped make
it a top-rated bike. Stout frame tubes gave dependable
precision, which allowed the tires to be taken right to
the edge of their grip without dire consequences. Body
weight was pushed low and planted firmly—a feature
which, when combined with the Italian preference for
longer stems and slacker angles, gave the Mortirolo
an advantage on the fastest descents. Moreover, there
was sufficient taper toward the tips of both ends of the
tubes to give the Wilier a distinctively buoyant ride.

Contributing to the exclusive feel of the Mortirolo
was Campagnolo Veloce componentry. The Italian gears,
with a combination of well-sculpted behind-the-brake
and side-of-hood shift levers, and a characteristically
solid shifting feel, were ideal for a frame which oozed a
class that belied its affordable price tag.

Fulcrum provided the super-smooth-riding Racing
7 wheels for a final stylish touch. The front wheel was
radially laced with twenty stainless J-spokes; the rear
wheel had sixteen three-cross spokes on the drive side
and eight radially laced on the other side.

Luxurious black-, white-, and red-highlighted livery
brought a real pedigree appeal, lifting the Mortirolo
above a host of raw carbon lookalikes. **GK**

COLNAGO Arte

2009 • Road bike • Italy • Sweeping alloy
mainframe with flexi-carbon seatstays

No longer produced, the Colnago Arte was a mid-
range bike, built from 6000-series aluminum alloy, that
offered a chance to enjoy the mystique of a Colnago
machine but without the usual eye-watering price tag.

The Arte was sourced from Giant Bicycles in
Taiwan and Shimano Ultegra SL-equipped, but with
many of Colnago's trademark touches retained. The
straight front fork, an element dating from the 1990s,
was included, along with the famous cloverleaf tubing
cross-section that stood out on Colnago's Master and
Dream frames. Curved seatstays, designed to improve
the comfort and balance of the ride, stood out as
among the most eye-catching features of the bike. The
bike was finished with a chainset by FSA (Full Speed
Ahead), who also provided the seatpost and handlebar.
Wheelsets varied, although the Mavic Aksium Race set
was a popular standard accompaniment.

The Arte stood out because it broke down
an economic barrier, allowing those with tighter
purse strings to enjoy one of the top brands in the
cycling world. Far from a lookalike, the Arte gave an
excellent ride, proving that even Colnago—a brand
that specializes in perfection—can turn its hand to
affordable bikes without losing the master touch. **DB**

NICOLAI UFO-ST

2009 • Downhill bike • Germany • Gravity-powered industrial heavy metal

If bicycles each had a soundtrack, the Nicolai UFO-ST would be accompanied by a raging storm of hardcore German industrial rock. This alpine-descending play bike, designed with adjustable travel allowing up to 8 in. (20.3 cm) of travel front and rear, is tough enough for the most technical descents and drops. Thanks to Nicolai's legendary experience in suspension design, a beefy single-pivot rear triangle tracks the ground to maintain grip and control, while still allowing effective pedaling on flatter sections. Also produced in a shorter-travel "DS" model for dual slalom and dirt riding, the UFO has aggressive geometry that spurs the rider to take every obstacle at full speed.

Nicolai's legendary welding skills—along with CNC-cut gussets and reinforcement, a tie rod to distribute the load of the fully compressed shock, and individually aligned wheel drop-outs for perfect tracking—produced a visually striking demonstration of the ethos "form follows function." When many of its competitors turned to mass-produced East Asian carbon fiber, Nicolai confidently stuck to handmade aluminum by experienced craftsmen at home in Germany. This has won the company a place in the hearts of many riders, and a good few engineers too. **KF**

PUCH E-Bike 8

2009 • Electric bike • Austria • Pedal/Electric hybrid bike

One of Europe's oldest bicycle firms was started by Johann Puch in Austria in the late nineteenth century. At its peak, Puch's bike-building division produced about 16,000 machines a year, but mergers and takeovers led to Puch being more closely associated with mopeds, most famously the Maxi. Now the mopeds have largely disappeared, but Puch has embraced the idea of electric bicycles, which are especially popular in the Netherlands.

The E-Bike 8 is technically an "electric-assistance bicycle." If the battery dies during a journey, the pedals can drive the back wheel via a chain in the normal way. Weighing more than 49 lb (22 kg), the E-Bike is not for sprinting, but it is a comfortable and stable ride. The power is supplied when the bike's system detects that pedaling is becoming labored. The power is delivered automatically, although the rider can select a low, medium, or high level of assistance.

The bike has a 250-watt Panasonic motor system powered by a rechargeable battery, while the three-speed automatic internal hub gears and lights work off the dynamo. A meter mounted on the handlebar tells the rider how much battery power remains. The normal range before recharging is about 43 mi (70 km). **SH**

NICOLAI Tandem

2009 • Mountain bike tandem • Germany • Double the trouble from the heavy metal bike brand

A Nicolai custom-built tandem costs more than $5,600 (£3,436) for the frame alone, but anyone who has ridden a tandem off-road would understand why people invest in the very best equipment. Only a select few brands have ever made successful mountain bike tandems because of the overwhelming amount of time and resources required to perfect such a niche product. Nicolai's knowledge of advanced metal manipulation was necessary in every one of its huge fishscale welds and machine-cut keystone sections. Long-term durability is assured though the use of the finest-quality materials. Nicolai, with its signature industrial approach, is unashamedly proud of its

"With aluminum we are still able to perfectly tailor the frame to the body of the rider."

Karl Heinz, Nicolai

underlying engineering principles and the fanatical approach that has won it ultra-loyal fans across the world.

Every Nicolai frame is hand built to the highest specification by highly skilled fabricators and welders. To secure the perfect fit and ride experience for both riders, every Nicolai tandem is a totally individual, custom-built special order. Individual specifications are taken for wheel size, full suspension or rigid rear ends, dropper seatpost compatibility, tapered head tube, and screw-through axle options, as well as custom geometry and the lengths of tubes throughout. It is only the choice of anodizing color that is restricted, and that is simply because the tandem frame is too big to fit into anything but the black or bronze anodizing tanks. **KF**

MERIDA Ninety-Six Carbon Team-D

2009 • Mountain bike • Taiwan • Ultra-lightweight mountain bike with a race pedigree

For years, Taiwanese bike-manufacturing superpower Merida has backed a high-profile and highly successful cross-country race team, providing state-of-the-art mounts. Many of its most exciting production bikes are directly derived from its race models, and that was certainly the case with the ultra-light, super-focused Ninety-Six Carbon Team-D.

Weighing in at 3 lb 14 oz (1.7 kg), for frame and shock the Merida is still one of the lightest full-suspension mountain bike chassis ever made. Double-chamber main tubes were sleeve jointed and wrapped into the oversized bottom bracket for stiffness, with a nano-particle bonding resin providing strength and titanium bolts ensuring minimum weight.

Merida did not cut any corners in suspension control either. While many race-bike makers use the smallest, shortest shock-absorber possible to save a few grams, the Ninety-Six has a full-sized DT Swiss shock. This gives a very low 2:1 actuation ratio and, combined with a much more "open" damping tune than most race shocks, delivers a very controlled, high-traction ride. With grip and rock impacts ably handled by the suspension, team riders are able to run faster-rolling, semi-slick tires of ultra-lightweight construction without worrying unduly about slipping and puncturing. As a result, the Merida became one of the first full-suspension bikes to be widely used by top-ten World Cup riders, who previously would have favored the brutal ride of an ultra-light fully rigid rear frame with its attendant zero power loss.

Team involvement in development gave the Ninety-Six a particularly focused and sometimes frightening handling character, though, something not helped by the long stem, narrow bar, and super-light Manitou R7 fork that was fitted as standard. **GK**

You'd be smiling on Merida's ultra-light Ninety-Six Carbon too. ▶

VAN NICHOLAS Euros

2009 • Road bike • Netherlands • Affordable titanium all-rounder

Van Nicholas (VN) was formed when the Dutch distributor of Airborne bikes bought the company and renamed it after himself. He also renamed the models, but kept the focus on economically priced, titanium-framed bikes.

The Euros wasn't the cheapest item in the VN catalog—that honor went to the Mistral—but, for the extra money, buyers got rear seatstays that were subtly curved for a compliant ride, rather than the simple straight stays that were fitted on the entry model.

The Euros was an immediate success: it was favorably reviewed, and soon became established as a top-value titanium bike that could comfortably compete with the growing number of affordable carbon fiber machines.

While the Mistral was available in only one specification, in order to ensure the best bulk discounts on parts, the Euros could be ordered with a range of different componentry via an online bicycle configurator. While such a facility is commonplace now, it was relatively rare in 2009, and helped to make the Euros popular all over the world.

Van Nicholas has since simplified its range by combining the straight stays of the Mistral with the curved seatstays and engraved headbadge of the Euros to create the Ventus. This is available as a fixed bargain build—the Ventus SE (Special Edition)—or as a Ventus frame with a variety of build options. In either form, it is an extremely impressive ride for an economical price. **GK**

VAN NICHOLAS Astraeus

2009 • Road bike • Netherlands • State-of-the-art titanium road bike direct from the Dutch master

Van Nicholas has long helped riders afford top-quality titanium bikes that normally would be far beyond their reach. By selling direct from Holland, not through traditional shops, and by concentrating only on titanium frames, it has cut costs to the minimum and passed those savings on to customers.

When the Astraeus frame was introduced in 2009, "hydro-formed" tubes (shaped by hydraulic oil under high pressure) were common in alloy frames but rare in titanium bikes because there the process was much more difficult. Hydro-forming gave the Astraeus an immediate edge because the tubing was perfectly tuned for the stresses and strains going through it in each part of the frame. By 2013, computerized Finite Element Analysis programs were used to refine the

frame further, resulting in larger-diameter main tubes and a tapered head tube for the latest generation of fork steerers. Van Nicholas' own super-light, smooth-riding VNT SLR fork is fitted as standard. A press-fit—rather than screw-in—bottom bracket and 3D drop-outs with tubular terminals beef up the power-transfer performance of the bike too. The frame is compatible with both mechanical and electronically triggered shifters and mechs.

Van Nicholas sells a frame and fork package in six sizes for $2,699 (£2,195). A comprehensive custom function on its website allows buyers to choose almost every component they want to create a perfect ride. Price is kept competitive with generic alloy or lower-grade carbon frames from big-name brands. **GK**

GENESIS Croix de fer

2010 • Road bike • UK • Steel disc-equipped all-rounder and round-the-world bike

Carbon frame bikes might dominate the technological spotlight, but rugged, versatile machines that combine many different bike elements are becoming increasingly popular with riders who are more interested in exploration and adventure than outright performance. The Croix de fer is a great example of this type of sports utility bike, and it has some impressive achievements under its steel belt to underline its versatility.

While some carbon fiber race frames might be only one-third of the weight of this chassis, the Croix's slim steel tubes give an extremely smooth and sure-footed ride that comes into its own when the tarmac runs out and the adventure begins.

Bike explorers in remote lands have long favored steel frames because they can be repaired with traditional brazing or welding technology. This made the Croix a wise choice for Vin Cox as he took on the rough tracks of South America and Africa to set an 18,000-mi (29,000-km) round-the-world record in 2010. The Croix de fer was also used in 2011 by the Montane Icemen (Pete Sissons and Paul Cosgrove), who set a record for circumnavigating the relentlessly rugged 1,600-mi (2,500-km) coast of Iceland.

It's a tribute to the design that the Croix de fer is equally at home zipping through city streets and exploring local lanes and bike paths. In both areas, the larger-than-normal cyclocross tires and smooth steel frame help cushion rough dirt tracks. Mountain bike-style disc brakes mean wet surfaces won't affect your ability to stop safely either. **GK**

FORME Vitesse

2010 • Road bike • UK • Practical "bike to work" scheme racer

With cycling going through a boom period in the UK in recent years, thanks to the high-profile success of riders such as Mark Cavendish and Bradley Wiggins in the Tour de France and the Olympic Games, it's been an extremely fertile period of growth for new brands. Many of these brands are being created by established companies that normally import bicycle components from overseas but want to add a bike line to their range. Forme is one such new name; it is the associated brand of UK parts importer Moore Large.

The Vitesse has further benefited from the enthusiastic public response to a government-backed "bike to work" scheme to ease urban traffic congestion by encouraging commuters out of four wheels and onto two. Companies may receive up to 40 percent off the purchase price of bikes for their staff, who effectively lease the machines from their employers as they pay for them by installments. The bikes have to cost less than $1,600 (£1,000), a limit that has focused the minds of bargain-bike producers on the true upper price limit of their market.

After some adverse criticisms of its first Vitesse bike, Forme devoted considerable attention to sorting out the details on the 2010 model. The frame—built by Taiwanese aluminum specialist Kinesis—was stiffened and reinforced around the cranks, making the bike considerably easier than its predecessor to ride uphill. The frame and fork were also upgraded with mudguard fitting mounts to keep riders clean in the rain, which regular British riders inevitably have to cope with. **GK**

INSPIRED Skye

2010 • Street trials bike • UK • Danny MacAskill signature bike

April 2009, the work of BMX enthusiast Dave Sowerby, is a film lasting 5 minutes, 38 seconds that shows bike mechanic Danny MacAskill performing street bike stunts in Edinburgh. Posted on YouTube in 2009, the video caused a sensation: It has since been viewed more than 34 million times.

MacAskill, a young man from Dunvegan on the Scottish Isle of Skye, can be seen doing things never seen before on a bike. In one particularly memorable scene, he rides along the top of spiked railings.

Once established as an online celebrity, MacAskill starred in a Volkswagen TV commercial, worked as a stunt rider in Hollywood, and was nominated for the Action Sportsman of the Year Award.

Sowerby then shot a follow-up video, *Way Back Home*, which followed MacAskill as he performed even more hair-raising stunts on a ride from Edinburgh back to Skye. At the time of publication of this book, that 7-minute, 43-second clip had had over 29 million views.

With so many fans and such an exciting reputation, it was only a matter of time before Danny MacAskill developed a signature bike. And it was no surprise when it was a highly specialized street trials bike.

The Skye from Inspired is based on a super-strong frame. The geometry is completely geared to stunts, so it's a heavy bike, weighing 26½ lb (11.95 kg), but strong enough to cope with the biggest jumps. There are bolt-through axles for stiffness and security, and the drivetrain components are tucked on the wheel side of the chainstay to protect them from the inevitable stunt bangs.

MacAskill is now one the best-known riders in the world, and rides for the Red Bull and Inspired Bicycles teams. His videos demonstrate some of the best stunt techniques ever seen. **SH**

KONA Lacondeguy Inc

2010 • Slopestyle bike • USA • Signature slopestyle bike for crazy Spaniard

Andreu Lacondeguy signed for Kona in 2007 at the age of seventeen, and proceeded to take the slopestyle world by storm. In the same year's edition of the 26TRIX slopestyle contest in Leogang, Austria, Lacondeguy became only the third person in history to land a double backflip in competition.

In 2008, he took gold at Crankworx Whistler in Vancouver, British Columbia. This was the highest accolade in the sport at the time. In the following year, he and his brother Lluis appeared in the tenth film in the *New World Disorder* series, shortly after signing a fresh two-year deal with Kona. In 2010 came the long-awaited Lacondeguy Inc signature dirt jump frame.

> *"I really wanted a bike that was clean and simple . . . specifically for really aggressive tricks."*
> Andreu Lacondeguy

Lacondeguy was pushing the limits in slopestyle, so he had the designers choose an air-hardened Reynolds 835 chromoly steel tubeset to give the bike the feel of steel. The bike is low-slung, and its outsized extra-stiff tubing gives it an aggressive look. The rear is short at 15⁷⁄₁₀ in. (39.9 cm), giving the rider control when pinning or flipping the bike. Lacondeguy is only 5 ft 3 in. (1.6 m) tall, so the steeply sloping top tube and low seat tube give him freedom of movement in the air, key for the more technical tricks. Coming in an all-black paint finish with understated branding, the Lacondeguy Inc personified the man himself, who favored black clothes and black tattoos. The Lacondeguy Inc was sold as a frameset for only one year, as Lacondeguy moved onto Mondraker later in 2010. **CJ**

GIANT Glory

2010 • Downhill bike • USA • Danny Hart World Championship-winning bike

In 2010, Giant redesigned the Glory from the ground up. The previous bike was a privateer racer's favorite—strong, powerful, and cheap. The new Glory held fast to these core principles, while at the same time evolving, losing weight, and refining its chassis. And it really does come prepared for anything: It's one of the best bikes to buy in the morning and race in the afternoon.

The frame used Giant's own ALUXX SL aluminum tubesets for incredible stiffness when battling the roughest downhill tracks. It also featured a new version of the Maestro Suspension system, giving 8 in. (20.3 cm) of predictable rear travel for easy shock-tuning. Added for the benefit of Giant's downhill World Cup race team was the OverDrive steerer tube, which, Giant says, provides "supreme front-end stiffness and control."

In 2011, team rider Danny Hart won the World Championship in Champéry, Switzerland, in a race run that will go down in history as one of the great downhill displays of all time. In torrential alpine rain, on the steepest racetrack of the series, Hart won by 11.69 seconds—a time gap almost unheard of in a sport where milliseconds usually separate the top five. Hart's Giant Glory was an only slightly tweaked "Danny" version of the standard large-sized chassis. It featured slightly slacker, slower steering, and had a lower bottom bracket height, but was otherwise totally stock. His suspension also came from the revered SRAM BlackBox race program and was custom tuned for Danny's style, but, those modifications apart, he genuinely won on the Giant Glory that you can pick up in your local bike shop. **CJ**

CANYON Nerve AL

2010 • Mountain bike • Germany • Phenomenal-value all-round mountain bike

When it comes to the amount of pedaling per head of population, few countries can rival Germany, which is one of the biggest and most important bike markets in the world. This makes competition between brands extremely fierce: Pricing in Germany is much more aggressive than in the rest of Europe and elsewhere. German bike magazines are known for their fastidious, technically based reviews, which often feature the results of stress and stiffness tests carried out in the renowned EFBe laboratory near Dortmund.

This all creates a high-pressure but effective environment for forging some of the world's best-performing, best-value bikes. Canyon bikes are prime examples. The company first became established globally through direct sales of bikes that cost

significantly less than other brands. But the keen pricing was not achieved by downgrading the product; on the contrary, bikes like the Nerve AL are some of the best-quality frames around.

The Nerve AL's Hydro 14 frameset is a showcase of subtle, hydraulically shaped tubing that delivers a stiff structure with internal cable routing, and a hard, anodized surface treatment rather than paint to preserve its good looks and save weight. Radial pivot bearings give very smooth and long-lasting movement of the suspension, while the handling is balanced to give an enthusiastically versatile overall character that's as happy traversing the Alps as circuit racing. The original Nerve AL was later joined by the Nerve AL+, the carbon fiber Nerve CF, and the big-wheeled Nerve AL 29. **GK**

CHARGE Duster

2010 • Mountain bike • UK • Steel-frame cross-country range

Based in Somerset, England, Charge formed in 2006 under the technical guidance of industrial designer (and former teenage Young Inventor of the Year) Nick Larsen. After first producing well-regarded mountain bikes, Charge helped fuel the hipster bike boom by making single-speed jobs that were popular with city couriers. Reaping the benefit of being in at the start of the "fixie" boom, Charge soon expanded into road bikes and titanium frames.

The popularity of the Charge Duster showed, perhaps surprisingly, that in the first decade of the twenty-first century there was still a market for an old-style mountain bike. Appearing in a variety of complete bike guises, the lightweight steel-framed Duster gives a solid ride that's certainly comfortable enough to deal with the daily grind to and from the office. But one of Larsen's stated aims is to bring mountain biking to the general public, and it would be a great shame if—as is the fate of so many similar bikes—commuting was the only hard graft you had in mind for your Duster. When you get it off-road and down and dirty, the bike really begins to shine. Kitted out with a fine RockShox fork and Avid brakes, the springy Duster is tailor made for a flat-out cross-country blast. **TB**

NUKEPROOF Scalp

2010 • Downhill bike • UK • The bike that brought Aussie racer Sam Hill back to the podium

Created by celebrated British designer Brant Richards, the Nukeproof Scalp features a single-pivot, Fallout Linkage suspension system that uses dog-bone links to give the bike a multi-stage travel progression over more than 8 in. (20.3 cm).

The main chassis is built from 6061 T6 aluminum with Nukeproof's double smooth welds; the head angle is 63 degrees, and the wheelbase a little more than 47 in. (119 cm).

The Scalp was built to be raced, and in 2013 Nukeproof signed double overall World Cup champion Sam Hill to its World Cup team. Before the 2013 World Cup season even kicked off, Hill had won all three of the Australian national rounds, setting the stage for his return to glory. He raced on the Pulse, Nukeproof's top-end version of the Scalp, developed over two years using feedback from the race team. The frames of both bikes are almost identical, featuring interchangeable drop-outs to adjust chainstay length, and teardrop twin links to increase stability throughout the suspension travel. Sam Hill took the Pulse to the third step of the podium at the 2013 World Cup round in Andorra after qualifying first the day before, his first top-three World Cup finish since 2010. **CJ**

LYNSKEY Pro 29

2010 • Mountain bike • USA • Titanium 29er with unique helix tubes

According to Mark Lynskey, the signature twisted-helix tubes of Lynskey's Pro 29 frame were created by chance: "We were shaping some square-section tubing, and we just decided to twist it gradually as it came out of the machine. The twisted tube looked really cool, but it took us ages to use this twisted piece as a down tube. The results were really surprising too, until we thought about what the twist was actually doing. It basically creates a very stiff square-section tube where the specific performance of each part of the pipe can be tailored by where the twist is. This enables us to create a distinctively stiff but smooth riding frame that's unlike any of our round-tubed bikes."

The helix tube was particularly useful when Lynskey set out to design an accurate and aggressive-riding race frame based on the popular 29 model. It stiffened both top and down tubes to counteract the extra leverage of the larger wheels and longer fork. Skinny rear stays and cantilevered, adjustable wheel-holding sections meant the super-smooth ride feel of titanium was still very much in evidence. The unique tubing also looks amazing—particularly in the high-polish versions—and the full custom-sizing options make the Pro 29 a true superbike. **GK**

WATTBIKE Pro

2010 • Training bike • UK • The ultimate stationary training bike

Since the Millennium, the Great Britain track cycling team has won multiple Olympic and World Championship titles. One of the key components in the success of riders such as Chris Hoy, Victoria Pendleton, Sarah Storey, Laura Trott, and Jason Kenny is this stationary trainer, developed by Wattbike in conjunction with British Cycling, the UK governing body.

Stationary trainers, for use when weather prevents outdoor riding, are nothing new. While many are simple machines relying on mechanical resistance, the most advanced units have evolved into high-tech, computer-linked, power- and pulse-measuring devices.

The Wattbike combines the convenience of an exercise bike with the most advanced ride simulation, training feedback sensors, and software. Monitoring thirty-nine key performance measures up to 100 times a second, the Wattbike can immediately give full variations of speed, power, pace, pulse, and pedaling speed (cadence). It also measures the power developed by each leg to help users refine their pedaling style, show inconsistencies in strength between legs, and find their ideal pedaling rate. It'll even generate a specific training plan based on preset tests, making it the ultimate indoor training machine. **GK**

PINARELLO Dogma

2010 • Road bike • Italy • Italian finesse meets British brawn

In December 2009, Team Sky held a press conference to unveil its new team leader. As predicted, the rider chosen by manager Dave Brailsford was Bradley Wiggins, who had finished fourth in that year's Tour de France while riding for the Garmin-Slipstream team.

Pinarello had already been announced as Sky's official bike supplier for the team's debut season, but this was the first time man and machine were pictured together. Wiggins, dressed smartly in a suit, posed with the bike that Britain hoped would carry him to success in the 2010 Tour.

Pinarello—owned by the Treviso, Italy-based family that had built bikes for the likes of Miguel Indurain and Jan Ullrich—believed that it had really raised the bar in terms of design with the Dogma. The bike's revolutionary, asymmetric layout was calculated to improve both the overall balance and the control from the uniquely profiled fork to the variable section and size of the rear stays.

The rounded diamond shape—which used ultra-high-quality 60HM1K Torayca carbon fiber—certainly looked sleek, and was rounded off with Shimano's top-of-the-range Di2 electronic components. The Dogma's curved "lady legs" front fork, an eye-catching feature of Pinarello's entire series, also featured, with the frame weighing in at 2 lb 1½ oz (0.9 kg).

Prologo provided the saddles; Deda supplied bars and stem. Italian finesse and British brawn took two years to reach their ultimate goal, but in 2012 Wiggins finally became the first Briton to win the Tour de France. In an interesting example of Wiggo's renowned unorthodoxy, it was only on the final stage of the Tour that he first used the Sky Team's preferred Shimano 11-speed groupset, having previously raced with his own favored 10-speed set-up. **DB**

FLEET VELO Joust

2010 • Polo bike • USA • Custom-built mountain-bike-wheeled polo bike

The Joust did away with everything that polo cyclists had come to hate in traditional polo bicycles. Annoying things like toe overlap, wheel flop, polo mallet jam, ridiculous turning circles—all the flaws that had riders worrying more about coming off than the finer points of their unconventional but increasingly popular sport.

The Joust had 26-in. (66-cm) wheels for a tighter wheelbase, a performance fork, reinforced head tube, a raised bottom bracket to eliminate pedal contact with the ground on sharp turns, 4¾-in. (12-cm) rear spacing to align with available track hubs, V-brake mounts for sharper braking, and minimal toe overlap on its redesigned pedals. This made the Joust an extremely

"Bike polo is not newfangled. It was . . . an exhibition sport in the 1908 London Olympics."

Matthew Miller, columnist

popular bike among polo riders, but Fleet Velo didn't stop the evolution of its bikes there.

The Joust Wide followed and, as its name suggests, it uses a wider 5³⁄₁₀-in. (13.5-cm) rear hub spacing, and a wider 2⁹⁄₁₀-in. (7.3-cm) bottom bracket shell, in order to sync with the wider mountain bike hubs.

The Wide also lets riders use MTB equipment on the new frame. Fleet Velo upgraded the tubing to super-light True Temper OX platinum with multiple wall thicknesses. The rear drop-outs were lengthened to permit sufficient wheel movement for either polo-sized rear cogs or smaller street cogs to be used without changing the length of the chain. Custom geometry and S & S Couplings facilitate easy transport, and make the Joust truly the ultimate polo steed. **BS**

IMPERIAL Custom 4-Stroke

2010 • Motorized bike • USA • In the world of Imperial Cycles, everything old is new again

Custom motorized bicycle manufacturers have been with us ever since a single-cylinder commercial steam engine was attached to a Pierre Michaux iron-framed pedal bike in 1867. It is only when you see motorized bikes such as this Imperial, by Eric Soriano, that you realize just how far the concept has come—not so much in terms of the mechanics, but in the design.

The Custom 4-Stroke has pin-striped, all-black, outsized Schwalbe tires, and a chrome bullet headlight. It is powered by a 50-cc motor with 4G belt-drive transmission using a direct-drive, forty-tooth sprocket. Its chopped and lowered chrome springer front end imparts an aggressive, crouching stance. The

". . . things in my head I want out so was just doodling and came up with a new design."

Eric Soriano

wonderfully retro gas tank and shortened handlebars recall the café racers of the 1960s, bikes designed to get you quickly, noisily, and none too comfortably from one cup of coffee to the next. This bike is a fitting homage to that genre.

Imperial excels in reinvigorating fads of yesteryear. Some of its other creations are inspired by the board track racers, which, in the 1920s, competed on oval tracks with inclined surfaces made from wooden boards.

Imperial's motorized bike frames are vintage Schwinn, its fuel tanks bare metal, and its seats leather-sprung Brooks. Some of the frames are co-designed with Shorty Fatz, the design and art studio of Samuel Rodriguez. There is much to be said for motorized bikes, but don't buy one if you love pedaling. **BS**

MOREWOOD Sukuma

2010 • Mountain bike • South Africa • All-mountain trail tamer

While Patrick Morewood has left his self-named brand to set up Pyga Industries, Morewood Bikes is still turning out new designs, the most recent of which at the time of publication was the Sukuma.

This 6-in. (15-cm) wheel-travel all-rounder was first shown as a bike show concept chassis in 2011 (the prototype was created in 2010), but it took two further years of development to raise it to a level that satisfied the South African designers.

The hydro-formed alloy front end certainly ticks all the dropper-post remote-control cable and chainguide mount boxes. The handling angles are perfect for taking the trail by the scruff of the neck too, with the distinctive crooked seatpost allowing a short, fast-reacting rear end. The Sukuma also gets carbon fiber seatstays to reduce weight, while a Syntace X-12 rear axle screws directly into the frame for maximum stiffness and wheel security.

The rear of the bike features the Dave Weagle-designed split-pivot suspension system that is also used by Devinci of Canada and Beistegui Hermanos (BH) of Spain, and which is similar to Trek's ABP setup. It uses a seatstay-to-chainstay pivot that is concentric with the rear axle, effectively removing the influence of brake torque from the suspension. However, this system is sensitive to the chainring that's being used, and some professional reviewers reported a weird out-of-sync bobbing sensation when pedaling a Sukuma with a triple chainset. Using the bike with the sort of double chainset for which it's designed produces much better results, and the complete weight—28 lb (12.7 kg), which is relatively light for a bike with a mixed SRAM stem and Fox forks—also helps on the hills.

Sukuma is a Zulu word meaning "arise." However, there's no doubt that this bike's real talents are best showcased when you let it go with the gravity flow. **GK**

Its "Morewood by name, more fun by nature" with the Sukuma. ▶

PASHLEY Princess

2010 • Road bike • UK • Elegant ladies' roadster

Some of Pashley's most popular twenty-first century bikes are the two retro Princess roadsters, which are based on designs that predate the Second World War. Both the Princess Classic and the more luxurious and expensive Princess Sovereign are traditionally styled ladies' touring bicycles.

The Princesses are based around an elegant frame with a "loop" top tube and relaxed geometry. They are bikes for pottering to the shops, going on a picnic, or cruising quiet rural lanes.

They are sturdy too, with a lugged tubular steel construction, including a hand-brazed set of tubular crown forks. The frame comes in three sizes.

The gears are from Sturmey Archer. There are five of them on the Sovereign, and three on the Classic. Brakes are fully enclosed hub units, again from Sturmey Archer, and the 26-in. (66-cm) wheels have polished rims. The saddle is a classic too—a well-sprung, antique-brown leather Brooks B66.

All-weather protection involves chunky enameled mudguards front and rear, a full chain cover, and even a retro-style skirt guard on the back wheel. Other traditional features include a deep wicker basket sitting on its own mounted metal carrier at the front, and a proper "ding-dong" bell mounted on the chrome-plated raised handlebars.

The Pashley Sovereign offers even more standard extras, including a built-in rear-wheel lock that secures the bike at the push of a lever, a dynamo-powered front and rear lighting system, and an additional tubular load-carrying shelf at the rear. The tires are Schwalbe puncture-resistant Marathon Plus rubber with reflective sidewalls.

The two Princesses are available in suitably regal Buckingham Black or Regency Green color schemes—the finish crowns the work. **SH**

"The quintessential English town and country bicycle with timeless traditional looks and impeccable build quality."

Pashley sales material

TREK Remedy 9.9

2010 • Mountain bike • USA • A thoroughbred carbon flagship

Trek's Remedy long-travel trail bike had been around in alloy format since 2007, but it was this 9.9 that finally established the marque as an all-time classic.

The big difference between the 9.9 and previous mountain bikes was its incorporation of Optimized Compaction Low Void (OCLV) carbon. By using extremely high molding pressures and careful carbon fiber sheet arrangement, the finished frame walls could be densely packed for maximum strength. The high pressure also expelled from the lay up any voids and gaps that would have weakened the structure.

OCLV carbon had previously proved its resilience in Trek's road bikes and lightweight race mountain bikes. However, the company realized that a full mountain bike would have to be even tougher than its previous

offerings, so the parts of the 9.9 that were likely to be hit by flying rocks were strengthened with rubber armor, and alloy was retained for the rear end tubes to reduce the risk of chain slap damage.

At 25 lb 15 oz (11.75 kg), the resulting frame was heavy for a carbon bike, but its strength and ability to shrug off everyday abuse more than compensated for the extra ounces. Trek confirmed the bike's resilience in exhaustive tests by firing 5-oz (150-g) stones at it at 23 mph (38 kph).

The combination of a Fox TALAS travel-adjustable fork and Trek's unique Fox-developed DRCV shock at the rear gave a balanced ride on the most technical trails, and pulled off the difficult trick of dealing with major jolts and minor bumps with equal aplomb. **GK**

CUBE Aerium HPC Pro

2010 • Multisports bike • Netherlands • Steel disc-equipped all-rounder and round-the-world bike

Encompassing short-draft legal races, longer solo races, flat speed courses, and hilly events, triathlon is such a diverse form of cycling that it can be difficult for riders to find a bike that fulfills all the sport's requirements.

While many manufacturers had addressed this problem, Cube was the first to produce a multisport bike in a budget format.

At first glance, the Aerium HPC Pro was just a ready-built version of the conventional road bike with added clip-on tri bars. More detailed inspection, however, revealed that Cube had purpose-designed every part of the frame. The 75.5-degree teardrop-section seat tube and matching seatpost split the difference between the conventional 73–74 degree seat angle and the steeper 77–80 degrees found on dedicated

triathlon bikes. The aero profile with internal cable routing was stable enough to ride confidently in a turbulence-reducing tucked position, but it was not so slow that steering became a liability on short, twisty courses or in training packs.

Cube's decision to retain on the Aerium a conventional handlebar with integrated gear and brake levers, rather than mount the gear shifters separately on the tips of the tri bars, enabled riders to change gear easily when climbing or accelerating.

The clip-ons that could be unbolted to make the bike legal for group races completed a truly versatile machine that, when matched with a high-value componentry spec, became an overnight success that other major brands have since copied. **GK**

FIETSER WAW

2010 • HPV • Belgium • Super-aero enclosed velomobile

The Fietser WAW is a velomobile—a fully enclosed human-powered vehicle. Like Charles Mochet's pedal cars and velocars of the 1930s, the Fietser is designed to be driven in everyday motorized traffic. It is as aerodynamic as a bullet, its carbon fiber frame and tough, Kevlar fiber supports combining to provide its occupant with both shelter from the elements and protection in a road smash. It was developed by Dries Callebaut from an idea of Frederik van de Walle.

The materials used in the construction of the WAW make it one of the lightest vehicles of its kind. There are three versions—the Ultralight at 53 lb (24 kg), a commuter vehicle weighing 62 lb (28 kg), and a hybrid bio-electric at 73 lb (33 kg)—all of which have very compact turning circles. Each model is 9 ft. 2 in. (2.8 m) long and 29½ in. (75 cm) wide.

The extended nose section and the tail are detachable for repairs and maintenance, and also serve as crumple zones. The overall roof canopy is removable, and can be stored when not required in the front or rear trunk of the WAW. There are two tiny rearview mirrors to compensate for the lack of space that prevents the driver from turning his or her head. The visor is adjustable to help prevent fogging and maintain visibility in the rain.

Although the WAW is much heavier than a conventional bike, Fietser claims that the velomobile, with its far-superior aerodynamics, uses only 0.5 kWh per 62½ mi (100 km) traveled at a constant speed of 31 mph (50 kph). This is less than 20 percent of the energy required to propel an upright bicycle. The WAW is as fast as an automobile in congested urban conditions and, of course, it is vastly more environmentally friendly than any such fossil-fueled machine. **BS**

DELTA 7 Arantix

2010 • Mountain bike • USA • Pioneering twisted carbon fiber spiderweb frame

The open latticework frame of this machine makes it one of the most eye-catching bikes available.

Both the Delta 7 Arantix mountain bike and the Ascend road bike use pioneering technology to produce maximum strength with minimum weight—just 2 lb 11 oz (1.24 kg) and 2 lb 5 oz (1.05 kg), respectively.

The frame looks like some sort of child's building toy, but it's more clever than that. The patented Iso Truss tubes are formed by heat-curing a series of intersecting triangles of twisted carbon fiber and synthetic Kevlar.

The efficient strength-to-weight framework design originated from scientists at Brigham Young University in Provo, Utah. It is claimed that Iso Truss is twelve times

> *"If you see a Delta 7 Arantix Ascend once, you'll remember it for life."*
>
> Road Bike Action Magazine

stronger than steel, while weighing ten times less. The technology, developed for NASA, was licensed to Delta.

Riders report that the tubes remain more rigid under strain, survive bigger crashes, and are even more responsive than their solid metal equivalents.

The downside for mountain bikers is that the tubes can get clogged with mud. Delta provides "lizard skin" neoprene tube covers to help avoid this, but these add to the weight and detract from the appearance.

All this cutting-edge technology is expensive: a Delta 7 frame costs around $5,000 (£3,100), while a complete bike loaded with top-quality peripherals will be around $10,000 (£6,200). But it's so eye-catching that *Road Bike Action* magazine advised owners to "prepare a short speech," such is the attention that it will attract. **SH**

Delta 7's radical tubing is clear to see and clear to see through. ▶

PINARELLO Graal

2010 • Road bike • Italy • Bradley Wiggins' original Team Sky time trial bike

Bradley Wiggins first teamed up with the Graal in 2010 during his first season at Team Sky. That year Wiggins didn't really meet expectations at the Tour de France, and when he crashed out of the race a year later it briefly looked as though his fourth place in the 2009 edition of the race would be as good as it got.

However, in 2012 Wiggins couldn't put a foot wrong, winning time trial after time trial, and stage race after stage race. It culminated in a Tour de France victory where Wiggins was competitive in the mountains and unstoppable in the long individual time trials.

The Graal was used by several other riders within the peloton at the time—Pinarello also supplied the Movistar team in 2012—but Sky made a number of alterations to the bike to suit Wiggins' needs.

First, the team used its track technology to provide a custom-made one-piece stem-and-bars ensemble. Wiggins also plumped for mechanical shifting and his trusted Osymetric chainrings. Although these had created a few mechanical problems for him in the past, they were reliable through the Tour de France. The frame itself was full carbon, with asymmetric layers of 60HM1K carbon fiber complete with external ribbing on the down tube to micromanage airflow and reduce overall turbulence.

Although the Graal was officially replaced in Wiggins' arsenal by the new Bolide aero bike at the 2013 Giro d'Italia, Wiggins famously jumped back onto his favored Pinarello machine halfway through a stage on his ultimately unsuccessful campaign. **DB**

KUOTA Kueen-K

2010 • Triathlon bike • Italy • Carbon fiber time trial bike

Italy has always been in the vanguard of bicycle design. It's not just established brands such as Bianchi, Colnago, Pinarello, and Wilier that lead the way, but also relative newcomers, such as Cipollini and Kuota. Kuota hasn't been shy about trading on its technology or the sponsorship of top teams and riders to give it wider recognition on the race circuit.

Its flagship Kueen-K triathlon bike is named after the Queen Ka'ahumanu Highway that forms a major part of the traditional Ironman World Championship route on Big Island, Hawaii. The machine uses the full range of Kuota composite materials know-how, which includes the use of nanotechnology resins. Here the bonding glue used to consolidate and join the carbon fibers—first into sheets, and then into the

complete structure—is infused with microscopic carbon fiber tubes to act as a super-lightweight filler, reducing overall weight and increasing stiffness within the bonding agent itself. The aerodynamically profiled tubes of the Kueen-K are also tapered to concentrate strength around high-stress areas, while minimizing weight where stress isn't so high. Kuota increased the mechanical advantage of the frame by using an oversized crank-bearing area, and a fork with a larger-diameter lower-steering bearing. To minimize aerodynamic drag, the tube forms follow the rear wheel, the brakes are hidden behind the forks, the saddle is fixed directly to the frame, and the gear cables are routed inside the tubes. This bike is every bit as ready for the Queen K Highway as its name suggests. **GK**

SANTANA Exogrid

2010 • Tandem • USA • The ultimate titanium and carbon tandem

Tandems inspire a fanatical riding passion among their fans that exceeds the enthusiasm of even the most evangelical solo riders. And for the vast majority of performance-tandem fans, only one tandem builder can deliver the ultimate ride. Santana, founded in California in 1976, has only ever made tandems (along with "triplets," "quads," "quints," and even six-seater "hexes"). The vast majority of Santana bikes are beautifully made in oversized aluminum or steel tubing, depending on the purpose of the bike and the depth of the buyers' pockets. Some fortunate teams might be able to afford the smooth, lightweight strength of a titanium-frame tandem, but the ultimate upgrade is the Exogrid titanium tubeset.

This elaborate building technique, first introduced in a collaboration between bike company Titus and composite specialists Maxm, involves a super-thin titanium outer "exoskeleton" sleeve over an inner carbon fiber tube. The titanium sleeve is machined away in a lattice design in the center portion of the tube, effectively making it into a continuous lug for a seamless joint and deliberately engineered flex for comfort. Santana equips its team tandems with custom carbon cranks, bars, and front fork to minimize the extra weight added by a second rider. The result is a two-seat speed machine that weighs barely more than a top-quality solo, but with twice the power and not much more aerodynamic drag. A map-shrinking, single-rider-crushing cruising speed is the default performance setting of this stunning machine.

The fact that the carbon visible through the titanium lattice produces a totally unique, ultra-high-tech look does not hurt the appeal of this ultimate tandem either, but at $11,395 (£7,600) for the chassis alone, you would expect something special. **GK**

ISLABIKES Creig 26

2010 • Kids' bike • USA • Cutting-edge mountain bike downsized for junior riders

As Islabikes has flourished, founder and lead designer Isla Rowntree has been able to expand into more specific areas of bike making without diluting her passion for giving children the best possible performance. As a top mountain bike racer and multiple national champion, Rowntree is particularly focused on making off-road and trail riding as easy and as much fun as possible for junior riders.

Designed for riders of eight years and older, Creig bikes receive more attention to detail than most adult machines. The aluminum alloy frames are very light and designed to give plenty of standing clearance and maneuverability on tight trails. The short-travel

> *"I . . . occasionally still race and I've never run out of gears on proper off-road trails."*
>
> Isla Rowntree, Islabikes founder

suspension forks are custom tuned with new damping circuits for the relatively light body weights of riders who may not have even reached high school age. The forks are a far cry from the clanking, barely mobile compromise forks featured on most lookalike children's bikes, and they give the Creig genuine confidence-boosting control on rough off-road trails.

Creig componentry suites also include many cutting-edge trends that most major manufacturers have not yet addressed. These include a single-ring crankset and chain guide matched to a wide-range rear gear cluster to give a simple, effective, and easy-to-use transmission for trail use. This makes the Creig 26 a kids' bike that shames many adult machines when it comes to practical performance detailing. **GK**

Islabikes' Creig is small in size but big on detail. ▶

RIBBLE New Sportive

2010 • Road bike • UK • Cost-effective carbon fiber "bike to work" champion

While the $1,500 (£1,000) mark has always been a significant break point in the buying comfort of many riders in the UK, it has now become even more important thanks to a government subsidy. Under the so-called "bike to work" scheme, an employer can buy any bike costing less than £1,000 and effectively lease it to an employee. The employee gains a substantial saving on the list price and pays back the balance gradually as a salary deduction. Consequently, UK makers and overseas brands have scrambled to produce bikes for just under that four-figure sum.

Few UK companies have had as much success in this price bracket as the Merlin bike store in Lancashire and its Ribble New Sportive frameset. The Ribble is designed around a noticeably relaxed, taller front-end geometry for comfort on long rides. The frame tubes are also deliberately curved for a slightly more springy ride than that of a conventional race bike, with the result that the frame is as easy on the rider's body as on their wallet. But this is certainly no mushy, low-quality carbon fiber mess. Tracking is usefully tight and obedient, and the New Sportive is always eager to join in the attack on any climb, or contest the obligatory sprint for village signs on group rides. **GK**

SCOTT Foil

2010 • Race bike • Switzerland • Tour de France-dominating aerodynamic road racer

When race cycling's governing body put a 15-lb (6.8-kg) minimum weight limit on race bikes, makers looked for different ways to make their machines faster. There was an explosion of aerodynamically enhanced "AiRoad" machines with thinner, deeper, wind-cheating tube shapes, but these frames were often heavier and more flexible than traditional designs. Scott, taking a new aerodynamic approach with sprinter Mark Cavendish in the Mercedes-Benz Grand Prix wind tunnel with its project FO1, did not forget to keep the bike light and stiff.

"Virtual foil" tube shapes are chopped off bluntly at the back, causing the swirling wind in the rider's wake to create a "virtual" tail of air. The tail naturally bends around if there is a crosswind, making the bike more efficient in those conditions; it also makes the Foil an absolutely beautiful, seriously fast yet obedient descender, which is very rare in an aero road bike.

Broad, thin-walled HMX Net carbon fiber tubes deliver excellent weight and stiffness too, so the Foil does not struggle on climbs or through corners. Mark Cavendish switched to a Specialized Venge aero bike courtesy of Omega Pharma Quick-Step, but he was certainly a big fan of the Foil when he rode it. **GK**

RITTE Muur

2010 • Road bike • USA • Frame combining stainless steel and carbon

Ritte Bicycles' name was inspired by young Belgian racer Henri "Ritte" Van Lerberghe, who, legend has it, turned up on foot at the start of the 1919 Tour of Flanders. Borrowing a bike from a local, he was soon winning by such a margin that prior to entering the velodrome to take the flag, he stopped off at a bar for a few beers. He was eventually tracked down by an official who coaxed him back onto his bike. Ritte still managed to win the race by a clear fourteen minutes.

The Ritte name was to reemerge in Venice, California, almost ninety years later. Although it is a champion of stainless-steel frames, Ritte acknowledges that steel bikes cannot match carbon for efficiency and power transfer, and that making the frame lighter causes it to be too flexible. The answer, exemplified by the Muur, was a design using carbon tubes to stiffen and lighten the frame, combined with an entire back end built from stainless steel. As modern road bikes go, few could offer more comfort than the Muur, but the stainless-steel elements of the frame push the weight up to 37 lb (17 kg), making it less than ideal for competitive racing. Sadly, production of the Muur was suspended in 2013 when Ritte experienced difficulties in sourcing materials. **TB**

ORBEA Orca

2010 • Race bike • Spain • Spanish carbon racer

Orbea's flagship bike was ridden by the Euskaltel-Euskadi pro team's Samuel Sánchez to gold in the Men's Road Race at the 2008 Beijing Olympics.

The Orca's chunky but ultralight monocoque frame was made of two types of carbon fiber. The tubes had wide, fat joints, including a big wishbone arrangement in which the seatstays merge, and a bulky tapered head tube where the top and down tube joined. The construction also featured an oversized bottom bracket and a sturdy rear triangle. Some of the tubes had angled cross-sections. In its black color scheme with red flashes and white details, the Orca looked purposeful, fast, and very rigid.

Orbea's carbon experts had engineered "nerves"—long strands of carbon that stretched right around the frame, but which varied in thickness as appropriate to their position. These nerves smoothed the ride of the Orca, which was widely praised for its comfort.

Such advanced production techniques are not cheap, and Orbeas are correspondingly expensive. Complete Orcas cost between $5,800 (£3,700) and $9,175 (£5,800). All the builds feature high-quality parts, of course, ranging from Shimano Ultegra and RS80 wheels to digital transmission and Dura Ace wheels. **SH**

SPECIALIZED Cancellara

2010 • Race bike • USA • Race bike alleged to have a secret motor

The allegation was bizarre but very specific: Swiss pro racer Fabian "Spartacus" Cancellara was winning races by employing a tiny electric motor hidden inside his bike frame. In 2010 a controversial YouTube video linked state-of-the-art developments in electric cycle motors and batteries with "bike doping." Cancellara was shown pulling away from the field in various races with a sudden turn of speed that was alleged to be "unnatural." The film footage focused on some unusual hand movements just before each burst of acceleration. The rumors spread, particularly in the Italian press and broadcast media, and both Cancellara and the Union Cycliste Internationale (UCI) were forced to deny any cheating through the use of electronic assistance. The sport's governing body took the allegations seriously, but Cancellara himself was roundly dismissive of them, calling the whole idea "plain stupid."

At the time of the scandal, Cancellara was riding a typically ultra-light and aerodynamically sleek Specialized S-Works Road bike, which the manufacturer claimed was its stiffest-ever model. It had huge chainrings, plus customized brake levers and gear shifters. Even the action of the brake calipers could be fine-tuned from the handlebar. Some people said that this unusual configuration provided an innocent explanation for Cancellara's suspicion-arousing hand movements on the bars.

In 2010 Specialized unveiled a spoof electric race bike at a presentation in Colorado. Called the Specialized Roubaix 2011, it had a 430-watt Duracell "mechanical doping battery" clamped to the down tube. Perhaps ironically, Specialized now markets an electric-assist performance bike, the Turbo S, that really does have a battery pack hidden in the frame. **SH**

SWOBO Sanchez

2010 • Utility bike • USA • Stylish and affordable urban fixed-gear road bike

Swobo calls its simple Sanchez fixed-gear machine the "classic street bike." The stripped-down design is available as a frameset for $250 (£170) or as a complete bike for $679 (£455).

Swobo has maintained a cool image through three incarnations. The original company made cycling clothes, mostly with Merino wool. That went bust, but was revived as a bike and clothing brand. Again, it went out of business. Then two entrepreneurs, Justin and Peter Discoe, moved the operation from California to Fort Collins, Colorado, and concentrated on producing high-quality cycling clothes and affordable bikes. Most of the products are made in

"Comfortable, fast, absolutely silent when underway, and incredible fun."

Consumer review, 2010

the town, and the Sanchez is assembled from mostly U.S. components. The brightly colored Sanchez frame, available in three sizes, is made from tungsten inert gas (TIG)-welded, custom-specified, galvanized double-butted steel chromoly tubing. As a complete bike, the Sanchez comes with good-quality components: 28-in. (71-cm) Velocity Deep V rims; Kenda Karvs tires; a Tange headset; Origin cranks; and Swobo's own steel seatpost. Buyers can specify Tektro front brakes or, if they are hardcore fixie fans, they can choose to do without brakes altogether.

The Sanchez comes either with a dedicated fixed hub or Swobo's own "flip-flop" rear hub, which can be switched from fixed to freewheel single-speed simply by putting the wheel in the other way around. **SH**

HARO Porter

2010 • Slopestyle bike • USA • Mountain bike legend Eric Porter's signature slopestyle bike

In 2010, the original BMX brand Haro boasted a formidable mountain bike slopestyle team that included Eric Porter, Greg Watts, and Phil Sunbaum. That year Watts—following his Crankworx slopestyle win in 2009—won the best trick contest at Crankworx Whistler on a prototype Haro Porter. His backflip double tailwhip had never been seen in competition.

When it came to market in 2010, the production Haro Porter was built to the same spec as Porter's personal bike, including a specially shortened 4-in. (10-cm) travel Fox Float 36 RC2 fork, and a Fox Float rear shock giving the bike 4½ in. (11.5 cm) of travel through a tough single-pivot suspension system. The paint job, a collaboration between Haro and Porter, featured a collage of beer labels using actual labels created by

Haro for Porter's own homebrew beer. What better way to brand your own signature bike than with labels from your homemade beer?

With the top-of-the-line signature model costing $3,200 (£2,150), Haro decided in 2011 to offer some more affordable builds of the Porter. The Porter Comp, still featuring the Porter 4½-in. (11.5-cm) travel frame, cost $1,305 (£870) and made use of less-expensive components such as the Marzocchi Dirt Jumper 2 fork and Marzocchi Roco R coil rear shock. These and other substitutions allowed Haro to offer the complete bike for a very reasonable price. The line ended in 2011 when Porter moved to new sponsor Diamond Back, but Watts still rides the Porter in competition, even though it has ceased to exist in the Haro lineup. **CJ**

SCOTT Scale RC

2010 • Mountain bike • Switzerland • Ultra-light big-wheeled mountain bike

Scott's road and mountain bike ranges have always had a very strong race focus. The Scale RC was one of the first truly lightweight, race-competitive, 29-in. (73.5-cm) wheeled bikes, and has racked up an impressive tally of results to prove it.

At less than 1 kg (2 lb 2 oz), the Scale RC frame is truly lightweight, even with its alloy seat collar, rear derailleur fixtures, and bottle-cage bolts in place.

These are the only metal parts of the entire structure. The steering and crank bearings mount directly onto carbon fiber surfaces, and the drop-out sections that hold the rear wheel are also made of carbon fiber—and not just any carbon fiber, but HMX Net, Scott's lightest, stiffest grade of the material, for the maximum effect.

Scott weighs every frame after production to ensure that it hits the target; frames that fail the test are used for the cheaper Scale Pro model. Even after the addition of all the exotic parts, the complete Scale RC bike weighs only 21 lb (9.7 kg).

However, weight is not the sole preoccupation of the makers of the Scale. The bike's front end and lower stays are designed for optimal steering precision and power delivery, yet the flat-profile SDS (Shaft Drive System) rear stays are surprisingly effective at smoothing out rough terrain.

With its relatively relaxed handling character, Scott's Scale RC is more than just a pure racing machine—it is an impressively capable and extremely enjoyable all-round trail bike. **GK**

WILIER Twin Blade

2010 • Time trial bike • Italy • Radical carbon aero road bike with extended H fork

Italian bike designers are famous for their flamboyantly stylish attitude toward aero bikes—the iconic Cinelli Laser with its blended TIG-welded tube junctions; the Rossin Crono with its motorbike-style fairing; Francesco Moser's Colnago Pista track bike with its radical short wheelbase design and twin Campagnolo discwheels; the swooping monocoque lines of Miguel Indurain's Pinarello Sword. All are sculpted by artistry as much as by wind flow, and the Wilier Twin Blade is no different.

The mainframe of the Twin Blade follows conventional smooth slipstream etiquette with deep teardrop tube shapes helping the ride to slice cleanly through headwinds. The fork channels the airflow instead of just cutting through it; wider spacing of the lower legs means less turbulence between the fork

and the spinning wheel surface and spokes. The legs continue upward outside the frame (rather than inside) before ending in a direct mount on the handlebar. Rather than let the turbulence spill off the surfaces of the tubes, this "twin foil" design forces air over the frame to minimize its overall aerodynamic profile, creating the feeling of an extremely fast machine.

But what really marks out the Wilier among its clock-beating contemporaries is its remarkably cultured and comfortable ride. That gives it a clear advantage over slavishly wind-tunnel and wattage prioritized punishment machines from other brands, particularly in long-distance events. The Twin Blade is a pure-pedigree machine in the fine tradition of stylishly speedy Italian bikes. **GK**

SALSA Fargo

2010 • Hybrid touring/mountain bike • USA • Steel-frame adventure bike

What exactly is this, then? Mountain bike? Tourer? Cross-country? Dividing the opinions of riders ever since its introduction, the Salsa Fargo has been able to delight and confound in equal measure. Is it the ultimate adventure bike, as Salsa would claim, or a jack-of-all-trades that does nothing with any great flair?

Whatever the truth, the Fargo is undeniably a visually striking piece of kit. A first glance at the frame reveals a well-equipped steel mountain bike with 29-in. (73.5-cm) wheels. The complete bikes are built up with rigid steel forks and road bike-style drop bars. The impressive spec includes a chromoly frame with rigid fork, Avid cable disc brakes, Shimano XT transmission with bar-end shifters, and low-tread WTB Vulpine tires. The bike is also nicely equipped for long hauls with no fewer than six bottle cages, so there is little danger of dehydration on a long trek.

How does Salsa's claim that the Fargo "will take you where you want to go" stack up? Well, for high-mileage commuting, or touring that takes in a variety of surfaces, from tarmac to light woodland tracks, this bike will do the job with some panache. It may be a little jarring in wilder terrain because the supersized rigid fork can calm down rougher parts of your ride only so much. The more adventurous rider might want to research the availability of spares before going too far into the outback, and also pack some spare 29-in. (73.5-cm) tires and disc brake spares. Those parts will be especially hard to find in middle-of-nowhere locations if they wear out in the wilderness. **TB**

DECADE Virsa

2010 • Mountain bike • UK • Contemporary version of a classic steel hardtail

The Decade bike brand came into being as a steel-frame alternative to the highly popular aluminum alloy Kinesis Maxlight range of U.K. distributor and designer Upgrade. The two bike families are similar in that their frames are designed to be used with forks in the 4- to 5-in. (10- to 12.7-cm) travel range for general cross-country and trail riding. The Virsa's 1¾-in. (4.4-cm) diameter head tube is compatible with straight or tapered steerer forks, depending on the bearings you install, and is reinforced with an extra wraparound gusset piece to cope with heavy landings. Interchangeable Swopout drop-outs at the rear give a broad choice of transmission options, from geared

"A great hard-riding cross-country frame with single-speed or geared compatibility."

Bikeradar.com

to single-speed or hub gears, depending on the end pieces you fit. The rear disc mount is slotted, letting you slide the brake back and forward to position a single-cog setup perfectly. Typically for a well-designed British bike, the vertical clamping slot for the seatpost binder faces forward rather than backward, to prevent mud from the rear wheel sneaking inside the frame and causing corrosion, and the "wishbone" rear stays are widely spaced to allow plenty of mud clearance, even with a 2½-in. (6-cm) wide tire. The seat tube is "bulge butted" for extra strength with a longer seatpost.

The Virsa mainframe features Tange Prestige JPN double-butted tubing for the top tube and down tube. This minimizes weight, and maximizes the sprung feeling that riders seek in a steel-tubed frame. **GK**

BIXI "Boris Bike"

2010 • City bike • UK • The bike of London's first public sharing scheme

Although these iconic public-hire bikes are named for Boris Johnson, the London mayor who oversaw their launch, the idea of the project—to provide Londoners with an affordable and environmentally friendly form of transport—was formulated by Johnson's predecessor, Ken Livingstone. When the plan was announced in 2007, London was a long way behind cities such as Paris, France, and Copenhagen, Denmark—the former launched its highly regarded Vélib network in 2007.

A total of $187.5 million (£125 million) was poured into the project, with 315 bike stations spread throughout London, and an initial total of 5,000 bikes. At first, the scheme required users to pay registration and membership fees, but by the end of 2010 that had changed, and cyclists were allowed to use the bikes even if they were not members—the system became pay-as-you-go. A further 3,000 bikes added to the total over the following two years, and by March 2012 more than 19 million journeys had been recorded.

Despite becoming a London icon, the bikes and their stations were designed and built in Canada. They feature puncture-resistant tires; a twist grip-operated, low-ratio internal three-gear shift system; and an adjustable seat height. Dynamo-powered front and rear lights and small cargo basket complete the bike.

At 50 lb (23 kg), the bikes were exceptionally heavy, and some riders were disappointed with their handling. However, the "Boris Bike" was, and still is, an overall success as a city initiative. A record of 47,105 bikes were hired in a single day during the 2012 Olympics. Criticism of "Boris Bikes" is focused mainly, not on the scheme itself, but on the current paucity of cycle lanes that are safely separated from motor traffic. In this regard, London has much to learn from the bike-friendly highways of the Netherlands. **DB**

Conceived of by Ken Livingstone, but "Boris Bike" just sounds better. ▶

SPECIALIZED Stumpjumper FSR Evo

2010 • Mountain bike • USA • Rally-prepped limited-edition play bike

Specialized has always prided itself on a strong riding culture among its staff, based around legendarily competitive lunchtime ride sessions. President Mike Sinyard is a regular pace setter and also leads an annual multi-day employee and VIP ride from the company's headquarters at Morgan Hill, California, to the Interbike trade show in Las Vegas. Brandon Sloan, head of Specialized's research and development team, is also an extremely skilled and aggressive race rider whose influence is very clear in the brand's Evo series of bikes.

At first glance the Evo is almost identical to the standard Stumpjumper FSR bike, but a closer look reveals that the geometry is subtly altered to lower ride height and stabilize steering, with an increased front

and rear suspension stroke. A shorter stem and wider bar give more leverage and control to the feel of the steering, while the double-ring crankset gets a roller and guide to keep on the chain in chaotic situations. Grippier tires underline that extra control and the dampers are tuned more for a downhill than a pedal-focused performance.

On the Stumpjumper FSR Evo's release, an outrageously confident and playful ride character led to rave reviews all over the media and the more alert stores began to stock them immediately. With the success of the Evo concept came similarly modified and similarly exciting Evo versions of the Enduro, Epic, and even Stumpjumper hardtail, as well as more radical limited-edition models from other brands. **GK**

KINESIS Maxlight XC130

2010 • Mountain bike • UK • Highly evolved and exciting UK-designed mountain bike

Smaller, national rather than global bike brands are often quicker and more flexible in their reaction to subtle local nuances in consumer tastes. That is especially true when the designers are riding the same trails as their customers. A case in point is Upgrade Bikes' designer Dom Mason and his range of Kinesis-frame bikes. Leading aluminum alchemist Kinesis makes the frames in East Asia using advanced hydraulic tube-forming technology, but the bike shapes are purely up to Dom and his design team.

The Kinesis XC series started as affordable, lightweight, mountain bike race frames designed to work best with a short-stroke, 4-in. (10-cm) suspension fork. The bikes were popular with riders looking for a cost-effective competitive chassis to complete to their own specification, partly because, despite their short suspension, the frames proved surprisingly tough in do-or-die race-winning descents. Over the years the Kinesis reputation for lightweight strength grew, and so did the length of the forks people were fitting into the frames.

Luckily, Mason and prototype test specialist Paddy Blake were regularly meeting cross-country riders on weekend trails and races. Able to react quickly and order small production runs, they were perfectly placed to keep pace with developments. That evolution led directly to the Kinesis XC130. Aluminum tubing shaped for steering stiffness and strength is balanced with a 5-in. (12.7-cm) fork to achieve smoothness in the saddle, perfect for seeking out the best trails all day long. **GK**

IBIS Tranny

2010 • Mountain bike • USA • Innovative carbon hardtail with an adjustable chainstay length

Scot Nicol of Ibis Bicycles has never been one to follow convention if he can see a better way of doing things, as the development of the Tranny testifies.

Gears undoubtedly make riding hilly terrain a lot easier, but many riders prefer a single-gear setup for its simplicity, reduced maintenance, and lower weight. Single-speeding and the visceral, often violent struggle of a single cog against crowding contours on technical climbs, is unique in its purity of purpose.

However, running a single gear is not quite as simple as it looks. Unless you have a clumsy chain-tensioning pulley, the rear wheel has to stay in exactly the right position to keep the chain tight and prevent it from dropping off. Having some way to adjust its position is vital. The horizontal slotted drop-outs of

track bikes work in a pure single-speed setup, but riders wanting to go back to gears often find the drop-outs lack derailleur compatibility. Bolted drop-outs, on the other hand, are ugly and have a nasty habit of coming loose and letting the wheel slip.

In response, Ibis created the Tranny's totally adjustable rear frame section, which slides in and out of a socket to change the chain length without losing any wheel security. The lightweight carbon fiber construction reduces the complete chassis weight too, to get the most out of every one of those single-minded pedal revolutions. The whole rear end can be unbolted and removed, so you can pack it very small for transport. With any transmission or travel setup, the Tranny is an extremely versatile mountain machine. **GK**

SCOTT Voltage FR 10

2010 • Freeride bike • Switzerland • Highly adjustable and versatile hardcore mountain bike

Scott's Swiss Army knife—or the Voltage FR 10, as the bike is officially known—was a bolt of lightning in the thunderstorm of the 2010 freeride world.

This new all-round fun machine set the standard for super-versatile bikes. The frame can be adjusted between 5½ in. (14 cm) of travel for a slopestyle slayer up to 7 in. (17.8 cm) for a downhill dominator. Its very long compatible shock offers 6½–7 in. (16.5–17.8 cm) of adjustment. Two other shorter-stroke shock options can be fitted using separately obtainable add-on kits, so that you can get down to a 4-in. (10-cm) travel fork with 5½ in. (14 cm) out back, and still have the ideal geometry for dirt jumps.

The hydroformed tubing is secured at the head tube using the "full Nelson" weld technique—a straight weld with a tongue-and-groove junction—to create a super-strong joint. An interchangeable drop-out system can be used to increase or decrease the chainstay length by approximately ½ in. (1 cm) from the stock 16¾-in. (42.5-cm) setting, and to adjust the configuration of the axle.

The Coastal Crew of British Columbia, Canada, developed the Voltage with Scott and immortalized it in its ten-part website series over the winter and summer of 2010. In 2012, Scott signed World Cup racer Brendan Fairclough, who rode the Voltage FR until Scott released its new Gambler DH bike in 2013. In spite of this development, the Voltage FR series remains available to cyclists in search of wonderful all-round do-it-all bikes. **CJ**

WHYTE 146

2010 • Mountain bike • UK • Super-light carbon fiber endurance racer

The Whyte 46 had scored perfect reviews, so creating the follow-up bike was a tall order, especially as Jon Whyte himself had left the company. Young designers Ian and Pat Alexander had a blank sheet of paper and big expectations to fulfill, but they did not panic. Digging deep into their carbon fiber construction expertise and combining it with their belief in the benefits of radical downhill bike-bred geometry, they came up with a bike every bit as benchmark-setting as the 46.

With lightweight wheels and carbon components, the 146 was lighter than most contemporary short-suspension bikes at less than 26 lb (12 kg). The "Quadlink" design prioritized pedaling performance, so it could sprint between tricky race sections and stomp up the steepest climbs, but still delivered nearly 6 in. (15 cm) of controlled wheel movement to deal with rocks and jumps on the way down. It even featured a remote-controlled seat dropper to give riders room to fly freely in extreme situations.

The 2011 Whyte 146X took this ready-to-rage bike to even more focused extremes. It is a tribute to the Alexander brothers' design that, with the benefit of yearly evolution, the 146 is still seen as a cutting-edge enduro downhill race bike in today's market. **GK**

NICOLAI Helius FR

2010 • Freeride bike • Germany • Engineering masterpiece from a über-cool German bike maker

Austrian Horst Leitner worked for many years to resolve the issue of chain torque in bicycle and motorbike suspension designs. His eventually patented four-bar "Horst Link" pivot became the most widely used suspension design. A young German, Karlheinz (Kalle) Nicolai worked under him on the design team, and many credit Nicolai with helping to perfect the application of the Horst Link to the bicycle.

Frames designed by Nicolai, labeled as Mongoose for sponsorship reasons, began to win world championships in 1995. He then started to produce frames under his own name, and this model, the Helius FR, continues his development of the Horst Link he helped create. The design allows effective pedaling with minimal feedback, or "bob," and perfect tracking of the ground during descents. The bike is assembled from the finest-quality aluminum, with Nicolai's characteristic bold welds and an attention to detail that borders on the obsessive. Drop-outs are CNC-machined to perfection out of solid aluminum billet, the five-year warranty covers racing, and specs include anything from crud-catcher mounts to fully customized geometry. The Helius is a sure-footed, ultra-tough, and highly individualistic freeride bike. **KF**

Nicolai's Helius bikes can even be ordered with a radical Pinion internal gearbox. ▶

SANTA CRUZ Driver 8

2010 • Downhill/Freeride bike • USA • Reinvention of the Santa Cruz VP Free

After a decade of hype, the mountain biking world realized that a massive freeride bike is not what you want to pedal uphill. People had had enough of claims of miraculous all-rounders that actually did most things okay but none really well. Riders wanted either a bike that was great uphill and fun downhill—a trail bike—or a downhill bike best suited to jumping off things.

In 2010, Santa Cruz ended production of the VP Free and launched the Driver 8, a bike that looked like a smaller version of its World Cup-winning downhill bike, the V10. Mike Ferrentino, Santa Cruz's marketing director, wanted to stress that "this is not a replacement VP Free," mainly because he felt the VP Free had a "kinda funky bottom bracket height and it didn't steer well."

Santa Cruz did not want to repeat that mistake. It already had the Nomad, which rode very well uphill while feeling better than the VP Free on the downhills, making it a true trail bike. The Driver 8 rode downhill like the V10 but had a little less travel—8 in. (20.3 cm) to be precise)—so was more playful and fun in the freeride arena. The Driver 8 featured double-row cartridge bearings in the bottom linkage of the VPP (Virtual Pivot Point) system, while the upper link was carbon fiber and had oversized cartridge bearings. All the linkages had grease ports to ease servicing and prolong the life of the bearings. All in all, the Driver 8 was an everyman downhill/freeride bike, built to last and with a lot of passed-down technology from its big brother, the V10. **CJ**

TIME Speeder Veloce

2010 • Road bike • France • Top-end performance from an affordable bike

French company Time is best known for its top-end carbon fiber frames and its clipless pedal range, but its new Speeder frame was more than just an exercise in name trading. Despite being designed for "cyclotourism" and clocking in at a relatively weighty 18½ lb (8.4 kg), the Speeder was actually a lot more positive when pedaled than that would suggest. The naked carbon finish made the smooth construction clearly evident, and each tube of the mainframe and rear subtriangle was carefully tapered and shaped, delivering a ride quality way above that expected for the affordable price.

Reviewers of the time were particularly impressed with the handling, which was notably sure-footed and stable at all speeds but particularly outstanding on long, fast, twisting descents. The position was lower than that of most similar "sportive"-styled machines of the time, and full-depth bars—rather than sets with a compact curve—let the rider drop down really low on the bike, a real advantage when it came to maximum-speed descending. Even with the relatively aggressive position and spirited ride, the Speeder was a comfortable, friendly companion on long rides. Much of this was because of Time's vast experience of carbon fiber composites, but Selcof's seatpost and Selle Italia's XR saddle could also take some of the credit.

Journalists at *Cycling Plus* were so taken with the Time that it was immediately placed on the magazine's long-term test roster. They came away as big fans of the Speeder after riding it extensively for six months. **GK**

COVE G-Spot

2010 • Mountain bike • Canada • Cove hit the G-Spot long ago, but found it again for 2010

In its original form, the G-Spot was a classic for more than eight years before the appearance of this redesign.

The manufacturer, Cove Bikes, was founded by Chaz Romalis, a pioneer of the North Shore, a riding area outside Vancouver, British Columbia, that is full of incredible trails, wooden ladder bridges, and massive jumps and drops. At the Cove Bike Shop in North Vancouver, while you're waiting for pro riders like Eric Lawrenuk to fix your bike, you may see mountain bike heroes like Thomas Vanderham and Wade Simmons stop in for coffee.

The new G-Spot is built from custom-drawn 7005 alloy tubing with a 1½-in. (3.5-cm) head tube. The bike features a floating pivot-point suspension system that uses the same Dual Link as the Cove Shocker downhill bike. This produces an especially stiff rear end, which is perfect for any trail workhorse. The 6 in. (15 cm) of rear travel designed around a 2.6:1 leverage ratio creates a supple riding feel.

Cove believes passionately that all its ancillary suppliers should be local. Thus the G-Spots are welded by Yess Products right in the Vancouver suburb of Surrey. Built entirely in Vancouver, and shaped by the city's world-renowned trails, the G-Spot is not just another all-mountain bike; it is a true freeride machine. Capable of being pedaled up long and arduous ascents, yet super-controlled and stable at speed, and nimble in the air once pointed downhill, it handles steep, rough, and fast terrain like the perfect combination of a mini downhill bike and a heavyweight all-mountain machine.

In an online review, *Vital MTB* summed up the G-Spot with succinct accuracy: "You will not find a more capable all-mountain bike anywhere." It's easy to see why Lawrenuk himself always rides the G-Spot at large slopestyle competitions. **CJ**

". . . free from the constraints of the tube ratio rules of the UCI, the massively deep down tube becomes the focus."

Bikeradar.com

Cove's G-Spot starts making sense when the trail stops. ▶

2011

WAGON WHEELS
AND WIND-CHEATERS

29ers and wind tunnels take the lead.

SANTA CRUZ Tallboy

2011 • Mountain bike • USA • Super-light yet tough big-wheeled carbon bike

Some bike makers exude cool naturally, while others strain to achieve little or none of the same effect.

High on the list of those that do is Santa Cruz of California. Ever since the company introduced the Tazmon in the early 1990s, its model timeline reads like a Who's Who of super-significant bikes. When Santa Cruz rocked up to the 29er full-suspension party in 2010, it didn't come in quietly through the back door.

Rather than getting consumer feedback on its design by introducing an easily altered aluminum frame first, Santa Cruz was confident enough to commit to a full carbon fiber frame straightaway. It took a no-holds-barred approach to the Tallboy build, using details such as molded (rather than riveted or glued) cable stops, and top-quality fibers in flowing, asymmetric lines. The result was an extremely stiff and strong frame at a stunningly low weight of well under 6 lb (2.75 kg) for frame and custom Fox Racing shock-absorber. In case people failed to note the spec, they painted the bike bright orange.

The Tallboy was as good as it looked, and soon pushed the boundaries of what people saw as acceptable behavior for a 29-in. (73.5-cm) wheeled bike with 4 in. (10 cm) of suspension. **GK**

FW EVANS/PASHLEY SE

2011 • Touring bike • UK • Tourer built to celebrate the heritage of an expanding bike shop chain

Evans Cycles store chain is the Starbucks of the UK cycling revival, with (at time of writing) fifty retail outlets nationwide and a thriving mail-order business. It has become one of the first points of call for serious cyclists and newcomers alike.

Frederick Evans opened his original workshop on London's Kennington Road in 1921, producing high-end lightweight steel racing and touring cycles. In 1925, he produced an innovative quick-release precision drop-out, which allowed a double-cogged wheel to be flipped around to change gear in a matter of seconds. His shop was notable for its "top-to-toe" approach to equipping the rider; supplying not only hand-built frames, custom produced in any size on a pioneering universal frame jig, but also its own ranges of luggage, shoes, accessories, and made-to-measure clothing.

The Special Edition (SE) is a throwback to past times. Built in collaboration with Pashley, which produces its own range of retro-style rides, it uses a classic hand-built, lugged and brazed Reynolds 531 steel frame, a chainset by Stronglight, Rigida rims, a Brooks saddle, Dia Compe center-pull brakes, and old-fashioned bar-end shifters. Add a Carradice saddlebag, and you're off! **SE**

COVE Hooker

2011 • Slopestyle bike • Canada • Hardcore four-cross or slopestyle all-rounder

The Hooker, first released in 2004, was a 4-in. (10-cm) travel four-cross race machine-cum-slopestyle slayer. It was Cove's answer to aggressive, short-travel, full-suspension bikes such as the Specialized SX Trail and the Kona Bass, which you could build to ride slopestyle, race four-cross, or ride fun trails flat out. The Hooker is thus a very versatile bike.

It is built of Easton RAD tubing that starts with square cross-sections at the head tube and morphs into cylindrical tubes toward the bottom bracket. The rear suspension comes via a custom-tuned four-bar linkage with the main pivot placed just above the bottom bracket. The low 2:1 leverage ratio gives the

"The best fun and most solidly built 4-in. [10-cm] travel thrasher we've ridden."

Bikeradar.com

rear suspension an incredibly plush feel, and the short chainstays, coupled with the low-slung feel adopted from Cove's Foreplay hardtail, make the Hooker the perfect shape for slopestyle. The bike also gives the rider the feel of an aggressively responsive hardtail with rear suspension backup when required.

The Hooker has been used in slopestyle events such as Crankworx Whistler by team riders Geoff Gulevich and Eric Lawrenuk. Lawrenuk appeared aboard a Hooker in the mountain bike film *Alchemy*, which he also directed. Gulevich featured in the stunning freeride film *Roam*. The Hooker has been refined over the years, but in 2013 it still looks very similar to the original, which just shows that Cove got it right the first time around. **CJ**

NS Surge

2011 • Jump bike • Poland • Super-tough hardcore hardtail

By the end of the first decade of the twenty-first century, Poland had emerged as the latest big player in the design and production of ultra-tough, highly acrobatic jump bikes and other hardcore machines. At the head of this resurgence has been Gdansk-based NS Bikes, whose Surge model is proving to be a popular and cost-effective choice for anti-gravity junkies all over the globe.

The essential requirement for every jump bike is strength. After all, you can launch almost any bike off a ramp, but it's landing it repeatedly—and often very roughly, after multiple whips and flips between takeoff and touchdown—without damage to machine or rider that separates success from failure, winners from write-offs. With this in mind, NS has followed the lead of the toughest BMX bikes, and constructed the Surge from a chromoly steel tubeset.

While the exact tubing details are a closely guarded secret, neat strengthening features are clear to see. The seat tube penetrates the top tube, with the rear stays extending along the side of the junction to add strength. That's because this area is particularly vulnerable to damage if the bike bounces off the saddle in a cartwheeling crash.

The front of the frame also needs to be extremely tough to cope with nosedive landings onto the fork. As a result, the Surge gets an extra welded gusset plate to reinforce the head tube. The down tube is a large-diameter pipe that enables the frame to be used with a travel fork of up to 6³⁄₁₀ in. (16 cm). That's a serious amount of travel for a bike with a rigid rear end, but then, in spite of its fun image, the Surge is a serious machine that is capable of taking on the world. *Bikeradar* called it "an absolute blast" and, with a frame costing only $390 (£240), "an absolute bargain." **GK**

NINER JET 9 RDO

2011 • Mountain bike • USA • Big-wheeled bike that just loves to climb

Big-wheel evangelist Niner is determined to put 29ers at the top of the pile. When it comes to getting to the top of mountains, few bikes are faster than the Jet 9 RDO (the initials stand for "Race Day Only").

The Jet 9 uses a smoothly sculpted, premium carbon fiber mainframe and swingarm with a carbon fiber CVA suspension linkage to join them. Making sure the two halves pivot with ultimate smoothness are Enduro Max cartridge bearings, which are normally fitted as an after-market extra even on the most expensive frames from other brands. Complete Niner RDO bikes also come with similarly super-light carbon fiber bars and seatposts, which ensure you're carrying the minimum amount of bike up the mountain with you.

It's not just the low weight of this super-expensive flagship machine that makes it one of the most talented climbers on the trails. By using a steeper-than-normal seat angle, the rider's weight is pushed forward, which stops the front wheel popping up and losing control on really steep climbs. It also puts the rider in the perfect position to drive back and down through the bike from the nose of the saddle, keeping the rear wheel in constant contact with the ground, regardless of the amount of torque. Moreover, the frame deliberately rides higher than on most bikes to stop the pedals from smashing into the ground if you keep the power on up rocky or rooty climbs. And the CVA suspension works with whatever chainring you're using to get the right gear. This JET is ready for takeoff. **GK**

TURNER DHR

2011 • Downhill bike • USA • Dave Turner's fourth-generation DHR downhill bike

Released in 1999, Turner's first single-pivot suspension design downhill bike, the DH Javelin, was one of the first bikes with built-in ISCG tabs for a chain-retaining roller guide.

In 2000, its name was changed to the Turner DH Racer or DHR. The 2013 is radically different from this original, but it still bears the marks of its heritage. Back in 2000, the DHR had a twin top tube design, which was retained until 2004, when it was superseded by box-section tubing. In 2008, Dave Turner began a collaboration with suspension designer Dave Weagle, and henceforth used the latter's DW Link on all his full-suspension bikes. However, the DHR did not receive its DW Link upgrade until 2010, at the end of two years of research and development and the construction and

testing of five prototypes. Unfortunately, the makeover bikes had to be recalled in late 2010, because the head tubes were cracking; after the addition of a head tube gusset, the DHR was re-released in 2011.

The 2011 Turner DHR came with some of the most extreme geometry of any off-the-peg downhill bike: a super-slack 63-degree head angle, and a low 13½-in. (34.25-cm) bottom bracket. This gave the bike an incredibly stable feel when riding at speed or on rough trails. The DW Link has a serious pedigree, being the suspension linkage in the Iron Horse Sunday on which Sam Hill dominated the World Cup Circuit in 2006, 2007, and 2008. The linkage had be reworked to suit the modified design, but retained Weagle's anti-squat suspension characteristics. **CJ**

ORBEA Alma G

2011 • Mountain bike • Spain • Purist hardtail racing machine

French rider Julien Absalon is one of the most successful cross-country mountain bike racers of all time, with gold medals at the 2004 Olympics in Athens, Greece, and the 2008 Games in Beijing, China, four consecutive World Championship titles (2004–2007), and multiple World Cup race wins. Nearly all these victories were achieved aboard bikes manufactured by Orbea. The flagship of the Spanish company is this remarkable hardtail.

The Alma G's carbon fiber monocoque frame had maximum stiffness to accommodate the Frenchman's aggressive riding style. Unlined internal control cable routing reduced weight and friction for the quick

> *"I love being with Orbea; they offer me reliability, the best bikes and a great team."*

Julien Absalon

gear changes that are crucial in cross-country racing. During races, Absalon is supported by SRAM's Black Box suspension and transmission racing program, which develops cutting-edge, race-only performance components, such as the carbon fiber and magnesium RockShox SID World Cup XX fork, and the SRAM XX 10-speed transmission. Innovations proven on the racetrack are then passed on to production parts that the wider public can buy.

Absalon's lightweight wheels—from French manufacturer Mavic—are 26 in. (66 cm) in diameter. Most riders currently use 29ers, but Absalon prefers the smaller size because it reduces weight. And it certainly doesn't seem to slow him down. In 2012, Absalon left Orbea and moved to the BMC Racing Team. **GK**

BTR FABRICATIONS Belter

2011 • Mountain bike • UK • Tough downhill hardtail

Burf and Tam met as students at the University of Oxford, and became friends through their shared love of cycling. They talked a lot, as undergraduates do, agreed that the bikes currently on the market didn't cater for their own riding styles, and decided to start their own bike company. They called it Burf and Tam Racing (BTR), and established their operation headquarters in Burf's garden.

The BTR Belter is a steel hardtail frame built from seamless 4130 tubing to take the knocks, but with downhill racing-specific geometry. With a lack of big hills and big downhill courses near their homes in gently undulating southern England, the two developed a love of riding hardtails, and firmly believed that riding without full suspension was more fun and a better way to learn bike-handling skills. They wanted to build a hardtail for downhill racing that was enjoyable to ride on smaller trails, but which could also handle the big trails.

Ignoring contemporary trends, and instead looking at what they wanted the bike to do, they took from the current technology of downhill bikes what they believed was genuinely useful, and applied it to a hardtail, cutting out everything that they regarded as superfluous—they strove constantly to maintain the distinction between the features that real bikers really want and those for which big companies' advertising agencies try to create demand. In short, their aim was to produce a bike that was good enough to succeed without being hyped.

The Belter is long, low, and slack, and looks very different from most hardtails. "The first time Tam showed me the geometry, I was pretty shocked, to be honest," admits Burf, "but when I got on it, I couldn't believe how good it was." **MH**

LAPIERRE Xelius FDJ

2011 • Road bike • France • Tenth-anniversary bike of long-time team tie-up

In the turbulent world of pro bike racing, the relationship between French manufacturer Lapierre and the Française des Jeux (FDJ) team has been remarkably long-lasting. The tenth anniversary of their partnership was marked by the introduction of the Xelius, which featured a head tube, down tube, and top tube that were all tapered for extra steering stiffness, and an outsized BB30 crank axle. The rear stays were thin to act as a comfort-increasing leaf spring so that riders would feel fresh enough to sprint, even after more than 125 mi (200 km) in the saddle. The carbon frame had internal wiring ports and an external battery mount for Shimano's Dura Ace Di2 electric shifting system. All this weighed only 1 lb 13 oz (850 g).

"Buy if you've won the lottery and fancy a light, efficient yet hard-edged cruiser."

Bikeradar.com

The distinctive livery included the maker's name on a stripe along the full length of the fork leg and the lower half of the head tube.

As well as providing the FDJ team with custom-equipped machines, Lapierre was one of the first bike manufacturers to provide consumers with their own bike customization menu. The company's W-Series website allows buyers to cherry-pick their ideal specification. Lapierre then builds the bike to these requirements, before delivering it to each customer's local dealer, who performs the setup before the final handover.

Meanwhile, back on the racecourse, the Xelius has made the relationship between Lapierre and FDJ stronger than ever. **GK**

CANYON Aeroad CF

2011 • Road bike • Germany • Aerodynamic multi-race-winning machine of Philippe Gilbert

Road race bikes with an extra aerodynamic edge to help solo riders escape the chasing pack are often referred to as breakaway bikes. Canyon's Aeroad is a prominent example of the type. After extensive wind-tunnel tests, it was ridden to great effect by Belgian final-furlong breakaway specialist Philippe Gilbert in the 2011 race season.

By slimming down the head tube and fork blades, and using aero-profile down tubes, seat tubes and rear stays, plus a neat, flush-fit, rear seatpost clamp and internal cable routing, Canyon claimed a 20 percent reduction in drag compared to its conventional CF SLX road frame.

Most significantly, while many aero bikes suffer from a much harsher ride because of their deeper, drag-dodging tube shapes, the Aeroad uses specific carbon fiber layups, including VCLS basalt fiber elements, to create a discernibly smoother ride than the CF SLX road frame. This smoothness made the frame particularly suitable for racing over the rougher courses of the early season Classics, and Gilbert exploited that suitability to the maximum. His first win came in the Montepaschi Strade Bianche race in Italy, so called because of the inclusion of nearly 44 mi (70 km) of rough gravel "white roads" through Tuscan vineyards.

Returning to his native Low Countries, the Belgian star promptly won the Brabantse Pijl, the Amstel Gold, the Flèche Wallonne, and the Liège–Bastogne–Liège Classic races. Later in the year, he added the victories of the opening stage of the Tour de France, the San Sebastián Classic, an ENECO Tour stage, and the Québec Grand Prix, finishing the season as the top-ranked rider by a massive points margin. The Aeroad CF had further competitive successes in 2012 and 2013 with the Katyusha Russian pro team. **GK**

Canyon's Aeroad is a winning balance of smoothness and speed. ▶

SPECIALIZED McLaren S-Works Venge

2011 • Road bike • USA • Ultra-successful Formula One-collaboration race bike

On the outskirts of Woking, England, the handful of press gathered at McLaren's Formula One headquarters stood around anxiously ahead of a long-awaited presentation. They weren't there to see Lewis Hamilton perform donuts in the car park; in fact, this shindig had nothing to do with motor sport. Instead the event centered on one of the most eagerly anticipated road bike premieres in recent years.

After a nine-month collaboration between the motor racing giants and Specialized, the Venge was ready for its debut. Available in two models, it was the brainchild of Specialized's long-time R&D man, Chris D'Aluisio. D'Aluisio had taken a Specialized Transition out for testing one day in 2006. Having lowered the bars, he was shocked by the speed of the new fit. He

then outlined to his employer the idea of creating the first aero road frame.

From these discussions came the S-Works Venge, which first appeared in 2009. It weighed 4 lb 13 oz (2.18 kg). In the same year McLaren took the concept of the Venge and created a frame with cambered airfoil cross-section seatstays and a tapered head tube and steerer. The result was a full aero road bike that tipped the scales at 4 lb 9 oz (2.07 kg).

A week after the launch, the Venge won the 2011 Milan–San Remo Classic under Australian Matt Goss. Since then the bike has never looked back, with Mark Cavendish, Tom Boonen, Alexander Vinokourov, and a host of other racing stars racking up repeated wins in numerous events. **DB**

GIANT Trinity Advanced SL

2011 • Triathlon bike • Taiwan • Ultra-aggressive angular aero bike

Minimizing aerodynamic drag is a key design aim for any bike designed for solo riders in time trials or triathlons. Even among the latest breed of aero superbikes, Giant's Trinity Advanced SL was an extreme example of pure wind tunnel-bred performance. The problem with the design, though, was that it fell foul of the regulations of the Union Cycliste Internationale (UCI).

One of its contentious features was a structural section below the stem that contravened the ICU's 3:1 tube depth ratio. Specialized first tried this on its Shiv, but then dropped it from the time trial bike, though it remained on the triathlon version. Giant tried to dupe the UCI by pulling the stem down over the front of the bike, but the "beard" thus created had to be significantly trimmed on road-legal bikes. The bayonet

fork design still winds all the gear and brake controls tortuously around the various bearings and tubes of the front end to minimize drag. In common with many aero superbikes, the Trinity Advanced SL also gets a custom fixed-position aero handlebar with adjustable extension sections to keep the rider comfortable in a tucked position. The influence of Cervélo is clear throughout: The radical wheel-hugging curve and vertical seatpost section recall the P3, while the large keel section is very reminiscent of the P4.

Whatever the similarities, the Trinity is blisteringly fast in its own right, and is regarded as one of the quickest bikes on the pro racing circuit. But compromises in handling balance and braking control mean it's not a machine for the faint of heart. **GK**

ROSE Granite Chief

2011 • Mountain bike • Germany • High-value, high-performance all-mountain bike

With its straight tubes, the Granite Chief flew in the face of then-current fashion for curved and curled hydro-formed tubes. Also unconventional was the manually activated Kind Shock dropper seatpost, which was standard on the 8 model. Hydraulic, remote-control, RockShox reverb posts were available on more expensive versions of the bike. Lightweight frame tubing and DT Swiss wheels made the 5½-in. (14-cm) travel comparable with much shorter-travel bikes in terms of overall weight and climbing performance. The Granite Chief also came with a progressive short stem and wide bar combination when most bikes—particularly German ones—still compromised control with a cross-country-style hand position.

Optional equipment included SRAM's super-light, carbon fiber-rich X0 transmission, and mega-powerful brakes from Italian hydraulics specialists Formula. Suspension was handled with fork and rear damper from U.S. control kings Fox.

Some riders found that the suspension tune undermined the consistent control and traction levels. As a result, more recent Granite Chief models have come with a range of rear shock and suspension fork tuning options. **GK**

KUIPERS Sawyer

2011 • Kit bike • Netherlands • Limited-edition self-assembly kit bike

In 2013, Dutch designer and sculptor Jurgen Kuipers, who had previously made a tricycle from the branches of an apple tree, won the International Bicycle Design Competition in Taipei, Taiwan, with his Sawyer lowrider, a ready-to-assemble kit incorporating a custom-made, beech-plywood frame and components attached to an injection-molded sprue.

Kuipers began with a piece of foamboard on which he figured out the bike's geometry; he then drew on his experience as a BMX rider. Next, he bought a piece of standard builder's plywood and went straight to his jigsaw. It is form that enthuses him, not function or aerodynamics—hence his lack of concern that the Sawyer's bulky frame might make the bike hard to maneuver in city traffic, or that riding a plywood bicycle in the rain might not be a good idea. In his view, aesthetics are more important than utility.

Yet the Sawyer is practical, with front suspension and a refreshingly comfy bucket seat above a sculptured wooden frame that, unlike aluminum or carbon, exudes warmth and character. Does Kuipers worry about termites? He replies: "I think they prefer wood that stays in the same location and doesn't move around so much. And, probably, they're not fast enough." **SH**

COMMENÇAL Supreme DH

2011 • Downhill bike • Andorra • Multi-World
Cup-winning bike raced by the Atherton family

The Supreme DH first appeared in 2006, when Cédric Gracia moved from Cannondale to Commençal in order to become involved in the design of its downhill race bike. In the same year, Commençal also signed the Athertons, the first family of downhill mountain biking, who took the Supreme DH to World Cup overall and World Championship wins. Accordingly, the bike was offered for sale in the Atherton team colors and a Team Replica guise.

This versatile downhill bike has a head angle that is adjustable between 65 and 63 degrees, and an adjustable wheelbase that allows riders to tailor the bike to their specific requirements. Eight in. (20.3 cm) of suspension are delivered through Commençal's Contact suspension system—a single pivot positioned above the bottom bracket in line with the top of the chainring to neutralize pedal feedback while maintaining a low center of gravity.

In 2011, the bike gained a triple-butted 7005 aluminum frame with floating shock suspension linkage that reduced pressure on frame and shock, and gave the bike a slightly rearward axle path. These changes led to more wins for Commençal, including Rémi Thirion's triumph at the 2013 Andorra World Cup. **CJ**

GALLUS Paris Brest Randonneur

2011 • Road bike • USA • Classic frame for
long-distance audax events

The Paris–Brest–Paris (PBP) Audax race is a grueling 750-mi (1,200-km) ride across France. First held in 1891, it is the oldest biking event still held regularly on the open road anywhere in the world.

Entrants ride the route from the French capital to the westerly Atlantic port and back, around the clock. The 90-hour time limit means that even the first past the post is not guaranteed a medal.

Like all the other PBP competitors, Jeremy Shlachter, of Fort Worth, Texas, trained hard for the 2011 event. Unlike the other competitors, however, Shlachter built his own bike to ride in the marathon event. He finished it only a day before he flew to France. Although previously a fan of skinny-tired road bikes, he designed his PBP with classic touring features—relaxed geometry, large tires, mudguards, generator lights, and a front rack.

His stainless steel randonneur bike was coupled, so that he could take it on a plane. The KVA tubing was jointed with decorative lugwork, and the components were mostly Shimano. The cranks were IRD, the brakes Paul's, and the rims Velocity 650Bs.

Shlachter finished the PBP in 78 hours 31 minutes, well inside the cutoff limit. **SH**

14 BIKE CO. Custom

2011 • Road bike • UK • Signature bike from online hipster custom shop

This is no heritage-laden, ancient family-owned bike business; 14 Bike Co. is cutting-edge trendy.

The company is based in the old Truman Brewery in Brick Lane in the über-hip East End of London. Most sales, however, are online.

The bikes are hand built in the UK to customer specifications, and can feature all sorts of head-turning innovations, such as weight-saving paint borrowed from Formula One motor racing, and lightweight Columbus Zonal steel tubing.

Customers can browse the frame styles and shapes on the company's website. The base bikes have typically "urban" names like the Pimp 43 or John 33. Alternatively, buyers can choose from an extensive list of components, ranging from an untreated raw steel frame to white randonneur tires—a 14 Bike Co. machine is meant to be seen and admired. Features include bar ends with gold logos, brightly coloured tires and pedals, and elaborately decorative lugs. Other options include nineteen different saddles, seven types of wheel, and five different cranks. The biggest choice of all is in the palette of dozens of colors for every component, so buyers can create a truly unique custom bike.

As an example of 14 Bike Co.'s cool urban credentials, the company recently held a club night at a "secret location" in East London. Company founders Andy Ellis and Ted James then welded and built bikes for each of four DJs on stage while the music was played. The event was broadcast live on the Internet. **SH**

TREK Speed Concept

2011 • Time trial bike • USA • Innovative luggage-equipped aero machine

Having developed aero machines since 2000, Trek made a great leap forward with the Speed Concept, the design of which has since been copied by several other brands.

The Speed Concept featured a leading-edge or bayonet fork with a split fork steerer, and the shrouded brake and integrated stem and base bar concept that first appeared on Specialized's Shiv. The front end of the Trek was particularly slim and clean, splitting the wind like a carbon fiber scalpel. Rather than continuing the smoothness and curved sections right through, the Speed Concept introduced a radical trailing-edge aerodynamic concept borrowed from the automotive industry. The Kammtail concept is based on the idea of a virtual foil formed by chopping off the tail

of a teardrop tube to create a blunt rear edge. This generates swirling vortices in the wake of the tube, but the turbulence results in a smoother flow for most of the air streaming back off the surface of the truncated tube. Because this virtual foil is entirely fluid, it can also curve sideways when influenced by a side wind, making the frame more efficient and less prone to gusting than a conventional teardrop design.

Trek further increased the aero advantage of the Speed Concept by remaking in hard-case format the various frame bags used by long-distance triathletes to store food and tools behind the saddle and stem and in the crook of the mainframe. This effectively made them into extended fairings that further reduced drag to make the Trek one of the fastest machines around. **GK**

PIPEDREAM Sirius 650B

2011 • Mountain bike • UK • Steel-frame
hardtail for British trails

The Sirius was the first frame produced by Pipedream
Cycles, a company set up by Alan Finlay and Stuart
Davies, who were dissatisfied with the hardtail
mountain bikes on the market so decided to design
and build their own.

The original Sirius (2006) was made from 4130
chromoly, and had head tube and seat tube angles that
were slacker than the then-typical 71 and 73 degrees,
so that the bike could better utilize the increasing
amounts of travel available in suspension forks.

Five years later, a new and greatly improved Sirius
was unveiled. This incarnation retained chromoly for
the seatstay and chainstays, but introduced stronger,
lighter Reynolds 853 on the main triangle. The updated
frame gained a tapered head tube, and even greater
mud clearance, thanks to bridgeless chainstays and
a curved seatstay bridge. The new Sirius was also
furnished with sliding drop-outs to make it capable of
being run as a single-speed as well as with either 26-in.
(66-cm) or 27½-in. (70-cm) diameter wheels.

The original Sirius was a steel hardtail trail bike that
was good enough to go up against its full-suspension
equivalents. The latest version was generally agreed to
be even better and more versatile. **RB**

TOMAC Diplomat

2011 • Enduro bike • USA • 29er enduro bike
from the legendary John Tomac

Tomac bears the name of ten-time U.S. national
mountain bike champion John Tomac. Owned and
operated since 2007 by John and his business partner,
Joel Smith, the company currently has a range of nine
models, all of which are designed and developed in the
United States.

The Diplomat—Tomac's first full-suspension 29-in.
(73.5-cm) wheel bike—was so named in the hope that
it would stop cyclists arguing about the comparative
merits of this wheel size and the 27½-in. (70-cm)
alternative. Tomac claims that, in terms of fun, there is no
difference between the two.

Built from butted aluminum and weighing 6 lb
12 oz (3 kg), the frame is lightweight and as strong as
Tomac's 26-in. (66-cm) bikes, with sloping tubes and
tapered head tube combining to create a notably stiff
chassis. To keep the ride nimble, Tomac maintained
short chainstays by designing a removable seatstay
arch, and attaching the front derailleur to the chainstay
yoke. The unified rear triangle delivers 4⁷⁄₁₀ in. (12 cm)
of travel through Tomac's IAS rocker-actuated, single-
pivot suspension design. Because of the large wheels,
the Diplomat is available only in three sizes, but each is
equally worthy to bear the name of the grand master. **CJ**

SANTA CRUZ Highball Alloy

2011 • Mountain bike • USA • Affordable alloy counterpart of its cutting-edge carbon sibling

The Highball Alloy debuted in Sedona, Arizona, at the same time as the carbon fiber and alloy versions of the new long-travel Tallboy LT bike, as well as a 29er version of Santa Cruz's classic Superlight frame. This less expensive version of the earlier Highball Carbon didn't take long to create its own avid fans who appreciated the balance of encouragingly responsive handling. The frame could be supplied with conventional geared drop-outs or angle adjustable drop-outs for tensioning the chain on a single-gear setup. Handling could also be fine tuned by installing either a 4½-in. (12-cm) or 4-in. (10-cm) travel fork, depending on the rider's preference for racey or more relaxed riding. The ability of the tough and stoutly built custom-tubed frame that could take a lot of relentless trail punishment drew inevitable parallels with Santa Cruz's evergreen Chameleon hardcore hardtail, with the added smoothness, rolling speed, and traction of the larger 29-in. (73.5-cm) diameter wheel format.

While it was fairly expensive compared to more mainstream competition, as the cheapest bike in the Santa Cruz lineup it enabled aspirational riders to get astride a machine from this famous brand at a more affordable price, and it has proved consistently popular ever since it first appeared in the Arizona desert. **GK**

TREK Slash

2011 • Mountain bike • USA • Trek's all-singing, all-dancing enduro bike

Marketed as "an enduro bike for downhillers," the Slash incorporated some of the features developed on two previous Trek machines, the Remedy cross-country bike and the Session 9.9 downhill bike, and took account of rider feedback from team members Andrew Shandro and René Wildhaber. The makers also took due precautions to ensure that the product would withstand rough handling.

It is constructed from Trek's Alpha Platinum Aluminum with an E2 tapered head tube to increase front-end stiffness and a 5⅗-in. (142-mm) rear axle to increase lateral stiffness. Among the components are a custom-for-Trek Fox DRCV shock, which sits in a Full Floater suspension system and uses a hub-centric rear pivot to allow for active suspension under braking. A Mino Link chip gives the rider 0.6 degrees of geometry adjustment, just enough to make a difference. The Slash also has internal routing for cables, and was the first bike on the market to be compatible with RockShox's Stealth Reverb dropper seatpost.

The Slash had only just made its public debut when René Wildhaber rode one to second place in the 2012 Crankworx Mountain of Hell enduro downhill event in France. **CJ**

SPECIALIZED Crux Pro

2011 • Cyclocross bike • USA • State-of-the-art
CX racer

In the runup to the 2010–2011 cyclocross race season,
the Union Cycliste Internationale (UCI)—the sport's
governing body—gave riders the go-ahead to use
disc brake-equipped bikes in competition. At the time,
Specialized was developing the Crux Pro, its all-new
high-performance cyclocross bike. The alloy-frame
Crux Pro was designed to be a lightweight and razor-
sharp version of Specialized's Tarmac SL road racer.
It made its debut in 2011 with traditional cantilever
brakes; they were replaced by disc brakes by 2012.

An official disc-brake version of the Crux Pro
appeared in 2013, as well as a carbon fiber-frame
version, the Crux Pro Carbon. Although significantly
lighter, this new frame retained the exceptional
stiffness and sharp steering accuracy of the alloy
original. The Pro Carbon kept cantilever brakes to
minimize weight. It also featured so-called "nu skool"
geometry, derived more from mountain bikes than
cyclocross. In particular, a low bottom bracket made
handling stable and sure-footed—ideal for controlling
slides through slippery corners and staying upright in
deep sand. The top tube was carefully shaped to make
shouldering the bike easier whenever riders needed to
run around obstacles impossible to ride over. **RB**

STORCK Raddar

2011 • Electric bike • Germany • A bike
combining German precision and Swiss craftsmanship

There is much to praise about the German-built Raddar
Pedelex E-bike—including its motor, which was
custom built in Switzerland. It is a gloriously functional
piece of engineering, a 250-watt sports model set
within the rear wheel that delivers some truly smooth
torque. A patented torque sensor can tell how much
pressure is being applied to the pedals.

Power delivery, via a thumb throttle on the
handlebar, produces a constant torque level right
through the range, regardless of terrain and without a
sound. Even gradients of 1 in 10 or more are overcome
with only modest effort. The rider selects a slightly
higher gear than they might otherwise, and the sensor
detects that they are under pressure and calculates
how much assistance it needs to deliver. It therefore
assists riders rather than simply pulling them along. The
24-volt, 10-amp lithium polymer battery weighs less
than 4½ lb (2 kg) and may be charged within five hours,
either on or off its frame mount.

Of course, there is more to this bike than its motor.
It has Schwalbe Big Apple tires, front and rear hydraulic
disc brakes, and 27-speed Deore derailleurs. And it
has its share of awards too, including the International
Forum Product Design Award in 2011. **BS**

VELOCITE Magnus

2011 • Road bike • Taiwan • Super-stiff full-carbon sprint platform

The design brief for the Velocite Magnus was simple: Make the world's stiffest carbon fiber road bike. The Taiwanese company wanted a bike for sprinters, one rigid enough to withstand the immense pedaling forces of the biggest, most powerful riders.

Three types of carbon fiber were used to construct the monocoque frame. Lateral flex was almost entirely eradicated by optimizing the shape of each tube and reinforcing the areas under the greatest stress—such as the head tube, down tube, bottom bracket shell, and chainstays—with up to thirteen layers of carbon.

Maximum stiffness was the main priority for the Magnus, but the real challenge was hitting that target while keeping it lightweight and comfortable. After all, sprinters may ply their trade in the short distance before the finish line but, like everyone else, they still have to ride all day to get there. Thus, a patented seatpost clamp design keeps it flush with the top tube and exposes more of the seatpost, allowing greater flex where it has little effect on pedaling efficiency.

Velocite is one of the newest brands in bike manufacturing—the company was established in 2008—but it has quickly made a name for itself thanks to high-end highly focused bikes like the Magnus. **RB**

THE LIGHT BLUE Kings

2011 • Road bike • UK • Classic-looking steel road bike

The Light Blue Kings is a slim-tubed steel frameset with elegant looks that hark back to a bygone era. The brand, founded in 1895 by John Townsend in Cambridge, England, was resurrected in the twenty-first century by Ison Distribution, a company run by one of Townsend's descendants and still based in Cambridge. The light blue referred to in the brand name is that associated with Cambridge University—in contrast to the dark blue of archrival Oxford—and "Kings" refers to the University's well-known King's College.

The main tubes of the Kings are made from double-butted Reynolds 853 steel, while the seatstays and chainstays are double-butted chromoly steel. The lugged frame has everything brazed together, with gold-painted "lug lines" adding to the classic look. The frame tubes are very slim by modern standards, as are the legs of the triple-butted chromo fork.

Buyers who want the complete retro package can build up The Light Blue Kings with traditional down tube shifters thanks to the brazed mounts. Those who like the classic looks but would rather go for the convenience of modern bar-mounted shifters can fit "stop covers" on the down tube mounts instead, and so enjoy the best of both worlds. **MB**

HP VELOTECHNIK Grasshopper

2011 • Recumbent bike • Germany • A good-looking recumbent bursting with speed and strength

Honored with the 2007 Eurobike Award for innovative design and product quality, the HP Velotechnik Grasshopper is, thanks to its pair of 20-in. (50-cm) wheels, wonderfully compact at just 63 in. (160 cm) long. Cunning design makes it fast and stable even when fully loaded to its impressive weight capacity of 275 lb (125 kg), which includes up to 110 lb (50 kg) in the optional panniers. The bike folds up efficiently inside sixty seconds. Its "No-Squat" suspension design maintains a constant chain length over bumpy surfaces, preventing "pedal bobbing" at slow revs, yet still floats over rough trails. In other words, the wheels handle the rough, rather than the rider.

The Grasshopper possesses the geometry, and therefore the feel, of a full-fledged tourer/commuting bike because of the low-slung seat just 21 in. (54 cm) above the ground. With the seat height lying 5 in. (12.7 cm) below the bottom bracket, the bike has a low center of gravity. As a result, handling at speed is wonderful, and it is very easy to balance and get your feet down when you stop. The steering too is normally configured in an under-bar style for maximum stability and comfort, although this can cause problems in terms of ground clearance when the bike turns sharply at low speed. Consequently, an above-seat steering configuration is offered as a build option.

Other accessories include a headrest and the options of either a body-link or an ergo-mesh net seat, and very cool-looking black rims may be substituted for the standard rims. **BS**

USED Scooterbike Roadster 1.5

2011 • Recumbent bike • Germany • Chopper-influenced, small-wheeled recumbent

When Klaus Schroeder began designing bicycles in Cologne, Germany, in the mid-1980s, he had long grown weary of the pain associated with upright riding. He met Bob Giddens in 2002, and the pair began a series of long discussions on the form and future of pedal-powered vehicles. The birth of USED, in 2004, was the result—and, if you believe the hype, a ride on a Scooterbike Roadster 1.5 is just what Schroeder always wanted cycling to be: "as soft as a feather bed."

The Scooterbike was designed and built on two guiding principles: simplicity and comfort. It has front and rear hydraulic-damped suspension as standard, panoramic visibility, and a truly comfortable broad seat with lumbar support. Everything is close at hand: handlebars, gear changer, and front wheel are all close

and accessible, and conform to the USED philosophy that function need not come at the expense of style.

Options include automatic lighting, hydraulic brakes, and even a rearview mirror to keep an eye on curious onlookers behind. The Scooterbike's handlebars are adjustable by 4 in. (10 cm) in all directions, and the suspension has a spring element that can be preloaded to offset the bike's load.

The Scooterbike was designed with an array of add-on features to suit the needs and quirks of its owners. USED values and uses owner input in the development of its range, which includes urban and touring versions of the bike, and an urban trike that rides in reverse. All of them represent USED's vision for a stylish—and very comfortable—future. **BS**

ISAAC Muon

2011 • Time trial bike • Netherlands • Radically angular wind-cheater from Newton-inspired brand

When Isaac Newton, musing on the nature of gravity, famously watched apples dropping from the tree above him, there were no bicycles to distract him from his thoughts, and it was a long time before the first boneshakers were striding out along the roads. Yet he would certainly have approved of this angular aeronaut from the Isaac company in the Netherlands.

Given the pace of change in aero bikes, the Muon still looks remarkably fresh for a bike introduced in 2010, and updated in 2011. When it first appeared, the radically angled machine looked dramatically different from the flowing, wind-sculpted lines of the competition. The Muon has now been joined on the start lines of time trials and triathlons by other angular bikes from Scott, BMC, and Trek, but it is hard not to suspect that the Muon was an influential introduction.

The forward-thinking frame design is still up to date today. The front brake might be conventionally mounted, rather than hidden in or behind the fork legs, but the big square-section Isaac stem gives maximum steering stiffness and control. The rear brake and gear controls plug vertically into a large hump behind the stem on the top tube, which keeps them out of the way of the wind. The top tube's cross-section is aggressively triangulated for a seamless sync with the similarly geometric seat tube, which itself features a deep "wheelhugger" cutout to shield the rear tire from the wind and reduce overall drag. The rear wheel drop-outs are fully replaceable and horizontally slotted for micromanaging the wheel position.

Buyers can alter the rider position by ordering either the very steep, triathlon-style "Type A" seatpost or the more conventional rear-setback "Type B" model. Add a power-efficient press-fit-style bottom bracket, and the Isaac remains a force to be reckoned with when it comes to high-speed science. **GK**

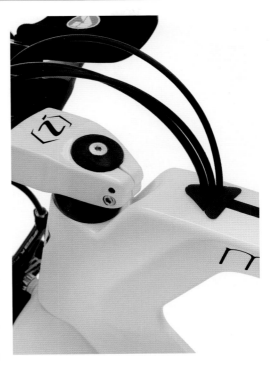

> *"[It] has a surefooted stability and assured authority that refused to get flustered however fiercely we spun the pedals."*
>
> Triathlon Plus magazine

◄ Isaac's Muon is aerodynamic science in motion.

HARVEY CYCLE WORKS Rapha Continental

2011 • Touring bike • USA • Custom bike for long-distance challenges

Rapha is an upmarket global cycling-clothing brand that has gradually diversified into accessories, books, and even travel. It also sponsors race teams and events. In 2007 it launched the Rapha Continental, a series of challenging long-distance road bike routes used as a way of promoting the Rapha brand. Rapha has linked up with various big-name makers over the years, and custom builders have also produced special custom bikes to take part in Rapha Continental rides.

In 2011, former ProTour mechanic and current VeloNews technical editor Nick Legan was given a brand-new Harvey Cycle Works bike to tackle one of the Rapha-selected routes: the USA Pro Cycling Challenge course. Legan produced words and images for the magazine as he made the weeklong journey

across some of Colorado's toughest roads. The perfect performance of the black-and-pink fillet-brazed S&S-Couplings bike prompted the experienced cyclist to write a passionate defense of traditional steel bikes.

The Rapha bike was well fitted out. It featured a special black-and-pink fi'zi:k saddle, SRAM gearset, and a wheelset built by Sugar Wheel Works of Portland using pink Chris King hubs, black DT Swiss rims, and Michelin Optimum tires. Sturdy stainless steel bottle cages and handy seat bags came from Arundel.

Bike maker Kevin Harvey mixes old and new technology in all of his bikes. Perhaps that is because he works as a machinist for the high-tech Andretti car racing team. Only in his spare time does he get around to building his highly rated steel bikes. **SH**

RENOVO R4

2011 • Road bike • USA • High-performance wooden-frame road bike

While metal and carbon fiber account for the vast majority of bike frames, a growing number of specialists are producing wooden frames. Renovo, based in Portland, Oregon, has already sold hundreds of its high-end wooden road and mountain bikes.

Wood is expensive, but enthusiasts praise the natural material for its smooth, stiff, and responsive handling. Renovo claims a wooden frame can "easily exceed the stiffness of a carbon frame by 15 percent." Wood also provides a near-silent ride that naturally absorbs shocks, unlike any man-made material.

Each frame is customized by hollowing wooden tubes to varying degrees of thickness. The tubes are made in two halves using computer-controlled cutters, then the halves are epoxy-glued together. Customers can specify a precise balance of stiffness for precision and flexibility for comfort. The type of wood may be selected, although all the tubing types are said to be extremely damage resistant yet easy to repair. Cables are routed inside the frame.

The R4 was launched as Renovo's top-of-the-line road bike. It has a beautifully finished, stiff, lightweight-but-powerful frame with an arched top tube and finely carved wooden stays. It is available in sustainable tropical woods such as wenge, padauk, and sapele, or "Appalachian woods" like black walnut and maple.

Aluminum is then used for the drop-outs, seatpost clamp, and derailleur hanger; steel for the head tube insert; and carbon for the forks and seatpost. Complete bikes cost from $5,100 (£3, 350). **SH**

BOARDMAN AiR TT 9.8

2011 • Time trial bike • UK • Aerodynamic
superbike from world record-setting designer

By 2011, Olympic- and World Championship-winning Chris Boardman had established an extremely successful cost-effective range of road and mountain bikes. There was one type of bike that was missing from the lineup, though: Boardman was not going to release an aero bike until he made sure it was one of the fastest available from any manufacturer.

As well as spending months in the wind tunnel, the Boardman team ran many different tube shapes and equipment positions through various computer simulations to create the slipperiest bike it could. The resulting bike included a radical "hidden" front brake behind the front fork, internally routed gear and brake cables, and wing-profile stays and fork legs to drag air away from the turbulent surfaces of the wheels. The frame was compatible with oversized crank axles for maximum power output. The aerodynamic seatpost could be reversed to give conventional time trial bike angles or a forward-set triathlon-style seating position for easier transition into the run section of the race.

A full range of component options was provided across four bikes, from the affordable AiR TT 9.0 to the no-expense-spared 9.8, which won the Hawaii Ironman World Championships in 2012 under Pete Jacobs. **GK**

BOARDMAN AiR 9.8

2011 • Aero road bike • UK • Olympic and
multiple World Championship-winning race machine

The data Chris Boardman gained during testing for the Air TT triathlon bike put the Olympic gold medalist turned bike designer in the perfect position to create an aero road bike. Many of the design cues from the TT are very obvious in the AiR road bikes. They do not have the hidden front brake fork, but the head tube and main tube shapes are very similar. The seat tube and seatpost sync in matched aerodynamic sections, and the flat-inner curved-outer stay sections actively pull airflow away from wheel turbulence.

Boardman then added the ultra-sure-footed handling of the SLR road bike to keep it totally safe at speed. Knowing the bike was likely to be a favorite of riders with a tendency for long, high-velocity solo escapes, he also spliced direct oversized crank axle power delivery with impressive comfort levels.

To say the resulting ride has been a success would be a huge understatement. Despite being the youngest bike in the range, the AiR 9.8 has already become the most competitively successful. With both the all-conquering Brownlee brothers saddling up on the Air 9.8, it has already won Olympic Gold and Bronze medals, plus World Championship and multiple World Cup wins in triathlon. **GK**

Boardman's World Championship-winning AiR 9.8 uses the best equipment. ▸

PAULUS QUIRÓS Reynolds 953

2011 • Touring bike • UK • Welsh polished-steel retro road tourer

Paulus Quirós is a two-man operation run by Jonathan Paulus and José Quirós in the remote western seaside town of Burry Port in Carmarthenshire, Wales. All its bikes are built as one-off custom commissions.

Like a classic sports tourer of decades gone by, this Paulus Quirós handmade bike reeks of sunny days exploring quiet country lanes. It has a retro look, but with modern techniques and kit too. For example, the bike has Reynolds 953 steel tubing throughout, but this is a modern stainless steel created with a special new aging process that builds in high-tensile strength.

The 953's joints are expertly silver brazed and finished with finely carved matching polished stainless steel lugs. Even the fork blades are made of polished 953. The makers have added brazed bosses all over the frame, for mudguards, brake cables, bottle cages, and luggage carriers. The seatstays are linked by a distinctive curved bridge that also acts as a mount for the rear brake cable. The aluminum mudguards are highly polished too, to match the rest of the bike. The tan leather saddle with copper studs comes from Brooks, of course, and is color matched to the leather handlebar tape. The finished bike has a 10-speed Campagnolo gearset, crank, and cassette. **SH**

WOODRUP Bantel Retro

2011 • Race bike • UK • A limited-edition bike made from a forgotten batch of Reynolds 531 tubing

In the 1950s, Stephen Maurice Woodrup had a small bicycle shop at 111 Burley Lodge Road in Leeds, England. A 10-mi (16-km) English national road champion, Woodrup built his first frame in 1960, and in no time acquired an enviable reputation for frame building. He taught his son everything he knew, and in the mid 1970s Stephen Jr. took over the family business. One day, somebody packed away in an upstairs storeroom dozens of sections of Reynolds 531 tubing, complete with Nervex lugs and Campagnolo and Zeus drop-outs, where they remained—untouched and largely forgotten—for nearly forty years.

In 2011, during a tidy-up of that upstairs storeroom, the tubing was rediscovered. In the 1970s, a small team of frame builders produced almost 800 frames a year and supplied frames for the top UK professional racing team, Bantel. Labels found still intact on the boxes suggested that their contents were purchased to fulfill a Bantel contract. Needless to say, the frames are now in short supply. The tubes were mitered and the joints tacked, never pinned. They were brazed with hand-held torches using Sifbronze and had few exotic angles as the Woodrups paid little attention to fashion. They just don't make 'em like this anymore. Literally. **BS**

PACE RC129

2011 • Mountain bike • UK • Gorgeous steel big-wheeler from classic UK brand

According to Isaac Newton, every action has an equal and opposite reaction, and what goes for physics also goes for tastes in mountain bikes. As most such machines have become more and more complex, more and more riders have deliberately gone for a cleaner, simpler style of riding, and a bike to match. Pace's RC129 rigid single speed is one of the leading reactionaries.

The frame uses Reynolds 853 steel, which is TIG-welded and then fillet-brazed before the joints are hand sanded to create totally seamless junctions. The rear stays are chromium plated for corrosion and scratch resistance, with the driveside chainstay and offside wheel and brake mounts unpainted to let the chrome shine through. The wheel can also slide forward and backward to take up chain slack if the rider prefers a single-speed system to conventional gears.

The RC129 is also available with rigid steel forks, and a single-piece stem and handlebar "stembar" unit color-coded to the frame, which echoes the original RC100 of 1989. The fork and stem of the RC100 were color-coded too, although then Pace chose neon yellow rather than the subtly retro Morris cream of the modern machine. These beauties bookend the story of one of the UK's smallest but most significant brands. **GK**

GREENSPEED Anura

2011 • Recumbent trike • Australia • Reversed-layout recumbent

Developed in conjunction with a focus group, Greenspeed's Anura project—codenamed "Frog" ("Anura" is the biological name for the amphibian family to which the frog belongs)—aimed to create an appealing alternative to the traditional delta-style trike.

Primarily intended for older and disabled people, the Anura is a recreational trike with a high seat that eases mounting and dismounting and gives the rider a better view—and higher visibility—in traffic.

Abandoning the conventional two front wheels–one rear wheel format, the designers removed the cross-member in front of the seat, which was set at a height of 17 in. (43 cm). The trike's welded aluminum frame and front boom are robust if a little utilitarian, and its underseat steering configuration is via width-adjustable bars with a turn limiter beneath the frame. A differential prevents sideways skating of the front wheel, and ground clearance has been increased by the addition of a Schlumpf speed drive. There are disc brakes all round.

The RANS seat has a nice lumbar support, but its shallow shape can cause sliding with spirited cornering, confirming the Anura as a cruiser rather than a rapid racer. If a more relaxed and friendly ride is what you're after, though, this frog is well worth hopping onto. **BS**

ARGON 18 E-118

2011 • Triathlon bike • Canada • Aggressively sculpted aerodynamic superbike

Cervélo is the company most bike enthusiasts would probably think of first if asked to name a Canadian bike manufacturer. However, Argon 18 of Montreal, Quebec, has meanwhile been quietly filling its trophy cabinet with an impressive array of honors and awards, and carving itself a very loyal international following in the process.

While Argon might not blow its own trumpet too hard in terms of hype, it certainly isn't shy about creating extremely striking-looking bikes, and the introduction in 2011 of the new flagship E118 frame confirmed the brand as one of the hottest around.

The angular front end is built around a bayonet-style leading-edge fork fairing that helps split the wind around the rest of the frame as efficiently as possible. The front brake is tucked behind the fork, and the back brake sits behind the cranks to keep drag to a minimum; the back wheel sneaks forward against a curved wheel hugger cutout on the teardrop-shaped seat tube. The integrated handlebars use an aggressively low gull-wing design to keep the rider aero efficient even when cornering or climbing. In fact, every part of the frame was computer profiled with airflow-simulation software before being validated in a wind tunnel.

Argon 18 has been careful to ensure that its frame conforms to the strict requirements of the Union Cycliste Internationale (UCI) so it can be used for professional road race time trials as well as triathlons. A sticker on the bike frame confirms that it abides by the governing body's rules.

The E118 isn't just about aerodynamics: The evolved AFS fit system provides far better comfort and handling balance than most superbikes, so it's no surprise that this bike has already left a string of rave reviews—as well as rival riders—in its wake. **GK**

Argon's AFS fit system includes radical gull-wing handlebars. ▶

WHYTE 901

2011 • Mountain bike • UK • Super-fun, affordable all-rounder

The Whyte company—named for its original designer, ex-Formula engineer Jon Whyte—made suspension bikes—including the PRST1, the 46, and the 146—that were outwardly radical in their overall design and equipment, and concealed some of their sharpest features beneath their hardtail exteriors. The semi-suspension 901 puts many of these qualities into a more affordable package with an alloy frame.

At 26 lb (12 kg), the Whyte 901 is light enough to pick up speed quickly, and comes into its own on descents. The stem is short, but there's adequate space between the tips of the trail width bars. The tapered head tube is capable of handling a stiffer, tapered fork. Among the features are a closed seat clamp, two bottle mounts, and threaded mounts for a rear rack.

The equipment, which comes partly from Whyte's own brand and partly from the SRAM component family, includes the Maxle Lite through-axle version of the RockShox Recon fork.

Whyte's determination to hold the price of the 901, in spite of the rising costs of tire rubber and frame materials, has necessitated some economies in the spec—the rear brake is old-school International Standard (IS), for example, and there is no adjustable drop-out feature—but, perhaps surprisingly, these cost-cutting measures have done nothing to impair the bike's performance.

The 901 struck a blow for riders on a budget, and demonstrated plainly that trail bikes don't have to be expensive to be enjoyable. **GK**

SANTA CRUZ Highball Carbon

2011 • Mountain bike • USA • Tough and versatile 29er carbon hardtail

Having had only one hardtail in its range throughout the first thirteen years of its existence, Santa Cruz could definitely be seen as a company that focused mainly on its extremely popular suspension bikes. In 2011, however, it answered the calls from fans who wanted an ultra-efficient racer that was even more purposeful than the 4-in. (10-cm) travel, ultra-light carbon fiber Tallboy suspension frame.

This was the dark and deadly-looking Highball Carbon. Despite being built around 29-in. (73.5-cm) wheels for extra rolling speed, the custom carbon frame was less than 2½ lb (1.1 kg), thanks to the best-quality materials and most exacting construction processes.

Unsurprisingly for a bike that Santa Cruz declared was "designed to do two things: 1. Race. 2. Win." the

high-class hi-tech Highball Carbon was an immediate with racers looking for ultra-low weight and uncompromising power delivery. A tapered head tube that accommodated oversized lower bearings and a screw-through (6 x ½ in.) 14.2 x 1.2 cm rear axle, plus a curved seat tube that set up a short rear end despite the bigger wheels meant the Highball Carbon was as sturdy as it was light.

Riders such as DH World Champion Steve Peat of Santa Cruz's Syndicate team used the Highball Carbon to devastating effect, even in short-course DH races such as the Sheffield Steel City event. Its high velocity, versatility, strength, and unexpected chaos capability has made sure it has remained a popular performance option in the Santa Cruz lineup ever since its introduction. **GK**

MIJL VAN MARES Stretch Cycle

2011 • Novelty bike • Netherlands • The world's longest bike

In 2002, students from Delft Technical University in the Netherlands established a world record for the longest bike: Their stretch cycle was 92 ft 2 in. (28.1 m) long.

This feat inspired the organizers of an annual cycle race at Maarheeze near Eindhoven to try to build a bike that was even longer. The Mijl van Mares team unveiled its creation in August 2011. It was an astonishing 117 ft. 5 in. (35.79 m) from stem to stern, 27 percent longer than the Delft bike.

As this book goes to print, the Mijl van Mares bike still holds the Guinness World Record in this bizarre field of human endeavor. It is officially and undisputedly the longest true bicycle that works with only two wheels and no stabilizers.

The bike has enough room to accommodate an army, but it can ridden by only two people, one of whom sits at the front and steered, while the other sits more than 100 ft (30 m) behind and does the real work.

The main section of the bike is constructed from a cube-shaped welded lattice of black tubing. The front and rear ends with seats and all components are bolted to either end of this box section. A wide, roller-style rear wheel extends on forks behind the rear seat.

The bike is driven by the rear rider, who operates treadle-style pedals that turn a chain sending power to the rear axle.

No details for the weight of the Mijl van Mares bike have been released, but it must be substantially greater than that of the Delft bike, which was 881 lb (400 kg), and had to be hoisted into position by a crane.

To qualify for inclusion in the Guinness book, both bikes had to prove that they were real working machines. The stipulated test distance was 328 ft. (100 m), which is less than four bike lengths for the Mijl van Mares machine. **SH**

SPIN Spitfire

2011 • Road bike • UK • Affordable bike made from aspirational material

Spin is a British company founded by Drew Gill, who, after having ridden other people's titanium frames for years, decided that he could make better ones himself.

Gill's self-confidence is reflected in his company— Spin isn't afraid to lay the hype on thick when it comes to bigging up its bikes, but there is no doubt that its cut-price titanium machines have some impressive features to back up the marketing claims.

The entry-level Spitfire is more than an ultra-basic-budget build. The down tube is cold-worked into a teardrop shape, and its seat tube is double-butted to minimize weight. The head tube is outsized for extra strength, and the Spin logo is machine-carved into

"High-quality titanium bike with exceptional production values; a smooth-riding eye-catcher."
Road.cc

the front face—not an easy process on titanium. Even harder 6Al 4V titanium is used for the chain hanger pip on the driveside seatstay. This feature is normally reserved for custom steel and titanium machines, not cost-conscious, off-the-peg bikes.

The weight of the Spitfire is within 2 oz (60 g) of Spin's top-level Supermarine frame, with which it shares classic Grand Tour geometry. In spite of its race potential, the Spitfire Mk1 is still equipped with hidden mudguard mounts to make it a great choice for both daily commuting and winter training. Spin also provides a whole menu of matching titanium finishing components, including stem and seatpost, to ensure that its machine really is the ace when it comes to the discount titanium dogfight. **GK**

ON-ONE Dirty Disco

2011 • Cyclocross bike • UK–Taiwan • Minimalist self-supported long-distance expedition racer

Most Dirty Disco bikes have happy but generally uneventful lives as versatile all-rounders. The lightweight carbon fiber frames make them light enough to race short, sharp cyclocross events, but they're tough enough to take on the roughest roads. Confident handling also keeps them safe in extremes of terrain or fatigue.

That's what made a Dirty Disco the ideal choice for Mike Hall, who rode one to victory in the World Cycle Race 2012 and broke the world record for circumnavigating the Earth by bicycle—200 mi (320 km) a day every day for three months.

Hall's bike was not a standard-issue machine, though: it was specially modified for his purpose. It had the same light aerodynamic carbon Reynolds rims

as those used in the Tour de France, but customized with thirty-two spokes rather than the standard twenty, for additional strength to withstand ninety-two consecutive days of hard riding. The bike had disc brakes to save wearing out the rim walls and risking a blow-out. The baggage racks—which carried all the equipment and supplies Hall needed for the whole journey—were lined up with the rider's position in the saddle to minimize drag and make the machine as aerodynamically efficient as possible.

The result was astonishingly effective. In Hall's own account: "Even with all my luggage on, the bike was almost as fast as a regular road bike. Incredibly the wheels didn't go out of true in the 18,000 mi [29,000 km], although I did wear out a few tires." **MH**

CANNONDALE SuperSix Evo

2011 • Road bike • USA • Sublimely smooth yet super-light superbike

Modern bikes are so well designed and engineered that the differences between most of them are absolutely tiny. Occasionally, a bike appears that puts all the others in their place with a truly outstanding mix of performance and charisma. One such is Cannondale's SuperSix EVO Hi Mod.

The name is a mouthful but contains a biography of the bike itself. The all-carbon SuperSix was introduced in 2008, superseding the Six 13 ("Six" being the atomic number of carbon; "13" that of aluminum). Then the arrival of the prototype Hi Mod in 2010 turned the SuperSix into a Giro d'Italia winner.

The entire SuperSix frame was remodeled by former Scott carbon-design guru Peter Denk. Each molded tube section was resized, and the direction and type of each carbon fiber sheet remapped. Ultra-light hollow frame ends were added, together with continuous high-modulus carbon fiber straps to reinforce the joints. Speed Save shock-absorbing areas were also included to reduce vibration and increase grip. This gave the bike fantastic handling as well as the highest stiffness-to-weight ratio of any bike at the time.

Denk saw that the concept's potential remained unfulfilled, so in 2012 he introduced the even lighter EVO Hi Mod, a bike that Cannondale team star Peter Sagan has used to phenomenal effect. For 2013, the EVO Black bike made another advance, saving $1^2/s$ oz (40 g) thanks to minute carbon fiber nanotubes in the bonding resin making the SuperSix EVO, at 1 lb 7 oz (0.65 g), one of the lightest production road frames ever. **GK**

ABICI Velocino

2011 • Urban bike • Italy • Remake of a classic Italian mini bike

The original Velocino was designed in the late 1930s at the behest of Italian fascist dictator Benito Mussolini, who wanted to give his nation a compact bicycle that was easy to carry and which could be folded and stored out of sight in the home. Unfortunately for the bicycle's mechanic–designer, whose name sadly seems lost to history, the era of the chic folding inner-city bike was still a long way off. When the entry of Italy into World War II forced the cancellation of the project, he took his own life.

That should have been the end of the story, but in 2011 a coterie of self-styled bike geeks-turned-entrepreneurs from northern Italy—Cristiano Gozzi, Stefano Stelleti, and Giuseppe Marcheselli—stumbled across a Velocino prototype in an old bicycle shop. Inspired by its aesthetic appeal, the trio decided to honor the memory of its anonymous creator and bring it back to life.

The reborn Velocino has a steel braze-welded frame and a back-pedal rear brake. Among numerous other idiosyncrasies are handlebars that can be turned through 180 degrees. This bike is plainly unsuitable for riders who regard a big front wheel as essential to their comfort and security, and the Velocino's weight distribution—the saddle is above the rear axle—makes it liable to launch into wheelies, a tendency that would be increased alarmingly with the addition of panniers or a rear rack. Just try not to lean back, if riding a unicycle isn't your thing. But on the plus side, there aren't too many bikes around capable of turning heads like this one can. Another attraction is the price—at the time of publication of this book, the Velocino retailed at €690 (around $950/£600). So even though the bike is not widely available, an adventurous cyclist with disposable income might easily be tempted to buy one without having tried it out first. **BS**

> *"Velocino showcases [Italy's] excellence in design and manufacturing . . . Simple and harmonious."*
>
> Blackle Mag

The Velocino is about style, not speed. ▶

MONDRAKER Podium

2011 • Mountain bike • Spain • Radical integrated-stem race bike

Inspiration for bike designs can come from a remarkably wide range of sources in both the natural and human worlds. Looking at the latest race bike from Spanish performance manufacturers, Mondraker, it's not surprising that designer Cesar Rojo cites modernist architect and Bauhaus director Ludwig Mies van der Rohe as a major influence. There's certainly a lot of evidence that Mies' signature statements that "God is in the details" and "less is more" have been taken to heart. While early carbon fiber frames mostly used smooth, organic lines to make them easy to manufacture without damaging individual fibers or leaving potentially frame-killing voids in the structure, the latest techniques allow angular tube shapes. Mondraker took advantage of this with the Podium, using faceted geometric tube sections for every

part of the frame except the cylindrical seat tube. The way the pipe punctures the flat rear stays is a key part of the frame design, but it's the front end of the bike that creates a real impression. Integrated stems that fit flush with deeper-than-normal "hunchbacked" top tubes had been used on road time trial bikes for aerodynamic reasons for a while. But Mondraker and French brand Look are the only companies to have transferred the concept onto their mountain bikes, and while they claim lower, stiffer front ends for better ride positions and accuracy despite tall 29-in. (73.5-cm) wheels, there's no doubt that the edgy cosmetic appeal is a factor.

The Podium also uses the latest extra-large crank axle standards and through axle wheels for a ride that's as fast and aggressive as it looks. **GK**

DECATHLON Rockrider

2011 • Mountain bike • UK • A top bike for a bottom price

Rockriders established their maker, French sports hypermarket Decathlon, as home to some of the biggest bike bargains in Europe. The Rockrider 5.2 certainly got off to a good start with the 6061 series alloy frame that used subtle tube shapes and reasonable dimensions to produce a light and durable chassis. It cost only around $300 (£200), but unlike most products at this super-cheap price point it wasn't so stiff that it would shake and batter the rider on rough surfaces. It even featured disc brake mounts for later upgrading, as well as mudguard and rack mounts.

Further features also belied the bargain purchase price. The Spinner Grind fork was more controlled than most low-cost units of the time. Shimano EZ Fire gears were fitted to produce smooth and instinctive shifting

through the usefully broad gear range. Properly treaded tires rather than the center ridge or semi-slick rubber usual on budget wheels made the Rockrider a machine that you could take off-road with real confidence.

While most bikes costing less than $400 (£300) are loaded with cheap steel componentry, the bar, stem, and seatpost of the 5.2 were all alloy, helping to keep weight to an impressively low and usefully responsive sub-29 lb (13 kg) level. Quick release rather than bolted wheels made puncture repairs or disassembly for transportation quick and simple, confirming this French flyer as a proper mountain bike and an incredible bargain, nothing like the over-heavy, under-performing mountain bike-style mess that one might expect at such a rock-bottom price. **GK**

2012

Carbon fiber evolution and the artisan reaction.

HIGH MODULUS AND HANDCRAFTED

SHAND Stoater

2012 • Touring bike • UK • Versatile Scottish-built adventure bike

Shand is a small traditional framebuilding and bike manufacturing company based in Livingston, Scotland.

Shand frames are made by traditional fillet brazing methods that bond the tubes together with a torch-melted metal filler, which is usually brass but may be silver alloy on the highest-quality products.

The melted filler flows into the gaps between the precision-cut ends of the tubes and the junctions, and is then built up to produce smooth-flowing joints between the tubes that are both strong and aesthetically pleasing. Because of the low melting point of the filler materials, the steel of the tubes is never heated to a temperature that might weaken it and compromise its strength or resilience.

The tubes are carefully selected for their suitability to the purpose and ride feel of each bike. The owners of Shand have professed a preference for adventure, so this Stoater model has been designed as a versatile "go anywhere" bike. It has disc brakes and space for larger tires that make it comfortable for anything from touring to rough path exploration. Rack eyelets are fitted, and the geometry is focused on long-distance comfort and an ability to shrug off poor-quality surfaces. The bike is a delightful combination of luxury and practicality. **KF**

PEGORETTI Responsorium

2012 • Road bike • Italy • Perfect blend of style and tradition from one of cycling's greatest names

Dario Pegoretti learned framebuilding through twenty-five years working for his father-in-law, Luigi (Gino) Milani, one of the most iconic framebuilders of the modern age. Like most Italian greats, Pegoretti spent years making the finest custom frames for professionals who wanted something their sponsor could not offer, before stepping into the limelight himself.

Pegoretti specializes in steel and aluminum frames, making only a few hundred frames every year at his factory in the Italian Dolomites. Despite his traditional background, he certainly isn't afraid to embrace the latest technology. He was one of the first European builders to embrace TIG welding, working closely with steel manufacturers Excell, Dedaccai, and Columbus to develop lighter tubesets and materials. Pegoretti has been an outspoken critic of the proliferation of mass-produced carbon frames, which force riders onto stock sizes and prioritize manufacturing ease over harnessing the best attributes of the material.

The Responsorium has the most comfortable and responsive frame possible, made from Stainless Columbus XCr custom tubing with longer butting and thinner walled tubes to minimize weight but maximize frame stiffness and power transfer. **KF**

RACER Rosa

2012 • Road bike • Italy • Custom bike with an Italian twist from London-based shop

Racer Rosa is a London-based bike shop that has thrived in the current British riding renaissance. As well as standard machines from mainstream manufacturers, Racer Rosa sells custom and off-the-peg frames and complete bikes from its Italian suppliers.

The steel frames are handmade by a small Italian family framebuilder, founded in 1947 by Giovanni Taverna and continued first by his son Ferruccio and more recently by his grandson, Antonio. The family subcontracted for Cinelli, Colnago, and Pinarello until those companies turned to Asia for mass-produced carbon frames. The Taverna family now maintains the old tradition by supplying classic steel tube set frames constructed both by lugged methods and low-temperature fillet brazing.

Racer Rosa also produces frames to order in carbon fiber, aluminum, and titanium. The shop focuses on customer service, measuring each buyer and designing the frame to cater precisely to his or her requirements and preferences. This means that a frame can be made for criterium racing, touring or track, in any size or color, with specific cable routing or braze-ons—a range of choice that big brand off-the-peg manufacturers cannot hope to provide. **KF**

VELO ORANGE Polyvalent

2012 • Road bike • USA • Versatile urban bike that can also turn its hand to light touring

Velo Orange's mission statement is music to many riders' ears: "Most cyclists don't race, yet they ride uncomfortable racing bikes and try to go too fast, and so miss much of the world around them. Our emphasis is on a more relaxed and comfortable style of riding, and on refined bikes that are comfortable on a century ride, an inn-to-inn tour, or even on a ramble down your favorite dirt road."

The company was founded by Chris Kulczyck, a civil engineer, to import European parts and accessories specific to the niche cycle touring market, from full metal mudguards through to blocks of French soap (yes, really). It later expanded into frames and components.

The polyvalent (general purpose) model shown here is a Taiwanese-made TIG-welded steel frame designed as an urban bike with touring credentials. It is made for the increasingly common 650B standard wheels, with room for touring tires and mudguards. Its reliable and weatherproof uninterrupted cable runs, horizontal drop-outs, and full rack mounts combine to create a setup that is sturdier and more resilient than that of traditional touring bikes, and is thus equally well suited to the often unpaved back roads encountered on long-distance U.S. tours. **KF**

FLAT FRAMES Wooden Frame

2012 • Road bike • UK • A challenge to convention

In recent years there has been a real resurgence in the use of wood for bicycle frames. In some ways you could see this as a throwback to the wooden-beamed dandy-horses of the early nineteenth century, but it's not just about retro appeal. Several timber frame builders contend that wood is Nature's own composite frame material. After all, it features extremely strong carbon-based fibers, held together with a strong natural adhesive. Used sensibly it can produce a great-riding bike that is more competitive with other materials than one might expect.

Mike Cubbage of Flat Frame Systems has spurned his traditional wooden chair-making skills for advanced birchwood ply laminate construction. This can be CNC-machined into almost any shape and size from only four pieces of wood, and given an exterior cosmetic veneer in a variety of finishes. Riders have praised the steady handling and road-taming characteristics of the material, as well as its radical flowing curves.

There is huge potential for this new branch of frame building—interesting noises have been made about nanocellulose, a wood pulp-based composite material that is environmentally friendly and claimed to be even stronger than conventional carbon fiber. **KF**

GENESIS High Latitude Alfine

2012 • Mountain bike • UK • Rugged steel-frame hub-geared mountain bike

One of the beauties of bicycles is the wide range of materials that can be used to make them. Carbon fiber is the lightest option for competitive riders; alloy is stiff, light, relatively cheap, and easy to make into any shape a designer desires. Between them, they make up the vast majority of frames on the market. Not every rider strives to get to the top or bottom of the hill first, however; for a lot of bikers it's the journey that matters most.

Consequently there is a growing return to steel frames by riders who prefer the "warm" smoothly sprung ride and retro appeal of slimline tubes. Genesis is a brand that provides excellent alternatives to alloy anonymity. The High Latitude is built on classic steel mountain bike lines with modern features. The 29-in. (73.5-cm) wheels are a smooth-rolling match for the sprung frame tubes of this minimum-maintenance mileage hunter. Genesis is also one of the few brands to use Shimano's excellent Alfine hub gears in a mountain bike format. The totally enclosed 11-speed gearing system is a perfect answer to the relentless rain and mud of winter biking on its native British trails. There's even extra room around the tires to prevent mud from clogging them up. This all makes the High Latitude an amazing bike on which to head off into the hills, whatever the weather. **GK**

BIANCHI Oltre Super Record

2012 • Road bike • Italy • Flagship bike for the world's oldest bike manufacturer

Italian brand Bianchi started in 1885, making it the oldest manufacturer in cycling with a rich heritage and an enviable list of top-end bikes. From its revolutionary 22-lb (10-kg) track bikes at the turn of the twentieth century to bikes for Fausto Coppi, Felice Gimondi, and Marco Pantani, Bianchi has been integral to the development of racing bikes and cycling worldwide.

There's no doubt that any bike lucky enough to have the Bianchi stamp on its head tube or the signature celeste blue paint job has a tough act to follow. In 2012 and 2013, the Oltre, later supplanted by the Oltre XR, has been ridden by the Vacansoleil DCM World Tour team, and the Oltre remains one of the most respected flagship bikes in the world racing peloton.

The full-carbon monocoque diamond frame uses X-Tex, Nano-Tube, WMP, and UTSS technologies to create a 14-lb (6.25-kg) bike, and the Oltre has enough standout features to remain unique. The wing-bladed front fork and aero-shaped head tube and seatpost, along with the slightly curved top tube and bladed seat post, are up there with any of the contemporary aero road bikes. The Campagnolo Super Record gearset is also available in an EPS electronic format, marking another forward step in both technology and price. **DB**

GIANT Twist Esprit Power Double

2012 • Electric assist hybrid bike • Taiwan • Efficiently integrated battery-powered pedal boost

The 2012 version of the Giant Twist allows a mix of pedaling and battery power, extending the range of this mass-produced hybrid bike. It was upgraded with a Shimano Nexus 8-speed internal hub transmission for more reliable gearing and two 36-volt lithium ion batteries to give a greater range to the electric motor. Giant estimates that it can keep going for around 87 mi (140 km). The electric motor system is well integrated. The battery pack is hefty but it is neatly placed on one side of the rear rack. The batteries can be removed to be charged, then locked back onto the bike. The Giant Sync Drive motor itself is hidden in the front hub. Casual glances may not reveal it's an electric bike at all.

The Power Double is not meant to be a head-turner. The aluminum frame is available in gray or black and in two sizes: 19¾ and 21½ in. (50 and 55 cm). Comfort is taken care of thanks to Giant's adjustable telescopic suspension forks and the Post Moderne seatpost with integrated suspension. There are Shimano twist shifters and brake levers, and an aluminum stem and handlebars. The 622 double wall rims are aluminum too, and are shod with Schwalbe Energizer tires. There is also an integrated lock, luggage carrier, and LED front light. **SH**

GENESIS Fortitude Race

2012 • Mountain bike • UK • Stripped-back-to-basics 29er for maximum feedback fun

UK brand Genesis deliberately injects its own distinct character to distinguish itself in an increasingly crowded market. The Fortitude Race is a prime example, delivering many of the features you'd normally get only from a bespoke bike in an affordable off-the-peg format.

The frame is built from Reynolds heat-treated-and-butted 725 chrome molybdenum steel-alloy main tubes. The rear stays are custom drawn to match the elastic feel of the mainframe, but the most dramatic aspect of the Fortitude Race is the frame geometry. Pretty much every other hardtail frame in existence can be used with a suspension fork. Most rigid forks are also built to include the extra length of adding suspension so the geometry stays correct. Genesis has deliberately used its own short-length rigid steel 29er fork and based the frame geometry around it. This produces a ride that's as close to engineered suspension as you'll get without using an elaborate truss-style frame and fork. Add large-volume and round-carcass tires from Continental, and while the Fortitude might be a jackhammer down steps or rocky descents, it floats over roots and smaller rocks. The lack of suspension and simplified drivetrain offset the weight of the steel tubes compared to alloy, making the Fortitude a tempting left-field choice for swift and skillful riders. **GK**

ALCHEMY Arion

2012 • Road bike • USA • State-of-the-art custom frame

While most riders can find a near-perfect fit and ride performance from the vast number of off-the-peg frame and bike options available, some aficionados want the tuned perfection of a custom bike. Builders like U.S. frame specialists Alchemy prove that made to measure doesn't have to mean sacrificing the latest technological innovations, as its stunning Arion road machine shows.

Alchemy based the Arion on its proven Xanthus model to give it the secure and confident handling often lacking in aero road bikes. It is possible to use gust-prone deep-rim aero wheels in a wide range of conditions without the risk of being blown off the road. The aerospace-derived shapes of the flattened-down tube and wheel-hugging seat tube also let the Arion slice through the air, whether you're conserving energy in a bunch or going for a solo kill.

The control cables are hidden inside the frame and it can be ordered optimized for conventional cables or Shimano Di2 electric controls. A tapered head tube guarantees precise response from the matching fork. As well as custom sizing options on every tube and angle, Alchemy also offer a full range of decals for the carbon frame or a range of custom paint colors: A true picture of personalized perfection. **GK**

GIANT TCR Advanced SL ISP

2012 • Road bike • Taiwan • Light but super-stiff and aggressive-riding race bike

Giant revolutionized road bike shaping when it adapted the MTB-style compact frame design for use in its Compact range.

The 2012 TCR Advanced SL ISP was an all-new design that upgraded the low-slung frame to create a truly outstanding ride. The most important addition was the oversizing of the whole front end of the bike. Giant's OverDrive 2 fork, head tube, and stem used a larger-than-normal 1¼–1½-in. (3–3.5-cm) bearing setup to maximize steering stiffness. The Giant Contact SLR stem used a massive square carbon body for twist-resistance.

The result was a bike that dared riders to charge descents and rip through corners, relying on the unshakable stiffness and super-clear tire feedback to leave brakes untouched. The vast, square-section down tube joined the super-stiff front end to an outsized PowerCore press-fit bottom bracket block and thickset rear chainstays. Factor in super-low weight from Giant's Advanced SL-grade carbon fiber composite material, and the TCR exploded up hills and out of corners.

Excess weight was removed and a more compliant ride in the saddle was created by using a cut-to-fit aero-shaped seatmast extension of the seat tube, rather than a conventional separate seatpost. **GK**

TIFOSI CK7

2012 • Road bike • UK • UK all-rounder named after famous Italian bike fans

Tifosi is the name given to the famously passionate, well-informed, and loyal roadside fans of Italian cycling. While the CK7 might be designed in the UK and built in Taiwan, the Tifosi crew works hard to capture the classic Italian flair and performance that the company name suggests.

Little is radical about the 7005 series aluminum alloy frame, but it's light enough to ride well while remaining affordable, and it features Tifosi's retro graphics pack that gives it classic appeal. The straightforward tubeset also delivers a prompt power response on climbs or when sprinting for the finish line.

Tifosi has supplied genuine Italian componentry where possible. The crankset and wheels are from hub manufacturer Miche, while the tires are from Vittoria. The bars and stem are made by Dedacciai and the saddle is a manganese-railed model from Selle Italia. The combined shift and brake Ergopower levers deliver confidently robust gear changes under pressure.

The ride is reminiscent of the sure-footed and stable handling of classic Italian brands such as Colnago and Pinarello. While the harsher ride over rough surfaces might give its affordable quality away occasionally it's still a distinctive machine with an attention to detail that richly deserves its inclusion in this book. **GK**

RIDLEY FAST

2012 • Road bike • Belgium • Radical aero road bike with integrated brakes

Belgian bike manufacturer Ridley has always been involved in pro bike racing, and that gives it more reason to maximize the performance of its flagship machines. The latest evolution of its Noah road bike draws heavily on innovative aerodynamic cues from its Dean time trial bike to create a bike that's truly as FAST as it sounds.

Ridley has adopted the split blade "F Split" fork legs developed by renowned aerodynamicist John Cobb. The idea is that by slotting the forks, airflow is actually sucked away from the turbulence created by the front wheel. All the frame tubes are aero profiled and Ridley even includes strips of rough material on the sides of the more vertical parts that is designed to smooth overall airflow by disturbing the airstream right against the frame.

While brake arms hidden by the structure of the fork and frame are increasingly common, the FAST extends the carbon fiber from the fork and rear stays into the brake arms, making the arms an integral part of the fork. This removes the weight of separate pivots and creates the smoothest airflow possible. The brakes are also very powerful, making sharp stopping a signature of the FAST.

The stiff frame means the Ridley has no trouble getting up to top speed either, but it's the bike's ability to hold that speed that makes it exceptional. **GK**

CANYON Nerve AL 29

2012 • Mountain bike • Germany • 29er version of Canyon's 2010 successful MTB

Canyon's Nerve full-suspension bikes had already proved an all-conquering mix of a highly detailed, hydraulically shaped, lightweight frame and fantastic value-for-money componentry since their introduction in 2010. However while Canyon had the direct-buy 26-in.- (66-cm-) wheeled market sewn up from its German HQ right across Europe, the 29-in. (73.5-cm) wheel was increasingly becoming the go-to size for the efficient, long-distance riding that the Nerve excelled at providing.

It was no surprise when Canyon unveiled a 29er version of the Nerve. Despite having larger wheels, careful tube shaping meant that it had 4¼ in. (11 cm) of wheel travel at either end compared to the 4½ in. (12 cm) travel on a 26-in.- (66-cm-) wheeled bike. It used the same neutral, easy pedaling, high-traction asymmetric four-bar suspension system managed by a Fox Shox damper, and Fox also provided the Float fork upfront.

Canyon carefully picked the componentry that made the biggest difference to the overall ride character. In the case of the top 9.9 SL version, that was the inclusion of super-stiff yet lightweight and "tubeless" airtight C29Max wheels by Mavic. The agile ride was a coup for Canyon and ensured the Nerve AL 29 became a popular all-round trail bike as soon as it was launched. **GK**

Canyon's Nerve 29er is an impeccably balanced trail-blasting bargain. ▶

KONA AfrikaBike

2012 • General-purpose bike • USA • Updated version of tough utility bike for African charity project

Kona's idea was simple: build a rugged, sensible bike that would appeal to traditional cyclists all over the world. Then for every two that are sold, donate one to healthcare workers, schools, water monitoring officers, and good-will organizations throughout Africa.

It worked. Since Kona first launched its AfricaBike program in 2006, originally to assist those treating HIV and AIDS patients, it has donated nearly 4,000 bicycles to Africa. The bikes mean that local workers can be much more productive than they could be on foot—which means that they can help more people.

The bike itself is designed to handle the rough roads of Africa in a stable and smooth way. The Kona's frame has a sturdy, step-through, top-tube design so that people of all ages and abilities can ride easily and

safely. The tubes are chunky, plain-gauge chromoly with Kona's ultra-proven P2 forks. The tough 26-in. (66-cm) wheels wear 1¾-in. (4.5-cm), puncture-resistant rubber, and there's a Nexus three-speed gearset, although the bike is also available as a single-speed. Standard features include a rear luggage rack and folding front basket, mudguards, a single-speed internal coaster brake, rear-wheel lock, and a kick-stand. There are wide Kona Riser handlebars for a very relaxed upright riding position, and the big Viscount saddle is also oriented toward comfort.

At over 42 lb (19 kg), this isn't a performance machine, but it is good at steady, comfortable cruising on rough roads and tracks. It's tough, easy to maintain, and cost-effective—perfect for its mercy mission. **SH**

KONA Entourage

2012 • Freeride/Downhill bike • USA • Big-hitting freeride bike designed with mountain star Graham Agassiz

The Entourage was Kona's product manger Chris Mandell's baby ever since the release of the highly successful Operator in 2011.

The idea was to build a short-travel downhill bike to allow for more fun riding. A bike you could pop around the trail, trick off jumps, and generally play around on more than a full out-and-out downhill bike. Kona's wonder kid and Monster Energy athlete Graham Agassiz was the perfect human guinea pig for the Entourage. His riding style is aggressive and powerful and he takes no prisoners. In short, if the bike stood up to the Agassiz treatment, it would be ready. After taking the bike for a tour of every type of riding Graham could think of, including huge 360s off jumps, incredibly steep chutes, and top-speed downhill runs, he was super-happy.

The Entourage is built for the rider who wants their bike to just work day in and day out. The big, durable pivots on Kona's walking-beam linkage and deep-interface hardware are designed to last without having to pull them apart and grease them every few rides. The 65-degree head angle and 13½-in. (34.25-cm) bottom bracket give you a happy medium between a playful-feeling ride and a stable downhill platform.

The bike also has 16⅓-in. (41.5-cm) chainstays that are shorter than the original Kona Bass Slopestyle bike, showing that the Entourage is not just meant for downhill duty. The Entourage is a true all-round bike whose purpose is defined by the rider aboard it: Downhill, big mountain, dirt jumps—it will happily eat them all up. **CJ**

PELIZZOLI Curdomo Pista

2012 • Track bike • Italy • True hand-built
artisan Italian frame

Giovanni Pelizzoli was born in Curno, Italy, in 1942, the
son of a bicycle mechanic. By his teens he had raced
bikes, repaired bikes, and managed junior teams,
but more than anything he wanted to build his own
machines. He founded the brand Ciocc in 1969 and
built the first frames under his own name in 1983.

This bike is typical of the Pelizzoli approach—a
classically lugged frame built to order and handmade
from Columbus SL tubing with crowned fork, chromed
front and rear dropouts, and ornate bottom bracket
shells. It is available in either track-specific or road
geometry; both versions have Pelizzoli's trademark
stunning paintwork and decals. (Pelizzoli still brazes all
of the steel frames himself!)

Pelizzoli's factory in his hometown is low key; two
small signs on the gate are the only hint you've arrived.
Inside, frames of Gilco tubing lie covered in dust, and
on the walls there are photographs of old bicycles and
the champions who rode them. All painting is still done
in-house: The decals are cut there, the fillets on the
aluminum frames and the miters on the steel tubes are
all handmade, and the dropouts are all filed by hand. As
a result, no two frames are exactly alike—so no one has
a Curdomo Pista quite like yours. **BS**

RITCHEY Breakaway Ti

2012 • Mountain bike • USA • Titanium MTB
with split travel frame

Folding bikes are often damage limitation exercises—
trying to minimize the bad consequences of having a
hinge in the middle of the frame. Ritchey's Breakaway
Ti is a much higher performance machine than most,
however, thanks to a clever but effective system that
uses just three bolts to dismantle the frame.

Once a collar around the tube end flanges has been
unbolted, the down tube pulls away from a socket at
the bottom bracket. The seatpost is then removed, and
the tube separates from the seat tube joint, splitting
the frame into two halves. The wheels and the two
frame halves then fit into a specially made padded case
measuring 31 × 26½ × 8½ in. (79 × 67 × 22 cm), well
within most airlines' carry-on limits.

The bike weighs 15 lb (6.8 kg), so even when the
case is filled with riding kit, it is light enough to pass as
cabin baggage. Tom Ritchey claims that his frame-locking
mechanisms contribute only 4 oz (100 g) to the total.

The frame is made of unpainted titanium tubes
with carbon fiber rear end and forks. These tubesets
come in six sizes, but that sort of sophistication isn't
cheap. The frameset comes without any wheels,
tires, groupset, or saddle, but still costs around $3,000
(£1,960), although steel versions are cheaper. **SH**

BLACK MARKET Killswitch

2012 • Slopestyle bike • USA • BMX-inspired slopestyle bike designed by pro rider Carter Holland

In 2012, southern California-based, pro rider-founded company Black Market Bikes unleashed the Killswitch. It was a 4-in. (10-cm) travel, full-suspension slopestyle and dirt jump bike built around a 6061 T6 custom aluminum frameset and the lowest ride height of any full-suspension bike of that time. This, combined with a 69-degree head tube angle and low 13-in. (33-cm) bottom bracket, made the Killswitch ideal for jumps and tricks, which isn't surprising considering its designer.

Carter Holland—a pro mountain bike and BMX rider—started Black Market Bikes with the MOB hardtail that *Decline* magazine hailed as "the most influential hardtail ever made." Following the success of the MOB, Holland wanted to build a full-suspension version. He teamed up with Pablo Tafoya—the man behind Corsair Bikes—to design the Killswitch. They designed the Hammer Link suspension system, which allowed them to create a low-profile suspension frame with short 16-in. (40-cm) chainstays that keep the rear end stiff and controllable. The main pivot revolves around the bottom bracket, allowing the rider to use single-speed or geared setups without complicated chain issues. Suspension company X-Fusion created a custom tube for its RCX shock especially for the Killswitch. **CJ**

NINER Air 9 RDO

2012 • Mountain bike • USA • Outstandingly good-looking large-wheeled race bike

The Niner brand, established by Chris Sugai, is a totally single-minded setup when it comes to wheel size. Every bike in its range is—and always has been—designed around larger-diameter 29-in. (73.5-cm) wheels.

Of all the bikes in its sculpturally formed range, nothing matches the Air 9 RDO for sheer speed and gorgeous looks. An evolution of the already show-stopping Air 9 Carbon, the "Race Day Only" slims down the curving, smoothly organic carbon tubes of its older sibling. It also uses a slimmer Press Fit 30 bottom bracket than the Press Fit 86 of the Carbon, which removes the need for alloy reinforcing rings. The steering bearings are also fitted directly onto the carbon head tube without alloy platforms, which together with the tubing changes, removes over ½ lb (0.25 kg) from the 2½ lb (1.1 kg) chassis. It's no wilting willow, though, as the oversized bottom bracket increases drivetrain stiffness and the rear brake is mounted inside the rear stays for clean routing and precise stopping feedback. The head tube is designed for a stiffer tapered tube fork and the headbadge includes entry ports for internal gear cable routing. Hiding the cables also gives the full beauty of the frame's gracile tubes and the luxuriant vivid green–black or pure white–black two-tone paint job choices. **GK**

EVIL Undead

2012 • Downhill bike • USA • A full-carbon evolution of the Evil Revolt DH bike

After two years of problems with the aluminum Revolt downhill bike, Evil had had enough. The constant battle with manufacturing incompetency, delivery issues, and final complete breakdown of communication and business relationships left Evil Bikes out in the desert, with many loyal customers waiting to hear whether they would get a warranty for their poorly welded Revolt.

Evil started again from the ground up. New design, new factory, and new carbon fiber material. As soon as Evil released the photos of the aptly named Undead, all wrongs were righted. The promise that everyone with a warranty-worthy Revolt would receive a brand-new Undead frame left people stunned. The new design still focused around Dave Weagle's DELTA (Dave's Extra Legitimate Travel Apparatus) link suspension design. This unique linkage allows the rider to adjust the geometry of the bike without altering the suspension characteristics. The frame is molded using unidirectional carbon with custom-tuned chassis flex. The bike was ridden in 2012 by Red Bull Rampage winner Cam Zink and World Cup racers Brook MacDonald, Luke Strobel, and Wyn Masters. Filip Polc also won Red Bull's Descenso Del Cóndor urban downhill race in Chile on his Undead in 2012 to mark Evil's return to the top of the podium. **CJ**

FOCUS Cayo Evo 1.0 22-G Chorus

2012 • Road bike • Germany • Production bike designed by custom builder

Whatever the industry, there's an inevitable "trickle down" of features introduced on premium-priced flagship items down to lower-cost, mass-market ones. Bikes like the Focus Cayo Evo are a fantastic example of the kind of bargain buyers can get by biding their time.

In the 2012 Focus road range, the Cayo Evo played second fiddle to the Izalco frame, but it certainly wasn't short of state-of-the-art features. The lean-legged fork used a tapered top to add steering stiffness and accuracy without excess weight or component matching issues. Tapering main tubes tailored stiffness and strength throughout the frame, with a pressed-in bottom bracket in the belly for maximum pedaling response. Focus also produced dedicated frames for both mechanical and electric gear-shift systems.

The Chorus 1.0 pictured here uses a Chorus gearset from Campagnolo to steal another march on competing bikes. That's because although SRAM and Shimano have since followed suit, in 2012 Campagnolo were still the only manufacturers producing an 11-speed rear gear cassette. Combined with a carbon fiber-armed chainset up front, this gave the Cayo twenty-two gears (hence the "22-G" suffix) against the twenty of most bikes at this price point. **GK**

◁ Evil's aptly named Undead is a carbon fiber comeback king.

High modulus and handcrafted **651**

COOPER T100 Spa

2012 • Urban single-speed bike • UK • The Spa reprises a famous motoring marque

It can be a 1956 Chevrolet Bel Air or a Harley-Davidson Fat Boy—it doesn't really matter. Whenever you apply a copious amount of chromium to things that move, something magic happens; a truism for motorcars, motorcycles, and bicycles such as the Cooper T100 Spa.

Cooper first began manufacturing bicycles in 2009, with the unveiling of the T100 Monza and Sebring at the Earls Court Cycle Show. They were followed by the T200 series, bicycles inspired by the lightweight racing bikes of the 1960s. The Spa was named after the famous Grand Prix circuit in Belgium of the same name, the track where the Australian Formula 1 racing car driver Jack Brabham clinched the 1960 World Championship in his Cooper Climax. Cooper's two-wheeled chrome homage to Brabham's achievement is an all-rounder, ideal for

commuter jaunts, leisure, and track, with a double-butted Reynolds 520 frame, Sturmey-Archer crankset, Brooks B15 swallow saddle set above its chromed rail, and all with an aggressive, tracklike styling including classically shaped handlebars reminiscent of the tour bikes of the early 1900s, wrapped in racing green Brooks bar tape. It has both single-speed freewheel and fixed-gear options, and the ride is smooth, thanks to its matte black Alex R475 rims and responsive Continental tires.

The extent and perfection of the Spa's chrome work gives it an allure few bikes can hope to match. And if you're tempted to buy one but are thinking of holding out in the hope of finding a cheaper production bike with a similar finish, take note of the words of John Cooper himself: "You buy cheap, you buy twice." **BS**

NS Soda Slope

2012 • Slopestyle bike • Poland • Bombproof Polish jump and stunt bargain

The NS Soda Slope was designed with slopestyle rider Martin Söderström in mind. He had been riding for NS Bikes for a few years and was rapidly rising up the ranks of the slopestyle circuit. In 2010, NS Bikes released the Soda at Eurobike, explaining that it would be the bike on which Martin would continue his winning streak in 2011.

Unfortunately that winter Martin signed with Specialized Bicycles, leaving NS with a brand-new slope bike and nobody to ride it. Then along came Monster Energy rider Sam Pilgrim, who signed with NS in 2011 and took the Soda Slope to the top of the podium nine times in 2011, coming third overall in the Freeride Mountain Bike World Tour.

The Soda Slope is based on the Soda full-suspension family, which includes a trail bike and a freeride bike. The

difference with the Soda Slope is that the suspension system uses a concentric bottom bracket, meaning the suspension pivots around the bottom bracket. This allows the rider to run the bike as a single speed or with gears. The classic slopestyle 4 in. (10 cm) of rear suspension, along with super-stiff rear end and hardtail geometry, make the Soda Slope exactly what a slopestyle rider wants. The chainstays are some of the shortest available on a production full-suspension bike, and the linkage's machined elements keep the whole bike incredibly stiff—something you undoubtedly need when landing 360s over huge jumps. Sam Pilgrim went on to win another five rounds of the 2012 FMB World Tour, finishing fifth overall and continuing his success in slopestyle competition on his Soda Slope into 2013. **CJ**

PIVOT Mach 5.7 Carbon

2012 • Mountain bike • USA • All-round
suspension machine using signature suspension system

Pivot Cycles was founded in 2006, but president Chris Cocalis has been in the industry longer than most of his peers. After attending a maintenance class in his local bike store at the age of nine, he started to spend every spare minute in its workshop. By 1987, he had built his first frame, and he co-built his first titanium frame with a local aerospace welder a year later, before they launched Titus cycles in 1991. Over the course of the next seventeen years, he developed the Titus brand and built flagship bikes for many prestige U.S. brands. He also helped develop composite frame-building techniques with his Exogrid, Isogrid, and MaxM technologies.

Cocalis launched Pivot into a crowded mountain bike market, and bought in help from suspension designer Dave Weagle. By evolving his signature DW Link suspension system, Weagle built the perfect base for an efficient, high-control trail bike. The aluminum Mach 5.7 chassis created by Cocalis' team proved the versatility of the almost 6-in. (15-cm) suspension movement design. Cocalis thought the bike still hadn't hit its full potential, so he set about prototyping a carbon frame. The result is the Mach 5.7 Carbon, with a lightweight flowing chassis of high-pressure molded carbon fiber and the same powerful DW Link performance as its alloy sibling. **GK**

LABYRINTH Agile

2012 • Mountain bike • France • Tough and
agile newcomer to the Enduro scene

Labyrinth was formed in 1991, but only recently has its reputation spread globally. This is in no small part because of the performance of the aptly named Agile.

Designed for the increasingly popular Enduro racing scene—which fuses elements of DH and technical cross-country events to create a truly testing multi-stage format—the Agile provides 6 in. (15 cm) of suspension travel. The way this travel is delivered really cements the Agile's reputation as one of the best bikes in its category. The Adapt Link System suspension is based on a conventionally placed single pivot but uses a distinctive linkage system to drive the vertically mounted rear shock absorber. As the back wheel moves through the travel, the shock leverage changes from smooth and easy, through a consistent linear spring rate in the middle part of the stroke, to a dramatic final ramp-up that stops the biggest hits from causing a blunt impact. The Marzocchi Roco shock is custom-tuned to cope with the varying leverages too.

The frame uses triple-butted 7005 aluminum that's heat-treated after welding, and the linkages are cold-forged for maximum strength. Chain device mounts and a tapered head tube mean it's compatible with all that aggressive riders need for a winning time. **GK**

CANNONDALE SuperSix Evo Tourminator

2012 • Road bike • USA • Custom-painted race bike of unstoppable Slovakian sprinter

A full custom paint job certainly says you've arrived in the pro peloton, and few riders have arrived with greater force than young Slovakian powerhouse Peter Sagan. The Team Liquigas–Cannondale star didn't just have his bike handed to him, though: he had to earn it. After he won an unprecedented four stages in the 2012 Tour of California, team staff told him that they'd give him a custom-painted bike if he managed to win a fifth. Sagan promptly delivered on his side of the bargain, so a Cannondale Super Six Evo with Sagan's custom geometry—a large front end matched to a small rear end for maximum sprinting stiffness—was duly despatched to custom-paint specialists Artech Design in Italy.

Sagan's established "Terminator" nickname—firmly underlined by his seemingly unstoppable performance in California—was adapted later that year to "Tourminator" in the confident expectation that he would excel in the forthcoming Tour de France. Artech picked up on this in its custom paint job for the prize bike, which included a superbly detailed Terminator skull on the face of the head tube, cunningly painted so that the internal cable routing morphed neatly into the sinister brow lines. To match Cannondale–Liquigas colors and Sagan's intention to take the overall points jersey, the head was given blazing green eyes. The same vivid green was used to create a fuzzy LCD computer display effect behind the big "Tourminator" slogan panels on the top tube and the Cannondale logos on the down tube and fork. The remaining logos were picked out in suitable metallic silver. Lever hoods, crank axle caps, and Speedplay pedals were all color-coordinated too.

Sagan lost no time in consolidating his reputation, taking his stunning new machine to victory on the very first stage of the 2012 Tour. **GK**

> *"The tradition of bike brands giving select riders custom-painted bikes continues with the stunning Tourminator."*
>
> road.cc

Peter Sagan rides his Super Six at the 2012 Tour de France. ▶

ONIX RH

2012 • Road bike • UK • Start-up road bike brand developed with top rider input

The appeal of creating your own bike brand has always been strong among people bewitched by riding but bored with their current jobs. In the United States, that seems to generally involve moving to Portland, Oregon, and making painstakingly detailed steel frames. In the United Kingdom, sourcing a carbon frame from the Far East and building a website to sell it seems the more popular option. When lifelong printer Craig Middleton set up his own brand, however, he recruited one of Britain's most successful riders, Rob Hayles, as a development consultant, and top TV bike pundit David Harmon to promote it. And rather than just picking a frame and fork from an open mold catalog, he worked carefully with the best Far Eastern carbon companies to create an optimum blend from the available options.

The Black RH was perfect for recreational riders like Middleton himself, who often start a ride stiff and fatigued, and do not want or need a brutally rigid race bike. This bike had a slightly taller head tube and more relaxed handling feel than a pure racer, so you could breathe easy on long climbs and technical descents. A top-quality fork and oversized BB30 bottom bracket meant it still felt solid in the right places, and at just over 15 lb (6.8 kg), it was no slouch on climbs. **GK**

VAN NICHOLAS Aquilo

2012 • Road bike • Netherlands • Electronic shift-compatible titanium all-round roadster

Dutch titanium specialist Van Nicholas produces a whole range of corrosion-proof rides, from road bikes to hardcore mountain machines. Its Aquilo frame is ready for the latest transmission technology, and features all Van Nich's usual high-quality detailing on a plain gauge titanium tubeset.

While the 3AL 2.5V titanium alloy tubes don't have the variable wall thicknesses of the top bikes in the Van Nicholas range, they are shaped to accommodate a range of loads with a subtly flared, integrated bearing head tube and outsized press-fit bottom bracket for extra stiffness. The rear drop-outs are connected to the rear stays with neat perpendicular tube sections that maximize the weld contact area without adding weight or stress to the structure. The tubes are also drilled and ported for the electronically controlled shifting systems and their batteries, making them upgradable with a wide range of custom-build kit options.

The frame has a lustrous hand-brushed finish, but it's not just aesthetics that have made Van Nicholas so popular. The company consistently produces bikes that offer a glove-like fit and friendly yet inspiring handling, and the use of titanium enables it to offer frames for life at an affordable cost. **GK**

The Aquilo frame is loaded with neat signature detailing. ▸

AEROSPACE GRADE

NUKEPROOF Mega AM

2012 • Enduro mountain bike • UK • Lightweight long-travel hell-raiser for grueling gravity races

The Nukeproof brand name was first applied to hubs and a few other components in the early boom years of mountain biking. It reappeared recently as a hardcore riding-oriented house brand of the Northern Irish cycling super-shop Chain Reaction.

The Mega frame was designed to tackle extreme endurance downhill events such as the French Mega Avalanche races. However, while the downhill bike-style geometry and cost-effective kit selection of the original 2011 bike showed the potential of the aptly named Mega, the frame was too flexible to deliver essential accuracy in the most dangerous and dynamic situations.

This led to a redesign of the Mega AM tubeset in 2012, using outsized square-section tubing and super-strong forged and machine-sculpted "keystone" sections

around the bottom bracket, main pivot, rocker link mount, and other high-stress areas.

The low chassis geometry put the center of gravity close to the ground, which meant the bike felt extremely grounded when pushed hard through corners. The long front end helped the wheel self-correct if it was knocked off-line by roots or rocks, and the kit included a stubby stem and wide bar for a power-assisted steering feel.

While the suspension architecture was a simple low-pivot swingarm with separate shock strut and shock-driving swing link, the revised shock sucked traction and smoothness out of even the roughest trails. Add a similarly controlled long-travel Rock Shox Lyrik fork and a very well-priced complete build, and the Mega AM was a genuine smash hit with aggressive gravity riders. **GK**

KIRKLEE 29er Dream Machine

2012 • Mountain bike • USA • Lefty fork carbon custom

The specialist high-end builder KirkLee makes bikes only from carbon. That specialization allows it to concentrate on the multitude of intricate carbon bonding and molding techniques to create excellent lightweight frames.

The KirkLee 29er Dream Machine is a hardtail mountain bike using those big wheels and tires within a very specialized frame structure. Take, for example, the rear triangle. KirkLee has molded independent seat- and chainstays. These are precisely ovalized and hour-glassed. This allows them to combine strength and style with perfect heel and chain clearances. The aluminum drop-outs are custom-machined for each frame too. These are designed carefully so they can deal with the structural stresses between the drive-side and non-drive-side stays. They also include provision for

mounting an electronic gear shift system if the customer chooses one—and it would have full internal routing.

Other features demonstrate the KirkLee attention to detail. The integrated seatpost is round in section but slightly tapered, the head tube uses a Cannondale stem and steer tube system with integrated bearings, and the front fork is a distinctive left-side-only unit. The fork can be more conventional if customers request it. Note also how the rear brake cabling is routed through the tubing for a protected and cleaner look to the bike.

The frame weighs 2 lb 14 ounces (1.3 kg), while a made-up bike would weigh around 19 lb (8.6 kg), depending on components used. KirkLee prides itself on fitting 100 percent American parts to its bikes. Final cost? The frameset alone is $5,000 (£3,300). **SH**

NORCO Aurum

2012 • Downhill bike • Canada • Super-successful Canadian downhill bike

The Norco Aurum was so vastly different in style, design, and technology from anything Norco had released in the past ten years that people found it hard to believe it was a Norco bike. It was designed predominantly by former Rolls-Royce aerospace engineer Owen Pemberton: "From the outset this project had one goal: to create a top-class downhill race machine, a bike capable of handling the harshest terrain the World Cup circuit can serve up without breaking a sweat. Building on the success of our 2011 ART (Advanced Ride Technology)-equipped bikes such as the Range and the Shinobi, the bike employs our ART philosophy optimized to suit a downhill race application. Suspension kinematics were tailored to give a perfect balance of small bump compliance, square edge performance, and pedaling efficiency."

Gone from the Aurum is the Specialized FSR suspension that Norco had been using for the past decade. Gone too is the previous North Shore-inspired geometry and build. The Aurum is built purely to win downhill races, and its angles show it; slack for stable steering and with a low center of gravity for supreme grip. The new ART suspension system also gives the rear wheel a rearward axle path, allowing it to move up and out of the way of block and rock obstacles and improving braking. Other small frame details, like integrated front suspension bumpers and built-in seatpost clamp, show the Norco design team's dedication to detail. The *Dirt Mountainbike Magazine* Norco DH team raced the Aurum in the 2012 World Cup season along with Bryn Atkinson and Red Bull athlete Jill Kintner. **CJ**

NORCO Sight SE

2012 • Mountain bike • Canada • All-rounder mountain bike designed by Rolls-Royce engineer

Norco has always delivered rock-solid free ride bikes, and former Rolls-Royce aerospace engineer and Sight designer Owen Pemberton, who came to bike design via an unconventional route, actually started working for Norco in its hire shop at the world-famous Whistler Mountain bike resort north of Vancouver. It's exactly this experience of working in one of the harshest—but most fun—bike-testing environments on Earth that enabled him to create a trail bike that became an award-winning benchmark as soon as it appeared.

By using a smoothly sculpted, hydraulically shaped aluminum alloy frame, he was able to shift the heavy weight problems that had always dogged Norco's all-rounder bikes. Smart design of the stays and linkages plus the latest wheel-tightening ½-in. (12-mm) hollow axle at the rear meant it was still stiff enough to take speed and stunts to the limit.

Pemberton's ART suspension modified a classic rocker linkage design to make it more stable under pedaling but also more responsive to big hits when freewheeling. The resulting bike felt energetic through the pedals yet carried speed and control through rocky, rooty, or rutted sections superbly. The handling of the Sight was also informed by Norco's long experience with super-confident gravity bikes, making the Sight supremely sure-footed.

The frame was lightened for 2013 and joined by a 650B wheeled version, which Owen described as "a bit of a different beast to the 26-in. [66-cm] Sight, it still has the same soul, but it's like its rowdier big brother." **GK**

SPA CYCLES Audax

2012 • Touring bike • UK • Titanium frame
provides strength and lightness for all-day rides

Half the density of steel yet every bit as strong, titanium
had a rocky introduction to the world of cycling. Some
early manufacturers, emboldened by how thin titanium
could be made, went too far in the pursuit of lightness,
and their titanium frames developed a reputation for
excessive flexing. It took a while for designers to realize
they could increase the frame's wall thickness and still
achieve the balance of lightness, strength, and flexibility.

The Audax comes with SRAM Apex 20-speed
compact double gearing, which provides a gear range
comparable to many road triple groupsets and often
leaves a gear or two in reserve, even on the steepest
ascents. And though its Schwalbe Durano tires aren't
road-race thin, they're durable and shock-absorbent,
not to mention mounted on nicely crafted Rigida Chrina
eyeleted rims with thirty-six Sapim spokes.

With the Audax, Spa targeted a specific niche: the
less competitive middle-aged rider who wants a road
bike more attuned to big days out than bunch sprints.
Not everything is Ti, however—the forks are carbon—
as tapering forks are too costly to produce in Ti for small
manufacturers. The Audax may look a tad utilitarian, but
unlike some of its competitors it can take a mudguard,
and a rear rack, and there's no toe overlap, either. **SH**

BMC Timemachine TM01

2012 • Time trial bike • Switzerland • Radical
angular time trial specialist

Conventional aerodynamics and carbon construction
tend to breed smooth, flowing lines, but the latest
structural and wind-tunnel research is producing a
whole new breed of more angular aeronauts. Few bikes
showcase this better than BMC's radical Timemachine.

The "Sub A" aerodynamics start with a bayonet-style
fork that runs up the front of the conventional head tube
to deepen the front end of the frame for minimal drag.
The deep down tube, stepped triangular top tube, and
wheel-hugger seat tube with matching seat post are
fully wind tunnel profiled too, while the bladed rear stays
dogleg off the back of the mainframe with an angular kink.

The Timemachine also features extensive component
integration, such as the P2P stem that uses multiple
interlocking sections that can be rearranged to give a
wide range of potential positions for the bars. Custom-
designed linear pull brakes are set into the leading edge
of the fork, while the second set are inset under the rear
chainstays for smooth airflow. On bikes using Shimano's
latest Di2 electronic shifter gears, the battery is built into
the base of the seatpost. Add top-flight components,
such as deep-section carbon wheels and Shimano Dura
Ace transmission, and you've got a genuine time traveler
on your hands. **GK**

BMC Trailfox

2012 • Mountain bike • Switzerland • Versatile
Swiss all-mountain machine

While Swiss technologist BMC is better known for its road and time trial bikes and the eponymous team that rides them, it also produces a range of distinctive and well-detailed mountain bikes.

The Trailfox is based on BMC's own suspension system that delivers 6 in. (15 cm) of rear-wheel travel via a linkage-driven Fox shock-absorber. Like many European mountain bikes, this suspension is tuned toward the extremes of riding. It pedals extremely well on the long, smooth climbs that are characteristic of Swiss, German, and Austrian mountain events. It also uses its full-suspension travel easily over rolling bumps and compressions on less technical, high-speed descents.

The underlying handling geometry of the bike is very good, with a relaxed head tube giving confidently stable self-straightening steering at speed. The heavily shaped alloy tubes produce a stiff and precise frameset, with accuracy boosted by screw-in axles through both front and rear wheels. Easton provides the well-shaped cockpit kit, while Shimano takes on the transmission duties.

The original alloy version has now been joined by a lighter but considerably more expensive carbon fiber version for those Trail Foxes who want to get up the hill or out of corners a bit faster. **GK**

BMC Fourstroke FS01 29

2012 • Mountain bike • Switzerland • Ultra-stiff
Swiss race machine

BMC's carbon road bikes are renowned for their precise and high-velocity performance, and BMC has transferred those strengths onto the cross-country trail arena.

The Fourstroke is based around a savagely stiff angular-tubed carbon frame. A massive down tube locks the head tube and crankset area together to allow you to recruit shoulders as well as legs into any fight with gravity. The split top tube and slim seat tube keep overall chassis weight low to make sure every watt you muster has maximum effect on acceleration. With screw-through axles holding both front and rear wheels very securely, that precise feedback and control is transmitted straight from rider to trail, and vice versa. Unusually for a European-configured race bike, the cockpit equipment is based around a short stem and reasonably wide bar of the type normally reserved for more radical riding. As a result, there are few short travel bikes so determined to power their way through problem sections and come out at the far end on line and with entry speed totally intact.

Short, tight connecting linkages mean the back end follows the front as accurately as possible, so you can carve aggressive lines through corners. The suspension is tuned so that it only moves over bigger impacts too, which leaves pedaling firm and very efficient. **GK**

PASHLEY Classic

2012 • Touring bike • UK • Elegant
retro roadster

Not everyone wants the latest full-suspension mountain bike or super-light carbon fiber racer; some cyclists want to take more leisurely rides in the genteel style of yesteryear.

Whether commuting to work or pottering around a village, the Pashley Classic is a retro bike that captures something of a golden age of traffic-free country lanes and never-ending summer days.

With its big, 28-in. (71-cm) wheels, this Stratford-upon-Avon-built machine is an imposing but comfortable riding bicycle. Pashley sales material called it "the King of the Road." The cyclist certainly enjoys an upright riding position and a well-sprung, high-quality black leather Brooks saddle.

The hand-built, traditionally lugged and brazed steel frame comes in a choice of three sizes. The largest frame, at 24½ in. (62 cm), comes with a double top tube (one above the other) for extra structural rigidity. The forks have a tubular crown and are hand-brazed in classic style.

The on-board components are equally traditional. Sturmey Archer supplies a three-speed hub gear system and front and rear hub brakes. There is a full chain case and large front and rear mudguards to shelter the rider from mud and puddles. In addition, the rear mudguard incorporates a feature not often seen on modern bikes: a "coat guard" to prevent the rear wheel from soiling trailing garments.

The Pashley roadster's extras include a steel rear luggage carrier above the rear mudguard and a sturdy fold-down two-legged stand. The character of the bike is completed with the raised chrome handlebars with black grips and a traditional "ding-dong" bell. The Classic is available in one very sedate period color scheme—all black. **SH**

CIELO Sportif Racer

2012 • Road bike • USA • KVA Stainless steel
all-rounder

Stainless steel takes the attributes of normal steel and adds more strength, hardness, and beauty. That's why more and more bike builders have started using it, despite the expertise and time needed to work with this demanding material.

Cielo's Sportif Racer uses high-quality 410 stainless steel tubing from the American supplier KVA. This is a particularly hard and lightweight form of steel, and some say it makes the ride a bit crisper than standard steel. Whether it does or not, the aesthetics win over most doubters, and the majority of owners choose to leave the bike unpainted to let the eye-catching raw stainless-steel finish shine.

"Ideal for performance-minded road riders who want . . . immediate power response."

cielo.chrisking.com

The Sportif Racer itself is classically designed for road speed. Note the short chainstays, short-reach caliper brakes, and a shorter head tube, plus that light but strong stainless frame.

Cielo founder Chris King had become renowned as a high-end bike component maker before he launched the bike brand in 2008. But this "return to the torch," as Cielo calls it, was King reviving a frame-building career he had enjoyed thirty years before in California. (The Santa Ynez Mountains feature as the company brass logo, even though Cielo now operates from a factory 1,000 miles away in Portland, Oregon.) King's component firm provides ultra-high-end bits for the Cielo bikes. These include precision headsets, bottom brackets, plus dropouts, and forks that can't be found on any other bikes. **SH**

FUJI Altamira

2012 • Road bike • USA • Carbon performance from one of the longest-running U.S. brands

Named after the Japanese national mountain, whose iconic profile forms the headbadge on its frames, Fuji cycles is actually one of the longest-established U.S. brands. Founded in 1899, it has been through many twists and turns but it's still producing both affordable utility bikes and high-performance machines such as the carbon fiber Altamira range.

While many modern road bikes are soft rollers, this mountain-monikered machine lives up to its sometimes rocky but sky-searching promise. The 73-degree parallel handling angles set up a classic ride in terms of poise and balance. The stout-legged, full-carbon-fiber fork with oversized lower steering bearings gives an acutely accurate feedback of grip levels in corners. Even though the rear stays are

sculpted and flat like the leaf spring designs of many soft-riding bikes, there's plenty of clarity feeding through from the rear of the bike, too.

The Fuji uses a relatively long and low seat position to let riders wring the maximum possible wattage out of their muscles and onto the road. That stance is matched by the ability of the solid-feeling frame to get that power from the pedals to the road with very little dilution of drive. The stiffness in the frame does come at the expense of weight and comfort, though. As a result, reviewers commented on the fact that an out-of-saddle riding approach often helped when tackling hills or rough surfaces. The Altamira continues to be a stalwart of the Fuji range, though with a much lighter Altamira SL1 now added as the flagship line. **GK**

REVOLUTION Belter

2012 • Urban bike • Scotland • Belt-driven single-speed

Simplicity and convenience are at the heart of the Revolution Belter, which is why it has neither gears nor a chain. By ditching the derailleurs in favor of a single-speed set-up, and swapping the chain for a Gates Carbon Drive belt system, the Belter boasts a transmission that's ideal for fuss-free urban cycling.

The absence of shifters, gear cables, derailleurs, and unnecessary sprockets keeps maintenance to a minimum. The use of a belt instead of a chain results in a near-silent drivetrain that doesn't leave indelible oil stains on you or your clothing.

Scotland's Edinburgh Bicycle Cooperative is behind the Revolution brand and the design of the Belter's aluminum frame and steel fork. The Carbon Drive belt system comes courtesy of the Gates Corporation, an engineering company that began in Colorado over a century ago and has grown to become the world's biggest manufacturer of power transmission belts. The reinforced carbon-fiber band is driven by teeth made from tough polyurethane or alloy. The belt is approximately half the weight of a typical chain and durable enough to last twice as long.

But although the Carbon Drive simplifies gearing, it's not without complication because, unlike a traditional chain, a belt can't be split. Therefore, in order to fit one, you need a frame that can be split so the belt can be threaded through the rear triangle. To achieve this, the Belter uses a removable drop-out on the drive side. Taking it out separates the seat- and chainstays to create an opening through which the belt can pass. **RB**

HERCULES Roadeo

2012 • Mountain bike • India • Mountain bike with Anglo-Indian heritage

The Hercules Cycle Company had been a popular British bike manufacturer since 1910. Much later it became absorbed into the giant Raleigh bike-making empire.

As part of an international collaboration with Raleigh, the Indian manufacturing group TI Cycles started producing Hercules bikes in India in 1951. Eventually, the Hercules name disappeared in the United Kingdom. By the start of the twenty-first century, Hercules bikes lived on only in the products of its Indian manufacturer.

The old British brand thrived in its new South Asian location. Hercules introduced the subcontinent's first suspension bike in 1993, and the company helped

"The faster, cooler, and wilder ride to reach your dreams . . . will turn heads and steal hearts."

Hercules promotional literature

inspire a mountain biking craze in India, particularly among young people. Thus, in commercial terms, the move from Britain was doubly beneficial: it reduced Hercules' production and labor costs while increasing the size of its market.

The Hercules Roadeo is promoted as "India's most stylish mountain bike." The youth-oriented styling—with bright graphics, fat tubes, and extreme frame geometry—has inspired the advertising slogan: "Beats other bikes even when parked."

All Roadeos come with steel and alloy frames with full suspension and Shimano components. The flagship model, the A-300, features full suspension, front disc brakes, 21-speed gears, double wall alloy rims, alloy stem and pedals, and a quick-release seatpost. **SH**

DESALVO Steel Cross

2012 • Cyclocross bike • USA • Hand-built steel thoroughbred from Oregon

When Mike DeSalvo was twelve years old, the 7-Eleven cycling team visited his California hometown and inspired him to get a job at the local bike store. His enthusiasm grew from there. Later he enrolled in a bike-frame-making course at the United Bicycle Institute (UBI) in Portland, Oregon, and after graduation hung out on both bikes and skis in the Outward Bound resorts of Colorado. Later he returned to UBI as a teacher.

Eventually, DeSalvo set up his own company in Oregon to design and build bike frames. He subsequently established a reputation a top-quality independent custom bike maker—a hard job in a state that was already teeming with successful bike builders.

DeSalvo was soon making frames for leading pro racers, including Barry Wicks and Carl Decker. DeSalvo's frames—and in particular his welding—have won awards at prestigious bike shows, and he still conducts classes and seminars on frame building at UBI.

DeSalvo works in titanium or steel, but the bike featured here as an example of his outstanding workmanship is one of his steel designs. The Steel Cross bike is versatile enough to tackle tarmac expeditions, off-road trails, or urban adventures. DeSalvo cyclocross bikes have a raised bottom bracket for increased pedal clearance on rough terrain and the option of a lower top tube for more stand-over clearance.

Buyers have a choice of Columbus tubing depending on their size and requirements. There's a choice of size and geometry, too. It's all TIG-welded by DeSalvo himself, and the steel forks are built by hand too.

The Steel Cross was widely acclaimed. Brett Luelling, for example, described the bike as "fun to ride whether I'm doing hill repeats, or racing cross-country." Of the maker, he declared: " DeSalvo lives up to his reputation as a high-end builder and delivers a fantastic product." **SH**

Desalvo's Steel Cross combines retro aesthetics with cutting-edge performance. ▶

KELSON R.A.D.

2012 • Versatile all-rounder • USA • Road, asphalt, and dirt bike

The village of Ashton is in a sparsely populated area of southeastern Idaho, bordering the Yellowstone and Grand Teton National Parks in the United States' rugged Northwest. Bike builder Brian Williams moved there to set up his company, Kelson Custom Cycles. To explore the high desert, rolling farmlands, and mountain trails, Williams took all-day rides across every type of surface using road, mountain, and cross bikes. He reckoned none of these coped with all the various surfaces adequately, so he set out to build a bike that does. The result was his new R.A.D. series. He claims these bikes are perfect for a long day on the back roads or in a road-and-gravel race like the legendary "Crusher in the Tushar."

The most unusual feature is the mix of titanium and carbon in the R.A.D.'s frame. Using his expertise in both materials, Williams has been able to create a machine with a head tube, down tube, and chainstays made of titanium, while the top tube, seat tube, and seatstays are carbon. And the whole lot is strengthened by hand-wrapped carbon lugs. The R.A.D. also has custom carbon fiber cable stops and guides, and a bladder-molded bottom bracket. Brakes are discs, and cables are routed externally. The geometry is a mix of road, cross, and mountain. Williams claims the titanium resists big impacts, and the carbon helps with higher-frequency damping. The wheelbase is somewhere between a road and a cross bike.

Williams builds all the bikes to order by hand, including hand painting, and the finished frame weighs just 3 lb 2 ounces (1.4 kg). **SH**

VITUS Vitesse Sean Kelly

2012 • Road bike • Ireland • Relaunch of classic brand with star rider signature model

Sean Kelly was one of the dominant sprinters of the pro cycling world: a hard-as-nails farmhand from rural Ireland who excelled in the toughest races on the calendar with multiple wins in the Spring Classics, including the legendary cobbled course of the Paris–Roubaix. Most of his victories were aboard a Vitus bike, so when Irish Internet bike megastore Chain Reaction revived the brand, who better to act as consultant?

Unlike many riders of his time, Kelly had experience of riding an at-least-partly-carbon fiber frame, but the super-light yet stiff monocoque-framed Vitesse is a totally different beast from the flexible plug-and-lug Vitus frames of twenty-five years ago.

There are many other differences too. The tires are now high-performance clinchers with an easy-to-repair inner tube rather than glue-on tubulars. There's a choice of twenty gears rather than ten or twelve, and you can shift them swiftly and safely without your hands leaving the bars—a far less frightening prospect than fishing around for down tube levers a few inches from your front wheel as a bunch sprint hits the last few hundred meters. As Kelly told *Cycling Plus* magazine in 2012: "Of all the things on this bike I wished I'd had when I was racing, it would be the STI shifters. A gear change can win or lose you a race."

True to his no-nonsense reputation, Kelly didn't go mad with the kit on his signature model, concentrating on cost-effective alloy components rather than flashy carbon fiber. The result is a tough, race-ready bike that will stand the test of time as well as Kelly has. **GK**

MATTHEWS Touring 29er

2012 • Off-road tourer • USA • Custom bike to tackle Grand Divide route

The Grand Divide bike trail is the world's longest off-road route—2,745 miles (4,418 km) between Banff, Alberta, Canada, and Antelope Wells, New Mexico. Most of the arduous course runs along the mountainous continental divide of North America. To tackle the trail, riders must conquer a constant succession of climbs and descents, negotiate dirt trails and jeep tracks, and cross valleys, deserts, and badlands from the Canadian Rockies to the Mexican plateau. Around ninety percent of the Grand Divide bike trail is off-road.

Riders take an average of three weeks of sixteen-hour, self-supported days to complete the unmarked route. Along the way they must tackle more than 200,000 feet (60,960 m) of elevation. Some competitors do it as a lone challenge; others enter one of the regular timed events.

Chauncey Matthews is a custom bike maker based in Belen, New Mexico, near the southern end of the Great Divide route. His bikes have a great reputation for strength and aesthetics: they are as tough as they come, and eye-catchingly good to look at. Matthews has made bikes for other Grand Divide riders and for himself.

Matthews' own bike for the Grand Divide was a geared custom machine with 29-in. (73.5-cm) wheels and rigid forks, which he made by hand. A remarkable synthesis of several different styles, it had the bars of a road bike, the racks and mounts of a tourer, and the discs, wheels, and tires of an off-roader. The frame was neatly constructed from steel tubing with an elegantly curved top tube.

Sadly, the Matthews Touring 29er was never tested to the limit, because the rider twisted his ankle after an encounter with a snowdrift in Canada, and was forced to quit before he had even made it across the border into the United States. **SH**

MATSUDA Keirin

2012 • Track bike • Japan • Track racer for Keirin events

Keirin is a type of track bike racing that originated as a gambling sport in Japan after the Second World War. It has now developed to become a recognized sport at the Olympic Games. Keirin races are only around 1¼ miles (2 km) long, and start with up to eight riders following a motorbike or tandem that gradually increases its speed then leaves the bikes to their own devices with about 656 yards (600 m) left to ride. This means there's a mad sprint for the finish line at around 40 mph (64 kph).

In Japan, the sport is tightly regulated. Riders must attend a special Keirin school, and bikes must conform to strict technical regulations. Builders must be approved,

". . . all about speed and power. They are designed to work as a single unit with the cyclist."

Matsuda publicity

and all parts must be stamped by the sport's authorities. Matsuda made this bike precisely to the exacting requirements of the Keirin governing body. It is an exact copy of the bike ridden by Japanese star Kazuya Narita, winner of the 2012 Keirin Derby.

The bike is built around a frame of Kaisei 8630R chromoly steel tubing—a very high-quality, heat-treated, double-butted tubeset. (Around sixty percent of Japan's Keirin frames are made of Kaisei tubing.)

Keirin events are all about pure speed, so the machines that take part in them are stripped back to the barest minimum. Thus, this Matsuda has no brakes and a high-ratio fixed gear, as per track bikes in general. The tires are handmade from silk rather than rubber, to minimize weight and facilitate fast speeds at very high pressures. **SH**

Japanese Keirin racing is a uniquely colorful but competitive sport. ▶

MOSAIC XT-1 Small Batch

2012 • Cyclocross bike • USA • Custom bike builder's own team bike

Mosaic Bespoke Bicycles is a small bike builder at the foot of the Rockies in Boulder, Colorado. The small team is led by master metalworker and frame builder Aaron Barcheck. In 2013 it launched a small cyclocross race team with a group of like-minded local companies. Team Small Batch is a twelve-strong amateur team that promotes cycling and community projects.

The Small Batch bikes are based on the company's XT-1 cross bike. This is an acclaimed machine that won the Best Cyclocross Bike award at the 2013 North American Handmade Bike Show.

The XT-1 is a custom titanium cross bike with disc brakes and some flashy finishing touches. Its custom geometry, butted tubeset, integrated seatmast, and 1¾-in. (4.4-cm) head tube all add to the rugged all-terrain versatility. Brake cables are routed internally and there's internal wiring for an electronic shift system if the customer requests it. The bike is ready for disc brakes too.

Mosaic bikes have a neat line in modern bling finishes. To create a matte effect, the titanium frame is bead-blasted, but only after the logos have first been masked off. These logos appear much classier than decals, and can be painted or left as bare polished metal when the masks are removed. **SH**

MUSE Mezzaluna Mixte

2012 • City bike • USA • City cycle award winner

The elegant design of the Mezzaluna Mixte won Best City Bike at the 2012 North American Handmade Bike Show. It has an innovative frame design in which the twin curved top tubes swoop right past the seat tube and curve onto the end of the rear mudguard.

The bike was created to be user friendly. So there's a comfortable upright riding position and easy step-through geometry. The front and rear integrated racks provide sturdy baggage capacity, and a dynamo lighting system keeps it all safe after dark. Muse fitted a Gates carbon belt instead of a normal chain. It's quieter, simpler, more durable—and not covered in black grease.

Disc brakes provide reliable stopping power in all conditions, and the cables are routed internally through the frame tubing. A Shimano 8- or 11-speed internal hub means a more reliable, neater gear system, and a premium-quality Chris King headset is installed, making for a lifetime of easy and responsive steering. The distinctive frame is made from double and single-butted aircraft-grade steel. These tubes are either TIG-welded or joined with traditional silver brazing lugging techniques.

A new city bike has to look chic, so it is finished in a two-tone liquid paint job with painted-on logos. Then it is given a clear gloss protective layer. **SH**

Even the cargo racks are integrated into the sculptural Mezzaluna frame. ▶

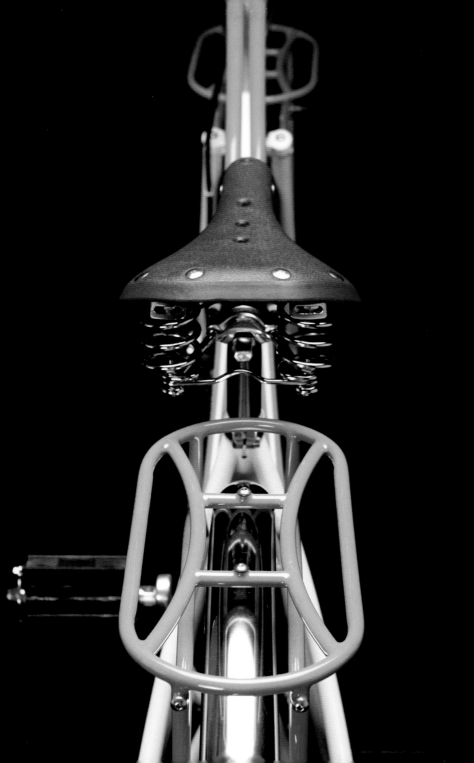

ONDERWATER Family Tandem

2012 • Family tandem • Netherlands • Practicality and plain good looks combined in a bicycle built for four

Ronald Onderwater began building his own bicycles in 1998 after moving to Amsterdam. He was, in his words, "pleasantly surprised" by the number of bike parts and even frames that people in that bicycle-obsessed city had thrown out or otherwise discarded for one reason or another: "I used the rear triangle of a bicycle frame I found, cut some tubes off, and welded some on and made my first Filibus look-a-like, which I still have." Friends and acquaintances liked what Onderwater cobbled together, and what began as a hobby has been a thriving business ever since.

Onderwater now designs and builds a range of traditional Dutch cargo bikes, work cycles, and tandems, including his elongated masterpiece, the Family Tandem. Suitable for children from four to eight years, two children sit in front of the rider, giving adults the option of choosing not to pedal and letting the kids do all the work! Because the front drivetrain is independent, when the lead cyclist's little legs grow weary, they can simply stop pedaling and rest their feet on the foot pegs. And if two seats aren't enough, a third can be fitted to the rear carrier behind the rider. The Family Tandem's frame is powder-coated steel; its tires are flat puncture resistant 2-in. (4.7-cm) Schwalbe Marathons; it comes with either a Shimano 3-, 7-, or 8-speed gear hub; and it has roller brakes front and rear, an LED headlamp and taillights, fully enclosed chains, and easily adjustable saddle heights. The bike is well balanced and surprisingly good on inclines, and it has a great aesthetic appeal; not something all tandems can boast of. **BS**

LANDESCAPE Direct Lateral

2012 • Tandem • UK • Adaptable all-rounder tandem from specialist builder

There's something about tandem bikes that creates a particularly strong, almost addictive pull to certain riders and designers. That's certainly the case with premium UK bike builder Pete Bird, who has been a multi-rider bike fanatic since he finished training as a goldsmith in 1979. He designed his first tandem for Chas Roberts the same year and organized the first British tandem event in 1980 before starting Swallow cycles in his parents' shed in 1981.

Bird started innovating both tandem frame design and components such as air-cooled hub brakes for long double-rider descents, and he soon became the world's youngest frame builder qualified to use ultra-thin walled Reynolds 753 steel. By 1985, a full range of tandem-specific parts were added to the Swallow lineup and the fixed-componentry, made-to-measure frame Toucan

tandem was introduced. Bird and partner–builder Rob continued to innovate both their tandems and two-up events like the Tandemania festival, but Swallow closed in 1999 to allow Bird to explore other avenues.

His passion for producing bikes didn't stay dormant for long, and in 2005 he launched Landescape Tandems. In 2012, his initial single-frame design was joined by a frame using a stiffer, taller "direct lateral" frame for larger riders and loaded touring. Landescapes use custom parts to create super-versatile twin-seat machines that can be used for anything from road racing, to loaded touring, or off-road exploring. With major manufacturers such as Cannondale and Trek dropping tandems from their ranges, the Landescape couldn't have come at a better time, and it has become an instant success. **GK**

SPEEDHOUND Only One

2012 • Cyclocross bike • USA • Changeable transmission all-rounder

The Only One is so named because it is the only bike that uses the Speedhound Dropout System (SDS). This innovative and unique feature allows riders to change their drop-outs quickly and easily, the benefit of which is that it allows them to replace the complete drivetrain for use in different weather conditions, seasons, terrain, and riding styles. The SDS also allows riders to switch from a chain to a belt-drive system, fit different hubs, or convert the bike to a single-speed or fixed-gear transmission. Moreover, owners can switch between road- and mountain-style derailleurs: the bike is therefore celebrated for its almost infinite adaptability.

SDS works through the use of converters that are permanently attached to the True Temper butted chromoly steel frame, and which hold a series of replaceable drop-outs that are supplied with the frame. These make it simple to change from track-style horizontals to derailleur vertical-style attachments. They also allow riders to adjust the spacing between the drop-outs to fit different types of hub. The split in the drive-side drop-out receiver allows a belt or an unbroken chain to fit into the rear triangle.

This all means that the owner of a Speedhound Only One bike—which is built by hand in Minneapolis, Minnesota—can adapt it to become almost any type of machine. This versatility is the inspiration of the corporate slogan: "Go your own speed."

The frame itself is in the widely deployable cross-bike style, with a wide fork crown and bent chainstays that can accommodate tires as big as 27½ x 1½ in. (70 x 3.5 cm) in diameter. The Only One's frame includes studs for cantilever or linear-pull brakes (discs are an option, too), plus mudguard and rack eyelets and two pairs of bottle bosses. In addition to all that, the bike comes in five sizes and eight colors. **SH**

SIX-ELEVEN CX/Brevet

2012 • Cyclocross bike • USA • Steel all-rounder frame with brass details

The economic recession of the early twenty-first century has not destroyed the market for high-end custom bikes, but modern customers are increasingly seeking even better value for their money, and demanding one bike that does everything.

In response to this market trend, Six-Eleven's cross bike is an all-purpose construction that can handle most riding styles, terrains, and conditions.

The CX/Brevet has one of Six-Eleven's smallest frames to date. It is built for 26-in. (66-cm) wheels, but with wide clearances to allow the fattest tires to be fitted. The frame angles are relaxed enough for touring and long-distance racing, but the bike has sharp

"Imparting ingenuity into each and every frame . . . a unique work of exquisite craftsmanship."
North American Handmade Bicycle Show (NAHBS)

enough handling to tackle short cyclocross challenges, too. The brakes can be disc or cantilever—there are frame mounts and eyelets for either system. There's a lightweight steel frame and a custom-built composite fork, but brass is used for the chainstay guard and paint protectors. The finished bike now features Six-Eleven's black and gold branding decals.

Six-Eleven bikes are produced by Aaron Dykstra in a small workshop in Roanoke, Virginia. Dykstra is a former student of master Japanese frame maker Koichi Yamaguchi. Now he cuts and miters every piece of tubing for his Six-Eleven bikes by hand.

Roanoke's rural valley in the Blue Ridge Mountains was once a center for railroading. Dykstra's company is named after the 611 J-Class steam locomotive. **SH**

◀ Gates Carbon Drive belt system or gears, fixed or braked; Speedhound have it sorted.   High modulus and handcrafted   **681**

STINNER 29er Rohloff Belt Drive

2012 • Mountain bike • USA • Fillet-brazed,
belt-driven, one-sided fork freak

Young Californian custom bike maker Aaron Stinner pulled
out all the tricks he could with this custom mountain
bike built for one of his customers. Little wonder that
Stinner displayed the belt-drive lefty at American bike
shows in 2012 to help promote his brand.

The bike is a 29er steel mountain bike in a striking
yellow finish, hand built in the Santa Barbara, California,
workshop. The front of the bike features Stinner's first use
of a Cannondale Lefty fork, while the back end has an
elegantly bent seatpost to allow more clearance for those
big 29er rims and all that Racing Ralph rubber.

The bike uses a low-maintenance, high-durability
14-speed Rohloff internal hub, which is held in place
by a set of Paragon stainless steel and aluminum rocker
dropouts. The chunky black Rotor cranks turn a neat dry
and clean Gates Carbon Drive belt system. Handlebars
are by Syntace, and the disc brakes are from Formula.

The rear brake hose and twin Rohloff cables are all
neatly routed through the frame tubing by Stinner. This
is an unusual touch but a good way of cleaning up the
appearance of the tail of the bike.

The frame, in comparison to the features list, is rather
traditional. It's made of light steel tubing joined by fillet
brazing, one of Stinner's favorite techniques. **SH**

STRONG Twentieth Anniversary

2012 • Road bike • USA • Twentieth-
anniversary, limited-edition bikes

Strong Frames' twentieth year in the bike-building business
was worth celebrating. Carl Strong marked this event by
building twenty limited-edition anniversary frames. The
first two went to Strong and his wife, Loretta, and the
other eighteen were to be bikes for customers, finished
to their custom specifications in the normal Strong way.

The bikes were built on a handmade steel road
frame and featured all Strong's favorite ideas and parts
from the previous two decades. The bikes feature a
distinctive handmade silver headbadge by artist and
cyclist Mike Cherney, a metalworker renowned for
making headbadges for many bike companies.

Strong's twenty-year career had seen his bike-
making operation grow to a large company with its own
factory. Almost 1,000 frames a year were being churned
out at the height of the turnover. But Strong wasn't
particularly happy with that direction, so he deliberately
shrank back down to himself and Loretta, working
quietly in a small shop in his backyard in Bozeman,
Montana. Strong prefers to work hands on with the
frames rather than be immersed in administration.

The flipside of Strong's downsizing means the
waiting time is now around eight months, but plenty of
Strong enthusiasts are prepared to endure it. **SH**

SYCIP Java Boy

2012 • Road bike • USA • Custom retro steel cruiser

Check that date. It's really 2012, not 1912. Yet the Sycip Java Boy looks like it really could be from 100 years ago.

The Sycip brothers, Jay and Jeremy, wanted to produce a machine in homage to the elegant European commuting bikes of that bygone era. Their creation, the Java Boy for men (and Java Girl for women) evoked a different time with the relaxed, upright riding position, the easy swept-back handlebars (the hand-bent Wonderbar), and appealing curved tubes. The choice of color-coordinated or wooden mudguards and the chunky luggage racks or bespoke panniers also evoked vintage English touring bikes or American cruisers.

The Java Boy is designed as an urban bike, but it combines the road manners of a 700C with the practicality of a tourer, so gentle rambles down country lanes sound just right too. The custom-bent chromoly steel tubing is a good start, as it allows for good ergonomics and cute retro styling. The frame comes in various combinations of curved and straight tubing.

The bike can be built up as a single-speed or with an internally geared hub, for period simplicity and durability. Some customers also opt for a belt-drive system. The Java Boy looks especially fetching with wooden rims, white wall tires, and a traditional brown leather saddle. **SH**

TWENTY2 650B Mountain Cross

2012 • Cyclocross bike • USA • Belt-driven intermediate wheel all-rounder

Twenty2 launched the glamorous Mountain Cross machine to immediate critical acclaim. It is capable of being used as a standard mountain bike, a cross race bike, or even a long-distance bike-packing tourer. The frame design is meant to handle everything from steep mountain trails to flat gritty roads.

Twenty2 has packed the bike with interesting features. First, it's all built up on that sexy polished titanium frame. Then those fat wheels, which use the inbetweener 650b size, fitted with big Schwalbe Rocket Ron rubber. The stays and forks can take 29ers if you prefer bigger wheels, although you'd need to use narrower cyclocross tires.

The bike's drivetrain appears to be built to handle anything the elements can throw at it. Drive happens via a tough Gates Carbon Drive belt system and that acts on a protected Rohloff internally geared hub. Those gears are selected by a single retro twist shifter on the bars. There are Avid disc brakes but no springs on this frame, as the rigid front carbon fork is the aptly named Rock Solid from White Bros. Internal cable routing keeps the bike looking tidier and frees up space to fit touring extras like racks and bags. Note also the retro touch of flared drop bars. **SH**

VENTUS Carbon/Ti

2012 • Touring bike • USA • Custom retro titanium frame

Nebraska firefighter Mark Kargol had always longed to make his own bike frames. As a trained artist and bike enthusiast, he had been asked to paint many frames and eventually he planned to make his first bike. His debut Carbon/Ti machine was displayed at the North American Handmade Bike Show in 2012 to great acclaim. The bike was so well made it seemed extraordinary that this was Kargol's first effort.

Kargol virtually made two separate frames for this bike. One was ENVE carbon, and the other, with wider tubes, was titanium. Kargol cut the titanium tubes into substantial lugs, including an integrated seatmast, and slotted the carbon tubes into this metal skeleton.

> "[The bike] wasn't necessarily built for me, but it is my size."
>
> Mark Kargol

The geometry was loosely based on a cyclocross bike with the top tube adjusted to be horizontal and the bottom bracket dropped ⅝ in. (1.5 cm). This established the basis of his retro-styled 11-speed touring bike, but there were plenty more interesting features to spot, from the internally routed cables to the Wheel Fanatyk wooden rims and plastic Crud wraparound mudguards.

Kargol used high-end parts but restyled them to his own designs. For example, many of the components were 2012 Campagnola Athena. These were all stripped back to bare metal and polished, and then the brand logo was re-engraved into them. The Origin-8 brakes were also adapted by Kargol, then polished to a steely shine. The bar tape was custom ordered from Australia to match the brown leather of the Brooks saddle. **SH**

VICTORIA Hot Rod Cross

2012 • Cyclocross bike • USA • Custom fillet-brazed all-rounder

Bike lover Dave Hill admits he has been a "dreamer of fine bicycles" for more than thirty years. The trouble was that he didn't actually get around to making the dream come true until a lot more recently.

Eventually the former racing rider enrolled as a student on the United Bicycle Institute's frame-building courses, in bike-mad Portland, Oregon. He emerged as another successful student full of bike ideas of his own.

Now Hill runs one of those high-quality, custom-building, one-man operations that have become so popular in the United States in the past decade. He now builds frames of all styles to his own designs, using exclusively high-quality steel tubing with traditional lugs and fillet-brazing techniques. His company, Victoria Cycles, is based in Salida, Colorado.

This striking cyclocross bike was built for a customer who requested a fully functional cross racing bike, but with bags of style and added individuality. The combination of a flame paint job on the race-geometry frame and the polished steel lugs certainly achieves that.

Cyclocross bikes evolved out of a need for winter training bikes for European road racers. The important features were lightness for portage, ruggedness for muddy conditions, and versatility to take different tire sizes and different brake systems. Hill has built all this into the Hot Rod Cross design.

Its frame is light enough to carry over serious obstacles, and it's got chunky off-road tires and a sufficiently tough build to cope with all conditions and surfaces. As for attention to detail, note how Hill has designed the rear cables to be routed along the top of the top tube, keeping them safely away from any splattered mud. **SH**

YIPSAN Road Adventure

2012 • Touring bike • USA • Custom Rohloff bike with shifter stub detailing

Renold Yip, the man behind YiPsan bikes, was born in Hong Kong. He earned an engineering degree in the United Kingdom, then emigrated to the United States. His business is now based in Fort Collins, Colorado.

Yip has joined the new wave of young American custom bike makers, but insists on using traditional materials and techniques. His frames are made from fine steel tubing, and his tube-shaping mitering is all done by hand. Some of his most popular bikes have been commuters or touring machines.

This Road Adventure, which was displayed at the 2012 and 2013 North American Handmade Bike Shows (NAHBS), typifies Yip's recent work. This sort of modern

"A bike that is pleasing the eye of the rider gets more miles and smiles."

Renold Yip

touring bike has integrated lighting, front and rear racks, mudguards, and water-bottle cages. Yip designs them with a hint of cyclocross, too. The tires are wider—1½ in. (3.5 cm) across—and the frames are designed to handle most surfaces. It's a modern take on the hybrid bike.

The Road Adventure comes with a Rohloff internally geared rear-hub system. Yip's unusual twist-grip shifter is positioned on the side of the stem, not on the bars. Brakes are cantilever style. The bike is finished with a cool, metallic-blue paint job with brown leather saddle to match the bar grips and bare metal mudguards.

Yip—who was named Renold after a British motorcycle manufacturer by his bike-mad dad—now jokes that, to maintain the family tradition, he may call his own children Shimano or SRAM. **SH**

WINTER L'Arrotino

2012 • Cargo bike • USA • Retro knife-sharpening bike

During the Clinton boom of the 1990s, people threw away knives and scissors when they became blunt, and bought new replacements. The disposable society ended the careers of itinerant implement grinders who, fifty years previously, had toured around homes offering blade-sharpening services. Many of these tradespeople used bike-powered grinders that both transported the equipment and turned the grinding wheel. The system was simple: the bike was placed on a stand, and the grinder pedaled hard while the machine remained stationary. Drive was transferred to the grinding stone by an extra belt. The stone turned and sharpened the blades. Most of these machines have long since disappeared, but a few have been preserved in museums.

However, the global economic recession has made people thriftier, and, instead of disposing of worn-out tools, they increasingly prefer to mend them. Unfortunately, there was a lack of knife sharpeners.

Into this breach stepped fine-art metalwork sculptor Eric Estlund, who now creates steel-framed, all-season bikes at his workshop in Springfield, Oregon.

L'Arrotino—which is Italian for "knife-grinder"—was commissioned by one of the few remaining mobile knife sharpeners still plying his trade. Estlund based it on a 1940s' example from Rome, Italy. It features an integrated, pedal-powered, sharpening stone that uses an ingenious drive system. The bike rides in the normal way with the pedals turning a chain to drive the rear wheel, but the rear rack can be lowered when required to form a sturdy and stable stand for the rear wheel. The chain is then disengaged from the crank, and an alternative chain fitted. This links to a geared transfer wheel between the two top tubes, which drives a chain turning the grinding wheel. **SH**

Winter's work bike is truly cutting edge in spite of the 1940s-influenced design. ▶

DA VINCI Carbon Tandem

2012 • Tandem • USA • Carbon tandem with independent coasting drivetrain

Riding a tandem can be a complicated business. Normally the two riders have to find some common pedaling strategies to coordinate their efforts. With the latest Da Vinci tandems, that's a far less crucial factor, as Da Vinci has invented the "Independent Coasting Drivetrain," known as the ICS.

This patented innovation allows either the captain or the stoker to stop pedaling at any time, but the other rider can carry on. Alternatively, both riders can pedal, or both can coast. The two sets of cranks can be positioned however you want—they operate on the drivetrain separately. This means either rider can start or stop pedaling, or take a rest for a drink or to soak up some scenery. Either can adjust their seat or even stand up on the pedals to stretch their legs.

This system makes it easier to combine two riders' efforts to drive the tandem. Starting, stopping, and cornering are less stressful and it is easier to avoid obstacles or deal with awkward terrain.

The ICS is a complex arrangement that uses an intermediate driveshaft mounted 6 in. (15 cm) in front of the rear bottom bracket and two single-speed freewheels. This system transfers the pedaling input to a four-speed converter, which then drives the bike. The ICS has spin-off advantages, like smoother gear shifts, a bigger gear range (up to 32 speeds), more ground clearance, and less strain on the chain when changing gear.

The Da Vinci tandems are available in steel, aluminum, titanium, and carbon, and with and without S & S Couplings for ease of transport. **SH**

XTRACYCLE Cargo Joe C21

2012 • Cargo bike • USA • The world's first folding cargo bike takes practicality to a new level

It can carry you, it can carry your stuff, it can even carry your kids, and it folds up so you can carry it—maximum functionality in glorious harmony with minimal footprint. In fact, it might just be the world's most practical thing on two wheels.

A collaboration between Xtracycle and Tern, a world leader in folding-bike technology, the Cargo Joe C21 longtail is a hybrid—a morphing of Xtracycle's Free Radical Classic with the folding bike platform of Tern's 26-in. (66-cm) Joe C21. The result is the world's first folding cargo bike, capable of carrying anything from groceries to passengers. It can also be folded or unfolded inside of ten seconds, and its cruiserlike geometry provides a "normal bike" feel even when under load. This is aided by a 21-speed Shimano drivetrain, and its performance

leaves little room for arguing in favor of taking the family car on those daily shopping runs.

The compact folding design allows the bike to fit in the storage racks of an urban bus or on the back seat of your car. Its WideLoader cargo kit attachment allows you to pile on the weight—up to 400 lb (181 kg) according to The Gear Caster blog—while an optional LongLoader lets you carry stuff like surfboards and ladders in an alignment that keeps them well away from its pedals. If taking your children for a ride is your idea of parent–child bonding, there are Peapod infant seats for toddlers, and the means to upgrade to footrests, handlebars, and even a stoker tandem conversion kit for when they get a little bigger and you're pedaling them to school. **BS**

NEIL PRYDE BURAsl

2012 • Road bike • UK • Ultra-light race bike from famous wind-surfing brand

"The stiff and ultra-lightweight road bike. It's not just about the weight, but what you do with it."

neilprydebikes.com

While the crossover between bike manufacturers and car and motorcycle brands dominated the development periods of both industries, there are other areas with a lot of shared heritage. Neil Pryde is the latest wind-surfing and sailing brand to develop a bike brand, following Orange mountain bike founders Tushingham and other companies such as Surf Sales and Windwave off the water and onto dry land.

Aerodynamics are obviously every bit as important to driving wind-surf rigs forward as they are in stopping race bikes being driven backward. The increasing use of composite technology in both cycling and sailing also makes for an easy link between the sports. That's certainly the case with Neil Pryde, which has been using composite materials in its sailing range for twenty-five years—far longer than most competing cycle brands.

The BURAsl design—an evolution of the award-winning DIABLO—is a fantastic showcase of the company's technological expertise too. While the 1½-lb (0.7-kg) frame weight is certainly the headline statistic of its flagship bike, the BURAsl is also designed to be extremely stiff. Neil Pryde has achieved this by using its highest modulus (most concentrated fiber ratio) carbon material and external strengthening ribs—known as Exoskeleton technology—in key areas of the mainframe. The junction sections also use a proprietary molding process that ensures ultra-accurate positioning of each carbon fiber sheet, with no slippage or "fiber wash" during the forming of each piece. In another very advanced design application, the rear stays of the bike are also made in one continuous molded piece to reduce fiber overlap. This means every fiber is positioned exactly where it should be to give the bike one of the best strength-to-weight ratios in the industry. **GK**

AWARD E Stay

2012 • Mountain bike • UK • Elevated-stay MTB from ex-Formula One designer

This hand-built titanium 29-in. (73.5-cm) wheeled mountain bike incorporated a collection of design ideas from the past and present, plus a few new touches. The brainchild of Formula One vehicle designer and engineer Adrian Ward, who was also involved in the designs of Marin and Whyte suspension bikes, the Award frame managed to mix a very short back end with big wheels and a massive amount of room for the biggest tires. While 29ers are great when it comes to a smooth roll along bumpy trails, most big wheelers end up with a very long wheelbase that often makes them noticeably less nimble than 26-in. (66-cm) wheeled bikes. The raised chainstays and curved seat tube of Award frames maintained the short back end and nimbleness of a smaller-wheeled bike, focusing further

on the no-fuss, no-handling compromise approach by being built with a tooth-belted, rather than chained, single-sprocket drivetrain. The raised chainstays join to the seat tube/down tube juncture just above the crankset, making a front-gear mechanism impossible, but overcoming the bottom bracket flex that afflicted so many previous raised-stay bikes. A very clever adjustable chain was ideal for taking up drive belt slack on a single sprocket rear hub, ideal for riders looking to either a hub-geared or minimum-weight single-geared setup. At the time of writing, only a few Award bikes exist, but with the renewed interest in single-chainring drivetrain configurations and titanium frames, it would seem likely that some of Ward's unique design ideas will surface again in the near future. **SW**

DEMON Hermes

2012 • Track bike • UK • A striking showcase of fastidious lugwork in a clean, crisp style

Frame builder Tom Warmerdam is renowned for his individual machines, and two things set this track bike apart from the steel-fixie hipster herd. The first is its unique aged-copper finish, something Warmerdam achieves by accelerating the oxidation process of the copper plating, causing it to patina. Perhaps more striking, though, is the lugwork in which he invests so much of his time. After building many bikes using bought-in lugs, he now makes all his own—and won't use anyone else's. As he says, "You basically build the bike twice, you build the frame once over, chop it up, carve the lugs, and then use those lugs to build the finished bike."

One of his signature bikes, the Hermes, won the prize for Best Track Bike at Bespoked Bristol in 2012. It features two types of head tube lug, as does the Manhattan

model, which won Best Road Bike at the North American Handmade Bicycle Show in the same year. They both have Art Deco styling and are the product of many hours of cutting, filing, and polishing to get the perfect detail. Warmerdam starts by machining down stainless steel pipe to the correct gauge. The sections are then TIG-welded before the weld fillets are smoothed and the shape is cut. Warmerdam uses a staggering amount of tools in the process and goes through hundreds of saw blades, needle files, and drill bits. The lugs are left unpainted with a brushed finish, and their bright, sharp edges contrast with the tarnished copper. The lugs are joined to the frame using 56 percent silver and the rest of the tubes are joined using fillet pro, a brazing rod that was specifically developed for bicycle fabrication. **MH**

VUELO VELO Vuelo 8

2012 • Road bike • Australia-USA • Australian-designed, U.S.-built custom Ti bike

After retiring from the Australian National team, rider Marty Renwick set up a custom bike company in Sydney and created the Vuelo 8.

The frame is welded by Black Sheep Bikes in Fort Collins, Colorado. The tubing—butted FeatherTech high-performance titanium—comes from Colorado, too.

Renwick's design philosophy is well thought out. His curved seat tubes make the rear end as short as possible. The short chainstays create a very lively response. This bike is built for climbing, sprinting, and sharp handling.

The curved seatpost acts as an automatic frame adjustment for taller and shorter riders. As the seat goes up it also goes farther back, and vice versa. The curved seatstays help shock absorption.

The Vuelo 8 is full of top-end components, including slick electronic Dura-Ace Di2 sprint shifters powered by a Calfee internal battery hidden in the seatpost. Note also the Mad Fiber wheels, SRM power-measuring versions of the Dura Ace cranks, and ENVE Composites bar, stem, fork, and seatpost.

The built-up bike weighs in at 13.9 lb (6.3 kg). And the price? Including these components, the bike will cost around an eye-watering $17,000 (£11,100). **SH**

FEATHER Rapha Continental

2012 • Road bike • UK • Smart classic-modern road bike for long-distance fashionistas

Ricky Feather is one of the new breed of British frame builders who have reignited the custom bicycle building scene in the United Kingdom.

Ricky began his career as a fabricator in heavy industry, working in sheet metal and building trailers for articulated vehicles. However, he quickly showed he had a flair for design and was attentive to detail in lighter materials. His special interest in bikes—he was a BMX rider—inspired him in 2009 to leave his factory job and set up Feather Cycles at his home in York, England.

He soon became a major force at Bespoked, the UK's hand-built bike show, winning Best Track Bike in 2011, Best Road Bike in 2012, and Best in Show in 2013. His bikes caught the attention of designer cycle clothing maker Rapha, which commissioned Ricky to build this bike to feature in a series of marketing videos shot at inspiring cycling locations around the world.

The continental frame was a traditional lug construction, but with a clean, modern look, internal cable routing, and outsized head tube to allow carbon forks to be used. The Columbus XCR stainless steel tubing makes the bike forgiving over long distances but light and racy enough to be no slouch when you've got speed in mind. **MH**

Ricky Feather knows how to create a classic bike frame. ▷

CERVÉLO S5

2012 • Aero road bike • Canada • Fifth-generation ultra-fast carbon race bike

By blending the versatile position and light weight of race bikes with the advanced aerodynamic advantages of time trial bikes, aero road bikes have become an extremely popular race bike for many disciplines.

This fifth-generation aero road bike from the pioneers of the genre is widely regarded as one of the finest ever produced. The wraparound wheel-hugger seat tube and almost vertical seatpost are translated from the iconic P3 time trial bike design, while the skinny fork, dropped down tube, and vertically inserted internal cables come from the P4. Among the new features on the S5 were flattened sections to smooth airflow around the water bottle, and rear stays specifically shaped to hide the rear brake from the wind.

The S5 is a great improvement on the previous S3. At any given speed, the S5 uses nine fewer watts than the S3, and 32 watts less than a conventional round- or square-tubed frame. That represents up to ten percent of the power output of an average rider, and is worth well over a minute an hour at 25 mph (40 kph).

To cope with the power output of legendarily strong riders like Norwegian Thor Hushovd, the S5 is also built with oversize rear frame members and extra-wide crank axle bearings for maximum torque transfer. **GK**

KALKHOFF Endeavour

2012 • Fitness bike • Germany • Innovative bike from one of the great names in German cycling

In 1919, sixteen-year-old Heinrich Kalkhoff became a postal worker in Cloppenburg, Germany, delivering mail on his bike. Soon tired of punctures, he bought some spare tires, and then wondered if local farmers might also need them. His bicycle parts business grew rapidly, and four years later, in partnership with two friends, Heinrich was making his own bicycles. Demand was high: by 1939 he had 70 employees, and the company had made 700,000 frames. In 1950, with a workforce of 1,200, production reached 5,000 hand-welded frames per day, and in 1972 Kalkhoff made its five millionth bicycle. In the 1970s, the company diversified into home exercise bikes and sports and fitness equipment, but the venture was disastrous: Kalkhoff filed for bankruptcy in the 1980s, and the company was absorbed into Derby Cycle Werke, which kept the name alive.

The Endeavour 14-G has a light, smooth-welded all-aluminum frame, Rohloff gears, a magnesium suspension fork with an air/oil shock-absorber, Magura hydraulic rim brakes, and a remote control fork lockout. It is also available with electric assist from a Bosch 36-volt, 350-watt Xion drive motor. The BS10 model comes with an 11AH battery that produces speeds of 28 mph (45 kph) over 80 mi (130 km) off a single charge. **BS**

CUBE Litening

2012 • Road bike • Netherlands • Premium performance, affordably priced racer

Cube's Litening Super HPC Pro frame made its debut at the start of the 2011 season, but it was with the release of the 2012 season bike that it really realized its practical potential, and opened itself up to a much wider customer base.

The main part of the original Cube frame wasn't altered or dumbed down in any way for the production model. The twin-mold monocoque carbon fiber structure still started with a tapered head tube for accurate steering, pushed its power through an oversized bottom bracket with press-fit bearings, and then sucked out road rumble with super-thin seatstays. It also had the same premium, full carbon fiber EC90SL fork from composite construction legends Easton. Instead of the built-in seatmast that needed to be

permanently cut to the right length by the first owner, the 2012 season bike had a conventional, top-class Syntace P6 carbon seatpost. This immediately made the bike easier to set up, store, transport, share, and ultimately sell on to a different-sized rider.

The price of the complete bike was kept within the bounds of reason by the incorporation of a conventionally controlled Shimano Ultegra component suite, rather than the only other viable option, a top-of-the-range Shimano Dura Ace Di2 transmission system.

The top-quality Syntace carbon bar and seatpost still kept weight impressively low at 16 lb 8 oz (7.5 kg), and the smooth-spinning Fulcrum wheels were shod with premium-quality Schwalbe Ulremo ZX tires. **GK**

DEDACCIAI Nerissimo

2012 • Road bike • Italy • Award-winning carbon bike from tubing specialist

In 2013, BikeRadar.com voted the Nerissimo its Bike of the Year—quite an accolade for Dedacciai, a company better known for making tubing than complete bikes.

One look at the Nerissimo's monocoque frame, however, and you realize that tubing expertise is at the heart of this machine. The down tube, for example, is one of the fattest in this book—4 in. (10 cm) in diameter. That amount of high-modulus 7000-grade carbon certainly promises a sturdy link between the front end and the bottom bracket.

The top tube is more subtle—it tapers from a chunky front end to flow delicately into the box-section seat stays. The chainstays are fatter, but with a boxy cross-section, too, and the straight seat tube is neatly picked out from the rest of the frame with a contrasting color.

Other design details include full carbon drop-outs, and broad, stiff, but straight carbon forks from Dedacciai itself.

Patriotically, Milan-based Dedacciai has kitted out the bike with all-Italian components: a Campagnolo Veloce groupset, a Khamsin twenty-eight-spoke wheelset, fat Vittoria Rubino tires, a Selle Italia SL Team saddle, and Dedacciai's own bar, stem, and post.

The frame weighs just 2 lb 8 ounces (1.15 kg). The full build is around 18 lb (8.2 kg), making for a fast, nimble, and responsive bike that still absorbs plenty of the round buzz that carbon bikes often transmit unrelentingly to their rider's hands and bottom. So at well under $3,200 (£2,000) for the whole bike, it's easy to see why BikeRadar experts chose Nerissimo. **SH**

KIDDIMOTO Scrambler

2012 • Children's wooden bike • UK •
Motorbike-styled, wooden teaching bike

The Kiddimoto range of wooden bikes is designed for children aged two through six years to help develop their sense of balance and get them ready for larger children's bikes. There are no pedals on a Kiddimoto—they only get in the way—and no stabilizers, because all they do is hinder development by encouraging complacency. The brakes come later too, along with the pedals. Foot braking is all that's needed here.

The Scrambler—Kiddimoto's version of an off-road motocross bike—comes with all the appropriate design features: a stylish, sculpted tank, fairings, a rear swingarm, rotating handlebars, an exhaust pipe beneath the seat, a round plate at the front on which to mount a favorite number, and tires that are pneumatic and knobbled.

In addition, there are Kiddimoto helmets, gloves, spare inner tubes and tires, and replacement parts, just in case mom or dad back over it in the driveway. The accompanying manufacturer's brochure contains a list of dos and don'ts: don't leave it against a heater; always patch any scuffed or exposed areas with either paint or wax to protect the wood; always wipe it dry after a wet ride; don't leave it out in the rain; and, above all, don't let your parents ride it no matter how much they may plead with you to do so. **BS**

TERN Swoop

2012 • Folding bike • Taiwan •
Precision-engineered Taiwanese folder

Tern has come a long way in a very short time since it began manufacturing bicycles in Taiwan in 2011. With a lawsuit in the wake of a bitter family feud now firmly in the past, it looks to be here for a long time to come.

The commuter-ready Swoop uses a 20-in. (50-cm) wheeled, step-through aluminum frame with the top tube just 11 in. (28 cm) off the ground. This frame is fitted with a high-tensile steel front fork, V-brakes, oversized tires to absorb the bumps, a rack with common-sense built-in cords, and a scuff guard guaranteed to keep clothes clean and that doubles as the bike's carry handle when folded. It has a quick and simple fold mechanism (10 seconds max). Posture is upright and relaxed, and its high-set handlebars can accommodate all but the tallest riders. At 30 lb (13.6 kg), it isn't the lightest folder around, but it gives a solid ride without noticeable flexing.

The Swoop is available in two models; the Duo and the D7i. The Duo has minimal cabling and a 2012 Eurobike award under its belt, and the D7i has a Shimano Nexus 7 integrated hub. They both feature a patented OCL joint design that makes folding easier and increases stiffness, and a unique double truss that transforms the rear of the bike into a three-dimensional structure that all but eliminates torsional forces. **BS**

JULIANA Origin Primeiro

2012 • Mountain bike • USA • Simple but very popular women's suspension bike from the "Queen of dirt"

The long and very productive relationship between Santa Cruz bikes and legendary 1990s racer Juliana Furtado started after injury ended her all-conquering MTB career. While Furtado had achieved her race success with Yeti and then GT bikes, joining Santa Cruz as their marketing chief was an obvious move for this Santa Cruz native. As well as driving the marketing of the expanding conventional line, Furtado also developed one of the first female-specific full suspension bikes, the eponymous Juliana. It was an immediate hit and remained a staple of the Santa Cruz range for over a decade, receiving the same incremental upgrades as its Superlight sibling.

In 2012, Juliana Bicycles was launched as a separate entity, with the aptly named Origin Primeiro as the lead model. Again it was based largely on the proven template of the Santa Cruz Superlight, which uses a single pivot system introduced on Santa Cruz's original Tazmon bike in 1996. Like the other bikes in the Juliana range, the Primeiro has a female-specific saddle, a shorter handlebar span, and smaller grips. Furtado thought carefully about the aesthetics of the bike, with different models using lotus, flame, and wolf designs as well as the "Queen of Dirt" crown from Juliana's racing past. "I wanted it feminine but not silly." Furtado says. **GK**

GT Stay Strong

2012 • BMX • UK • Injured rider support T-shirt that became a state-of-the-art Olympic BMX race bike

UK-born BMX star Stephen Murray was one of the most flamboyant and progressive riders of his era, famous for the most dangerous freestyle dirt jump tricks such as double and 360-degree twisted back flips. Unfortunately he miscalculated a double back flip in the finals of the BMX Dirt competition of the Dew Action Sports Tour in Baltimore, Maryland, in 2007, and broke his back, paralyzing him below his shoulders.

Other pro riders and supporters immediately started wearing "Stay Strong" T-shirts, the proceeds from the sale of these going toward his medical rehabilitation. The product range increased to include bike accessories, but GT's Stay Strong race frame has gained the most publicity for this worthy cause.

It was a top-class frameset, using a low and long design with a heavily reinforced hydroformed head tube, an oversized bottom bracket shell, and distinctive square section rear stays with a reversed wheel dropout design. UK star Shanaze Reade signed with the Stay Strong team for 2012 and the frame was used for her London Olympic Games BMX bike.

Murray has Stayed Strong too: with the help of the doctor who worked with Hollywood actor Christopher Reeve, he has recently regained the use of his arms. **GK**

SPECIALIZED Turbo

2012 • Electric road bike • USA • Designed specifically to be "the fastest and best electric bike ever"

Specialized has been a pioneer in mountain biking and road racing for decades, so it was only a matter of time before the company turned its attention to the E-bike market. Founder Mike Sinyard never does anything by halves, and his first venture into the rather utilitarian world of electrical bikes certainly caused a stir.

Unveiled in 2012, the Turbo boasts a top speed of 28 mph (45 kph), a run time of around an hour, and a battery recharge time of under three hours. The sweeping top tube, internal cable, and hidden battery also make the Turbo one of the most stylish bikes in the category. The concealed battery was an integral part of the design, as Specialized wanted the bike to look as stylish as possible, and for all intents and purposes unlike a typical E-bike.

Other features included carbon fiber Magura MT series disc brakes with a regenerative charging feature, and a wireless handlebar computer unit that displays power level and battery status as well as speed and distance. All this technology was mounted onto a lightweight alloy frame, with top-level transmission componentry provided by SRAM.

The project took three years to complete, but all that planning and technology could not prevent one major oversight. As if the cost wasn't a stumbling block in itself—the bike retails at around $5,900 (£3,700)—the maximum speed was also an issue. As product manager Marc Faude admitted at the launch, "Due to regulatory requirements, there are many markets, including the USA, where the Turbo is simply too fast to be legal." **DB**

LAND ROVER Nitride 2012 ED

2012 • Mountain bike • UK • Pedal-powered offshoot of the famous 4x4 brand

Skeptics feared that the Land Rover 4x4 mountain bike range might be merely another rebadged import from Southeast Asia. Their fears proved unfounded. Unlike some other automotive manufacturers, Tim Higgins and the design team at Land Rover thought long and hard about what they wanted their ultimate off roaders to have in terms of equipment: top-of-the-range Shimano XTR drivetrains and brakes, premium Black Chili compound Continental Mountain King tires, Marzocchi forks, and WTB saddles and rims—as good as anything you'll find on their competitors. Land Rover then decided to go one better (three microns better, to be precise) by incorporating all the best components of its Experience range of mountain bikes into a titanium-framed, titanium nitride-clad wonder called the Nitride.

Covered in a three-micron-thick layer of vaporized titanium that's one-fifth of the thickness of a drop of mist, the Nitride is totally scratch- and corrosion-proof. Gossamer-thin titanium spray—the material used to coat the 2012 London Olympic torches—envelops a bike that is custom made to suit the build of its owner, and that takes eighteen weeks to construct.

Jaguar Land Rover sales director Scott Hillyard was predictably enthusiastic about the product: "A titanium bike has timeless looks, is understated and above mere fashion; it feels supple, springy, and fast, and flows over the terrain, feeding back information to the rider without sting or vibration." Maybe so, but while it is undeniable that Land Rover execs love their new creation, that's still a lot to ask of just three microns. **BS**

SPECIALIZED Epic S-Works Kulhavý

2012 • Mountain bike • USA • Olympic gold medal-winning, full-suspension bike

Specialized's automatic suspension Epic bike has always been a (literally) firm favorite with racers. Its position as one of the most successful race bikes of all time was underlined when Specialized team rider Jaroslav Kulhavý surged past Nino Schurter in the last few metres of the 2012 London Olympics to blast his big-wheeled, Brain-equipped neon red bike over the line in first place.

This gold-winning bike was even more specialized than Specialized's top showroom model. The frame at its heart was the company's flagship S-Works model with a high-modulus Fact 11R carbon front triangle. The top tube on the larger frame model used by Kulhavý also had an additional reinforcing strut ahead of the extended seat tube. The rear stays and offside drop-

> ## "Seamless transition from efficient pedaling on smooth terrain to fully active on rough."
>
> Worldxcmtb.com

out are all FACT carbon fiber too, while a tapered head tube, BB30 bottom bracket, and screw-through 5⅗ x ½-in. (14.2 x 1.2-cm) rear axle all add baseline stiffness.

The unique advantage of the Epic is the minimalist shock under the down tube that links to a Brain bump sensor at the rear wheel. This lets it move automatically as soon as it detects rough terrain, but keeps it locked for maximum power transfer on smooth surfaces. The front fork is also a custom Brain-equipped version of the superlight Rock Shox SID XX 29er fork, which uses a carbon-fiber crown and steerer tube for minimal weight.

Kulhavý was one also of the first athletes in the world to get a Black Box development version of SRAM's radical 11 speed XX1 transmission, which he definitely turned up to 11 to blast his Epic to gold-medal glory. **GK**

◁ Jaroslav Kulhavý on his way to gold.

STANTON Slackline

2012 • Mountain bike • UK • Super-tough trail steel or titanium hardtail

Dan Stanton isn't the first rider to get bored with bikes that didn't quite suit him and decide to design his own. However, few have been as successful in gaining significant recognition, since the Slackline has been featured in the highly influential annual "Top 100" product selection of *Dirt Mountain Bike* magazine three times.

Stanton combines elements of both long-travel fork trail geometry and the agile, compact characteristics of 4X and slalom racing bikes. He underlines the qualities created by the frame angles and tube lengths by picking the right materials to make the bikes come alive. The most popular options are two Reynolds steel tubesets; 853 and 631. 853 is premium non-stainless steel alloy and was the first bicycle tubeset to actually increase its strength when welded. The frame is surprisingly light and naturally sprung but still tough enough to race multi-stage Enduro downhill events. Double-butted Reynolds 631 is a steel tubeset that maintains the liveliness of the Slackline for less money but with a little more mass. The flagship of the range is the Titanium Slackline, which is even lighter and livelier than the 853. Whatever material your wallet can cope with, you still get chain guide mounts and a dropper-post-compatible seat tube to handle the most hardcore riding demands. **GK**

CINELLI Saetta

2012 • Road bike • Italy • Cost-effective bike from classic Italian marque

Established by pro rider Cino Cinelli in 1947, the Cinelli company has always been among the most iconic and pioneering of Italian bike and component brands. The curvaceous Saetta proves the company is still one of the best, even when operating at a bargain price.

A noticeably sprung feel is the first obvious trait of the frame, thanks to the "Progressive Flexion Control" curve that forms a flat-leaf spring effect through the flat centered top tube and the wishbone seatstay top. This doesn't just smooth out road shock, it also creates a momentum surge between accelerations. In spite of the spindly retro looks of the chainset, the octagonal down tube, big bottom bracket, and chainstays mean the bike still climbs and accelerates enthusiastically. It's not as sharp and firm in its progress as the most solid bikes because of its heavy wheels, but it performs well whether spinning the compact rings in the saddle or stomping and shouldering a big ratio over the top of a climb.

While the tall head tube and straight steerer Columbus forks mean it's not anchored into the ground, overall balance is good and there is enough feedback to foster trust. While blunt riveted guides for the external cable routing don't exactly purr "premium product," the sleek lines still drew admiring comments. **GK**

CONDOR Pista

2012 • Road bike • UK • Single-speed
street bike

The Pista—Italian for "track"—is much more than a
single-speed racer: most Pistas are used as hardcore
street bikes.

The frame is ideal for city couriers who need
something stronger than aluminum. It consists of a
super-lightweight Italian Dedacciai SAT 14.5 triple-
butted steel (with different thicknesses, at each end
and in the middle of the tube to save weight and add
strength where needed) that is heat-treated and has
bosses for bottle fitments on the down tube, plus cable
guides for the front and rear brakes. It comes in olive,
cream, or gray with a choice of five sizes: 18, 19, 20, 23,
and 24 in. (46, 49, 52, 58, and 61 cm).

London-based Condor began making its own
components to go with the frame, and promoted the
finished product as a traditional fixed-gear machine
for ultimate simplicity with the option of fitting a
freewheel to make it easy to work in towns.

In 2013 Condor also released the World Series Pista,
a limited-edition frameset to celebrate the eightieth
birthday of company founder Monty Young and the
success of Condor-backed riders. The World Series is
available in five color combinations, each featuring a
color of cycling's world-champion rainbow. **SH**

LAST Herb 160

2012 • Trial bike • Germany • Downhill-style
enduro bike

Last has gone for a customizable approach with the
Herb Trail, which can be bought in either 6³⁄₁₀- or 7¹⁄₁₀-
in. (16- or 18-cm) travel configurations, although
either can be converted into the other by swapping
the main rocker link. The frame is built from custom-
butted aluminum. The wall thicknesses and the rear
triangles are different on the right and left sides to
handle the different forces of braking and chain pull. The
65.5-degree head angle, 16⁷⁄₁₀-in. (42.4-cm) chainstays,
and the long wheelbase give the Herb a distinctly
downhill feel but, with a weight of 33 lb (15 kg), it rides
light and nimble on climbs and descents.

The suspension system is a rocker-actuated single
pivot placed directly above the bottom bracket to
neutralize as much of the pedal force as possible. This
system gives the rear wheel a vertical and rearward path
as it travels through the suspension, allowing the bike to
accelerate through rocky terrain because the wheel can
move away from impact as it moves through the travel.

Last focused on every detail of the Herb frame, using
crimson anodizing on the linkage, headset, and rear axle.
The mainframe has been anodized black to increase its
lifespan and provide a more durable finish than regular
paint. **CJ**

LYNSKEY Pro29 FS-120

2012 • Mountain bike • USA • Full-suspension mountain bike from the legendary Ti builders

Lynskey had been working in ultra-high durability metals such as titanium for the aerospace, engineering, and industrial sectors for decades, before a happy accident steered the family into titanium bike manufacture.

While its product portfolio changes every year as the company discovers new ways to improve the ride and performance of their Chattanooga, Tennessee-made machines, the debut of the Pro29 FS-120 at Interbike trade show in 2012 was extremely significant. Having previously relied almost exclusively on the inherent spring and compliance of titanium to soften the ride of the bikes and add control and comfort, creating a full-suspension bike was a radical departure for the brand.

"Pretty much anywhere I took the Pro29, the suspension systems reacted well."

Jon Pratt, dirtragmag.com

Lynskey stuck with 3V 2.5AL titanium alloy for the tubeset, using their signature twisted-box-section helix forming process to stiffen the massive down tube for "stomp and go power transfer." A press-fit bottom bracket tube was used to create the biggest possible junction area with the down tube.

To complement the light weight and create a lively, responsive ride, travel was kept to 4½ in. (12 cm) using a short swing link to add lateral stiffness and drive the Fox rear shock. Large 29-in. (73.5-cm) wheels helped sustain speed over choppy, rocky terrain far better than smaller-wheels. The seat tube was also sized to take dropper seatposts for more body movement space on steep and technical trails. The result was a bike that added a whole new bloodline to Lynskey's illustrious lineage. **GK**

BRITISH CYCLING Olympic Bike

2012 • Keirin track bike • UK • Sir Chris Hoy's gold-medal winning bike with "round wheels"

The British cycling team's medal haul at the London 2012 Olympics prompted some jealous suspicions from the French team. The French team director was particularly concerned that the British track team's wheels may not have met regulations.

As a retort, the British cycling chief told a French interviewer that their team's secret was the use of "specially round wheels." The reporter failed to spot the humor, and Britain's new "round wheels" were seriously reported in the following morning's edition of the French national sporting paper, *L'Equipe*.

"Round wheels" became one of the great cycling jokes of the year, and the term was soon emblazoned on biking T-shirts. In fact, the joke was doubly on the French, because the British track bike team's wheels were actually normal off-the-shelf items made by Mavic . . . in France.

To be precise, Sir Chris Hoy's gold-medal-winning Keirin track bike used a Mavic Comete Track disc at the rear, and a five-spoke at the front. Pursuit riders used discs on the front, but Hoy needed the extra stiffness for the sudden and violent changes of direction in Keirin.

The British bikes were made by UK Sport, which published details of their machines. In accordance with Olympic rules, all the parts were available for the public to buy, so it was easy to confirm that Hoy's bike was built up on a 3-lb (1.4-kg) Mark III carbon frame.

UK Sport's own carbon chainset was claimed to offer twice the stiffness of a Shimano Dura-Ace crank while being 7 oz (200 g) lighter.

At speeds over 70 mph (112 kph), every aerodynamic detail can be important. Narrow front area is crucial. So Hoy's sprint bars were integrated with the stem in one ultra-stiff piece of carbon that was distinctively shaped for low drag resistance. **SH**

The stealth bikes were a big part of Team GB's incredible 2012 Olympic success. ▶

SPECIALIZED S-Works Demo 8

2012 • Downhill • USA • World Champion developed carbon fiber downhill bike

The launch of the Specialized Demo 8 Carbon marked the acceptance of carbon fiber as a suitable material for mass-production downhill bikes.

The relative strengths and weaknesses of carbon fiber and aluminum have been argued over by cyclists of all kinds, but the most animated discussions have always occurred in the downhill arena. GT was the first to produce carbon downhill bikes—first the STS, and then the Fury—in 1999, but it was more than a decade before other manufacturers followed suit. In 2010, GT tried again with the Santa Cruz V10 Carbon, but two more years passed before Specialized decided it was ready to make the leap.

". . . the world's fastest downhill machine . . . oozes premium downhill performance."

Specialized.co.uk

Determined not to release the bike until it was totally proven, Specialized had its World Cup racers Sam Hill and Troy Brosnan race the carbon frame for a year while monitoring how it dealt with the World Cup circuit. It was so happy with the bike's performance that it pushed the production button on an almost unchanged version of the team bikes.

In fact, the S-Works Demo 8 Carbon Team Replica is almost identical to the test bikes ridden by Hill and Brosnan. It looks like a Ferrari that has been transformed into a bicycle. The matte black and gloss red paint job oozes beauty; the magnesium link is 2 oz (50 g) lighter than the regular model; the alloy rear end features a ½ x 5³⁄₁₀-in. (12 x 135-mm) axle length, as opposed to the ½ x 6-in. (12 x 150 mm) of the standard Demo 8 Carbon. **CJ**

JERONIMO Slütter Ti X

2012 • Cyclocross bike • Spain • Tenerife-made Ti cyclocross bike

Pedro Jeronimo is a custom bike builder based in Tenerife, in the Atlantic Ocean off the coast of North Africa. Tenerife is great biking terrain, with steep slopes around Mount Teide, a volcano that, at 12,198 ft (3,718 m) above sea level, is the highest point in Spain.

In his effort to make a bike that was as flexible as possible, Jeronimo hired designer Jerome Slütter to produce the framework for a go-anywhere sort of machine—one that could be changed from a mountain bike into a road bike simply by changing the wheels. All other parts and features would be equally appropriate for both forms of use.

To many commentators, this sounded like an impossible dream, but the finished product more than lived up to the manufacturer's hype: the Slütter features a really eclectic mix of road-, cross-, and mountain-bike components. It comes with a Gates carbon belt-drive system, a Shimano Alfine internal rear hub, and Avid mechanical disc brakes. The wheels are 27½ in. (70 cm) in diameter, the handlebars are flat, and there are mountain bike-style shifters and levers. In addition, the Slütter has a pure carbon fork and a traditional leather saddle.

But the coolest part of this undoubtedly cool bike is the frame. It's all made of grade-9 double-butted titanium, which is aircraft-quality material. The neat tube tungsten inert gas (TIG) welds are made using pure titanium as solder. The whole frame is then finished in an attractive satin matte. This build makes the bike strong, lightweight, and shock absorbent. And it will never rust—this is perhaps the most useful quality of a bike born in the middle of the Atlantic.

The Slütter's design is striking and purposeful too, with a bent top tube and a curved integrated seatpost, although the final tube angles are chosen by the customers themselves. **SH**

SPECIALIZED P Slope

2012 • Slopestyle bike • USA • Full suspension slopestyle stunt mountain bike

Specialized took two years to develop the P Slope in consultation with two of the world's best slopestyle stunt athletes, Martin Söderström and Darren Berrecloth. It took all the aspects of the popular P series hardtail dirt jump bikes and built them into this new rear-suspension chassis.

Söderström says, "In slopestyle we only need suspension that saves us for certain moves." Specialized took this feedback and developed the P Slope to have incredibly progressive suspension that allows the bike to feel like a hardtail on the takeoff but still gives enough suspension for hard landings. The suspension pivots around the bottom bracket, allowing riders to run single-speed setups on the bike without adverse effect. RockShox suspension developed a custom-tuned

Monarch RT3 rear shock with a super-stiff dampening profile for Söderström's P Slope, but it is available on the bike you can buy off the shelf too, giving the customer truly world-class performance.

Just two weeks after taking delivery of his new P Slope, Söderström took it to second place in the world's biggest slopestyle competition, Crankworx Whistler.

This bike is not just for slopestyle maestros—it has race pedigree too. Mitch Ropelato won the 2012 Crankworx pump track competition on his P Slope, even though he'd had it for only three days. So whether you are into slopestyle, dirt jumps, dual slalom, or pump tracks, the P Slope will step up to the plate. As Berrecloth says: "I can't even begin to explain how stoked I am to have a bike like that." **CJ**

SPECIALIZED Status
2012 • Downhill/Freeride bike • USA • Specialized's cost effective "Big Hit" replacement

The Status takes the place of the Big Hit, the bike that thrust Specialized into the downhill/freeride limelight. The Status is a long way from the old 24-in. (61-cm) rear-wheeled Big Hit that first appeared in the Specialized lineup in 2003. This bike changed the freeride mountain bike movement from people with no fear blindly jumping off huge cliffs to the incredibly dexterous and skilled moves seen in competitions like the Red Bull Rampage. The Status marked the end for the Big Hit, but a new beginning for a bike to make its place in history.

Built from Specialized's M4 alloy with clear parallels with the company's Demo 8 and SX Trail bikes, the Status reeks of style and poise. The Status idea was first tested under the feet of Brendan Fairclough in Whistler, where he was riding his Specialized SX Trail with a lowered RockShox BoXXer front suspension fork. It shares many of the previous SX Trail bike's traits, including a 5½-in. (13.5-cm) rear axle, Specialized's proven FSR suspension system, and 6-in. (15-cm) head tube. The very relaxed 64.5-degree head angle gives the Status a confidence-inspiring ride, and the low 14-in. (35.5-cm) bottom bracket means it has a lot of grip in corners. Specialized's U.S. Gravity team—Brad Benedict and Red Bull athlete Curtis Keene—use the Status on the downhill World Cup circuit instead of Specialized's bespoke downhill race bike, the Demo 8, to show the world and potential Specialized consumers that you don't need the most expensive bike to win. The devolved technology of the Status has made it an unsurprisingly popular bike with riders on a budget. **CJ**

INTENSE Carbine Carbon

2012 • Mountain bike • USA • Powerful, agile, and lightweight mountain-biking weapon

There are all sorts of inspirations for bike names, but some companies definitely follow themes. In the case of Intense Cycles, weapon-related tags have always been common for their tough trail bikes.

The Carbine was originally launched in 2002, when it joined an Intense line-up that already contained the Tracer (as in bullet) and the Uzzi, which, with the addition of an extra "z" to avoid copyright infringement, had almost the same name as an Israeli high-powered submachine gun.

The bike was one of the first Intense products to use the VPP (Virtual Pivot Point) suspension technology co-developed and shared with Santa Cruz. Its name appropriately summed up its performance. The original carbines were compact rifles designed to enable soldiers on horseback to fire full-sized bullets. Both the term and the design principles were maintained after cavalry units swapped their horses for tanks, but still faced the same issues of restricted storage space and movement.

Thus the Intense Carbine was extremely powerful but compact and responsive, with an aggressive ride character that divided opinion like few other bikes: people either loved it or avoided it at all costs.

The alloy-framed, hand-built original was later joined in the Intense range by Asian-built carbon fiber frames based on the same travel, geometry, and suspension systems. This represented a new departure for the firmly U.S.-rooted brand, but company founder Jeff Steber remains committed to building the aluminum alloy bikes with his thirty-strong team in Temecula, California. Although he acknowledges that the expertise for carbon fiber frames lies overseas, he sees that the ability to rapidly build new alloy frame designs, test them, and perfect them for production in either alloy or carbon is a vital part of his process. **GK**

TRANSITION Bandit

2012 • Mountain bike • Canada • Burly trail bike with a no-nonsense reputation

"Rider-owned" is a term often associated with the grassroots, back-street world of BMX, but Kevin Menard and his crew from Transition Bikes are rightly proud that their company is run by real riders for real riders. Transition's emphasis on getting the most out of every ride came to fruition in 2010 with the launch of the Bandit, a bike designed to rob the trail of any dullness.

The outward simplicity of this no-nonsense bike belies the amount of thought and design experience that went into the carefully designed tubes and the machined sections that join them. The result is a frame that can be built up light enough to toe the start line at a rough cross-country race, but tough enough to let

> ". . . the Bandit certainly has an air of solidity to it that we don't see from all trail bikes."
>
> *Brad Walton, pinkbike.com*

you armor up and let rip on the rowdiest downhill. The optimized pivot placement and carefully calculated leverage curves of the suspension make for consistently balanced traction and pedal delivery performance. Just 5½ in. (13 cm) of travel is enough to handle the biggest drops and hits under a skillful rider, but not so much that it sucks all the life out of the bike when you're sprinting. Add confidently progressive handling geometry, and this bike lets you take any route up or down the trails without having to compromise.

As well as a frame-only build-up, there are three complete bike options available. The original 26-in. (66-cm) wheeled bike now comes in a range of three 29-in. (73.5-cm) bikes for those who want more traction and smoothness in their Banditry. **GK**

◁ Intense's latest Carbine matches big wheels with big confidence for massive speed.　　High modulus and handcrafted　**715**

PAKETA D2R

2012 • Tandem • USA • Magnesium tandem with electric gears

When Beth Graff won gold medals at the 2011 U.S. Masters National Championship in the Mixed Tandem 110 and Time Trial, she knew whom to thank for her triumphs. Her Paketa bike was "so fast," she said, that she and her partner flew through the course "as a result of having such superior equipment."

Paketa is a small, Denver, Colorado-based company that, since its foundation eleven years previously, had gradually refined the art of making customized high-performance bikes from magnesium. It's a tricky—and unusual—material to work with, so not many builders use it. Paketa is one of the top mag bike makers in the world. The tubing it uses is AZ61, which is ninety-three

". . . a Paketa tandem will be the smoothest ride you have ever experienced."

roadbikereview.com

percent magnesium, six percent aluminum, and one percent zinc. According to Paketa, this alloy mix provides the best strength-to-weight ratio and best vibration damping, not just of any magnesium tubing, but of any bike frame material currently in use.

Paketa builds all sorts of bikes, but has had most success with racing tandems. The V2R magnesium two-seater was the first two-person machine to use a right-side timing belt drive. It has been winning races all over the world since its launch, and weighs just 21 lb (9.5 kg). The D2R is the latest evolution of the V2R. It has two couplings, so that it can be dismantled for easy transportation. It uses the Gates Carbon Drive belt system, and a compact crankset. The frame is finished in a new ceramic coating, which is very thin but scratch resistant. **SH**

PRATIK GHOSH Cycle Rickshaw

2012 • Rickshaw • India • Classic pedal-powered taxi

Cycle rickshaws first appeared in Japan in the late 1860s, when they began to be used in place of the covered sedan chairs of the Meiji period. Their use spread to India, China, and throughout Southeast Asia, and they were enthusiastically welcomed as a major leap forward over older, hand-pulled rickshaws. They were also a boon to the poor, who could not afford to travel on the increasingly common, though expensive, auto-powered rickshaws that charged three or four times the price per mile of their pedal-powered cousins.

Traditional cycle rickshaws have the operator sitting in front of his or her passengers, who sit side by side in a two-person carriage with an awning above. It is a timeless concept, and although there's a worldwide push to develop new, efficient "pedicabs"—cycle rickshaws with electric-assist motors—the argument for pollution-free cycles remains a strong one.

In 2012, Kolkata, India-based engineer Pratik Ghosh designed a new-generation cycle rickshaw that, it is claimed, harnesses the weight of its passengers to help push it along by having its chassis set at an angle of ten degrees to the ground, sloping forward so that the shock generated by the bumps and movement in the road is transferred into the frame—a forward component to assist propulsion.

"Since the rickshaw pullers will be able to travel long distances with high speed effortlessly," Ghosh explains, "it is presumed that these rickshaws will be able to replace autos to some extent, and reduce dependence on fuel-based vehicles."

At the time of writing, the concept remained unproven, but with the cost of gasoline constantly increasing, and the congestion in some of Asia's cities reaching saturation point, it is worth persisting with further development. **BS**

PAWTREKKER Rufftrax Evolution

2012 • Specialist bike • UK • Scooter bike for dog racing

The sport of dog scootering or "bikejoring" requires at least one dog hitched up to either a mountain bike or a specially designed dog scooter. The dog helps pull the rider along off-road tracks against other dog bikes. As the activity grows in popularity, more manufacturers are launching more specialist products.

Pawtrekker, based in Southampton, England, has a range of machines specifically designed to be pulled by dogs. The Rufftrax Evolution is its top model.

The design is a cross between a scooter and a mountain bike, with a 26-in. (66-cm) wheel at the front with SR Suntour alloy front-suspension forks and a 20-in. (50-cm) wheel at the back. The front and rear wheels are quick release, with Shimano hubs and rims. The spec includes a front and rear mechanical disc braking system with "two-finger" levers from Shimano. The frame is made of lightweight alloy, and there's even a braze-on mounting for a water bottle holder.

The hardtail Evolution has a unique "brushbow" attachment. This is a quick-release arm fixed to the head tube that allows dog harnesses to be fixed to the bike without the dogs fouling on the front wheel or interfering with the steering.

These scooters are often preferred to bikes among bikejoring fans. The rider can quickly and safely step off the bike if the dogs become distracted, and the low center of gravity makes the ride more stable over rough terrain. An optional extra is the Sidewalker attachment, which clamps onto the side of the bike and allows your dog to run alongside you, rather than in front. **SH**

KTM Lycan 652

2012 • Mountain bike • Austria • State-of-the-art trailwolf

Austrian bike brand KTM might have split from its motorcycle brethren a while ago, but it is still based in the same town and still delivering high-performance two-wheelers.

The Lycan 652 proves KTM is still a driving force in terms of innovation, too, by adopting the new 650B wheel size far earlier than most major manufacturers.

Interestingly, 650B wheels are far from a new development for mountain bikes, as some of the earliest off-road lash-ups used this intermediate-sized wheel some thirty-five years before the Lycan. Tire and rim availability meant more readily available 26-in. (66-cm) wheels were accepted as the default standard instead, and it's only since 2012 that these availability issues have been overcome.

The new wheel size potentially offers a compromise between 26-in. (66-cm) and 29-in. (73.5-cm) wheels. They are larger than the former, so they have a shallower contact tire angle and roll better over momentum-sapping blunt objects on the trail, such as rocks and roots. A longer directional footprint on the ground also adds traction. However, they're not so large that acceleration is noticeably dulled or flex in wheels increased, as can be the case with 29-in. (73.5-cm) wheels.

KTM have taken all this into consideration with the Lycan. With smoother-rolling wheels, a Fox suspension shock, and RockShox fork, it's a very sure-footed machine. The advanced aluminum frame with screw-through wheel axles adds lightweight pep and precise handling to create a state-of-the-art all-rounder. **GK**

HP VELOTECHNIK Streamer

2012 • Recumbent • Germany • Aerodynamic all-season faired recumbent

The Streamer by HP Velotechnik is instantly recognizable by its teardrop-shaped front fairing. Constructed of strong, transparent plastic, it comes complete with its own lightweight aluminum mounts.

It's far from a full-fairing "velomobile," as the screen covers the rider's legs only from the knees down, and is open at the sides. There is no upper-body protection, but neither is there any obstruction to easy, "foot-down" stopping. The design also reduces the danger of the fairing acting like a sail to destroy steering control in gusty conditions.

The curved structure still covers the whole front aspect of the bike, and thus contributes significantly to speed efficiency. Because drag is the biggest drain of

". . . protects . . . from the elements and . . . slips through the air with minimum effort."

hpvelotechnik.com

driver energy, and wastage increases exponentially with speed, the fairing makes even more sense for faster or longer-distance riders.

The superstructure is attached to the standard Velotechnik frame on two struts: the front is on the bottom bracket, and held in place with a fast-release lever; the rear is on the main boom. Both are adjustable, so that riders of all sizes can see the road ahead.

Users report a noticeable absence of rattle or vibration on the road, as the screen is extraordinarily thin, and weighs just 3 lb (1.45 kg). Aluminum spars are held onto the inside of the fairing with Velcro for crash safety. Because of its inherent flexibility, the screen is resilient, and can even be dropped without cracking. **BS**

YETI SB-66

2012 • Mountain bike • USA • Patent-swerving switch-suspension superbike

By 2012, innovation in the mountain-bike world was totally choked with suspension-licensing deals and savagely protected patents. It looked like there was no possible way to make a rear-wheel move in relation to the mainframe without paying someone a pot of cash or risking a lawyer turning up on your doorstep. Designers seemed to be spending more time in court than out on the trails testing.

Yeti, however, has always prided itself on an unconventional approach, and the Switch Technology suspension it introduced on its SB-66 (SB stands for "superbike") was a totally fresh design. By combining a main pivot set in a rotating eccentric drum and an upper rocker linkage, the aptly named system actually changes the way the suspension works halfway through the stroke. The first half of the 6½ in. (16 cm) of movement is arranged to give fantastic grip and firm pedaling, while the second stage is super-smooth to suck up the biggest hits without registering even a blip on your ride radar. The result is a bike on which you can charge up climbs or away from start lines without worrying that you'll never get the full value out of your suspension.

Not only is the frame impressively stiff, but its smoothly curved lines are also deliberately laid back low for unshakable confidence, no matter how chaotic the trails.

The SB-66 and its 29er sibling, the SB-95, have unsurprisingly proved a literal runaway success too, especially when carbon-fiber versions of both frames appeared to lop a huge chunk of weight off the aluminum frames. The result is hell on your wallet, but absolute heaven when you hit fast, technical trails flat out. **GK**

Yeti's Superbike 66 is ideal for exploring the wildest riding possibilities. ▶

YETI 303 WC Carbon

2012 • Downhill bike • USA • Carbon incarnation of Yeti's winning 303 design

The all-black 303 World Cup (WC) Carbon follows in a long Yeti tradition of manufacturing the world's most awe-inspiring race machines for some of the world's best riders, including John Tomac and Missy Giove.

To maintain its status as a maker of modern classics, Yeti puts its top-end bikes through a race program for at least two years, to ensure that every design kink is ironed out before the machines go on sale to the public. For the development of the 303 WC Carbon, the company engaged the services of its longest-serving racer, Jared Graves.

There are few better testers than Australian Graves, who in 2008 reached the BMX finals at the Olympic

> *"The new Yeti 303 WC Carbon is one of the most alluring of this special breed we've seen."*
>
> bikeradar.com

Games in Beijing, China. In 2009, he won both the 4X World Championships and the World Cup 4X series overall, and retained the latter title in the following year. With sixteen years' experience, he is one of the most revered racers on the planet.

Graves returned to downhill racing in 2012 with Yeti's brand-new 303 WC Carbon. The bike is based on the aluminum version, but because of the carbon fiber mainframe it is almost 1 lb (0.5 kg) lighter. The suspension uses Yeti's famous rail system to control the leverage ratio, and a shock extender to create a varying suspension feel throughout the wheel movement. This system is coupled with custom-built Fox suspension to tailor the bike to each racetrack and provide as smooth a ride as possible. **CJ**

GRAEME OBREE Beastie

2012 • Track • UK • World-record-breaking machine

Graeme Obree has long challenged convention in the often stuffy world of cycling. He came to reluctant fame in the 1990s during a legendary cut-and-thrust fight between himself on his home-made bikes and British Olympian Chris Boardman on his Lotus-built carbon composite machines. After retreating back into obscurity in 2011, Obree launched a training manual that laid out a simple, back-to-the-roots plan for fitness. That year also saw him announce his aim to break a world record in 2013, using a typically radical machine named Beastie.

In this unusual, prone-position bicycle, the rider lies on his belly, with his nose only inches from the front wheel. The chainset is turned by linkage-driven push rods rather than conventional pedals. Obree kept up his reputation for gradually dismantling the kitchen workspace around him by utilizing an old saucepan to make the shoulder supports, with the frame built of steel, a variety of spare parts, retractable stabilizers made from an old pair of roller skates, and the whole package encapsulated in a molded outer skin for maximum aerodynamic efficiency.

In September of 2013, Obree rode the Beastie at 56.62 mph (91.12 kph) on a timed flat section of highway at the World Human-powered Speed Challenge in rural Nevada, a world record for prone recumbent cycling, but still some way off the overall two-wheel human-powered vehicle (HPV) record of 83 mph (133.57 kph). The bike is a stunning example of a human surrendering conventional notions of comfort to a purist engineering approach, but it also speaks volumes about Obree. Having fought to overcome personal demons, he has talked about his passion for personal challenge and adventure, and his determination always to do the best that he can. **KF**

COLNAGO C59 Disc

2012 • Road bike • Italy • Road bike with hydraulic disc brakes and redesigned carbon frame

With hydraulic front and rear disc brakes set over a 5½-in. (14-cm) diameter disc, electronic shifting, redesigned forks, chainstays, seatstays, Artemis Disc wheels with carbon composite rims, and disc-specific hubs, the C59 fully justified Colnago's claim that it was "a bold step toward the future of road bike evolution."

The advantages of the C59's discs are many. There's no rim damage and less rotating inertia, no braking track heat to affect tire pressure, and the same braking efficiency in all weather conditions. The C59 has fully internal brake routing, its hydraulic calipers are lighter than mechanical cabling and behave better in muddy conditions, and its fork drop-outs have been reversed to prevent wheel rejection.

Perfection cannot be hurried, and even on a busy day at the Colnago factory in Cambiago, Italy, only sixteen C59s are made. Each carbon-fiber frame is set on a special alignment jig, and the company that produces Ferrari's Formula 1 racing car chassis makes the C59's lugs and tubes from raw carbon. Hand-painted colors include Maserati Blue and NATO Green, and those carbon tubes are beautifully bonded into carbon lugs. If money were no object, you'd surely want one. But at just under $16,000 (£10,000), an object it will most likely remain. **BS**

COLNAGO K.Zero

2012 • Road/time trial bike • Italy • State-of-the-art aero race machine from legendary brand

While some major bike manufacturers make one or two technological breakthroughs and then stagnate, Colnago continually looks for ways to improve. In view of both the increasingly tight technical regulations of cycling's governing body, the UCI, and the global economic recession that has necessitated a drastic reduction in research and development budgets, it was a mammoth accomplishment when Colnago announced its K.Zero time trial bike in Taipei in 2012.

Colnago's thirst for innovation is underlined by the fact that its K.Zero launch came soon after unveiling its revolutionary C59 disc brake road bike. The K.Zero is also a completely new bike, not just an update of the hugely successful Flight TT. New features included an integrated bar–stem combination, a full set of internal cable routing, and all-new tube profiles. The front fork setup was improved to allow for better airflow, while a brake system courtesy of TRP was also built in. The new tube profiles reduced drag, while increasing stiffness and improving energy transfer from rider to bike. Aesthetically, the bike more than holds up too, and chief designer Davide Fumagalli definitely delivered on his ambition for the K.Zero to become a standard-bearer for time trial bikes across the planet. **DB**

◁ Colnago's C59 led the way in the use of road discs.

BOARDMAN SLR 9.8

2012 • Race bike • UK • Classic all-round race bike from legendary UK racer-turned-designer

Chris Boardman started designing his own bikes when he worked with maverick carbon construction innovator Mike Burrows to create the single-sided, Lotus-badged, hour-record-breaking "superbike" in 1996. He's also been involved with the development and evolution of the bikes used by the British cycling team ever since.

Boardman's long professional experience is also obvious in the handling DNA of the SLR, which is slightly slower and more stable than most road race bikes. In fact, one early reviewer described the handling as too slow for cut-and-thrust circuit racing. However, he found himself immediately and very publicly corrected on an attached forum by none other than Boardman himself, who pointed out the same geometry had already won

world and national championships, plus an Olympic road-race gold under Nicole Cook MBE.

As the name suggests, the SLR (Super Light Race) is the only bike in the Boardman Elite range where aerodynamics are not a priority. Internal control cables keep things neat, but otherwise the frame is based on large, square, and rectangular tube sections for maximum stiffness at a sub-kilo frame weight. Massive rear stays help squeeze undiluted power out of the oversized axle BB3 crankset to make it a ferociously fast climber and descender.

Unlike many machines that really reveal their full potential only in their most expensive complete bike formats, even the entry-level SLR 9.0 shares the 9.8's enjoyable, rapid, and responsive ride. **GK**

OLYMPIA Ego

2012 • Road bike • Italy • Full-carbon racer

The Ego has evolved quickly since it first appeared in 2012. The full-carbon chassis arrived with a clear leaning toward performance thanks to its traditional race-bike geometry, but in the short time since its debut, the Ego has undergone further enhancement.

Additions such as a tapered head tube for superior steering precision, an oversized bottom bracket shell for greater stiffness, and full internal cable routing for improved aerodynamics have all put an even finer edge on its already sharp competition credentials.

The cutting-edge bike design and engineering are enough to make it appealing, but being from an Italian maker adds the allure of the expertise and craftsmanship that have been built up as a result of bike racing and building being so deeply ingrained in the country.

Olympia may not immediately inspire the same reverence as names like Colnago, Pinarello, or De Rosa, but it has a far longer history than all of them. Olympia was established in 1893, and of all the high-profile Italian brands, only Bianchi has been making bikes longer.

And while many bike makers have shipped some or all of their manufacturing overseas, Olympia prefers to rely on the experience and mastery built up during its 120-year history. If a frame bears the Olympia name, it will have been designed and made in its factory in Piove di Sacco, just over 12½ mi (20 km) southwest of Venice.

Retaining that exceptional heritage but also building on it by employing modern materials and designs to produce new and better bikes is an ideal approach the Ego embodies perfectly. **RB**

MERIDA Big.Nine

2012 • Mountain bike • Taiwan • Super-light World Championship-winning race mountain bike

Taiwanese bike building powerhouse Merida derives a large number of development and marketing benefits from its Multivan Merida World Cup cross-country race team.

The Big.Nine—the latest weapon to be added to the team's impressive lineup—has already proven itself capable of delivering a sharp dose of speed that puts it out ahead of the pack, with a Marathon World Championship and European Cross-Country championship already in the bag.

A key part of the Big.Nine's success is its super-light carbon mainframe, which weighs only 2 lb 6 oz (1.1 kg). This is not just a gram-saving exercise, though: the ride character of the bike has been tuned to the demands of the pro team by careful shaping and material composition. In particular, the rear stays are flat and curved to create a leaf spring effect at the rear of the bike, and the seat tube tapers down to a super-slim 1¹⁄₁₀-in. (2.72-cm) diameter to increase the amount of flex between frame and saddle and thus enhance rider comfort.

Merida has also added flax fibers into the carbon-fiber construction sandwich in order to reduce vibration and rattle through the frame tubes. This advanced, multi-aspect damping is pronounced enough to leave riders fresher and better able to contest the last-lap charge and the final 100-meter sprints that conclude so many top-level races, even 62-mi (100-km) marathons.

Naturally, the frame still needs to be stiff enough to take the fastest possible racing line and put down that final kick to the finish without losing any vital wattage. That's why Merida has installed an outsized X-Taper head tube at the front, and a wider wheel axle, measuring 5³⁄₅ in. x ½ in. (14.2 x 1.2 cm), that is hollow and screws into the frame at the rear. **GK**

"Good geometry, a decent riding position, and a comfortable, if flexy, ride are all present and correct."

MBR UK

SURLY Krampus

2012 • Mountain bike • USA • The first twenty-nine-plus go-anywhere bike

If you've put two radical ideas into production that have proved surprisingly popular, why not combine them for a third tilt at the prize? That's exactly what Surly did when it launched the Krampus bike in 2012.

It was already among the first brands to produce an off-the-peg 29er, the Karate Monkey, and it started the production-Fatbike frenzy with the Pugsley, so a large-tired 29er was an obvious development.

The Krampus uses 2-in. (5-cm) rims to support specially made 3-in. (7.5-cm) tires with a shallow, arrow-style tread that rolls fast but grips in turns. Extra-wide rear stays and fork on the steel frame mean plenty of clearance when churning through snow or plowing through marshy ground, but they're still narrow enough for a normal crank rather than a Fatbike axle.

The Krampus rides much more like a standard 29er than a Fatbike. Conventional cranks mean it feels less freaky between your feet than the latter, and the lack of suspension keeps the weight reasonable for an enthusiastically responsive ride.

Surly claims that "when bicycles and insects have merged their lineages and become the dominant, unstoppable race on the planet Earth, Krampus will no doubt be this new species." We look forward to it. **GK**

QUINTANA ROO Illicito

2012 • Triathlon bike • USA • Innovative single-sided aero frame

While single-sided wheel fixings work fine on motorized road vehicles and airplanes, bikes require a much finer balance between weight and stiffness. But that hasn't stopped Quintana Roo from using the latest carbon-fiber technology to create a radical asymmetric triathlon bike that literally bends the rules of aerodynamics.

Because the crankset and gear on the driveside of any bike are less aerodynamic than those on the cleaner offside, the Illicito has been designed to push wind flow around the left-hand side of the frame.

This is a development of Quintana Roo's Shift fitting system, which first emerged in 1989 on the original Superform. It works by shaping the down tube and the keel around the cranks. This pulls more air down the offside of the bike to reduce the overall drag coefficient.

However, the real difference between the Illicito and other bikes is its lack of a diagonal seat stay strut, which has been omitted in order to maximize airflow efficiency.

While the massive chainstays on both sides of the Illicito mean it isn't a fully single-sided bike, they eliminate the flex and wobble problems that often afflict such designs. It's a remarkably comfortable bike though, which is a relief for Ironman athletes still facing a 26.2-mi (42.2-km) run when they unclip their pedals. **GK**

STEVENS Sonora

2012 • Mountain bike • Germany • Race-focused big-wheel bike from popular brand

German mountain bike makers tend to focus on minimizing weight and maximizing stiffness.

The Sonora, from the highly successful Stevens brand, is a prime example of this. The same carbon fiber frame is used throughout a family of bikes that spans equipment selections ranging from a relatively modest Shimano SLX-based bike to an ultra-light SL-R flagship that comes complete with a DT Swiss rigid carbon fork and costs more than $9,500 (£5,800).

Whichever model you choose, you're getting a state-of-the-art frame. In addition to a high-modulus carbon construction that gives excellent stiffness-to-weight statistics, you get a tapered head tube to maximize fork-to-frame control without adding weight. Gear cables are also routed internally to keep lines tidy and protect shifting performance from mud and water. Unusually, the hydraulic hose for the rear disc brake is also routed internally, popping out of a port on the chainstay just ahead of the caliper itself.

Steep handling angles and a relatively racy choice of Steven's own Scorpo-brand cockpit components mean that the extra-clean back end is the only part of the Sonora that most riders will ever see on race tracks or climbing courses. **GK**

SANTA CRUZ Tallboy LTc

2012 • Mountain bike • USA • Game-changing big-wheeled carbon mountain bike

It was no surprise when Santa Cruz introduced the Tallboy Long Travel—the California superbrand had previously stretched the boundaries of big-wheel bike behavior with the original Tallboy frame—but few anticipated the Tallboy Long Travel Carbon. This was a real game changer, with 1 in. (2.4 cm) more wheel movement than the standard Tallboy. It was also stronger, stiffer to handle, and, with a weight of 5½ lb 8 oz (2.5 kg), lighter than its predecessor.

Santa Cruz head designer Joe Graney kept the Tallboy LTc as practical as possible. The VPP2 suspension bearings are easily adjustable with injection ports for pushing out dirty lubricant with clean grease. Santa Cruz also stayed with conventional screw-in rather than push fit crank bearings, and a clamp-on front derailleur for maximum options on custom builds.

The performance of the LTc on the trails led to perfect scores and Bike of the Year awards. The combination of race-bike weight with the smooth rollover of the big wheels and power-reactive suspension made it an outstanding climb and speed machine. Up to 5½ in. (14 cm) of suspension and rock-solid steering accuracy also meant it could challenge much heavier bikes on descents. **GK**

TREK Session 9.9

2012 • Downhill bike • USA • Aaron Gwin's 2012 UCI World-Cup-winning downhill bike

The Trek Session 9.9 began development in 2010, once again using long-standing Trek athlete Andrew Shandro to help advance the process and make sure the bike was going in the right direction.

All the testing was done on aluminum prototypes, but by summer 2011 Trek was ready to release the carbon Session 9.9 into the world for the 2012 season. It is a genuinely race-ready carbon downhill bike, and the new frame shed 2 lb (0.9 kg) to create a sub-35 lb (16 kg) overall bike weight. Trek employed an I-beam material layup and honeycomb composites to boast its highest-ever stiffness-to-weight ratio. The Session incorporates the same Mino Link switchable geometry seen on Trek's Remedy trail bike, and uses Cane Creek's AngleSet to allow the rider to

fine-tune the steering character. The frame gives 8¼ in. (21 cm) of rear travel, which was obtained through a new suspension-leverage ratio. This allowed Trek to develop a proprietary rear shock and fork with Fox suspension, meaning that the Session 9.9 is the only bike in the world with this suspension. The rear shock on the production bike uses the same custom tune as the one you will find on the World Cup race bike. The fork is a hybrid air unit that uses an air-assist and a metal coil spring. The proof is in the pudding: Trek set out to build a bike that would win races and, thanks to U.S. racer Aaron Gwin, it did just that! In 2012, Gwin was the first American to win the UCI World Cup overall, and the first man to win five World Cup races in one season, and he also won the U.S. Open Downhill championships. **CJ**

CARRERA Vulcan

2012 • Mountain bike • UK • Outstanding affordably priced mountain bike

Supermarket-supplied bikes generally have a really poor reputation for quality and assembly, with the tag "BSO" (Bike Shaped Objects) often used to describe them on bicycle-industry websites and forums. UK car and bike superstore Halfords has long bucked this trend by creating really sound bikes for remarkably little money, and the Vulcan has always been a champion of cost-effective mountain biking.

Designer Justin Stevenson has nearly two decades' experience in the industry. The obvious sign of his work is that while most brands churn out lower-cost bikes based on previous mid-price models without bothering to adapt the geometry and handling to current trends, Stevenson habitually fits longer forks, shorter stems, and wider bars to maximize control. Fitting properly functional rather than just price-appropriate suspension components and tires is also a key focus to underpin the performance of the bikes on the trail.

In the case of the Vulcan, that includes a reasonably controlled SR Suntour XCM suspension fork and tires from Maxxis motherbrand CST, both of which provide much more consistent connection to the trail than competing bikes. The short 3-in. (7.5-cm) stem keeps its steering reactions keen enough to catch any slips in control that do occur.

Very impressively for the price, Carrera also managed to include fully hydraulic-operated, self-adjusting disc brakes. These feel significantly more controlled under braking and don't require manually resetting to cope with pad wear. **GK**

High modulus and handcrafted **733**

AUDI WORTHERSEE E-bike

2012 • E-bike • Germany • A concept bike with Wi-Fi and a shaft drive motor

If the Audi Worthersee E-bike was ever mass produced, there'd be fewer cars on our congested roads. Who wouldn't want to ride it? It has an immobilizer that can be activated via Wi-Fi from your smartphone, a Segway-inspired "wheelie mode" that takes the skill out of looking cool, and five programmable pedal modes that blur the line between a traditional E-bike, where the bike provides all the power through an electric motor, and a "pedelec," where the bike merely supplements what the rider's legs contribute.

This bike, built for speed, has an ultra-light carbon fiber frame that weighs just 3.5 lb (1.5 kg), and wheels of carbon fiber-reinforced plastic. Its shaft drive motor produces 2.3 kW, and when in "pedelec" mode, can reach a speed of 50 mph (80 kph). Its e-Grip mode supplies power through a motorcycle-like, handlebar-mounted throttle control, and the wheelie mode (the angle of which can be lowered) provides power to the rear wheel so all you need do is concentrate on keeping the front wheel in the air. A trip computer is built into the frame and is connected to a fully integrated touch screen that can select the riding mode and measure the distance you've covered, your speed, the charge left in your battery, and the angle of any incline. **BS**

GREENSPEED X5

2012 • Recumbent trike • Australia • Top-end sports folding recumbent

The X5 is one of the world's top sports recumbents. With its low-slung mesh seat, low center of gravity, and scientifically cambered front wheels, it is clearly a machine for quick cornering.

It is equipped like a top racing bike, with sophisticated disc brakes, high-speed Schwalbe Stelvio tires, and carefully tuned chromoly steel tubular frame geometry. The front axles are slightly angled upward and backward toward the rider, giving the best compromise between strength, handling, and feedback. Lightweight aluminum is used for the handlebars, steering rods, and optional custom-made bike racks.

The seat may look like a trendy afterthought, but it is one of the most carefully designed components. The shape was decided following the advice of chiropractors for maximum body support. It is made of light and strong UV-resistant nylon mesh that has been specially laced with elastic cord to help absorb road shocks. On top of all that performance potential, it is a folding bike that breaks down and fits into a custom bike case.

Greenspeed is a small business run by enthusiast Ian Simms and four members of his family, who road test every trike before dispatching it to the customer. **SH**

◁ Audi's concept bike is jam packed with gagetry.

NICOLAI Pinion

2012 • Mountain bike • Germany •
Revolutionary internal gearbox mountain bike

Nicolai is a brand with an almost mythical reputation for its awesome execution and attention to detail, and an air of near-indestructibility. This model sees its radical approach to rethinking every stage of the design process come to fruition. Nicolai has thrown away the standards on the front and rear gear shifting and teamed up with another German company.

Pinion's internal gearbox sits at the lowest possible point on the bicycle to optimize the center of gravity, delivering eighteen sequential gears with no overlap, with a 600 percent range that can be changed even under load or while stationary. The gearbox is also completely contained inside a sealed unit, making for an ultra-reliable and nearly maintenance-free system. Further development and collaboration sees the replacement of the chain drive with a Gates Carbon belt system drive.

The rest of the frame is up to Nicolai's usual standard of perfection. Every Nicolai frame uses straight round tubes for the front triangle and rectangular sections for the rear end. This construction means the loads are exerted into the frame intelligently. Round tubes allow a minimum of material usage with maximum torsional stiffness, while a rectangular cross-section is the best shape to handle bending loads in the rear triangle. **KF**

DETROIT Madison Street Bike

2012 • Fixed-wheel bike • USA • Custom copper street bike

Designed, according to the makers, for "urban enjoyment," this is a street-smart bike with vintage track styling and copper plating on the forks, stays, decorative lugs, stem, pedals, and bars.

Steven Bock, the man behind the Detroit Bicycle Company, had already established his position in the vanguard of metal pedal machines. The basis of this retro fixed-gear road bike is a frame made of fine Columbus SL chromoly tubing. The rest of the components are high-quality too. Campagnolo supplies the seatpost, headset, bottom bracket, pedals, and cranks. The Vittoria Zaffiro tires and Velocity track wheels are also high-performance parts. The handmade leather saddle comes from Brooks of Birmingham, England, and the bars and stem are Cinelli products. An acid-etched headbadge finishes off the upmarket look.

This bike takes its name from one of the premium addresses in the city of Detroit. Despite this conscious attempt to bask in the reflection of the gloss and bling of the famous thoroughfare, there is no hiding the fact that this is a hardcore fixie bike with no brakes at all, so riders have to pedal backward to slow down or stop. The complete bike weighs around 20 lb (9 kg) and costs from $3,200 (£2,085). **SH**

Detroit's stunning Madison has appeared in fashion store showpieces. ▶

WHISTLE Modoc Sora

2012 • Road bike • USA • Entry-level road bike

The Whistle Modoc is an archetypal introductory road bike. Unlike the uncompromising race machines that are exclusively geared toward high performance, the Modoc is designed to give you a solid foundation upon which to start road riding.

Its frame is made from aluminum tubes that are triple butted for added strength. At the front, the fork's carbon blades and alloy steerer tube help keep you comfortable and in control. At the back, short chainstays make for a tight rear triangle to ensure as little of your pedaling power as possible is lost through flex.

But what the Modoc may lack in exotic materials and cutting-edge engineering, it makes up for with basic

"Every cyclist deserves a bike that provides maximum performance, at a reasonable price."

Whistle

dependability. To that end, the Modoc comes equipped with Shimano's reliable Sora groupset.

Designed in Colorado, Whistle bikes are made by Italian company Atala. Atala is based in Monza and has a history that not only stretches back to 1921, but also takes in several Italian national championship titles along the way. But the globetrotting doesn't end there, because Atala is part owned by the Accell Group, a Dutch company that, by virtue of the number of brands it owns, is one of the world's largest bike manufacturers.

The Modoc may be a bike for beginners but the people behind it are anything but. And although Whistle's roots may lie in the United States, the bikes that bear the company's name are built by drawing on a pool of experience that stretches around the globe. **RB**

DMO Element Bivvy

2012 • Off-road bike • USA • Custom wild-camping mountain bike

Fancy an overnight adventure on an off-road bike? If so, you'll need to combine all the luggage-carrying extras of a classic touring bike with the off-road capabilities of a mountain bike.

In 2012, young bike maker Olly Webb set about building just such a conveyance in his shed in the English countryside near Chippenham, Wiltshire. Webb's brand is DMO Frameworks and his bike is the Element.

It's a 29er designed for hardcore unsupported bivvy-biking—where the rider has to carry everything needed for days in the saddle and nights in a bivvy bag.

To start with, Webb opted for a simple, sturdy, and reliable basis to the bike. It has no suspension, and only one gear, and powerful disc brakes. The frame is a fillet-brazed arrangement of Reynolds 853 steel tubing with an appealing side-on geometry. The titan gray paint job leaves it looking clean and sleek.

But see the bike dressed up for a full expedition and it's a different beast altogether. "Full bivvy spec" means four fitted bags: one under the rear of the seat, one under the front of the handlebars, and the other two attached to each leg of the front fork. And that's not counting the full frame bag hanging from the top tube, which completely fills the front triangle. Once loaded up, the Element suddenly looks like it means business and could accompany you deep into even the most uninviting wilderness.

The creative process was anything but painless—on one occasion Webb accidentally stuck a red-hot brazing rod to his lip—but his previous experience with the Williams Formula 1 race car team, where he learned the arts of welding, machining, and fabricating, served him so well that the build quality of his DMO bikes was immediately acclaimed by reviewers and at British bike shows. **SH**

DMO's Element Bivvy is a true mountain bike. ▶

OYT Gelati

2012 • Tradesman's bike • UK • Ice-cream seller's bike

Some bikes achieve iconic status through engineering innovation, others through competitive success. Then again, some are famous because they are equipped to sell ice cream.

The classic ice-cream selling bike is really a trike. The salesperson pedals the rear end, while the front end has two wheels to support a square freezer section containing the ice cream. The two halves are connected by a robust hinge, and the whole unit is usually shaded by some sort of canopy or parasol.

The whole idea is thought to have started in the home of ice cream, Italy. The brightly colored "Gelati" mobile street vending units originated in the northern city of Varese and have become famous worldwide. Often, however, these are two-wheeled carts pushed along by someone who walks behind.

But genuine ice cream trikes are still popular. Many classic period trikes are hired out to add a glamorous touch to the catering for outdoor parties or weddings. And brand new ice-cream trikes are still being sold.

The Gelati—made by On Your Trike (OYT) from Tyne and Wear in the United Kingdom—is one of the most expensive machines in this book, with base models costing from $17,000 (£11,000). Among its extraordinary features are a canopy that incorporates solar panels to help power the fridge and a handmade mahogany container in which the ice cream is stored (you can choose from a selection of over 232 ice creams and sorbets, including 41 cocktail sorbets).

The rider steers with a fixed handrail on the back of the cart section. Extra-tough components include a motorbike chain and a car-style handbrake that applies drum brakes for heftier stopping power, which is needed because the bike can carry massive cargoes of up to 882 lb (400 kg). **SH**

THORN Me'n'U2

2012 • Triplet • UK • Extended bike for an adult and two children

Innovative English touring bike maker Thorn came up with a new and very specific cycling variant when it launched the Me'n'U2. This sturdy triplet machine was designed to be ridden by an adult with two children in the second and third seats.

Thorn was categorical about who the bike is meant for: the pilot should be an adult of 5 ft 4 in. (163 cm) or taller; the middle rider should be a child aged between seven and twelve; the third rider should be between four and ten years. In practice, the adjustable handlebars and seats mean that a small adult could sit in the middle.

The Me'n'U2 comes with touring extras such as mudguards, reflectors, a baggage rack, and a chainguard

"It's a supremely practical vehicle, making possible many journeys you just couldn't do otherwise."

Dan Joyce, Editor, Cycling Plus magazine

on the rear wheel. There is a hefty three-way braking system (two rim brakes and one disc unit) operated by the pilot. Other features include a versatile 24-speed, wide-ratio Shimano drivetrain with SRAM twist grip shifters.

The frame needed to be especially strong to cope with the extended wheelbase. Thorn used heat-treated chromoly steel with Reynolds crown forks. Other details are "comfort" alloy touring handlebars at the front, with straight bars on the back for the children (all with black grips), and five bottle mounts.

The Me'n'U2 doesn't come cheap, with a retail price of around $3,000 (£2,000). The built-in limitation of these bikes is that they are "in season" for only a few years before the children grow too big for them, which leads to a constant supply on the secondhand market. **SH**

HP VELOTECHNIK Scorpion FX

2012 • Tricycle • Germany • Folding long-distance touring recumbent

When it comes to comfortable recumbents and their all-important seats, it's hard to look beyond the Scorpion FX. HP Velotechnik has put a lot of thought into what makes a good seat: the BodyLink design adjusts itself to the natural S-shaped contour of the spine, and has a fully adjustable lumbar support. Lateral support hasn't been ignored either: this is provided by seat wings in the form of airflow-padded carbon-fiber hip supports. There's even an optional headrest for a truly relaxed long-haul ride. You can remove the seat in under a minute to fold the rear frame forward; to make the bike more compact, the front wheels are easily detachable using a simple Allen key. There's also an Ergomesh option that increases

". . . a great trike for the smooth trails and roads and when I am just looking for speed."

Gordon Cohen, Recumbent Journal

ventilation. These features produce a bike that suits both space-limited commuters and riders who don't want to be nursing a sore back at the end of a long ride.

The Scorpion FX has some serious suspension, with a shock and swingarm system familiar from mountain bike designs. It can come with either a plush steel spring or a lighter air shock with adjustable hydraulic damping. The 40-in. (1.2-m) wheelbase provides plenty of stability. The high seat allows for a lowrider rack made from ½-in. (1.2-cm) alloy tubing. Together with provision for up to four very cool-looking Moonbiker panniers, this delivers a carrying capacity of 110 lb (50 kg). Finally, HP Velotechnik has equipped the Scorpion FX with an ultra-wide range 81-speed gear system that helps make the bike the ideal recumbent tourer. **BS**

PEARSON Hammerandtongs

2012 • Road bike • UK • All-round ride from the world's oldest bike shop

In English colloquial parlance, to "go at" something "hammer and tongs" is to do it as vigorously as a blacksmith hammering hot metal while holding it in a metal grasping device.

Accordingly, the bike of that name is designed to do everything with brio. It is light, compliant, stiff, comfortable enough to cope with massive mountain rides, and aggressive enough to handle the cut-and-thrust of competition.

These qualities are notoriously difficult to incorporate into a single bike, but Pearson achieved the right balance by using its own mix of geometry, tube shapes, and tube sizes. The product may justly be described as the ultimate all-rounder.

The Hammerandtongs frame is made from carbon fiber, partly to keep weight down, and partly also because this material can be used to tailor the frame's performance in specific areas, such as the outsized down tube, the reinforced bottom bracket shell, and the straight forks, which together make the bike both rigid and responsive.

To these features are added a tall head tube, an arched top tube, and a slightly reduced seat tube angle to give the Hammerandtongs the compliance and riding position needed to make long, hard days in the saddle almost unbelievably comfortable.

The price is considerable but not exorbitant: at the time of publication of this book, the complete bike cost around $4,000 (£2,500); the frame alone retailed at $2,250 (£1,400).

The Hammerandtongs is a smart combination that draws on more than 150 years of experience in the industry. Pearson has been in business since 1860, and its retail outlet in London is officially recognized as the oldest bike shop in the world. **RB**

2013–

The machines of the aspirational riding revolution.

RIDING THE BIKING BOOM

AZUB Max

2013 • Recumbent • Czech Republic • A recumbent classic as much at home on a mountain trail as in a city

Azub began manufacturing recumbent bicycles in 2000 and quickly gained a worldwide reputation for durability, reliability, and superb design. The Max is one of its finest products, with sumptuous asymmetric curves, a TIG-welded frame, and state-of-the-art suspension provided by a triangulated swingarm that reduces flexing in the rear to soak up the bumps, and Rock Shox suspension forks. Optional extras include an electric motor, double-mount hardware for a front fairing, racks that can accommodate four panniers, disc brakes, and full fenders.

The Max comes in 24-in. (57.6-cm) or 26-in. (66-cm) wheel versions, with optional under-seat or over-seat steering. A two-wheeled recumbent's stability depends on the manufacturer getting its steering geometry

right, and Azub has done just that. A good thing too, considering the seat height is at a rather high 25 in. (63 cm), which can seem a long way off the ground if you're a recumbent novice. The carbon-Kevlar seat has an Ideal Position System (IPS), which can adjust its height, its fore–aft, and its nose up–nose down angles between 23 and 40 degrees. Azub knows that the secret of happy recumbent riding is a fully adjustable machine, and the IPS achieves this using just two simple clamping devices. A bike must adapt to the cyclist, not the cyclist to the bike.

The Max's standard of machine work, welds, and paint job are flawless. The bike is perfectly adapted to off-road conditions too, making it a truly versatile recliner ride. **BS**

AVD WINDCHEETAH HyperSport Series II

2013 • Recumbent • UK • If Batman designed a recumbent bike, it would probably look like this

This design first saw the light of day in the early 1980s, when designer Mark Burrows turned his attention to a three-wheeled trike that he thought might keep him fit (and upright) through an icy winter. He called his new recumbent Speedy, and liked it so much that he built a few more in his spare time. Then London-based American journalist Richard Ballantine bought one, and articles suddenly began appearing in cycling magazines. Speedy was gaining a reputation. Then someone thought it should be called the Windcheetah—and a legend was born.

In the mid-1990s Burrows went to work for Giant Cycles and gave the job of producing the Windcheetah to The Seat of the Pants Company in Manchester, England, where the recumbent continued its long

evolution into the HyperSport, the CompactSport, and the ClubSport. The Windcheetah range is now generally regarded as the finest in the world, and the flagship model is the HyperSport Series II.

A recumbent whose performance matches its looks, the HyperSport comes in three chassis and accessory pack versions: touring, leisure, and sport. A wisp with carbon frame tubes as thin as it's possible to make them, the bike is steered by a joystick on which can be found all the trike's controls except its park brake, which is a simple friction lever under the seat. A perfect synthesis of form and function, the HyperSport has set six major speed and endurance records, and has been exhibited in New York's Guggenheim Museum and Museum of Modern Art. **BS**

DOWNLAND Chris Hodge

2013 • Touring bike • UK • Bike built on a DIY course

Chris Hodge was an amateur cycling enthusiast who wanted to build himself a bike, so he enrolled on one of the renowned five-day courses in frame building organized by Downland Cycles in Canterbury, England. There he learned how to cut the tubing to the precise length required for his made-to-measure frame, and how to weld the joints.

The bright orange Audax tourer that he subsequently produced was so good that Downland displayed it at the 2013 Bespoked Bike Show in Bristol, where it received an enthusiastic reception—it was much more than just a creditable first attempt.

The account of the construction process that Hodge posted on his Internet blog, Mr O's Biking

"It rode like a dream . . . I felt like a peacock showing off his feathers."

Chris Hodge reports on his first ride

Bulletin Board, makes fascinating reading and will be of great practical assistance to anyone contemplating a similar undertaking in the future.

His machine was built around a traditional lightweight steel frame that was part lugged and part fillet-brazed. The bike used steel forks for comfort, and an FSA SLK carbon seatpost to minimize weight.

Hodge completed his bike with a selection of high-end components to provide versatility and long-distance comfort. These included a Shimano Ultegra 10-speed gearset, Mavic Open Pro CD rims, and a Shutter Precision PD-8 Dynamo hub with USB charging for GPS and cell phone. Stopping was courtesy of the latest cyclocross mechanical disc brakes. **BS**

GENESIS Volare 953

2013 • Road race bike • UK • Trend-bending stainless steel road race bike

Carbon fiber has long been the most widely used component of professional road racing bikes because no other material provides stronger, stiffer, lighter, and more aerodynamic frames and forks. However, left-field brand Genesis couldn't see the point of just following the peloton and producing yet another carbon bike, so it built a stainless steel frame and assembled its own team of young riders to prove that bikes don't have to be made of this material to be competitive.

While steel alloys have been used in bike frames for well over a century, stopping them rusting has always been a problem. Paint does an okay job for a while, and there was a big trend for chrome-frame extremities in the 1960s and 1970s. A totally stainless steel tubeset has always been the ultimate aim, but it has taken decades to perfect a method of shaping and joining iron alloys in tubes light enough to make maximum use of their strength. There are now many brands of stainless steel on the market, but Genesis plumped for that produced by British materials specialists Reynolds, whose 953 tubeset is even stronger than titanium.

The launch model of the 953 was fitted with top-grade components: Ultegra gears and brakes; PRO stem, bars, and seatpost; DT Swiss Tricon wheels with 27½ x 1-in (700 x 24-mm) Continental Grand Prix tires; a San Marco Regale saddle, and a Chris King headset.

Feedback from the Madison–Genesis racing team inspired three revisions in the first year—the later versions of the bike had a more sloping design and trimmed a significant amount off the original weight.

Continued development is under way to reduce the weight even further so that the Volare can become fully competitive with carbon—the Genesis approach to this extremely interesting development project is anything but rusty. **GK**

The Volare proves steel still has a very real future in the bike-manufacturing industry. ▶

MONDRAKER Factor XR

2013 • Mountain bike • Spain • All-mountain bike using standout Forward Geometry concept

Throughout history, bicycles have evolved to cope with changes in riding habits. That's been particularly obvious with the latest developments in mountain bikes designed for more radical riding. Even by the most progressive design standards, Mondraker's Factor XR bikes are a real leap forward.

With purpose-made recreational bike park trails becoming more like professional downhill racecourses, the handling characteristics of bikes have been changed to suit. Steering angles have been inclined backward to push the front wheel forward and make it more likely to self-correct and carry on straight than tuck under and trip you up. Frames have also been made longer and lower to increase stability through fast corners. So that potentially stubborn machines can still be turned, their

stems have been shortened and their bars widened to increase leverage and fine control.

Mondraker's Forward Geometry concept takes this longer frame, shorter stem idea to its ultimate conclusion. By bolting the bars directly on top of the forks they effectively create a zero-length stem, and the missing rider reach length is made up by an extended mainframe. The steering angle is also super-slack, which pushes the front wheel way out front.

The results are a startling amount of tire in front of the bars when you look down and, at slow speeds, steering that feels like you're pushing a wheelbarrow. But with the brakes off, the weird suddenly feels wonderful: the Factor gives a sure-footed ride that makes you feel like a mountain bike hero. **GK**

KONA Honzo

2013 • Mountain bike • USA • Hardcore hardtail 29er

Whether through marketing or the technical focus of the bikes they build, some brands, rightly or wrongly, end up associated with one particular facet of riding. Despite a long history of impressive race success in both cross-country and downhill events, Doug "Dr Dew" LaFavor and the rest of the laid-back management and design team behind Kona bikes have long been synonymous with the more irreverent, fun side of riding. When you ride bikes like this one, it's easy to see why.

The smoother rolling, increased traction, and boosted speed sustain of the 29-in. (73.5-cm) wheeled hardtails have made them must-have items for cross-country racers. Mountain bikers putting mobility and on-trail mirth before speed have generally stuck with 26-in. (66-cm) wheels because of their better

acceleration and direction-changing agility. This made the production release of the 2013 Honzo a big move for Kona, and the 29er obviously prioritized riding pleasure above race performance. The second-year evolution increased the swagger even further.

The steel frame provides a subtly sprung ride to take some of the sting out of the rigid rear end. It's also built with a relaxed head angle and low ride height for increased stability on steep or fast trails, while the rear wheel is tucked in tight to the curved seat tube for easy on-the-spot pivoting on switchback trails. Handling authority is reinforced by a very wide handlebar and short stem for total control of the most threatening descents, making the Honzo an outstanding bike for backcountry riding. **GK**

NINER RIP 9

2013 • Mountain bike • USA • The most popular bike in the Niner stable

Niner operates on the premise that 29-in. (73.5-cm) bikes are the best solution for almost every sort of riding (to date it hasn't produced a full-on downhill bike). It's no surprise that its best-selling bike is this dedicated do-it-all machine.

Typically for Niner, the frame of the RIP 9 is loaded with premium details: a tapered head tube that allows the maximum stiffness in the frame-to-fork connection without raising the bars too high above the already tall front wheel; a steeply sloped down tube that ensures the tall wheels do not affect standover clearance if you have to straddle the bike suddenly; and flared tube ends that increase weld area for strength.

"It's our passion . . . our one and only love, our heart and soul out there on the trail."

ninerbikes.com

The tubes are shaped with compressed air when heated to give more accurate shaping than traditional hydraulic pressure methods, so the whole alloy frame weighs just over ½ lb (0.25 kg) more than the carbon fiber RDO version. You still get tons of practical details such as chain guide mounts, direct attachment front derailleur and brake posts, and a screw-through 6-in. (14.2-cm) axle for maximum rear-wheel security.

Niner's unique CVA suspension is designed to work consistently with whatever chainring you're using. That means vital climbing traction when you're crawling up a steep slope in the smallest ring and smooth control when you're bombing back down in the big ring. Add 5-in. (12-cm) or 6-in. (15-cm) fork compatibility up front, and this Niner really is ready to RIP! **GK**

GIANT XTC Advanced SL 290

2013 • Mountain bike • Taiwan • Surprisingly smooth riding but super-light and crazy quick dirt racer

Despite running a very successful cross-country race team, Taiwan-based Giant was surprisingly slow to release a proper high-performance, big-wheel weapon to match those of other teams and brands. It has used the time it has taken extremely wisely, though, and the resulting machine is a proper superbike-category speed machine.

While the production model was released only in 2013, prototype versions of the frame have been raced for several years by Team Giant bikers such as Adam Craig. These bikes first showcased the massive, almost shoebox-sized down tube that was used on the first carbon 29er. This affordable machine used Giant's mid-grade Composite fiber and compensated for lost stiffness with increased tubing diameter. However, the use of Giant's in-house Toray T800-based Advanced SL level carbon fiber gives the frame an incredible strength-to-weight ratio. In response to racer feedback about the Composite bike being too stiff in some situations, Giant slightly downsized the massive beam. The tapering top tube, seat tube, and seatstays are slimmer too, creating a much more supple and subtle top note to the ride. In fact, the Advanced SL is so smooth in the saddle that it's easier to stay seated and keep the power down on rough trails on this hardtail than on many short-travel suspension bikes from other manufacturers.

These slimmer tubes are still bookended with Giant's oversized proprietary Overdrive 2 tapered head tube, fork-and-stem steering setup, and massive Powercore bottom bracket block. The chainstays are suitably sized to cope with the megawatt power outputs of professional racers, keeping the handling immediate and turning every muscle twitch into forward energy firing you down the trail. **GK**

◄ Niner's unique CVA suspension is 29er specific.

CANYON Ultimate CF SLX

2013 • Road bike • Germany • Top-of-the-range bike from German manufacturer

Canyon began in the back of a trailer, when Roman Arnold's father realized he could sell bike parts to other racers while his son competed in junior competitions. Business flourished, and by 1985 Roman had set up Radsport Arnold GmbH, which then set about transforming itself from supplier to manufacturer. The company rebranded in 2001 as Canyon Bicycles GmbH but remained outside the bicycling elite until Arnold created a test lab and hired designer Lutz Scheffer to create the Ultimate CF. This bike launched the business into the highest echelons of bike design and technology and powered a move into sponsorship. Among the top riders who came over to Canyon were Philippe Gilbert and his Lotto Bellisol team, and the Katusha team of Joaquim Rodriguez.

Unveiled in 2013, Canyon's Ultimate CF SLX featured several improvements on the original design, most notably a lighter frameset weighing just 27.8 oz (790 g) for extra stiffness and comfort. The bike also had a new down tube with a flat underside, which improved drivetrain and front triangle stiffness while making the front end more comfortable. Other standout Canyon features include the asymmetric Maximus seat tube, pencil-thin seatstays, boron composite VCLS seatpost, and the unique two-piece replaceable rear derailleur hanger. The result has been continued success for the Ultimate at the highest level of racing as well as a media trophy cabinet groaning with rave reviews from magazines and websites all over the world. **DB**

CANYON Speedmax CF

2013 • Time trial bike • Germany • Aero bombshell from Europe's leading direct-sell brand

Canyon certainly didn't skimp when it came to research and development investment in its new aero race machine, developed for time trial use by Dennis Menchov and the Katusha Pro Team.

Ten engineers, designers, and aerodynamicists worked with top time trialist Michael Rich and Katusha team members to create the initial concept. This was then refined in the Formula 1-standard Mercedes Petronas Drag2Zero wind tunnel with help from aero guru Simon Smart. The results led to a modified, slightly chopped tail, and an angled-shoulder "Trident" teardrop tube shape. This made the bike more stable and more drag-efficient in a wider range of wind angles than a pure teardrop tubed machine. It was also stiffer and lighter than Canyon's existing Speedmax CF bike.

Stability was enhanced by the integrated fork and custom handlebars, which kept handling friendly and predictable, even with a 3-in. (80-mm) deep front rim, and enabled riders to concentrate on pedaling smoothly and efficiently and hitting the fastest lines, rather than fighting against the wind. The flush-fit stem and internal cable routing meant minimal drag, but the combination of handlebar spacers and other adjustments, as well as a choice of conventional or triathlon-angled seatposts, produced a claimed 7,560 different setup options from just three frame sizes.

Show prototypes appeared in May 2012, ready for the Giro d'Italia, but the bike did not go on sale until early 2013. Its combination of blistering performance and bargain price made it worth the wait, though. **GK**

FOCUS Team Replica Izalco

2013 • Road bike • Germany • Team-issue road race bike

While the profile of professional cycling in Germany has been badly tainted by drug-taking scandals involving riders such as Jan Ullrich, German brands still have a strong tradition of supporting top teams with product.

Focus has been associated with Tour de France teams Milram, Katusha, Acqua & Sapone, and, most recently, AG2R. To give the latest team the best chance of success, Focus produced an SL (superlight) version of its award-winning Izalco frame. While the external shaping of the tubes was largely unchanged, the position of the carbon layers inside was tuned and altered so that less material could yield the same strength. Unique features such as built-in cable guide tubes inside the frame stiffened the thin wall tubes, while aluminum steering bearing holders were

dropped in favor of lighter holders molded directly into the frame itself. This reduced the frame weight to 7 oz (200 g) below the benchmark 2.2 lb (1 kg).

The frame was also fully ready for the Campagnolo Record EPS 22-speed electronically triggered shifting that the AG2R team used for most of 2012. Unfortunately, that season wasn't particularly successful for the team, with Sylvain George's stage win in the Tour of California the only real highlight.

As a result, a new Izalco Max bike was introduced in summer 2013. This used larger tube diameters throughout the mainframe to increase stiffness and further reduce weight, performance attributes that helped Cristophe Riblon win the double Alpe d'Huez stage of the 100th Tour de France. **GK**

PIVOT Les

2013 • Mountain bike • USA • Versatile hardtail from the Arizona suspension specialists

Chris Cocalis and his mountain bike design team at Pivot built their brand entirely on a range of suspension bikes, from the short-travel 429 marathon trail bike to the Phoenix DH. With help from suspension specialist Dave Weagle, Pivot's DW Link-equipped bikes earned a reputation for their tough, fast, and playful characters. A growing number of Pivot fans wanted this sort of bike feel in an ultra-fast, trail-connected hardtail format, and in 2013 they got exactly they wanted.

Knowingly called the Pivot Les, in reference to the pivotless non-suspension design, the new bike was built around the carbon-fiber, hollow-box, high-compression internal molding technology that Cocalis and his team had developed for their suspension frames. The frame—smoothed and compressed to extremely high tolerances, both internal and external—was extremely strong, but still race-light. Having sold the advantages of suspension for so long, Pivot knew a smooth-riding bike was also a massive advantage in terms of reducing fatigue and increasing control over longer, rougher races. As a result, the carbon-fiber layers and the material blends themselves were carefully chosen to provide a supple, rider-protecting ride without sacrificing power transmission. The frame was also designed to accommodate the largest available tires to smooth the ride. The long-distance credentials of the Les were firmly established when Pivot rider Mike Hall smashed the rest of the pack at the 2013 Great Divide Race, a 2,500-mi (4000-km) route through the Rockies from Canada to the Mexican border. **GK**

PIVOT 429C

2013 • Mountain bike • USA • Carbon-fiber
trail mountain bike with DW suspension

Translating a successful design from one material into another is a notoriously difficult enterprise, but Chris Cocalis made it look easy with his Pivot 429C.

Many manufacturers take the easy option of directly templating the handling and character of a proven alloy design into high-tech hand-knit fiber, but the 429C takes the 429 base and increases both performance and functionality.

Carbon fiber has a higher tensile strength than aluminum, and its use in the 429C makes it an extremely tough bike. Anticipating the demands that would be made on it, Cocalis fitted it with chain-taming fixtures normally reserved for downhill racing and freeride stunt bikes, despite its wheel movement of only 4 in. (10 cm). The 429C can also be equipped with a remote control seat-lowering seatpost to keep the saddle out of harm's way on chaotic trails.

What really sets the Pivot apart is its exceptional stiffness. By using wheel axles that screw directly into the frame and fork, and a twist-resistant chassis construction, the 429C has pinpoint accuracy on the trail. The result is a bike that has pushed the capability of short-suspension, big-wheeled mountain bikes to a whole new level for those who can afford it. **GK**

EVIL Uprising

2013 • Mountain bike • USA • Evil Undead DH
bike shrunk into all-mountain form

Evil started with the Revolt downhill bike, then moved on to the Undead carbon downhill bike. These were its only suspension bikes until the Uprising, which it claims is "the bike we have always wanted to make."

Like the Undead, the Uprising features a styled UD carbon frame, a DELTA link suspension system, and adjustable geometry via the Flip Chips. The Uprising is also interchangeable between 5.9 in. (14 cm) and 6 in. (15 cm) travel through the use of different linkage kits.

The Uprising is aimed at Enduro category mountain bikers, whose rapidly increasing numbers demand 5.9- to 6-in. (14- to 16-cm) travel full-suspension bikes that will climb like cross-country bikes and descend like downhill bikes. Evil's offering has already won races under the feet of Slovakian Red Bull athlete Filip Polc, and throughout its development Evil has pushed the bike to its limits. World Cup downhill racer Luke Strobel tested it on his home downhill training tracks, while Category One cross-country racers tested its climbing abilities. By using their feedback, Evil has created a truly world-class competitor for the Evil Vengence Enduro tour team, as well as privateer racers and riders looking for the ultimate all-rounder. **CJ**

PARLEE Z-Zero

2013 • Road bike • USA • State-of-the-art, fully customized carbon frame

Bob Parlee has cycled, skied, sailed, and rowed competitively and for fun. He began his working life in the boat industry, and built Olympic-class and One Design race boats. In his spare time, he designed bicycles. In 1998 he rented a corner in an aerospace prototype shop where he developed the carbon technology for which he is now renowned. In 2000 he founded Parlee Cycles.

His company's products were ridden in the Tour de France and other major races, and demand for them began to grow. In 2004 Parlee started selling through independent shops worldwide. His bicycles won a string of awards, and in 2010 he built a new factory and design studio in Beverly, Massachusetts.

For ultimate performance a bicycle must fit its rider perfectly, but the cost of carbon molds means there are few fully bespoke options. Parlee's Z-Zero uses an exclusive tube-joining process to produce a completely customized frame for each rider. The secret manufacturing process allows total shape and performance management without the addition of material and weight. The result is a truly "ultimate" bike that's on the wish list of riders all over the world but between the legs of only a very lucky few. **GK**

CANNONDALE Super X Disc

2013 • Cyclocross bike • USA • Ultra-light, disc-braked, carbon cross bike

Having produced what are widely regarded as the best road bikes in the world, Cannondale set out to create a cyclocross machine to the same standard. The Super X Disc has a wealth of top-grade features loaded onto one of the finest frames available.

While cyclocross races are typically through mud or sand, rather than over the rocks that characterize mountain courses, the sheer ferocity of the competition means that the frames have to be extremely tough. Hence the Super X blends the construction methods and materials of both Cannondale's Flash mountain bike and its Super Six Evo Hi Mod road bike. Ballistec base carbon fiber is stiffened with Hi Mod carbon fiber sheets in high-stress areas, and the whole frame is strapped together with long, continuous fibers. The result is a strong frame that maximizes traction and control on rough courses but still rides smoothly.

Cannondale redesigned the frame and fork in order to accommodate disc brakes, which produce greater stopping power than conventional cantilever disc brakes in muddy terrain. The investment was costly, but it paid dividends when Tim Johnson won his first two races on the prototype. Disc brakes were fitted as standard on the production model for 2013. **GK**

HUFFY Fat Bike

2013 • Cruiser • USA • Super-cheap Walmart snow bike with a surprising race history

Magazine testers ride the best bikes in the world, but occasionally they take a perverse pleasure in seeing how far they can push the most basic and unsuitable bikes. A memorable recent example was the Huffy Fat Bike raced by *Bike* magazine at the 2013 Sea Otter Classic in Monterey, California.

At nearly 50 lb (22.5 kg) with 4-in. (10-cm) tires and a single gear, the Huffy Fat Bike—$199 (£132) from Walmart—certainly isn't a first-choice competitive machine. The single rear coaster brake had to be augmented with a front brake to comply with U.S. race regulations, although its painted rims meant it was useless. The only other modification was a stronger handlebar to survive the jumps of the downhill course.

The lack of performance didn't stop Manuel "The Beast" Beastley entering every race of the weekend. In the cross-country event, he led the pack off the line for several yards; in the cyclocross, he was one of the few riders to consistently clear the hop obstacles.

The Beast went on to complete the head-to-head dual slalom and celebrity log-pull events despite a badly bent crank axle and a bent front fork, entering Sea Otter legend and proving that the cost of your bike is never an obstacle to competing. **GK**

SENSA Giulia

2013 • Road bike • Netherlands • Dutch-built digital shifting speed machine at an affordable price

Dutch road riders are renowned for relentless power that's honed in the face of wind blasting off the North Sea. If you combined their strength and determination with sheets of carbon fiber composite, the result would probably be very like the Sensa Giulia. At 2 lb 10 oz (1.2 kg), its Generation 5 unidirectional carbon fiber monocoque frame is muscular in build. The stout frame tubes, with their smoothly blended joints, match with big-diameter rear stays and chunky cut carbon fork legs. Feedback from the wheels is clear and precise. A BB86 press-fit bottom bracket keeps the cranks locked in place no matter how much power you put through them. Dual mechanical or electrical shifting compatibility provides a full choice of original or upgrade material.

The frame is meaty enough to keep a big gear-turning tempo no matter how turbulent the headwind, and you'll soon understand what riders mean by "going Dutch." The default equipment selection of the Sensa includes a Continental pro-style long-stem cockpit that enables you to stretch out for maximum lung expansion. The seatpost and seat tube are built for big legs to push big gears from the saddle rather than for soaking up road vibrations. **GK**

HOY Sa Calobra .002

2013 • Road bike • UK • Signature bike of legendary Olympian

Eleven times a world champion, Chris Hoy's haul of six gold medals at Beijing and London make him Britain's most successful Olympian. The modest Scotsman announced his retirement in April 2013, a month before the launch of his own signature range of bikes. His partner in the venture was Evans Cycles—one of the major retailers in Britain's recent bike boom—whose chief designer, James Olsen, was previously responsible for the Genesis brand. Naturally there were concerns that this was merely an attempt to cash in, but the product turned out to be well worthy of its famous name.

The Hoy range kicked off with a trio of road bikes named after the fiendish Sa Calobra climb in Majorca, Spain, where Hoy and his Team GB colleagues trained during the winter months. At around $1,275 (£850), the Sa Calobra .002 is a well-appointed entry-level model with a lightweight triple-butted 6061 aluminum frame and full carbon fork; gearing comes from the versatile Shimano Tiagra 20-speed set. These features place the Calobra in direct competition with some of the alloy-framed models from the lower end of the Cannondale Synapse range. Broadly similar in appearance, the .002's siblings, the .003 and .004 models, offer frames built from sturdier, lighter, and costlier 6066 aluminum, providing a nice selection of options for anyone in the market for a mid-price road bike.

With a big marketing budget that includes television advertising, Evans clearly hopes to establish Hoy as a significant brand. **GK**

RAGLEY Marley

2013 • Mountain bike • Ireland • Alloy-framed all-rounder mountain bike

Ragley has always been a no-nonsense, fun-for-your-money brand, and this Marley hardtail consolidates its reputation for characterful cost-effectiveness.

Beneath the suitably Rastafarian red, gold, and green color details over black or bright acid green paintwork is a 7005 heat-treated frameset with a relaxed head angle for laid-back Reggae-style handling. The 1³/₄-in. (4.4-cm) head tube can take either straight or tapered top forks, while the trademark Ragley split plate "Three Finger" bridge means it can roll with the biggest rubber available. The complete bike comes with some of the most popular all-round trail tires—Maxxis' High Rollers. You also get a bashguard on the crankset to protect the chainrings if your log roll or rock hop doesn't end as well as you'd hoped, and tabs are provided on the frame to carry the roller guide that'll keep your chain in place if you're really making merry.

The RockShox Sektor does an outstanding job of making sure that rocks and drops don't cramp your style without costing an arm and a leg, and a through-axle front wheel keeps steering precise and secure. Simple but effective SRAM gearing and Avid brakes give robust stop/go performance at a bargain price, and Ragley's own wide bar and short stem cockpit make the most of the confident handling when things get really fast and loose.

Add Ragley's own bolt-on grips and a color-coded Cheeky saddle, and you have the ideal bike for getting your groove on down technical trails without breaking the bank. **GK**

TURNER Czar

2013 • Mountain bike • USA • Alloy alchemist finally releases a carbon fiber frameset

Throughout his first twenty years in business, Dave Turner patriotically manufactured all his bikes in the United States, first in California, and later in Oregon. To make this possible, Turner bikes had always been made from custom alloy tubing and meticulously machined alloy subsections. Yet although Turner and collaborators such as SAPA and Zen took the potential of available metals to the limit, top-end competitors were increasingly using composite materials.

In 2013 Turner and his team finally bowed to pressure, and produced this super-light carbon fiber machine as their XC racing and long-distance trail option. The Czar retains many of Turner's signature features, including Zerx grease injection inserts that allow the rider to flush the solid-state journal bushings with fresh grease between rides, rather than having always to clean and dismantle them. The result is far longer periods between part replacement than the cartridge bearings typically used by other brands.

The Czar also retains the DW Link suspension system specially designed for Turner by Dave Weagle. This delivers a naturally buoyant, terrain-following ride that allows the rider to forget about specific pedaling and power application techniques, and to concentrate entirely on the trail to get maximum speed and fun out of every section.

The switch to a high-modulus, Toray carbon fiber frame was also carefully considered, with the proprietary C6 Turner carbon construction deliberately designed to offer what the makers describe as "a snappy, yet controlled ride experience" rather than a frame that feels "like a block of wood with a harsh ride." It saves significant weight over the equivalent alloy frame, and with 29-in. (73.5-cm) wheels, the Czar is properly ready to rule the trails. **GK**

NORCO Range Killer B

2013 • Mountain bike • Canada • 650B-wheeled all-mountain bike

The 26-in. (66-cm) wheel has been the default size for mountain bikes since the late 1970s, but only fortuitously. Early pioneers adopted it because it was the standard diameter on the beach cruisers they converted for racing down California mountains.

More than thirty-five years later, this original size came under serious threat from bikes such as this.

While 29-in. (73.5-cm) wheels work well for fast rides over long distances and for tall riders, they have less manoeuvrability and stiffness than 26ers, and are harder to fit into frames without restricting suspension movement. However, the new 650B wheel size—which, at 27 in. (68.5 cm), sits in between the two—combines

> *"I don't mind saying I will NEVER go back to 26 in. [66 cm] for trail/all mountain."*
>
> Owen Pemberton

the smoothness and traction of the 29er with the responsiveness of the smaller traditional alternative. In the Range Killer B, designer Owen Pemberton created a bike that is very easy to flick and jump around on the trail, and which also has responsive suspension. Pemberton says, "To me this is the beauty of 650B. There is no geometry compromise with 650B, but you get the same advantages of a 29er, just not quite to the same extent."

The Range Killer B also features ART suspension architecture, which helps smooth out big hits and keeps it keen to pedal, rather than wallowing about and wasting energy. Its ability to roll with the punches on the rockiest trails, and to pull maximum traction out of rough and smooth corners alike, has gained it a lot of praise from professional reviewers. **GK**

Norco's Range Killer B was one of the first hardcore 650B machines. ▷

GHOST Lector AMR 9500

2013 • Mountain bike • Germany • Ethereal specter at the piste

Ghost's Lector name spans a remarkably wide range of products, including both mountain bikes and road bikes, but the AMR is very much a serious off roader. The 9500 is the flagship model of the AMR family. It shares the same layout and suspension system as the entry-level alloy framed versions but uses a fully carbon fiber chassis. This saves significant weight over the metal bikes and the carbon front/alloy rear bikes that make up the mid-price AMR range. Ghost has also gone all out to save weight elsewhere in the bike with a top-of-the-range spec. The Fox fork and rear shock get the most advanced CTD Trail Adjust tuning settings as well as the super-smooth and eye-catching gold-colored Kashima anodized coating on their shafts. Shimano's top-dog XTR groupset provides impeccable

featherweight transmission performance underlined by Easton wheels and Schwalbe tires. German hydraulic and composite specialist Magura also supplies its top-level MT8 disc brakes for maximum power and minimum weight stopping.

The result is a light but capable descent and single-track all-rounder, but its origins are clear in its distinct slant toward climbing. The stem is relatively long, and the shock is tuned to move less than most when pedaling, which is perfect for the long fire road climbs typical of European MTB marathon events, but not so good at fine traction control. It deserves inclusion in this book as a great example of a state-of-the-art European tour mountain bike that's ready for anything a fit, speed-hungry rider can throw at it. **GK**

DEVINCI Dixon

2013 • Mountain bike • Canada • Carbon-fiber update of versatile mountain bike

Even a cursory glance at contemporary road bikes will show that carbon is the default frame material on most complete premium models. That's been the case for several years now, with few carbon-related scares to undermine consumer confidence.

The change to carbon has taken a lot longer in the world of mountain biking, primarily because of concerns over the longevity of the material if crashed or ridden too hard. However, as carbon-fiber pioneer Peter Denk said when he launched his radical Ransom carbon freeride machine: "If someone buys a carbon-fiber bike and they crash it and break it, they think, 'I shouldn't have bought carbon fiber.' But if they had exactly the same crash and result on an alloy bike they would say, 'I should have ridden more carefully!'"

Times are changing, and with most professional downhill racers now riding carbon-fiber frames, manufacturers who were previously alloy-only are now switching to hand-woven construction.

Devinci is among the recent converts to the carbon copy process. Rather than just transfer its designs to a Far Eastern fiber manufacturer, Devinci brought the whole process in-house to its Canadian factory. The benefits are obvious, with the previously highly rated but slightly heavy Dixon trail bike dropping more than 12 oz (3.5 kg) in carbon format. Impressively, Devinci have made the switch without dropping its existing lifetime warranty. The result is a state-of-the-art all-round mountain machine that's as comfortable climbing as it is on downhill tracks. **GK**

MONGOOSE Teocali Comp

2013 • Trail • USA • World-famous trials rider Chris Akrigg's do-it-all bike

Mongoose was an extremely successful BMX maker that—like many other similar brands, such as the GT and the Diamond Back—also developed a comparably profitable line in mountain bikes.

First released in 2005, the Teocali has been a champion in the lower-price range full-suspension market for many years; its success based largely on Mongoose's own Free Drive suspension. This design is driven by a high main pivot isolated from the bottom bracket by a lower link, allowing for the suspension to work free of chain growth. This effectively means that as the suspension compresses, the opposing force of the chain does not restrain it. Another significant advantage of the bottom bracket being free of the front and rear triangles is that the rider can be in any gear without affecting the suspension.

On the Teocali Comp's first appearance, former BMX Pro and World Cup 4-Cross Champion Eric Carter confidently asserted that it was "a true all-mountain bike that can do everything." His judgment has stood the test of time. Fast forward seven years to 2013, and Mongoose's professional trials riding legend, Yorkshireman Chris Akrigg, was still competing on a modified Teocali Comp.

After eight years of incessant refinement, the Teocali Comp retains its unique looks thanks to its hydroformed aluminum chassis. The 2013 model has 6 in. (15 cm) of rear travel, a tapered head tube, a rear axle measuring ½ in. by 5⅓ in. (1.2 cm 13.5 cm) to increase lateral stiffness, and an evolved Free Drive suspension system. Akrigg not only rides his Teocali on regular trails but also has his own brand of trail riding, including trials-style sections that require extreme technical skill and ultra-accurate bike control. Negotiating such courses on a full-suspension bike truly exhibits the Teocali's versatility. **CJ**

"Out of all the years I've been riding for Mongoose this is probably the most fun and versatile bike I've ever ridden."

Chris Akrigg, 2013

◁ Nobody rides their Mongoose more radically than Chris Akrigg.

SARACEN Zen

2013 • Mountain bike • UK • State-of-the-art 650B wheeled mountain bike

The riding conditions in the United Kingdom and the often idiosyncratic preferences of the nation's cyclists have presented mountain bike designers with a unique set of challenges. Commercial necessity being the mother of invention, these problems have inspired some very distinctive and characterful bikes that have often served as a catalyst for evolving global trends. Saracen's Zen is a good case in point. It is loaded with a full deck of distinctively British features and strengths to make it a classic UK trail bike.

Because Britain is dominated by wooded hills and steep-sided moorlands rather than massive mountains, most downhills don't last more than a couple of minutes. That's created a riding scene devoted to taking the most tortuous, technical, slow-but-still-scary route down any slope to maintain the excitement for as long as possible. In such terrain, hardtails are a great choice for skillful riders, especially if, like the Zen, they're equipped with long stroke suspension forks and big handlebars for maximum control leverage. The absence of rear suspension also keeps the bike light and agile in really tight "hop and pop" trials, and keeps maintenance to a minimum.

Given that the wheels of British bikes are likely to be covered in mud most of the time, disc brakes became a must-have item in the United Kingdom while other countries were still happy with rim pull brakes. It is consequently unsurprising that a British company, Hope, led the development of the first cable-operated and then hydraulic disc brakes to provide all-weather anchorage.

Although the long-running Zen series was named to evoke images of Asian mysticism, the bikes that carry the label are as distinctively British as John Bull, The Beatles, and bad weather. **GK**

LAPIERRE XR 729

2013 • Mountain bike • France • Ultra-smart electrically controlled "intelligent" suspension bike

Since the arrival of the Internet, it has become hard for companies to keep the lid on technological advances until they're ready to launch. However, in summer 2012, even the most savvy sleuths were blind-sided by a top-secret collaboration between the Lapierre/Ghost/Haibike bike group, RockShox suspension, and Abus Electronics.

The XR 729's EI (Electric Intelligence) suspension works by putting a vertical accelerometer and a wheel-speed gauge sensor on a conventional front fork together with a crank rotation sensor in the frame. These send speed, pedaling, and fork-movement data to a computer on the bars that works out the ideal rear

"Do you get off every time you want to change the resistance or let this system deal with it?"

gizmodo.com

shock setting for the next stretch of trail before the back wheel even gets to it. A servo motor on the shock then adjusts the valves in the damping circuit of the damper up to 200 times a minute.

Pedal hard on a smooth surface or steep climb with little or no fork movement and the rear suspension locks to give direct drive. Keep pedaling on rolling trails where the fork moves a bit and you'll get rear movement exactly when you need it and firm power when you don't. Start smashing the fork through a boulder field or freewheel off a dropthrough and the computer will flick the rear shock open allowing maximum oil flow to cope with the impacts.

The result is an outstanding ride with fluid control and punchy power delivery. **GK**

The rear shock servo motor and battery are obvious on the XR 729 frame. ▶

BOTTECCHIA Emme 2

2013 • Race bike • Italy • State-of-the-art pro bike

Bottecchia started as small family bike-making business in Cavarzere, Italy. Legendary Italian racer Ottavio Bottecchia helped it develop its bikes until his mysterious death in 1926, whereupon the Carnielli family took his name for their business.

Today the company specializes in top-end race machines, although its range of around seventy models also includes road, mountain, city, touring, BMX, folding, cyclocross, and electric bikes.

Bottecchia sponsored the Acqua & Sapone team, which in 2011 used Bottecchia Emme 2s. Their successes that year included the green jersey for Stefano Garzelli in the Giro d'Italia.

The specialist race team at Bottecchia continued to fine-tune the Emme, and the 2013 bike is said to be the best yet: the recently slightly shortened seat stay reportedly improves the stiffness of the frame by 5 percent.

The bike has a 2-lb (0.9-kg) (unpainted) handmade carbon frame that is stiffened to reduce energy waste. There is an integrated headset to hold the carbon forks and carbon drop-outs to hold the wheels. The latter have been strengthened and the cables routed internally through the tubing for a neater look. The Emme also comes in five frame sizes—17, 19, 20, 21, and 22 in. (44, 48, 51, 54, and 57 cm).

Buyers can choose from a range of supplied kit on the finished bike; options include high-quality parts such as Swiss carbon tubular wheels, Campagnolo EPS electronic gear shifting system, and the latest Vittoria tubular Corsa Evo CX II tires. **SH**

ARGONAUT Carbon

2013 • Road bike • USA • Full-carbon custom bike

Ben Farver began making bikes with steel—"because that was my favorite material to ride"—but gradually realized the material has limitations. He started using carbon fiber and hasn't looked back since, although he gives credit to his steel years for teaching him how to make great bike frames.

The main reason carbon fiber is better, he claims, has nothing to do with fashion, style or even weight. He says that carbon allows him to meet customers' unique demands by "tuning not just your frame's external geometry but what ultimately matters most: the material inside your frame." Any bike builder can change the length of the chainstays, but only carbon builders can change the composition and orientation of the fibers inside them.

Argonaut uses a production facility in the Pacific Northwest that has been using composite materials for more than thirty years and has some of the finest machinery and expertise. The workshop makes all its own tubing and the tooling used in its creation.

Farver took that skill and directed it at frame building. Initially he worked to mimic the exact characteristics of high-end steel tubing, then worked on every section of that tubing to adjust its stiffness, aiming to produce the perfect ride.

The carbon tubing is bonded together at the joints, and Farver even creates his own compression-molded carbon drop-outs, which link to the frame via custom-machined titanium plates. None of this comes cheap: custom Argonauts start at $6,500 (£4,360). **SH**

BMC Time Machine Road TMRO1

2013 • Road racer • Switzerland • Aero road bike

After Swiss premium manufacturer BMC launched the blisteringly quick and angularly eye-catching Time Machine time trial/triathlon bike, it was only a matter of time before it turned that technology loose on the regular road race peloton. The resulting bike is an equally innovative, high-velocity weapon.

First looks confirm that much of the "Sub A" aerodynamic innovation of the Time Machine has been inherited by the TMR. The fork uses a conventional internal steerer and normal stem, but a fairing is extended up the front of the head tube to hide brake and gear cabling from the wind. It uses the same super-powerful flush fit brakes built into the face of the legs. The forks, head tube, and seat tube also use BMC's Tripwire feature. This breaks up the rounded nose of the

teardrop aerofoil section with a small ledge that creates turbulence over the tapering surface of the tube. This sounds like a disaster on a bike designed to be as drag-free as possible, but by roughening the boundary layer airflow, the overall airflow runs more smoothly over and behind the tube. The low-set angular bladed stays, chainstay-mounted brakes, inset clamped aero seatpost, and wheel-hugger seat tube are all carried over from the TM too.

The TMR's mainframe tubes are also chopped off bluntly at the rear to create a virtual aerofoil shape using the eddying wind. This makes the bike more efficient in a crosswind than a full aerofoil frame, and keeps the handling from becoming too stubborn for fast steering reactions at high speeds in a tight race pack. **GK**

BMC Gran Fondo

2013 • Road bike • Switzerland • Comfortable racer for cobbles and sportives

The Spring Classics are the most savage one-day events in the cycling calendar. The mix of cobbles and short, steep climbs that litter the routes pushes the riders and their bikes to the limit, frequently leaving both lying broken by the roadside.

Simply surviving these races is hard enough, but excelling in them takes not only a special type of rider but also an extraordinary bike. Like the sort that Swiss manufacturer BMC set out to make when it began developing the Gran Fondo—a bike that combines simple and sophisticated approaches to solve the problems presented by the cobbled Classics.

The sophisticated approach led to flex being designed into the seatstays, seatpost, and fork. By determining the most suitable sizes, shapes, and angles for these tubes, as well as carefully choosing and aligning the carbon fiber used to make them, BMC's engineers gave the Gran Fondo shock-absorbing capabilities to cushion its rider to the maximum.

Simplicity is present in the slightly longer-than-normal wheelbase and in the tires, which, at 1.1 in. (2.8 cm), are broader than the standard diameter to take the sting out of harsh road surfaces.

The Gran Fondo was developed with help from Norway's 2010 World Road Race Champion Thor Hushvod. On its Paris–Roubaix prototype debut in 2012, it was ridden to third place by Italy's 2008 World Road Race Champion Alessandro Ballan. The blend of cushioning, stability, and performance makes the Gran Fondo equally good for amateur long-distance racers. **RB**

MODA Interval

2013 • Time trial bike • UK • Aerodynamic specialist

". . . a competent ride and decent-value package . . . offers good control in gusty conditions . . ."

bikeradar.com

With triathlon going through a boom in the UK in recent years—thanks mainly to the high-profile success of riders such as Chrissie Wellington and the brothers Alistair and Jonathan Brownlee in Ironman, World Cup, and the Olympics—the twenty-first century has so far been an extremely fertile period for the creation and growth of new brands.

Moda was one of the first such brands, with a range designed from the outset to provide cost-effective performance bikes for racers and enthusiast fitness riders in all riding disciplines.

Moda already had a successful Interval time trial and triathlon bike in its lineup, but the 2013 introduction of an all-new machine bearing the same name really upped the ante. The frame is built from a high-modulus grade of carbon fiber to provide a balance of strength and stiffness that's competitive at the top level of racing. The contemporary aerodynamic treatment of the frame really gives the Interval an edge, both metaphorically and literally. The front brake is conventionally mounted for effective braking, rather than being hidden, but the drag-reducing fork is synced neatly into a notch on the head tube of the frame. Another notch on the shoulders of the frame contains the entry point for the wind-cheating internal cable routing, and there's a flush-mounted stem option to complete the slippery low-profile front end. Both wheels are also set into curved wheel hugger cutouts to keep overall airflow smooth over the aerodynamic American Classic wheels that are supplied as standard with the frame.

For maximum customer satisfaction, Moda is willing to change the rest of the specification from a wide range of SRAM, Shimano, and Campagnolo kit in order to suit personal rider preferences or to match a particular price. **GK**

Moda delivers a professional performance at an amateur price. ▶

BILENKY Ephgrave Tribute

2013 • Road bike • USA • Decoratively lugged road frame

In the early 1960s, British bike maker Les Ephgrave created a bike with memorable finely filed decorative joining lugs that featured intricate swallows' tails and arrowheads. Some of these bikes were imported to the United States and have since become collectors' items.

At the start of the twenty-first century, Stephen Bilenky—already renowned for his quirky but high-end, handcrafted framesets and complete bikes—turned out his masterpiece: the Ephgrave Tribute Road.

The special steel frame of this bike featured delicately decorative lugs modeled on the original Ephgrave products. Staff at Bilenky's workshop in north Philadelphia fabricated the lug blanks themselves, then carefully cut them by hand with a jewelry saw. It took several weeks to carve them all but, just like the originals, they feature elaborate cutouts, arrowheads, and swallows' tails.

The beautiful lugwork was highlighted to great effect on the unpainted Bilenky frame that was entered into one of the top U.S. custom bike exhibitions, the Handmade Bicycle Show. Not surprisingly, the Bilenky Ephgrave Tribute won the award for the best lugged frame on display.

Bilenky's Cycle Works began producing acclaimed custom bikes in 1983. Its principal component was steel, but it also occasionally used titanium. The workshop specializes in frames with steel couplers for easy dismantling. Over the years, the Cycle Works claim to have built and installed around 10,000 of them. **SH**

BISHOP Road

2013 • Road bike • USA • Handmade mixed-steel custom bike

Baltimore bike courier Chris Bishop took frame-making lessons from two masters of the art—Steve Garn of Brew Bikes and Koichi Yamaguchi of the U.S. Olympic/National team—and then set up his own business.

Four years later, he gained the crowning accolade when one of his creations won the Best Road Bike award at the 2013 North American Handmade Bike Show (NAHBS).

The triumphant Road showed Bishop's mastery of many traditional steel-frame construction techniques, including bi-lamination, custom handcut lugs, fillet-brazing, and sleeved seat stays.

Beneath the classic, elegant exterior, this machine is built from a complex mix of different custom-swaged Reynolds steel tubes. Internal brake and rear derailleur routing keeps the shape looking sleek. The stiff bottom bracket, KVA stainless steel chainstays, and lightweight top tube created a frame that the NAHBS judges admired for its lively feel—stiff around the bottom bracket but supple where needed.

The Road was completed with an array of high-quality international components from ENVE Composites, Brooks, and Nitto. The steel forks were made by Bishop himself. The bike's understated looks won the judges' approval too: a three-color metallic paint job that neatly picks out the lugs, sleeves, and stainless steel sections.

Bishop's title was not an isolated accolade: in the previous year he won Best Steel Frame, Best Fillet Construction, and Best Lugged Construction. **SH**

BLAZE 29er

2013 • Mountain bike • USA • Lugged steel big-wheeled mountain bike

Traditionally, most mountain bikes have been fitted with 26-in. (66-cm) wheels, but manufacturers are increasingly choosing the 29-in. (73.5-cm) alternative.

The bigger rims divide opinion. Their advantages include easier rolling over obstacles and greater momentum; their drawbacks include the extra weight and extra steering power required. They are more suited to larger riders; smaller riders struggle to find a frame that fits both them and the wheels.

Prominent among the companies that favor the 29er are Blaze Bicycles, which produces custom machines in the mountains in Moab, Utah. Owner Pierre Chastain is a former guitar maker and film animator who now concentrates on building one-off bikes from scratch, one at a time, for high-performance biking enthusiasts. His range includes everything from roadsters to hardcore MTBs. Chastain designs the frames and forks himself.

Like all Blaze bikes, the 29er is built using lightweight chromoly steel tubing from Reynolds, Columbus, and True Temper. The 29er also features True Temper OX platinum tubes fillet-brazed together. The rear triangle features an A-bend seat and chainstays for extra structural rigidity. The hardtail frame comes with disc brake mounts and a hard-wearing two-color paint job. Options include additional colors, internal cable routing, steel couplers, and curved tubing.

Blaze says its 29ers are "made for adventure," and tests them on the bike tracks around Moab, "in the middle of a cycling paradise." **SH**

BREADWINNER Arbor Lodge

2013 • City bike • USA • Fully equipped modern city bike with integrated lock

State-of-the-art bike building doesn't necessarily mean creating ultra-light racers or oversized, full-suspension, all-terrain machines. The Arbor Lodge is simply a stylish but classic town bike. It won't jump over canyons or win a sprint stage, but it is an expertly designed and well-built bike for commuting in urban environments.

Its looks are elegant and understated, with a classic saddle and a selection of six striking colors. Custom paint is available as an optional extra. There's a big, sturdy front rack that is reminiscent of postwar delivery bikes. Want to cycle to work whatever the weather? The Arbor Lodge has full mudguards to protect the rider. Dynamo-powered lights are another option, while hydraulic disc brakes give all-weather stopping power.

The drivetrain uses either a single speed or clothing-friendly internal hub gears. The frame is prepared for racks, lights, pumps, reflectors, and bottles to be fitted. Like all other Breadwinner bikes, the Arbor Lodge uses a TIG-welded steel frame and is assembled in Portland, Oregon, with primarily U.S.-made components.

Urban bikers will appreciate the award-winning integrated lock system that is another Breadwinner optional extra. A key inserted into a hole on the head tube locks a supplied U-section hasp into holes on the top tube and head tube, making it easy to clamp the bike to a post or bike rack.

Breadwinner is a collaboration between long-established bike builders Ira Ryan and Tony Pereira. **SH**

BLACK SHEEP UIMA Phat Bike

2013 • Snow bike • USA • Truss-framed snow bike for art exhibition

Black Sheep Bikes lives up to its name by building machines that stand out from the crowd. Since the company launched in 1999, it has earned a reputation for extraordinarily curvaceous titanium products, some of which look more like cartoon drawings than the top-quality artisan bikes they really are.

This bike was specially commissioned by the University of Iowa, and is now permanently displayed at the Museum of Art in Iowa City—hence the name.

A single-speed machine with a complex curved titanium frame, TIG welds, and enormous "phat" tires, it also features elaborately supported tubular titanium luggage racks at front and rear, and a frame that is easily disassembled for transportation.

The front forks have an unusually complex double-truss structure, and the seat tube/top tube junction features the most flamboyant arrangement of tubing shown anywhere in this book.

There were no bizarre color schemes, but a cool "brite brush" polished titanium finish. The bike was topped off with a classic leather Brooks saddle.

The UIMA Phat Bike won the award for best titanium construction at the 2013 U.S. Handmade Bicycle Show in Denver. **SH**

BOB KELLER Fat Bike

2013 • Fat bike • USA • Eye-catching, half-painted show bike

After 20 years of building up his metalworking expertise, who could begrudge Bob Keller a chance to show off his skills? The Michigan-based bike maker produced a special show frame with one side painted red with yellow decals and the other left bare. The idea was to showcase his ultra-neat, fillet-brazed joints, which are normally hidden by paint.

Keller usually makes bikes with steel tubing jointed by fillet brazing, a technique that involves melting a filler metal onto two surfaces that bond together as the molten material cools and hardens.

The show bike frame was only Keller's third fat bike. The first two were for customers. Later came a fourth, which he made for himself, having become a fat bike fan while struggling to commute through Michigan snows to his day job as an automotive designer.

The 2013 North American Handmade Bike Show was Keller's first time as an exhibitor, so he wanted to offer something different on his stand.

The fat bike frame featured an elegant concave top tube that was mirrored by curved cantilever seatstays extended all the way along it to join the down tube. The chainstays were curved too, allowing huge tires to be fitted. **SH**

◁ Black Sheep's snow bike includes a custom titanium rack and flask.

CALFEE Dragonfly Gravel

2013 • Gravel race bike • USA • Project bike for magazine feature

The Dragonfly Gravel was custom built for *Road Bike Action* magazine so one of its writers could ride it in Utah's Crusher in the Tushar, an arduous 69-mi (110-km) gravel race over loose rock tracks and tarmac roads that includes 10,500 ft (3,200 m) of climb.

The geometry was stretched to create a longer wheelbase for greater stability and tire clearance. The frame, forks, lugs, and even the seat were all made of carbon, which was the main component of a Calfee bike that had been a Tour de France stage winner.

The magazine editors also had design input, opting for titanium drop-outs with disc brake mounts and carbon forks. Additionally, they chose Calfee's special seatpost with integrated battery for the Shimano Di2 electric gear changers. The seatpost includes a charging point to top up the battery without the need to remove any components.

Disc brakes gave the bike serious stopping power regardless of mud, rain, or dust. The wheels used lightweight carbon ENVE rims with handmade tubular low-pressure Schwalbe tires to deal with the gravel terrain of the race. The neatest component was Calfee's one-piece carbon BarStem with an integrated mount for a Garmin GPS unit.

The total weight was 17 lb 10 oz (8 kg), and the total cost around $13,700 (£9,200).

In the hands of retired pro Neil Shirley, the magazine's bike performed fantastically in the Crusher. Shirley won the King of the Mountain stage and finished the race in second place. **SH**

BOO Glissando Townie

2013 • Hybrid town bike • USA • Bamboo and titanium bike

Although bamboo bikes are in the present day often touted as a recent innovation, frames were made from this sustainable natural material at least as long ago as 1894. Sadly, however, bamboo was largely forgotten in the twentieth century, during which most bikes were made of steel.

So far in the new millennium, the first-choice alternative to metal has almost always been carbon fiber. Colorado-based Boo built racing-standard bamboo-and-carbon bikes, and then developed the Glissando Townie, a concept creation that uses bamboo laminate as a shock absorber in a frame with a curved titanium backbone.

The bamboo component flows all the way from the head tube to the rear drop-outs. This not only contributes to the graceful overall shape but also performs an important practical engineering function, as the bamboo flexes with the load from the front and rear axles. The seatpost is isolated from this process by an unusual joint in which the vertical pole rises directly from the bottom bracket, and is linked to the two bamboo struts only by a pivot.

The Townie provides a comfortable ride over any surface. It is stylish too, thanks to the raw unpainted finish of the wood and the metal, which complement each other to pleasing effect. The bike won the Best Alternative Material award at the 2013 U.S. Handmade Bicycle Show. Many people would like it to be made widely available, but at the time of publication of this book there were no plans to put it into production. **SH**

CALETTI Adventure Road

2013 • All-rounder • USA • Large-tired road or rough bike

Take a standard road-racer-style bike, then give it a stronger steel fork and longer-reach brakes so you can slap on some larger, tougher tires. That's basically the secret recipe behind John Caletti's Adventure Road, a versatile machine that is equally at home in rough lanes and on smooth dirt tracks.

Okay, there's a bit more to it than that, of course. Caletti is an established high-quality custom-bike builder based in Santa Cruz, California, and his bikes are known for being well planned and executed.

Caletti certainly arranges things carefully: the Adventure Road's frame geometry is fine-tuned for each individual buyer's comfort and also to keep the ride stable on rougher surfaces. Nevertheless, its road-bike origins mean that the Adventure Road still has the agility to twist through a tight downhill or dodge the traffic in an urban environment.

Caletti's frame and fork will fit large tires and come with medium-long-reach caliper brakes, disc brakes, cantilever- or mini-Vs. Taller head tubes are available for more comfortable riding positions.

The frame itself is made from butted high-strength steel alloy or high-cost titanium. Both include Caletti's distinctive stainless steel square headbadge featuring a cutout seagull and the letter C.

Options include preparing the bike for an electric shifter Di2 drivetrain with internal wiring; rack and mudguard mounts, and a selection of forks. The Adventure Road can be bought as a frameset or a complete bike. **SH**

DEAN Ace FS4.0

2013 • Mountain bike • USA • Particularly fine TIG-welded titanium bike

TIG welding is a way of joining metals; it is commonly used for thin steel, titanium, or aluminum. The process uses a tungsten electrode, electricity, and an inert gas to create an arc of energy that is applied to the surfaces to be welded.

TIG is harder to get right and more time consuming than other welding methods. It gives the fabricator more control over the welding joints, which, as a result, are usually stronger and neater. It's also a more versatile method of joining bike tubes than the classic fillet brazing or lugging techniques.

Racing cyclist John Siegrist became a bike builder after he sold his precious titanium race bike to buy his first TIG welding kit. In almost a quarter-century since then, Siegrist's company, Dean, has gained a reputation

for finely welded frames with perfectly neat and durable joints. Around 125 of them are built per year; Siegrist welds them all. Most are titanium.

Based near Boulder, Colorado, Dean specializes in mountain bikes and makes all its own titanium or carbon and titanium forks.

For his renowned and award-winning frames, Siegrist uses what he calls a "two-pass" welding process: he first makes a root weld to hold the joint in place, then a second weld with a titanium rod to fill and anchor the joint.

We've picked Dean's Ace FS4.0, with 4-in. (10-cm) of suspension travel and interchangeable transmission, as well as a choice of 26-, 27.5-, and 29-in. (66-, 70-, and 73.5-cm) wheel compatibility. **SH**

JAMIS Xenith

2013 • Time trial bike • USA • Affordable and smoothly comfortable solo speedster

The Xenith is a characteristically smooth Jamis design for the single-minded pursuit of solo speed.

The makers have minimized the effects of drag on the lone rider with no one to shelter behind. The aptly named Windshield carbon fiber fork swells from the tips, growing large enough to enshroud the rear-mounted TRP brake at the top of the wheel. All control cables plug into the skinny top tube to keep them out of wind's way, while the short head tube enables the bars to be dropped into an aggressive aero position.

The seatpost uses an aerodynamic teardrop cross-section, held in place with a neat twin-bolt clamp at the far end of the top tube. A fat 1⅕-in. (30-mm) crank axle slots into the BB30 bottom bracket shell, while a U-brake is mounted beneath the skinny chainstays, aft of the cranks, to stop it creating extra turbulence. Accurate but safe positioning of the rear wheel, close to the curved wheel-hugger seat tube cut-out, is assured by small stop screws set into the track bike-style drop-outs at the rear of the frame.

American Classic wheels and a fully carbon fiber cockpit from Profile Design keep weight low. The cloven, John Cobb-designed saddle complements the comfort of the ductile frame. **GK**

ALLIANCE Steel Coupled Allroad

2013 • Utility bike • USA • Handmade custom coupled travel roadster

American bike builder Erik Rolf refuses to classify his products as "road" or "mountain" machines. They are all custom made after consultation with the buyers about the other bikes they've owned, their pedaling style, and the riding conditions they anticipate encountering. Because of this, many of Rolf's bikes are versatile enough to ride on or off road.

Rolf served a two-year apprenticeship at Bozeman, Montana, under the guidance of Carl Strong, then worked on 180 frames for the Strong Frames brand. He later established his own company, Alliance, in Ketchum, Idaho—an area crisscrossed with hundreds of miles of bike trails through forests.

The most distinctive feature of the Allroad is a pair of steel S&S Coupling links to allow halving of the frame and make it easier to pack and transport. The couplings are built into the top tube and down tube, and the buyer has a special spanner to loosen and tighten the links. This means it takes only a few moments to disassemble and reassemble the bike.

Coupled bikes like this allow owners to fit them in a car trunk or take them on airplanes. The steel couplings are light but very strong, and advocates insist they remain as strong as a standard frame. **SH**

ANDERSON 4 Seasons Stainless

2013 • Road bike • USA • Semi-polished U.S. custom roadster

Perhaps the most important recent trend in the bike world has been the proliferation of small, exclusive, custom-bike builders, particularly in the United States.

One of them, St. Paul, Minnesota-based Dave Anderson, is so hands on with his work that no one else touches the bike from the moment the tubing arrives in his workshop to the moment the finished bike is dispatched to the customer. Everything that happens in between he does himself.

Although Anderson builds a variety of bikes to match his buyers' different needs, one of his most popular special creations is the 4 Seasons, a versatile steel-framed road bike that is suitable for year-round use. The tubing, lugs, and drop-outs are all lightweight Reynolds 953 stainless steel. The design allows for mudguards, water-bottle cages, and most combinations of brakes and tires.

The looks are understated yet classic, and this is definitely a multi-use machine. One set of wheels could make it into a race bike; another would make it into a long-distance road bike. Install a rack for touring, add fenders for winter riding, or change the tires to tackle off-road trails. The bike is even available with an S&S Coupling system for easy transportation and storage. **SH**

APPLEMAN Custom CX

2013 • Cyclocross bike • USA • State championship-winning custom carbon fiber crosser

It was a dream order for any imaginative bike builder: a customer from Thailand asked for a custom bike that was "as unique as possible." At his workshop in Minneapolis, Matt Appleman set out to create "the last carbon frame [the buyer] would ever want." He used the flag of Thailand as his inspiration for the design. According to the Appleman website, the customer said "it's the best frame I've ever ridden."

The same would undoubtedly said by this bike's rider Eric Thompson, if he were not too busy dominating the local race scene. It's a truly state-of-the-art cyclocross machine custom built to Thompson's needs.

The stiff, light yet smoothly compliant frame features assymetrical seatstays with extra tyre clearance to cope with the muddiest race courses. Disc brakes are a no-charge option on all Appleman's bikes but they are particularly suited to off-road use. The transmission is an electric-shift Di2 Shimano setup for instant, silent gear changes. It's then completed with HED carbon wheels, carbon ENVE shallow drop bar and stem, and a distinctive kinked seatpost from Thomson. In short, another stunning bike for a lucky customer of Matt Appleman's one-man custom bike workshop and definitely one to dream of riding. **SH**

DAWES Discovery Twin

2013 • Tandem • UK • Popular two-person tourer

Dawes makes some of the most popular tandem bikes, and its Discovery Twin is a typically well-thought-out product. It's not the cheapest, but the price is justified by the aluminum alloy frame with tandem-specific, high-tensile steel forks, which cope admirably with the extra structural stresses of maintaining the handling capabilities of a two-person machine.

The Discovery Twin is aimed at leisurely days out rather than high-speed road work or all-terrain adventures. Riders are treated to Dawes Comfort saddles, Kraton Comfort grips, and front and rear chromoplastic mudguards to keep them comfortable, clean, and dry. Impressive quality components include slick Shimano Acera 24-speed EZ-Fire gears with Shimano derailleurs, precision Truvativ Firex Gigapipe cranks, and strong 48-spoke, double-wall 26-in. (66-cm) wheels with quick-release hubs. Safe stopping is assured by Tektro alloy linear spring V-brakes with Shimano levers.

It may be an off-the-peg tandem, but the details—such as the alloy pedals with rubber insets and quality Tioga tires—are unfailingly impressive.

The Discovery Twin comes in two frame sizes—21/17 in. (54/40 cm) and 19/15 in. (45/36 cm)—both of which have alloy stems front and rear for handlebar-height adjustment. The alloy seatposts are also micro-adjustable.

Despite all this equipment, the finished bike weighs only 40 lb (18 kg), much less than two equivalent solo bikes. **SH**

CO-MOTION Periscope Torpedo

2013 • Tandem • USA • Family tandem with telescopic seatpost

How do you adapt a tandem to fit both a toddler and a basketball player? The Periscope Torpedo has the answer.

The key to the bike's flexibility is that Co-Motion fits double-telescopic seatposts at the rear. This micro-adjustable system copes with a huge range of height differences very quickly and easily. The tandem stoker can be 3 ft (0.9 m) tall, then in a matter of seconds a 6-ft (1.8 m) adult can take over.

The front seatpost and rear handlebars are also telescopically adjustable, albeit with a normal single extension. The top-tube geometry means standover height is reduced, which further helps make the bike family friendly for all shapes and sizes.

Periscope bikes come in two sizes: one for the tiniest tots, the other for supersized captains. Most people, however, can ride either version, especially as there are also nine choices of front stem and two adjustable stoker stems, plus different crank lengths as options to fine-tune the tandem's fit.

The Periscope Torpedo has a performance dimension too: it is built on a handmade lightweight chromoly steel tubing frame with sophisticated zonal butting and heat treatment for extra strength. Components include high-quality Avid disc brakes, a Shimano 10-speed gearset, and Velocity rims. A high-spec option shaves 2 lb 12 oz (1.25 kg) from the weight by swapping in carbon forks and timing belt, plus even lighter wheels.

The Torpedo can come with four S&S Couplings, making it easier to transport than standard tandems. **SH**

CREMA Rapha Continental

2013 • Road bike • USA or Germany • Custom bike for clothing brand event

---

Since 2007, a series of top-end custom bikes have been produced by various independent builders for Rapha, a boutique cycle clothing retailer with headquarters in London and its biggest outlet in Portland, Oregon. They are all part of the Rapha Continental-sponsored high-speed long-distance road event campaign that has also inspired a series of cycling videos.

The bikes produced for the Continental series are all painted black and pink and branded in Rapha style. The bike maker's own logos appear too: this is all part of the cross-fertilization of branding that is a big part of modern bike marketing.

Rapha Continentals are also usually excellent examples of modern cycle making.

In 2013 Crema joined the Rapha collection with its own one-off road bike. Crema is a German bike maker based in the Bavarian Alps, but whose bikes are hand-built from top-quality steel tubing in the United States.

The Rapha Continental is based on Crema's road bike, the Doma. It has a compact steel frame turned out in the standard black-and-pink finish with Rapha branding, but the important technical details are quite specific to the Crema bike.

The outsized tubing features a simple and elegant racy geometry for "the perfect blend of light weight and stiffness with an emphasis on performance to produce a surrealistically stable ride," according to Crema.

Other features of all Crema road bikes include stainless steel STI cable adjusters, ENVE 1¼-in. (3.2-cm) tapered fork, stainless steel drop-outs, and a 1¾-in. (4.4-cm) head tube.

The company's declared aim is "to rediscover the lost spirit of cycling." While not everyone agrees that it's gone missing, few would dispute that Crema has a great deal of it. **SH**

CASTLE Singlespeed

2013 • Mountain bike • USA • Super-rapid retro-looking off-road racer

---

Eric Coury worked for ten years in a bike shop as a salesman and mechanic before deciding to retrain as a welder and metalworker. First he built cars; then, after buying a bike from acclaimed custom builder Carl Strong, he switched to making bikes. Coury was not the first bike builder to cite Strong as an inspiration.

Coury formed Castle Frameworks and started building his own frames in high-quality steel and titanium. The business is based in Hailey, Idaho, prime mountain territory with spectacular bike trails.

Castle's range of machines now includes road, track, touring, jump, and mountain bikes. They are all custom built by Coury after a detailed interview with each purchaser to determine a host of personal details, such

> *"I . . . have always found that fit quality and craftsmanship . . . transcend fads."*
>
> Eric Coury

as shoulder-to-wrist measurement, length of femur, preferred brake mounts, and position of water bottle.

This mountain bike takes tuneability to a new level thanks to fully adjustable rear wheel dropouts. Because they can be moved backward and forward in the frame, they can take up slack in the chain for a purist single-speed transmission. While some swappable dropouts allow you to retrofit gears, this frame is totally committed to one cog. It is built without gear stops for ultra-clean lines that are picked out in the bold yellow and pinstripe detail livery. The chainset is also a specific single-ring model and the only control on the handlebars apart from the brakes is the hydraulic lock-out for the RockShox SID XX forks. **SH**

Eric Coury's custom mountain bike is a true performance puritan. ▶

ENGIN CYCLES Ti Singlespeed 29er

2013 • Mountain bike • USA • Simple but beautiful single-gear titanium 29er

Would people pay $3,250 (£2,150) for a simple hardtail bike frame that could use only one gear? American boutique bike builder Engin thought they would, and the Singlespeed 29er may well have the credentials to justify that eye-watering price tag.

The 29er's frame is elegantly made from high-quality titanium tubing with a lightly brushed finish. No printed decals here; the Engin logos are expertly etched into the metal itself. Yet no one could accuse the Ti 29er of being flashy. Like most of Engin's output, it has an understated, simple, but classic design.

Engin is the brainchild of bike builder, designer, and cycling enthusiast Drew Guldalian. He started

". . . to build bicycles that appeal both as a work of craft and as machines that can be ridden . . ."

Engin mission statement

working in a bike shop immediately after leaving college in 1995, and his business grew from there. It is now an established and successful operation based in Philadelphia.

At the start of his career, Guldalian worked mainly in steel, but, in response to demand and fashion, he launched a range of road, mountain, and cyclocross titanium bikes in 2013. These Ti bikes were characterized by attractive build quality, including neat welds and custom-machined parts such as drop-outs and seatposts. Guldalian himself bent the chainstays by hand and the head tubes and bottom brackets were also made in-house. The bikes are finished with high-end componentry, including Shimano gearsets and Schwalb Racing Ralph tires. **SH**

DONKELOPE Steampunk

2013 • Concept bike • USA • Brass-clad frame, internal hydraulic brake plumbing

With a distressed brass-clad head tube, polished wooden mudguards, and copper hydraulic car brake pipes, the Steampunk bike created a flurry of interest when it appeared on the Donkelope stand at a 2013 bike show.

All over the bike were striking retro features: a Stanley square-sided water bottle and cage; elegantly sweeping curved twin top tubes, and a heavily sprung black leather saddle (from Brooks, of course).

The Steampunk design added a wealth of details such as small reflector pods at the rear ends of the top tube, a double stem system linking the handlebars to the headset, and straight retro bars with custom-made leather grips and a classic shiny metal bell.

The gaslight at the front looked like something borrowed from an early-twentieth-century steam locomotive, but within the ancient-looking housing was an LED light unit powered from the front generator hub—the new encased in the old.

The wooden fenders were held in place by unique little curved brackets of steel, the lugs were covered in brass, and the chainguard was made of wood.

Creative constructor Greg Heath began building Donkelope bikes in Bellingham, Washington, in 2002. His frames are made from steel tubing, either silver-brazed or TIG-welded. They are usually, but not always, more conventional than this machine.

Although strikingly nostalgic, not all of the Steampunk's components were evocative of a bygone era—the bike featured Shimano's state-of-the-art Di2 electronically shifting internal hub system. The hydraulic disc brakes were modern too, although they were controlled via a twisting arrangement of copper piping from a car that coiled around the handlebars and was ducted through the frame. **SH**

⊲ Monogram gear hangers are one of the many signature details on Engin bikes.

ENGLISH CYCLES Nuvinci Cruiser

2013 • City bike • UK–USA • Innovative relaxed cruiser

Successful time trial racer Rob English normally builds the hottest performance machines, but this bike is his take on a more relaxed type of cycling. In fact, the Nuvinci Cruiser is probably the heaviest, slowest bike that he has ever built. However, it cleverly targets a whole new audience with its selection of features that prioritize comfort and style.

The 30-lb (13.6-kg) bike has big, soft, 29-in. (73.5-cm) tires, and these, along with the flexible frame and Gates Carbon Drive belt system, give the Nuvinci a super-smooth, clean, and silent ride.

Of course, the elegantly swooping frame is nothing like English's racing bikes. Note the unusual double-

> ". . . sometimes it is good just to sit up, ride easy and watch the world go by."
>
> *Rob English*

blade forks, providing strength and suppleness in spite of the wide clearance required for those bigger wheels and mudguards. There are delicate twin-spar top tubes that become seatstays, and then seem to curl around into the chainstays, too.

Inside the rear hub, English has installed the latest Fallbrook continuously variable planetary gear system, which enables riders to twist a dial on the bars until the pedaling rate is comfortable, rather than flick between preset ratios, as on a normal gearset.

The Oregon-based designer has also managed to squeeze all the disc brake and gear cables inside even the narrowest parts of the frame for hidden internal ducting. Beautiful polished wood fenders from Creative Openings in Washington State complete the look. **SH**

SOULCRAFT Tradesman

2013 • Mountain bike • USA • Off-the-peg mountain bike from top custom designer

In the early part of the second decade of the twenty-first century, some business commentators noted that the bike market appeared to be polarizing: at one extreme, there were top-end, hand-built custom machines from boutique manufacturers; at the other, cheap, high-volume, off-the-peg bikes from larger brands. There were concerns about the apparent reduction of choice for customers in search of something in between.

The Tradesman is an attempt to bridge that gap by Soulcraft, Sean Walling's custom bike-building business based in an old farm building in rural Petaluma, California. Walling's acclaimed bikes are normally built individually to order, carefully taking into account customers' personal details, such as their weight, height, and riding styles.

This new 29er has the same quality and materials as the custom bikes, but is offered only in stock sizes, as either a frame or a complete bike. That gives customers the chance to get a top-end bike at a reduced price, just so long as they can find the right fit.

So the TIG-welded frame comes in four sizes—small, medium, large, and extra-large—with different tube lengths, but the forks, head and seat angles, and chainstay length remain the same whatever size you choose.

Thus, off-the-peg buyers have to compromise, but they still get several top-end features, such as internally and externally butted head tubes, a replaceable derailleur hanger, stainless steel water bottle bosses, and a frame drain hole at the bottom bracket. The Tradesman also comes with a removable aluminum seatpost clamp, reinforced seat collar insert, and stainless steel cable stops and cable guides. The frame is pretreated with iron phosphate before a two-coat powder paint finish. **SH**

WHYTE 829

2013 • Mountain bike • UK • Trail-tough big-wheeled hardtail

With big wheels appearing in pretty much every manufacturer's lineup, 2013 was undoubtedly the year of the 29er. Typically, British brand Whyte produced its own trail-tangent approach with the all-new 829.

The 69-degree head angle is relatively slack, to give a long front center, while a generous top tube offsets the short-reach cockpit. The curved seat tube and super-wide chainstay yoke keep the back end as short as possible, with Whyte's swinging drop-out system changing the effective chainstay length by up to ⅘ in. (20 mm), thus enabling owners to run a single-speed setup without a tensioner. Continuous outer cable routing and Crud Catcher mudguard mounts provide filthy weather protection. Whyte used bigger wheels only on the 18½- and 20-in (47- and 50.8-cm) frames in its hardtail range, keeping smaller wheels for smaller riders. It also introduced own-brand wheelsets to save weight. Fox's 15QR axle F29 fork was a benchmark all-round control unit, while the Shimano XT transmission included a 36-tooth sprocket at the back.

Once you're rolling or no longer fighting gravity, the 829 takes the ball and runs with it. It's a fun and dynamic bike to ride, rather than just a roll around cross-country bike like most 29ers. **GK**

GANGL Record Strada 753

2013 • Road bike • USA • Steel frame built by experienced racer

Richard Gangl hardly qualifies as one of the new wave of American boutique bike makers. He's been around since before some of them were born, and has been building professional-quality bikes since 1979.

Back then, Gangl was a world-class racer who had amassed more than 100 victories on road and track. He returned to his home state of Colorado to establish a bike workshop in which he created steel, carbon, aluminum, and titanium bikes that, over the following three decades, have won at least as many races as Gangl himself did. Today he specializes in traditional lugged or fillet-brazed steel and TIG-welded titanium frames, mostly for road bikes. It's definitely a one-man operation: Gangl designs, welds, and paints the bikes himself. He even designed and built the paint oven and frame jigs.

The 753 Reynolds lugged-steel road bike is a great example of Gangl's quality craftsmanship. It features a delicately lugged and lightweight frame designed for racing in the high mountain passes of the Rockies that Gangl knows so well. Its retro feel is completed by a Campagnolo Super Record Titanium groupset from the mid-1980s. The bike weighs in at a remarkably light 16½ lb (7.5 kg). **SH**

GAULZETTI Cazzo

2013 • Road racing bike • USA • Reinforced steel hardcore road race frame

Niobium is a metallic element that vastly increases the strength of steel. Alloys containing it have been used in the nozzles of Apollo spacecraft, and to reinforce Columbus Uber Oversize PegoRichie tubing steel, one of the bike world's finest materials.

Craig Gaulzetti chose niobium-strengthened metal for the frame of this hardcore race bike. The tubing was designed as a joint project between U.S. bike steel expert Richard Sachs and renowned Italian frame builder Dario Pegoretti. It is lightweight, easy to work with, and corrosion resistant. Frame makers consider it the best material for machining, welding, and finishing.

The large-diameter tubing was chosen for its stiffness and resistance to flexing, whatever the stresses. The slight increase in weight was worth it, according to Gaulzetti. The Cazzo (the word is an Italian profanity) was designed to be ridden fast on the worst terrains that wild road cyclists have to face. It's snappy and responsive, but has a less nervous ride over bumps and holes than similar lightweight racers.

The Cazzo is handmade, with premium features that include special drop-outs made by Richard Sachs and an ENVE carbon fork. It currently costs around $12,000 (£8,000). **SH**

GEEKHOUSE Mudville CX

2013 • Cyclocross bike • USA • Belt-driven single-speed cross bike

Marty Walsh founded Geekhouse in 2002. The company began making tungsten inert gas TIG-welded steel frames but later expanded into building and selling whole bikes.

Mudvilles are highly customized to suit each individual purchaser, and can cope with everything from off-road demands to city commuting. Their features and options include fender and rack mounts, S&S Couplings, disc brakes, and ENVE carbon forks. The frame is normally built from an extra-durable, double-butted steel tubeset, but is also available in ultra-light True Temper OX steel. The bikes are finished off in bright nontoxic paint at the in-house "Sugarcoat" paintworks. With all American-sourced parts and materials, the bike is proudly labelled as "100 percent made in the USA."

The specification of the Geekhouse Mudville CX includes the Gates Carbon Drive belt system, Chris King single-speed hubs, SRAM crank, and Avid disc brakes. The frame has been customized to feature a tapered head tube and internally routed rear brake cable. Among other striking features are the chunky Luxe Wheelworks wheelsets from Justin Spinelli's workshop, which, like Geekhouse itself, is based in Boston. **SH**

GROOVY Frankenstein X

2013 • Mountain bike • USA • Reborn bike
with monster paint job

Groovy Cycleworks owner Rody Walter was on a wild group-biking adventure on some hairy trails in Colorado. One of the riders, piloting a brand-new custom Groovy, misjudged a small jump, fell, and could only watch as his titanium bike tumbled 500 ft (150 m) over a cliff.

The next day, the party rappeled down into the canyon to retrieve the bike. On the way, they saw the wreck of another MTB dangling from a tree. When they found what they were looking for, Walter noted that the titanium frame had sheared in two. The bars were torn from the stem, the internal cables ripped in two, the fork and axle bent, the rims smashed, the seatpost was crushed, and the hydraulic fluids had bled clean.

"Most stories have a happy ending if you are willing to work at it hard enough."
Rody Walter

Back at his Ohio workshop, Walter felt that he "couldn't toss it back in the bin," so he tried to fix it. He stripped and cleaned the parts, then slid a 5-in. (12.7-cm) insert into the tubes to bind the fracture, and welded it in place. A broken fork was repaired and fitted, and further strengthening work was carried out on the frame. Finally, the bike passed a 225-lb (102-kg) drop test.

Walter finished the new bike with a lighthearted Frankenstein paint job that featured fake stitches, dripping blood, and a decal with the legend "It lives." He then added some top-end components, including Rohloff drop-outs, internal cable routing, and belt drive.

Walter then declared that the bike would now "live out its days under my fat ass and less demanding riding style (if you can call it style)." **SH**

FESTKA Motol Chrom

2013 • Track bike • Czech Republic •
Extraordinary-colored chrome bike

Exhibitors at the North American Handmade Bike Show (NAHBS) normally display smart, new, understated products, and earnestly admire each other's lugwork. Then suddenly a bike like this appears and redefines everyone's idea of what is normal.

Festka designs and builds unique custom bikes and accessories in a workshop in the center of Prague, the capital of the Czech Republic. The company claims to "combine precise handcrafting with high technology and art."

The Motol Chrom is an extraordinary-looking multi-purpose track, road, and urban bike that is certainly not for faint-hearted cyclists. It is the work of progressive young designers Michael Mtoureček and Ondřej Novotný.

The mechanical basics are that it is a fixed-gear speedster with a high-performance frame made from Columbus steel tubing and fitted with carbon forks, bar and wheels, and an aluminum stem. The tires are from Tufo but the wheels are built in-house.

All that technical detail pales into insignificance beside the multi-layered, sprayed-on, colored chrome finish. Somehow, the repeated coating and cleaning of the chrome have resulted in a striking look unlike that of any other bike in this book. Even the saddle, handlebars, and drop-outs have received the colored-chrome treatment. The bar tape and drivetrain are almost the only chromed parts of the bike.

This might be one of those bikes you see once and never hear of again. Then again, it might not. At the time of writing, Festka was planning major expansion into international markets, and has arranged distribution in the United States. A Festka race team is planned too, so perhaps we can look forward to seeing more of the company's head-turning designs. **SH**

Few bikes are as eye-catching as Festka's Motol Chrom. ▶

LITEVILLE 301

2013 • Mountain bike • Germany • Fastidiously built German suspension bike

While many big-brand manufacturers' bikes are carefully developed to have universal appeal for maximum global sales, specialist builders often deliberately design their bikes for the distinctive and sometimes idiosyncratic tastes of their local market. The latter is certainly the case with the ultra-fastidious engineering and multiple shock, tune, and travel options of the Liteville 301, which is unmistakably German in design and ride feel.

As an example of the level of detail Liteville goes into, the company doesn't use a single off-the-shelf tube from a third-party manufacturer. Every tube in its frames is custom shaped to the exact dimensions and wall thicknesses Liteville needs to make a super-stiff yet lightweight frame. We're not just talking single or double changes in thickness, either. The top tube on the 301 has no fewer than five different steps to handle different loads at different points. All the bearings are top-quality double-sealed units, held in place with titanium bolts.

The frame carries an unprecedented 10-year guarantee, but Liteville owners are unlikely to need to claim on it because the whole structure is bombarded with metal shot between being heat treated and electroplated to give the surface the toughest, most crack-resistant finish possible. Alternatively, buyers can choose from more than 650 thick painted colors. Liteville and partner component brand Syntace have also developed the 5⅗ x ½-in. (14.2 x 1.2-cm) rear screw axle and hub size that's become the default dimension for all current rear wheel attachments.

The 301 has always been renowned for its adaptability, but this eleventh manifestation of the series surpasses all its predecessors. It is so versatile that it has a justifiable claim to be the best engineered mountain bike in the world. **GK**

"Maybe we are bike enthusiasts. Or maybe we're just a little bit bike-crazy."

Liteville.de

Liteville's 301 makes the impossible possible.

HEROBIKE Bamboo

2013 • Utility bike • USA • Community bike built from local bamboo

Alabama's Black Belt region is one of the most deprived areas of the United States. The nonprofit organization Hero has worked there since 1994 to alleviate rural poverty through job training and cheap housing schemes.

In 2009 Hero launched Herobikes, which builds custom bicycles and trains teenagers in green technologies and manufacturing. It is based in Greensboro, a city at the center of the "Alabamboo" scheme to develop sustainable bamboo crops. Hero linked with this project and started building a range of bikes using bamboo instead of tubing. Locally grown stalks are dried with a propane torch and the joints are made using carbon fiber and epoxy resin.

Bamboo has been used successfully for years as a lightweight bike-building material—many urban messenger cyclists swear by the material's durability and longevity, and some riders contend that its natural strength and structure give a smoother ride than aluminum, steel, or carbon.

There are currently five types of Herobike: a single-speed, a 7-speed, a 14-speed, a 20-speed, and the Coaster shown here. The last named is the top seller. It has classic swept-back handlebars, soft cushy grips, a wide saddle, and 1 1/10-in. (2.8-cm) tires that are ideal for comfortable cruising around town.

The bike parts are also available as a mail-order package to assemble yourself at home. Some people sign up for build-your-own courses in Alabama and come away with a custom bike they have created themselves. **SH**

KISH 650B Mountain Bike

2013 • Mountain bike • USA • Custom mid-sized wheel MTB

With a diameter of 27½ in. (70 cm), the 650B wheel is halfway between the traditional 26 in. (66 cm) and the modern 29 in. (73.5 cm). It combines the former's maneuverability and low center of gravity with the latter's rollover abilities, traction, and consistently smooth ride.

Despite these qualities, Jim Kish, one of the United States' best-known and most experienced bike builders, remained skeptical about 650Bs but was eventually persuaded to create a frame for these in-betweeners. He tried the product out on a few trails, and not long afterward became an enthusiastic convert. "I've grown to like this wheel size a lot," Kish says. "It's not too small . . . and not too big. It's just right. I'm really hoping this size catches on."

Kish's mountain bikes are normally built on a straight-gauge frame, but on the 650B he adopted a more sophisticated butted titanium tubeset which produced a frame weighing only 3 lb (1.36 kg) to maximize performance.

After being completed with a mix of SRAM XX and XO parts, White Brothers' Loop fork, Industry Nine wheels, and Thomson stem and post, the bike was displayed at the 2013 North American Handmade Bicycle Show.

Although the original drawback of 650Bs was the lack of choice, that is no longer a problem because bigger brands have now introduced them into their ranges and component manufacturers have increased the range of parts that work with mid-sized rims. **SH**

KISH Titanium MTB

2013 • Mountain bike • USA • Handmade curved-tube titanium bike

Former bike tour leader Jim Kish became a custom frame builder who pioneered titanium frames and later ran courses in the use of this metal in cycle construction. He also makes complete bikes that are remarkable for their strength-to-weight ratio, their lively but comfortable ride, and their complete freedom from rust.

Kish hand builds his company's bikes in the famously liberal community of Carrboro, North Carolina. After sales, he keeps in touch with all of the buyers, to monitor the progress of his machines, which he guarantees for life.

All Kish bikes use U.S.-made titanium or steel tubing. Bottom brackets, drop-outs, and braze-ons are also sourced domestically.

The Kish mountain bike frame is the most eye-catching. It is available with an elegantly curved rear end including S-bend chain and seatstays with a hand-brushed titanium finish. The MTB frames are built one at a time, not in batches, and each is designed specifically for the dimensions and requirements of each buyer. Completed bikes are either single-speed or in geared format. Parts usually come from Shimano or SRAM, tires from Schwalbe, and wheels from Industry Nine Tail or Stan's.

Kish's mainframe triangle is carefully made with outsized tubing that has optimized wall thicknesses and diameters. The details are impressive too: features include a welded seat-tube reinforcement sleeve and welded bottle-frame bosses and cable stops. **SH**

IRIDE Volatore

2013 • Road bike • Italy • Family-built Italian roadster

The advertising slogan explains the bike's design concept well: "High-speed fun is practical." The Volatore is a road racer with a soft side. It is built with top specifications and components that would enable owners to go straight into competitions, even though in reality they are much more likely to ride off to the local stores instead.

Iride bikes have been produced since 1919 in the Veneto of northeast Italy, at a picturesque old ocher-washed factory where both the office and the attic are crammed with awards accumulated over nearly a century. The Gemmati family who owns the company is expert in a wide range of traditional construction methods. Among the trade secrets passed down from generation to generation is a technique of hand brazing with a low flame to give the molten bronze and brass longer to run deeper and more effectively into the joints.

The family has moved with the times in other ways, though. The materials used are modern: the Volatore's frame tubing is triple-butted Columbus niobium steel with individually cast lugs. It's an 18-speed roadster sporting traditional looks but with state-of-the-art ultra-light Miche Race wheels featuring bladed spokes and Vittoria Zaffiro Pro 35½ x 10-in. (700 x 25-cm) Kevlar beaded tires. The factory may be traditional and peeling, but the components are completely up to date, including a Columbus full-carbon fiber fork, Campagnolo Veloce derailleurs, and a Miche Race compact crankset. **SH**

OWEN Softride Wood

2013 • Road bike • USA • Wooden boat builder's dream beam bike

Ken Stolpmann is a vastly experienced wooden boat builder based in Michigan. When he decided to make himself a bike, it was only natural that he should construct it from the material with which he was most familiar.

The bike shown here is his second attempt. The first had what he called "flex issues," but this Softride is much stronger and very light, and it looks pretty cool, too. The ride is described as "lively but stiff."

It is built in the style of beam bikes, which have long been Stolpmann's favorites. The chunky down tube is mahogany, sculpted like an aircraft wing for aerodynamism, and built in two halves, which are then joined around a honeycomb core. The head tube is aluminum covered in a wooden veneer.

That beam-style double top tube is made of hickory. Structurally, it is only glued to the down tube with epoxy. The only frame bolts are used to join the seatpost to the top tube and the drop-outs to the chainstay, which is carved to shape from ash, and inlaid with fine marquetry using slivers of differently stained wood. The drop-outs, head tube, and seatpost were all machined by hand from aluminum.

There is also a small integrated bag behind the Forte saddle, and behind that a couple of water bottle cages. Note also the "flip-flop" fixed or freewheel hub that Stolpmann usually rides on the fixie side.

Stolpmann has adopted the Owen trade name in honor of Owen Woolley, his late woodcraft mentor in his native New Zealand. At the time of writing, he seemed undecided about whether to produce bikes like this on a commercial basis. Although he claims that bike building is no more than a hobby, he exhibited his work at the 2013 North American Handmade Bicycle Show (NAHBS) in the hope of getting orders. **SH**

DON WALKER Crazy Legs Cycle Cross

2013 • Cyclocross bike • USA • Aero-industry techniques on steel bike

Don Walker spent much of his early life working as a skilled mechanic on USAF and Navy bombers and private executive business jets. When he finally changed careers, he set up his own bike-building business and launched the North American Handmade Bicycle Show (NAHBS), which has grown into one of the world's top exhibitions for small independent companies.

Walker's own business is certainly small. In fact, it's a one-man operation based in rural Kentucky. But his reputation for building fine high-performance bikes has grown each year. He makes all types of frames as well as complete bikes, and there's a waiting list for his products.

> "There is nothing more sexy in the bike world than a custom steel frame done just right."
>
> Nik Borem, DW team rider

Since Walker set up his company, his bikes have been successful in national and international races, with top American riders including Erin Hartwell, Allie Dragoo, and David Wiswell all singing their praises.

Crazy Legs CXs are versatile bikes that are equally at home on and off the road. They are ridden by the company's successful cyclocross team of thirteen riders.

Their frames are handmade from Reynolds 853 custom steel. The top-end components include carbon forks by Ritchey Logic, and bars, stems, posts, and clamps from LH Thomson of Georgia. Paul Component usually supplies the Neo-retro brakes, and Shimano provides Ultegra CX groupsets. The wheels from Shimano are wrapped in Continental rubber. The Crazy Legs CX is finished in Walker's gold-and-black paint scheme. **SH**

Beautiful bikes deserve beautiful components, such as this Curtis Odom chainset. ▷

LITTLEFORD Daily Driver 3.0

2013 • City bike • USA • Split frame all-rounder

MOOTS IMBA Bike

2013 • Mountain bike • USA • Dedicated trail maintenance machine

When Jon Littleford decided that his own everyday bike needed updating, he thought he'd incorporate some of the features that he installed on the bikes he made for other people. The project began as "a little updating," but soon grew into something much bigger.

He rebuilt the rear rack and updated the rack struts to mount right through the seatstays. He changed all the attachment points on the frame and racks into stainless steel. Then he asked himself, why stop there?

Next he installed a completely new front rack— an integrated front lowrider baggage shelf for serious touring—and eyelets on the outside of the front fork crown in case he ever needed a randonneur-style basket shelf. Then he added a detachable wooden trunk to use when he was pottering around his home city of Portland, Oregon.

After that came a new paint job in deep red to match his beloved old leather Brooks saddle. All the lugs were repainted with a four-toned faded theme.

Finally Littleford installed S&S Couplings to allow him to carry the bike in a suitcase-sized holder. He gave the derailleur cables their own couplers too, so they could be disconnected just above the bottom bracket during the folding process. **SH**

This self-contained, all-in-one maintenance bike is a fully rideable off-road machine that can carry all the tools that trail builders and maintainers need.

The bike itself is very lightweight because of all the equipment it must carry: its frame, racks, and fork are all made of titanium. Extras include a chainsaw with a titanium chainguard mounted on the rear rack, a fuel bottle on a special mount behind the seatpost, and a tool pouch hanging from the top tube holding a foldable hacksaw, pruners, and gloves. Mounted at the front is a specially made foldable shovel with a leather sheath and titanium handle, and a generous rack that could hold essential water supplies—or perhaps even a six-pack of beer.

To cope with all this additional loading, the IMBA has an extended wheelbase like a cargo bike with big 29er wheels to spread the weight.

Moots displayed this one-off concept bike at the 2013 North American Handmade Bicycle Show, where it was voted The People's Choice for the whole event. Moots now lends it out to organizations such as the International Mountain Biking Association, who helped design it, to assist in trail projects around the United States. **SH**

This unique workhorse even includes a custom chainsaw rack. ▸

RETROTEC Triple 29+

2013 • Mountain bike • USA • Instantly recognizable triple top-tube frame

Curtis Inglis began producing Retrotec bikes in 1993. In 2012 and 2013, he beat bigger, better-known operations to scoop Best Mountain Bike awards at the North American Handmade Bicycle Show (NAHBS).

In his workshop deep in the Napa Valley in California, he produces both Retrotecs and more conventional Inglis bikes. Retrotec was originally founded by Bob Seals, who had wanted to capture the appeal of early Schwinn cruisers—hence the swooping top tube design.

Inglis worked for Seals, then took over the company himself. He found that extending the original idea to a triple-tube arrangement allowed him to use

> *"It is smooth as silk and absorbs all the rough hits with aplomb but yet climbs just like I wanted."*
>
> oldglorymtb.com

much thinner tubing and reduce the weight of the bike while retaining its strength. It also looked cool.

This triple frame can be ordered with any of the Retrotec bikes, and the third tube can be either curved or straight. But Inglis's recent 29er has grabbed the most headlines of all his triples. The clearance required for this bike's chunky 3-in. (7.5-cm) wide tires meant that the split top tube needed an extra wishbone, breaking the normally sleek swooping lines of the top tube/seatstays. For the same reason, a special bridge component was needed for the chainstays.

At the NAHBS, the 29+ cruiser was finished in a sumptuous chocolate-and-cream color scheme with appropriately retro lettering that caught and retained the attention of passersby. **SH**

VIVELO Arc

2013 • Road bike • Bulgaria • Custom-colored, pro-looking road machine

In the increasingly crowded carbon fiber bike market, brands use every possible attraction to get buyers to choose their bikes ahead of rival products. Vivelo of Bulgaria uses pro team-style color options for frame, wheels, and other components to tempt riders onto its Arc all-rounder.

After several years supplying bikes to local teams in order to obtain development feedback, Damyan Nikolov set up his Vivelo brand in 2009. The company's involvement in increasingly higher-rated teams continued as its bike range developed, and in 2012 it achieved a stage win with the Spanish Caja Rural team in the Vuelta a España.

The Arc draws inspiration from top aero road-racing machines such as Specialized's Venge. The straight tapered leg forks plug into a short head tube to allow an aggressively low front position. The deep triangulated down tube gives the bike a purposeful appearance, and conceals the gear cables to improve aesthetics and aerodynamics. Color-matched flashes on frame and wheels are carried up onto the aero profile seatpost and bottle cages for a very slick "pro" look. While the mainframe is a meaty affair, the skinny rear tubes have the largest influence on the ride, noticeably taking the sting out of rough roads and making the Arc comfortable on potholed surfaces. As well as different color options, complete bikes are available in a wide range of specification options to suit riders' desires and pockets.

The strengths and shortcomings of the Arc were well summarized in *Bike Radar*'s review, which praised the bike's appearance and ride but expressed reservations about its heavy frame. However, its overall verdict was that the bike is ideal for riders who want a comfortable high-mileage cruiser. **GK**

SHAMROCK Celtic Cross

2013 • Cross bike • USA • Award-winning stainless steel lugged frame

With the arrival of sexy new materials like carbon, titanium, aluminum, magnesium, and even wood, is steel finished? Not a chance, according to Tim O'Donnell of the Shamrock custom bike frame workshop.

"No material can match the ride quality, durability, and life cycle of good-quality steel," says the award-winning bike builder. Although the days of heavy, clunky steel bikes are gone, today's steel can be as light as any of the exotic materials that grab modern headlines.

And that's why this award-winning cross bike is built on a KVA steel tubeset and jointed with classic decorative lugwork. The frame is treated with a frame-saver spray on the inside before jointing, virtually eliminating the risk of rust. O'Donnell also claims that steel is the easiest material to repair.

The Celtic Cross offers all the versatility of the best cross bikes, with various configurations available to order. It can be specified as a pure cyclocross race bike or a total all-rounder. All Celtic cross bikes have wide-spaced stays that allow fatter tires to be fitted.

The Shamrock frame is approved by the Union Cycliste Internationale (UCI) for cyclocross events.

The Celtic Cross's build is typically high standard, with plenty of custom options available. Some details are fixed, however. The tubing is from KVA, Columbus, or True Temper; lugs are from Llewellyn in Australia. The main tubes slide into these steel sleeves and are silver-soldered in place. There are vertical drop-outs to ensure the wheel never slips under hard pedaling, and S&S Couplings are available for easier transportation. **SH**

SHED 6 Stroopwafel

2013 • Town cruiser • UK • Custom newcomer from humble origins

Bike-building company Shed 6 is based in one of a row of small lock-up garages and workshops in Leeds, England. It's the sixth shed in the row, and has a simple number 6 hand painted on the door.

Humble though this structure appears, it is nevertheless the global headquarters of Shed 6 bikes, which are conceived, built, and sold by sole operator Felix Fried.

In 2013, Fried travelled to the North American Handmade Bicycle Show in Denver, to display the fourth bike that he had built—the Stroopwafel. A traditional cruising town bike with some great practical touches, it is named after a thin and syrupy Dutch waffle, in reference to the fact that it was at least partly inspired by bikes in the Netherlands.

Fried uses the Stroopwafel as his own city transport around Leeds, so he designed it to cope with the unpredictable Yorkshire weather that can change from rain to sun or ice to fog—all in one day.

The frame was made from Reynolds 631 steel tubing. Features include an integrated dynamo hub system powering lights that are secured to the frame to deter thieves. The rear light in particular is an ingenious masterpiece: a patchboard of red LEDs built into the frame between the seatstays. There's an on-and-off switch behind.

Cables are routed inside the top tube for a neater profile. The rear cables emerge from the seatstay right next to the rear derailleur. And the final urban flourish is the classic brass bell from Danish company Sogreni. **SH**

STEVE POTTS Mountain Bike

2013 • Mountain bike • USA • Race mountain bike from legendary builder

Steve Potts was a prime mover of mountain biking, which developed after he and his friends started racing the Repack downhill trail in Marin County, California.

Steve built his first bike as a way to get out into the wilderness to go fishing. In 1980, he began to build and sell his own frames. Then, with other members of the Repack gang, he formed Wilderness Trail Bikes (WTB), which became one of the most innovative companies in the industry, producing high-end components, and licensing out designs such as the original mountain bike water-bottle cage, and Greaseguard headset and hubs, which had grease-injection ports that enabled riders to refresh the bearings without dismantling them.

"Impeccable . . . It is so simple. Everyone needs a singlespeed in their stash of bikes. "

Mountainflyer magazine

An early leader of the 29er movement, Steve Potts understands as well as anyone the relationship between the geometry of the frame and the wheel size, and the way they both interact with the terrain. However, some people may never forgive him for the appearance of a spate of drop-bar mountain bikes in the late 1980s.

After leaving WTB, Steve Potts continued to build top-quality mountain and road frames in his Point Reyes workshop. At the time of publication of this book, he was the only one of the original gang still manufacturing and selling his own bikes. His frames are constructed exclusively from titanium, a metal he extols not only for its reliability and strength, but also for its resistance to corrosion. **KF**

VENDETTA Dark Soul

2013 • Road bike • USA • Gothic-style Italian-tubed racer

Columbus Spirit for Lugs (SFL) steel tubing is made in Milan, Italy, for use in competition-standard bike frames. It is a lightweight, triple-butted, niobium alloy, fine-tuned by the PegoRichie partnership for optimum strength, weight, and flexibility.

So when you see that a manufacturer has built its frame with SFL, you might expect a classic race bike. Instead, Vendetta has presented this bizarre but striking Gothic creation.

The SFL frame is here transformed by a specialist liquid paint job, featuring solid black with House of Kolor Purple Ice Pearl Glass and Purple Passion highlights. The ice pearl effect is created in-house by spraying small pieces of glass over a color base to give added depth. There are custom-painted stenciled logos along the tubes, too.

The Dark Soul has some classic features, though, including curvy steel stays and a polished stainless steel headbadge. The fork crown and drop-outs are also polished stainless steel. Head-turning polished steel lugs and bottom brackets are available as an option.

The quality of this machine is demonstrated by its components, which are a luxurious mix of high-end Campagnolo, White Industries, and Chris King parts.

Vendetta is a two-man operation, formed in 2004 by old friends Garrett Clark and Conor Buescher. It is based in the U.S. cycle capital of Portland, Oregon. The bikes are usually built to a visual theme with evocative names such as The Abyss, Mad Max, and Screaming Eagle. The Portland duo make every frame by hand, file every lug, paint every inch, and assemble every bike themselves. The Vendetta catchphrase—"a touch of royalty"—might normally be dismissed as marketing hype, but in the case of this company, it has an almost authentic ring. **SH**

Vendetta's Dark Soul is a gorgeously Gothic Batbike. ▷

DYNAMIC BICYCLES Easy Step 8

2013 • Utility • USA • Minimal-maintenance shaft drive bike

The problem with the metal links in bicycle chains is that in order to operate efficiently, they require oil, which attracts dirt that then gets onto your clothing. And it's a fact of cycling that sooner or later it's going to get on you. That is unless, of course, you're riding a Dynamic shaft drive bike.

Shaft drives—which use bevel gears to permit the axis of drive torque from the pedals to turn through 90 degrees—first emerged in the 1890s. However, the number of gears was limited.

But since then technology has advanced, and the fourth-generation Sussex Shaft Drive System (SDS) used on the Easy Step 8 and every bike in the Dynamic range is the lightest and most efficient SDS in the world. It uses heat-treated spiral chromoly gears to transfer drive from the pedal crankshaft to a Shimano Nexus 8-speed internal gear hub in the rear. The whole shaft drive system is fully enclosed inside an aluminum alloy casing. This means no mess, no noise, and no contamination of clean transmission components with outside dust and dirt. As a result, Dynamic claims that its SDS bikes require 90 percent less maintenance than a conventional chain-driven bike.

The Easy Step 8 is built around a handmade frame of aircraft-grade 7005 aluminum for strength and stiffness, and has 35½ x 1½-in. (70 x 3.5-cm) tires that get you comfortably over a variety of riding surfaces. The seatpost has its own built-in shock-absorber, there's front fork suspension, and the stem provides up to 6 in. (15 cm) of handlebar adjustment. **BS**

ATOMIC ZOMBIE Aurora Delta Racing Trike

2013 • Mountain bike • Canada • DIY three-wheeler bike plan

The Aurora is an ultra-low-slung racing trike that costs a fraction of a normal machine. That's because you have to build it yourself. Buyers don't get the bike—they just get plans and instructions.

Readily available components and standard-diameter steel tubing produce a three-wheel machine that gives extraordinary handling on and off road. Steering is an under-the-seat system that puts the recumbent rider's hands in a lowered, relaxed position.

Rear suspension and a low climbing gear range make for a comfortable ride, while the low center of gravity and aerodynamic profile give racing potential.

Gears and suspension parts are the same as those on standard mountain bikes. Dual front disc brakes and an optional rear brake provide stopping power.

Buyers are encouraged to make their own modifications, such as installing a rear cargo box behind the seat or an electric battery pack to power a motor for climbing hills. All-weather fairings are another option.

Bike builders are given detailed instructions, including welding techniques and the use of a hand-held grinder. Costs are kept to a minimum by using electrical conduit pipes instead of chromoly tubing.

Atomic Zombie is the trade name of bike creators Kathy McGowan and Brad Graham. In 2003 Graham's SkyCycle—14 ft 3-in. (4.34-m) high—was officially acknowledged as the world's tallest rideable bicycle. Atomic Zombie also sells DIY plans for choppers, unicycles, and two-wheel recumbent cycles. **SH**

AIRFRAME A frame

2013 • Folding bike • USA • Aluminum-framed folding bike

The Airframe lightweight folding bike was originally designed by British architect Grahame Herbert in the late 1970s. Niggling design problems and production difficulties delayed the commercial release of the cycle until 1984. Again it was beset by manufacturing hiccups, and was relaunched in 2002.

This later version—built with help from a specialist tube manufacturer in Dunstable, Bedfordshire, England—was favorably reviewed. Sadly, the Airframe disappeared again, and at the time of writing it is unclear if it is still in production.

The bike itself is ingenious, if a little flawed. It is a very lightweight folding machine with an aluminum alloy frame that has its own unique folding geometry. The standard version was fitted with four-speed Shimano gears with twist-grip changers; an eight-speed Super 8 was also available. Other features included caliper brakes and 16-in. (40.5-cm) wheels.

The Airframe's distinctive rust-free frameset looked interesting and cooler than most folding rivals. The adjustable handlebar and seat heights compensated for the lack of frame-size choice.

There were, however, some riders who found the frame too flexible for anything other than the shortest trips. This was because the folding system was fairly elaborate, with several nonlocking joints that affected the rigidity of the bike in use. Some hinges were made of plastic. Folding could be awkward but could also be accomplished quickly with practice. The bike's folded shape was long and thin, making it easy to carry or store. The sales literature claimed it could fit in a car boot, tennis bag, or cabinet. There was also another folding mode, in which just the handlebars and pedals were quickly folded flush with the bike frame, making it convenient to store in a hall or corridor. **SH**

AIRNIMAL Joey

2013 • Folding bike • UK • The super-versatile Joey is a folding-bike chameleon

The ingenuity of Airnimal's Joey design is in the folding of the bike: an initial fold takes about thirty seconds and leaves a compact package that can be wheeled or picked up in one hand, and an additional fold takes a few minutes more and gets the Joey configured so that it can fit neatly inside its chic "Joey Bag." The options about how far to fold it cease to be interesting once you've ridden it, though, because the last thing you'll want to do is put it away. The Joey is one of the coolest, fastest folding bikes you'll never want to fold.

It flies along on the road on skinny high-pressure tires that make onlookers wonder if it really is a folder,

> *"I took one for a spin. Two minutes later I handed over my cash."*
>
> Phil Wigglesworth, bicycle reviewer

because it doesn't look like one. The lack of a crossbar takes a little getting used to (though the down tube is massively oversized to compensate), and the default bars are flat, which creates a slightly upright riding position, but make no mistake: It rides like a bike, sprinting and cornering hard; you can even slide the back end out.

Custom builds are commonplace for the Joey because of its wide range of options, but essentially six versions are available. These range from a sports model with an 8-speed derailleur through to a commuter-friendly Joey with a Shimano Nexus 8-speed hub and smaller, fatter wheels. Racks, mudguards, and panniers are available too, but they inevitably complicate the folding process. **BS**

DONHOU 100 mph Bike

2013 • Experimental bike • UK • Experimental speed monster

Disenchanted with creating "perfume bottles, toys, and other tat that people will just throw away," commercial product designer Tom Donhou gave up his day job and set off from England with some friends to drive to Mongolia. He took his bike and, once they reached Ulaanbaatar, he pedaled off alone, heading south through Asia. One night in a tent by the side of a road somewhere between the Gobi Desert and the jungles of Laos and Cambodia, he saw in a dream that what he really wanted to do with the rest of his life was to build handmade bikes. After that revelation, what had until now been a meandering tour became an urgent mission. He hurried to Singapore, from where he flew back home to Hackney in East London so he could get on with turning his vision into reality.

Donhou's passion led him to create Donhou Bicycles, which were soon acclaimed for their simple, bold styling, clean lines, and attention to detail. Still not satisfied, Donhou had long harbored a desire for speed, which became apparent at the 2013 Bespoked Bristol, the UK handmade bicycle show, where he unveiled this machine, which is designed to achieve around 100 mph (160 kph). To this end, it is fitted with a giant 104T chainring produced by UK precision-component engineers Royce and a fixed 13T sprocket. The custom-made handlebar is stable but allows Donhou to duck behind the draft vehicle. Outsized high-stiffness Columbus Max steel tubes keep the deliberately low-slung, high-stability handling on track too, while Avid disc brakes deal with deceleration. **MH**

VIBE Lincoln

2013 • Fat bike • USA • Copper-plated snow bike

The current wave of American independent small-scale custom bike makers is accelerating design and innovation faster than at any time in the past hundred years. New ideas are bursting out from little workshops all over the United States. The best place in the world to catch the latest innovations has become the North American Handmade Bicycle Show (NAHBS).

Among the bikes that turned heads at the 2013 NAHBS in Denver was this offering from Vibe, a company based in Boise, Idaho, and run by former racers Dave and Christi Kelley. It is an unusual steel-framed, copper-plated fat bike with a distinctive twin-top-tubed curved frame.

Among its innovative details is a snowflake-shaped rear light, which is cut from a sheet of steel that sits between the seatstays with a red light fitted behind. The switch, which is hidden behind the stays, is a chunky great magnet on a cord that needs pulling off or sticking back on—a device so simple that even someone wearing gloves could use it.

Internal cable routing is just used among today's top custom builders, but this is another neat example. Having a second curved top tube isn't common, but it looks rather cool on this bike. Evidently it's there to add more stiffness to the frame.

Vibe's hip-flask-style bottle has a huge version of an Abe Lincoln penny like a logo on the outside. Also noteworthy are the copper chain and copper-studded pedals. Even the Surly Rolling Daryl rims have been copper plated. **SH**

CHERUBIM Ranger

2013 • Utility bike • Japan • Innovative city bike concept that blends artistry and utility

Founded in 1965 by Hitoshi Konno, Cherubim built the track frames that brought gold medals to the Japanese team in the 1968 Olympic Games in Mexico City. The oldest Nihon Jitensha Shinkokai (Japanese Bicycle Association; NJS)-certified frame builder still in operation, Cherubim is now run by Konno's son, Shinichi, and based in Machida-city, Tokyo, Japan.

While Cherubim's lineage is in track bikes, Shinichi continues to innovate, blending lightweight custom tubesets from Japanese manufacturer Kasei with aesthetic forms to create elegant machines that combine form and function, with form often taking precedence in some of his more conceptual works.

This single-speed bike stole the show at the 2013 North American Handbuilt Bicycle Show, winning both the Best City Bike and the President's Choice awards. Combining several ideas, the Ranger is both artistic and utilitarian. The twin top tubes arc gracefully into the seatstays with an integrated rack, and the dramatic bar-and-stem combination features many different hand positions to accommodate both upright riding and aggressive speed work. The lines are kept clean and simple by the use of a coaster brake in the rear hub. **MH**

FIELD Takashi

2013 • Road bike • UK • Ultra-detailed Sheffield-built road machine for a Japanese bike blogger

Every frame produced by Sheffield, England-based Field Cycles is unique. In addition to bespoke fit and build details, buyers can have custom-designed and often complex paint schemes such as that on this road bike built for Japanese blogger Takashi.

Field Cycles is a collaborative enterprise. "I would hesitate to call us a 'company'," says Harry Harrison, one of three main participants. "We're definitely not businessmen. We just like doing what we do." Harrison, a part-time lecturer in Design Technology, is the engineer and frame builder. Graphic designer Tom creates the aesthetics, and the paint is applied in Field's "Cromaworks" by restorations expert John.

A bare frameset can take up to a week to prepare cosmetically, and the actual application of the paint is a very small part of that process. Most of the time is spent prepping, masking, and polishing. Every line, word, and graphic on a Field frame is rendered in paint. No decals are used.

Harrison declares that Field's goal is "to build something sustainable, to get to a place where we can make the most unique and beautiful things we can, and have people pay us a fair wage to produce that. We don't want to end up working in a bike factory." **MH**

CERVÉLO R5CA

2013 • Road bike • Canada • Ultra-expensive road bike hand built by the designers themselves

Some bike designers are happy to let manufacturers deal with production. Others are convinced that only by building at least the prototypes themselves can they acquire a real understanding of how the design can be refined. Cervélo takes the latter view. However, it doesn't just make a few hand-built prototypes to prove its ideas; it actually sells the bikes built in its California office to anyone who can afford $10,000 (£6,600) for just the frame and forks.

A look inside the frame shows that the R5CA is a proper artisan build: there are none of the dollops of excess resin, rough edges, or small creases and folds found in mass-produced frames, just smooth tube walls that are as perfect as the external surfaces. Cervélo takes its Project California bikes to the limit in terms of attention to detail and, with a weight of 1½ lb (0.7 kg), the R5CA's medium-sized frame is one of the lightest available. The front fork even gets a microscopic nickel alloy coating on its steerer: this reduces its weight to below 10½ oz (0.3 kg).

The Cervélo R5CA punches sprints like a heavyweight, charges climbs like gravity got turned off, and glides over rough roads like a limousine. But then, at this price, it should. **GK**

MERCIAN King of Mercia

2013 • Touring bike • UK • Flagship custom hand-built touring frame

Ever since Mercian started in Derby, England, in 1946, most of its bikes have been customized to each buyer's measurements—length of torso, forearms, and legs; even shoe size. Of all the models they produce, none has been more popular than the King of Mercia.

Every King of Mercia frame is made from Reynolds lightweight steel, which Mercian believes is the finest available, and worked on by a single builder whose identifying number is etched into each bottom bracket shell. Tubes and lugs are fitted and pinned together as the frame is brazed in an open hearth. There are no production lines here.

The bike can be fitted with oversized or conventional tubing, according to individual stiffness preferences, and can be presented in either a touring or a racing configuration. The luxurious finish can be in any combination: among the most attractive is Leaf Green Pearl with white enamel on the head tube and Mercian's signature seat tube bands. Other options include an extra set of bottle cage bosses, vertical drop-outs, and built-in threaded rack mounts front and rear. No matter what your choice, you'll be in good company, because as the headbadge says: Mercian cycles can be found "The World Over." **BS**

CERVÉLO P5

2013 • Aero road bike • Canada • State-of-the-art aerodynamic race bike

As bikes have become more complex and the margins between success and failure have become narrower, computer and engineering technology have played an increasing part in the birth of any performance bike. Canadian bike company Cervélo was started by two engineers and now employs a higher percentage of engineers than any other major manufacturer. No surprise then, perhaps, that its machines have a reputation as some of the most advanced available. Its latest P5 aero road bike comes with unique hydraulic brakes and in two distinct versions to comply with both the tight regulations of time trial and the looser rules governing triathlons.

Although hydraulic rim and disc brakes have been increasingly common in mountain biking since the early 1990s, the P5 is the first road bike to be designed specifically around Magura's radical hydraulic RT8 brake. While control and power are both increased over conventional brakes, the major advantage on an aero bike is that the hydraulic lines aren't compromised by tight turns and tortuous routing in the same way as conventional cables are. That allows minimal drag mounting under the frame and fork shroud of the P5 without any consequent reduction of braking power and control.

The deep-legged, shrouded front fork of the Triathlon P5 extends right up to the custom P5 cockpit with internally plumbed controls to create a phenomenally aerodynamic front end. The frame is similarly slippery in the maximum range of wind angles, and Cervélo has even designed the frame to carry custom-built aerodynamic storage boxes for tools and fuel on longer rides. Add outstanding frame stiffness, and the P5 is definitely one of the fastest bikes ever built. **GK**

BOBBY HUNT Minivelo

2013 • Novelty bike • Russia • Record-breaking tiny working bicycle

In 2006 the A-Bike, designed by British inventor Sir Clive Sinclair, was acknowledged as the smallest bike in the world. A full-production machine weighing 12 lb (5.5 kg), it is just 35 in. (8.9 cm) long when in operation, and can fold down to half that size for carriage and storage.

In 2009, the A-Bike lost its title to the Moosshiqk, an electric machine built in India by motorbike racer Santosh Kumar. The Moosshiqk is a mere 12 in. (30 cm) high and 18 in. (45 cm) long. It can drive forward and backward at up to 9 mph (15 kph), and can carry an adult for 1,000 yards (1 km).

These are the smallest bikes on the market, but they are enormous giants in comparison to American

> " . . . a full-sized adult, properly trained, should have no problems riding it . . ."
>
> techeblog.com

circus performer Bobby Hunt's homemade micro bike. This is 7¾ in. (20 cm) tall with a 3-in. (7.5 cm) wheelbase. To ride it, Hunt holds the handlebars with just three fingers and places two toes on each pedal.

This was the ultimate in tiny two-wheelers until 2013, when a Russian video appeared online at www.youtube.com/watch?v=SSkBRskWdzs.

The footage showed an unidentified man remove from his backpack a bike which, even though it was no bigger than his shoe, he proceeded to mount and pedal down a street. At the time of writing, no one knew the name of the rider or the machine, although the latter became known as the Minivelo: all that can be stated with certainty is that this appears to be the world's smallest bike. **SH**

© Cervélo's P5 is a race winner straight from the wind tunnel.

BIRIA Easy 7 Comfort Bike

2013 • Commuter bike • Germany • "Step-through" bicycle that is big on comfort and style

The Easy Boarding range of bicycles, designed in Germany, threatens to redefine how a bicycle should look. With their unique "step-through" aluminum frames and absence of a traditional high crossbar, riders in the 50-plus age bracket no longer need to worry about sustaining a groin injury every time they casually throw a leg over. Mounting is now a breeze; you can simply step "into" the bike and up onto the seat. And if you should happen to come off the seat unexpectedly, there's considerably less risk of incurring an embarrassing personal injury.

The Biria Easy 7 comes with a Shimano 7-speed derailleur (there is also a single-speed cruiser and several other options), and a chainring guard to keep grease off your clothes, while fenders and a rear rack are optional. But the oversized aluminum tube on the front half of the frame is the heart of this bike, allowing for a "standover" height of just 6 in. (15 cm). The handlebar stem is adjustable too, which means that people of varying girths—and those with hip complaints—will be comfortable on the Easy 7 and the other models in the Easy Boarding range, although if you're in excess of 6 ft (1.8 m) in height, you might want a taller seatpost and stem.

Everything about these bikes oozes comfort, from their large leather seats to their thick, flat-resistant belted tires for extra stability when riding over uneven terrain. At 34 lb (15.4 kg), however, they are undeniably heavy, so you might want to keep your rides a little on the short side. **BS**

BIKE FRIDAY Pocket Llama

2013 • Folding bike • USA • High-quality folding mountain bike

Paying $2,000 (£1,200) for a folding bike? It may sound extreme . . . but then, so is the performance of this top-end, handmade folder from Oregon-based Bike Friday.

The Pocket Llama Select Group has a list of components worthy of properly serious MTBs. It includes 27-speed SRAM transmission; Avid disc brakes, cables, and levers; a Cane Creek Thudbuster seatpost; and Bike Friday flat MTB silver-polished aluminum bars.

There's a flexible water bottle cage with white water bottle supplied, while the 20-in. (50-cm) wheels are black Alex DM18s wearing Schwalbe Big Apple K 2¼-in. (5.7-cm) tires. The small wheels mean it also uses a large-ratio FSA Gossamer crank in a choice of three arm lengths—6½, 6⁷⁄₁₀, and 6⁹⁄₁₀ in. (16.5, 17, and 17.5 cm).

The chromoly streel frame is tough but light, and the low center of gravity ensures nimble handling. The small wheels get the Bike Friday up to speed very quickly, making it just as effective in cities as off-road. The bike can be folded down to fit in a bag or suitcase that can double as a trailer, making the Friday a truly versatile bike for any day of the week.

Buyers select a frame size from three basic options—a 20-, 22- or 24-in. (50-, 56- or 60-cm) top tube—and a frame color of Flag Red, Green Gear Green, Cream Soda Blue, or Ink Black, as well as one of seven decal/cable housing color options.

Selection and purchase can be done online via the Bike Friday website, which helps you to choose the best frame size for your height and body weight. **SH**

CIPOLLINI Bond

2013 • Race bike • Italy • Latest bike from flamboyant Italian racer

Colorful Italian racer Mario "Cipo" Cipollini, often called "Super Mario," was one of the world's best sprinters during his long and eventful career. The self-styled ladies' man was famous for often refusing to tackle arduous climbing sections, instead releasing photos of himself lounging on a beach at the time of the stage.

In 2010, he released his own brand of bikes. They were extreme top-end machines and were promptly used by an Italian race team. Company publicity claims that Cipollini tests the products himself on the roads of Tuscany "every day," and that he personally subjects the frames to "grueling laboratory tests."

The Bond is more restrained than his earlier offerings, although its release was accompanied by an over-the-top James Bond-style video with Cipollini

himself playing the role of 007, outracing an assassin on a motorbike and escaping with a girl on a speedboat.

The Bond is a carbon-bonded frame, with seatstay and chainstays made separately then bonded to the T700 monocoque mainframe. There's a traditional adjustable seatpost, and the chainstay mold section includes a bottom bracket and drop-outs, giving the rider a very direct drive to the rear wheel.

The Bond is available either as an ultra-light frame weighing 2 lb 5 oz (1.05 kg) or made up into a complete bike (often with Campognolo Record components). Wheels are usually Vision Trimax Carbon.

Cipollinis are nearly all-Italian: they are designed and assembled in Verona, engineered in Milan, and molded in Venice; extra parts are made in Florence. **SH**

RIVENDELL SOMA San Marcos

2013 • Road bike • USA • Affordable twin-tube collaboration

Rivendell, named after a fictional refuge in J.R.R. Tolkien's *The Lord of the Rings*, is a specialist stock and custom-bike builder based in Walnut Creek, California. Soma is a San Francisco-based frame builder producing quality affordable bikes.

The two joined forces to create this bike. Rivendell's Grant Petersen designed the sturdy twin-tube frame; Soma builds and sells it.

The San Marcos is a modern take on a classic sports touring bike. It's meant to be more comfortable and durable than a lightweight racer. It can carry some loads but does not have the full panniers of a hardcore touring bike.

The details are a mix too. The tubing is light enough to give a bit of zip on the tarmac but it has fatter, softer, more comfortable tires than normal, and there are bolt holes to fit mudguards and a rear luggage rack if required. This bike could tackle smooth off-road trails with a 20-lb (9 kg) load. It is also designed to operate in rougher weather conditions than a normal road bike.

The old-fashioned frame geometry pushes the handlebars higher for a relaxed riding position. The anti-vibration handlebar plugs and plush bar tape add to the softer feel. Soma uses a traditional threaded-steel fork for easy height adjustment. A distinctive second top tube adds only a few ounces in weight, but Soma claims it makes the bike sturdier, more rigid, and more durable.

Soma either sells the frame or makes up complete bikes with any groupset, so it can be targeted at road work or touring. **SH**

ROCKY MOUNTAIN Element BC

2013 • Mountain bike • Canada • Fast and loose large-wheeler with an extra dose of attitude

Based in the radical riding hot spot of Vancouver, Canada, Rocky Mountain is ideally placed to spot new trends in progressive riding. This BC (for "British Columbia") adds dynamic fun to the smooth ride of the big-wheeled Element cross-country trail bike.

The actual frame of the bike hasn't been changed. The front half is still the lightweight carbon fiber. The rear end uses a tapered and shaped alloy tubeset with a screw-through 5⅗ x ½-in. (14.2 x 1.2-cm) axle for high stiffness at a reasonable price. A classic FSR-style suspension setup delivers 4 in. (10 cm) of wheel movement to boost control and speed sustain. Large-diameter 29-in. (73.5-cm) wheels make short work of stutter bumps and slippery surfaces with their decreased impact angle and increased inline contact

patch. The result is a tight, light, and tough machine that's ready for most things the trail can throw at it, but relatively conventional and calm in character, not a natural hell-raiser.

The twist comes in the use of a 4¾-in. (12-cm) Fox fork up front to slacken the head angle and increase the stability of the steering on fast, steep, technical, and fun trails. The BC also gets a hydraulic remote-controlled RockShox Reverb seat dropper post to get the saddle out of your way and totally liberate your body movement to boost control in more chaotic moments.

The result is a bike that's perfect for the fantastically fun and challenging cross-country trails of Vancouver, Squamish, and Whistler, as well as for epic single-track events like the British Columbia Bike Race. **GK**

WHYTE 929

2013 • Mountain bike • UK • Hardcore trail-riding 29er

While rear-suspension mountain bikes have been in production since 1983, hardtails with only front suspension and fixed rear frames are still a big part of the mountain-bike landscape.

The lack of complex shock-absorbers and pivots gives hardtails an edge in terms of weight, cost, and maintenance, and makes them particularly suited to cash-strapped or high-mileage riders. The introduction of larger 29-in. (73.5-cm) wheels, with their smoother rolling performance on rough terrain, has given them a new lease of life recently, and the cross-country race scene in particular is now dominated by lightweight, big-wheeled carbon hardtails.

Whyte's mountain bike range includes several race-style hardtails, but tucked away at one end of

the line is this genuine riding renegade. The 929 uses a tough aluminum frame designed to take serious knocks, and a longer suspension fork up front than the race bikes. Bigger tires take the sting out of rocky trails, and Fizik's Gobi saddle has a reputation as one of the most comfortable places to put your rump on a long day out. Dependable Deore XT gears from Japanese component specialists Shimano are another classic tough rider's choice. Whyte has gone radical with the gear ratios, and fitted a downhill racing-style single chainring with plastic guide block.

In effect, Whyte has taken an already fast and fun bike, stripped it down, toughened it up, and turned it into what may fairly be described as the pedal-powered equivalent of a rally car. **GK**

EARLY RIDER Spherovelo Juno

2013 • Child's bike • Australia • Teaches the basics of riding to children as young as twelve months

"The Spherovelo is a revolution in the physical development of young children—the world's first ride-on that helps the coordination of motor system and sensory perception in early toddlerhood."

Early Rider brochure

When asked what it takes to ride a bike, most adults who have mastered the technique would probably give a one-word answer: "balance." But that is an oversimplification. Having examined the question in great detail, the designers at Early Rider offer a more scientifically rigorous reply that breaks down "balance" into its essential components—equilibrium, sight, and the application of pressure. These aspects need to be nurtured individually in young children as they strive to make connections between their senses and their still-developing motor systems.

Thus, learning to ride a bike is not so much balancing, but more about coordinating muscles in response to what can be felt and seen. "Finally," the thousands of twelve- to twenty-four-month-olds out there must be thinking, "finally, there are some grown-ups who understand where we're at!"

The design philosophy of the Spherovelo is reflected in its two "wheels," which, instead of being traditional in shape, are spherical and thus able to simulate all the characteristics of a wheel while providing a high degree of lateral safety. It is almost impossible for a child to fall off one of these charming conveyances. The rear sphere is free for "turn on the spot" maneuverability. Unlike a wheel, which is prone to tipping over to one side if its rider makes any fundamental errors in judgment while steering, this sphere merely revolves. An additional safety feature is the low center of gravity.

With lovely birch handlebars and a curvy, edge-free jellybean shape, it's hard to think of a toddler who wouldn't jump at the chance to ditch the pram and make the Spherovelo his or her preferred mode of travel. There's no doubting it: the Spherovelo is the most forgiving thing on two wheels you'll ever ride; it's all downhill from here. **BS**

Learning to ride doesn't get any easier than when using a Spherovelo. ▶

SCOTT Scale 710

2013 • Mountain bike • Switzerland • Replica of Swiss World Champion's mountain bike

Building replicas of race bikes for mere mortals to buy has always been a good way for manufacturers to get the most from sponsoring a team.

While there's a limited-edition Nino Schurter race version with tweaked geometry and super-light SRAM XX componentry, the 710 gets a slightly heavy but totally bombproof Shimano XT 2x10 drivetrain and matching brakes. Fox provide the 4-in. (10-cm) travel fork, but thankfully the remote control is Scott's discreet Twinloc lever rather than Fox's CTD (Climb Trail Descend) oars. Scott house brand Syncros complete the rest, including DT Swiss-based 27½ in. (70 cm) wheels, with Schwalbe's tubeless triple "Pace Star" compound Rocket Ron tires.

How does the Scott ride? One word: Incredibly. As you'd expect for a 22 lb (10 kg) bike, it's instantly reactive,

but it's also super-stiff in terms of power delivery and steering. Punch the pedals and acceleration is shocking. You have to work a bit harder than on a 29er to stop it skipping on rough or loose tracks, but otherwise it'll leave similarly light wagon wheelers feeling soft-boiled or stiff ones feeling difficult to get going. Traction levels are noticeably better than a 26er too, with more rollover on roots or rocky crux sections and smoother skim over rubble or braking bumps.

Cornering is outstanding too. You can hit corners full-on Moto GP-style, with fork crushed and back tire either off the ground or skittering sideways. Thorough axle frame stiffness means it never felt out of control, and it's instantly responsive to traction or line correction like no 29er is. **GK**

SWIFT Detritovore

2013 • Mountain bike • Netherlands/Germany • Bringing time-trial standards to off-road trails

Swift founder Mark Blewitt is a former professional road racer, so it is perhaps no surprise that his brand should be best known for top-quality carbon fiber and time trial machines.

But there is more to his company. The Detritivore takes race performance off the road and onto the trail. If you think that would mean a super-harsh, overmuscled power machine, you would be mistaken. Thin rear stays combine with a narrow diameter—1⁷⁄₁₀₀ in. (2.72 cm)—carbon seatpost to put a fair amount of spring between the rider and the rocks. The built-in compliance makes for a comfortable ride, and aids traction by letting the bike flex and mold to remain in contact with rough ground, rather than kicking about off every little lump. Screw-in axles at the rear of the frame and the fork

tips mean tracking and steering obedience never become too out of shape as the bike flows down the roughest trails.

The handling character is deliberately rapid too, responding immediately to any line corrections and letting the rider leave corner entry to the last split-second despite the large 29-in. (73.5-cm) wheels.

The smooth lines of the meticulously constructed carbon frame include very generous mud room around the rear tires, and a seat tube that pierces the broad top tube. The backward curve of the seat tube also puts the seat in the right position despite a comparatively short and quick-turning back end. The result is a distinctively smooth yet rapid racer that expands the Swift performance into a whole new area of riding. **GK**

SCAPIN Morgan

2013 • Mountain bike • Italy • Sculpturally designed super-light suspension bike

The full-suspension Morgan maintains Scapin's reputation for immaculate aesthetics. The lines of the bike's ultra-light carbon fiber frame—which is of the same type as that used by parent company Olympia—are dominated by a top tube that sweeps back from the tapered head tube in a shallow S shape. It splits at the seat tube end to allow room for the RockShox Monarch shock to sit partially inside the tube, and thus provides perfect stress-spreading alignment of the shock and the forward section of the top tube. The bottom bracket uses a supersized Press Fit BB92 standard for maximum crank options, while the DMD front mech mounts directly onto the frame. The rear disc brake nestles in the crook of the tapering rear stays, which end in chunky alloy drop-out sections locked together with a 5⅜ x ½-in. (14.2 x 1.2-cm) axle.

The gear-mounts and rear drop-outs are fully replaceable in case of damage, while a distinctive extended seatpost clamp locks separately onto both frame and post rather than just nipping them both together. Scapin detailing extends beyond the sumptuous paint job: the rear shock linkage is formed in the shape of a stylized Scapin "S."

The Morgan isn't just a pretty face, either. Scapin's FMT (Fluid Molding Technology) uses a hydraulically driven mandrel inside the mold to ensure every last drop of heavy excess resin is wrung out of the frame before baking to set it. This gives the Morgan a frame weight of less than 4 lb 6 oz (2 kg). The 650B wheels provide an excellent balance between the agility of 26-in. (66-cm) wheels and the smooth speed of 29-in. (73.5-cm) wheels.

Reviews of the Morgan were highly positive. *Bikeradar* called it "a thoroughbred," while *Northern Ride* judged it "Italian cycling at its best." **GK**

ORBIT Routier Ultimate

2013 • Tandem • UK • Versatile, patriotically equipped tandem

Tandems potentially deliver twice the fun of a solo bike, but if they're not designed correctly they can cause more than double the grief.

Ruth and John Hargreaves' passion for two-up riding was so great that they gradually outgrew the shop—JD Cycles in Ilkley, Yorkshire, England—in which they stocked tandems from all the leading global brands, and opened another specialist outlet in 2010 in the neighboring village of Gargrave. At the same time, they bought the tandem side of the established Orbit brand name and designed a complete new range of twins, the pick of which is their Routier Ultimate.

> *"Tandem riding is social and fun, and the shared teamwork brings couples closer together."*
>
> Ruth Hargreaves

The lightweight, cross-braced alloy frame is built to Orbit's design by leading frame factory Kinesis, with a massive 8-in. (20.3-cm) rear disc brake and a strong but light cargo rack as standard, plus a front disc brake as an optional extra. Super-tough Shimano mountain bike gears cope with double the usual pedal power, while the Ultimate gets patriotic propulsion from handmade UK Middleburn cranks. The heavy-duty wheels are made just over the hill from Gargrave in the Hope Technology works in Barnoldswick, and the bikes are also built locally. The Routier Ultimate is available in three standard sizes and with either a metallic blue or glossy black paint job.

The result is a smooth-riding twin machine that's perfect for days out for couples. **GK**

◁ Scapin even sculpt their intial into the suspension linkage.

CYCLES MAXIMUS Cargo Trike

2013 • Utility bike • UK • Part cargo bike, part rickshaw, part urban van—the Cargo Trike can do it all

Though buoyed by the success of its first pedal-powered rickshaws in 2000, Cycles Maximus supremo Ian Wood and his chief designer Tom Nesbitt did not rest on their laurels—they redoubled their efforts, and created a broad new range of pedal-powered and electrically assisted trikes that represent the cutting edge of cargo bike evolution.

Hand built with a space frame capable of carrying an impressive 551 lb (250 kg), the Cycles Trike comes with differential drive, hydraulic brakes, 24-speed transmission, a ventilated rubberized seat designed to disperse water, and a waterproof cover for the tray. Which all add significantly to the weight, of course—a daunting 165 lb (75 kg) even before the rider hops on. In response to this problem, they created the Cargo Trike.

This power-assisted version of the basic trike comes with either a Heinzmann motor in the front wheel or a beefier, chassis-mounted Lynch Powerdrive at the rear, each of which will help you to get those loads up hills with 20 percent gradients. Built to carry a standard-sized European pallet measuring 47½ x 31½ x 5⅜ in. (120 x 80 x 14.5 cm), the Cargo Trike comes with spoked, composite, or alloy wheels and moped-strength tires, and its continuous gearing means you can change gears even when at rest.

The current price of $7,650 (about £4,995) for the Lynch power-assisted version may sound steep—the pedal version is a slightly less daunting $4,450 (£2,900)—but remember that with a Cycles Maximus Cargo Trike you'll run no risk of parking tickets and will have no road taxes or compulsory insurance to pay for. What you will have is a vehicle that requires minimal maintenance and is every bit as efficient as a van around city centers. **BS**

PYGA OneTen29

2013 • Mountain bike • South Africa • Tough trail-taming big-wheeler from new South African brand

Pyga is a new name on the scene, but the men behind it are some of the best-known and respected innovators in the southern hemisphere, if not the world.

Patrick Morewood created the brand. His partner in Pyga, Mark Hopkins, is a key player in the C-SIXX component company and a co-founder of Leatt, which makes whiplash neck guards for downhill racers. Given their backgrounds, it's no surprise that their bikes have a more robust attitude than the wheel sizes suggest.

While a 4.3-in. (11-cm) travel, 29-in. (73.5-cm) wheeled bike from most companies would generally be a lightweight race machine, the Pyga OneTen takes a no-holds-barred approach to the trail.

> "Ignore the short travel, the Pyga is a proper sawn-off shotgun."
>
> MBUK Magazine

With the tapered head tube cleared to handle a 4.7- or 5.1-in. (12- or 13-cm) stroke suspension fork, it's got a confident, self-correcting steering feel. The smooth, hydraulically shaped alloy frame tubes keep stiffness high and center of gravity low. Add a Syntace X-12 screw-through rear axle to keep the back wheel on track, and this is a bike that loves to put its shoulders low into corners or blast its way through and over rough sections.

The same gung-ho attitude is even more evident in the 29er's 650B-wheeled sibling, the OneTwenty 650. The slightly smaller wheels give a more agile, fast-reacting feel, and are also more playful on the trail, while a 5½-in. (14 cm) fork up front means it's ready to tackle trouble head-on. **GK**

Pyga's bikes are bred to blow any aggressive riding doubts into the dust. ▶

QHUBEKA Buffalo

2013 • All-terrain bike • USA • 40,000+ Buffalos overcome the tyranny of distance for rural Africans

When the designers at World Bicycle Relief in Chicago developed a tough-as-nails bike to haul heavy loads over the most rugged tracks and terrain in Africa, they sought a brand name that would convey durability and strength—hence the Buffalo.

Built to serve the needs of communities whose livelihoods depend on durable bicycles, the Buffalo comes with heavy-gauge spokes and steel rims, puncture-resistant tires, weather-proof coaster brakes, a heavy-gauge steel frame with an angled, "one-size-fits-all" top-tube, a high-capacity stand, and a rear rack capable of carrying loads up to 220 lb (100 kg). In addition to the heavy stuff, this bike is also able to take a child to school or to the doctor, potentially cutting travel time by 75 percent.

There's more to Buffalo manufacturer Qhubeka than just building and selling bikes. Its Field Mechanics Training Program trains local people to carry out maintenance, and helps students with marketing and even setting up and running small businesses.

Team MTN-Qhubeka—Africa's first Professional Continental race team—had a podium finish at the 2013 Milan–San Remo, after which their next objective was to become the first African team to race the Giro d'Italia and the Tour de France. They hope thereby to raise awareness of the Qhubeka Foundation, the driving force behind the Buffalo and a new generation of mobile, terrain-conquering young Africans who together are doing their bit to solve the age-old problem of transport in rural Africa. **BS**

FELT AR1

2013 • Road bike • USA • Aero road bike from the famous triathlon brand

While most road bike manufacturers now have an aerodynamic racer in their range, few brands' headwind-beating technology can compare with that of Felt, whose AR series bikes are some of the most sought-after high-speed rides around.

Having provided the world's leading triathletes with super-fast solo-ride aero bikes for nearly twenty years, Jim Felt's design team was uniquely positioned to deliver the fastest possible "breakaway" bikes for professional racers. The new line made its impressive debut in the 2008 Tour de France with the Garmin Slipstream team.

While professional road race bikes have to adhere to tighter restrictions on shape and dimensions than triathlon bikes, Felt put its wind tunnel experience

with the former to good use in the development of the latter, producing a slim-finned, wheel hugging, internal cable frame shape that can save a minute per hour in a solo breakaway at typical pro-race pace.

Unlike many aero bikes, the latest 2013 AR1 is also impressively light, thanks to a combination of advanced modular construction techniques and materials. By making the frame in sections, the tube formers can squeeze every last gram out of each section of the frame using internal and external formers before baking it. Felt also uses super-tough, featherlight nano-particle-enhanced resin in the carbon fiber panels to deliver maximum strength and stiffness with minimum weight. Add a suite of electrically triggered transmission from Shimano, and this is the ultimate speed machine. **GK**

VOODOO Bizango

2013 • Mountain bike • UK • Standout big-wheeled mountain bike bargain

The Voodoo name has long been associated with designer Joe Murray, who was a big influence in the original sloping top tube bikes introduced by the Rocky Mountain and Kona brands in the late 1980s. Murray started his own Voodoo brand in the 1990s, and produced some typically innovative yet practical bikes.

The mid-1990s was a period of consolidation in the bike industry, and Murray was among many one-man brands that were absorbed into bigger bike groups. In Joe's case, the Voodoo brand was effectively licenced for UK use by auto and cycle supermarket Halfords, which has repositioned it as an aspirational but still affordable headline brand.

Murray is no longer involved in the business, but Halfords has remained true to the pioneering spirit of his brand in this 29-in. (73.5-cm) version of the Bizango, which has a tough and well-shaped frame and a host of details that would often be upgrades on more expensive bikes. The generously fat Maxxis Ardent tires have a fast-rolling, low-profile tread that offset high bike weight but are tough enough to tackle rocky terrain, and the Suntour fork uses a ⅗-in. (1.5-cm) diameter hollow axle to maintain accurate control of the bigger wheels. **GK**

SARACEN Ariel 142

2013 • Mountain bike • UK • Highly entertaining DH-shaped trail bike

These bikes re-established Saracen as innovators rather than just a bargain brand.

In 2012, both the 5½-in. (14-cm) and 6³⁄₁₀-in. (16-cm) suspension-travel bikes used a new tubeset producing a lighter, stiffer version of the same low-slung, tapered head tube, chainguide mount-equipped mainframe. The 6¼-in. (16-cm) version also got a slacker head angle of 66.5 degrees, rather than the usual 68 degrees, and a longer back end for increased stability.

Equipment included gold anodized Kashima-coated Fox shocks and Shimano brakes, but it was the shape of the bike rather than its spec that made it popular. Some aspects of the performance were strong, too: the Fox 36 set a gold standard in line holding and impact control, and the bike sucked up square edges and held speed well, even on rock trails. The geometry was speed friendly, but the Ariel didn't realize its potential when pushed hard through corners. The frame and narrow linkages allowed a lot of flex between the front and rear of the bike, and the hard-compound Schwalbe tires were low on traction. Bolt loosening in the suspension was a problem on production models too, but happily these issues were resolved in this 2013 version, which realizes the bike's full potential. **DB**

SARACEN Kili Flyer

2013 • Mountain bike • UK • Totally up-to-date rebirth of a classic bike name

Every established bike brand has a model name that's become central to its identity. Specialized has its Stumpjumper, Orange has its Five, Turner has its Burner. For Saracen, it is the Kili Flyer.

The name comes from one of the earliest epic two-wheel adventures—a 1984 ride on Saracen bikes by explorer Nick Crane and his cousin Richard Crane to the summit of Mount Kilimanjaro, at 19,341 ft (5895 m) the highest peak in Africa.

Since the Cranes' achievement, the Kili Flyer has come and gone from the Saracen range as the company's fortunes have ebbed and flowed, but the current owners have now made sure that this slice of mountain bike history gets the living memorial it deserves. The 2011 Kili Flyer—a beautifully built, traditional fillet-brazed frame made from Reynolds 853 steel—was deliberately designed with reference to the original Crane bikes.

The latest Kili Flyer has been created by designer Simon Wild to make almost every part of any mountain an absolute blast to ride on. Built around the latest 650B wheels, with downhill bike-style angles, this full-suspension Flyer sits at the summit of current mountain bike performance. **GK**

SANTA CRUZ V10 Carbon

2013 • Downhill bike • USA • The world's lightest-production downhill bike

The refined V10 Carbon is officially the lightest, and, makers Santa Cruz claim, the strongest downhill bike available. It certainly has an impressive pedigree: since its inception, the V10 has taken 64 World Cup podiums, 14 wins, and 2 overall titles.

The first V10 Carbon appeared in 2010, and although it has since remained externally unaltered, Santa Cruz subsequently brought in several new features developed in secret with its Syndicate World Cup racing team. In fact, their South African Greg Minnar won the 2012 World Championships without anyone noticing that he was riding on a bike with a new frame, which features a carbon swingarm in place of the previous aluminum one. It also has a completely new carbon layup in the front triangle, reducing the total weight of the frame and the rear shock to less than 8 lb (3.6 kg).

Unlike nearly all other carbon bike manufacturers, Santa Cruz lay up their frames as one piece, using proprietary internal mandrels to stretch the carbon ply tightly over the entire structure. The V10 Carbon has 10 in. (24 cm) of rear wheel travel, although this can be reduced to the more usual 8 in. (27.2 cm) by riders who think that less is more. **CJ**

LONGWISE EU Bike

2013 • E-bike • China • Electrically assisted urban bike

Chinese company Longwise is one of the first Far Eastern companies to commit to electrically assisted "E-bikes" with a complete range of rides from full-suspension mountain bikes to EU utility bikes.

With an annual production of 800,000 units, Longwise is a big player in the rapidly expanding power-assisted bike market, and it is fully compliant with the latest certification standards.

As the name suggests, the EU bike is aimed at the massive European utility market. Its features include tall, swept-back bars and a comfy sprung saddle to create an upright, high-visibility riding position. Luggage racks are pre-fitted front and rear. Full guards, including a plastic chainguard, keep road and chain grime off clothes, a dynamo light system gives

nighttime safety, and a double-sided kickstand makes for easy parking.

Although the frame is alloy, which is lighter than steel, the bike is heavy, but fortunately it also has a 250-watt motor powered by a lithium ion battery mounted behind the seat tube. This gives a maximum speed of 15 mph (22 kph) and a range of 27 mi (43 km) from a three- to five-hour recharge. The motor is controlled through an LCD screen on the bars which gives speed, distance, and battery data, as well as speed control. More conventional power comes through a 7-speed Shimano Nexus derailleur system, which is controlled through a twist shifter on the right-hand side of the bar.

The result is a cost-effective, comfortable, and practical budget E-bike with global sales potential. **GK**

DOLAN Tuono SL

2013 • Road bike • UK • Super-light carbon fiber racer from top UK designer

Terry Dolan has been synonymous with bikes for Britain's top riders since Chris Boardman started breaking records on them in the early 1990s. Every Dolan product—be it a classic with steel tubes or the latest carbon fiber composite machine—reflects and benefits from his vast experience with velocipedes.

That's certainly true of this model. With an Asian-built frame weighing less than 2 lb 3 oz (1 kg) and a fork weight of under 14 oz (400 g), it's a super-light machine, and yet, even fully loaded with SRAM's flagship Red transmission, it costs less than most competing framesets sold separately. With a total weight of 14½ oz (6.6 kg), this bike absolutely begs to be blasted up hills without so much as a glance back at the chasing pack.

Neither does the low weight come at the cost of limp power delivery. Outsized mainframe tubes and rear stays, together with the much stiffer feel underfoot of the new-generation SRAM chainset, catapult this bike over contour lines with utter contempt for such minor obstructions. Even at this weight, front-end stiffness through the alloy bar and stem is good enough to bully hills into submission while standing on the pedals—and the fun doesn't stop when you reach the top; descents are every bit as exhilarating.

While flyweight bikes are often a scary prospect as slopes steepen and corners tighten, the Tuono SL is happy to turn and burn with the best of them. There's no wonder that it started winning awards from professional testers as soon as it appeared. **GK**

CANYON Ultimate AL
2013 • Road bike • Germany • Ultra-responsive racer proves alloy can still match carbon

While Canyon follow the majority of brands in making their flagship models out of carbon fiber, the 2013 model of its top-level alloy-frame machine is truly worthy of the "Ultimate" badge it sports on its tough black anodized flanks. At 2¾ lb (1250 g) for a medium-size frame, the Ultimate was only fractionally heavier than the carbon frames of similarly priced bikes.

Canyon partnered the Ultimate frame with the same One One Four SLX full-carbon fork and Acros Ai integrated composite headset as their top-line bikes, bringing full chassis weight in under that of many more expensive carbon bikes. Canyon also wove basalt fibers into its VCLS forks and seatposts to reduce vibration

> ## "Powerfully punchy, infectiously combative, inspiringly responsive package at a great price."
> bikeradar.com

transmission to the rider and offset the generally more harsh ride of large-diameter tubing. Buyers could also choose Canyon's unique split shaft Post 2.0 suspension seatpost to provide even more saddle float.

Canyon's buy-online model also provided extremely good spec levels on complete bikes, including components such as Mavic wheels and superlight Ritchey kit. The German designers hadn't skimped on design features either. The neat Acros bearing head tube backed onto a big down tube that swelled to swallow the oversized press-fit bottom bracket. Vertical torque control was assured by the asymmetrically shaped and sideways offset Maximus seat tube to convert the low weight into dramatic launch out of corners or up climbs in any gear. **GK**

THORN Raven
2013 • All-rounder bike • UK • Versatile on- and off-road tourer

Possibly the ultimate rough-stuff all-rounder, the Raven tackles the current age's two most popular types of cycling in a new way. Buyers don't have to choose between one bike that is uniquely adapted for use off road and another that will only really work on tarmac: They can here get a bike that fulfills both functions.

The manufacturer, Thorn, is a touring specialist based in fantastic cycling country on the Somerset Levels in England's West Country. The company was founded by Robin Thorn in 1984, and has gradually refined the design of its bikes ever since. The Raven is a sturdy but lightweight tourer that is equally at home on and off the road.

Part of the secret of the Raven's versatility is the range of optional extras. The wheels are always tough 26-in. (66-cm) units, but buyers can choose between drop or straight handlebars, long or short wheelbases, and a massive selection of ten different frame sizes.

The basic design and build of the Raven are also important. The frame is made of high-tensile, heat-treated, double-butted chromoly steel chosen for its strength, durability, and repairability. It's also good at accommodating touring extras, such as water-bottle holders, trip computers, and load carriers.

Derailleurs are swapped for a 14-speed Rohloff Speedhub system that is more expensive and noisier than normal gears but acclaimed for its reliability, low maintenance, and stationary changes. With no dangling derailleurs, the bike is easier to transport too. The Rohloff hub is operated via a grip shifter on the straight bars or a new twist shifter that can be fitted to drop bars near the stem.

In its sales literature, Thorn claims that the Raven is "the most versatile bicycle on the market," and no one has yet gainsaid them. **SH**

STIJL Lear's All Fast Mountain 29er

2013 • Mountain bike • USA • Custom single-speed steel leftie

When advertising agency executive Mike Lear wanted a new bike he knew who to commission to make it: Hinmaton Hisler of Stijl, a builder of extreme mountain bikes for Cirque du Soleil performer Lance Trappe.

Lear's machine had several distinctive features suited to his desire for the "feel" of his previous big mountain bikes but with more aptitude for cross-country racing.

The result was this striking bike, fitted with 29er-size wheels for that big-bike feel. The frame was lightweight and responsive, thanks to fillet-brazed steel from Columbus and True Temper. The custom geometry included a slack head angle of 69 degrees for confident descending and a very tight rear triangle for pin-sharp cornering.

Other special features included a Gates Carbon Drive belt system instead of a conventional chain, and the latest carbon Lefty fork from Cannondale.

The components included Rocker drop-outs from Paragon Machineworks, a tapered head tube from Loco-Machine, and a carbon crankset from Specialized S-Works. Ritchey supplied the bars and stem, while pedals and disc brakes are Shimano XT. Wheels are Stan's Race Gold laced to custom Industry Nine hubs wearing fat Specialized Ground Control tires, sealed with Stan's tubeless sealant. The understated paint job was by Sonny Naylor of Naylor Finishes.

For purity Lear chose to have his off-roader built as a single-speed. But as the fully-built bike only weighs 20.7lbs (9.4kg), it still tackles gradients easily. **SH**

SANTA CRUZ Bronson

2013 • Mountain bike • USA • Carbon fiber 650B-wheeled superbike

The current speed of innovation across the biking world is constantly forcing manufacturers to make difficult choices about their response to new technology: should they embrace it, ignore it, or come up with something totally different of their own?

When it comes to wheel size or frame changes, these questions are even more awkward if they are building in carbon fiber. Alloy frames can be altered fairly easily after initial production, but carbon incurs far greater tool costs. Once they've been made, carbon molds are impossible to change apart from minor tweaks, which is why most firms like Santa Cruz do the prototype riding with hand-built alloy "mules."

Having finished that phase of development, however, Santa Cruz banished its doubts and committed wholeheartedly to the new intermediate 650B wheel size with this full-carbon frameset that weighs an ultralight 5⅓ lb (2.4 kg), despite outstanding stiffness.

The Bronson also features 6³⁄₁₀ in. (16 cm) of suspension stroke to make it very fast rolling yet chaos capable. It follows in a long line of successful similar Santa Cruz bikes, such as the Bullitt and the Nomad. If proof were needed of the new contender's performance, it came only a month after it was launched when it was ridden by ex-World Champion Steve Peat of the Santa Cruz Syndicate team to a place on the podium at the Sea Otter Classic in Monterey, California.

An alternative version of the Bronson offers the same package on an alloy frame at a more affordable (though still premium) price. **GK**

STORCK Aernario Platinum

2013 • Road bike • Germany • Ultra-advanced, test-beating über-bike

The German bike market has always been heavily influenced by press reviews, particularly those that appear in *Tour* magazine, which scientifically tests a wider range of features—including weight, stiffness, and, more recently, aerodynamics—than, it is generally agreed, any other publication.

Ever since he founded his company in 1995, Marcus Storck has produced nothing but unashamedly performance-oriented, cost-no-object superbikes. Models like the Scenario and Fascenario have kept Storck at or near the top of the *Tour* test charts throughout their history, despite increasing competition from rival brands.

In 2013 Storck introduced the Aernario Platinum frame, a properly premium flagship machine based on the Scenario and taking many design cues from the extremely successful Fascenario. The ultra-high-quality, hand-laid carbon fiber sheets of the new bike's frame meant that, despite its aerodynamic shaping, the chassis remained extremely light and stiff. When *Tour* magazine scientists got their hands on it, they found that the wind resistance was between 1.1 and 1.5—the lowest recorded by the magazine in more than twenty years of testing.

The ride tests were equally auspicious: handling and comfort levels set new benchmark levels. Summarizing their findings, the editors—who do not go in for frothy hyperbole—declared that the Aernario Platinum had "the best frame ever . . . with a dreamlike ride quality." **GK**

PINARELLO Dogma Visconti

2013 • Road bike • Italy • Scorer of a memorable Giro d'Italia victory in its home city

While back-to-back Tour de France wins under Team Sky riders Bradley Wiggins and Chris Froome were the most prestigious honors taken by Pinarello's flagship Dogma race bike in the 2012 and 2013 seasons, they were not the only ones. Equally remarkable in its way was Giovanni Visconti's solo victory for the Spanish Movistar team on Stage 17 of the 2013 Giro d'Italia.

This was not Visconti's first win in that year's event—he had previously triumphed at the summit of Col du Galibier on one of the Giro's rare excursions over the border into France. While this stage victory represented an emphatic return to form for the rider after a troubled 2012 season, which had ended in suspension, Visconti's second win had even greater symbolic significance for Pinarello, because the finishing line was in the company's home city of Vicenza. It is also the base of Campognolo, which was celebrating its eightieth anniversary in that year, and had supplied the wheels for the victor's Dogma 65.1 Think 2 bike.

Visconti's performance helped to ease misgivings about the Dogma's handling, the quality of which had been questioned after the crashes that would eventually see Bradley Wiggins retire from the Giro.

Thus when Visconti, having broken free of the pursuing pack with 10 mi (16 km) to go, and pushed his advantage home on the twisting final descent, crossed the line first, he scored an unusually holistic victory for himself, his team (their third in that year's Giro), and the makers of his bike and equipment. **GK**

SPECIALIZED Venge Cav 100

2013 • Road bike • USA • Unique custom machine to mark landmark 100th victory of Mark Cavendish

British professional road-race sprinter Mark Cavendish is known as "The Manx Missile" because he was born in the Isle of Man, whose natives are termed "Manxmen" and "Manxwomen." When he achieved his landmark 100th professional race victory in Stage 12 of the Giro d'Italia in May 2013—a dash to the head of the pack to the finish line in a rain-lashed Treviso—his bike sponsors marked the occasion by presenting him with a custom version of what was described as his "normal" S-Works Venge.

"Normal" is not really the right word, however, because even the standard Venge is a truly outstanding machine. The constructors of the S-Works variant have taken the Venge features that enable Cavendish to accelerate quickly to speeds of more than 40 mph (64 kph)—advanced aerodynamic profiling of the downtube, curving top tube and seat tube—and then reduced the overall weight and increased the stiffness through the use of carbon fiber construction techniques developed in partnership with renowned British Formula 1 motor racing team McLaren.

The result is a phenomenally fast all-rounder. Structurally, the frame of this special edition is no different from that of the "normal" bike, but it has a matte black-and-gray base coat and a top tube streaked with graphic and text strips celebrating Cavendish's greatest victories. Along the frame tubes a green pinstripe matches the color of the Points Winner jersey the rider claimed at the 2012 Tour de France.

An identical frame—with the addition of Cav's signature on a decal on the bottom bracket block—was made available for sale as a limited edition chassis through Specialized flagship stores. Ironically, Cavendish's voracious appetite for victory meant the bike was soon out of date, as he scored his 101st victory only a few days after becoming a centurion. **GK**

"It's a bike that I believe is the fastest bike in the world."

Mark Cavendish, 2013

◁ Cavendish crosses the finishing line at the Giro d'Italia in May 2013.

MERLIN Extralight

2013 • Mountain bike • USA • Rebirth of classic titanium mountain bike

Back in the late 1980s, the pioneering days of early titanium mountain bikes, Merlin was a world leader. Merlin Metalworks, as it was called then, was one of the first to introduce titanium as a material for mountain bikes and bring the world outsized titanium tubesets and S-bend chain- and seatstays.

Merlin road bikes were pioneers too, as they were among the first to have titanium butted tubing.

Fast forward a quarter of a century and carbon is the material of choice for many pro riders. Merlin had all but disappeared under a succession of different owners but has now been revived under a new parent company. So what material should the new Merlin bikes use?

"We've never lost our feelings for the simple elegance and precision of Merlin frames."

Competitive Cyclist, new owners of Merlin

The Extralight is the answer. It's a classic titanium mountain bike. It may not be as light as the top carbon machines but has ride quality, comfort, and great handling in its favor. And it's got that retro touch to take riders back to Merlin's glory days.

The new owners of the Merlin brand, Competitive Cyclist, arranged for the Extralight to be built by Form Cycles of Arizona using double-butted brushed titanium oversized tubing of aerospace quality. It's an all-American product, featuring an ENVE composite carbon fork, Chris King headset, and PressFit bottom bracket. There are S-bend chainstays, and tubing diameters and angles that are tuned for each different frame size. The company claims this creates a custom feel and a more compliant ride than any previous Merlin. **SH**

MERIDA Scultura

2013 • Road bike • Taiwan • Pro team road bike from bike superpower

As the Western bike industry moved most of its production to Taiwan in the 1980s and 1990s, Merida was one of the manufacturers that grew to support the sudden increase in production. Its own range of bikes peaked in public profile when it replaced renowned Italian brand Wilier as supplier to the Lampre Pro Tour team for the 2013 season.

The Scultura SL capitalizes on Merida's extensive carbon fiber experience to produce a smoothly sculpted 29-oz (0.8-kg) frameset and a similarly lightweight fork. The frame incorporates the latest press-fit crank-bearing design to enable it to handle the sprinting power of some of the strongest riders in the world. The Scultura design isn't all about stiffness, though: the carbon fiber includes "bio-flax" fiber sheets sandwiched into the structure to soak up high-frequency buzz from rough road surfaces. The ⅜-in. (1-cm) rear stays are the minimum allowed in racing, and the fork is shaped to keep supple and connected to the road on fast descents, rather than skipping about as super-stiff bikes sometimes do.

A detailed look at the team-issue Scultura SL also reveals some interesting tweaks designed to help the bike withstand the buffeting that it will routinely take from a pro rider. To cope with the continual drinking needs of team riders on 125-mi (200-km) race days, the water bottle bolt positions are reinforced with additional material. The frame is strengthened at the points where it will be clamped to team car racks, and the front derailleur hanger is stiffer too.

This bike may not be a world-beater—it is neither sharp nor stiff enough under full-power stomping—but it offers a superb ride, especially at the budget price, which at the time of publication was just under $2,500 (£1,500). **GK**

Merida bikes and the Lampre pro team have proved a winning combination. ▣

TREK Stache

2013 • Mountain bike • USA • Rugged trail 29er

One of the most refreshing things about bicycles is that some of the biggest brands got where they are through continual innovation rather than by bland mass-market unit selling. That's certainly the case with Trek's Stache big wheeler, which is the latest in a line of category-blurring, rule-bending hardtails from one of the industry's most eclectic and experienced array of in-house thinkers.

The eye-catching bright rust color of the Stache's frame harks back to the deliberately in-your-face Trek 96, which featured a 29-in. (73.5-cm) front wheel and a 26-in. (66-cm) rear wheel on a single-speed alloy frame, with a long-travel Maverick fork plugged in the front. A comparable level of unorthodoxy has been applied to the new series by the principal developers—longtime

Trek racers and test riders Travis Brown and Andrew Shandro.

While the wheels are both 29ers, the rear one is positioned as close to the center of the frame as possible in order to keep it responsive on tight trails. The seat tube is shaped to leave enough room between tire and tube in muddy conditions, and has an exit port for an internally routed saddle dropper seatpost if you need to get your seat out of the way on the steepest descents. The surprisingly nimble but never nervous handling is the work of mountain bike pioneer Gary Fisher.

The whole ride is cushioned on big tires from Keith Bontrager, a mountain bike pioneer who joined the Trek organization in 1995. **GK**

TREK Domane 6.9

2013 • Road bike • USA • Radical scissor-framed road smoother

---

The Domane is something of a game changer in the road bike market. While many companies have used specific carbon fiber layups to reduce the transmission of road vibration, Trek has introduced a totally new and radical aid to smoother riding performance that has been a massive hit with reviewers, riders, and even top-level racers.

The soft-riding composite layup of the fork is immediately noticeable in the way it deals with the normal hammer of potholes, frost damage, and wrist- and shoulder-fatiguing asphalt acne. It uses an extended forward rake for greater shock absorption, while gel pads are built into the IsoSpeed handlebars.

The really radical part of the Domane is the joins between the IsoSpeed main tubes. Instead of

a conventional solid junction between the almost vertical seat tube, horizontal top tube, and seatstays, the "decoupled" seat tube uses a cartridge bearing to leave it free to pivot in relation to the top tube and stays. This decoupler junction allows the seat to flex vertically by 50 percent more than Trek's conventional (but still notably comfortable) Madone model for an extremely smooth ride.

On rough sections, riders can stay comfortably seated rather than bouncing around in the saddle or hovering above it. This was clearly demonstrated when Trek-sponsored Classics legend Fabien Cancellara powered his top-of-the-range 6 Series Domane to victory across the punishing cobbled sections of the epic Paris–Roubaix race in 2013. **GK**

WHYTE 109S

2013 • Mountain bike • UK • Rapid and outstandingly agile 29er

While the 4-in. (10-cm) travel, 29-in. (73.5-cm) wheel segment is generally associated with bike makers who rank efficiency higher than playfulness, Whyte has made a deliberate decision to create a fun bike rather than just a fast one. The hydro-formed alloy frame is tough, stiff, and tipped with a 5⅗ x ½-in. (14.2 x 1.2-cm) screw-through axle. The chainstays are super-short despite decent tire space, the bearings are warranted for life, and it's dropper-seatpost ready too. The Fox CTD shock and fork prove why they're the benchmark dampers every time you hit a rough section, and the single-finger XT brakes keep a firm grasp on your speed. The clutch mech-stabilized shift of the XT transmission is light but accurate. Whyte's own carbon-rimmed wheels are shod with fast-rolling Maxxis Ikon tires.

The Fox shock is perfectly tuned for the new Whyte suspension too, with the "trail" setting consistently screening out chatter and rubble far better than its efficiently firm pedaling feel suggests it should.

The combination of smooth suspension, ultra-short back end, and long and relatively slack front end makes the Whyte 109S handle quite differently from almost any other 29er. With the back end tucked in tight, the front end lifts easily off drops or for hauling round climbing hairpins, so you can ride it really dynamically on lip, hip, pump, and jump trails. The excellent balance and tight tracking also let you pick fights with tree roots or off-camber sections in a most un-29erish way to give the 109S a fantastically agile and lighthearted feel. **GK**

CUBE Stereo HPC SLT

2013 • Mountain bike • Germany • Big, super-light suspension Alp bike

The success of Cube's ultra-light Stereo HPC SL is a clear reflection of a strong modern trend in the German mountain bike market.

Traditionally, most of Germany's vast legions of mountain bikers rode in mass-participation marathon events and epic stage races such as the famous TransAlp Challenge. Bike makers catered for them by producing machines with lots of suspension that were tuned for maximum efficiency when pedaling up brutally long climbs.

Since the late twentieth century, however, tastes have changed, and a significant number of German riders now prefer downhill courses. Manufacturers have responded accordingly by installing the softer suspension feel of British and French Alp bikes.

Weight and efficient drive are still important, though, and it is these considerations that have inspired the creation of the phenomenal Stereo HPC SLT.

This bike combines a 4½-lb (2.08-kg) frame with a cost-no-object carbon fiber-rich SRAM, Reynolds, and Race Face equipment list to keep total weight below 22 lb (10 kg). This would be impressive even on a 650B-wheeled hardtail bike, but the Stereo delivers more than 6¼ in. (16 cm) of wheel movement at either end. Screw-through wheel axles front and rear also underline the excellent stiffness of the frame to make this a bike that can climb Alps as quickly as the fastest race machines and match downhill bikes on the descents. This bike is the rare product that is better than the hype claims it is. **GK**

OLYMPIA Rex

2013 • Touring bike • Italy • Forward-thinking manufacturer's moment of nostalgia

Italy's second-oldest bicycle maker after Bianchi, Olympia started business in Milan in 1893, and has been renowned ever since for its ability to merge craftsmanship with style. The company manufactures everything from mountain bikes to lightweight racers, and in 2013 added to its range this retro cruiser, a wonderful synthesis of modern technology with the classic beauty of a bygone age.

The Rex looks like it would be quite at home touring the streets of 1950s Rome. It comes with drawn-steel tubes connected by seamless joints and an 1895 Olympia logo prominently displayed on the fork headset. The touring handlebars have eye-catching chrome work, as well as punched Olympia brake levers and rod brakes. The spokes are stainless steel, and the lovely saddle is a Brooks Model B67 Aged Leather (the grips are Brooks as well). Optional (but why be without them?) canvas bags attach to the rear rack.

Relatively unknown outside Italy, Olympia was the first European manufacturer to produce aluminum and carbon frames, and the first Italian company to make mountain bikes. Today it is a world leader in hydro-formed alloys and fluid-molded carbon frame-making techniques. Olympia continues to buck the trend of outsourcing frames to the Far East by continuing to make all its bicycles in Piove di Sacco, a small town near Venice in northeastern Italy. Few manufacturers can boast such an intimate connection with the evolution of the bicycle as Olympia has enjoyed over more than a century. **BS**

GLOBE Work 3

2013 • Commuter bike • USA • Individually styled urban ride

Designed as a city commuter and errand runner, the Globe Work 3 comes with a long head tube, a short, high stem, and handlebars swept back at an angle of 16 degrees. This configuration makes good urban sense because it allows riders to sit in an upright position with arms not overly extended, so they can do all the scanning around and behind that urban cycling requires without needing to make a chiropractor as their final stop at the end of the day.

The Work 3 has an aluminum frame and a Shimano Nexus 7-speed internal gear hub that makes for easy shifting and low maintenance—the perfect recipe for a town bike, although it could perhaps benefit from having a larger sprocket. And its Infinity tires—width a shade less than 1½ in. (3.8 cm)—come with puncture-resistant belts and reflective sidewalls. Because commuter bikes are often left outside office buildings during working hours, the Work 3 also features specialized bolts to secure the seatpost, stem, and handlebars.

It also is available as a step-through, and both versions come with all the mounts needed to accommodate a range of urban accessories as well as full fenders and a (partial) chainguard, so you don't have to fiddle around with annoying cycle clips.

This bike neither is nor aspires to be the conveyance for cyclists who burst into vigorous sprints the moment the light turns green. Conversely, sedate riders looking for comfort may find that the Globe Work 3 is just the bike they've been looking for. **BS**

MSC Blast

2013 • Mountain bike • Spain • Super-light
carbon fiber Spaniard

MSC began in Barcelona, Spain, in 1999, when father
and son Luis and Ferran Marias started designing light
but affordable kit for racers.

Their first bike project was the F1 downhill model,
which has racked up four World Championship titles
since its introduction in 2003.

In spite of the F1's success, it was MSC's opening
of a carbon fiber production line in Taiwan that
really launched its range onto the world scene. The
prime mover of its rapid growth has been the Blast
4⁷⁄₁₀-in. (120-mm) travel all-rounder. This bike's current
incarnation was co-developed with students in the
AMADE Tech Center of Girona University, and their
influence and design dedication are obvious in the
carbon fiber frameset, which is so light that complete
bikes built around it are lighter than most race hardtails,
let alone proper full-suspension bikes with remote-
controlled rear shocks.

Carboflex rear stays let the back end move enough
to permit full travel, but without the extra weight.
Transformer rear drop-outs enable the frame to be
fitted with either conventional quick-release or screw-
in axled rear wheels. The oversize BB30 makes it easy to
fit any crankset you want, too. **GK**

SCOTT Genius 700/900

2013 • Mountain bike • Switzerland • Light,
remote-controlled shape and suspension change bike

A decade after the appearance of the original Genius,
Scott released a totally new bike that's available with
either 27½-in. (70-cm) or 29-in. (73.5-cm) wheels.

Based around an implausibly light 5-lb (2.2-kg)
frame and shock, the flagship SL models also get a
top spec that includes Syncros carbon fiber wheels,
handlebar, saddle, and stem, plus SRAM carbon cranks.

The unique Equalizer shock gives an "Open"
downhill mode, a "Traction" mode for climbing, and a
"Locked" mode for sprinting; changes are made at the
flick of a handlebar-mounted button.

The 650B "inbetweeners" on the 700 series allow
just under 6 in. (15 cm) of wheel travel, and thus
provide better agility on really tough tracks and trails.
The 700s also get remote-control saddle droppers so
you don't injure yourself on the seat when the bike is
bouncing around underneath you on a crazy downhill.

The larger 900SL has less clearance between tire
and frame, and its suspension is limited to just over 5 in.
(13 cm). It's an amazingly fast bike for blasting along
rocky trails or up challenging climbs.

Both bikes also come in more affordable alloy-
framed versions, but the carbon fiber SL bikes are the
real showstoppers. **GK**

◁ MSC's Blast looks great on the trails and the weighing scales.

SCOTT Gambler 10

2013 • Downhill bike • Switzerland • Developed with British racer Brendan Fairclough

Introduced in 2008, the original Gambler remained largely unaltered, apart from a different coat of paint every season, until 2012, when Scott hired World Cup racer Brendan Fairclough to develop a new version.

Launched in the following year, the Gambler 10 is much more than an update; it is a complete redesign, with a new suspension system, new geometry, and an all-round new look.

The original Gambler was highly adaptable. You could adjust the suspension from 7 in. (17.8 cm) to 9½ in. (24 cm); you could lengthen the wheelbase using a different set of drop-outs, and you could alter the head angle using an adjustable head tube sleeve.

The new Gambler has retained these features within a more refined package. The bottom bracket

height is adjustable though a chip on the bottom shock mount and the chainstay length is also changeable through Scott's IDS X drop-out system. The overall aim is to allow riders to tailor their ride to their own requirements.

Another innovation on the Gambler 10 is Floating Link, a suspension system very similar to Dave Weagle's DELTA link. It gives the suspension a dual progressive curve by using shorter actuating links and a main single pivot. The result is not only one of the fastest and most easily tunable off-the-peg downhill race machines on the market, but also the weapon of choice for the Scott Gstaad race team. Scott's collaboration with Fairclough has produced a truly World Cup-level bike for a worldwide clientele. **CJ**

SCOTT Plasma

2013 • Aero bike • Switzerland • The fastest Tour de France bike in history

Scott's Plasma family has always been at the forefront of aero bike development, and this is the model that in 2013 won the fastest-ever Tour de France stage.

This triumph came in the team trial event in Nice as Australian Simon Gerrans led his Team Orica Green Edge over the line in less than 26 minutes for the 17-mi. (27 km) course.

The Plasma has ultra-thin straight-bladed forks extending upward into an integrated stem that fits flush with the flat top tube. The headbox junction is extended as far back as race regulations allow. The seat cluster uses super-broad rear stays that sync with the top of the seat tube and top tube in a wind-cutting wing above the wheel-hugging curve of the lower section. While most of these features are shared with

other top-end aero machines, the Plasma's chainstays are particularly distinctive. Staying parallel to the wheel spokes for most of their length, they suddenly kick outward and upward ahead of the hub, shrouding the spinning cassette and the turbulence it creates.

The bike ridden by Gerrans has extras found only on a pro bike. Shimano's electric Di2 aero shifting buttons make it possible to change gear on both the tri-bar extensions and the conventional base bars. This was a massive advantage on the twisting, turning Nice course. However, Shimano hadn't released an update of the system to cope with the new 11-speed Dura Ace gears used by Orica Green Edge, so a 10-speed Ultegra Di2 rear mech was used, with the battery mounted under the saddle to minimize drag. **GK**

ELECTRA Flatfoot

2013 • Leisure bicycle • USA • Super-cool limited-edition cruiser

For most of the twentieth century, cruisers were the only bikes that sold in significant numbers in the United States. These single-speed, coaster-brake machines certainly weren't designed for speed. Balloon tires and big saddles combined with swept-back bars to give a very relaxed Harley-Davidson-style ride; many frames even had fake fuel tanks fitted to complete the motorbike illusion. Cruisers spawned the first mountain bikes, but that didn't mean the parent breed died out. On the contrary, its health has been maintained by dedicated cruiser companies, one of which, Electra, now offer it in both classic and contemporary versions.

Electra's Flatfoot series cruiser bikes are particularly interesting because they take the already relaxed ride position of a conventional cruiser and make it even more caricatured. Handlebars measuring 28 in. (71 cm) curve right back round toward the rider for a super-upright position. The cranks have been moved forward in the frame: this not only increases the Harley effect but also means that the rider's feet can sit flat on the floor with the saddle at riding height—hence the name Flatfoot. Alloy frames and fast-rolling balloon tires mean these bikes aren't slow, but their major selling point is the limited-edition designs.

Not content with a massive range of hand-painted finishes, from the hot rod-flamed "Ghost Rider" to the floral pattern "Daisy," Electra goes all out with accessories that include frame-design matched saddles, grips, and two-tone bells, handlebar tassles, and even a range of baskets and racks. **BS**

FELT DA

2013 • Triathlon bike • USA • Electric shift-equipped aero bike

Felt has dominated the triathlon bike scene ever since Jim Felt built an Ironman-winning bike for Paula Newby-Fraser in 1991. The current flagship DA model is a truly cutting-edge machine for people who want to get maximum solo speed out of their ride.

While wind-cheating, extended frame-and-fork combinations have become commonplace on top-flight aero superbikes, Felt was one of the first brands to produce the cunning "bayonet." This design splits the upper end of the fork so it sits both inside and in front of the mainframe with a direct mounted stem on top to hold the bars with minimum interruption of airflow. The DA1 also uses super-narrow tubes with "wheel hugger" cutouts to keep wind flow onto the spinning rims as drag-free as possible. The rims themselves are state-of-the-art, bulged-profile, deep-section Firecrest designs from fellow aero innovators Zipp; in combination with the frame aerodynamics, these rims can slice minutes off an Ironman bike leg.

True to its finger-on-the-pulse reputation, Felt was also one of the first companies to fit the triathlon version of Shimano's radical Di2 transmission onto an off-the-peg bike. The triathlon version is a proper game changer too, because extra shift buttons can be added to the conventional base bars as well as the extensions. This means that riders can change gear while going into or coming out of corners or climbing without letting go of the bars.

Add a superbly balanced, comfortable ride, and the DA1 is a true benchmark in triathlon bike design. **GK**

PAUL HEWITT Grampian Rohloff

2013 • Touring bike • UK • Versatile custom tourer with Rohloff 14-gear hub

Every Paul Hewitt bike is built by hand in Leyland, England, to the customer's precise specifications.

In the case of the Grampian Rohloff, the buyer wanted a lightweight touring bike with sufficient clearance for larger tires and mudguards, a green frame, and red anodized components.

The bike's specification was based around a TIG-welded frame with Reynolds 725 tubing made of heat-treated thin-gauge, tight-tolerance seamless chrome molybdenum steel.

The bike was finished in a zinc-primed, lacquered green powder coat. The final decorative touches were individually designed red and silver transfers and a brass headbadge, hand made by Jen Green in Philadelphia. The Rohloff 14-speed hub gear system had a red anodized finish, which matched the Hope headset, headset spacers, stem, and skewers.

The speedhub and disc brakes were built into DT trekking rims, custom built by Hewitt himself using high-quality DT Swiss spokes. The rims were then shod with Schwalbe Marathon touring tires. The machine was completed with USE Summit aluminum bars, Tubus rear carrier, SKS P-45 mudguards, Selle Italia Max Flite Gelflow saddle, and a black Hope seatpost. **SH**

MAWIS Custom

2013 • Mountain bike • Germany • Handmade custom titanium bike

For a commercial undertaking that exists in order to sell its products, Mawis is remarkably publicity-shy. It doesn't publish its street address or phone number because it doesn't want its craftsmen to be disturbed. It can be contacted only by email.

The man behind the company is Mathias Scherer, who keeps an equally low profile, preferring to let his high-end bikes do his talking for him. Perhaps that's understandable when the bikes look as good as this.

Scherer works only with TIG-welded titanium frames and, undisturbed by the telephone, creates machines for road and mountain that are highly desirable but nameless: "We don't do models named 'Mountaingoat' or 'Lightning,'" says Mawis. "Your frame carries your name on its top tube, and that's the only name it will ever get."

The bikes are hand built after extensive discussions with the prospective client, the taking of full measurements, and computer-aided design. Then all sorts of options are possible, from simple fixies to sophisticated groupsets and S&S couplers.

Mawis bespoke frames start at $3,000 (£1,900) for a road frame and $3,300 (£2,000) for a mountain bike. Extras and parts add considerably to this total. **SH**

SANTA CRUZ Chameleon
2013 • Mountain bike • USA • Latest version of an original hardcore classic

The Chameleon was one of the first truly versatile hardcore hardtails, and its continued evolution means the latest bike is every bit as much belligerent fun as the original.

While Santa Cruz's carbon fiber bikes have been getting most of the limelight in recent years, the Chameleon has been aggressively reworked to prove that alloy frames can still stand up to hi-tech knitted machines. A switch to a new high-pressure oil-shaped hydro-formed tubeset has enabled the Californian designers to shave 1 lb (450 g) off this Asian-built frame. To keep its truly versatile credentials intact, the rear of the frame can still be fitted with either fixed- or adjustable-position wheel mounts for tuning chain tension and handling geometry. This no-holds-barred frame comes with built-in mounts for a chain-retaining roller device which you'd normally see only on dedicated downhill machines. Santa Cruz has even made the frame strong enough to take a 6³⁄₁₀-in (160-mm) fork.

This latest Chameleon has been given a slacker steering angle for more grunt when holding a line, even when rocks, roots, and ruts are trying to snatch the tires from underneath the rider. It is a worthy successor to its much-loved predecessors. **GK**

WHYTE 909
2013 • Mountain bike • UK • Lightweight yet tough showcase for the latest wheel sizes

The 26-in. (66-cm) wheel became the norm in mountain biking for no better reason than that it was the size used by the beach cruisers that formed the basis of early Frankenstein-style lash-ups. As pioneers such as Keith Bontrager started to cut down road racing rims to use in lightweight mountain bike wheels, and tire manufacturers such as Araya started to make dedicated off-road rubber, its position as the preferred wheel size was cemented for the next thirty years. Twenty-nine-inch (73.5-cm) wheels gradually gained ground with cross-country riders in pursuit of faster, smoother-rolling performance. The process of designing and refining properly competitive components in the new wheel size took over a decade after Gary Fisher first pushed the concept with the backing of parent company Trek. Even then, 29ers were still regarded as a niche segment for specialist usage.

That makes the sudden popularity of 650B or 27½-in. (70-cm) wheels all the more surprising.

The 909 hardtail is a fine example of the new breed. It combines the traction and stability of the 29er 829 with the agility and responsiveness of the 26er 19, to which Whyte has added 11-speed SRAM components to maximize performance on punishing trails. **GK**

CYFAC Absolu

2013 • Road bike • France • High-end French carbon road racer

Francis Quillon was an amateur sprint racer who made the French national team. As a sideline, he worked in one of his sponsor's workshops, repairing his teammates' bikes. Quillon progressed to painting frames with sponsors' names, and then to building complete new machines for pro racers. Eventually he was supplying sets of frames to whole professional racing teams.

In 1982 Quillon opened his own business, Cyfac. The name is a mix of abbreviations and initials that roughly translates as "handmade bike frames." Since then, Cyfac bikes have been ridden to many race victories, including Paris–Roubaix, Liège–Bastogne–Liège, and the Giro d'Italia.

"This is an extremely versatile, 'do-anything' machine of a decidedly superior type."

Road Cycling UK

The Absolu V2 is the latest version of Cyfac's high-performance road frameset. It's made of Asian-sourced carbon fiber tubing with chunky Kevlar reinforcements. The geometry is conventional, with a parallel top tube, but carefully weighted with a tapered and outsized front end to give a more reactive ride and to hide the bearings.

With the frame alone costing more than $6,200 (£4,000), the Absolu is packed with sophistication: its features include sub-10½-oz (300-g) carbon forks, full-carbon rear drop-outs with alloy strike plates for increased durability, a replaceable derailleur hanger, internal rear brake cable routing, and painted carbon cages. Off-the-shelf bikes come in five sizes, or custom builds are available at extra cost. **SH**

HOBO Weirdy Beardy

2013 • Road bike • UK • Handmade mix of classic and modern styling

The booming UK handmade bike scene is certainly innovative in one respect—the names of its products.

Maker of the Weirdy Beardy, Hobo is a Coventry-based outfit whose bikes are designed by Alexander Hatfield and Mike Mudd and built by the city's long-established frame-maker, Lee Cooper.

Hobo's stated aim is to provide "traditional English touring and street bicycles with a true sense of style." So the Weirdy Beardy is not that weird after all. In fact, it's clearly designed to be a traditional touring bike, with a frame geometry that can carry big loads over extensive distances. It has all the makings of a comfortable, durable bike for long commutes, day trips, or far-flung expeditions.

The Weirdy is made with outsized tubing for strength and looks; its buyers have a choice of Reynolds 631 or the more expensive 853. The design details include capped seatstays, front and rear stainless steel drop-outs, and cast lugs at the joints. The bottom bracket features integral cable routing and is cast too.

The oval chainstays and wide-cast fork crown create clearance for bigger tires and mudguards. And the Weirdy Beardy has a very comprehensive collection of stainless braze-ons: down tube bosses, four-point pannier mounts (front and rear), three pairs of bottle-cage bosses, and various mudguard mounts and pump mounts behind the seat tube.

Prices for the frame and fork start at around $1,700 (£1,100). Complete bikes are made up with mostly Velo Orange components, such as the VO rims and crankset, although the mudguards come from Honjo, and the bike rolls on Campagnolo hubs.

Incidentally, other Hobo bikes have similarly eccentric names, like Cous'n Jack (a fixie) and Bushwacker (a mountain bike). **SH**

Hobo's Weirdy Beardy mixes a 1980s aesthetic with modern steel. ▷

18 BIKES Pinion Hardtail

2013 • Mountain bike • Germany • Handmade custom machine with oil-bath gear system

In classic mountain biking territory, deep in England's Peak District National Park, Matt Bowns has been building custom bikes and frames since 2006. His company, 18 Bikes, is best known for producing hardtail mountain bike frames.

Bowns builds each bike one at a time, producing only about twenty a year by hand, as well as teaching workshop courses.

His normal frame material of choice is Reynolds 853, top-of-the-line lightweight steel. This tubing is heat-treated to increase fatigue resistance in spite of its thinness. The composition of 853 includes a precise recipe of carbon, manganese, chrome, molybdenum, silicon, and copper. This creates a particularly fine-grain material that gains strength from being air-cooled immediately after welding. (Other steel alloys would be quenched in water or oil, but these processes compromise their final strength.)

One of Bowns' star creations was this pioneering 853 hardtail. It was one of the first British bikes of its type to use the innovative 18-speed German-made gearbox, which is mounted in the bottom bracket. The cogs are sealed in a compact, lightweight box, and they run in a bath of oil. This automobile-like system requires less maintenance, and has better weight distribution and a wider range of ratios.

Bowns had to learn to weld aluminum to mount the Pinion brackets to his 853 frame. He also needed to fit Paragon Machine Works rocker drop-outs to tension the chain, a job normally done by the rear derailleur. **SH**

OGRE Monocoque

2013 • Concept bike • Japan • The only deliberately ugly bike in the whole book

Ogre bikes is the cycle branch of Eiji Konishi's Weld One specialist titanium parts company and it produces a range of beautiful conventionally framed mountain and road machines. Fans of motorised two wheelers will also be drawn to the distinctive rainbow heat burst finish on the tubes of the bikes. While this occurs naturally on high-performance titanium exhaust pipes, Eiji uses deliberate heating to decorative effect on the main tubes of his bikes. For the 2013 North American Handmade Bicycle Show he wanted to create a bike that nobody would miss. Enter the aptly named Ogre.

The multisection main spar was formed from seemingly random titanium plates welded together along their seams to create a crooked polygonal monocoque. The rear end of the bike was created by two curved tubes at either side of the wheel, each braced by a lattice of short stub stays. Up-front the fork legs used long splints of titanium crudely tack-welded together and connected to a unique one-piece cockpit. This was created by splicing two titanium tubes together to form the "stem" with the tubes then splitting apart to form the left and right sides of the bar.

The saddle was then mounted at the end of an upswept carbon fiber beam that cantilevered off the shoulders of the main spar just behind the head tube. Eiji wasn't just content with any normal fiber either; gold powder and spun gold fibers were fused into the carbon layup for a unique gilded detail. The same finish was also applied to a carbon fiber clutch bag rather randomly displayed alongside the bike. **GK**

BROTHERS 117

2013 • Town bike • UK • Custom-built retro steel road bike

Brothers Cycles was formed in London in 2008 by Will and James Meyer, siblings who restored vintage bikes, and now design and build small runs of bikes for track and road. Brothers frames sell at very affordable prices and are particularly popular among the no-gears fraternity all over the United Kingdom and in several countries across Europe.

This town bike was built in 2011 by James Meyer, who was originally taught frame building by Dave Yates. It was displayed at the prestigious Bespoked Bike Show in Bristol, where it was well received by afficionados, and then sold to the boss of a leading British cycle-wear company, who gave it to his wife for city travel and nicknamed it "Olive" for its distinctive color scheme.

The one-off design was loosely based on the Brothers' Classic track frame. This uses traditional double-butted 4130 chromoly steel tubing and a lugged construction. The tight geometry, however, makes it a responsive and nimble machine in urban surroundings, while remaining a steady and comfortable ride.

The Brothers' Classic normally works as a single-speed fixie, but in this instance was built up with a Sturmey 3-speed hub, in the style of a popular city road bike of the 1950s and 1960s. For period style, the saddle had to come from Brooks, of course—it's a B18 "lady sprung" saddle. Hand-built wheels with gumwall tires and an old-school pulley wheel for the hub gear cabling add to the retro feel of the machine. **SH**

FAGGIN Primavera
2013 • Road bike • Italy • Leather-covered steel frame

Marcello Faggin (pronounced *fah-jeen*) set up his bike workshop in Padua, Italy, in 1945. His business survived the adverse economic climate of the late 1940s and early 1950s, and is today run by his four daughters, who have been brazing and welding Faggin designs since their teens. Meanwhile Faggin's former apprentice, Massimo, married one of the daughters and is now the company's main frame builder.

Faggin bikes have become famous among Italian pro racers. After Endrio Leoni won the prestigious Venice Stra race in the 1980s, he presented the winner's bouquet to Marcello's widow in gratitude for the company building his bike. Over the years, the Faggin family kitchen has become a meeting place for many distinguished cyclists, including Eddy Merckx and Gino Bartali, who employed Faggin to build his own Bartali brand of pro-spec race bikes.

The small family company has managed to stay ahead of developments in frame building, and now includes world-class carbon frames with its more traditional steel offerings. Whatever the material, the bikes are still made individually by hand.

The Primavera is one of Faggin's most distinctive creations. It has an elegant steel frame completely sheathed in leather. Customers choose whether to cover the Columbus Thron tubing and forks in brown or black hides. The dark leather contrasts with the neat white lugwork and stitching. There is a matching bar tape and retro-style copper-riveted Brooks leather saddle with a small bag at the rear for essentials. **SH**

BRICK LANE BIKES La Poivra Air Frame

2013 • Fixed-gear bike • UK • Alloy fixie from ultra-trendy Londoners

"Trendy" doesn't adequately cover it. Brick Lane Bikes (BLB) is über-cool in every way. First, it is based in London's fashion-conscious and expensively revived East End district, and named after its most famous thoroughfare. Second, it is a sought-after clothing retailer, featuring its own chic cycling range developed with Swedish clothing giant H&M; it also stocks many top designer brands.

Moreover, BLB has oodles of urban street cred: It was launched by a former bike courier, and has become a pioneering specialist in fixed-gear and single-speed city bikes. It also stocks a unique collection of vintage classic European track and road bike frames, as well as distributing the hottest components and bikes from some of the best-known U.S. handmade companies.

Amid all this razzmatazz and gloss, it may come almost as a surprise to discover that BLB actually makes its own bikes too. The orders and measurements are taken at the London shop, although the actual frames are constructed in Poland by acclaimed bike builder Rych Tarski.

There are various BLB styles and options available. Custom road, track, and mountain bikes can be built around its La Poivra framesets, but some of these are also available as off-the-peg bikes. One of the latest stock designs is BLB's La Poivra Air Frame.

This very affordable but spectacular-looking road frame uses top-grade aluminum alloy outsized Columbus 7005 T6-grade tubing with very smooth welded joints. Design details include a hydraulically-formed fluted seat tube with very tight rear wheel clearance, distinctive angled top tube, chunky wishbone rear end, and integrated headset. The frame alone can cost less than $620 (£400). **SH**

TI CYCLES CarGoAway

2013 • Utility bike • USA • Titanium electric-assisted cargo bike

Ecospeed normally makes electric motor kits to convert bicycles to pedal-electric hybrids. Ti Cycles normally makes high-performance titanium bikes. The two companies got together, and this eccentric utility cargo bike was the result.

The CarGoAway was certainly unusual, but it was also innovative enough to scoop a prize at the prestigious 2013 North American Handmade Bike Show (NAHBS). The CarGoAway won the Belt Drive category. Perhaps the judges were influenced by the fact that it uniquely includes not one but two Gates Carbon Drive Belt systems. It also shows off Ti's engineering expertise. As well as the two belts, there

". . . a monster of a cargo bike, with a serious motor to help push an insane load."

Dirt Rag *magazine*

are two head tubes and three headsets. The EcoSpeed 1300-watt powertrain supplies enough grunt to get the bike up hills, and enables it to cruise at a steady 20 mph (32 kph), even fully loaded. It can also operate in an assist mode, combining with the rider's pedaling. That is why there are two carbon belts—one for the motor, the other for the crankset.

The bike also features a Light-On! dynamo and battery-powered lighting system plus four piston TPR disc brakes. Ti created its own universal hydraulic brake line couplers to stretch the full length of the bike.

The steering linkage system operates under the large front cargo box without intruding into the load space. The smaller rack at the back can carry loads or double as a seat for extra passengers. **SH**

This collaborative cargo bike is the ultimate pedal-powered pickup. ▶

LEGEND Queen

2013 • Road bike • Italy • The man behind the professional custom bikes creates his own company

Marco Bertoletti spent many years as the craftsman hidden behind the logos of other people's companies, but despite his lack of public recognition he was the builder to whom top pros and even whole teams turned when they were dissatisfied with their official bikes or needed special geometry. Bertoletti's work would then be painted to look like their sponsor's bikes. Other brands even went to him to build flagship models that they then put on general sale. In 2009, Bertoletti came out from behind the scenes to take the credit he deserves as one of the world's finest builders of high-end custom frames.

In the Legend factory near Bergamo, Italy, Bertoletti employs unique construction techniques to tune each frame to suit rider preferences. The Legend Queen frame shown here is meticulously hand-welded from high-grade titanium alloy. A custom-made carbon seat tube and carbon drop-out inserts are then bonded in, before the whole frame is hand finished and fitted with a matching custom carbon integrated fork. The bike is then completed with the customer's choice of components to produce a peerless performance frame that carries the classic lines of a traditional roadster but packs the punch of the latest speed machines. **KF**

CHAS ROBERTS Women's Audax

2013 • Road bike • UK • Custom high-performance road tourer for women

If the builder uses pre-cast lugs to build a bike frame, they are restricted to using the angles of the lugs. Given the biased economics of the bike world, these are normally suited to the geometry of a man's bike. Likewise, bike frame tubing comes in specific dimensions optimally designed for a male-sized frame.

Chas Roberts tackled these problems head on with the design of his latest dedicated women's bike. Roberts commissioned Reynolds to make special 853 steel tubing with which to create smaller frames without compromising on the performance or quality of the bike. Secondly, he used lugless fillet brazing so there is no restriction to the angles of the joints. Note how the geometry features a sloping top tube and low-slung seatstays. This aims to create a more comfortable ride without losing any responsiveness to pedaling.

The Women's Audax is a mix of racer and tourer. It is photographed on the Roberts website with drop bars and a luggage rack, mudguards, and water-bottle cage, but it is ideal for a variety of riding.

Sadly, this type of bike is considered too specialist to be mass produced so female riders have to buy from more costly custom builders. This frameset alone is priced between £1,225 and £1,395 ($1,952 and $2,225). **SH**

MOOTS Vamoots RSL

2013 • Road bike • USA • Beautiful Colorado-built road bike

When Colorado-based titanium specialist Moots established its reputation for beautifully crafted off-the-peg and custom frames with mountain bike designs, it wasn't long before riders were knocking on the door of the company's Steamboat Springs headquarters asking for road bikes with ethereal weight and ride quality.

The result was the cleanly conventional Vamoots frame, which is still a staple of the Moots line. As customer demands and road riding nuances changed, the Vamoots line expanded into three other models. The Mootour (now called the Vamoots LT) was introduced as a light touring machine with space for fatter tires. The Vamoots CR had a more modern, slightly sloping geometry for greater seatpost extension and a tighter ride feel on climbs. The Vamoots RSL, the flagship of the range, has an ultralight yet stiff tubeset. The main triangle tubes are double-butted 3Al 2.5V titanium alloy with thicker walls at the ends than at the center to reflect riding stresses. A custom-painted, full-carbon tapered fork slots into a 1¾-in. (44-mm) diameter headtube, and an outsized BB30 bottom bracket ensures precise handling. The seatstays use super-thin 6Al 4V titanium alloy tubes to keep the ride floated yet still ferociously fast. **GK**

WINTER Tenga Track

2013 • Track bike • USA • Japanese-style track bike

This deceptively simple-looking machine was judged Best Track Bike at the 2013 Bespoked show in Bristol, England. In truth, of course, there's nothing simple about Erik Estlund's one-off creation: It's a beautifully conceived state-of-the-art tribute to traditional Japanese track bikes. And that means there are no gears or brakes to clutter up the design.

The bike's sprint frame is constructed from True Temper steel tubing with neatly finished joints that use crisp modern cast lugs. The closer you look at the bike, the more its elegance reveals itself: Estlund, who is based in Portland, Oregon, has made very neat cast drop-outs and an internally lugged fork crown; the end of the stem facing the rider features a delicate metal-worked floral pattern.

The Tenga Track's components are a pleasing mix of old and new styles. There's a new custom-built Winter stem, and a vintage Fujita saddle from Texas-based Recovered Saddles. There are classic Campagnolo parts, and new Curtis Odom hubs laced to specially made Velocity rims.

The frame may look like bare metal, but it's actually a very discreet "evening orchid" paint job with a period drop-shadow Winter logo. **SH**

DONHOU Tourer

2013 • Touring bike • UK • Customized
Reynolds-framed road bike

Tom Donhou had just cycled across the Gobi Desert and was somewhere to the west of Beijing, lying in a tent being kept awake by a procession of coal trucks passing by. Suddenly he realized that all he wanted to do in life was build bikes.

This was evidently a shock to him, but it can't have come as much of a surprise to his friends. Donhou had grown up as a BMX addict, then became a teenage road racer, and won the first national mountain bike race he entered. He had studied design, worked as a bike courier, and gone surfing with his Schwinn and a homemade trailer to carry the board. His career arc had an air of inevitability about it from the start.

Donhou is now an established, award-winning bike builder in Norwich, in the flatlands of England's East Anglia region. Perhaps it was that fast cycling environment that inspired him to build a dedicated speed bike as a sideline to his normal business. It has one massive 17-in. (43-cm), 104-tooth Royce chainring. Donhou himself has ridden this bike at up to 102 mph (165 kph) on a rolling road.

As a more typical example of his work, we've featured here one of his custom builds for a particular client. Steve's Bike is a modern take on a touring concept. It is based on the Donhou Rapha Continental design but with the addition of a rear rack and a special paint job.

The frame is constructed from Reynolds 853 Pro Team, and the bike has disc brakes, touring drop-outs, and a steel rack with carbon slats that match the Wound Up fork. Components are mostly high-end, with a SRAM Force groupset, Avid brake calipers, and various parts from Chris King and Thomson. The final touch was a paint job inspired by the customer and his girlfriend's favorite chocolate. **SH**

GURU BICYCLES Photon

2013 • Road bike • Canada • Handcrafted
high-tech custom-built performance carbon bike

Set up by an engineering student in 1993, with the aim of building bikes to perfection, Guru has moved to the leading edge of custom-built frame production. The micro-brand prides itself on its ability to tune every aspect of frame construction to individual riders' needs. To do this, it produces frames in alloy, steel, titanium, scandium, and carbon fiber. It is with the last named material that the company has really made its reputation, having set about developing a proprietary method of laying up the fibers seamlessly to produce a lighter, stiffer frame.

Many companies' top-end carbon bikes are merely large-scale, offshore factory production frames.

"To start with the thing felt just too light to lean—surely it will fall over?"

Guy Pearson, Pearson Cycles

Although the choice of brands may appear daunting, the range of differences is actually very narrow, and it is consequently difficult for riders to find the size, layup, and stiffness that best suit them.

By contrast, Guru makes each frame by hand in its own factory, and makes every one of its products an exact fit for the customer. Indeed, the Montreal-based company is one of only a handful of manufacturers in the world that pays this level of attention to detail in carbon, and most such products are not available to the public.

The Guru Photon is one of the world's lightest production frames, with medium-sized versions weighing just 1 lb 10 oz (750 g)—the minimum achievable without compromising performance. **KF**

Guru perfects rider fit with its own custom-sizing rig. ▸

OAK Touring Bike

2013 • Touring bike • UK • Versatile modern custom tourer

The 2013 award for the best tourer at the Bespoked bike show in Bristol, England, went to a machine built by Ryan McCaig, whose company is called Oak Cycles.

This custom build was a versatile 29er on a steel frame made of custom Reynolds 853 tubing.

Similar frames and forks, with relaxed touring geometry and load-bearing capabilities, later went on general sale; these are each customized to the purchaser's requirements. McCaig's measuring sessions are famously exhaustive—they each take several hours and cost around $2,000 (£1300).

McCaig decided to open his own workshop while on a bike expedition. He had finished his own frame the week before he left on a marathon ride over the European Alps, through the deserts of Syria, and down to Cairo, Egypt. He has since become a specialist in these adventure bikes. His company first hit the news in 2011, when former cycle courier/blogger Emily Chappell began a round-the-world tour on one of his hardcore expedition tourers.

The award-winner shown here has the features of an off-road tourer, a road tourer, and a 29er mountain bike combined. The seat tube is carefully kinked to shorten the wheelbase and allow for fat 2½-in. (6.3-cm) tires, although it normally wears 28-in. (71-cm) road tires. For touring there are water-bottle mounts and frame, saddle, and bar bags sourced from Wildcat Gear. For cross-country there are those big 29er wheels, and front suspension forks with just over 3 in. (80 mm) of travel can also be fitted. **SH**

WHYTE T129S

2013 • Mountain bike • UK • Tough, fun, fast yet affordable 29er trail bike

Twenty-nine-in. (73.5-cm) wheels certainly haven't been an overnight success in mountain biking, but they've slowly grown in popularity as more people find out how much faster and more controlled a big-wheel bike can be than a traditional 26-in. (66-cm) wheeler.

Because the large wheels hit obstacles at a shallower angle, bumps feel smaller and the bike rolls over them more smoothly and loses less speed in the process. Longer tire contact patches with the trail also mean more grip. The wheels themselves have more gyroscopic stability once they're rolling, and bike weight is lower in relation to the wheel axles, so the whole bike feels more sure-footed.

With their heavier wheels, however, 29ers can feel sluggish on twisty trails, and it is there that Whyte has scored a real coup with its T129S. Both this bike and its lighter, shorter suspension sibling, the M109, use slack steering angles and long front ends for totally assured on-trail authority.

A short stem and rearward rider position keep the Whyte feeling remarkably agile and poised for a big wheeler. A saddle dropper post included as standard allows the rider maximum body movement potential on descents and tight technically challenging trails. Fast-rolling but tough Maxxis Ardent tires give the ride real pep under power, and its light steering makes it an absolutely great bike to throw around.

Few riders were surprised when the T129S was the clear Trail Bike of the Year 2013 winner in the British *What Mountain Bike* magazine. **GK**

ENIGMA Excel

2013 • Road bike • UK • Double-butted high-grade titanium frame

British bike builder Enigma gets these off-the-shelf frames built to order in Taiwan using some of the highest-grade titanium available. The double-butted tubing is grade-five AL-4V, the same as that used for supercar components. It's as light and stiff as you can get.

This top-notch alloy is 17 percent stronger, 10 percent lighter, and 8 percent stiffer than other Enigma products made with lower-grade titanium. Little wonder then that the frame alone comes with a hefty $3,125 (£2000) price tag.

Cycling Weekly reviewed the Enigma over some of the UK's 2014 Tour de France route. The testers fitted the frame with Enigma's own monocoque carbon fork, plus top-notch parts from SRAM, Forza, and Challenge. The verdict: "It performed exceptionally, compliant enough to soak up road buzz but stiff enough to climb and not feel wallowy in steering or flex under twisting load."

This Enigma flagship machine comes in five stock sizes; there is also a premium customized option. The variety of finishes available includes a full mirror polish or a two-color paint job. Full Excel bikes can be made up for customers using components such as hand-built Mavic wheels, Campagnolo Record EPS groupsets, and ENVE carbon forks. Naturally, this level of parts boosts the price to superbike levels.

Is it worth it? Enigma says the Excel is "reassuringly expensive and very exclusive." *Cycling Weekly* said: "It's one to take home to meet the parents, the classy one that everyone will admire from afar. It's one that will quite possible outlast you." **SH**

BRIAN ROURKE Custom 953 Stainless Oversize

2013 • Road bike • UK • Latest steel bike from father-and-son builders

This is a genuine father-and-son business, with dad Brian Rourke designing bikes since 1972, and his boy Jason growing up to become his specialist torch-wielding accomplice.

Brian Rourke was an accomplished cyclist. His 25-year racing résumé included national road and track championships, three rides in the UK Milk Race, and five veteran road race titles.

Now the Stoke-on-Trent duo produces hundreds of handmade bikes every year. The Rourkes specialize in made-to-measure racing frames, hand built from Reynolds 953 steel, and readily distinguishable by their wrap-over seatstay joints.

The Brian Rourke TT bike from the 1980s, as ridden by top road racers Ian Cammish, Phil Griffiths, and Kevin

Dawson, was nominated as one of the 50 greatest bikes of all time by *Cycling Weekly* magazine. Nicole Cooke won the 2000 World Junior Road Champion on a Brian Rourke machine.

In spite of Brian Rourke's pedigree, his latest road frameset, in 953 stainless steel with carbon forks, costs from only $2,600 (£1,655)—substantially undercutting many big-name rivals.

Complete bikes are made up to order with high-end components from Shimano, Campagnolo, SRAM, and Mavic. Rourke's workshop is alongside the company's own cycle shop, which features a pub—Kelly's Bar, named after sprinter Sean Kelly. All the walls are covered with cycling memorabilia, including a collection of trophies won on Rourke bikes. **SH**

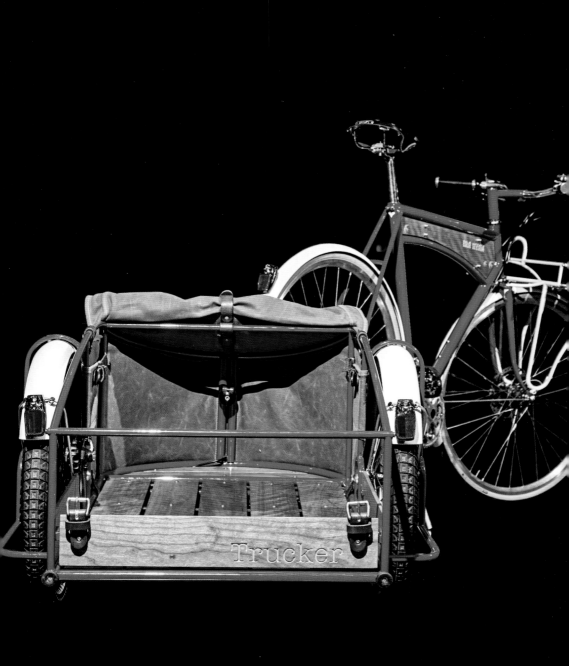

IRA RYAN/TRUCKER Ned Ludd

2013 • Cargo bike • USA • Custom bike with trailer

This striking load-carrying bike was built specially for the Ned Ludd Restaurant in Portland, Oregon. Chef and owner Jason French needed something to take to the local farmers' markets to collect fresh produce for his kitchen. Since the city is the U.S. cycling capital, the method of transportation had to be a bike.

When acclaimed local bike builder Ira Ryan, a former bike courier, came into Ludd's restaurant to eat one evening, French took the opportunity to pitch his idea. Local leather-wear company Tanner got involved too, as it wanted to expand its range with a selection of bike bags. Trucker Racks, also of Portland, added its luggage-carrying expertise to the project.

The outcome was this cool and practical way of transporting the restaurant's ingredients. Note how the trailer is heavily protected with a dedicated waxed canvas-and-leather cover. Tanner added a special dedicated front bag, which sits on a wooden slatted rack conceived by Trucker. The trailer, which is made mostly of wood, can be unfixed alongside the rear drop-outs, leaving a usable trader's bike.

There's also a wood panel between the top tube and the lower cross tube, which is added for strength. This gives a chance for the trader or the bike builder to display his or her branding.

The rest of the bike featured Ryan's top-end lugged steel frame and a variety of quality components. For example, the classic leather saddle is from Brooks, the slick gearset is from Shimano Ultegra, and the legendary American parts maker Chris King supplied the hubs. Modern features include full-size mudguards and disc brakes.

The custom project was entered in the North American Handmade Bike Show (NAHBS) in 2012, and won the best city bike category. **SH**

SEVEN Sola SLX

2013 • Road bike • USA • Ultra-light titanium bike developed from an Olympic race machine

The origins of Seven can be traced to Merlin Cycles, the pioneers of titanium mountain bike construction. Rob Vandermark refined his trade as Merlin rose to become the most prestigious brand in the rapidly expanding mountain bike market. When he felt that Merlin's upward curve was starting to flatten, he stepped aside to set up Seven Cycles in January 1997.

It wasn't just Vandermark's technological expertise that set Seven apart. His company introduced an ultra-detailed "Custom Kit" interview system for all clients who wanted a bespoke bike. Each customer's responses then formed the basis for the tubeset design of the titanium frames, which used pipes shaped to

> *"Whatever a person's reasons for having a relationship with bikes . . . they're all good."*
>
> Rob Vandermark

deliver precisely the ride that suited each customer. By 2004 Seven had won numerous awards and expanded its workshop in Watertown, Massachusetts, bringing paint and tube-butting processes in-house as it prepared to finish its 10,000th bike. When Seven's sponsored rider, multiple U.S. national champion Mary McConneloug, was selected for the U.S. Olympic mountain bike team, the company created a suitably special version of its Sola race frame for her. This "ultra-butted" frame has since evolved as titanium construction techniques have become more refined into a 3-lb (1.4-kg) masterpiece with few if any equals.

For customers who want a perfectly sized and shaped bike, but who cannot afford titanium, Seven also produces the Sola S in steel. **GK**

◁ Nothing illustrates Portland's eclectic culture better than this bike-and-trailer combo.

TOKYO FIXED Wide Open

2013 • Road bike • UK • Lightweight sporty tourer

Tokyo Fixed is a London bike shop and online retailer that has diversified into building its own bikes.

The Wide Open is its ultra-versatile steel road bike. The company says it can cope with everything from commuting to audax racing. It's meant to go fast—the short-wheelbase frame geometry is sporty, and the mix of Columbus Zona steel and chromoly tubing is responsive and lightweight. And it's all put together with smoothly finished fillet brazing.

In winter the bike can be adapted to wetter conditions—there's ample room for mudguards and chunkier tires. And this is a frame that's built to carry panniers and racks full of luggage on long touring rides.

This do-anything machine is fitted with the Shimano 105 groupset, a lightweight, smooth-shifting system with built-in toughness. The wheels work for various types of riding: Ambrosio Excellence low-profile rims are laced with double-butted spokes to Ambrosio racing hubs with bearings that are sealed against the worst weather. Handmade Japanese tires from Panaracers are smooth enough for the best tarmac, but are also designed to glide over gravel or dirt tracks. Those semi-enclosed drop-outs are tough enough for that sort of action too.

Extra class is provided by the set of silver Nitto Randonneur bars, Brooks Swift saddle and bar-tape, and a retro racing green-and-gold paint job kept neat with internal cable routing. And for serious touring riders there are brazed-on fittings for the mudguards, front and rear racks, and water-bottle cages. **SH**

RAPHAEL CX

2013 • Cyclocross bike • USA • Custom-built racer

Rafi Ajl had always loved riding bikes, but when a college friend showed him a crude bike he had built himself, he decided he wanted to build them too.

He moved from his native Brooklyn to California, worked as a bike mechanic, built his own fixie, undertook epic long-distance rides, and taught on a bike fabrication course. Eventually he set up his own bike company, Raphael Cycles, in San Francisco. Today his custom bike range includes everything from track machines to rugged, fat-tired adventure bikes.

Ajl had built only around twenty bikes when a client commissioned this striking cyclocross racing bike. It's a fast, single-speed machine that was designed to be strong, light, and nimble. Ajl brazed the frame from low-weight Columbus PegoRichie steel niobium

tubing, then completed it with a Paragon Machine Works bottom bracket, and Rocker adjustable drop-outs and head tube. Note also the tapered steerer tube for the ENVE carbon fiber fork. Finishing touches included disc brakes front and rear, black grips and saddle, and that eye-catching purple satin paint job with the white maker's logos.

Ajl described it as "a racing bike designed to be ridden hard with no bells and whistles." Before it was delivered to the customer, the bike was exhibited at the North American Handmade Bike Show (NAHBS) in 2012. It was Raphael's first appearance there, and this was the company's only bike on display. Reaction was good. Show-goers particularly admired (and even stroked) the super-smooth fillet brazed joints. **SH**

PASSONI Top Force W

2013 • Downhill bike • Italy • Luxury carbon–titanium road racer

In the 1980s, Italian amateur rider Luciano Passoni and his son Luca founded a company that set out to make some of the most sought-after frames in the world. Today, the small boutique manufacturer, based just outside Milan, is still turning out some of the world's finest titanium bikes, and trying to show that titanium racers are a match for carbon machines.

This exclusivity and expertise don't come cheap: the Top Force W is a fully custom product that costs around $8,600 (£5,500) for just the frame, fork, and headset. A complete bike is around $15,600 (£10,000).

Titanium is notoriously hard to work with, but the Passoni's tubing is arranged in various diameters and

". . . the Top Force responds instantly to tiny changes in body position, speed and direction."

Stuart Kerton, Road.cc

specially strengthened with machined higher-grade metal at key stress points: head tube, bottom bracket shell, and drop-out. This bike is clearly built for stiffness, not comfort. Note how the frame tubing is ovalized toward the joints for extra strength. The welds are perfectly smoothed. In addition, there are standard-fit Columbus carbon forks, and the frame is hand polished. Even the logos are beautifully created, by sandblasting through a stencil.

The W stands for "wired"—this version uses an electronic shift. The Shimano Di2 system is controlled via completely internalized wiring. Other high-end kit includes super-light Marchisio carbon wheels, grippy Veloflex handmade tires, and Passoni's own carbon bars, alloy stem, and titanium seatpost. **SH**

CANNONDALE Slice RS

2013 • Aero bike • USA • Distinctive ultra-narrow drag machine

In recent years. increasingly realistic wind tunnel data has replaced theoretical design cues for top-end aero bikes designed purely for solo speed in triathlon and time trial events. As a result, recent superbikes have increasingly abandoned the smooth, flowing lines and textbook teardrop cross-sections in favor of much sharper, more angular frame architecture.

Few bikes have thrown that in the face of onlookers as blatantly as Cannondale's Slice RS. The most obvious angle of the whole bike is the sharp triangular tail formed by the rearward extension of the seat tube and horizontal top tube. The dramatic shape is further enhanced by the fact that the super-narrow bladed shaft seatpost itself is offset significantly forward to the front edge of the seat tube. Up front Cannondale has made the bike as narrow as possible to truly "Slice" through the air.

Rather than a conventional fork slotting into a broad head tube, the Slice direct-mounts the bearings in the frame, and the fork then screws straight into them, allowing further reduction in the width of the front end. The stem syncs directly into the top of the fork, and lies flush with the top tube for minimal airflow disturbance. The handlebars are state-of-the-art, wind-cheaters with a low base bar and a high tri-bar; they are the work of Cannondale team co-sponsor FSA. The ultra-narrow legs also hide the front brake, while shock-absorbing stays guarantee the excellent ride quality that primarily distinguishes current 'Dales from all other bike brands.

Before the Slice went into production, Slovakian speedster Peter Sagan rode an early model in the 2012 Tour of Switzerland, and brought it home ahead of Swiss star Fabian Cancellara to win a 4½-mi (7.3-km) time trial. **GK**

DEMON Manhattan

2013 • Road bike • UK • Award-winner with decorative lugs

Demon is new to the bike scene, but its creations are traditional in style. The Reynolds steel frames are individually brazed and welded by Tom Warmerdam in his workshop in Southampton, England.

Warmerdam originally worked with bought-in lugs, but has now developed his own decorative lugs that are painstakingly created by hand and customized for each buyer—those on one of his creations was matched to the design of the customer's wrist tattoo, an undertaking that took a whole month and required 120 saw blades, numerous needle files, and 30 drill bits.

The Manhattan is one of Warmerdam's Signature frame series, with individually-made stainless steel head lugs that are left unpainted with a light brushed finish. The head tubing is TIG-welded and smoothed before the lugs are welded to the frame using a mix containing 56 percent silver. The rest of the frame is fillet-brazed using the latest techniques that avoid overheating the tubing and thus reducing its strength. Customers have a choice of three types of Reynolds tubing and carbon or steel forks. The overall frame can be finished in brushed unpainted steel or a mirrorlike polish.

The Manhattan won Best Road Bike at the 2013 North American Handmade Bike Show (NAHBS). **SH**

FIELD Cross Classic

2013 • Cross bike • UK • Custom bike for both road and cross conditions

---

Inspired by the quirky bikes that compete in the Paris–Roubaix race, Field's Cross Classic is an artful variation on the usual theme, with a striking purple-blue-yellow-black-gray paint job and a highly polished stainless steel brazed badge with the maker's name on the front of the stem.

The frame geometry is a mix of road and cross bikes, with reinforced fillet-brazed joints to cope with heavy knocks. It has clearances for 1⅖-in. (35-mm) off-road tires for rough tracks and potholed roads. Its sophisticated mix of Reynolds 853 (down tube and top tube), 631 (head tube) and 4130 chromoly (seat tube, seatpost top, and stem) makes for a fast, comfortable ride. The integrated seatpost allows 1⅛ in. (30 mm) of saddle height adjustment.

The rear triangle comes from Columbus. The chainstays have the S-bend design, while the more delicate seatstays are strengthened by a 4130 X-brace. Unusually the rear brake cable is externally mounted, but passes right through a hole drilled in the seat tube.

Field is a cooperative venture by friends from various disciplines in Sheffield, England. Its bikes are built by Harry Harrison, who says he made this one just for himself. **SH**

DON WALKER Stayer Bike

2013 • Paced track bike • USA • Custom retro derny race-style bike

In paced track racing, cyclists follow a derny, a motorized pace bike, and stay as close to it as they can. On the back of the derny is a frame with a roller bar to minimize the impact if a following rider misjudges the distance and bumps into it.

When Don Walker set out to build a retro mid-1950s steel track bike for derny racing, he adopted the classic geometry for such a frame. Note how the forks curve backward, shortening the wheelbase, allowing the use of a smaller front wheel, and helping to absorb any impact with that roller bar. The steeper head angle allows the bike to get closer to the derny and thus maximize the slipstream effect.

The distinctive feature is that enormous chainring with 66 teeth, which can cope with speeds of up to 70 mph (112 kph) but needs a Herculean effort to start from a standstill. (The ring was made by retro parts specialist Curtis Odom; hence the "CO" pattern in the spokes.)

Other retro details include the Odom aluminum–stainless steel hubs, Wheel Fanatyk wooden Ghisallo rims in place of modern disc wheels, and Campagnolo bars, pedals, and headset. Note how stayers often have very long adjustable stems to allow different riders to use the same bike. **SH**

ENGLISH CYCLES Single Sided

2013 • Custom road bike • UK • Innovative one-sided design

English Cycles' bike builder Rob English says he's always up for a design challenge. A customer in Arizona provided the brief: they wanted "something extraordinary." Using computer-aided-design and his own engineering skills, English then managed to expand on the concept of a leftie fork and create a whole "rightie" bike.

This meant the fork has a single blade, on the right. This is strong enough to do all the work of two regular forks plus carry the internally routed brake cable and mount the disc brake, which needed a modified caliper to work on the right side of the wheel. English machined a special aluminum axle and used a one-piece stem and steerer.

The rear was more complicated. English's custom-machined hub extended enough to allow the belt drive to be mounted on a cog outside the single chainstay. For balance, the chainstay needed to be as close to the bike's center line as possible, and this enabled the belt to be completely outside the frame.

After adding other custom features, English sent the bike to professional artist Geoff Mcfetridge for a striking paint job in lime green with custom graphics all over the frame. The final bike weighed in at just 16 lb (7.25 kg). **SH**

PEACOCK GROOVE Voltron Red Lion

2013 • Track bike • USA • Custom bike builder's extreme race bike

Custom bike builder Erik Noren of Peacock Groove in Minneapolis isn't joking when he says of his workshop's output: "Everything is super-deep custom."

From an Evil Dead machine with skull wheel inserts, to a bike with a special holder to fit a six-pack of beer, Noren has gained a reputation for ultra-creative concepts. His back catalog bikes include Motörhead lyrics on the rims, copper frames, and "Peacock Groove Forever" cutouts on a chainstay. One show bike had a tube logo made of crushed stone, and most of his machines feature distinctive decorative head badges and drop-outs. Although there was never any doubting Noren's business acumen, some of his bikes stretched

> ## "We are making track bikes that look like the Lions from Voltron."
> *Erik Noren*

his creative powers and his sense of humor to the limit. However, he is well within his comfort zone with this Red Lion, one of a series of five track bikes built to celebrate the robots in the Voltron anime cartoons of the 1980s.

Note the beautiful finish on the chunky Columbus steel frame, and the adoption of the popular track tactic of a bent top tube and seat tube to create a shorter wheelbase for more power. Eye-catching features include the front wheel's twelve-spoke set with bizarre lacing; decorative rims specially built by H+ Son Wheels; a paint job by airbrush artist Brad Gavlin of Dirt Design Graphics in Minnesota, and a saddle embroidered with a Transformers logo by Paul Smith of Stoke Seats in Wisconsin. **SH**

RUSBY Olly's

2013 • Road bike • UK • Former sculptor turns his hand to frame building

London-based James Rusby used to be a sculptor, and he typifies the new blood that has rejuvenated British frame building. Retro revivalists have made their mark by blending traditional methods with modern designs to breathe life back into steel, while big manufacturers concentrate on factory-made carbon.

The history of custom steel bikes is long and prestigious. To many, the adaptability of steel to tubes of different diameters and thicknesses to suit both the fit and the feel of a frame to the rider remains its true beauty. This could be done in an almost endless variety of ways that cannot be achieved with an off-the-shelf frame. As new tubing options become available, small manufacturers such as Rusby are making the most of their skills to maximize the opportunities.

For example, this custom-built model uses revolutionary Reynolds 953 tubing. This is an innovative blend of stainless steel with outstandingly high tensile strength and stiffness that combine to bring a hitherto unknown level of resilience to the frames made from it, even though this type of steel is harder to work with than previous forms.

This is an area in which a small company can compete with big name manufacturers because it can take greater care and pay more attention to detail.

The fact that customization is economically unviable for mass-production companies has created a gap in the market for true craftsmen with businesses that are small and need to remain that way in order to give buyers the personalized service for which they are prepared to pay a premium. This opportunity has enabled custom steel to return to the forefront of performance cycling machinery. Products made with this material by such painstaking methods are expensive, but one look at the Rusby shows why people think it's worth every cent. **KF**

GIANT Trance 29X

2013 • Mountain bike • Taiwan • Big-wheeled version of popular all-rounder

The Trance had been one of the best-selling all-round trail bikes in the world. By 2013 the long-running design was starting to look slightly dated.

Giant responded with a complete redesign of the Trance chassis, to which it added big, smooth-rolling 29-in. (73.5-cm) wheels rather than the more common 26-in. (66-cm) wheels. This modification required the use of a heavily curved seat tube that kinked the seat backward so that the rear wheel could be brought closer to the mainframe without reducing clearance.

The Trance 29X is very agile for a big wheeler, and it gained additional kudos for its keen and enthusiastic ride character on more technical trails. Giant used its vast aluminum frame-building expertise to produce a frame that was stiff enough to track satisfactorily, even

with a conventional quick-release rear axle. The frame also used a very short head tube to keep the front end low, notwithstanding the big front wheel. This was where Giant's extra-large Overdrive 2 tapered headset standard came in particularly useful to keep steering accurate in spite of the shorter stack height.

The hydraulically-shaped alloy tubes brought the weight of the Trance very close to that of a lot of the carbon-framed competition, but at a much more affordable price.

The Trance X also benefited from the expansion of Giant's own-brand wheel range to include TRX wheels, which completed a cost-conscious but high-performance rolling chassis that was then loaded with a range of high-value specification options. **GK**

ROBIN MATHER Commuter

2013 • Utility bike • UK • Seemingly understated single speed from a pragmatic artisan

Robin Mather tells of his route into frame building as though it was an almost inevitable process: "I grew up in the countryside so the only way to get anywhere was on a bike. My A Level (High School) project was a recumbent tricycle and that got me a bench, a vise and some files and then I got some tubes off Dave Yates to build a proper bike."

Considering his pragmatic entry into frame building, it's perhaps unsurprising that he specializes in versatile, hardworking, everyday bikes for his growing client base.

These humble words don't give any hint of the exquisite levels of detailing that Mather's frames display. His ornate lugs are hand filed for hours for an ultra-clean finish and he loves to create custom monogrammed sections or ingenious mounts for any add-ons, such as custom stainless steel racks, ingenious Supernova dynamo lights, and scalloped metal mudguards.

At his first appearance at the Bespoked Bristol show, Mather's pale blue Camponneur won both the judges' and public's "Best of Show" votes. He returned the following year with several bikes including this salmon-pink single-cog commuter. The single color was chosen to showcase Mather's seamless finishing at every joint and his intricately hand-shaped lugs on main tubes and fork crown. The seat lug included tall curved points at front and rear that seemed to caress rather than just clamp the waisted Campagnolo seat pin. The rear drop-outs were also beautifully detailed with a raised slot for the sliding axle and conical thumbwheel set screws to stop the rear wheel shifting under power. **GK**

SOUPLESSE Bamboo

2013 • Road bike • Uganda • Custom bamboo bike frames made in Africa

Through the history of bicycles we have seen frames made of wood, metal, plastic, and carbon. But grass? Surely not! As the largest member of the grass family, bamboo has plenty of green credentials. It's extremely fast-growing, it is widespread across the world, it's cheap, and it's one of the few potential bike materials with a positive carbon footprint.

Since as early as 1894, manufacturers have experimented with bamboo frames, working with both the advantages and challenges of an entirely natural product. The organic growth means that every frame piece has to be judged and then used according to its strengths—a selection process that requires real skill. On the plus side, bamboo has an inherent ability to absorb vibration and transfer energy through its complex fibrous structure, and can thus create a ride of exemplary smoothness.

Souplesse exploits this quality to the maximum in its custom frames. It takes precise measurements from the customer, and then uses them to set the correct dimensions for the build. Each frame is manufactured in Uganda by dedicated craftsman who carefully select stem size and thickness to match the weight of the rider and the intended purpose of the bike. The cured bamboo stems are carefully mitered and joined, then combined with alloy contact inserts for the headset, seat tube and bottom bracket. This is all done by hand-wrapping each piece with layers of Kevlar and setting in resin, producing a frame with a unique blend of nature and the latest man-made materials. Each join is finished with a layer of dyed tree bark cloth before being immaculately hand filed, sanded, lacquered, and deep polished to reveal a beautiful marbled effect, before finally being finally shipped to the United Kingdom for testing, assembly, and final delivery. **KF**

INTENSE Tracer 275

2013 • Mountain bike • USA • Super-stiff trail bike

One of the great advantages for Intense of being among the last genuine in-house bike builders in the United States is that it can create new models very quickly. The company demonstrated that emphatically when it beat most of its rivals into the mid-sized wheel market with this celebrated version of the Tracer.

Within the Intense range, the Tracer has always been a pivotal model, combining all the best elements of the company's lightest race-style bikes with the strength and attitude of its legendary gravity machines.

Unlike many first-generation 27½-in. (70-cm) wheeled bikes, the Tracer betrays no signs of an uneasy compromise between stiffness and handling integrity.

"This bike is made to ride up, down, sideways, and everything in between."

Intensecycles.com

Reviewers and riders alike have commented on the toughness of the multi-section, semi-monocoque frame that's shaped and welded in Temecula, California.

The super-strong frame sections are joined with short, stiff linkages that form the 5½–6-in. (14–15-cm) travel VPP2 suspension layout that Intense shares with Santa Cruz. These provide the Tracer with a punchy, pedal-reactive character that suits the added rolling speed of the wheels but still makes the most of their agility, which is greater than that of any 29-in. (73.5-cm) wheeler. Add confidently relaxed steering angles and screw-through axles at the front and rear, internal dropper post cable routing, and built-in mounts for a chain-taming device, and the Tracer is truly ready for anything its rider or the trail can throw at it. **GK**

Intense's Tracer has always been a highlight of its range. ▶

FEATHER Cross

2013 • Cross bike • UK • Handmade steel cross bike

Few frame builders will ever match the meteoric rise of Ricky Feather in the handmade bicycle industry.

He worked in a factory making parts for diggers and lorries until he decided to become a bike maker during a trip to New York City, where he "saw gorgeous bikes everywhere." He taught himself the requisite techniques and, only four years after he started, won awards three years running at the Bespoked bike fair in Bristol, England: Best Track Bike in 2011; Best Road Bike in 2012, and in 2013 Best in Show and the public vote for his semi-painted Ultimate.

Even after these successes, Feather still works where he has always worked: in a humble wooden

"People like things that are built by hand rather than knocked up in a factory."

Ricky Feather

shed at his father-in-law's home. This out-of-the-way rural location, 10 mi (16 km) north of York, has now predictably become a magnet for cyclists in search of the perfect ride.

The bike you're most likely to find Feather himself riding and racing is his own cyclocross machine. This standout gloss black and fluorescent yellow creation is completed with perfectly color-matched saddle and stem and red anodized component detailing. Lines are kept ultra-clean by rear brake cables and electric shift cables neatly routed through the frame; the Shimano Di2 battery is also hidden internally. Unlike most of Ricky's bikes, it uses a lugless design with totally smooth joints between the tubes. The integrated seatpost is naturally custom-built to Ricky's requirements. **SH**

VELOCITE Geos

2013 • Road bike • Taiwan • Big-boned road bike with a surprisingly warm heart

Velocite is a Taiwan-based brand but with global ambition, and its affordable carbon fiber frame Geos bike comes in a range of complete bike options.

The frame is the heart of every bike, and Velocite has made sure the Geos is a frame that gets your heart pumping. The curved leg forks, head tube, and down tube certainly get things off to a very positive and precise start, with reviewers reporting that the Geos is particularly firm in terms of its grip of tight lines on technical descents. Perhaps that inevitably comes at the expense of a smoothly comfortable ride up front, and the same reviewers report that keeping a wary eye for potholes is a wise precaution.

The big tubes and oversized 1¼-in. (3-cm) axle-compatible bottom bracket shell aren't as still as you might expect, however. While the large-diameter seatpost transfers rattle from the road to the rider without much damping, the overall ride of the Geos is comfortable enough for the most epic of days.

A carbon fiber bearing seat and full-carbon drop-outs keep the frame reasonably light considering its relatively affordable cost. That makes it an efficient climber whenever the road turns upward, but the Geos comes alive on twisty descents. The combination of stiff front end and short overall wheelbase makes for a very accurate and agile approach on any downhill, particularly those with lots of corners or limited clean tarmac where the accuracy of the bike can be used to maximum advantage.

The build quality of the frame is excellent too, with near-perfect reports from workshop strip-downs that form part of the most thorough magazine bike performance tests.

The Geos can be bought direct from Velocite or via your local bike store for pro setup and sizing advice. **GK**

◁ This stunning cyclocross bike is Ricky Feather's own ride.

BILENKY Townie

2013 • City bike • USA • Custom-built retro town bike

Not everyone wants a bike to climb mountains or race long distances. Some cyclists simply want a likeable and attractive machine to potter around their neighborhood—something practical with a bit of style.

Sadly, not many of today's large companies produce bicycles like that, so people in search of traditionally styled urban riders have to turn to custom bike builders.

This machine from Bilenky Cycle Works hits the mark—it is utilitarian with pleasing hints of retro. It has a beautifully finished and polished lugged steel frame with a long wheelbase and relaxed geometry.

It isn't for riding standing up or bent over the bars; it's clearly for cruising in a sitting position. Yet there is a mix of some of the best modern additions too, such as

the Rohloff internally-geared hub, the all-weather disc brakes, and the oil-free Gates carbon belt. These up-to-date, low-maintenance features combine with the classic style of details such as the neat leather saddle and the gloss black luggage racks front and rear.

The decorative touches are definitely less obvious. Only the unpainted stainless steel tubing with decorative lugwork catches the eye, contrasting with the gloss black full-size fenders and black Bilenky logo strip. Internal cable routing keeps it all looking tidy.

The Philadelphia-based bike builder is better known for its extreme creative machines. It hosts an annual cyclocross race in a neighboring scrapyard. But perhaps this more understated and considered Townie shows the company's craftsmanship more clearly. **SH**

SAFFRON Butcher's Bike

2013 • Utility bike • UK • Award-winning fixed-gear bike

By scooping two top bike show awards in 2013, Matthew Sowter's Saffron Frameworks announced its arrival on the British biking scene with a fanfare. First it won Best Bicycle at Spin London. Soon after, it walked away with the Best Utility Bike award at Bespoked, Bristol.

The winning bike at the former show was a single-speed touring machine for a customer intending to ride it across Vietnam. It was made of a mix of Columbus 853 steel and chromoly tubing with a curved top tube and seatstays to add comfortable flexibility for endurance over challenging terrain.

The winner at Bespoked was Sowter's modern take on a traditional butcher's bike. It was a custom-built hub gear commuter bike for a barrister who wanted to transport all his documents to work with him every day.

To meet these requirements, the bike was given a massive stainless steel front rack with stained oak slats (to match the tan leather Brooks saddle). The client also specified an oil-free carbon belt drive, which added a state-of-the-art touch to the traditional design.

The bike's tubeset was a mix of Columbus SL and Columbus Spirit, which Saffron finished in-house in viper green. This was rounded off neatly with a silver-soldered polished steel lug-set and bottom bracket case, plus full-sized color-matched mudguards.

The build was completed with quality components, including an Alfine rear hub and Chris King front hub, and 650B Pacenti rims. The handmade cantilever brakeset was from Paul's Components, handlebars were Nitto Albatross, and headset from Chris King. **SH**

TONIC Epic 1 Crusher

2013 • Cyclocross bike • US • Rugged gravel racer

This was the bike built for Oregon racer Paul LaCava to compete in the grueling 2013 Trans Iowa Race over more than 300 mi (480 km) of rough gravel tracks.

LaCava is a former rider for the Giant team, but for the Iowa ordeal he chose to have a super-tough steel soft-tail bike built by the small independent handmade bike company Tonic Fabrication based in Portland.

The specially commissioned machine featured the Tonic soft-tail system: a shock-absorbing circular aluminum insert fitted between a crown that bridges to the two seatstays, and a short section of tubing to join the seatpost. Tonic says it takes the edge off the bumpiest rocky and gravel surfaces and adds traction to the rear wheel during climbs. The wishbone damper was originally developed by Tonic for a build to compete in the Crusher in the Tushar, the notorious 69-mi (110-km) bicycle race between Beaver, Utah, and the Eagle Mountain Ski Resort, which features equal parts of paved and unpaved sections, and involves climbs over 10,500 ft (3,200 m).

Everything from Tonic is made by the two-man team known only as "Landon and Tony." They do everything by hand, including custom tube-bending and machining their own drop-outs. They also specialize in making some of the toughest, most rugged frames for dirt and jump bikes. Tonic supplies an entire Japanese cyclocross team with bikes.

They usually avoid decorative features and even pointless brazing, preferring to keep the bike's lines uncluttered. In this case, however, they had to adapt their principles; LaCava asked for two water-bottle cage mounts on the forks plus the usual mudguard mounts.

The bike had disc brakes front and back, and was finished with a striking orange paint job with the Tonic Fabrication logo along the head tube and fork. **SH**

SEMESTER Citybike

2013 • Road bike • USA • Bamboo-framed community project bike

Who needs Reynolds 531 steel when you can use the bamboo stalks that grow wild just behind your factory? Slice them into strips, plane them flat, and bevel the edges. Then glue them around a carbon fiber mesh laid at 45 degrees to the bamboo fibers, to create uniform, ultra-strong, and lightweight hexagonal tubing. Then coat the whole lot in a protective clear fiberglass coating and trim to the length you require.

This sustainable alternative bike frame material is at the heart of a project by a group of design companies to help regenerate a deprived area of Alabama. The idea was to create jobs and develop skills by starting a handmade bike company using an idea from similar

". . . the mission is . . . to create a sustainable product . . . [and] new jobs in an area of need."

Designboom.com

projects in India. Expertise comes courtesy of the Hero Bike company, which specializes in bamboo bike production.

It's not all green materials, though; the Semester machine is decked out with powder-coated steel head tube, chain- and seatstays; the drive is single-speed with a 42-tooth chainring; the black deep-rim wheels are 29 in. (73.5 cm) in diameter and fitted with chunky 1 1/3-in. (35-mm) tires. There are porteur-style handlebars with custom woven cotton grips, twine wrapping, and cork end plugs. The saddle comes from Origin8. The brake system is a coaster rear hub—the rider has to backpedal to engage the brake.

Semester Citybikes come in three sizes and currently cost $850 (£525) each. **SH**

Semester's bamboo bike comes from a community building initiative. ▶

ICE Sprint

2013 • Tricycle • UK • Premium recumbent three-wheeler

In 1999, enthusiasts Chris Parker and Neil Selwood took over Trice, a small producer of recumbent trikes, and formed Inspired Cycle Engineering (ICE), which developed from its base in Falmouth, Cornwall, England, into a booming international business. The Classic trike has been the basic ICE model for years, having evolved from the original Trice model.

Recumbent bikes are powered by pedals mounted in front of the riders, rather than beneath them, as on conventional bikes. Trice was already a renowned builder in this specialist market, but, when it became ICE, its horizons broadened greatly: ICE's Works machine became one of the fastest human-powered forms of transportation.

The original Trice Recumbent was built with 20-in. (50-cm) wheels, with two at the front, and one at the rear. The design has since been regularly refined, most notably in 1988 with the introduction of 16-in. (41-cm) wheels and an easier system of leg-length adjustment.

Over the next few years, the hard seat was replaced with breathable mesh, the bike was made foldable, and the wheels went back up to their original size. New models were launched, including the X2 tandem trike and a mini commuter trike. Optional rear suspension and narrower bikes were added; then front suspension and adjustable seat angles. A carbon fiber seat and hydraulic disc brakes also appeared.

In comparison, the Sprint is fairly conventional, but has evolved into a very well-engineered machine. It features two 18-in. (46-cm) front wheels, and a 26-in. (66-cm) driven wheel at the back. This larger single wheel has been found to give a smoother ride. Standard kit includes cable-operated disc brakes, plastic tubes covering the chain, and a choice of three front wheel track widths. **SH**

JEFF TIEDEKEN Gravity Bike

2013 • Gravity bike • USA • Purpose-built freewheel free-fall bike

As their name suggests, gravity bikes rely solely on the force of gravity to propel them. They have no pedals, and no chains. All they need is a steep gradient, and a certain amount of weight—and the steeper and more technical the gradient, the greater the adrenaline rush for the rider. The first bikers to add weight to gain propulsion were BMX riders, but the method was soon widely adopted and evolved into a whole new genre comprising a lot of highly engineered, purpose-built machines capable of achieving speeds in excess of 81mph (130 kph).

One of the less overly-engineered examples of a gravity bike is this graceful exercise in minimalist

"If you're looking for a lesson in speed . . . take a good look at . . . the fastest one out there."

Meghan Young

design by Jeff Tiedeken, a builder of Penny-Farthings and employee of Disney Imagineering. Obviously it has no drivetrain, the crank has been locked, the pedals replaced with foot pegs, and the seat has been elongated to support the rider's body. The frame is made from chromium–molybdenum alloy steel, and the deceleration apparatus—without which any gravity bike is an accident waiting to happen—is a pair of Avid Elixr hydraulic disc brakes.

The International Gravity Sports Association was created in 1996 to foster, regulate, and administer competitions for gravity bikes and in gravity-related sports such as skateboarding. But because the sport is still in its infancy, most gravity bikes tend to be one-offs, put together in backyards and small workshops. **BS**

This Disney designer's bike can hit dizzying speeds without pedals. ▶

KTM Strada 5000 Di2

2013 • Road bike • Austria • State-of-the-art, carbon-framed, electronic-shifting road racer

The KTM name is more readily associated with motorbikes than bicycles, but the entirely separate KTM Bikes produces some impressively performing (and quiet) two-wheelers.

The Strada 5000 has a big down tube and deep chainstays on either side of the supersized press-fit bottom bracket at the lowest corner of a fully carbon fiber frameset. As a result, any increase of pressure from the sole of the rider's shoe produces an encouragingly positive reaction from the rear wheel and an immediate pickup in pace.

Some companies keep the price of their Ultegra Di2 bikes low by fitting heavy Mavic Aksium or Fulcrum wheels weighing around 6 lb 10 oz (3 kg), including tires, tubes, and cassettes. In contrast, the Strada's wheels are DT Swiss Spline R23s shod with Schwalbe Ultremo ZX-HD rubber; they weigh just over 5 lb 4 oz (2.4 kg) to give the Strada impressive responsiveness at every speed and gradient intensity. A full Ultegra setup—chain and cassette as well as the motorized highlights—keeps everything as flawlessly smooth as Shimano intended. The top-quality triple-compound rubber also means you can pull harder and later on the powerful Ultegra brakes or just leave them untouched and lean over further through corners.

The same frame and fork stiffness that helps on the ups gives crisp clarity on the descents for taking traction to the limits, and you've really got to be taking real liberties on very long, very fast hills to get the front end to flutter at all. **GK**

BMC TM02

2013 • Aero bike • Switzerland • Simplified version of the "fastest bike on earth"

While the latest carbon fiber frames are, for many, prohibitively expensive, the molds in which they are formed can easily be redeployed for the creation of cheaper carbon fiber mixes. The addition of budget features enables manufacturers to produce affordable bikes with near-premium performance.

That's the reasoning behind the Time Machine TM02 version of the brand's TM01 flagship. Instead of the complex leading-edge fork of the TM01—with its integrated, multi-section stem, twin steerer tube arrangement, and built-in brakes—the TM02 has a conventional plug-in fork with conventional brakes up front, and a conventional stem holding the bars.

However, the TM02's fork legs still get the original's "tripwire" boundary layer-disturbing detail on the

leading edge, and they sync neatly into a cutout on the mainframe.

From the head tube back, the TM02 is literally a carbon copy of the angular aero shapes of its more expensive sibling. The triangular top tube features a hidden clamping wedge for the deep tripwire-ledged aero seatpost, and uses the same multi-position saddle head. The sharp-profiled leading edge continues beyond the super-angular stays that kink off low on the rear wheel. The position of the rear wheel against the curved cutout shroud is micromanaged by built-in thumb-wheel set screws embedded in the drop-outs.

The TM02 also uses the TM01's brakes: flush-fitting, direct frame-fit sidepull arms hidden from the wind beneath the bottom bracket. **GK**

BRODIE Holeshot

2013 • Mountain bike • Canada • Flagship bike from premium Canadian frame builder

Many mountain bike designers are former artists or motorcyclists. Canadian frame-building legend Paul Brodie was both, and his background is still discernible in his creations nearly thirty years after he welded his first MTB frame in 1985.

While Paul's beautifully painted brass-welded frames built up a growing customer base through the 1980s, he made his greatest impact with his trademark "Vancouver" top tube that sloped down from a tall head tube to a shorter seat tube, thus making the frame stiffer and increasing the clearance for riders who had suddenly to straddle the bike if the rear wheel slipped on a climb.

Brodie then contributed his ingenuity and experience to the launches of the Rocky Mountain

and Kona brands in 1989. Since the 1990s, he has concentrated exclusively on his own Brodie brand, producing an increasingly wide range of bikes for the Canadian market.

With its titanium frame and aggressive hardtail line, the Holeshot Ti demonstrates that Brodie's innovative drive is undiminished. The signature sloping top tube is present and correct, and while titanium naturally keeps the frame light, it is tough enough to try anything.

The Holeshot is shaped and structured to take a 5½-in. (140-mm) stroke suspension fork at the front. The handling angles are also relaxed, in order to keep the steering stable, even on the steepest downhills. Brodie's reputation for building bikes for real riders is still very much alive. **GK**

FATBACK Snowbike

2013 • Snowbike • USA • Advanced aluminum-framed bike for snow riding

Founded by off-road biker and "wolf wrestler" Greg Matyas, Fatback is headquartered in Anchorage, Alaska, an ideal location for the development of snowbikes.

The company produces steel and titanium bikes, but it's the aluminum model that has created the greatest interest, especially after it won almost every major snowbike race of 2012.

It is sold either as a frame (in five sizes and five colors) or as a complete bike in two build options. Components of the complete builds include carbon forks, handlebars, and stem, hydraulic disc brakes, and Surly or 45NRTH tires. Fatback Snowbikes are built to take 2¾-in (70-mm) or 3½-in. (90-mm) rims, dependent on conditions. The rims have large circular holes drilled in them to minimize weight.

The wide wheels accommodate 3⅘-in. (9.7-cm) tires that distribute the weight of rider and bike across the largest possible area. The ultra-fat tires allow pressures as low as 10 psi (0.7 kg/sq cm), which give the bike unprecedented levels of traction.

The frame has Fatback's distinctive, kinked top tube design. This is to allow the use of a longer head tube, and to make it easier to get on and off in extreme conditions. It also looks rather cool.

The aluminum frame is very stiff, but its relaxed geometry makes for a controlled and stable ride, not just over the snow for which it was originally designed, but also over soft sand and pebble beaches—all of which are surfaces that would defeat a standard mountain bike. **SH**

INTENSE 951 Evo

2013 • Downhill bike • USA • Handmade in the USA, The 951 is Intense's World Cup race bike

Jeff Steber began Intense on his kitchen table in California in 1991. In 2013, he was still the company's president and managing director, and continued to build his bikes in the United States, one of the select few competitive bicycle brands still to do so. In the meantime, Intense sponsored some of the greatest downhill racers of all time, including Sam Hill, Chris Kovarik, Shaun Palmer, and Brian Lopes.

In 2013, there was a mass migration by all the major mountain/enduro bike companies to the 650B wheel, but few companies converted their downhill bikes in the same way. Among the exceptions was Intense, which based its Evo on the same platform as

". . . shaves seconds off your race run. Every second counts when your time is sub-three minutes."

Mike Dettmers, Intense sales director

the original 951, but applied numerous tweaks and redesigns to optimize the new wheel size. While it remains to be seen if the move is the beginning of a revolution in mountain biking, there is no doubt that Intense has here created another mighty machine.

The Evo chassis resembles that of the 951, but is completely redesigned, with 8½ in. (21.6 cm) of rear travel delivered through a re-curved virtual pivot point (VPP) suspension system. The slightly extended chainstay—⅕ in. (5 mm) longer than that of the 951—gives the Evo the snappy turning ability that is often lost on 26-in. (66-cm) wheels. The head angle—a super-slack 62.5 degrees—and the bottom bracket sitting at 13¾ in. (35 cm) show that this bike is built primarily if not exclusively to deliver speed and grip. **CJ**

SPECIALIZED S-Works Roubaix

2014 • Road bike • USA • Smooth-riding, disc-equipped superbike

Specialized introduced the first disc-equipped model of its high-comfort, high-mileage Roubaix road bike for the 2013 selling season. In 2014, the equipment suppliers backed up the bike brands that had adopted disc brakes with a proper range of rotary anchors.

Specialized's Roubaix SL4 Disc range is a great example of this strength-in-disc-brake depth. The Roubaix SL4 Expert was propelled with Shimano's Ultegra Di2 gears and stopped by Shimano Sora gears and cable disc brakes. However, it was the top-of-the-line S-Works Roubaix SL4 Disc Red that really showed what could be achieved without conventional brakes. The S-Works SL4 is the highest-grade frame in the Roubaix range, and uses the highest-grade fiber in its composite arsenal to maximize frame stiffness while minimizing weight.

The latest incarnation of the SL4 also sees the modification of the Roubaix's previously upright and pedestrian riding position into a significantly more aggressive, lower-fronted layout, with a sharper ride to match. Comparatively high levels of comfort are still assured by the carefully curved and shaped frame tubes, which have Zertz elastomer gel inserts designed to damp vibration between road and rider. The bike also gets fat gel handlebar tape, and the smooth-riding COBL GOBLR seatpost that Specialized designed for racing the rounded block "cobble Classics," in which the Roubaix has established an outstanding reputation for smooth speed in the worst conditions.

Specialized's supple S-Works Turbo tires, just over 1 in. (26 mm) wide, sit on disc-specific Specialized Roval Rapide carbon 40 rims to give a notably smooth and fast ride. SRAM's latest, disc-equipped, 11-speed Red 22 groupset really drops weight, and adds impeccable all-weather control to this super-versatile superbike. **GK**

⊲ Intense's 915 Evo leads the way in the downhill wheel size revolution.

CANNONDALE Synapse Hi Mod
2014 • Road bike • USA • Proof that endurance needn't be uncomfortable

With the launch of the Road Warrior in 2002, Cannondale became one of the first companies to introduce an increased comfort road bike with a short reach and a tall head tube. In 2006, this design was modified into the original carbon fiber Synapse. In 2014, the concept was thoroughly refreshed by the addition of the latest hi-modulus fiber technology of the all-conquering Super Six Evo race bike.

Synapse Hi Mods made their first appearance at the 2013 Spring Classics, where they were ridden by the Cannondale team that included the devastatingly fast Czech sprinter Peter Sagan. For all the bike's ability to win multiple podiums across Belgian cobbles, comfort and easy efficiency matter most to ordinary riders, and Cannondale has provided plenty of both by slightly

dropping and sharpening the handling and position of the new Synapse. The use of lightweight, super-stiff, ultra-high-modulus fibers in the BallisTec carbon fiber chassis also makes the bike stiffer and lighter.

Detailing is excellent, too. The skinny SAVE rear stays are curved, flattened, and swollen to allow fatigue-reducing flex in the back end. The internal seat clamp maximizes the exposed length of the super-slim FSA 1-in. (2.4-cm) diameter seatpost. A super-wide bottom bracket supports an innovative asymmetrically split base to the seat tube, with Cannondale's own Hollowgram cranks delivering ultimate power-to-weight ratio. Weight is minimized by internal cable routing and minute rear drop-outs. The result is an enthusiastic climber that will not exhaust the rider. **GK**

ZEALOUS 29er Hardtail

2014 • Hardtail bike • UK • Innovative 29er trail hardtail

Big-wheeled, hardtail mountain bikes have traditionally been built for racing. Recently, however, more trail-friendly rigid frames have been designed for riders who don't want the extra complexity or cost of suspension, but who do want the extra rolling smoothness and traction of bigger 29-in. (73.5-cm) wheels.

In the light of this new requirement, Zealous found new solutions to the old problem of the reduced agility of 29er bikes with extended wheelbases.

The company's 29er Hardtail has a split seat tube section that allows the crown of the tire to come forward into the central gap between the two legs of the tube. This feature gives a short rear end without sloping the seat tube excessively and disturbing the weight balance after adjusting the saddle. The same

principle may be seen elsewhere in this book, but the Zealous version is so special that the company has applied to patent it.

The lack of front gear-changer mounts and space for a mech commits riders to a single front ring transmission, but that's increasingly the choice of most aggressive technical trail riders, especially since SRAM's introduction of XX1 and X01 11 speed transmissions. The rear drop-outs are moveable to make it easy to tension the chain on a single-speed setup.

Maximum power delivery and crank compatibility are assured by the outsized BB92 Press Fit bottom bracket shell. The frame geometry and tapered head tube are designed around a 5½-in (140-mm) stroke suspension fork: this is a truly trail-ready machine. **GK**

GT Sensor Carbon Pro

2014 • USA • Mountain bike • Latest development of GT's all-trail all-rounder

"Less playful than the Force, but still a great handler for the day-long trail rider."

Oli Woodman, www.bikeradar.com

The Sensor has been the most popular all-round trail option in the GT bicycle range for many years, but, as is the case with many 2014 season bikes, that year's version was a complete redesign of the old machine.

GT is among the many brands that have jumped wholeheartedly onto the halfway-house, 27½-in. (70-cm) wheel-size standard bandwagon for both its mid- and long-travel trail bikes.

The GT Sensor has been re-imagined from the ground up, to fit the new wheels into the handling equation. With the 6-in. (15-cm) travel Force taking on more gravity-fueled duties, GT has deliberately kept the handling of its Sensor more neutral, so that the bike can function equally well on climbs and descents. The Angle Optimized Suspension installed on the bike is the latest evolution of GT's I-Drive system, which is one of the longest-established rear-end designs around.

The new PathLink joint helps to isolate pedaling forces from suspension action for a very smooth, high-traction ride. GT has also dropped the linkages and shock right down into the bottom corner of the carbon frame, in order to create a super-low center of gravity. Since the larger wheels put the bike lower in relation to the hubs anyway, this repositioning gives the Sensor a very sure-footed feel, even though it has steeper handling angles than numerous other bikes in the same category.

GT has always been among the leading users of carbon fiber frames in mountain biking, and the company's Fury Carbon DH bikes in particular have had massive success at the highest level of racing. It is therefore no surprise that the flagship Pro model of the Sensor frame has a carbon fiber mainframe and a swingarm with chunky dimensions designed to provide extra stiffness and strength, rather than maximum weight reduction. **GK**

GT's latest Sensor owes a lot to the Force Enduro bike. ▶

GIANT Trance

2014 • Mountain bike • Taiwan • Burlier, bigger-wheeled revamp of popular all-rounder

Giant's Trance has been a mainstay of mid-travel all-round trail biking ever since it was introduced. It's always been a very neutral riding bike in terms of suspension, and almost conservative in its handling and overall character. But in 2014 the manufacturers produced an aggressive and attitude-loaded version of the machine that was clearly intended more for maximizing gravity fun than for long-distance pedaling efficiency.

Giant massively slackened the steering angle, pushing the front wheel out in front for a naturally self-correcting ride that really helps control and confidence on rougher, faster trails. While the same super-neutral Maestro suspension system has been retained, rear wheel travel has been increased from 5 in. to 5½ in. (127–140 mm), a small alteration that makes a massive difference to what the Trance can now take in its stride.

The Trance also moves from 26-in. (66-cm) to 27½-in. (70-cm) wheels, to increase traction control, rolling speed, and smoothness without making handling and acceleration slow and ponderous. All the frames in the range also feature the now-obligatory aggro trail bike fixture list of internal cable routing, chainguide mounts, and a screw-through rear-axle setup. **GK**

WHYTE 109C Team

2014 • Mountain bike • UK • Semi-carbon evolution of fun alloy speed machine

According to everyone who reviewed and rode it, Whyte really hit the handling nail on the head with its 109S short-travel 29er marathon race bike, a well-priced machine that came in several cost-effective packages.

The only obstacle to race performance was the weight of the alloy frameset, but, with this bike, Whyte's designers showed that they knew exactly how to create a super-light carbon frame along the same lines.

They set about configuring a multi-sheet mainframe layup that dropped as much weight as possible without compromising stiffness and strength. The result was a hi-modulus, unidirectional carbon mainframe that weighed 1 lb 14 oz (800 g) less than the 6061 T6 mainframe. To keep cost reasonable—and because it was much harder to achieve the same level of weight saving here—the 109C Team's rear stays are the same alloy pieces as the all-alloy 109, complete with a screw-through rear axle for additional stiffness.

The full Team bike was equipped with Whyte's own-brand carbon fiber-rimmed wheelset wrapped in superfast Maxxis Ikon tires. Shimano XTR gears were fitted for maximum pedaling efficiency, together with an XT triple chainset for easy spinning, even on the steepest climbs. **GK**

KONA Carbon Operator

2014 • Downhill/Freeride bike • Canada • A leap into the future of the carbon downhill movement

This bike's unidirectional carbon fiber chassis features the walking-beam four-bar system with which Kona has become synonymous.

Many bike manufacturers make radical changes to their designs every year to entice new customers, but Kona sticks to its trusted formulae. As Kona's industrial designer Jack Russell puts it:

"Even though we started with that blank sheet of paper and looked at a lot of stuff, we found that this suspension design, which ends up being an evolution of our current Operator, was the best design out there for what we were trying to do."

The redesigned product has Kona genes, but it has evidently evolved from the 2013 aluminum version. The line of the carbon top tube bleeds straight into the line of the seatstay, while the narrow carbon tubing makes the bike lighter than its immediate predecessor.

The Carbon Operator will carry some of the world's leading bikers, including freerider Graham Agassiz and downhill racer Connor Fearon. Yet although the bike is designed to suit the best riders in the world, its launch price of only $5,599 (£3,399) underscored Kona's continuing support for privateer racers and fledgling freeride stars of the future. **CJ**

GIANT Propel Advanced SL

2014 • Road bike • Taiwan • Patient development produces outstanding aero road ride

While some brands pride themselves on innovation at all costs, Giant has always taken a slower but solidly researched approach to new projects. That's certainly the case with its Propel aero road bike, which went through no fewer than eighty different incarnations in design before the release of this definitive model.

The arduous gestation process was essential because the Propel is designed to deliver a perfect balance of several often inimical performance metrics: aerodynamics, stiffness, comfort, low weight, and handling. The Propel established new performance benchmarks for the genre. Practical aerodynamics included hidden mini V brakes that work well and are not so inaccessible that any adjustment takes a day out of the owner's life. The down tube is aerodynamic, even with a water bottle in place.

The outsized box-section Overdrive 2 stem, large-diameter fork steerer, and head tube—all borrowed from the legendarily precise TCR road race bike—give the Propel sure-footed, accurate handling, even with Giant's deep-section aero wheels fitted as standard. Power delivery is equally impressive, making it easy for riders to reach speeds at which aerodynamic profiling is worthwhile. **GK**

SCOTT Addict SL

2014 • Road bike • Switzerland • Second-generation bike even lighter than its predecessor

Some manufacturers boast that their road frames weigh less than 2 lb (1 kg), but the frame AND fork of Scott's Addict 2014 race machine weigh less than that when combined.

One of the major reductions came from the use of concentrated, high-strength T1000 carbon fiber. This "Toray" number refers to the tensile strength of the fibers in kilogram-force per square millimeter. Higher-tensile strengths are achieved by increasing the number of fibers per square millimeter, but while more fiber and less resin means higher strength, it also makes the material more brittle and harder to work with. Most manufacturers only use concentrates as high as T800 sparingly in their top-rated frames.

Another weight reduction in the bike's frame was achieved by bonding the carbon fibers with resin glue infused with microscopic nano-particles. These particles are lighter than the resin itself, and fill the minute gaps between the fiber more efficiently than adhesive alone.

Scott also included several drag-reduction elements that had previously proved themselves in the frame of the successful Foil, which was introduced in 2010. The down tube, for example, uses the same blunt-backed "Virtual Foil" shape that turns the turbulence generated in the bike's wake into an airflow-smoothing teardrop shape.

The design of the Addict's seat tube and rear stays is less obviously "aero" than that of the Foil, so its overall wind efficiency is slightly reduced. However, it is significantly smoother and more forgiving than the Foil on rough roads, while its handling is every bit as stable and safe as its predecessor's. A 3⅖-in. (86-mm) press-fit bottom bracket also gives excellent drivetrain stiffness, so that every bit of rider effort can take full advantage of the ethereal weight. **GK**

"Inevitably, there will be people who say there's no point in a bike being this light, but they're wrong. You can feel it and it does make a difference."

Jamie Wilkens, bikeradar.com

◁ Team Orica GreenEDGE had a phenomenally successful year aboard their Scott bikes.

TREK Fuel EX28

2014 • Mountain bike • USA • Bigger wheel size for Trek's fast trail bike

Trek was the first major manufacturer to put serious weight behind the previously niche concept of mountain bikes with 29-in. (73.5-cm) wheels. However, because of uncertainty about how these products would be received, the company initially marketed them under its left-field Gary Fisher sub-brand. Consequently, the Fuel EX and Remedy wagon-wheel bikes are Trek's first true 29ers.

They use the G2 custom fork crown and angles first introduced on the Fisher bikes, and they have inherited the full range of wheel and tire equipment from Bontrager, another Trek brand. The unique, dual-chamber DRCV Fox rear shock also first appeared on the Gary Fisher Roscoe bike. Both the cunning, axle-concentric ABP rear suspension, and the shock—

squeezed between linkage and chainstay tip Full Floater technologies—are taken straight from the previous 26-in. (66-cm) Fuel EX models. The range is restricted, but buyers can still choose between three extensively shaped and sculpted alloy-framed models, and two OCLV carbon fiber frames. This gives a price range from $2,500–$5,000 (£1,500–£3,000).

The Fuel EX 29 riding remit is similarly broad, thanks to a diverse selection of equipment. Trek's experience with big wheels shows in the adoption of relatively low-tread, fast-rolling Bontragers, which rely on an increased in-line contact patch for secure grip. The Fuel is designed to be ridden dynamically enough for an internally routed remote control seat drop post to be default equipment on more expensive models. **GK**

TREK Remedy 29

2014 • Mountain bike • USA • Bigger wheel size for Trek's technical trail bike

For all the publicity and development benefits of sponsoring top riders, when it comes to launching a new bike, nothing beats a first-time win at a major event. That's exactly what British Trek Enduro DH athlete Tracy Moseley did on her Remedy 29 at the first Enduro World Series event in Punta Ala, Italy.

On a seriously steep and technical course, Moseley took the view that the speed-sustaining, steamroller benefits of the bigger wheels would offset the potential agility advantages of her conventional 26-in. (66-cm) bikes. This decision was all the more remarkable because she had ridden the Remedy for only three days before race day.

Her enthusiasm for the new machine was amply rewarded when she came home nearly one minute ahead of her nearest rival. She also finished in the top fifth of the entire starting field, despite having ridden the whole 39-mi (62-km) loop in practice, rather than relying, like other competitors, on trucks to take her to the summits of the downhill sections.

Trek's engineers have done a great job of fitting larger wheels to the Remedy platform while reducing the travel by only ⅖ in. (10 mm) to 5½in. (140 mm). Stiffness is excellent, in spite of the inevitably longer levers holding the wheels at either end. Trek has added a wider bar and a shorter stem, to make the Remedy's handling more agile and controllable than that of smaller-wheeled bikes. Steering feel can be altered by a switchable insert in the Evo shock link; the seat drop post makes it easy to move body weight around. **GK**

TRANSITION Covert Carbon

2014 • Enduro bike • UK • A jack-of-all-trades with COCK and BALLS technology

In 2009, Transition of Ferndale, Washington State, launched the Covert, a 6-in. (15-cm) travel bike built from aluminum, which slotted neatly into the all-mountain/enduro market.

By 2013, the enduro world was increasingly adopting carbon fiber as its material of choice. The Covert was due for a revamp, and Transition decided that it would work well in the new material.

The frame is built using Completely Optimized Carbon Kinetics (COCK) to create a supremely strong carbon frame layup that incorporates neat internal cable routing. The Basically Aligned Linear Leverage System (BALLS) provides a linear suspension curve that allows riders to use the tune of the shock to keep their ride balanced and predictable.

Transition uses a long, 8½-in. (21.5-cm) custom-tuned Fox CTD shock to fully utilize the BALLS, and deliver 6 in. (15 cm) of suspension. The placement of the main pivot is higher than normal, to optimize the bike for 2 x 10 and 1 x 10 drivetrain configurations.

Transition is owned and operated by cyclists, and the pleasure of riding a Covert clearly shows that the machine was developed by people who love bikes and are passionate about riding them. **CJ**

SCOTT Solace

2014 • Road bike • Switzerland • Proof that more comfort needn't mean less speed

High-performance, high-comfort bikes for mere mortals who are not prepared to take the punishment that pro riders will endure for ultimate speed are the biggest growth sector in road cycling. The pace of technological change means that manufacturers have to refresh their ranges every few years to stay competitive. Accordingly, Scott produced this new bike to regain its place at the front of the sportive pack which its CR1 was no longer able to sustain.

Scott deliberately split the Solace frame into two sections. The lower section, the Power Zone, comprises deep chainstays, a big BB86 bottom bracket, an outsized down tube, and a tapered head tube. These create a stiff keel that ties the steering together front to back, and channels pedal and shoulder power to the rear wheel.

The upper Comfort Zone has thin tube walls and diameters to dissipate shock and vibration. The seatstays curve forward to blend into the side of the top tube. The rear brake is mounted beneath the thicker chainstays, behind the bottom bracket, to stop brake stress snapping the tubes. Syncros componentry includes a soft saddle, a flexible, carbon fiber seatpost, and back-swept handlebars. The bike has both electric and conventional cable gear shift capability. **GK**

CANYON Spectral AL 29

2014 • Mountain bike • Germany • Penthouse quality at a basement price

Canyon made a strong entry into the bigger-wheeled 29er market with its race hardtail and Nerve Al marathon bikes. The Spectral is for riders in search of a serious technical trail speed machine at an outstanding price.

The smoothly tapered and curved frameset follows the clean lines of the Nerve, but reworked linkages and a more pronounced seat tube curve squeeze another ⅘ in. (20 mm) of travel into the mix for a total of just over 5 in. (130 mm). The kinked top tube makes room for a fork with the same extended travel, and the frame has routing for a remote-control height adjustment post.

The top-of-the-line Spectral comes with Spectral AL 9.9 EX fork and Float X rear shock, complete with Kashima coated shafts and an additional external damper. The massively wide Fatbar handlebars and

unique clamshell stem come from British motocross motorbike specialists Renthal, and the E Thirteen single ring chainset is teamed with a matching chain-retaining device.

The Spectral is so cheap to buy that it is perhaps surprising that the frame is no throwaway piece of cheap tin. Asymmetric chainstays and a screw-through rear axle make it extremely stiff, no matter how hard you wrench it sideways, and the hourglass-shaped, tapered head tube keeps steering impressively accurate regardless of the amount of rider heave on the Renthal bars. Even the box in which Canyon deliver these bikes in is a masterpiece of cardboard origami, confirming the German brand as the Samurai of slashed-price quality. **GK**

PYGA OneTwenty650

2014 • Mountain bike • South Africa • Super-stiff and aggressive all-round MTB

On paper, the Pyga OneTwenty650 seems a mild-mannered, middle-of-the-road proposition. Its 4⁷⁄₁₀ in. (120 mm) of rear wheel travel theoretically puts it firmly into the all-day cross-country category, while its 650B wheels are a compromise between maximum-speed 29-in. (73.5-cm) wheels and maximum-toughness 26-in. (66-cm) wheels.

The Pyga is a "small travel, big capability" trail bike, rather than a fragile featherweight machine for distant summits. It is best suited to riders in crash-scarred knee pads and clothing as loose as the trails that it is designed to dominate.

To achieve this mastery, most of the frame's hydroformed tubes are as close as possible to the ground. The bottom bracket runs low enough to risk sumping

impacts on rocks, while the seat tube sticks right up above the kinked top tube, with a big vertical gusset plate at the front for stress protection. The already low-set, linkage-driven RockShox shock-absorber is mounted on the extended chainstay tips, rather than the frame itself. Hence the shock drops even lower as the back wheel arcs through its travel, slamming the Pyga right to the floor just when you need maximum stability.

The race-style tune on the Monarch shock means that the frame never wallows about needlessly, diluting control and feedback. Forged frame sections keep the frame stiff from the screw-through rear axle to the tapered head tube. This bike is at its best with brakes untouched on the most aggressive line through the most technical, rock-infested trails. **GK**

MARIN Mount Vision

2014 • Mountain bike • USA • Stiffer, lighter,
faster redesign of classic trail machine

The 2014 season opened a new chapter in the history
of Marin, as Indonesian financial backing enabled a vast
increase in research and development investment, the
results of which are evident in the new version of the
company's classic Mount Vision.

Innovations include a carbon fiber chassis in
place of the old alloy frame. The massive new frame
sections—particularly around the rear sub-frame—
increase stiffness to produce an extremely accurate
feel, no matter how hard the bike is thrown around.

While the lateral stiffness is brutal, the new design
builds vital vertical suspension flex into the rear stays,
which saves sufficient weight to accommodate a
piggyback reservoir rear shock for a more accurate feel
than a conventional, single-can shock. Rear travel of 5½
in. (140 mm) lets the bike tackle serious obstacles and
rough terrain at high speed without any worries about
losing control. A hydraulic, height-adjustable RockShox
Reverb seatpost is also fitted, complete with an internally
routed Stealth remote-control button on the handlebars
to get the seat out of the way when required.

The front end has super-stable DH angles, with a
short stem and wide-bar cockpit. The Mount Vision rolls
on 27½-in. (70-cm) wheels. **GK**

MARIN Attack Trail

2014 • Moutain bike • USA • All-new carbon
aggro bike from classic MTB brand

Marin's 2014 range redesign made maximum use of
investment by its new Indonesian owners, and the
aggressive-riding Attack Trail was a major beneficiary of
the new budget.

While this bike's frame and layout appear similar
to those of the Attack Trail and the Mount Vision, the
resemblance is only skin-deep. The carbon fiber chassis
is reinforced with extra layers of composite in high-
stress areas. The frame is based around the proven Quad
Link suspension system that Marin has used for several
years. It has been reworked to give a more neutral and
linear suspension feel than previous versions. The 6-in.
(150-mm) travel is managed by Fox's Float X piggyback,
damping-chamber-equipped Enduro DH shock for
maximum big-hit, high-speed control.

Up front, control is provided by a RockShox Pike
fork in a travel-adjustable format that allows the rider to
change between climbing and descending modes at
the flick of a switch. The RockShox Reverb seatpost can
be lowered or raised via a handlebar button.

The TRS+ Enduro equipment from E Thirteen
includes broad-rimmed 650B wheels, a twin-ring
chainset, a chain-taming device, and trail-gripping
Schwalbe Hans Dampf tires. **GK**

ORANGE Five 650

2014 • Mountain bike • UK • Refresh of classic British MTB

Part of the Orange range for many years, the Five became a favorite of British hardcore trail warriors who placed a premium on totally reliable and predictable character rather than smart suspension or low weight.

Then, after almost a decade of gradual evolution, this radical and largely unheralded change in the Five sent real ripples through the loyal fan base.

The frame of the 650 is a mix of hydraulically formed Reynolds alloy tubes and distinctive monocoque down tube and rear swingarm sections formed from two seam-welded, folded sheets held together by heavily sealed cartridge bearing pivots. The rear brake and gear control lines are routed inside the rear swingarm to minimize damage in a crash.

While almost indistinguishable in layout from the previous 26-in. (66-cm) wheeled bike, the new Five had 27½-in. (70-cm) 650B Mavic rims built onto tough hubs made by Hope in Barnoldswick, a small town near Orange's base in Halifax, Yorkshire, England. These slightly larger wheels gave the bike a new character, and the legs to roam effortlessly up and down hills, rather than just concentrating on descents, along which the longer-travel, punishment-proof Patriot is now the pick of the Oranges. **GK**

SANTA CRUZ Solo

2014 • Mountain bike • USA • A capable all-rounder with a wild side

When the long-travel, Enduro DH-targeted Bronson was launched in 2013, many people assumed that that was Santa Cruz's big launch for the year, but the designers and development riders of the company's Syndicate race team had another trick up their sleeves. They revealed it in an epic video shot in the wilds of the Scottish highlands just prior to the Fort William World Cup downhill race, with UK rider Steve Peat on a whole new bike platform.

Like the Bronson, both the Solo and the Solo Carbon are 650Bs—bikes with 27½-in. (70-cm) diameter wheels that give greater speed and grip than 26-in. (66-cm) machines, and fewer steering and flex problems than 29-in. (73.5-cm) wheels. Much of their geometry is the same as that of the Blur TR and TR Carbon. The bottom bracket is low for maximum cornering stability, but the steering angles aren't raked out too far, so the front wheel doesn't lose the line on climbs. VPP2 suspension delivers enough pedal feedback for positive traction control, but has a big appetite for swallowing speed-restricting impacts, and 5 in. (125 mm) of rear travel to keep wheel reaction tight and predictable. Although the frame weighs only 5 lb (2.27 kg), it is stout, stiff, and accurate, even at the ragged edge of control. **GK**

SALSA Beargrease

2014 • Fat bike • USA • Carbon fiber racer

Salsa is happier to plow its own furrow than to follow fashion trends. The company's individualism has created several bikes that were scoffed at when they first appeared but went on to be widely copied. Among the most popular Salsa innovations were fat-tired, disc-braked all-road bikes, and an extensive range of 29-in. (73.5-cm) wheelers long before most manufacturers got in on the act. The company was also instrumental in creating the current explosion in popularity of fat bikes.

These distinctive machines use specially widened rims and frames to accommodate low-pressure tires, 3–4 in. (7.5–10 cm) wide, that effortlessly cross surfaces into which conventional bikes would just sink.

A concept that at first found favor only in snowbound areas such as Alaska was later adopted as a fresh and fun way to tackle less severe trails. Since the bikes have become more readily available, there has been an increase in the number of fat bike events, and some ski resorts have opened up their cross-country routes to them.

The Beargrease is the latest in what has become a long line of Salsa bikes that appear to be acts of insanity at first glance, but which then turn out to be trail-blazing firsts. It has a fully carbon fat bike frame with internal cable routing and screw-through axles for maximum stiffness front and rear. Its handling is so responsive that you won't end up making snow angels if you start power sliding on the white powder. In addition to the complete bike, Salsa offers an SRAM XX1 build kit option. **GK**

SANTA CRUZ Heckler

2014 • Mountain bike • USA • The maker's gift to the world on its own eighteenth birthday

A direct descendant of Santa Cruz's original Tazmon suspension frame, the Heckler has always been a much-loved workhorse option in the Californian company's lineup. The Santa Cruz design team made sure it got to celebrate its eighteenth birthday properly with this total refresh of the classic single-pivot design. While the basic layout is essentially the same as that of the previous Heckler, smooth, hydraulically shaped and twisted tubes form the clean, unfussy front and rear ends of the frame. These are further stiffened by a tapered head tube at the front, and a 5½ x ½-in. (142 x 12-mm) screw-in axle at the rear. The two halves are joined by a fully adjustable and serviceable tapered collet bearing system bred from those introduced on Santa Cruz's classic Blur LT frame.

The handling angles are slacker than those of the previous Heckler, and thus produce a more confident feel through the bars. Most significantly, the new Heckler rolls on 650B wheels with 27½-in. (70-cm) diameters that offer better traction and rolling speed over rough terrain than 26-in. (66-cm) wheelers. They also lower the frame's center of gravity, further increasing stability through a pendulum effect, and making the Heckler sure-footed at speed.

The frame can be bought separately or as the centerpiece of a range of complete bike build kits from the affordable to the totally aspirational. To make sure the Heckler's dressed right for the trail, Santa Cruz also offers it in a 1990s retro vivid blue and neon green Club Tropicana paint job that'll brighten up any ride. **GK**

SCOTT Scale 700 RC Swisspower

2014 • Mountain bike • Switzerland • Replica of Swiss World Champion's mountain bike

Building replicas of race bikes for mere mortals to buy has always been an extremely good way for a bike manufacturer to get the most from sponsoring a team. Scott certainly backed a winner with multiple World Cup, World, and National Championship winner Nino Schurter, and this bike is pretty special too.

While most cross-country racers now use big, smooth-rolling 29-in. (73.5-cm) wheels to sustain their speed on rough race circuits, Schurter uses smaller 650B wheels. Team manager Thomas Frischknecht (a former World Champion himself) explains why: "Nino always had a hard time finding his position on the 29er because he has a very sporty position on his bike, having his handlebar very low," he said. "Even on his 26 in., he goes without spacers or anything and with the 29er he

had to compromise his position on the bike. He liked the wheels themselves but he could never get the position right for his size."

With the constant accelerations needed to make and respond to attacks, every extra gram on a race bike can be the difference between winning and losing. At less than 2¼ lb (1 kg) in weight, the Scale 700 RC frame is lighter than many road bikes and has certainly been a big part of Schurter's recent success. He also uses the lightest DT Swiss carbon wheelset with glue-on tubular tyres and a carbon fiber DT Swiss fork.

As this top-level frame is sold on its own, you'd have to decide what kit to put on yourself, but whatever your choices there's no doubting you'd be off to a flying start with this proven World Champion. **GK**

WHYTE G150

2014 • Mountain bike • UK • Meeting the latest challenges of mountain biking

Whyte has always produced radically handling machines that combine downhill-style confidence with cross-country weight. The G150 is perfectly placed to tackle the flat-out descents and physically demanding challenges of Enduro DH riding.

In France and Italy, an increasing number of Enduro events now feature epic, timed downhills and time-limited transfer stages to create full days—and, sometimes, full weeks—of nonstop, radical riding. In the United States, there are Super D races in which riders have to sprint to the top of massive technical peaks, before blitzing their way downhill on the same bike. As a response to these events, and as a process of natural evolution, trail bikes have become more and more downhill-capable, too.

Whyte's G150—the letter stands for "gravity," the number for the millimeters of travel (6 in.)—is the ideal bike for such competitions. The RockShox Pike fork is angled a long way forward. This makes it more likely to self-correct and straighten up if the front wheel gets knocked off line by boulders, ruts, or roots. With a short stem and wide handlebar, the bike is still quick enough to react to changes in traction or sudden slips. The low center of gravity makes it very stable and sure-footed through high-speed corners, while the short back end keeps it agile and quick to change direction at the rear.

The 650B wheels—diameter 27½ in. (70 cm)—maximize smoothness and traction, enabling the rider to hit corners fast, and carve or slide through them with complete confidence. **GK**

KINESIS Sync

2014 • Mountain bike • UK • Feature-loaded titanium mountain bike frame

With the Sync, Kinesis combined 27½-in. (70-cm) and 29-in. (73.5-cm) wheels into a new hardtail design for a ride that perfectly matched the machine with each individual rider.

The company's award-winning Maxlight FF29 hardtail had previously showcased the smooth-rolling, sure-footed ride advantages of big wheels—especially for bigger riders—but designer Dom Mason found them too cumbersome to work well with small frame sizes. As a result, he developed the smallest Sync frame option with 27½-in. (70-cm) wheels to give the advantages of increased rollover without disturbing the proportional balance and poise of the bike.

Not content with this innovation alone, Kinesis then loaded the bike with a host of other distinctive features. Rather than use carbon fiber, the company built the Sync from butted titanium, with some unique tubing profiles for highly fatigue-resistant strength and a smoothly sprung ride character. It then applied suspension fork strokes of 5 in. (130 mm)—a length significantly greater than most titanium frames could handle. The rear axle was a downhill-style 5⅗ x ½-in (142 x 12-mm) screw-in for maximum strength and rear wheel precision, rather than the often vague feel of titanium frames. Above all, Mason wanted the finished article to be about propulsion and getting the power down, while retaining the lively ride quality that is characteristic of titanium structures—in short, the best of both worlds.

The frame is fully ready for a remote-control seat dropper mechanism for easy body weight shift on steep and fast descents, and it also has internal gear-cable routing, which is extremely rare on titanium-framed bikes. The result is a true modern classic that combines many diverse elements into a genuinely trail-taming mountain bike. **GK**

"Tough enough for trail madness yet capable of racehead efficiency . . . a refreshingly different design."

bikeradar.com

◁ The Sync matches wheel size to frame size for perfectly balanced handling.

SPECIALIZED Epic World Cup

2014 • Mountain bike • USA • Stripped-down race machine based on an Olympic winner

After nearly a decade of race domination, Specialized's unique Epic platform stormed to an Olympic win in London in 2012. The lessons from the development of Jaroslav Kulhavy's stripped-down team bike have now been built into a race-focused machine.

The travel of the mass-market version has been reduced from the original 3⁹⁄₁₀ in (100 mm) to 3⁷⁄₁₀ in (95 mm), and the unique auto bump sensing Brain suspension has been retuned for racing. As a result, riders get maximum cornering control and power delivery, rather than a plush ride. The bike does not flow over small bumps in the manner of softer-tuned bikes, but locks out, hardtail-style, as soon as the trail becomes smooth, and needs a firm thump to get it moving again.

Power delivery has been made as direct as possible through the incorporation of chainstays so large that there's no chance of fitting a front mech. As a result, the complete bikes are totally committed to SRAM's XX1 single-ring drivetrain transmission. The BB30 bottom bracket gets Specialized's own carbon crank arms mated to an SRAM XX1 chainring. The chainstays have been slimmed down to increase heel clearance on rough ground, but a 5½ x ½-in. (142 x 12-mm) screw-through rear axle keeps the rear end stiff in spite of the extremely light weight of the frameset.

Fastidious racers will be delighted that the internal cable routing can be configured in four different ways. The repositioned rear shock creates room for two full-sized water bottles for longer races. **GK**

SPECIALIZED Enduro 29
2014 • Mountain bike • USA • Rule-breaking big-travel big-wheel bike

While most mountain bike manufacturers seemed to be shifting to mid-sized, 27½-in. (70-cm) wheels for their new longer-travel bikes, Specialized bucked the trend with a big 29-in. (73.5-cm) version of its classic Enduro long-travel machine. With just over 6 in. (155 mm) of rear wheel travel, and even downhill-style piggyback shocks on some models, the Enduro 29 is a proper trail tearaway with all the smoothness and grip associated with the largest wheel size.

Getting that performance from big wheels required some serious ingenuity from the Specialized design team. The major problem was providing sufficient frame clearance for the rear wheel to move without it contacting the frame or other components. By offsetting the seat tube forward, and curving it

around the back wheel, movement can be safely managed even with chainstays shorter than many bikes with only half the travel.

Specialized worked with SRAM to create a specific Taco curved plate mount for the front mech to prevent the tire hitting the back of the cage as the suspension compresses. This mount can also be used for chainguides when used with a single chainring.

Specialized has created three models. The S-Works and Expert models use carbon fiber mainframes and alloy rear ends, while the base Comp model uses an all-alloy frame to keep costs down. Initial reviews suggested that the gamble had paid off, and that the Enduro 29 is a truly outstanding gravity-biased fun bike, regardless of its wheel size. **GK**

GAFNI Cardboard Bike

2014 • Road bike • Israel • Ultra-cheap cardboard concept road bike

When experts told Izhar Gafni that a bike frame could not be made from cardboard, he determined to prove them wrong: this is, after all, supposed to be an age of recycled products.

In an interview with *Dezeen* architecture and design magazine, the Israeli engineer and systems developer explained: "The idea is like Japanese origami: you fold it once, and it doesn't become twice the strength, it's almost three times the strength. So I took it from there and did the same thing with cardboard."

After completing the folding process, Gafni cut out the shape, and then applied a waterproof and fireproof coating before a final coat of lacquer paint.

The complete bike is water- and humidity-proof—a section was submerged in a water-filled tank for months just to make sure—and it looks so good that it's hard to believe it's not made from some kind of lightweight polymer. And here's the kicker: it can carry up to 485 lb (220kg) and is stronger than carbon fiber. This may be difficult to believe, but it's true.

The bike costs less than $16 (£10) to manufacture, and Gafni expects it to sell for roughly twice that amount when it eventually enters production with the help of his business partner, the Israeli investment group ERB, which is helping with various fundraising initiatives. Of course, it's not all cardboard: the pedals, chain, and brake cables are made of metal. The tires are reconstituted rubber from old car tires. Tests showed that, although a little stiff, the ride is really not that different from that of many conventional bikes. **BS**

GIANT TCX Advanced 1

2014 • Cyclocross bike • Taiwan • Innovation-loaded, disc-equipped bike for racing or recreation

Giant's TCX Advanced cyclocross bikes don't just borrow disc brake technology from their MTB cousins, they're also the first mainstream production bikes to adopt screw-through front axles. This development is particularly welcome when accompanied by disc brakes, in view of some past incidents of front wheel quick-release skewer loosening, which were attributed to the torque force from rotor-based braking.

There's certainly no danger of losing the wheel with the MTB standard ⅗-in. (15-mm) screw-through axles used by Giant throughout its 2014 cross bike range. That's because the drop-outs on either side are totally closed, so that, even if the axle loosens, the wheel can't fall out. Mounting the brake on the fork tip also solves problems caused by independent frame

and fork flex interfering with control modulation on conventional cantilever brakes.

Giant keeps the carbon forks light even though they have to cope with extra stress at the tips. While most manufacturers equip only a few of their cyclocross bikes with discs, Giant fits hydraulic or cable-operated disc calipers to all its carbon and TCX SLR alloy frame bikes.

Hidden seatpost clamps and neat chainstay brake positioning are adopted from Giant's XTC Advanced SL 29. Advanced cyclocross bikes also use the oversized Overdrive2 headset, Powercore bottom bracket, and large-girth, square-section tubes.

The wheels are Giant's own brand, with carbon or alloy rims. SRAM Red or Force groupsets are cranked into action with Rotor 3DF chainsets. **GK**

PACE RC127

2014 • Mountain bike • UK • Excellent
mountain mix of retro and totally modern

Launched in 1989, Pace's first bike, the RC100, almost immediately gained legendary status. This ultra-integrated, machined alloy tube masterpiece was loaded with many features—threadless headsets, bolted fork crowns, direct-fit crank bearings, short-stem/long-top-tube geometry, direct-fit hydraulic brakes—that soon became industry standards.

In some ways, the RC127 frame pays homage to the ground-breaking introduction of the RC100 twenty-five years before. While the RC100 was one of the first alloy-framed bikes to break the stranglehold of steel-tubed frames, designer Adrian Carter returned to steel for the RC127. The Reynolds 853 tubes are a big advance from the pipes of a quarter of a century ago, however, using larger diameters and an ultra-high-tech, weld-hardening steel alloy. This creates a stiff yet light chassis that still has all the spring and zing of the best mountain bikes.

The RC127 has 650B wheels, with 27½-in. (70-cm) diameters. The increase from a diameter of 26-in. (66-cm) gives a shallower tire contact angle for a noticeably smoother ride, superb technical control, and better speed sustain over rough ground. Nevertheless, the wheels aren't so large that the slim steel tubes reaching around to the rear axle lose positive tracking and power delivery.

Although the ride of the RC127 has been rigged to suit the exacting requirements of Carter and his daughter, Sophie, both ultra-skillful and fanatical riders who design and test the prototype bikes, the slack steering angles and long stroke fork capability are perfectly suited to anyone determined to maximize fun on the most technical trails. Their bike started winning magazine tests and awards as soon as it appeared in prototype form. **GK**

LEXUS F Sport

2014 • Road bike • Japan • Packs more high-tech per ounce than its V10 automobile cousin

To mark the end of the 500-unit production run of the Lexus LFA, a 4.8-liter, V10-powered, two-seat supercar, the Japanese manufacturer decided to produce a high-tech sports bike made of the same carbon fiber-reinforced plastic as the automobile. Only one hundred of the bikes were made: fifty in pearl white, and fifty in a dark, exposed carbon fiber finish. They were originally for sale only in Japan.

The F Sport is only 14 lb 15 oz (6.8 kg), a lightness that is achieved by making almost everything from carbon fiber—not only the frame, but also the seatpost, the forks, the seat, the rims, the handlebars, and the crankshafts. And it looks good, thanks to three hours

"The frame design . . . makes full use of the vibration-dampening characteristics of the carbon."

Tsukasa Yoshimoto, bicycle reviewer

of hand-polishing per vehicle to achieve a remarkable glowing lacquer finish.

Lexus—the premium arm of Toyota—really knows how to accessorize, too, with a 22-speed Shimano Dura Ace Di2 electronic shift system that provides an instantaneous and jar-free click into gear every time, with shift paddles modeled after those used in Formula 1.

Some might suggest it's a bit of a comedown for the engineers and technicians at Toyota's secretive Motomachi Assembly Plant in Toyota City to go from assembling supercars to bicycles (the frame was actually made in Taiwan). After some debate at Lexus as to whether or not to follow BMW and Audi down the branded bicycle road, the Japanese caught up to their German rivals at the first attempt. **BS**

If you're sick of being stuck in traffic, don't drive a Lexus, pedal one. ▶

SPECIALIZED Tarmac SL4

2014 • Road bike • USA • All-round race bike that's a triumph of integration

Specialized's influence in professional road racing has grown as it has supplied increasing numbers of teams. The company's flagship Tarmac SL4 is one of the most successful top-end production bikes of all time.

The SL4 features a head tube, down tube, and top tube assembly that's built in a single section. The bottom bracket and seat tube are also built together for maximum stiffness.

Specialized has slimmed down the lower bearing in the bike's tapered head tube to give a better fiber wrap-over from the down tube. Great thought has gone into both the dimensions and the weight of the main tubes, so that the compliance and strength of each part can be accurately tuned to the weight and power of different-sized riders.

The same frame construction methods are used on the whole Tarmac range, from the most expensive to the cheapest, although the deeper you dig into your pockets, the better the composite materials. The top S-Works frames not only benefit from the lightest, stiffest, fiber mix, but they also get Specialized's unique carbon fiber-armed Functional Advanced Composite Technology (FACT) cranks and carbon Roval CLX40 rims. The frame is also easily switchable between Shimano's electronic Di2 and conventional, cable-triggered shifting setups, and both versions are available as complete bikes. The frame-only option is also offered in four different colorways, including the livery of the Saxo Tinkoff and Omega Pharma-QuickStep pro teams. **GK**

PIVOT Vault

2014 • Cyclocross bike • USA • Limited production cyclocross machine from top suspension MTB brand

A full-suspension MTB specialist based in the Arizona desert might seem an unlikely source of a state-of-the-art, dropped bar, cyclocross bike. Then again, this isn't a traditional cross machine.

The Vault developed from Pivot's work with its longtime collaborator, the Spanish bike brand Massi. The upward curved taper of the top tube and the way it blends around past the seat tube and into the rear stays are very reminiscent of the latter company's current crop of road bikes. Also Massi-inspired is the spring-loaded suspension, which reduces vibration on all surfaces, on- and off-road, and makes the Vault much more versatile than a brutally stiff, purist race bike.

And that was one of Pivot's key aims for the machine. While the Vault is smooth enough to take the roughest overtaking lines on frozen winter cyclocross courses without rattling its rider into pieces, it's also powerful enough to grind away from the opposition in the deep mud, sand, and snow that may make this sport so challenging.

Pivot has equipped the Vault with fixtures for either disc brakes or traditional cantilever brakes, and ensured that both types work with either electric or conventionally controlled gears. The BB386 bottom bracket allows for a very strong frame center, while still giving clearance for the fattest 700C cyclocross tires. That makes the Vault a classic example of the latest crossover-style bikes, but one that is more loaded than most rivals with performance potential and gritty "have a go" character. **GK**

BOARDMAN AiR 9.2 Di2

2014 • Road bike • UK • Aero race machine from a master of the craft

There's a very good reason why we invited Chris Boardman to write the foreword for this book, and his passion for creating and riding cutting-edge bikes couldn't be better illustrated than with this aspirational-yet-affordable machine from his latest Elite range.

This bike shows the obvious fruits of decades spent researching bike and rider airflow in wind tunnels. First, as part of the development of the Mike Burrows–designed Lotus Superbike that won Boardman his Olympic, Hour Record, and World Championship honors. Then as a key member of the "Secret Squirrel" track bike development team that reaped such incredible rewards for the Team GB athletes at the Beijing and London Olympics, and since then for the development of his own range of ultra-efficient time trial and road race bikes. This unparalleled personal crusade against aerodynamic drag is shown in the smoothly blended head and down tubes, and bladed seatpost and seatstays of the AiR 9.2. The seatpost uses a hidden clamp to secure ride height without any excess turbulence, the electric shift cables are all routed internally, and the rear brake is tucked under the bottom bracket in already "dirty" air.

Unlike many similar bikes, aerodynamics haven't outweighed safety or practicality on this model. The front brake is a very powerful conventionally mounted Shimano Ultegra unit and the frame and tapered fork are stiff enough for confident, aggressive handling even if the owner upgrades to deep-section wheels. The seatpost clamp gives four positions to suit relaxed road riding or an aggressive forward triathlon-style position.

Despite a surprisingly affordable price for a Shimano Di2 electric-shift-equipped bike, the 9.2 Di2 uses exactly the same top-grade carbon fiber frame as the flagship Air 9.8 Di2 ridden to devastating effect by Olympic and World Triathlon Champions Alistair and Jonathan Brownlee. **GK**

◁ Boardman's aspirational AiR 9.8 uses exactly the same frame as the AiR 9.2.

Index of Bikes by Model